Programming Games with Java™

A NetBeans IDE 11 Swing GUI
Game Programming Tutorial

11th Edition

Philip Conrod & Lou Tylee

KIDWARE SOFTWARE

KIDWARE SOFTWARE
PO Box 701
Maple Valley, WA 98038
www.kidwaresoftware.com

Published by:
Kidware Software, LLC
PO Box 701
Maple Valley, Washington 98038
1.425.413.1185
www.kidwaresoftware.com

Printed in the United States of America

ISBN-13: 978-1-937161-34-7 (Printed)
ISBN-13: 978-1-937161-33-0 (Electronic)

Copy Editor: Jessica Conrod
Book Cover by Stephanie Conrod
Illustrations: Kevin Brockschmidt
Compositor: Michael Rogers

About The Authors

Philip Conrod has authored, co-authored and edited over two dozen computer programming books over the past thirty years. Philip holds a Bachelor's Degree in Computer Information Systems and a Master's certificate in the Essentials of Business Development from Regis University. Philip has served in various Information Technology leadership roles in companies like Sundstrand Aerospace, Safeco Insurance, FamilyLife, Kenworth Truck Company, and PACCAR. Philip last served as the Chief Information Officer (CIO) for Darigold Inc for over a decade before returning to teaching and writing full-time. Today, Philip serves as the President & Publisher of Kidware Software LLC which is based in Maple V alley, Washington.

Lou Tylee holds BS and MS degrees in Mechanical Engineering and a PhD in Electrical Engineering. Lou has been programming computers since 1969 when he took his first Fortran course in college. He has written software to control suspensions for high speed ground vehicles, monitor nuclear power plants, lower noise levels in commercial jetliners, compute takeoff speeds for jetliners, locate and identify air and ground traffic and to let kids count bunnies, learn how to spell and do math problems. He has written several on-line texts teaching Visual Basic, Visual C# and Java to thousands of people. He taught computer programming courses for over 15 years at the University of Washington and currently teaches math and engineering courses at the Oregon Institute of Technology. Lou also works as a research engineer at a major Seattle aerospace firm. He is the proud father of five children, has six grandchildren and is married to an amazing woman. Lou and his family live in Seattle, Washington.

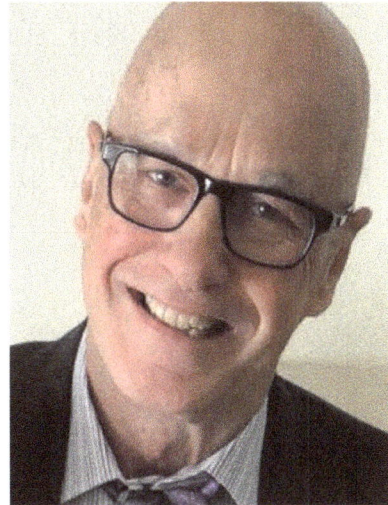

Acknowledgements

I would like to thank my three wonderful daughters - Stephanie, Jessica and Chloe, who helped with various aspects of the book publishing process including software testing, book editing, creative design and many other more tedious tasks like textbook formatting and back office administration. I could not have accomplished this without all your hard work, love and support. I also want to thank my best friend Jesus who always stands by my side giving me wisdom and guidance.

Last but definitely not least, I want to thank my multi-talented co-author, Lou Tylee, for doing all the real hard work necessary to develop, test, debug, and keep current all the 'kid-friendly' applications, games and base tutorial text found in this book. Lou has tirelessly poured his heart and soul into so many previous versions of this tutorial and there are so many beginners who have benefited from his work over the years. Lou is by far one of the best application developers and tutorial writers I have ever worked with. Thanks Lou for collaborating with me on this book project.

Contents i

1. Introducing Java

2. Java Program Basics

5. Debugging, Decisions, Random Numbers

6. Java Looping, Methods

7. Arrays, More Java Looping

8. Java Graphics, Mouse Methods

9. Timers, Animation, Keyboard Methods

10. More Topics, More Projects

Appendix. Installing Java & NetBeans for Windows or MAC

About The Authors

Philip Conrod has authored, co-authored and edited over two dozen computer programming books over the past thirty years. Philip holds a Bachelor's Degree in Computer Information Systems and a Master's certificate in the Essentials of Business Development from Regis University. Philip has served in various Information Technology leadership roles in companies like Sundstrand Aerospace, Safeco Insurance, FamilyLife, Kenworth Truck Company, and PACCAR. Philip last served as the Chief Information Officer (CIO) for Darigold Inc for over a decade before returning to teaching and writing full-time. Today, Philip serves as the President & Publisher of Kidware Software LLC which is based in Maple Valley, Washington.

Lou Tylee holds BS and MS degrees in Mechanical Engineering and a PhD in Electrical Engineering. Lou has been programming computers since 1969 when he took his first Fortran course in college. He has written software to control suspensions for high speed ground vehicles, monitor nuclear power plants, lower noise levels in commercial jetliners, compute takeoff speeds for jetliners, locate and identify air and ground traffic and to let kids count bunnies, learn how to spell and do math problems. He has written several on-line texts teaching Visual Basic, Visual C# and Java to thousands of people. He taught computer programming courses for over 15 years at the University of Washington and currently teaches math and engineering courses at the Oregon Institute of Technology. Lou also works as a research engineer at a major Seattle aerospace firm. He is the proud father of five children, has six grandchildren and is married to an amazing woman. Lou and his family live in Seattle, Washington.

Course Description:

Java for Kids is an interactive, self-paced tutorial providing a complete introduction to the Java programming language. The tutorial consists of 10 lessons explaining (in simple, easy-to-follow terms) how to build a Java application. Numerous examples are used to demonstrate every step in the building process. The tutorial also includes detailed computer projects for kids to build and try. **Java for Kids** is presented using a combination of course notes and many Java examples and projects.

Course Prerequisites:

To use **Java for Kids**, you should be comfortable working within the Microsoft Windows or Apple OS operating system environment. You will also need know how to find files, move windows, resize windows, etc. The course material should be understandableto kids aged 12 and up. No previous programming experience is needed.   If your student has previous programming experience, they can start this course as early as 10 years old with a parent or teacher's assitance. You will also need the ability to view and print documents saved in the Acrobat PDF format.

You also need to have 11th Edition of the Java Development Kit (**JDK**) and the 11th Edition of **NetBeans**, the Integrated Development Environment (IDE) we use with this course.

Complete download and installation instructions for the JDK and NetBeans are found in the Appendix (**Installing Java and NetBeans**) included with these notes.

Installing the Downloadable Multimedia and Solution Files

If you purchased this directly from our website you received an email with a special and individualized internet download link where you could download the compressed Program Solution Files.   If you purchased this book through a 3rd Party Book Store like Amazon.com, the solutions files for this tutorial are included in a compressed ZIP file that is available for download directly from our website (after registration) at:

http://www.kidwaresoftware.com/javakids11-registration.html

Complete the online web form at the webpage above with your name, shipping address, email address, the exact title of this book, date of purchase, online or physical store name, and your order confirmation number from that store. After we receive all this information we will email you a download link for the multi-media and source code solution files associated with this book.

Warning: If you purchased this book "used" or "second hand" you are not licensed or entitled to download the Program Solution Files. However, you can purchase the Digital Download Version of this book at a highly discounted price which allows you access to the digital source code solutions files required for completing this tutorial.

Installing Java for Kids:

The code for **Java for Kids** are included in one or more ZIP files. Use your favorite 'unzipping' application to write all files to your computer. The course is included in the folder entitled **JavaKids**.   The **JK Code** folder includes all the Java projects developed during the course.

How To Take the Course:

Java for Kids is a self-paced course. The suggested approach is to do one class a week for ten weeks. Each week's class should require about 3 to 6 hours of your time to grasp the concepts completely. Prior to doing a particular week's work, open the class notes file for that week and print it out. Then, work through the notes at your own pace. Try to do each example as they are encountered in the notes. Work through the projects in Classes 3 through 10. If you need any help, all completed projects are included in the **JK Code** folder.

Forward By Alan Payne, A Computer Science Teacher

What is "Java for Kids" ... and how it works.

The tutorial "Java for Kids" is a highly organized and well-indexed set of lessons meant for children aged 10 and above. NetBeans, a specific IDE (Integrated Development Environment) is used throughout the lessons.

The tutorial provides the benefit of completed age-appropriate applications for children and fully documented projects from the teacher's or parents' point of view. That is, while full solutions are provided for the adults' (and child learner's) benefit, the projects are presented in an easy-to-follow set of lessons explaining the rational for the form layout, coding design and conventions, and specific code related to the problem. Child-learners may follow the tutorials at their own pace. Every bit of the lesson is remembered as it contributes to the final solution of a kid-friendly application. The finished product is the reward, but the student is fully engaged and enriched by the process. This kind of learning is often the focus of teacher training. Every computer science teacher knows what a great deal of preparation is required for projects to work for kids. With these tutorials, the research behind the projects is done by an author who understands the classroom and parenting experience. That is extremely rare!

Graduated Lessons for Every Project ... Lessons, examples, problems and projects. Graduated learning. Increasing and appropriate difficulty... Great results.

With these projects, there are lessons providing a comprehensive, kid-friendly background on the programming topics to be covered. Once understood, concepts are easily applicable to a variety of applications. Then, specific examples are drawn out so that a young learner can practice with the NetBeans environment. Then specific Java coding for the example is provided so that the student can see all the parts of the project come together for the finished product.

By presenting lessons in this graduated manner, students are fully engaged and appropriately challenged to become independent thinkers who can come up with their own project ideas and design their own forms and do their own coding. Once the process is learned, then student engagement is unlimited! I have seen literacy improve dramatically because students cannot get enough of what is being presented.

Indeed, lessons encourage *accelerated* learning - in the sense that they provide an enriched environment to learn computer science, but they also encourage *accelerating* learning because students cannot put the lessons away once they start! Computer science provides this unique opportunity to challenge students, and it is a great testament to the authors that they are successful in achieving such levels of engagement with consistency.

My History with Kidware Software products.

I have used Kidware's Programming Tutorials for over a decade to keep up my own learning. By using these lessons, I am able to spend time on things which will pay off in the classroom. I do not waste valuable time ensconced in language reference libraries for programming environments with help screens which can never be fully remembered! These projects are examples of how student projects should be as final products - thus, the pathway to learning is clear and immediate in every project.

If I want to use or expand upon some of the projects for student use, then I take advantage of site-license options. I have found it very straight forward to emphasize the fundamental computer science topics that form the basis of these projects when using them in the classroom. I can list some computer science topics which everyone will recognize, regardless of where they teach – topics which are covered expertly by these tutorials:

- Data Types and Ranges
- Scope of Variables
- Naming Conventions
- Decision Making
- Looping
- Language Functions – String, Date, Numerical
- Arrays
- Writing Your own Methods (subroutines) and more... it's all integrated into the tutorials.

In many States or Provinces, the above-listed topics would not be formally introduced in Middle School computer studies, but *would* form the basis of most projects undertaken by students. With these tutorials, you as the teacher or parent may choose where to put the emphasis, to be sure to cover the curricular expectations of your curriculum documents.

Any further Middle school computer programming topics derive directly from those listed above. Nothing is forgotten. All can be integrated with the lessons provided.

Quick learning curve for teachers! How teachers can use the product:

Having projects completed ahead of time can allow the teacher to present the design aspect of the project FIRST, and then have students do all of their learning in the context of what is required in the finished product. This is a much faster learning curve than if students designed all of their own projects from scratch. Lessons concentrating on a unified outcome for all makes for much more streamlined engagement for students (and that is what they need, in Middle school, and in grades 9 and 10), as they complete more projects within a short period of time and there is a context for everything that is learned.

With the Java for Kids tutorials, sound advice regarding generally accepted coding strategies ("build and test your code in stages", "learn input, output, formatting and data storage strategies for different data types" etc..) encourage independent thought processes among learners. After mastery, then it is much more likely that students can create their own problems and solutions from scratch. Students are ready to create their own summative projects for your computer science course – or just for fun, and they may think of projects for their other courses as well! And what could be wrong with asking the students' other teachers what they would like to see as project extensions?

Meets State and Provincial Curriculum Expectations and More

Different states and provinces have their own curriculum requirements for computer science. With the Kidware Software products, you have at your disposal a series of projects which will allow you to pick and choose from among those which best suit your curriculum needs. Students focus upon design stages and sound problem-solving techniques from a computer-science, problem-solving perspective. In doing so, they become independent problem-solvers, and will exceed the curricular requirements of Middle schools and Secondary schools everywhere.

Useable projects - Out of the box!

The specific projects covered in the *Java for Kids* tutorials are suitable for students aged 10 and above.

Specific kid-friendly tutorials and projects are found in the Contents document, and include:

- Sub-Sandwich Party
- Savings Calculator
- Guess the Number Game
- Lemonade Stand
- Card Wars
- Blackboard Fun (GUI, meaning it has a Graphical User Interface)
- Balloons (GUI)

And, from the final chapter,

- Computer Stopwatch
- Dice Rolling
- State Capitals
- Tic-Tac-Toe (GUI)
- Memory Game (GUI)
- Pong (GUI)

As you can see, there is a high degree of care taken so that projects are age-appropriate.

You as a parent or teacher can begin teaching the projects on the first day. It's easy for the adult to have done their own learning by starting with the solution files. Then, they will see how all of the parts of the lesson fall into place. Even a novice could make use of the accompanying lessons.

How to teach students to use the materials.

In a Middle school situation, parents or teachers might be tempted to spend considerable amounts of time at the projector or computer screen going over the tutorial – but the best strategy is to present the finished product first! That way, provided that the adult has covered the basic concepts listed in the table of contents first, the students will quickly grasp how to use the written lessons on their own. Lessons will be fun, and the pay-off for younger students is that there is always a finished product which is fun to use!

Highly organized reference materials for student self-study!

Materials already condense what is available from MSDN *(which tends to be written for adults)* and in a context and age-appropriate manner, so that younger students remember what they learn.

The time savings for parents, teachers and students is enormous as they need not sift through pages and pages of on-line help to find what they need.

How to mark the projects.

In a classroom environment, it is possible for teachers to mark student progress by asking questions during the various problem design and coding stages. In the early grades (grades 5 to 8) teachers can make their own oral, pictorial review or written pop quizzes easily from the reference material provided as a review strategy from day to day. I have found the requirement of completing projects (mastery) sufficient for gathering information about student progress - especially in the later grades (grades 10 to 12).

Lessons encourage your own programming extensions.

Once concepts are learned, it is difficult to NOT know what to do for your own projects. This is true even at the Middle school level – where applications can be made in as short as 10 minutes (a high-low guessing game, or a temperature conversion program, for example), or 1 period in length – if one wished to expand upon any of the projects using the "Other Things to Try" suggestions.

Having used Kidware Software tutorials for the past decade, I have to say that I could not have achieved the level of success which is now applied in the variety of many programming environments which are currently of considerable interest to kids! I thank Kidware Software and its authors for continuing to stand for what is right in the teaching methodologies which work with kids - even today's kids where competition for their attention is now so much an issue.

Regards,

Alan Payne
Computer Science Teacher
T.A. Blakelock High School
Oakville, Ontario

A Brief Word on the Course:

Though this course is entitled "Java for Kids," it is not necessarily written in a kid's vocabulary. When we say "kid" we mean a strong reader who loves math and tehnology and who is internally motivated to learn Java programming. Highly motivated kids who are at least 12 years of age will enjoy this tutorial. Computer programming has a detailed vocabulary of its own and, since adults developed it, the terminology tends to be very adult-like. In developing this course, we discussed how to address this problem and decided we would treat our kid readers like adults, since they are learning what is essentially an adult topic. We did not want to 'dumb-down' the course. You see this in some books. Throughout the course, we treat the kid reader as a mature person learning a new skill. The vocabulary is not that difficult, but there will be many times the kid reader will need help from a teacher or parent. We recommend that this tutorial be facilitated by an experienced Java developer or teacher.

1

Introduction

Preview

In this first chapter, we will do an overview of how to build a Java project with a graphical user interface (GUI). You'll get a description of what is needed to complete this course, review the steps of building a Java GUI project and delve into use of an Integrated Development environment (IDE).

Introducing Programming Games With Java

In these notes, we will use Java to build many fun game projects with graphic user interfaces (GUI). The games are non-violent and teach logical thinking skills. They are appropriate for kids of all ages (even adults). The projects you will build are (in increasing complexity):

> ➢ **Safecracker** – Decipher a secret combination using clues from the computer.
> ➢ **Tic Tac Toe** – The classic game – one of the first programmed by Bill Gates!
> ➢ **Match Game** – Find matching pairs of hidden photos – you use your own photos!
> ➢ **Pizza Delivery** – A business simulation where you manage a small pizza shop for a night.
> ➢ **Moon Landing** – Land a module on the surface of the moon.

These projects will teach many of the skills needed to be a successful game programmer. You will learn about timing, multi-player games, scoring, simulation techniques and animation.

Each project will be addressed in a single chapter. Complete step-by-step instructions covering every project detail will be provided. Before beginning the projects, however, we will review course requirements, Java project structure and our approach to building a Java GUI project.

Requirements for Programming Games With Java

To complete the games in this course, you should have a basic understanding of the Java language and its syntax, understand the structure of a Java application, how to write and use Java methods and how to compile, debug and run a Java GUI application. You should be familiar with the Swing control library. We briefly review each of these topics in the course, but it is a cursory review. If you haven't built Java GUI projects before, we suggest you try our Java tutorial **Learn Java GUI Applications**. See our website for details.

Regarding software, you need two things: (1) the Java Development Kit (JDK) and (2) a development environment. The JDK is a free download from the Java website. Nearly all programmers develop their Java programs using something called an **Integrated Development Environment** (IDE). There are many IDE's available for Java development purposes, some very elaborate, some very simple. In these notes, we use a free IDE called **NetBeans**. If you are comfortable with another IDE, by all means, use it. Complete download and installation instructions are provided in the Appendix (**Installing Java and NetBeans**) included with these notes.

Testing the Installation

We'll use **NetBeans** to load a Java project and to run a project. This will give us some assurance we have everything installed correctly. This will let us begin our study of the Java programming language.

Once installed, to start **NetBeans**, double-click the icon on your desktop. The NetBeans program should start. Several windows will appear on the screen.

Upon starting (after clearing the **Start Page**), my screen shows:

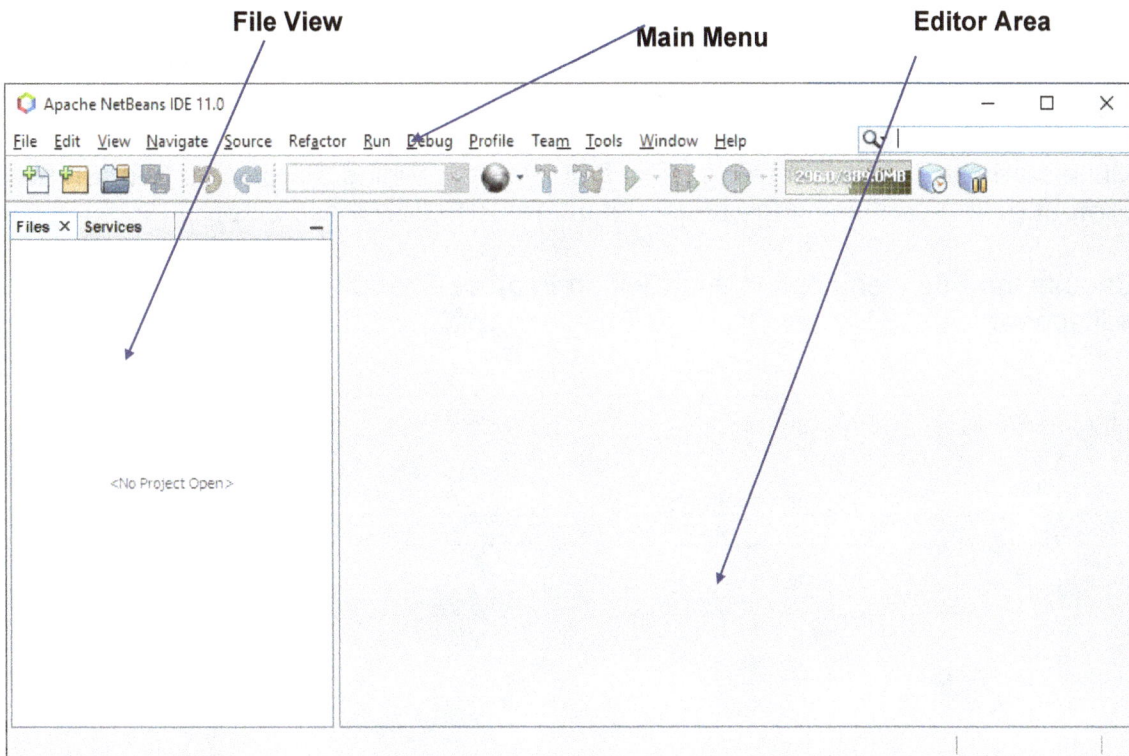

This screen displays the NetBeans **Integrated Development Environment** (**IDE**). We're going to use it to test our Java installation and see if we can get a program up and running. Note the location of the **file view** area, **editor** area and the **main menu**. The file view tells you what Java programs are available, the editor area is used to view the actual code and the main menu is used to control file access and file editing functions. It is also used to run the program.

What we want to do right now is **open a project**. Computer programs (applications) written using Java are referred to as **projects**. Projects include all the information in **files** we need for our computer program. Java projects are in **project groups**. Included with these notes are many Java projects you can open and use. Let's open one now.

Make sure **NetBeans** is running. The first step to opening a project is to **open the project group** containing the project of interest. Follow these steps:

Choose the **File** menu option and click on **Project Groups** option. This window will appear:

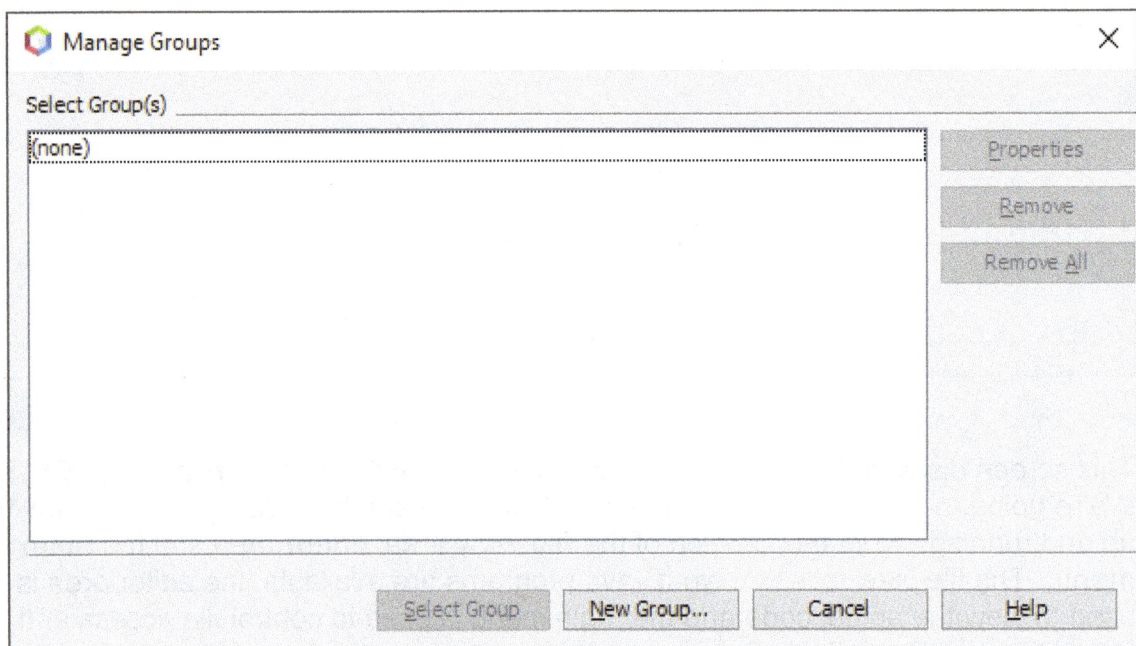

All projects in these notes are saved in a folder named
\KidGamesJava\KidGamesJava Projects**. Click **New Group, select **Folder of Projects**, **Browse** to that folder as shown. Click **Create Group**.

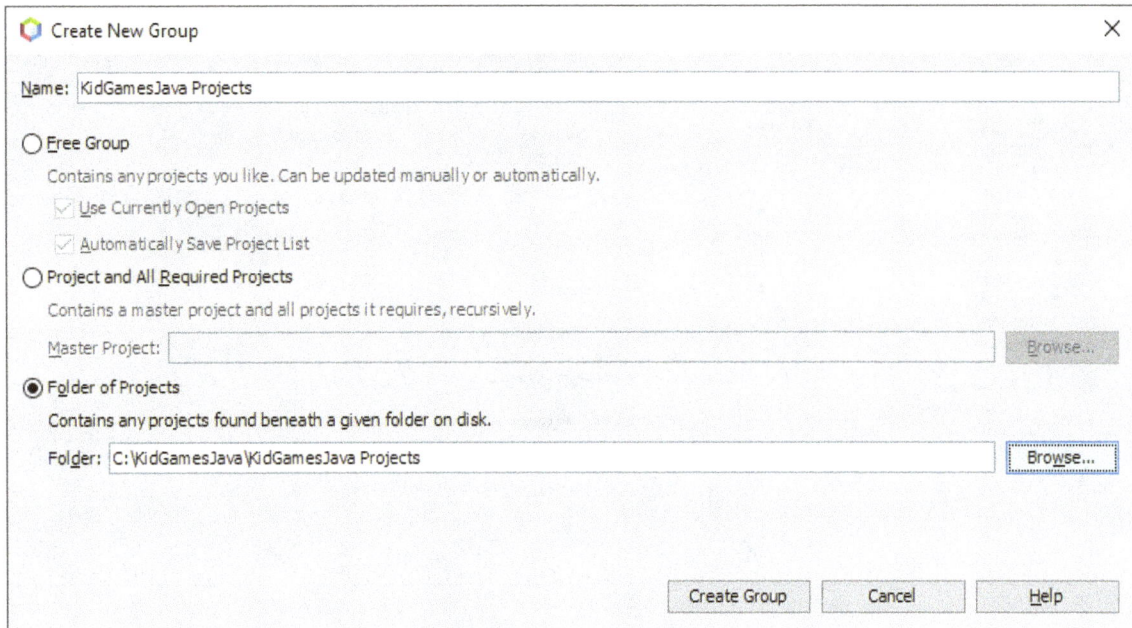

Create New Group   ✕

Name: KidGamesJava Projects

○ Free Group

    Contains any projects you like. Can be updated manually or automatically.

    ☑ Use Currently Open Projects

    ☑ Automatically Save Project List

○ Project and All Required Projects

    Contains a master project and all projects it requires, recursively.

    Master Project: [   ]   Browse...

◉ Folder of Projects

    Contains any projects found beneath a given folder on disk.

    Folder: [C:\KidGamesJava\KidGamesJava Projects   ]   Browse...

                      [Create Group]   [Cancel]   [Help]

There will be many projects listed in the file view area in NetBeans.

Find the project named **Welcome**. Expand the Welcome project node by clicking the plus sign. Open **Source Packages**, then **welcome**. Note there is one file named **Welcome.java**. If the file contents do not appear in the editor view area, double-click that file to open it.

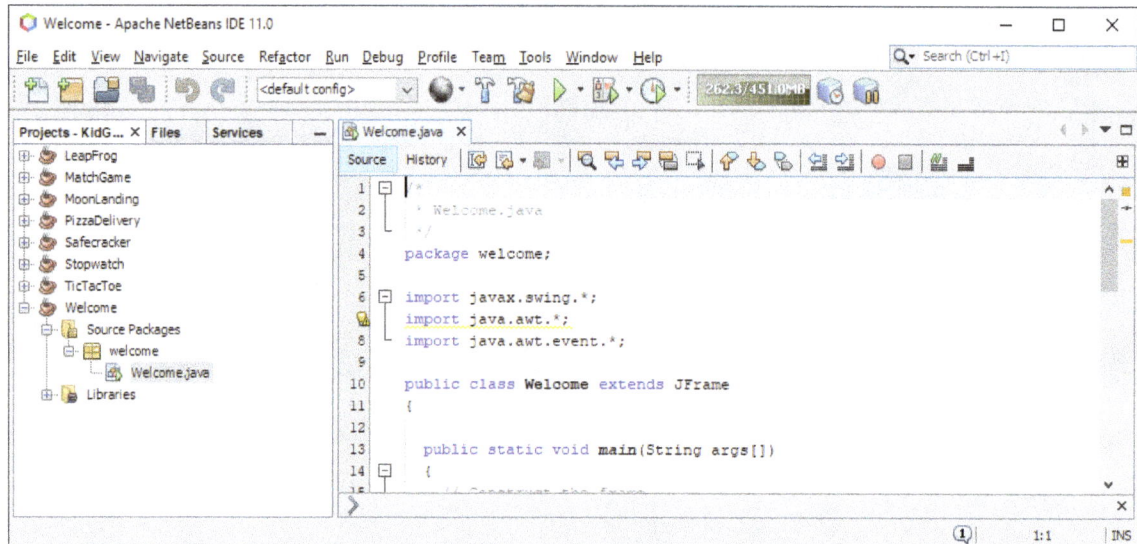

To run this project, choose **Run** from the menu and select **Run Project** (or alternately press <**F6**> on your keyboard or click the green **Run** arrow on the toolbar). An **Output** window should open and you should see the following Welcome message:

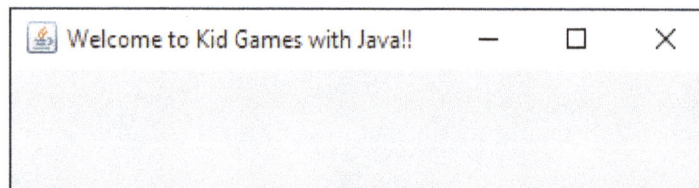

If you've gotten this far, everything has been installed correctly. If you don't see the Welcome message, something has not been installed correctly. You should probably go back and review all the steps involved with installing Java and NetBeans and make sure all steps were followed properly.

To stop this project, you click the boxed **X** in the upper right corner of the window. To stop NetBeans (don't do this right now, though):

 ➢ Select **File** in the main menu.
 ➢ Select **Exit** (at the end of the File menu).

NetBeans will close all open windows and you will be returned to the Windows desktop. Like with stopping a project, an alternate way to stop NetBeans is to click on the close button in the upper right hand corner of the main window.

Getting Help With a Java Program

As you build Java programs, there will be times when you get stuck. You will not know how to do a certain task using Java or you will receive error messages while compiling or running your program that you do not understand. What do you do in these cases? There are several options for getting help.

A highly recommended help method is to ask someone else if they know how to help you. Other Java programmers love to share their skills with people just learning the language. A second option is to look at one of the many Java books out there (you are reading one of them.

The **Java website** (http://www.oracle.com/technetwork/java/index.html) has a wealth of information that could possibly help. The problem with the website is that there is so much information, it can be overwhelming. There are tutorials, example, forums, … The Java **API** (application programming interface) documentation (on-line at the Sun website) is a great place to get help if you can wade through the difficult format. The Java website does offer search facilities. I often type in a few keywords and find topics that help in my pursuit of answers.

There are also hundreds of other Java websites out in WWW-land. Many websites offer forums where you can ask other Java programmers questions and get quick answers. A good way to find them is to use a search utility like **Google** or **Yahoo**. Again, type in a few keywords and many times you'll find the answer you are looking for.

As you progress as a Java programmer, you will develop your own methods of solving problems you encounter. One day, you'll be the person other programmers come to for their answers.

Structure of a Java Program

Java, like any language (computer or spoken), has a terminology all its own. Let's look at the structure of a Java program and learn some of this new terminology. A Java program (or project) is made up of a number of files. These files are called **classes**. Each of these files has Java code that performs some specific task(s). Each class file is saved with the file extension **.java**. The filename used to save a class must match the class name. One class in each project will contain something called the **main method**. Whenever you run a Java program, your computer will search for the **main** method to get things started. Hence, to run a program, you refer directly to the class containing this **main** method.

Let's see how this relates to **Welcome** project. This particular project has a single file named **Welcome.java**. Notice, as required, the name **Welcome** matches the class name seen in the code (public class **Welcome**). If no code is seen, simply double-click on the filename **Welcome.java**. If the project had other classes, they would be listed under the **Welcome** project folder. Notice too in the code area the word **main**. This is the **main** method we need in one of the project's classes.

That's really all we need to know about the structure of a Java program. Just remember a **program** (or project, we'll use both terms) is made up of files called **classes** that contain actual Java code. One class is the **main** class where everything starts. And, one more thing to remember is that projects are in **project groups**.

NetBeans uses a very specific directory structure for saving all of the files for a particular application. When you start a new project, it is placed in a specific folder in a specific project group. That folder will be used to store all files needed by the project. We'll take another look at the NetBeans file structure when we create our first project. You can stop NetBeans now, if you'd like.

Structure of a Java GUI Application

Let's look at the structure of a Java GUI application. In these notes, we tend to use the terms application, program and project synonymously. A GUI application consists of a **frame**, with associated **controls** and **code**. Pictorially, this is:

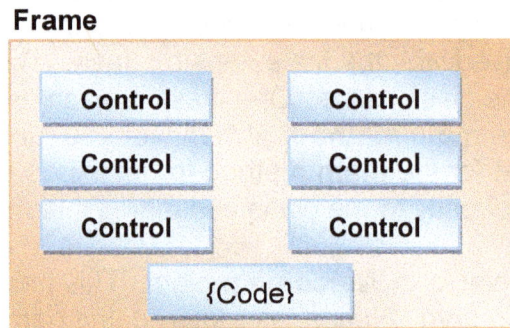

Frame

Control	Control
Control	Control
Control	Control

{Code}

Application (Project) is made up of:

> **Frame** - window that you create for user interface (also referred to as a **form**)
> **Controls** - Graphical features positioned on frame to allow user interaction (text boxes, labels, scroll bars, buttons, etc.) (frames and controls are **objects**.) Controls are briefly discussed next.
> **Properties** - Every characteristic of a frame or control is specified by a property. Example properties include names, captions, size, color, position, and contents. Java applies default properties. You can change properties when designing the application or even when an application is executing.
> **Methods** - Built-in procedures that can be invoked to impart some action to or change or determine a property of a particular object.
> **Event Methods** - **Code** related to some object or control. This is the code that is executed when a certain event occurs. In our applications, this code will be written in the Java language (covered in detail in Chapter 2 of these notes).
> **General Methods** - **Code** not related to objects. This code must be invoked or called in the application.

The application displayed above has a single form, or frame. As we progress in this course, we will build applications with multiple forms. The code for each form will usually be stored in its own file with a **.java** extension.

We will follow three steps in building a Java GUI application:

1. Create the **frame**.
2. Create the user **interface** by placing controls on the frame.
3. **Write code** for control event methods (and perhaps write other methods).

These same steps are followed whether you are building a very simple application or one involving many controls and many lines of code. Recall, the GUI applications we build will use the Java **Swing** and **AWT** (Abstract Windows Toolkit) components.

Each of these steps require us to write Java code, and sometimes lots of code. The event-driven nature of Java applications allows you to build your application in stages and test it at each stage. You can build one method, or part of a method, at a time and try it until it works as desired. This minimizes errors and gives you, the programmer, confidence as your application takes shape.

As you progress in your programming skills, always remember to take this sequential approach to building a Java application. Build a little, test a little, modify a little and test again. You'll quickly have a completed application.

Swing Controls

The controls we use in GUI applications will be **Swing** components. These components are defined in the **javax.swing** package and all have names beginning with **J**. Here, we briefly look at several controls to give you an idea of what they are, what they look like and what they do. You will see more Swing components in several of the projects.

JFrame control:

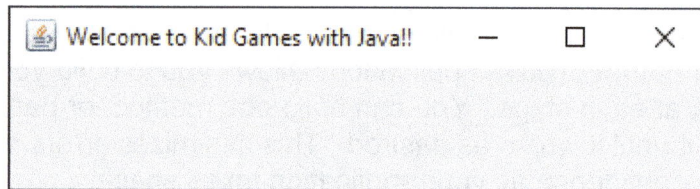

Welcome to Kid Games with Java!!

The frame control is the basic 'container' for other controls. It is the framework for a Java project. The **title** property establishes the caption information. Every application we build will start by building a **class** that **extends** the JFrame control.

JButton control:

JButton

The button control is used to start some action. The **text** property is used to establish the caption.

JLabel control:

JLabel

The label control allows placement of formatted text information on a frame (**text** property).

JTextField control:

```
JTextField
```

The text field control accepts a single line of typed information from the user (**text** property).

JTextArea control:

```
JTextArea
```

The text area control accepts multiple lines of scrollable typed information (**text** property).

JCheckBox control:

```
☐ JCheckBox
```

The check box control is used to provide a yes or no answer to a question.

JRadioButton control:

```
○ JRadioButton
```

The radio button control is used to select from a mutually exclusive group of options. You always work with a group of radio buttons.

JComboBox control:

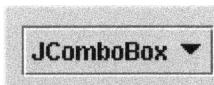

```
JComboBox ▼
```

Combo box controls are very common in GUI applications. Users can choose an item from a drop down list (states, countries, product).

JList control:

A list control is like a combo box with the list portion always visible. Multiple selections can be made with a list control.

JScroll control:

A scroll bar control is used to select from a range of values. The scroll bar is always "buddied" with another control related to the scroll bar selection.

JPanel control:

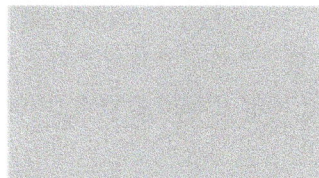

The panel control is a 'workhorse' in GUI applications – we will use many of them. It provides a convenient way of grouping related controls in a Java GUI application. And, the panel can also be used to host graphics.

Now, we'll start NetBeans and look at each step in the application development process, including using Swing controls. We will use a stopwatch application as an example.

Stopwatch - Creating a Java Project with NetBeans

We will now start building our first Java GUI application (a computer stopwatch). It might seem like a slow, long process. But, it has to be in order to cover all the necessary material. The more projects you build, the simpler this process will become. We begin by creating a new project and creating a frame. We will store all created projects in a separate project group named **Kid Games**. Create that folder now. If using Windows, you can use **Windows Explorer** or **My Computer** to that task.

If it's not already running, start **NetBeans**. The program group containing the **Welcome** project should still be there. We are going to remove this program group and create a new one. (You should only use the **KidGamesJava Projects** program group when you want to refer to the code included with the class notes. For all your projects, you will use your own program group).

Choose **File** from the main menu and select **Project Groups.** The **Manage Groups** window appears – choose **New Group** to see

---

Create New Group   ✕

Name: Kid Games

○ Free Group

    Contains any projects you like. Can be updated manually or automatically.

    ☑ Use Currently Open Projects

    ☑ Automatically Save Project List

○ Project and All Required Projects

    Contains a master project and all projects it requires, recursively.

    Master Project: [   ] Browse...

◉ Folder of Projects

    Contains any projects found beneath a given folder on disk.

    Folder: C:\Kid Games   Browse...

⚠ The list of projects currently open will be lost, unless you make a free group for them first.

             [Create Group]   [Cancel]   [Help]

As shown, click **Folder of Projects**, then **Browse** to your **Kid Games** folder. Click **Create Group**. The project group is displayed in the file view area (it is empty).

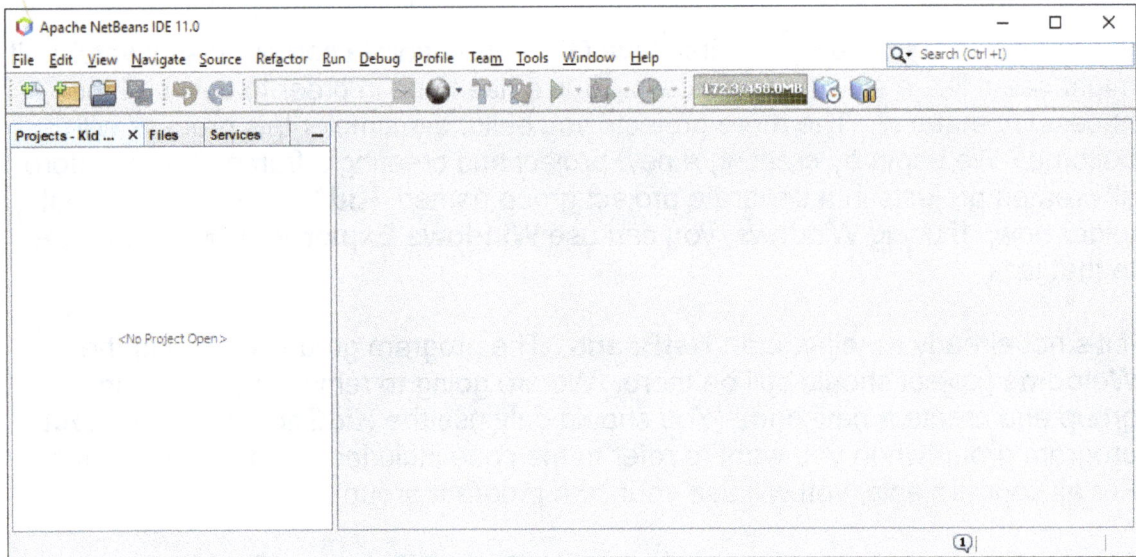

Now, we want to add a project to the project group. Pay close attention to these steps because you will repeat them every time you need to create a new Java project. Right-click the project group area in the file view and choose **New Project** to see:

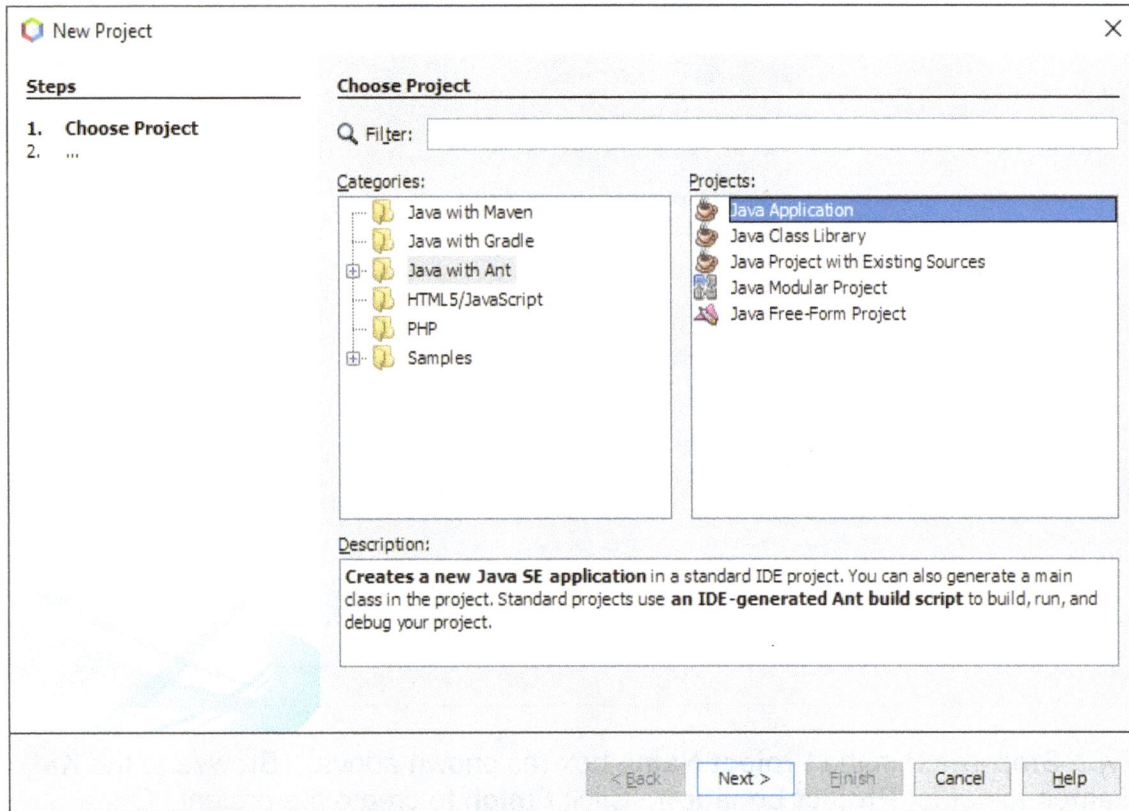

Select **Java with Ant** in **Categories** and **Java Application** in **Projects**. Click **Next**.

This window appears:

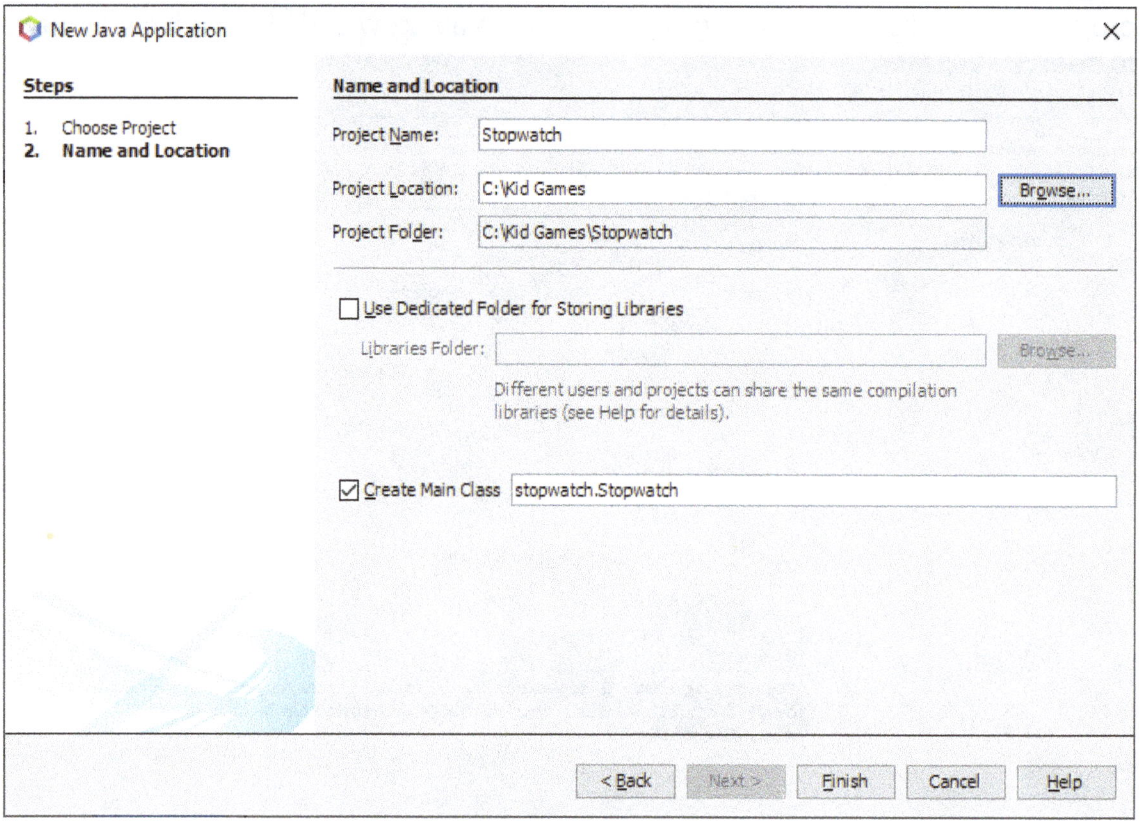

Type **Stopwatch** in the **Project Name** box (as shown above). Browse to the **Kid Games** folder for **Project Location**. Click **Finish** to create the project. Once created, click **Finish** in the resulting window.

The project group view window should now show a project (**Stopwatch**) in the project group (I've expanded all the folders):

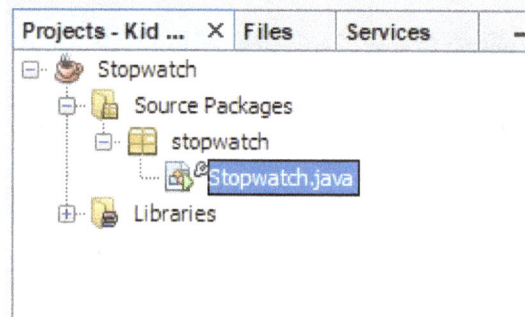

NetBeans uses a particular structure for each project you create. Under the Project main folder is a folder (**Source Packages**) with a **package** it names (in this case, **stopwatch**). In that package folder are the class files (**java** files) needed for your project. It creates a default class file (the one with your project name, **Stopwatch.java** in this case). You do not have to accept the default name (or default package name) – you can change it when creating the project, if desired. Just make sure there is a main class with the matching filename.

Double-click on the **Stopwatch.java** file to see a framework for the file in the editor view area:

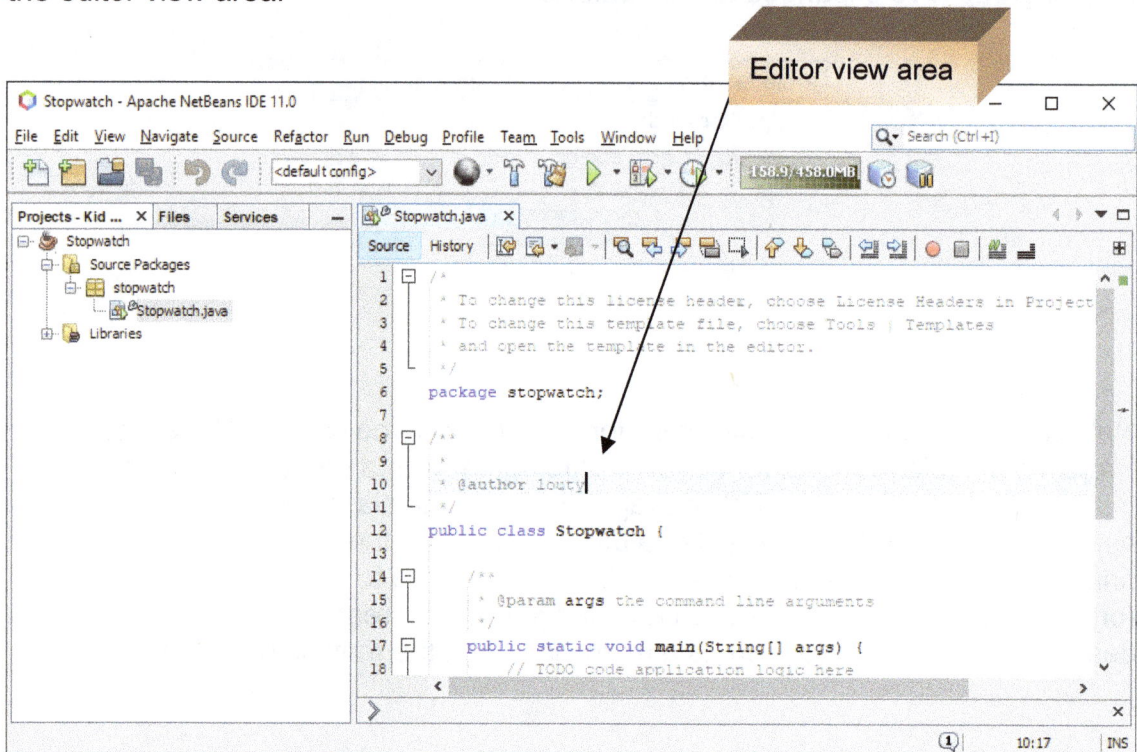

The default code created by NetBeans is:

```
/*
 * To change this license header, choose License Headers in
Project Properties.
 * To change this template file, choose Tools | Templates
 * and open the template in the editor.
 */

package stopwatch;

/**
 *
 * @author tyleel
 */
public class Stopwatch
{

  /**
   * @param args the command line arguments
   */
  public static void main(String[] args)
  {
    // TODO code application logic here
  }

}
```

We will always replace this default code with our own code (or you can modify it if you want to avoid a little typing). Delete the default code.

Recall, there are a few rules to pay attention to as you type Java code (we will go over these rules again in the next class):

> ➢ Java code requires perfection. All words must be spelled correctly.
> ➢ Java is case-sensitive, meaning upper and lower case letters are considered to be different characters. When typing code, make sure you use upper and lower case letters properly
> ➢ Java ignores any "**white space**" such as blanks. We will often use white space to make our code more readable.
> ➢ Curly **braces** are used for grouping. They mark the beginning and end of programming sections. Make sure your Java programs have an equal number of left and right braces. We call the section of code between matching braces a **block**.
> ➢ It is good coding practice to **indent** code within a block. This makes code easier to follow. NetBeans automatically indents code in blocks for you.

➢ Every Java statement will end with a semicolon. A **statement** is a program expression that generates some result. Note that not all Java expressions are statements (for example, the line defining the main method has no semicolon).

Stopwatch - Create a Frame

The first step in building a Java GUI application is creating a frame. At the same time we create the frame, we establish the basic framework for the entire program. The code (**Stopwatch.java**) that creates a frame within this basic framework is defined by a Java **class** of the same name:

```java
/*
 * Stopwatch
 */
package stopwatch;
import javax.swing.*;
import java.awt.*;
import java.awt.event.*;
public class Stopwatch extends JFrame
{

  public static void main(String args[])
  {
    // Construct the frame
    new Stopwatch().setVisible(true);
  }

  public Stopwatch()
  {
    // Frame constructor
    setTitle("Stopwatch Application");
    setSize(300, 100);
  }
}
```

Type one line at a time, paying close attention that you type everything as shown (use the rules).

As you type, notice after you type each left brace ({), the NetBeans editor adds a corresponding right brace (}) and automatically indents the next line. This follows the rule of indenting each code block. Like the braces, when you type a left parenthesis, a matching right parenthesis is added. Also, another thing to notice is that the editor uses different colors for different things in the code. Green text represents comments. Code is in black and keywords are in blue. This coloring sometimes helps you identify mistakes you may have made in typing.

When done typing, you should see:

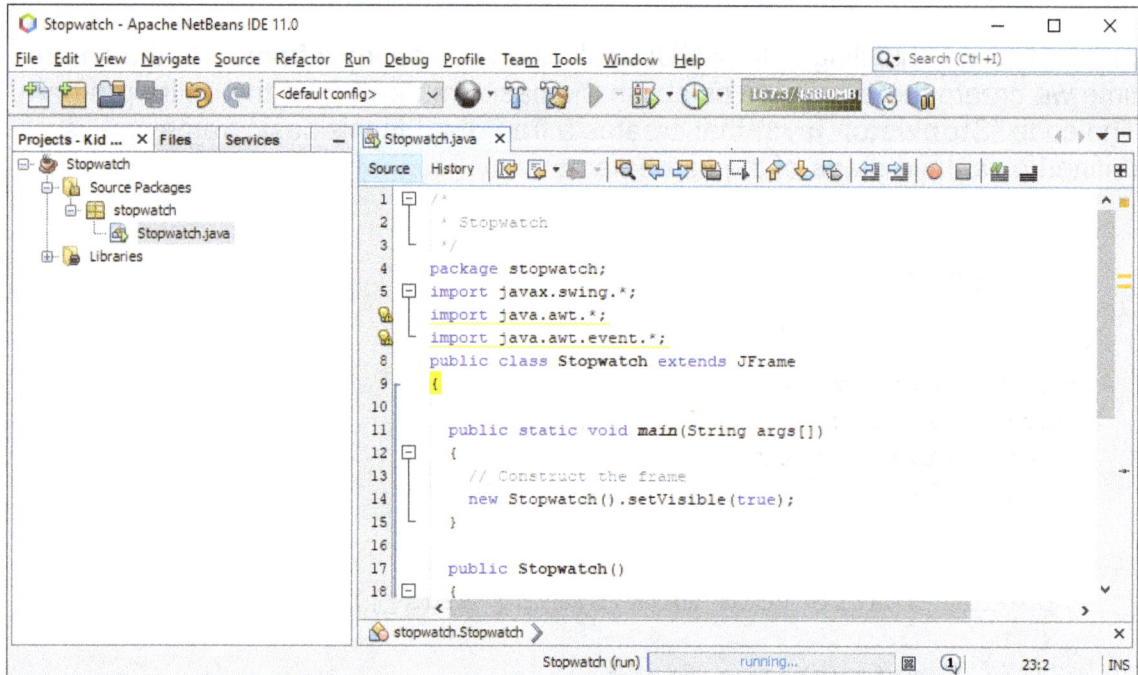

This code creates the frame by **extending** the Swing **JFrame** object, meaning it takes on all characteristics of such a frame. The code has a **constructor** for the **Stopwatch** object. You should see it executes two methods: one to set the title (**setTitle**) and one to set the size (**setSize**). The constructor is called in the **main method** to create the frame. We will use this same basic structure in every project built in this course. A constructor for the frame and all associated controls and control events will be built. The frame will be constructed in the main method.

Run the project (press <**F6**> or choose **Run**, then **Run Main Project** in the menu). You will see your first frame:

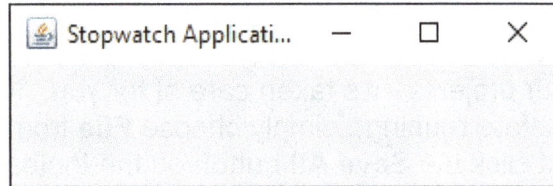

Saving Java Projects with NetBeans

Whenever you run a Java project, NetBeans automatically saves both the source files and the compiled code files for you. So, most of the time, you don't need to worry about saving your projects - it's taken care of for you. If you want to save code you are typing (before running), simply choose **File** from the main menu and click **Save All**. Or, just click the **Save All** button on the toolbar:

You do need to save the project group anytime you make a change, for example, if you add/delete files from a project or add/delete projects. This is also done using the **Save All** option.   If you try to exit NetBeans and have not saved projects, NetBeans will pop up dialog boxes to inform you of such and give you an opportunity to save files before exiting.

NetBeans and Java Files

So, how does all this information about program structure, files, compiling and running fit in with NetBeans, our development environment. We have seen that Java projects are grouped in project groups. And projects are made up of different folders and files.

Using My Computer or Windows Explorer (if using Windows), go to the folder containing the **Stopwatch** project you just built. There are many folders and files. In the **src/stopwatch** folder, you will see

Stopwatch.java

This is the source code that appears in the editor view area of NetBeans. In the **build/classes/stopwatch** folder is **Stopwatch.class**. This the compiled version of Stopwatch.java (this is the file needed by the Java virtual machine). Most of the other files are used by NetBeans used to keep track of what files make up the project.

Be aware that the only true Java files here are the ones with **.java** and **.class** extensions. The other files are created and modified by our particular development environment, NetBeans. If you want to share your Java program with a friend or move your Java program to another development environment, the only files you really need to transfer are the **.java** files. These files can be used by any Java programmer or programming environment to create a running program.

Create the User Interface

Having created a frame, we now create the user interface by "placing" controls in the frame. This placement simply involves several lines of logical Java code per control desired.

An object called a **layout manager** determines how controls are arranged in a frame. Some of the layout managers and their characteristics are:

FlowLayout	Places controls in successive rows, fitting as many as possible in a given row.
BorderLayout	Places controls against any of the four frame borders.
CardLayout	Places controls on top of each other like a deck of cards.
GridLayout	Places controls within a specified rectangular grid.
GridBagLayout	Places controls with a specified very flexible rectangular grid.
BoxLayout	Arranges controls either in a row or column.
SpringLayout	Arranges controls with positions defined by sprints and struts.

In this class, we will use the **GridBagLayout**. In our opinion, it offers the nicest interface appearance. As we work through the course, you will learn more and more capabilities of this manager. Study the other layout managers if you'd like.

A frame is actually made up of several different **panes**. Controls are placed in the **content pane** of the frame. The **GridBagLayout** manager divides the content pane into a grid of rows and columns:

	Column 0	Column 1	Column 2	Column 3	Column 4	Column 5
Row 0						
Row 1						
Row 2						
Row 3						
Row 4						
Row 5						

The top row is Row 0 and row number increases as you go down the grid. The left column is Column 0 and column number increases as you move to the right in the grid.

The **GridBagConstraints** object is used for control placement and positioning within the various grid elements. Controls are placed in this grid by referring to a particular column (**gridx** location) and row (**gridy** location). Rows and columns both start at zero (0). The grid does not have to be (but can be) sized. It automatically grows as controls are added. We will see that the GridBagLayout manager is very flexible. Controls can span more than one column/row and can be spaced (using **insets**) anywhere within a grid element.

A single line of code in our frame constructor is needed to specify we are using the GridBagLayout in the frame content pane:

```
getContentPane().setLayout(new GridBagLayout());
```

To place a control in the GridBagLayout grid, we follow these steps:

➤ **Declare** the control.
➤ **Create** (construct) the control.
➤ Establish desired control **properties**.
➤ **Add** the control to the layout content pane at the desired position.

In the projects we build, all controls will be declared with **class level scope**, meaning the controls and associated properties and methods will be available to any method in the class. Hence, all controls will be declared following the left opening brace of the class, before the first method.

We will also give **meaningful names** to controls. Accepted practice is to give the control a name beginning with some description of its purpose, then concatenating the type of control at the end of the name. Such a naming convention makes reading and writing your Java code much easier. Examples of names for button, label and text field controls (the ones we use with our stopwatch example):

```
startButton
stopButton
elapsedLabel
startTextField
```

To declare a control, you type the statement:

```
ControlType controlName;
```

In the Swing library, a button control is of type **JButton**. Hence, to declare our **startButton**, we use:

```
JButton startButton;
```

To create a previously declared control, use:

```
controlName = new ControlType();
```

For our start timing button, the Java code is:

```
startButton = new JButton();
```

The process of **declaring** and **creating** a control can be combined into a single line of code. We will always do this. For our example, the control declaration would be:

```
JButton startButton = new JButton();
```

The next step is to set any desired control properties. The format for such code is:

```
controlName.setPropertyName(PropertyValue);
```

Where **setPropertyName** is a method to set a desired property. When we discuss controls in detail, we will cover many of these methods. For now, we will just give them to you. As an example, to set the text appearing on the start timing button to "**Start Timing**," you would use:

```
startButton.setText("Start Timing");
```

The next step (yes, I know there are lots of steps) is to position the control in the **GridBagLayout** grid. First, we need to declare an object of type **GridBagConstraints** to allow positioning. Assuming this object is named **gridConstraints**, the declaration is:

```
GridBagConstraints gridConstraints = new
GridBagConstraints();
```

This statement is placed near the top of the frame constructor code.

Now, we use a three-step process to place each control in the grid. Decide on an x location (**desiredColumn**) and a y location (**desiredRow**). Then, use this code for a sample control named **controlName**):

```
gridConstraints.gridx = desiredColumn;
gridConstraints.gridy = desiredRow;
getContentPane().add(controlName, gridConstraints);
```

We will place the start timing button in the upper left corner of the grid, so we use:

```
gridConstraints.gridx = 0;
gridConstraints.gridy = 0;
getContentPane().add(startButton, gridConstraints);
```

To finalize placement of controls in the frame, execute a pack method:

```
pack();
```

This "packs" the grid layout onto the frame and makes the controls visible.

In summary, decide what controls you want to place in a frame. For each control, you need:

> ➢ a **declaration** and **creation** statement (class level)
> ➢ three lines of code for **placement** (in constructor method)

Once all controls are in the frame, you must execute a **pack** method to finalize placement. We'll clear this up (hopefully) with an example.

Stopwatch – Adding Controls

Continue with the **Stopwatch** example where we created a frame. We want to build this frame:

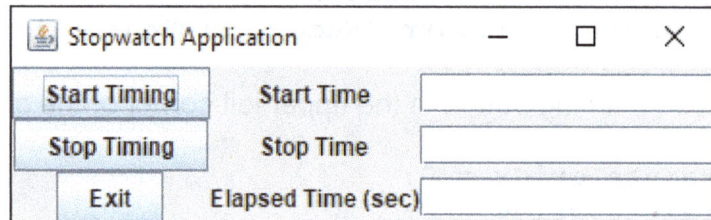

1. We will place nine controls in the frame: three buttons (**JButton** class), three labels (**JLabel** class) and three text fields (**JTextField** class). The buttons will start and stop the timing. The labels and text fields will be used to display the timing results: We will place these controls in a 3 x 3 array:

	gridx = 0	gridx = 1	gridx = 2
gridy = 0	**startButton**	**startLabel**	**startTextField**
gridy = 1	**stopButton**	**stopLabel**	**stopTextField**
gridy = 2	**exitButton**	**elapsedLabel**	**elapsedTextField**

Properties we will set in code:

startButton:
        text   Start Timing
        gridx   0
        gridy   0

stopButton:
        text   Stop Timing
        gridx   0
        gridy   1

exitButton:
        text   Exit
        gridx   0
        gridy   2

startLabel:
      text   Start Time
      gridx   1
      gridy   0

stopLabel:
      text   End Time
      gridx   1
      gridy   1

elapsedLabel:
      text   Elapsed Time (sec)
      gridx   1
      gridy   2

startTextField:
      text   [Blank]
      columns   15
      gridx   2
      gridy   0

stopTextField:
      text   [Blank]
      columns   15
      gridx   2
      gridy   1

elapsedTextField:
      text   [Blank]
      columns   15
      gridx   2
      gridy   2

2. First, type the code to declare the nine controls (recall these lines go after the opening left brace for the class definition):

```
JButton startButton = new JButton();
JButton stopButton = new JButton();
JButton exitButton = new JButton();
JLabel startLabel = new JLabel();
JLabel stopLabel = new JLabel();
JLabel elapsedLabel = new JLabel();;
JTextField startTextField = new JTextField();
JTextField stopTextField = new JTextField();
JTextField elapsedTextField = new JTextField();
```

3. Replace the **setSize** line in the constructor code with the line establishing the grid layout:

```
getContentPane().setLayout(new GridBagLayout());
```

4. The code to set properties of and place each of the nine controls (also goes in the constructor method):

```
GridBagConstraints gridConstraints = new
GridBagConstraints();
startButton.setText("Start Timing");
gridConstraints.gridx = 0;
gridConstraints.gridy = 0;
getContentPane().add(startButton, gridConstraints);

stopButton.setText("Stop Timing");
gridConstraints.gridx = 0;
gridConstraints.gridy = 1;
getContentPane().add(stopButton, gridConstraints);

exitButton.setText("Exit");
gridConstraints.gridx = 0;
gridConstraints.gridy = 2;
getContentPane().add(exitButton, gridConstraints);

startLabel.setText("Start Time");
gridConstraints.gridx = 1;
gridConstraints.gridy = 0;
getContentPane().add(startLabel, gridConstraints);

stopLabel.setText("Stop Time");
gridConstraints.gridx = 1;
gridConstraints.gridy = 1;
getContentPane().add(stopLabel, gridConstraints);
```

```
elapsedLabel.setText("Elapsed Time (sec)");
gridConstraints.gridx = 1;
gridConstraints.gridy = 2;
getContentPane().add(elapsedLabel, gridConstraints);

startTextField.setText("");
startTextField.setColumns(15);
gridConstraints.gridx = 2;
gridConstraints.gridy = 0;
getContentPane().add(startTextField, gridConstraints);

stopTextField.setText("");
stopTextField.setColumns(15);
gridConstraints.gridx = 2;
gridConstraints.gridy = 1;
getContentPane().add(stopTextField, gridConstraints);

elapsedTextField.setText("");
elapsedTextField.setColumns(15);
gridConstraints.gridx = 2;
gridConstraints.gridy = 2;
getContentPane().add(elapsedTextField, gridConstraints);

pack();
```

Notice how each control is located within the grid. Notice, too, how we set the number of columns for the text field controls. If we didn't do this, you wouldn't see the controls. I know there's lots of code here (and there will always be lots of code for GUI interfaces). You can choose to type the code or copy and paste from these notes into NetBeans. If you choose to type the code, notice much of the code is similar, so copy and paste operations come in very handy.

For reference, here is the complete **Stopwatch.java** code at this point (newly added code is shaded – the line setting the frame size has been deleted):

```
/*
 * Stopwatch.java
 */
package stopwatch;
import javax.swing.*;
import java.awt.*;
import java.awt.event.*;
public class Stopwatch extends JFrame
{
    // declare controls used
    JButton startButton = new JButton();
```

```java
  JButton stopButton = new JButton();
  JButton exitButton = new JButton();
  JLabel startLabel = new JLabel();
  JLabel stopLabel = new JLabel();
  JLabel elapsedLabel = new JLabel();;
  JTextField startTextField = new JTextField();
  JTextField stopTextField = new JTextField();
  JTextField elapsedTextField = new JTextField();
public static void main(String args[])
{
  // Construct frame
  new Stopwatch().setVisible(true);
}
public Stopwatch()
{
  // Frame constructor
  setTitle("Stopwatch Application");
  getContentPane().setLayout(new GridBagLayout());
  // add controls
  GridBagConstraints gridConstraints = new
GridBagConstraints();

  startButton.setText("Start Timing");
  gridConstraints.gridx = 0;
  gridConstraints.gridy = 0;
  getContentPane().add(startButton, gridConstraints);

  stopButton.setText("Stop Timing");
  gridConstraints.gridx = 0;
  gridConstraints.gridy = 1;
  getContentPane().add(stopButton, gridConstraints);

  exitButton.setText("Exit");
  gridConstraints.gridx = 0;
  gridConstraints.gridy = 2;
  getContentPane().add(exitButton, gridConstraints);

  startLabel.setText("Start Time");
  gridConstraints.gridx = 1;
  gridConstraints.gridy = 0;
  getContentPane().add(startLabel, new
GridBagConstraints());

  stopLabel.setText("Stop Time");
  gridConstraints.gridx = 1;
  gridConstraints.gridy = 1;
  getContentPane().add(stopLabel, gridConstraints);
```

```
        elapsedLabel.setText("Elapsed Time (sec)");
        gridConstraints.gridx = 1;
        gridConstraints.gridy = 2;
        getContentPane().add(elapsedLabel, gridConstraints);

        startTextField.setText("");
        startTextField.setColumns(15);
        gridConstraints.gridx = 2;
        gridConstraints.gridy = 0;
        getContentPane().add(startTextField, gridConstraints);

        stopTextField.setText("");
        stopTextField.setColumns(15);
        gridConstraints.gridx = 2;
        gridConstraints.gridy = 1;
        getContentPane().add(stopTextField, gridConstraints);

        elapsedTextField.setText("");
        elapsedTextField.setColumns(15);
        gridConstraints.gridx = 2;
        gridConstraints.gridy = 2;
        getContentPane().add(elapsedTextField, gridConstraints);

        pack();
    }
}
```

Run the project. The interface should look like this:

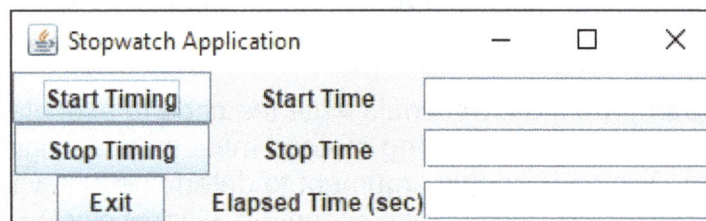

Notice how each control is located and sized in the layout of the frame. Save this project. We have no code to stop this project. To do this, select **Tools** in the NetBeans menu and choose **Stop Tool**.

Adding Event Methods

At this point, our interface has a finished look. What is missing is the code behind the control events. The next step in building a Java GUI application is to add this code. But, to add the code, we need a place to put it. We need to add event methods and their corresponding **listeners** to our application. There are two ways to add listeners, one for **AWT** objects and one for **Swing** objects. Listeners are added in the frame constructor code.

Java **event listeners** for AWT objects (primarily those for mouse and keyboard inputs) are implemented using something called **adapters** (also available from the AWT). The best way to see how to add such a listener is by example. In every project we build, we need to "listen" for the event when the user closes the window. The adapter that implements events for the frame (window) is called the **WindowAdapter** and it works with the **WindowListener**. There are certain window events that can be "listened for." In our case, we want to listen for the **windowClosing** event. The code that adds this event method to our application is:

```
addWindowListener(new WindowAdapter()
{
  public void windowClosing(WindowEvent e)
  {
        [Java code for window closing]
  }
});
```

This is actually one very long Java statement over several lines. It calls the **addWindowListener** method and, as an argument (all in parentheses), includes a **new** instance of a **WindowAdapter** event method (the **windowClosing** event). It's really not that hard to understand when you look at it, just very long!!

In the **windowClosing** method, we would write the code to execute when the window is closing. The **windowClosing** method must have a single argument (**WindowEvent e**). We can use this argument to determine just what event has occurred. In the stopwatch example, we assume a window closing event.

For Swing components, like the button, label and text field used here, event methods (**actionPerformed**) are added using the **ActionListener**. If the component is named controlName, the method is added using:

```
controlName.addActionListener(new ActionListener()
{
  public void actionPerformed(ActionEvent e)
  {
        [Java code to execute]
  }
});
```

Again, note this is just one long line of Java code. The method has a single argument (**ActionEvent e**), which tells us what particular event occurred (each control can respond to a number of events). For our stopwatch example, we will assume click events for the three button controls.

Note when we add a listener, we also need to add code for the event method. We could type the code at the same time we add the listener, but we take a different approach. When a method is added, the method code will be a single line of code invoking an "external" method where the actual code will reside. This separates the coding of method events from the code building the frame and makes for a "cleaner" code. For Swing components, we will name these external methods using a specific convention – the **control name** and **method name** will be concatenated into a new method name. Similar conventions are followed for AWT events. For our example above, the code adding such a method would be:

```
controlName.addActionListener(new ActionListener()
{
  public void actionPerformed(ActionEvent e)
  {
     controlNameActionPerformed(e);
  }
});
```

Once the method is added, the actual code is written in a method defined elsewhere in the program. The form for this method must be:

```
private void controlNameActionPerformed(ActionEvent e)
{
    [Java code to execute]
}
```

By separating the event method code from the code constructing the frame, editing, modifying and testing a Java GUI application is much easier. And, the naming convention selected makes it easier to find the event method associated with a particular control. The control event methods are usually placed after the constructor method.

Let's summarize the many steps to place a control (named **controlName** of type **controlType**) in a frame and add an event method:

➢ Declare and create the control (class level scope):

```
ControlType controlName = new ControlType();
```

➢ Position the control:

```
gridConstraints.gridx = desiredColumn;
gridConstraints.gridy = desiredRow;
getContentPane().add(controlName, gridConstraints);
```

(assumes a **gridConstraints** object has been created).

➢ Add the control listener:

```
controlName.addActionListener(new ActionListener()
{
  public void actionPerformed(ActionEvent e)
  {
      controlNameActionPerformed(e);
  }
});
```

➤ Write the control event method:

```
private void controlNameActionPerformed(ActionEvent e)
{
    [Java code to execute]
}
```

The first few times you add controls, this will seem to be a tedious process. As you develop more and more GUI applications, such additions will become second nature (and, you'll get very good at using the copy and paste features of NetBeans).

Stopwatch - Writing Code

All that's left to do is write code for the application. We write code for every event a response is needed for. In this application, there are three such events: clicking on each of the buttons.

1. Under the lines declaring the frame controls, declare three class level variables:

```
long startTime;
long stopTime;
double elapsedTime;
```

This establishes **startTime**, **endTime**, and **elapsedTime** as variables with class level scope.

2. In the frame constructor, add the **windowClosing** event method (every GUI project will need this code - place it after line establishing frame title):

```
addWindowListener(new WindowAdapter()
{
  public void windowClosing(WindowEvent e)
  {
    exitForm(e);
  }
});
```

And, add the corresponding event method code:

```
private void exitForm(WindowEvent e)
{
  System.exit(0);
}
```

This method is placed before the final right closing brace of the Stopwatch class (the normal place for methods). This one line of code tells the application to stop.

3. Let's create an **actionPerformed** event for the **startButton**. Add the listener (I place this after the code placing the control on the frame):

```
startButton.addActionListener(new ActionListener()
{
  public void actionPerformed(ActionEvent e)
  {
    startButtonActionPerformed(e);
  }
});
```

Then, add the event method after the constructor method:

```
private void startButtonActionPerformed(ActionEvent e)
{
  // click of start timing button
  startTime = System.currentTimeMillis();
  startTextField.setText(String.valueOf(startTime));
  stopTextField.setText("");
  elapsedTextField.setText("");
}
```

In this procedure, once the **Start Timing** button is clicked, we read the current time using a system function (in milliseconds, by the way) and put it in a text field using the **setText** method. We also blank out the other text fields. In the code above (and in all code in these notes), any line beginning with two slashes (//) is a comment. You decide whether you want to type these lines or not. They are not needed for proper application operation.

4. Now, add a listener for the **actionPerformed** event method for the **stopButton**:

```
stopButton.addActionListener(new ActionListener()
{
  public void actionPerformed(ActionEvent e)
  {
    stopButtonActionPerformed(e);
  }
});
```

Then, add this event method after the **startButtonActionPerformed** method:

```
private void stopButtonActionPerformed(ActionEvent e)
{
  // click of stop timing button
  stopTime = System.currentTimeMillis();
  stopTextField.setText(String.valueOf(stopTime));
  elapsedTime = (stopTime - startTime) / 1000.0;
  elapsedTextField.setText(String.valueOf(elapsedTime));
}
```

Here, when the **Stop Timing** button is clicked, we read the current time (**stopTime**), compute the elapsed time (in seconds), and put both values in their corresponding text field controls.

5. Finally, we need code in the **actionPerformed** method for the **exitButton** control. Add the listener:

```
exitButton.addActionListener(new ActionListener()
{
  public void actionPerformed(ActionEvent e)
  {
    exitButtonActionPerformed(e);
  }
});
```

Now, add the method:

```
private void exitButtonActionPerformed(ActionEvent e)
{
  System.exit(0);
}
```

This routine simply closes the frame once the **Exit** button is clicked.

For reference, the complete, final **Stopwatch.java** code is (newly added code is shaded):

```java
/*
 * Stopwatch.java
 */
package stopwatch;
import javax.swing.*;
import java.awt.*;
import java.awt.event.*;

public class Stopwatch extends JFrame
{

  // declare controls used
  JButton startButton = new JButton();
  JButton stopButton = new JButton();
  JButton exitButton = new JButton();
  JLabel startLabel = new JLabel();
  JLabel stopLabel = new JLabel();
  JLabel elapsedLabel = new JLabel();;
  JTextField startTextField = new JTextField();
  JTextField stopTextField = new JTextField();
  JTextField elapsedTextField = new JTextField();

  // declare class level variables
  long startTime;
  long stopTime;
  double elapsedTime;

  public static void main(String args[])
  {
    new Stopwatch().setVisible(true);
  }

  public Stopwatch()
  {
    // frame constructor
    setTitle("Stopwatch Application");
    addWindowListener(new WindowAdapter()
    {
      public void windowClosing(WindowEvent e)
      {
        exitForm(e);
      }
    });
    getContentPane().setLayout(new GridBagLayout());
```

```
    // add controls
    GridBagConstraints gridConstraints = new
GridBagConstraints();
    startButton.setText("Start Timing");
    gridConstraints.gridx = 0;
    gridConstraints.gridy = 0;
    getContentPane().add(startButton, gridConstraints);
    startButton.addActionListener(new ActionListener()
    {
      public void actionPerformed(ActionEvent e)
      {
        startButtonActionPerformed(e);
      }
    });

    stopButton.setText("Stop Timing");
    gridConstraints.gridx = 0;
    gridConstraints.gridy = 1;
    getContentPane().add(stopButton, gridConstraints);
    stopButton.addActionListener(new ActionListener()
    {
      public void actionPerformed(ActionEvent e)
      {
        stopButtonActionPerformed(e);
      }
    });

    exitButton.setText("Exit");
    gridConstraints.gridx = 0;
    gridConstraints.gridy = 2;
    getContentPane().add(exitButton, gridConstraints);
    exitButton.addActionListener(new ActionListener()
    {
      public void actionPerformed(ActionEvent e)
      {
        exitButtonActionPerformed(e);
      }
    });

    startLabel.setText("Start Time");
    gridConstraints.gridx = 1;
    gridConstraints.gridy = 0;
    getContentPane().add(startLabel, new
GridBagConstraints());

    stopLabel.setText("Stop Time");
```

```
    gridConstraints.gridx = 1;
    gridConstraints.gridy = 1;
    getContentPane().add(stopLabel, gridConstraints);

    elapsedLabel.setText("Elapsed Time (sec)");
    gridConstraints.gridx = 1;
    gridConstraints.gridy = 2;
    getContentPane().add(elapsedLabel, gridConstraints);

    startTextField.setText("");
    startTextField.setColumns(15);
    gridConstraints.gridx = 2;
    gridConstraints.gridy = 0;
    getContentPane().add(startTextField, new
GridBagConstraints());

    stopTextField.setText("");
    stopTextField.setColumns(15);
    gridConstraints.gridx = 2;
    gridConstraints.gridy = 1;
    getContentPane().add(stopTextField, gridConstraints);

    elapsedTextField.setText("");
    elapsedTextField.setColumns(15);
    gridConstraints.gridx = 2;
    gridConstraints.gridy = 2;
    getContentPane().add(elapsedTextField, gridConstraints);
    pack();
}
```

```
private void startButtonActionPerformed(ActionEvent e)
{
  // click of start timing button
  startTime = System.currentTimeMillis();
  startTextField.setText(String.valueOf(startTime));
  stopTextField.setText("");
  elapsedTextField.setText("");
}
```

```
private void stopButtonActionPerformed(ActionEvent e)
{
    // click of stop timing button
  stopTime = System.currentTimeMillis();
  stopTextField.setText(String.valueOf(stopTime));
  elapsedTime = (stopTime - startTime) / 1000.0;
  elapsedTextField.setText(String.valueOf(elapsedTime));
}
```

```
private void exitButtonActionPerformed(ActionEvent e)
{
   System.exit(0);
}

private void exitForm(WindowEvent e)
{
   System.exit(0);
}
```

```
}
```

Study this code to see where all the methods go.

Now, run the application (press <**F6**>). Try it out. If your application doesn't run, recheck to make sure the code is typed properly. Save your application. This is saved as **Stopwatch Project** in the **Projects** program group in **\KidGamesJava\KidGamesJava Projects** folder. Here's what I got when I tried:

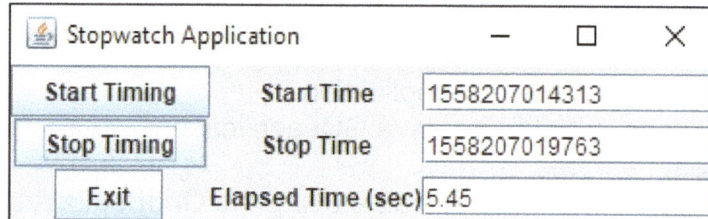

Stopwatch Application	— □ ✕	
Start Timing	Start Time	1558207014313
Stop Timing	Stop Time	1558207019763
Exit	Elapsed Time (sec)	5.45

If you have the time, here are some other things you may try with the **Stopwatch**. To make these changes will require research on your part (use web sites, other books, other programmers) to find answers. This is an important skill to have – how to improve existing applications by discovering new things. The solutions to the problems and exercises at the end of this class' notes can also shed some light on these challenges:

A. Try changing the frame background color.

B. Notice you can press the 'Stop Timing' button before the 'Start Timing' button. This shouldn't be so. Change the application so you can't do this. And make it such that you can't press the 'Start Timing' until 'Stop Timing' has been pressed. Hint: Look at the button **enabled** property.

C. Can you think of how you can continuously display the 'End Time' and 'Elapsed Time'? This is a little tricky because of the event-driven nature of Java. Look at the **Timer** class (do a little Java research). By setting the **delay** property of this class to **1000**, it will generate its own events every one second. Put code similar to that in the event method for the **stopButton** in the Timer class' actionPerformed method and see what happens. Also, see the exercise at the end of the class for help on this one.

Chapter Review

After completing this chapter, you should understand:

> ➤ The prerequisites for this course
> ➤ How to use NetBeans to build, run an application
> ➤ The structure of a Java GUI application
> ➤ The three steps in building a Java GUI application
> ➤ How to create a frame
> ➤ How to place a control on the frame using the GridBagLayout
> ➤ Proper control naming convention
> ➤ How to add event listeners and event methods
> ➤ How to add code to event methods

2

Safecracker Project

Review and Preview

We've completed our review of building Java GUI projects using NetBeans (or any IDE you choose). We now start building some kid games. For each project built, we provide step-by-step instructions in designing and building the form's graphic interface and detailed explanations of the code behind the projects.

The first project we build is a **Safecracker** that asks you to guess a secret combination of numbers using clues from the computer.

Safecracker Project Preview

In this chapter, we will build a **Safecracker** game. A bank safe is locked and can only be opened if you enter the proper combination. The combination can be 2 to 4 non-repeating digits (digits range from 1 to 9). After each guess, you are told how many digits are correct and how many are in the correct location. Based on this information, you make another guess. You continue guessing until you get the correct combination or stop the game.

The finished project is saved as **Safecracker** in the **\KidGamesJava\KidGamesJava Projects** project group. Start NetBeans (or your IDE). Open the specified project group. Make **Safecracker** the selected project. Run the project. You will see:

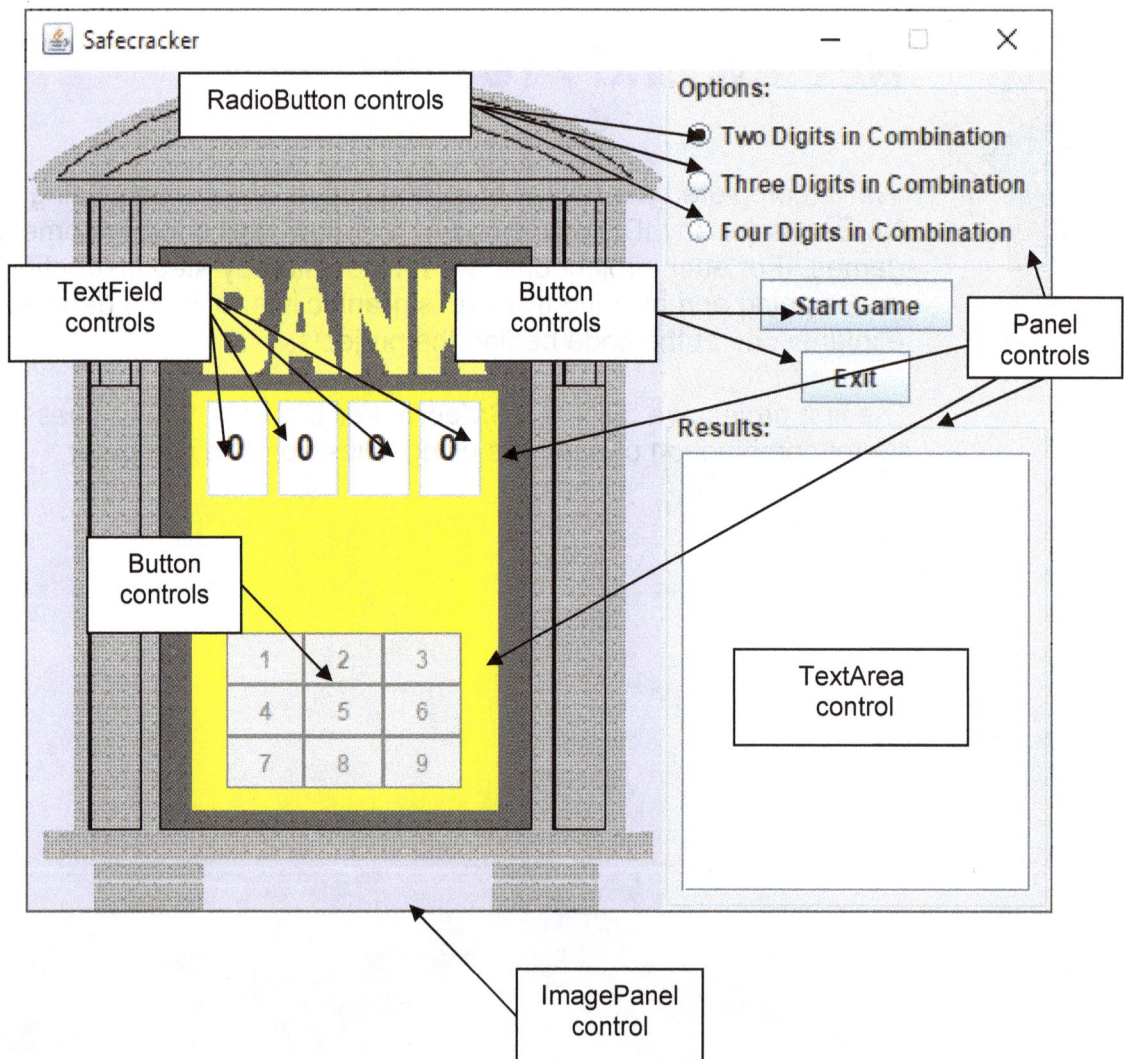

On the left is an image panel control displaying the bank safe (we will show you how to create such a control – it is a panel that hosts an image). A panel control holds four text field controls to display the entered combination and another panel contains nine button controls that form a keypad to enter the combination. On the right are two panel controls and two button controls. The first panel holds three radio buttons to select game options. The second panel holds a scrollable text area control to display the results of a guess. The two buttons are used to start and stop the game and to exit the program.

The game initially appears in its 'stopped' state, waiting for you to choose game options (how many digits in the combination and whether digits can repeat). The bank vault is disabled – no combination can be entered. I've selected 3 digits in the combination:

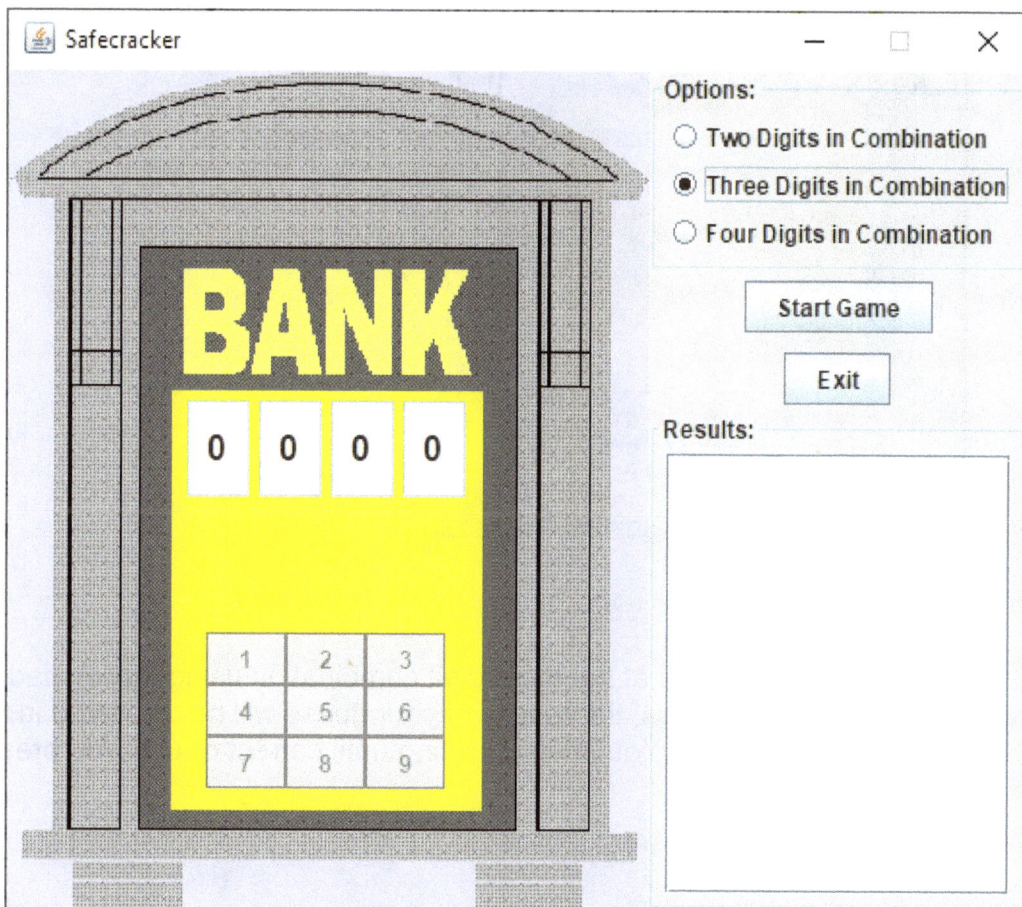

Click the **Start Game** button to start playing. Its caption will change (now reading **Stop Game**) and the **Options** panel and **Exit** button will become disabled. The panel control in the vault is now enabled showing a text field control for each digit in the combination and activating the 9 button keypad. We call this the 'playing' state:

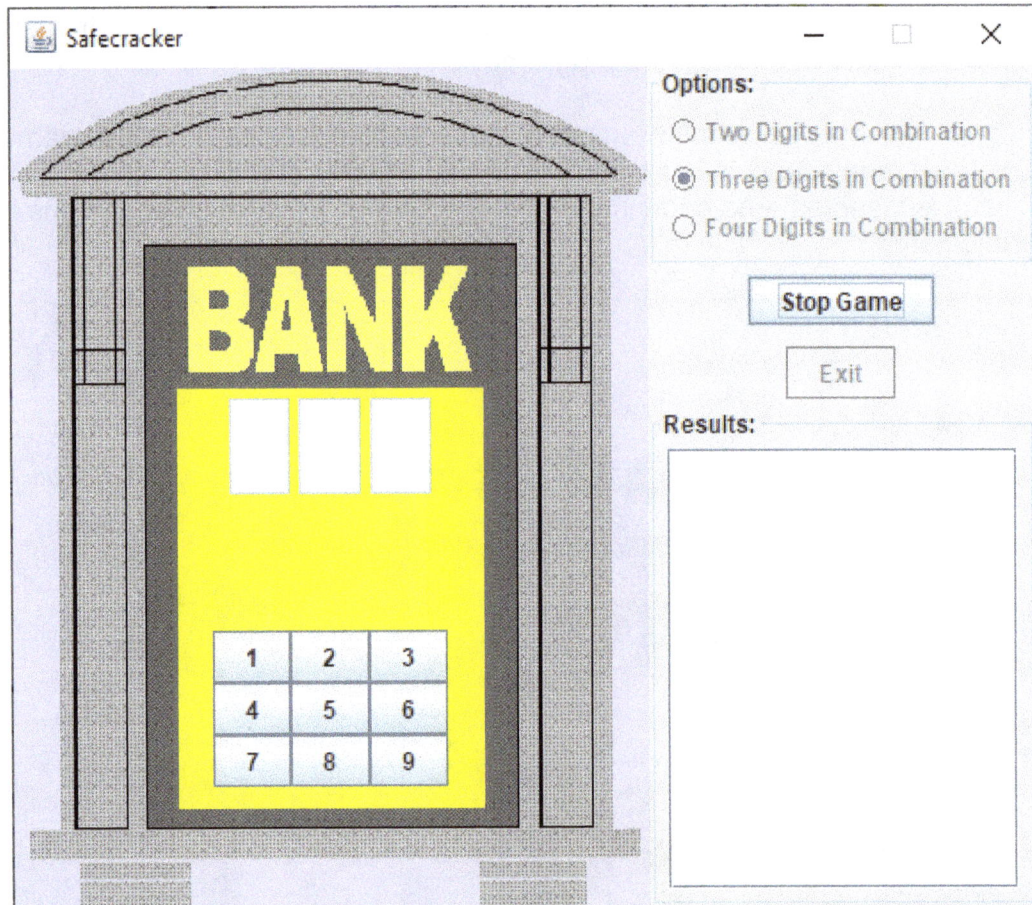

In this state, you make a guess at the three digit combination using the keypad in the bank safe. After each guess, the results of your guess will be displayed in the text box in the **Results** panel. You keep guessing until correct or until you press **Stop Game**.

Enter a guess; I entered 123:

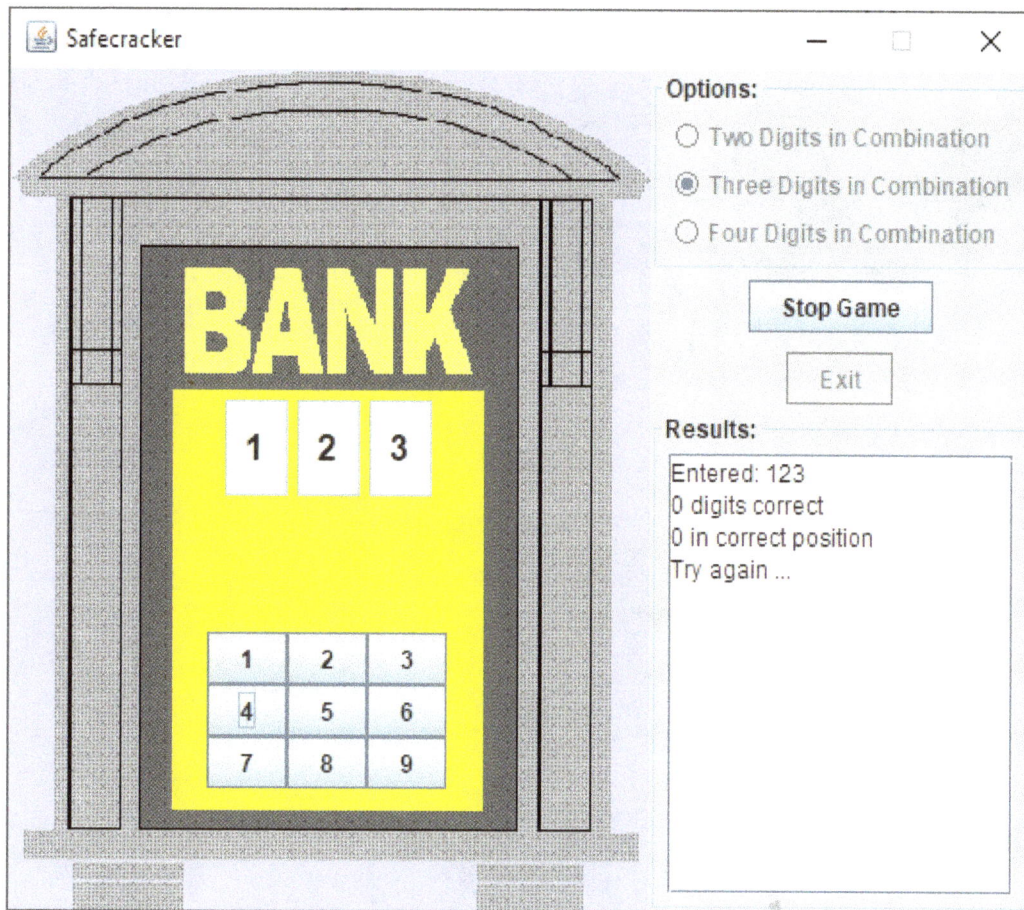

As a guess is entered, notice several things. Once a button is pressed, the corresponding digit appears in the proper text field. Also, the pressed button is disabled since the digits can't repeat. Once three buttons are pressed, the results are shown. You are told how many digits in your guess were correct and how many were in the correct position. If incorrect, you will hear an 'uh-oh' sound. Obviously, my guess was not very good!

When I try 456, I see:

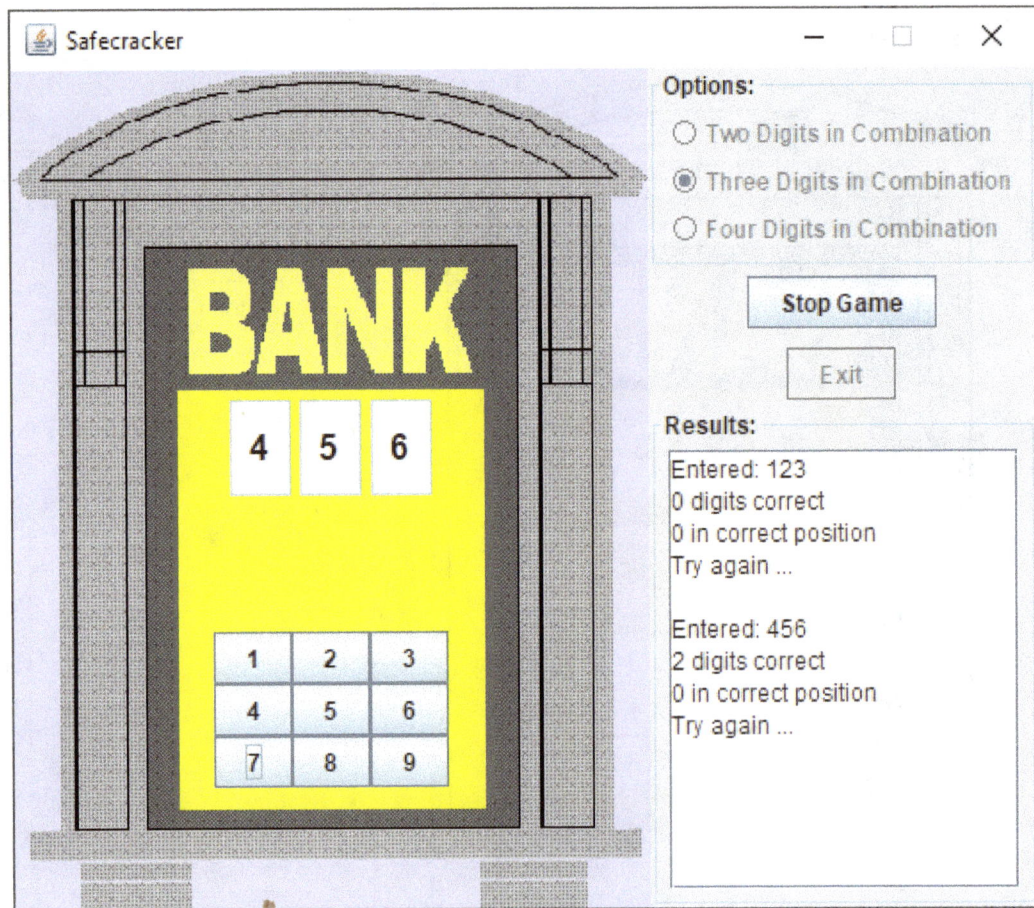

Much better. Now, I know that the combination has either a 4 and a 5, a 4 and a 6, or a 5 and a 6. I also know none of the digits are in their proper position.

What if I try 745 (I assumed the 4 and 5 should stay and shifted them over)

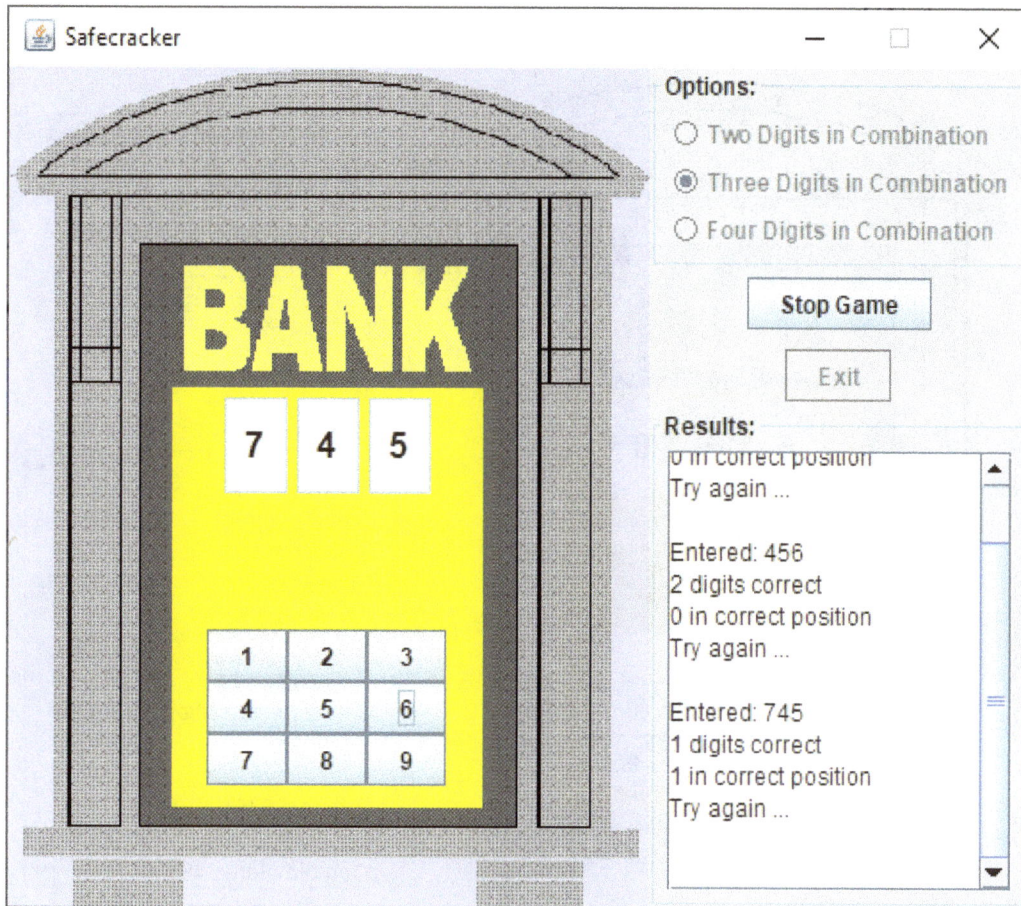

Since only 1 digit is now correct, I know the 6 is definitely in the combination. I think you're starting to see how the game works.

I continued playing until finally, after entering 648:

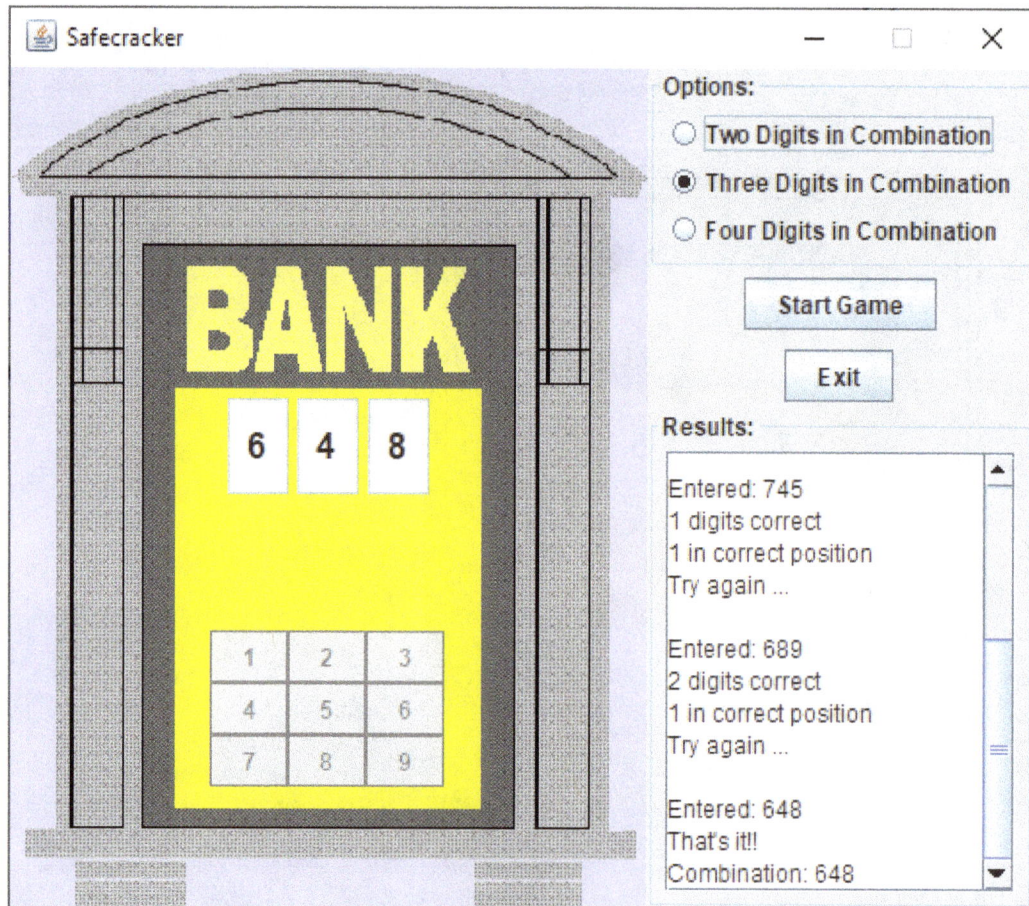

The correct combination was entered! A little celebratory sound is heard. The game returns to its stopped state to allow another game or to stop the program.

Continue playing the game to understand its operation. Click **Exit** when you're done to stop the game. Open the code file and skim over the code, if you like.

You will now build this project in stages. As you build Java projects, we always recommend taking a slow, step-by-step process. It minimizes programming errors and helps build your confidence as things come together in a complete project. This is the approach we will take on all projects in these notes.

We address **frame design**. We discuss the controls needed to build the frame, establish initial control properties and discuss how to change the state of the controls. And, we address **code design**. We discuss how to form the secret combination, how to gather user input and how to check an entered combination. We also discuss how to have several events invoke a single method. Before diving into this first project, however, we review some of the 'tricks' in using the grid bag layout manager.

Frame Design – GridBagLayout Manager

We use the **GridBagLayout** manager to set up our Java GUI projects (you can, of course, choose to use any layout manager you want). Recall, with this manager, a grid is used to place controls:

	gridx = 0	gridx = 1	gridx = 2	gridx = 3	gridx = 4
gridy = 0					
gridy = 1					
gridy = 2					
gridy = 3					
gridy = 4					
gridy = 5					

The **GridBagConstraints** object is used for control placement and positioning within the various grid elements. Controls are placed in this grid by referring to a particular column (**gridx** location) and row (**gridy** location). We have seen that the grid (and frame) automatically grows as controls are added. Column widths are set by the "widest" control in a particular column. And, row heights are set by the "tallest" control in a particular row.

There are other variables associated with **GridBagConstraints** that can be used to adjust control size and, hence, associated column, row, and frame size. A control can occupy more than one column or row. The number of columns spanned by a control is set with the **gridwidth** variable; the number of rows spanned is set with the **gridheight** variable. By default, a control fills one row and one column. If we have a GridBagConstraints object named **gridConstraints**, a control will occupy two rows and three columns, starting in the second column (gridx = 1) and fourth row (gridy = 3), with this code:

```
gridConstraints.gridx = 1;
gridConstraints.gridy = 3;
gridConstraints.gridheight = 2;
gridConstraints.gridwidth = 3;
```

In our example grid, this control would be placed like this:

	gridx = 0	gridx = 1	gridx = 2	gridx = 3	gridx = 4
gridy = 0					
gridy = 1					
gridy = 2					
gridy = 3					
gridy = 4		**Control goes here**			
gridy = 5					

A particular control may completely fill its region or may not. If the control is smaller than its allocated region, its dimensions may be adjusted to fill the region – use the **fill** variable. There are four values:

GridBagConstraints.NONE	Control is not resized (default value)
GridBagConstraints.HORIZONTAL	Control width fills display area.
GridBagConstraints.VERTICAL	Control height fills display area.
GridBagConstraints.BOTH	Control fills entire display area.

With our example **gridConstraints** object, a control will grow to fill the region width using:

```
gridConstraints.fill = GridBagConstraints.HORIZONTAL;
```

This control would look like this in its grid region:

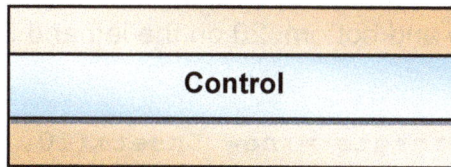

Control

Smaller changes in control size can be made using the **ipadx** and **ipady** variables. These determine how much a control size is to be increased beyond its minimum size (in each direction). To add five pixels to the width and height of a control using our **gridConstraints** example:

```
gridConstraints.ipadx = 5;
gridConstraints.ipady = 5;
```

If you choose not to expand a control to fill its area, its position within its allocated area is set with the **anchor** variable. There are nine possible values:

GridBagConstraints.NORTH	Control is centered at top
GridBagConstraints.NORTHEAST	Control is in upper right corner
GridBagConstraints.EAST	Control is at right, centered vertically
GridBagConstraints.SOUTHEAST	Control is in lower right corner
GridBagConstraints.SOUTH	Control is centered at bottom
GridBagConstraints.SOUTHWEST	Control is in lower left corner
GridBagConstraints.WEST	Control is at left, centered vertically
GridBagConstraints.NORTHWEST	Control is in upper left corner
GridBagConstraints.CENTER	Control is centered horizontally and vertically

To center a control (in both directions) in its display area, use:

```
gridConstraints.anchor = GridBagConstraints.CENTER;
```

This control would look like this in its grid region:

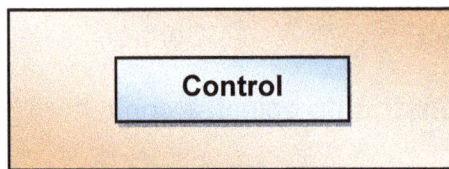

If a control completely fills its allocated display area, a border region (free space) can be established around the control using the **Insets** object. Four values are used to define the **top**, **left**, **bottom** and **right** side margins from the side of the display area. The default is **Insets(0, 0, 0, 0)**. With our example, if we want 10 pixels of space at the top and bottom, 20 on the left and 30 on the right, we would use:

```
gridConstraints.insets = new Insets(10, 20, 10, 30);
```

This control would look something like this in its grid region:

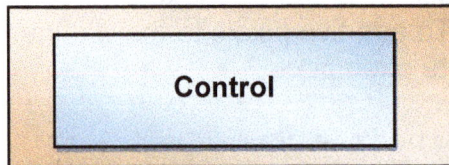

Once the **gridConstraints** are established for a control, it is added to the frame's content pane using the add method. If the control is **myControl**, the code syntax is:

```
getContentPane().add(myControl, gridConstraints);
```

Many times, we add controls to a panel control (with its own **GridBayLayout** manager) within a frame. If the panel is named **myPanel**, the code to add **myControl** is:

```
myPanel.add(myControl, gridConstraints);
```

I think you see the flexibility available with the **GridBagLayout** manager. You are encouraged to learn these ideas and use them to "beautify" your GUI interfaces. Remember to establish all grid constraint values before adding a control to the grid.

Building an interface is an "art," not a science. You will see the process involves lots of trial and error and adjustments. And sometimes, you get results you would never expect – components may not appear as you wish or may not appear at all! The bottom line is – once all adjustments are made, your completed frame size is established. Let's look at one final task - how to center the frame in the screen.

First, to place a frame (**width** by **height** in size) at a horizontal position **left** and vertical position **top**, we use the **setBounds** method:

```
setBounds(left, top, width, height);
```

All the dimensions are **int** types and measured in pixels. To center a frame in the computer screen, we need to know find **left** and **top**.

Programming Games With Java

To find the centering position, we need two things: the dimensions of the frame (use **getWidth** and **getHeight** methods) and the dimensions of the screen. The dimensions of the screen are held in the frame's '**toolkit**'. A **Dimension** object holds the information we need. To retrieve this object, use:

```
Dimension screenSize =
Toolkit.getDefaultToolkit().getScreenSize();
```

With this, **screenSize.width** holds the screen width and **screenSize.height** holds the screen height. So, the code to center the frame using **setBounds** is:

```
setBounds((int) (0.5 * (screenSize.width - getWidth())),
(int) (0.5 * (screenSize.height - getHeight())),
getWidth(), getHeight());
```

This code needs to be after the **pack** method in the code establishing the frame, so that proper frame size is used. We'll use this centering code in every application built in the remainder of this course. Any initializations for a project will be placed after this line in the frame constructor.

Safecracker Frame Design

We can begin building the **Safecracker** game project. Before starting, make sure you have established a project group on your computer for building Java projects. Always save your projects in this project group. Do not save them in the project group used in these notes (**\KidGamesJava\KidGamesJava Projects** folder). Leave this project group intact so you can always reference the finished projects, if needed.

Let's build the frame. Start a new project in your Java project group – name it **Safecracker**. Delete default code in file named **Safecracker.java**. Once started, we suggest you immediately save the project with the name you chose. This sets up the folder and file structure needed for your project. Build the basic frame with these properties:

Safecracker Frame:
    title   Safecracker
    resizable   false

The code is:

```
/*
 * Safecracker.java
 */
package safecracker;
import javax.swing.*;
import java.awt.*;
import java.awt.event.*;

public class Safecracker extends JFrame
{

  public static void main(String args[])
  {
    // create frame
    new Safecracker().setVisible(true);
  }

  public Safecracker()
  {
    // frame constructor
    setTitle("Safecracker");
    setResizable(false);
    addWindowListener(new WindowAdapter()
    {
      public void windowClosing(WindowEvent evt)
```

```
            {
                exitForm(evt);
            }
        });
        getContentPane().setLayout(new GridBagLayout());
        GridBagConstraints gridConstraints;

        pack();
        Dimension screenSize =
Toolkit.getDefaultToolkit().getScreenSize();
        setBounds((int) (0.5 * (screenSize.width -
getWidth())), (int) (0.5 * (screenSize.height -
getHeight())), getWidth(), getHeight());
    }

    private void exitForm(WindowEvent evt)
    {
        System.exit(0);
    }
}
```

We use similar code to start each project. It builds the frame, sets up the layout manager and includes code to exit the application. Run the code to make sure the frame (at least, what there is of it at this point) appears and is centered on the screen:

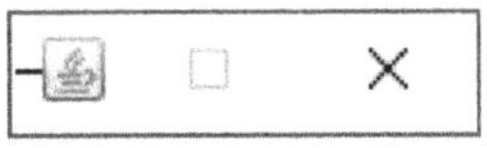

Let's populate our frame with other controls. All code for creating the frame and placing controls (except declarations) goes in the **Safecracker** constructor.

We start by putting four panel controls on the frame. The **GridBagLayout** is:

	gridx = 0	gridx = 1
gridy = 0		optionsPanel
gridy = 1	safePanel	buttonsPanel
gridy = 2		resultsPanel

We use lots of panels in building Java GUI projects. They are useful for sizing the frames and can be used to hold other controls. The **safePanel** will hold the safe graphic, the combination display and the keypad for combination entry. The **optionsPanel** will hold the radio buttons used to specify the number of digits in the combination. The **buttonsPanel** will hold the two button controls. The **resultsPanel** holds the text area displaying the results after entry of a combination. Each panel will be built individually We start with the **safePanel**.

The **safePanel** is an **ImagePanel** control, which is an extended version of the **JPanel** control. We want to use a background image (the safe) in the panel, but the JPanel control does not have an image property. We can get around this by using the object-oriented nature of Java by extending the JPanel control with a new **img** property. The code that does this is (found on the Internet by the way):

```
class ImagePanel extends JPanel
{
  private Image img;
  public ImagePanel(Image img)
  {
   this.img = img;
  }
  public void paintComponent(Graphics g)
  {
    g.drawImage(img, 0, 0, null);
  }
}
```

Add this code after the class describing the Safecracker project.

Let's construct the **safePanel** control (with graphic) and put it in the frame. Use these properties:

    safePanel (ImagePanel):

img	bank.gif (included in the **\KidGamesJava\KidGamesJava Projects\Safecracker** folder)
size	330, 420

Make sure to copy the bank.gif graphic file into the folder you use to build your project. The panel size matches the size of the graphic.

Declare and create the panel (goes after the class definition):

```
ImagePanel safePanel = new ImagePanel(new
ImageIcon("bank.gif").getImage());
```

The code to set the properties and place the panel in the frame (goes in the **Safecracker** constructor after the layout manager is defined):

```
safePanel.setPreferredSize(new Dimension(330, 420));
safePanel.setLayout(new GridBagLayout());
gridConstraints = new GridBagConstraints();
gridConstraints.gridx = 0;
gridConstraints.gridy = 0;
gridConstraints.gridheight = 3;
getContentPane().add(safePanel, gridConstraints);
```

As a reminder of where particular code segments go, here is the complete code at this point (additions are shaded):

```
/*
 * Safecracker.java
 */
package safecracker;
import javax.swing.*;
import java.awt.*;
import java.awt.event.*;

public class Safecracker extends JFrame
{
  ImagePanel safePanel = new ImagePanel(new
ImageIcon("bank.gif").getImage());
  public static void main(String args[])
  {
    // create frame
    new Safecracker().setVisible(true);
```

```java
  }

  public Safecracker()
  {
    // frame constructor
    setTitle("Safecracker");
    setResizable(false);
    addWindowListener(new WindowAdapter()
    {
      public void windowClosing(WindowEvent evt)
      {
        exitForm(evt);
      }
    });
    getContentPane().setLayout(new GridBagLayout());
    GridBagConstraints gridConstraints;

    safePanel.setPreferredSize(new Dimension(330, 420));
    safePanel.setLayout(new GridBagLayout());
    gridConstraints = new GridBagConstraints();
    gridConstraints.gridx = 0;
    gridConstraints.gridy = 0;
    gridConstraints.gridheight = 3;
    getContentPane().add(safePanel, gridConstraints);

    pack();
    Dimension screenSize =
Toolkit.getDefaultToolkit().getScreenSize();
    setBounds((int) (0.5 * (screenSize.width -
getWidth())), (int) (0.5 * (screenSize.height -
getHeight())), getWidth(), getHeight());
  }

  private void exitForm(WindowEvent evt)
  {
    System.exit(0);
  }
}

class ImagePanel extends JPanel
{
  private Image img;
  public ImagePanel(Image img)
  {
   this.img = img;
  }
  public void paintComponent(Graphics g)
```

```
  {
    g.drawImage(img, 0, 0, null);
  }
}
```

Run. The safe graphic should appear:

The **safePanel** will hold two other panel (JPanel) controls. The **GridBagLayout** for safePanel is:

	gridx = 0
gridy = 0	**comboPanel**
gridy = 1	**keyPanel**

comboPanel holds the controls used to display the combination, while **keyPanel** holds the buttons used to enter the combination.

The panel properties:

comboPanel:

size	160, 110
background	Yellow
gridx	0
gridy	0
insets	110, 0, 0, 0

keyPanel:

size	160, 100
background	Yellow
gridx	0
gridy	1

The sizing and position properties were obtained via trial and error.

These new panels are declared using:

```
JPanel comboPanel = new JPanel();
JPanel keyPanel = new JPanel();
```

The panels are placed in the **safePanel** using:

```
comboPanel.setPreferredSize(new Dimension(160, 110));
safePanel.setLayout(new GridBagLayout());
comboPanel.setBackground(Color.YELLOW);
gridConstraints = new GridBagConstraints();
gridConstraints.gridx = 0;
gridConstraints.gridy = 0;
gridConstraints.insets = new Insets(110, 0, 0, 0);
safePanel.add(comboPanel, gridConstraints);
```

```
keyPanel.setPreferredSize(new Dimension(160, 100));
keyPanel.setLayout(new GridBagLayout());
keyPanel.setBackground(Color.YELLOW);
gridConstraints = new GridBagConstraints();
gridConstraints.gridx = 0;
gridConstraints.gridy = 1;
safePanel.add(keyPanel, gridConstraints);
```

Add this code in the proper locations. Run to see:

The blank yellow panels appear on the safe graphic.

The **comboPanel** will hold four text field controls used to display the combination. The **GridBagLayout** for comboPanel is:

	gridx = 0	gridx = 1	gridx = 2	gridx = 3
gridy = 0	comboTextField[0]	comboTextField[1]	comboTextField[2]	comboTextField[3]

The text field properties:

comboTextField[i]:

size	32, 48
editable	false
background	White
text	0
horizontalAlignment	Center
font	Arial, Bold, 18
gridx	i
gridy	0

These text fields are declared using:

```
JTextField[] comboTextField = new JTextField[4];
```

The text fields are placed in the **comboPanel** using (place this code after the code positioning the comboPanel):

```
for (int i = 0; i < 4; i++)
{
  comboTextField[i] = new JTextField();
  comboTextField[i].setPreferredSize(new Dimension(32,
48));
  comboTextField[i].setEditable(false);
  comboTextField[i].setBackground(Color.WHITE);
  comboTextField[i].setText("0");

comboTextField[i].setHorizontalAlignment(SwingConstants.CE
NTER);
  comboTextField[i].setFont(new Font("Arial", Font.BOLD,
18));
  gridConstraints = new GridBagConstraints();
  gridConstraints.gridx = i;
  gridConstraints.gridy = 0;
  comboPanel.add(comboTextField[i], gridConstraints);
}
```

Add this code in the proper locations. Run to see:

We're making progress! The combination display is visible.

The **keyPanel** will hold nine button controls used to enter the combination. The **GridBagLayout** for keyPanel is:

	gridx = 0	gridx = 1	gridx = 2
gridy = 0	keyButton[0]	keyButton[1]	keyButton[2]
gridy = 1	keyButton[3]	keyButton[4]	keyButton[5]
gridy = 2	keyButton[6]	keyButton[7]	keyButton[8]

The text field properties:

keyButton[0]:
<pre>
    text   1
    gridx   0
    gridy   0
</pre>

keyButton[1]:
<pre>
    text   2
    gridx   1
    gridy   0
</pre>

keyButton[2]:
<pre>
    text   3
    gridx   2
    gridy   0
</pre>

keyButton[3]:
<pre>
    text   4
    gridx   0
    gridy   1
</pre>

keyButton[4]:
<pre>
    text   5
    gridx   1
    gridy   1
</pre>

keyButton[5]:
<pre>
    text   6
    gridx   2
    gridy   1
</pre>

keyButton[6]:
text	7
gridx	0
gridy	2

keyButton[7]:
text	8
gridx	1
gridy	2

keyButton[8]:
text	9
gridx	2
gridy	2

These buttons are declared using:

```
JButton[] keyButton = new JButton[9];
```

The buttons are placed in the **keyPanel** using (place this code after the code positioning the comboPanel):

```
for (int i = 0; i < 9; i++)
{
  keyButton[i] = new JButton();
  keyButton[i].setText(String.valueOf(i + 1));
  gridConstraints = new GridBagConstraints();
  gridConstraints.gridx = i % 3;
  gridConstraints.gridy = i / 3;
  keyPanel.add(keyButton[i], gridConstraints);
  keyButton[i].addActionListener(new ActionListener()
  {
    public void actionPerformed(ActionEvent e)
    {
      keyButtonActionPerformed(e);
    }
  });
}
```

Note how the loop index (**i**) is used to set properties.

This code also adds listeners for each button. The method called when a button is clicked is **keyButtonActionPerformed**. Add this empty method with the other methods:

```
private void keyButtonActionPerformed(ActionEvent e)
{
}
```

Add code in the proper locations. Run to see:

The keys appear. The **safePanel** control is complete. Let's move to the other three panels on the frame.

The **optionsPanel** will hold three radio button controls used to select the number of digits in the combination. The **GridBagLayout** for optionsPanel is:

	gridx = 0
gridy = 0	twoDigitsRadioButton
gridy =1	threeDigitsRadioButton
gridy = 2	fourDigitsRadioButton

The panel and radio button properties:

optionsPanel:
size	200, 100
title	Options:
gridx	1 (on frame)
gridy	0 (on frame)

twoDigitsRadioButton:
text	Two Digits in Combination
buttonGroup	digitsButtonGroup
selected	true
gridx	0 (on optionsPanel)
gridy	0 (on optionsPanel)
anchor	WEST

threeDigitsRadioButton:
text	Three Digits in Combination
buttonGroup	digitsButtonGroup
gridx	0 (on optionsPanel)
gridy	1 (on optionsPanel)
anchor	WEST

fourDigitsRadioButton:
text	Four Digits in Combination
gridx	0 (on optionsPanel)
gridy	2 (on optionsPanel)
anchor	WEST

These controls are declared using:

```
JPanel optionsPanel = new JPanel();
ButtonGroup digitsButtonGroup = new ButtonGroup();
JRadioButton twoDigitsRadioButton = new JRadioButton();
JRadioButton threeDigitsRadioButton = new JRadioButton();
JRadioButton fourDigitsRadioButton = new JRadioButton();
```

The radio buttons are placed in the **optionsPanel** (which is placed in the frame) using:

```
optionsPanel.setPreferredSize(new Dimension(200, 100));
optionsPanel.setBorder(BorderFactory.createTitledBorder("O
ptions:"));
optionsPanel.setLayout(new GridBagLayout());
gridConstraints = new GridBagConstraints();
gridConstraints.gridx = 1;
gridConstraints.gridy = 0;
getContentPane().add(optionsPanel, gridConstraints);

twoDigitsRadioButton.setText("Two Digits in Combination");
twoDigitsRadioButton.setSelected(true);
digitsButtonGroup.add(twoDigitsRadioButton);
gridConstraints = new GridBagConstraints();
gridConstraints.gridx = 0;
gridConstraints.gridy = 0;
gridConstraints.anchor = GridBagConstraints.WEST;
optionsPanel.add(twoDigitsRadioButton, gridConstraints);

threeDigitsRadioButton.setText("Three Digits in
Combination");
digitsButtonGroup.add(threeDigitsRadioButton);
gridConstraints = new GridBagConstraints();
gridConstraints.gridx = 0;
gridConstraints.gridy = 1;
gridConstraints.anchor = GridBagConstraints.WEST;
optionsPanel.add(threeDigitsRadioButton, gridConstraints);

fourDigitsRadioButton.setText("Four Digits in
Combination");
digitsButtonGroup.add(fourDigitsRadioButton);
gridConstraints = new GridBagConstraints();
gridConstraints.gridx = 0;
gridConstraints.gridy = 2;
gridConstraints.anchor = GridBagConstraints.WEST;
optionsPanel.add(fourDigitsRadioButton, gridConstraints);
```

Add this code in the proper locations. Run to see:

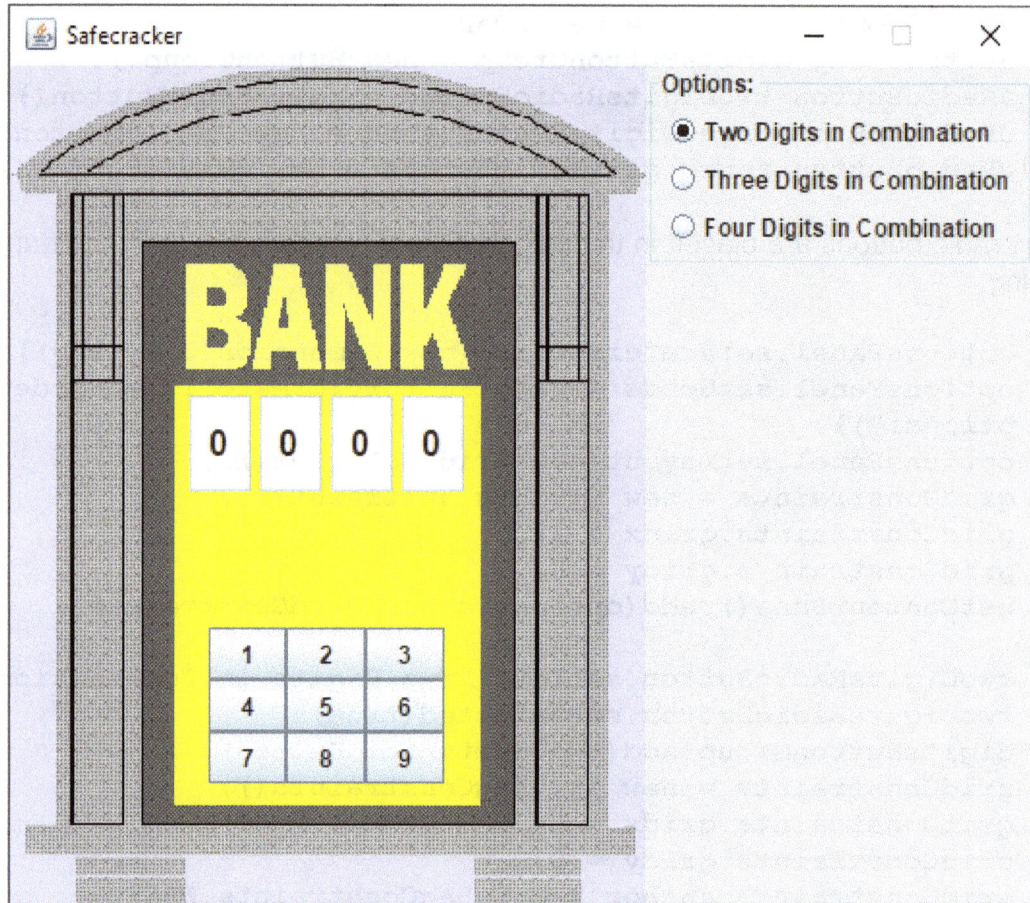

The options panel is displayed.

The **buttonsPanel** will hold two buttons used to control game play. The **GridBagLayout** for buttonsPanel is:

	gridx = 0
gridy = 0	**startStopButton**
gridy =1	**exitButton**

The panel and button properties:

buttonsPanel:
size	200, 70
gridx	1 (on frame)
gridy	1 (on frame)

startStopButton:
text	Start Game
gridx	0 (on buttonsPanel)
gridy	0 (on buttonsPanel)

exitButton:
text	Exit
gridx	0 (on buttonsPanel)
gridy	1 (on buttonsPanel)

These controls are declared using:

```
JPanel buttonsPanel = new JPanel();
JButton startStopButton = new JButton();
JButton exitButton = new JButton();
```

The buttons are placed in the **buttonsPanel** (which is placed in the frame) using:

```
buttonsPanel.setPreferredSize(new Dimension(200, 70));
buttonsPanel.setLayout(new GridBagLayout());
gridConstraints = new GridBagConstraints();
gridConstraints.gridx = 1;
gridConstraints.gridy = 1;
getContentPane().add(buttonsPanel, gridConstraints);

startStopButton.setText("Start Game");
gridConstraints = new GridBagConstraints();
gridConstraints.gridx = 0;
gridConstraints.gridy = 0;
buttonsPanel.add(startStopButton, gridConstraints);
startStopButton.addActionListener(new ActionListener()
{
```

```
   public void actionPerformed(ActionEvent e)
   {
     startStopButtonActionPerformed(e);
   }
});

exitButton.setText("Exit");
gridConstraints = new GridBagConstraints();
gridConstraints.gridx = 0;
gridConstraints.gridy = 1;
gridConstraints.insets = new Insets(10, 0, 0, 0);
buttonsPanel.add(exitButton, gridConstraints);
exitButton.addActionListener(new ActionListener()
{
   public void actionPerformed(ActionEvent e)
   {
     exitButtonActionPerformed(e);
   }
});
```

This code also adds listeners for each button. Add these empty methods with the other methods:

```
private void startStopButtonActionPerformed(ActionEvent e)
{
}

private void exitButtonActionPerformed(ActionEvent e)
{
}
```

Add this code in the proper locations. Run to see:

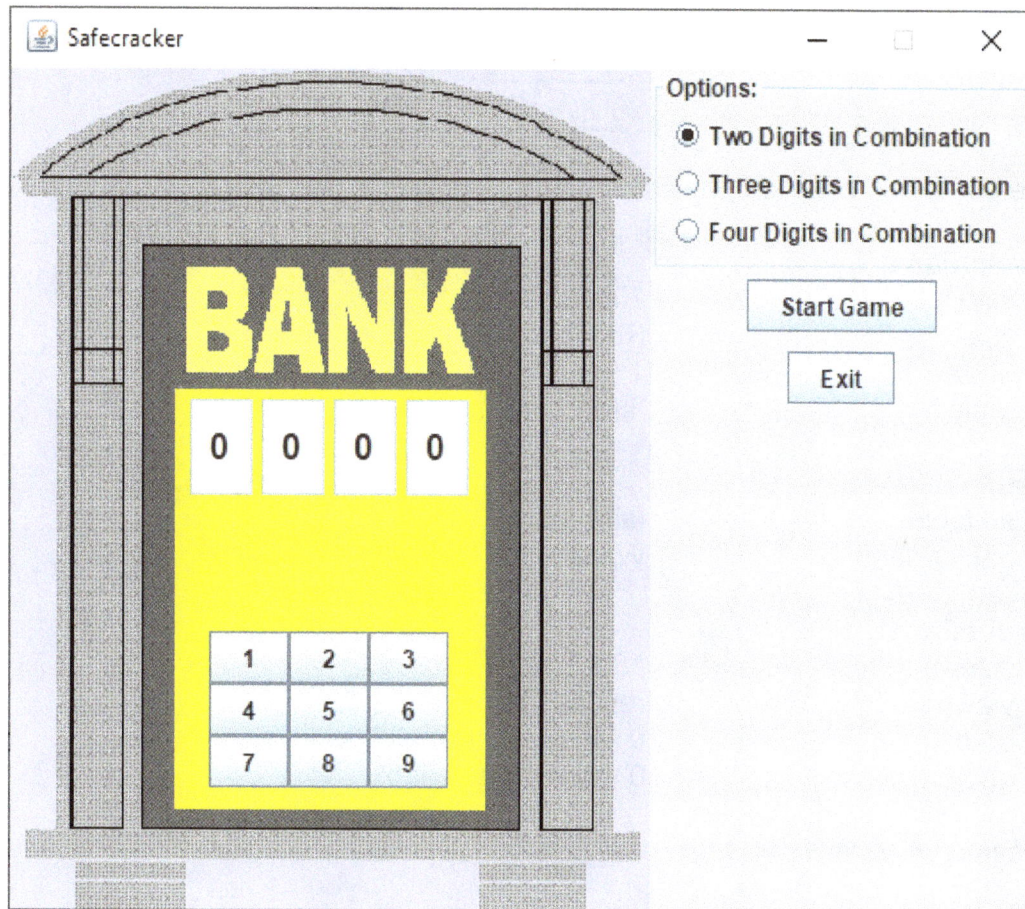

The button controls are displayed. One more panel and we're done with the frame design.

The **resultsPanel** will hold a scroll pane (which has a text area) used to display results of a combination guess. The **GridBagLayout** for resultsPanel is:

	gridx = 0
gridy = 0	**resultsPane**

The panel and pane properties:

resultsPanel:

size	200, 250
title	Results:
gridx	1 (on frame)
gridy	2 (on frame)

resultsTextArea:

editable	false
background	White

resultsPane:

size	180, 220
viewport	resultsTextArea
gridx	0 (on resultsPanel)
gridy	0 (on resultsPanel)

These controls are declared using:

```
JPanel resultsPanel = new JPanel();
JScrollPane resultsPane = new JScrollPane();
JTextArea resultsTextArea = new JTextArea();
```

The buttons are placed in the **resultsPanel** (which is placed in the frame) using:

```
resultsPanel.setPreferredSize(new Dimension(200, 250));
resultsPanel.setBorder(BorderFactory.createTitledBorder("R
esults:"));
resultsPanel.setLayout(new GridBagLayout());
gridConstraints = new GridBagConstraints();
gridConstraints.gridx = 1;
gridConstraints.gridy = 2;
getContentPane().add(resultsPanel, gridConstraints);

resultsTextArea.setEditable(false);
resultsTextArea.setBackground(Color.WHITE);
resultsPane.setPreferredSize(new Dimension(180, 220));
resultsPane.setViewportView(resultsTextArea);
gridConstraints = new GridBagConstraints();
```

```
gridConstraints.gridx = 0;
gridConstraints.gridy = 0;
resultsPanel.add(resultsPane, gridConstraints);
```

Add this code in the proper locations. Run to see:

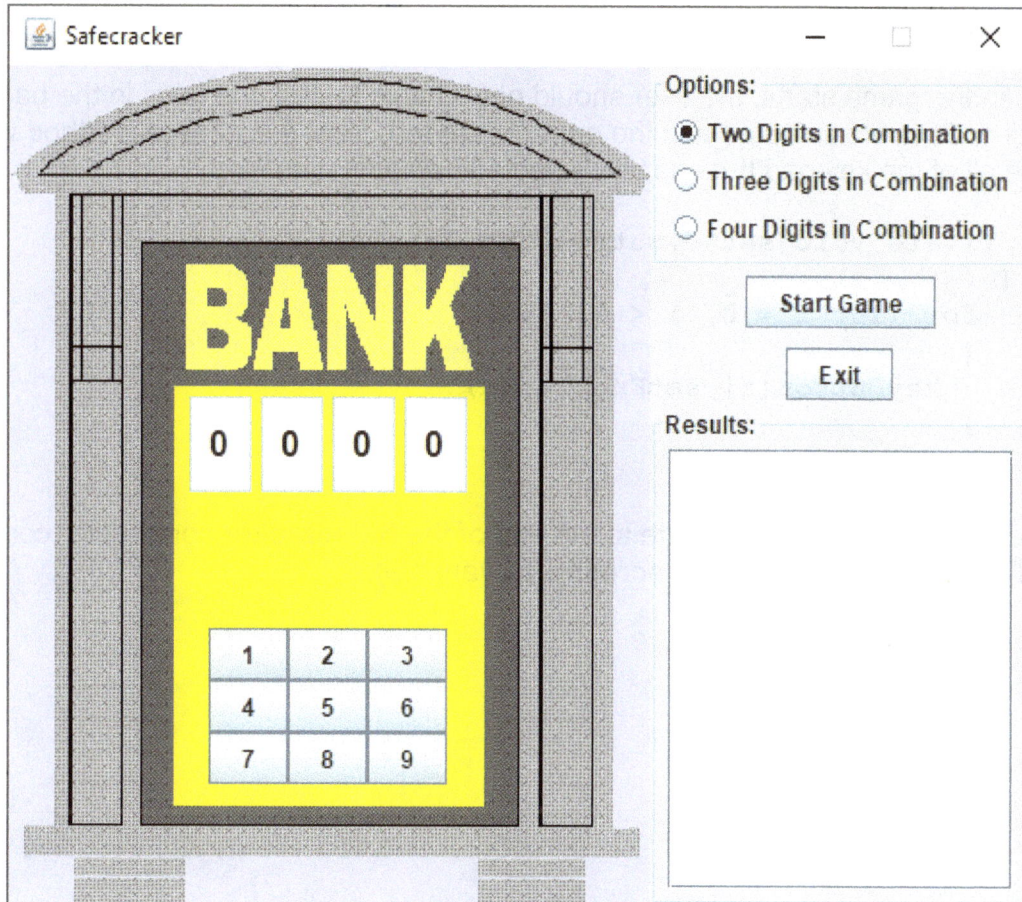

This completes the frame design. You should be able to identify all the controls in the game.

We will begin writing code for the game. We will write the code in several steps. As a first step, we will write the code that starts the game and establishes its 'stopped' state. Then, we look at how to go to 'playing' state following clicking of the **Start Game** button. During the code development process, recognize you may modify a particular method several times before arriving at the finished product.

Code Design - Initializing Stopped State

Any time we start a project, there are certain initializations that must take place. Let's look at the initializations needed in the **Safecracker** game. All initialization code is placed in the frame constructor after all the controls have been added to the frame.

When the game starts, the user should not be able to click the keys in the bank until options are selected and the game is started. Add this general method which sets all of the key pad buttons to a selected boolean state (**a**):

```
private void setKeyButtons(boolean a)
{
  for (int i = 0; i < 9; i++)
  {
    keyButton[i].setEnabled(a);
  }
}
```

Then, add this one line of code at the end of the **Safecracker** constructor code (following the line setting the **screenSize** variable):

```
setKeyButtons(false);
```

Run the project to make sure the frame is properly initialized. Do this and you'll see in the 'stopped' state (using default properties), the **Safecracker** game looks like this:

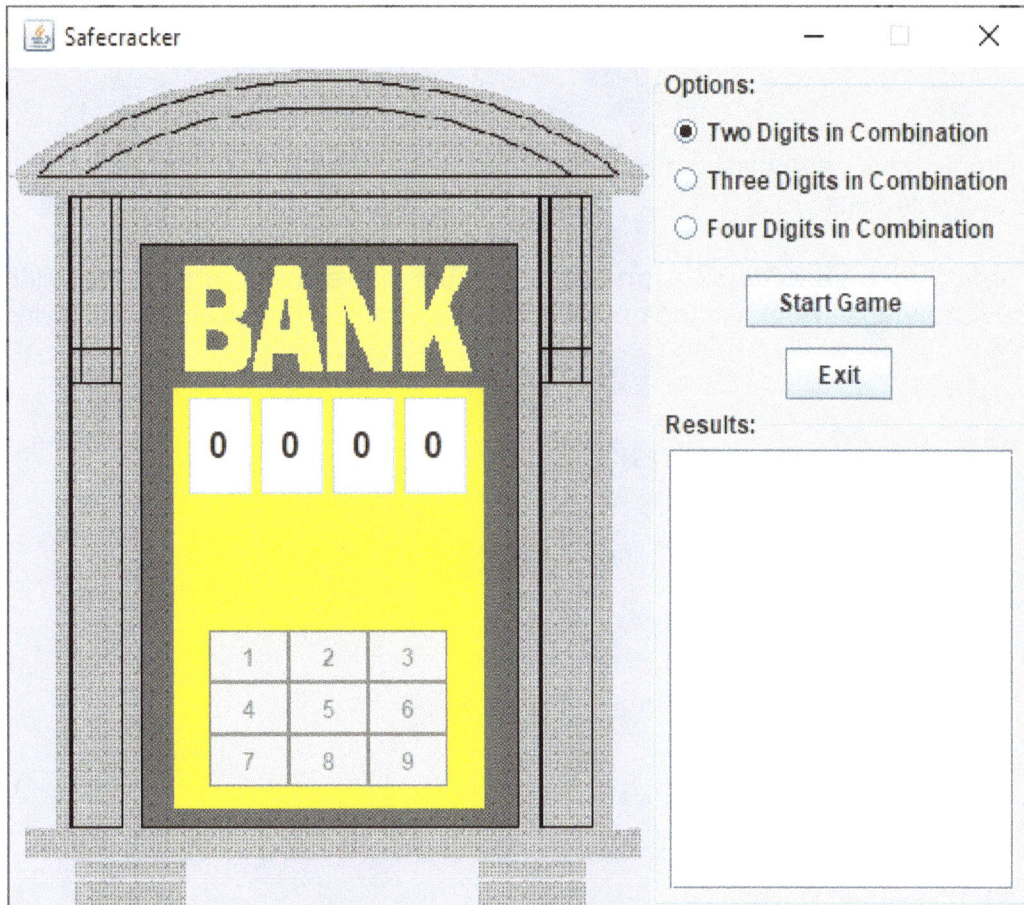

Note the keypad buttons are 'grayed-out' as desired. Try clicking one; you can't. We have two choices at this point – either choose some options and click **startStopButton** (the button with **Start Game**) or click **exitButton** (the button with **Exit**).

The code for exiting is simple. The **exitButtonActionListener** method (currently empty) is:

```
private void exitButtonActionPerformed(ActionEvent e)
{
  System.exit(0);
}
```

This simply says whenever the **Exit** button is clicked, the project closes. Add this code to the project.

The code for the **startStopButton** button is much more complicated. We will build it in several steps. First, we look at switching the game from stopped to playing state.

Code Design – Stopped to Playing State

When the user clicks the **Start Game** button in 'stopped' state, several things must happen to switch the **Safecracker** game to 'playing' state:

> ➢ Change the **text** property of **startStopButton** to **Stop Game**.
> ➢ Disable the radio buttons (don't allow selection of options while playing).
> ➢ Disable **exitButton**.
> ➢ Enable the keypad buttons (allow entering a combination)
> ➢ Blank out **resultsTextArea** (delete previous results).
> ➢ Display proper number of text field controls to show combination.
> ➢ Determine secret combination.
> ➢ Allow user to input combination.
> ➢ Check to see if input combination matches secret combination – provide results.

Right now, we will implement each of these steps <u>except</u> those establishing the secret combination and accepting and checking user input. Those steps will be addressed separately.

Add this line to the class level declarations to define a variable for the number of digits in the combination:

```
int numberDigits;
```

The code for the **startStopButtonActionPerformed** method that implements all but the last three steps in the above method is:

```java
private void startStopButtonActionPerformed(ActionEvent e)
{
  startStopButton.setText("Stop Game");
  twoDigitsRadioButton.setEnabled(false);
  threeDigitsRadioButton.setEnabled(false);
  fourDigitsRadioButton.setEnabled(false);
  exitButton.setEnabled(false);
  setKeyButtons(true);
  resultsTextArea.setText("");
  // determine number of digits and set up labels
  if (twoDigitsRadioButton.isSelected())
  {
    numberDigits = 2;
  }
  else if (threeDigitsRadioButton.isSelected())
  {
    numberDigits = 3;
  }
  else
  {
    numberDigits = 4;
  }
  for (int i = 0; i < numberDigits; i++)
  {
    comboTextField[i].setVisible(true);
    comboTextField[i].setText("");
  }
  if (numberDigits != 4)
  {
    for (int i = numberDigits; i < 4; i++)
    {
      comboTextField[i].setVisible(false);
    }
  }
}
```

Notice how the text field control array (**comboTextField**) is used to display the needed controls for the displayed combination.

Save and run the project. Click **Start Game** and the game should switch to 'playing' state (assumes 2 digits in combination):

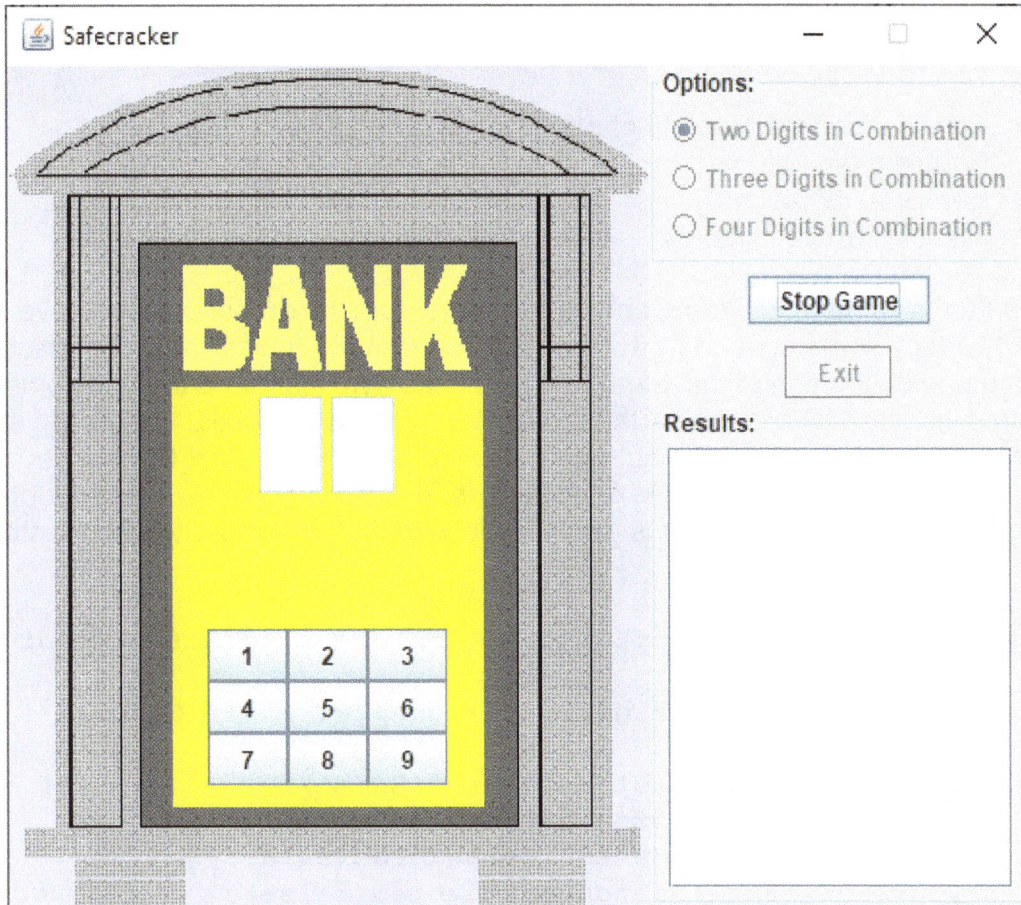

Make sure the number of text field controls displayed in the bank area match the option selected. Notice the **Stop Game** button does nothing at the moment. Let's fix that. Stop the project.

Code Design – Playing to Stopped State

When the user clicks the **Stop Game** button in 'playing' state, several things must happen to switch the **Safecracker** game to 'stopped' state:

➢ Change the **text** property of **startStopButton** to **Start Game**.
➢ Enable radio buttons.
➢ Enable **exitButton**.
➢ Disable keypad buttons.

The button now marked **Stop Game** is the **startStopButton** button. We have already added some code to its **actionPerformed** method. It is common practice to have one button control have multiple purposes - we just need to have some way to distinguish which "mode" the button is in when it is clicked. In this project, we use the text property of the button. If the text property is **Start Game**, we switch to 'playing' mode. If the text property is **Stop Game**, we switch to 'stopped' mode. The code that does this is (modifications to the current **actionPerformed** method code are shaded):

```
private void startStopButtonActionPerformed(ActionEvent e)
{
  if (startStopButton.getText().equals("Start Game"))
  {
    startStopButton.setText("Stop Game");
    twoDigitsRadioButton.setEnabled(false);
    threeDigitsRadioButton.setEnabled(false);
    fourDigitsRadioButton.setEnabled(false);
    exitButton.setEnabled(false);
    setKeyButtons(true);
    resultsTextArea.setText("");
    // determine number of digits and set up labels
    if (twoDigitsRadioButton.isSelected())
    {
      numberDigits = 2;
    }
    else if (threeDigitsRadioButton.isSelected())
    {
      numberDigits = 3;
    }
    else
    {
      numberDigits = 4;
    }
    for (int i = 0; i < numberDigits; i++)
    {
      comboTextField[i].setVisible(true);
```

```
      comboTextField[i].setText("");
    }
    if (numberDigits != 4)
    {
      for (int i = numberDigits; i < 4; i++)
      {
        comboTextField[i].setVisible(false);
      }
    }
  }
  else
  {
    startStopButton.setText("Start Game");
    twoDigitsRadioButton.setEnabled(true);
    threeDigitsRadioButton.setEnabled(true);
    fourDigitsRadioButton.setEnabled(true);
    exitButton.setEnabled(true);
    setKeyButtons(false);
  }
}
```

Save and run the project. You should be able to now move from 'stopped' to 'playing' state and back. Make sure you can display 2, 3 or 4 digits in the combination. Try the **Exit** button. We can now look at the three missing steps in the program: generating a secret combination and accepting and checking user input.

Code Design
Generating Secret Combination

A critical step in the **Safecracker** project is to generate the secret combination the game player is trying to guess. Using the options selected, we know the combination can be from 2 to 4 digits. We have also specified none of the digits can repeat.

Since repeated digits are not allowed, for each digit in the combination, we generate a random number from 1 to 9, but only add it to the combination if it has not been used before. The code snippet that accomplishes this for our game is:

```java
// determine combination
secretCombo = "";
int j;
boolean uniqueDigit;
for (int i = 0; i < numberDigits; i++)
{
  // select unique digit
  do
  {
    j = myRandom.nextInt(9) + 1;
    uniqueDigit = true;
    if (i != 0)
    {
      for (int k = 0; k < i; k++)
      {
        if
(String.valueOf(secretCombo.charAt(k)).equals(String.value
Of(j)))
          uniqueDigit = false;
      }
    }
  }
  while (!uniqueDigit);
  secretCombo += String.valueOf(j);
}
```

We'll step you through this code to see what's going on. A string variable (**secretCombo**) is used to store the combination. It is initially blank. One digit at a time (a total of **numberDigits**) is added to **secretCombo** using string concatenation.

A random digit **j** (from 1 to 9) is generated. We then look at the current digits in the code to see if this newly generated digit is unique. If so, it is added to **secretCombo**. If not unique, a new random digit is generated. All of this logic is implemented in a **do** loop. Study how we examine the individual digits in **secretCombo** using the **charAt** method. The returned values are **char** type, so we need to convert to **String** before comparing. Let's try this new code.

Since we are using random numbers, include this **import** statement near the top of the code listing (with the other import statements):

```
import java.util.Random;
```

Add these class level variable declarations to define the secret combination and establish the random number object:

```
String secretCombo;
Random myRandom = new Random();
```

Add the given snippet to the **startStopButtonActionPerformed** method as shown in the shaded code below:

```java
private void startStopButtonActionPerformed(ActionEvent e)
{
  if (startStopButton.getText().equals("Start Game"))
  {
    startStopButton.setText("Stop Game");
    twoDigitsRadioButton.setEnabled(false);
    threeDigitsRadioButton.setEnabled(false);
    fourDigitsRadioButton.setEnabled(false);
    exitButton.setEnabled(false);
    setKeyButtons(true);
    resultsTextArea.setText("");
    // determine number of digits and set up labels
    if (twoDigitsRadioButton.isSelected())
    {
      numberDigits = 2;
    }
    else if (threeDigitsRadioButton.isSelected())
    {
      numberDigits = 3;
    }
    else
    {
      numberDigits = 4;
    }
    for (int i = 0; i < numberDigits; i++)
    {
      comboTextField[i].setVisible(true);
      comboTextField[i].setText("");
    }
    if (numberDigits != 4)
    {
      for (int i = numberDigits; i < 4; i++)
      {
        comboTextField[i].setVisible(false);
      }
    }
    // determine combination
    secretCombo = "";
    int j;
    boolean uniqueDigit;
    for (int i = 0; i < numberDigits; i++)
    {
      // select unique digit
      do
```

```
        {
          j = myRandom.nextInt(9) + 1;
          uniqueDigit = true;
          if (i != 0)
          {
            for (int k = 0; k < i; k++)
            {
              if
(String.valueOf(secretCombo.charAt(k)).equals(String.value
Of(j)))
                uniqueDigit = false;
            }
          }
        }
      while (!uniqueDigit);
      secretCombo += String.valueOf(j);
    }
  }
  else
  {
    startStopButton.setText("Start Game");
    twoDigitsRadioButton.setEnabled(true);
    threeDigitsRadioButton.setEnabled(true);
    fourDigitsRadioButton.setEnabled(true);
    exitButton.setEnabled(true);
    setKeyButtons(false);
  }
}
```

We can now generate a secret combination, but have no way of seeing what it is.
Let's change that. Many times while developing a project, you want to check
results before the project is complete. This means adding temporary code just for
debugging purposes. Place this line after the closing bracket in the code
generating the combination:

```
System.out.println(secretCombo);
```

This will write the generated combination in the **Output** window of the the IDE
allowing you to see if the combination meets the requirements (proper number of
digits and proper repeating/non-repeating of digits).

Save and run the project. Click **Start Game**. Open the **output** window of your IDE and look at the generated combination. Make sure it meets the selected options requirement. Click **Stop Game**. Repeat this process for various combinations to make sure the combination is being generated correctly. When done, delete the debug line from the code. We're now ready to accept the player's guess at the secret combination using the 9 keypad buttons.

Code Design – Accepting Player Input

Once the secret combination has been generated, the next step is to allow the user to enter his or her guess at the combination. This is done using the 9 number buttons on the panel control in the bank graphic. The steps followed are:

> ➢ Click a button to enter a digit.
> ➢ If this is the first number in the combination, clear out any previous guess in label controls.
> ➢ Determine which button was clicked.
> ➢ Disable the clicked button since repeating digits are not allowed.
> ➢ Add the number on the clicked button to the user's input combination.
> ➢ Display the number in the proper label control.
> ➢ If all digits have been entered, enable the number buttons and compare the user's input to the actual combination, else repeat these steps.

The code to perform these steps will be placed in the method named **keyButtonActionPerformed** (currently empty). This method is set to handle a click event for all 9 buttons used for input (**keyButton** array).

Add these class level variables to store the combination entered by the user and the number of digits entered:

```
int digitsEntered;
String enteredCombo;
```

Initialize the value of these two new variables using the shaded code in
startStopButtonActionPerformed:

```java
private void startStopButtonActionPerformed(ActionEvent e)
{
  if (startStopButton.getText().equals("Start Game"))
  {
    startStopButton.setText("Stop Game");
    twoDigitsRadioButton.setEnabled(false);
    threeDigitsRadioButton.setEnabled(false);
    fourDigitsRadioButton.setEnabled(false);
    exitButton.setEnabled(false);
    setKeyButtons(true);
    resultsTextArea.setText("");
    // determine number of digits and set up labels
    if (twoDigitsRadioButton.isSelected())
    {
      numberDigits = 2;
    }
    else if (threeDigitsRadioButton.isSelected())
    {
      numberDigits = 3;
    }
    else
    {
      numberDigits = 4;
    }
    for (int i = 0; i < numberDigits; i++)
    {
      comboTextField[i].setVisible(true);
      comboTextField[i].setText("");
    }
    if (numberDigits != 4)
    {
      for (int i = numberDigits; i < 4; i++)
      {
        comboTextField[i].setVisible(false);
      }
    }
    // determine combination
    secretCombo = "";
    int j;
    boolean uniqueDigit;
    for (int i = 0; i < numberDigits; i++)
    {
      // select unique digit
      do
```

```
        {
          j = myRandom.nextInt(9) + 1;
          uniqueDigit = true;
          if (i != 0)
          {
            for (int k = 0; k < i; k++)
            {
              if
(String.valueOf(secretCombo.charAt(k)).equals(String.value
Of(j)))
                uniqueDigit = false;
            }
          }
        }
        while (!uniqueDigit);
        secretCombo += String.valueOf(j);
      }
      enteredCombo = "";
      digitsEntered = 0;
    }
    else
    {
      startStopButton.setText("Start Game");
      twoDigitsRadioButton.setEnabled(true);
      threeDigitsRadioButton.setEnabled(true);
      fourDigitsRadioButton.setEnabled(true);
      exitButton.setEnabled(true);
      setKeyButtons(false);
    }
}
```

Add this code to the **keyButtonActionPerformed** method.. This implements the needed steps to check the user's input:

```
private void keyButtonActionPerformed(ActionEvent e)
{
    String n;
    // determine which button was clicked
    // ActionCommand is text on button
    n = e.getActionCommand();
    // disable button since digits can't repeat
    keyButton[Integer.valueOf(n).intValue() -
1].setEnabled(false);
    // if first button in combo, clear out label boxes
    if (digitsEntered == 0)
    {
        comboTextField[0].setText("");
        comboTextField[1].setText("");
        comboTextField[2].setText("");
        comboTextField[3].setText("");
    }
    // add button to code
    enteredCombo += n;
    digitsEntered++;
    comboTextField[digitsEntered - 1].setText(n);
    // if all digits entered, check combo
    if (digitsEntered == numberDigits)
    {
        // reset combo buttons
        for (int i = 0; i < 9; i++)
            keyButton[i].setEnabled(true);
        // check combination
        System.out.println(enteredCombo);
    }
}
```

Notice the **getActionCommand** method returns the text property of the clicked button. This is the corresponding digit (the variable **n**). We have used a **println** statement to print the complete entered combination in the IDE **Output** window. Logic to check this combination is next.

Save and run the project. Make sure the entered combination looks correct (has the proper number of digits, in the correct order and following repeatability rules). Make sure the keypad buttons are re-enabled after entering a combination. Let's complete the game by comparing the player's input to the actual combination and displaying the results.

Code Design – Checking Player Input

We now have the capability to generate a secret combination and obtain the player's guess at that combination. We need the code that compares the two string variables and displays the results. If it's a match, great! If not, we tell the player how many digits are correct and how many are in the correct position. This is some of the trickier code.

Once the user has complete their input, we follow these steps:

> Display the user's guess (**enteredCombo**) in **resultsTextArea**.
> If user's guess (**enteredCombo**) equals the actual combination (**secretCombo**), return the game to stopped state and let the user know they guessed the combination.
> If incorrect guess, determine number of correct digits and number in correct positions. Display this information in **resultsTextArea**.
> Clear user's guess to allow another try.

All of the code to perform these steps is placed in the **keyButtonActionPerformed** method.

Place the shaded code in the **keyButtonActionPerformed** method to implement these steps (we deleted the **println** statement):

```java
private void keyButtonActionPerformed(ActionEvent e)
{
  String n;
  // determine which button was clicked
  // ActionCommand is text on button
  n = e.getActionCommand();
  // disable button since digits can't repeat
  keyButton[Integer.valueOf(n).intValue() -
1].setEnabled(false);
  // if first button in combo, clear out label boxes
  if (digitsEntered == 0)
  {
    comboTextField[0].setText("");
    comboTextField[1].setText("");
    comboTextField[2].setText("");
    comboTextField[3].setText("");
  }
  // add button to code
  enteredCombo += n;
  digitsEntered++;
  comboTextField[digitsEntered - 1].setText(n);
  // if all digits entered, check combo
```

```
if (digitsEntered == numberDigits)
{
  // reset combo buttons
  for (int i = 0; i < 9; i++)
      keyButton[i].setEnabled(true);
  // check combination
  resultsTextArea.append("Entered: " + enteredCombo +
"\n");
  if (enteredCombo.equals(secretCombo))
    startStopButton.doClick();
  else
  {
    numberRight = 0;
    for (int i = 0; i < numberDigits; i++)
    {
      n = String.valueOf(enteredCombo.charAt(i));
      for (int j = 0; j < numberDigits; j++)
        if
(n.equals(String.valueOf(secretCombo.charAt(j))))
          numberRight++;
    }
    // how many in correct position
    positionRight = 0;
    for (int i = 0; i < numberDigits; i++)
      if (secretCombo.charAt(i) ==
enteredCombo.charAt(i))
          positionRight++;
    resultsTextArea.append(String.valueOf(numberRight) +
" digits correct" + "\n");
    resultsTextArea.append(String.valueOf(positionRight)
+ " in correct position" + "\n");
    resultsTextArea.append("Try again ..." + "\n\n");
    // clear combo to try again
    enteredCombo = "";
    digitsEntered = 0;
  }
}
}
```

You should be able to follow the above code. It first counts the number of correct digits in the user's input. The code to see if digits are in correct position just compares each digit in **enteredCombo** and **secretCombo**. All the results are displayed in the **resultsTextArea** text box using the **append** method.

If the correct combination is entered, we want to return to 'stopped' state. An easy way to do this (and the way we did) is simply programmatically click on the **Stop Game** button using the **doClick** method. Using this approach, though, we need to add some code to the **startStopButtonActionPerformed** method. The new code is used to distinguish between stopping the game before guessing the combination and stopping because the combination has been guessed. Make the shaded changes to the **startStopButtonActionPerformed** method:

```
private void startStopButtonActionPerformed(ActionEvent e)
{
  if (startStopButton.getText().equals("Start Game"))
  {
    startStopButton.setText("Stop Game");
    twoDigitsRadioButton.setEnabled(false);
    threeDigitsRadioButton.setEnabled(false);
    fourDigitsRadioButton.setEnabled(false);
    exitButton.setEnabled(false);
    setKeyButtons(true);
    resultsTextArea.setText("");
    // determine number of digits and set up labels
    if (twoDigitsRadioButton.isSelected())
    {
      numberDigits = 2;
    }
    else if (threeDigitsRadioButton.isSelected())
    {
      numberDigits = 3;
    }
    else
    {
      numberDigits = 4;
    }
    for (int i = 0; i < numberDigits; i++)
    {
      comboTextField[i].setVisible(true);
      comboTextField[i].setText("");
    }
    if (numberDigits != 4)
    {
      for (int i = numberDigits; i < 4; i++)
      {
        comboTextField[i].setVisible(false);
      }
    }
    // determine combination
    secretCombo = "";
    int j;
```

```
      boolean uniqueDigit;
      for (int i = 0; i < numberDigits; i++)
      {
        // select unique digit
        do
        {
          j = myRandom.nextInt(9) + 1;
          uniqueDigit = true;
          if (i != 0)
          {
            for (int k = 0; k < i; k++)
            {
              if
(String.valueOf(secretCombo.charAt(k)).equals(String.value
Of(j)))
                uniqueDigit = false;
            }
          }
        }
        while (!uniqueDigit);
        secretCombo += String.valueOf(j);
      }
      enteredCombo = "";
      digitsEntered = 0;
    }
    else
    {
      if (enteredCombo.equals(secretCombo))
        resultsTextArea.append("That's it!!" + "\n");
      else
        resultsTextArea.append("Game Stopped" + "\n");
      resultsTextArea.append("Combination: " + secretCombo);
      startStopButton.setText("Start Game");
      twoDigitsRadioButton.setEnabled(true);
      threeDigitsRadioButton.setEnabled(true);
      fourDigitsRadioButton.setEnabled(true);
      exitButton.setEnabled(true);
      setKeyButtons(false);
    }
  }
```

Save and run the project. The game is now fully functional. Try playing it a few times to make sure things are working okay. It still needs just one more thing.

Sounds in Java

You may have never used sounds in your projects. Or you may have used the the one sound available with Java, a simple beep generated using:

```
Toolkit.getDefaultToolkit().beep();
```

This unexciting sound plays through the computer's built-in speaker, if there is one. Multimedia presentations and games feature elaborate sounds that take advantage of stereo sound cards. To play such sounds in Java involves just a bit of trickery.

We look at playing two particular types of sounds: **AU** files (a common Sun audio format) and **WAV** files. Most sounds you hear played in Windows applications are saved as WAV files. These are the files formed when you record using one of the many sound recorder programs available.

The Java sound capabilities are part of the **java.applet.*** package. This package is used to implement Java applications on the Internet. But we can still use these capabilities in our GUI applications. It just requires a little work. There are two steps involved in playing sound files: (1) load the sound as an audio clip and (2) play the sound.

A sound file is loaded using the **newAudioClip** method. If we name the sound **mySound**, the sound is loaded using:

```
mySound = Applet.newAudioClip(mySoundURL);
```

where **mySoundURL** is the "address" of the sound file. You may note that URL is an Internet address (universal resource locator) – this is because the sound utilities are part of the applet package. Does this mean our sounds must be stored on the Internet somewhere? No. By forming a special URL as the argument, we can load sound files from our project folder, just like we have loaded graphics files.

A URL for use in the **newAudioClip** method is formed using the Java **URL** method (in the **java.net.URL** package). If the sound file is **mySoundFile** (**String** type), the URL is formed with:

```
mySoundURL = new URL("file:" + mySoundFile);
```

The addition of the "**file:**" string tells Java the sound is loaded from a file rather than the Internet. This assumes the sound file is located in the project folder. If it is in another folder, you need to "prepend" the file name with the appropriate directory information.

We need to consider one last thing. The URL can only be formed within a **try/catch** loop to catch potential exceptions. Hence, the complete code segment to load a sound (**mySound**) from a file (**mySoundFile**) is:

```
try
{
   mySound = Applet.newAudioClip(new URL("file:" +
mySoundFile));
}
catch (Exception ex)
{
    [Error message]
}
```

Such code to create sounds is usually placed in at the end of your application's constructor with all sounds declared as class level variables.

Once we have created a sound clip, there are three methods used to play or stop the corresponding sound. To play **mySound** one time, use the **play** method:

```
mySound.play();
```

To play the sound in a continuous loop, use the **loop** method:

```
mySound.loop();
```

To stop the sound from playing, use the **stop** method:

```
mySound.stop();
```

It's that easy.

It is normal practice to include any sound files an application uses in the project folder. This makes them easily accessible. As such, when distributing your application to other users, you must remember to include the sound files in the package.

Code Design – Adding Sounds

The text feedback of the **Safecracker** game is a bit boring. Let's snazz it up a bit by adding sounds. In the **\KidGamesJava\KidGamesJava Projects\Safecracker** folder are two wav files that can be used for sound. The file **uhoh.wav** is an 'uh-oh' sound we'll use for incorrect guesses. The **tada.wav** file is a celebratory sound we'll use for correct guesses. These files will be loaded when the project starts. Copy the two sound files to your project's folder.

Add these **import** statements:

```
import java.net.URL;
import java.applet.*;
```

Add these class level declarations to represent the two sounds:

```
AudioClip wrongSound;
AudioClip correctSound;
```

Add these lines at the end of the **Safecracker** constructor (following the line that initializes the keypad status) to establish the sound objects:

```
try
{
  wrongSound = Applet.newAudioClip(new URL("file:" +
"uhoh.wav"));
  correctSound = Applet.newAudioClip(new URL("file:" +
"tada.wav"));
}
catch (Exception ex)
{
  System.out.println("Error loading sound files");
}
```

This code assumes the sound files are in your project's folder.

Lastly, play the two sounds at the appropriate (shaded) locations in the
keyButtonActionPerformed method:

```java
private void keyButtonActionPerformed(ActionEvent e)
{
  String n;
  // determine which button was clicked
  // ActionCommand is text on button
  n = e.getActionCommand();
  // disable button since digits can't repeat
  keyButton[Integer.valueOf(n).intValue() -
1].setEnabled(false);
  // if first button in combo, clear out label boxes
  if (digitsEntered == 0)
  {
    comboTextField[0].setText("");
    comboTextField[1].setText("");
    comboTextField[2].setText("");
    comboTextField[3].setText("");
  }
  // add button to code
  enteredCombo += n;
  digitsEntered++;
  comboTextField[digitsEntered - 1].setText(n);
  // if all digits entered, check combo
  if (digitsEntered == numberDigits)
  {
    // reset combo buttons
    for (int i = 0; i < 9; i++)
        keyButton[i].setEnabled(true);
    // check combination
    resultsTextArea.append("Entered: " + enteredCombo +
"\n");
    if (enteredCombo.equals(secretCombo))
    {
      correctSound.play();
      startStopButton.doClick();
    }
    else
    {
      wrongSound.play();
      numberRight = 0;
      for (int i = 0; i < numberDigits; i++)
      {
        n = String.valueOf(enteredCombo.charAt(i));
        for (int j = 0; j < numberDigits; j++)
```

```
          if
(n.equals(String.valueOf(secretCombo.charAt(j))))
            numberRight++;
      }
      // how many in correct position
      positionRight = 0;
      for (int i = 0; i < numberDigits; i++)
        if (secretCombo.charAt(i) ==
enteredCombo.charAt(i))
          positionRight++;
      resultsTextArea.append(String.valueOf(numberRight) +
" digits correct" + "\n");
      resultsTextArea.append(String.valueOf(positionRight)
+ " in correct position" + "\n");
      resultsTextArea.append("Try again ..." + "\n\n");
      // clear combo to try again
      enteredCombo = "";
      digitsEntered = 0;
    }
  }
}
```

Save and run the project. You should now have a complete, running version of the **Safecracker** game (the complete code listing is given at the end of the chapter). Have fun playing it! See if you can come up with some kind of winning strategy. Here's a game I played using 3 non-repeating digits. First, I tried 123 (obviously not a good guess) and heard 'uh-oh':

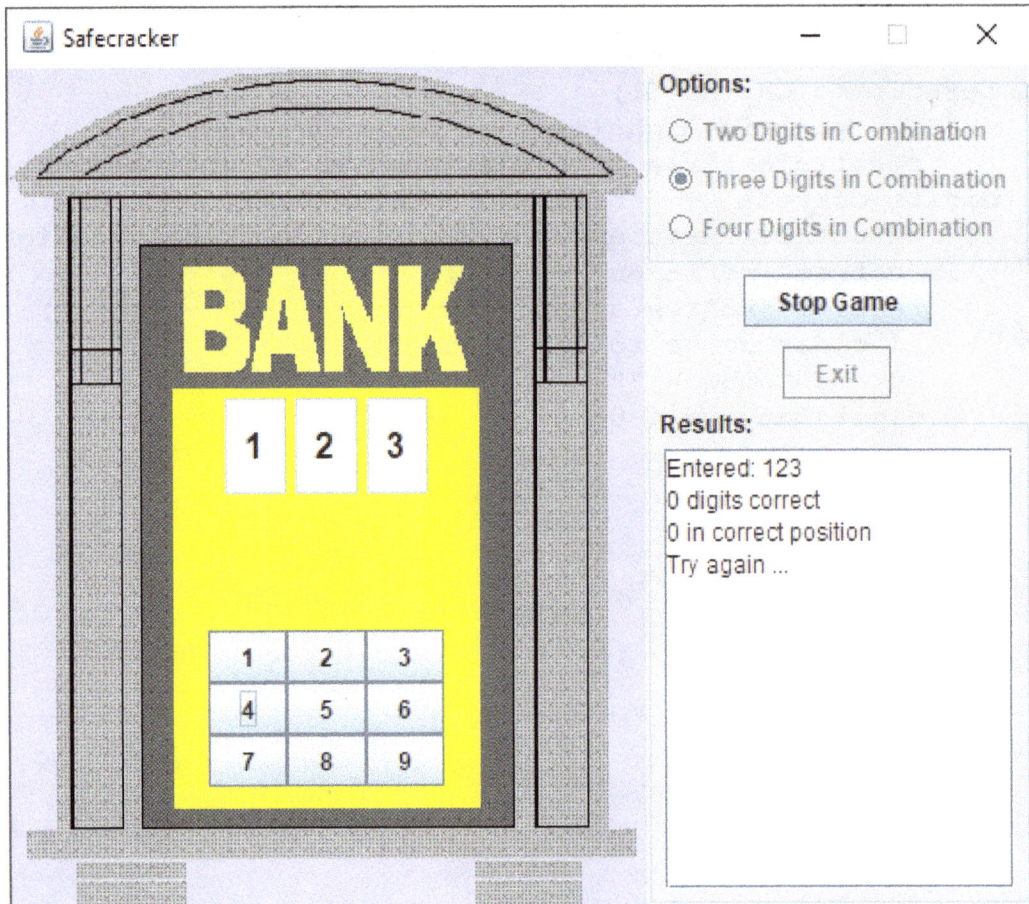

Next try was 456:

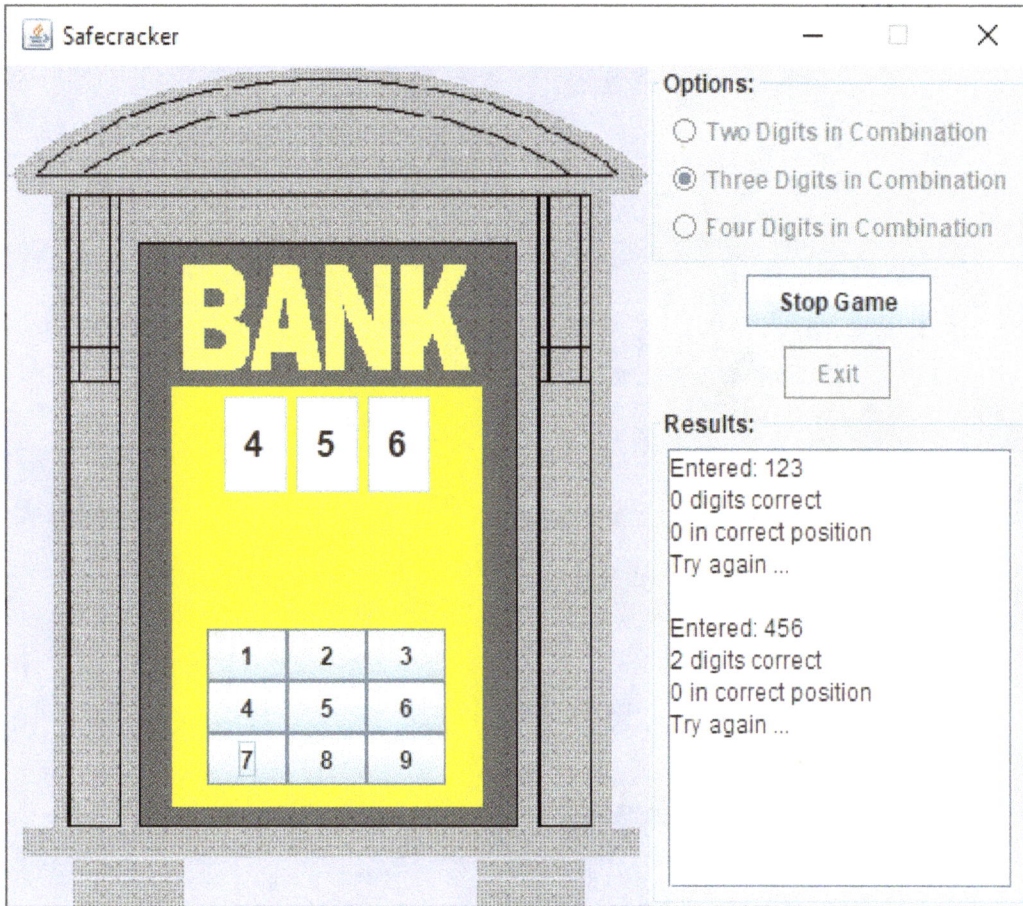

Much better – two digits are correct. I have some valuable information.

Next, I tried 745, digressing a bit:

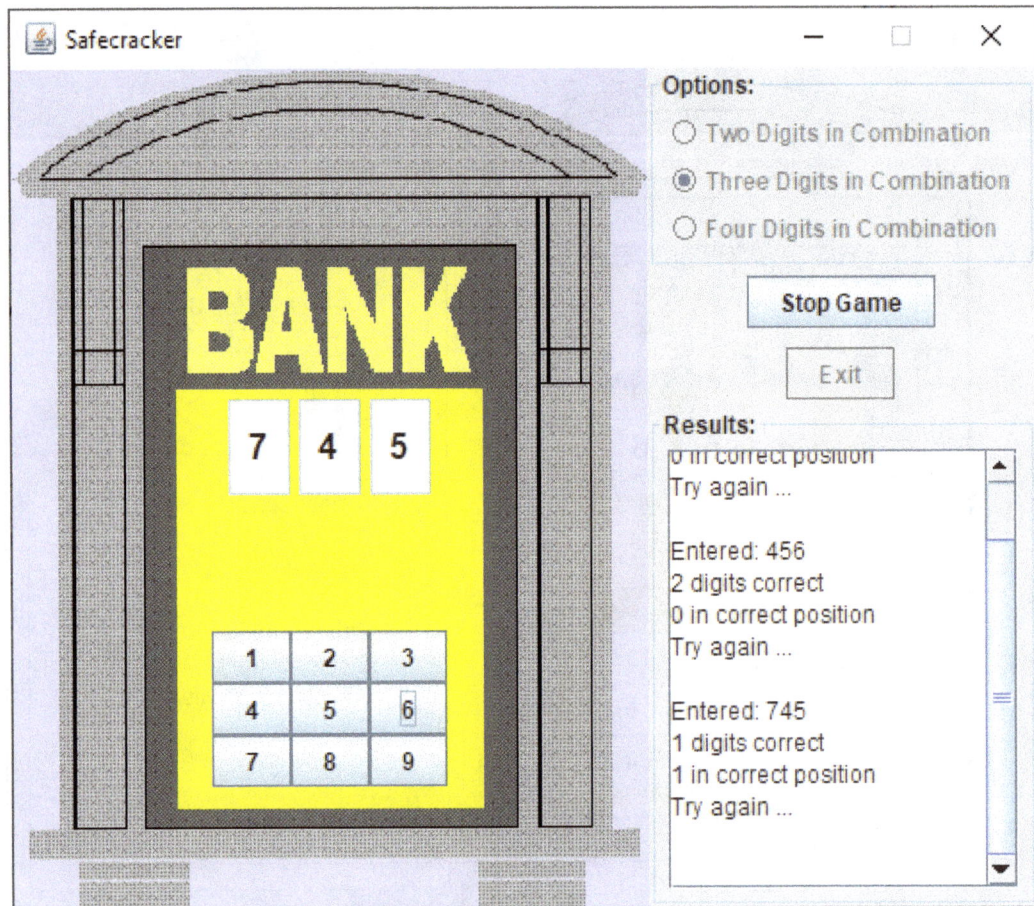

After another incorrect try (689), I entered 648:

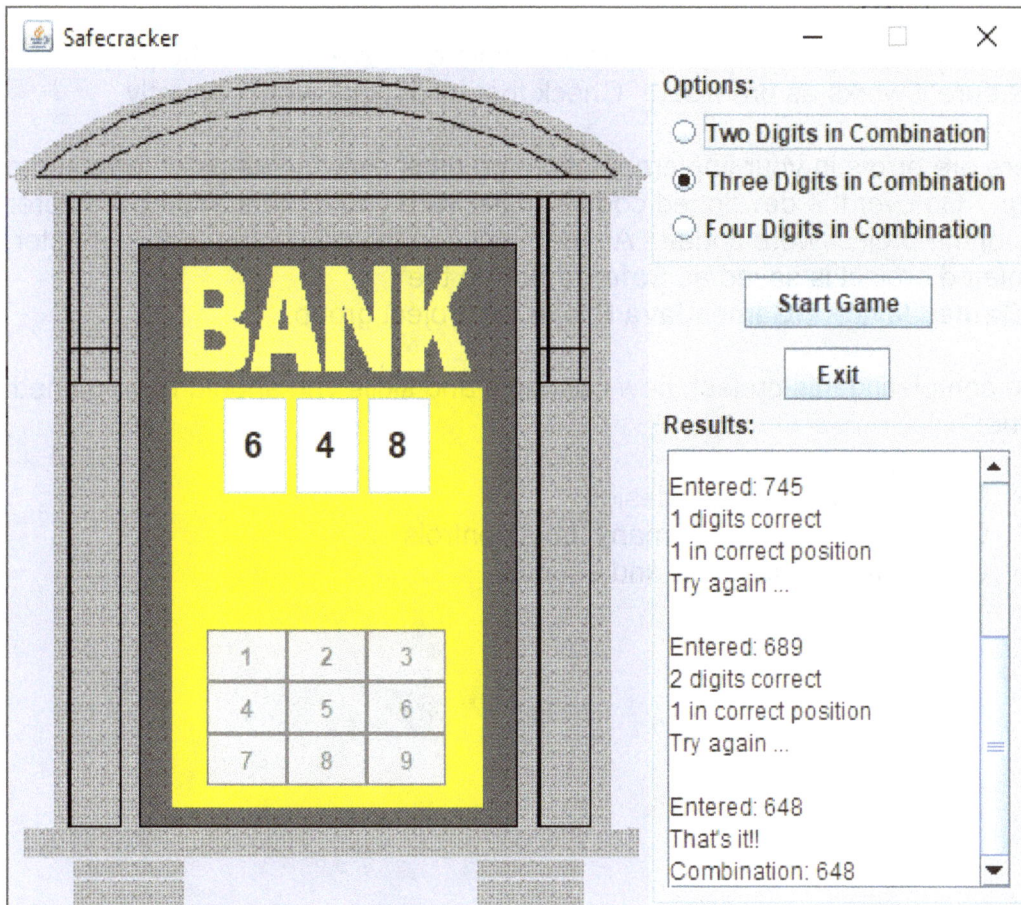

The correct combination was entered! A little celebratory sound was heard and the game returned to its stopped state.

Safecracker Project Review

The **Safecracker** game project is now complete. Save and run the project and make sure it works as promised. Check that all options work correctly.

If there are errors in your implementation, go back over the steps of form and code design. Go over the developed code – make sure you understand how different parts of the project were coded. As mentioned in the beginning of this chapter, the completed project is saved as **Safecracker** in the **\KidGamesJava\KidGamesJava Projects** project group.

While completing this project, new concepts and skills you should have gained include:

> ➤ Proper steps in project design.
> ➤ Capabilities and use of many Java controls.
> ➤ Using random numbers and sounds.

Safecracker Project Enhancements

There are always things you can do to improve a project. At the end of each chapter, we will give you some ideas for the current project. For the **Safecracker** game, some possibilities are:

> ➤ Add an option so the digits in the combination can repeat (perhaps use a check box control). You will need to modify the code that generates and checks the combination. You will also have to make sure the keypad buttons are not disabled after clicking. Do you see how such an option makes the game easier to play?

> ➤ To make the game simpler for smaller children, you might like to have combinations that use fewer than the 9 digits on the keypad. For example, a three digit code that only uses the numbers from 1 to 3 would be much easier to guess. You would need logic to decide which keys to keep on the keypad.

> ➤ After each guess, you might like to provide a hint on how to proceed.

> ➤ After a correct combination, maybe have more dramatic results. Perhaps, have the bank graphic disappear and a pile of treasure appear.

Safecracker Project Java Code Listing

```java
/*
 * Safecracker.java
 */
package safecracker;
import javax.swing.*;
import java.awt.*;
import java.awt.event.*;
import java.util.Random;
import java.net.URL;
import java.applet.*;

public class Safecracker extends JFrame
{
   ImagePanel safePanel = new ImagePanel(new
ImageIcon("bank.gif").getImage());
   JPanel comboPanel = new JPanel();
   JPanel keyPanel = new JPanel();
   JPanel optionsPanel = new JPanel();
   JPanel buttonsPanel = new JPanel();
   JPanel resultsPanel = new JPanel();

   JTextField[] comboTextField = new JTextField[4];
   JButton[] keyButton = new JButton[9];
   ButtonGroup digitsButtonGroup = new ButtonGroup();
   JRadioButton twoDigitsRadioButton = new JRadioButton();
   JRadioButton threeDigitsRadioButton = new JRadioButton();
   JRadioButton fourDigitsRadioButton = new JRadioButton();
   JButton startStopButton = new JButton();
   JButton exitButton = new JButton();
   JScrollPane resultsPane = new JScrollPane();
   JTextArea resultsTextArea = new JTextArea();

   int numberDigits;
   String secretCombo;
   Random myRandom = new Random();
   int digitsEntered;
   String enteredCombo;

   AudioClip wrongSound;
   AudioClip correctSound;

   public static void main(String args[])
   {
     // create frame
```

```java
    new Safecracker().setVisible(true);
  }

  public Safecracker()
  {
    // frame constructor
    setTitle("Safecracker");
    setResizable(false);
    addWindowListener(new WindowAdapter()
    {
      public void windowClosing(WindowEvent evt)
      {
        exitForm(evt);
      }
    });
    getContentPane().setLayout(new GridBagLayout());
    GridBagConstraints gridConstraints;

    safePanel.setPreferredSize(new Dimension(330, 420));
    safePanel.setLayout(new GridBagLayout());
    gridConstraints = new GridBagConstraints();
    gridConstraints.gridx = 0;
    gridConstraints.gridy = 0;
    gridConstraints.gridheight = 3;
    getContentPane().add(safePanel, gridConstraints);

    comboPanel.setPreferredSize(new Dimension(160, 110));
    safePanel.setLayout(new GridBagLayout());
    comboPanel.setBackground(Color.YELLOW);
    gridConstraints = new GridBagConstraints();
    gridConstraints.gridx = 0;
    gridConstraints.gridy = 0;
    gridConstraints.insets = new Insets(110, 0, 0, 0);
    safePanel.add(comboPanel, gridConstraints);

    for (int i = 0; i < 4; i++)
    {
      comboTextField[i] = new JTextField();
      comboTextField[i].setPreferredSize(new Dimension(32,
48));
      comboTextField[i].setEditable(false);
      comboTextField[i].setBackground(Color.WHITE);
      comboTextField[i].setText("0");

comboTextField[i].setHorizontalAlignment(SwingConstants.CENT
ER);
```

```
      comboTextField[i].setFont(new Font("Arial", Font.BOLD,
18));
    gridConstraints = new GridBagConstraints();
    gridConstraints.gridx = i;
    gridConstraints.gridy = 0;
    comboPanel.add(comboTextField[i], gridConstraints);
  }

  keyPanel.setPreferredSize(new Dimension(160, 100));
  keyPanel.setLayout(new GridBagLayout());
  keyPanel.setBackground(Color.YELLOW);
  gridConstraints = new GridBagConstraints();
  gridConstraints.gridx = 0;
  gridConstraints.gridy = 1;
  safePanel.add(keyPanel, gridConstraints);

  for (int i = 0; i < 9; i++)
  {
    keyButton[i] = new JButton();
    keyButton[i].setText(String.valueOf(i + 1));
    gridConstraints = new GridBagConstraints();
    gridConstraints.gridx = i % 3;
    gridConstraints.gridy = i / 3;
    keyPanel.add(keyButton[i], gridConstraints);
    keyButton[i].addActionListener(new ActionListener()
    {
      public void actionPerformed(ActionEvent e)
      {
        keyButtonActionPerformed(e);
      }
    });
  }

  optionsPanel.setPreferredSize(new Dimension(200, 100));

optionsPanel.setBorder(BorderFactory.createTitledBorder("Opt
ions:"));
  optionsPanel.setLayout(new GridBagLayout());
  gridConstraints = new GridBagConstraints();
  gridConstraints.gridx = 1;
  gridConstraints.gridy = 0;
  getContentPane().add(optionsPanel, gridConstraints);

  twoDigitsRadioButton.setText("Two Digits in
Combination");
  twoDigitsRadioButton.setSelected(true);
  digitsButtonGroup.add(twoDigitsRadioButton);
```

```
    gridConstraints = new GridBagConstraints();
    gridConstraints.gridx = 0;
    gridConstraints.gridy = 0;
    gridConstraints.anchor = GridBagConstraints.WEST;
    optionsPanel.add(twoDigitsRadioButton, gridConstraints);

    threeDigitsRadioButton.setText("Three Digits in
Combination");
    digitsButtonGroup.add(threeDigitsRadioButton);
    gridConstraints = new GridBagConstraints();
    gridConstraints.gridx = 0;
    gridConstraints.gridy = 1;
    gridConstraints.anchor = GridBagConstraints.WEST;
    optionsPanel.add(threeDigitsRadioButton,
gridConstraints);

    fourDigitsRadioButton.setText("Four Digits in
Combination");
    digitsButtonGroup.add(fourDigitsRadioButton);
    gridConstraints = new GridBagConstraints();
    gridConstraints.gridx = 0;
    gridConstraints.gridy = 2;
    gridConstraints.anchor = GridBagConstraints.WEST;
    optionsPanel.add(fourDigitsRadioButton,
gridConstraints);

    buttonsPanel.setPreferredSize(new Dimension(200, 70));
    buttonsPanel.setLayout(new GridBagLayout());
    gridConstraints = new GridBagConstraints();
    gridConstraints.gridx = 1;
    gridConstraints.gridy = 1;
    getContentPane().add(buttonsPanel, gridConstraints);

    startStopButton.setText("Start Game");
    gridConstraints = new GridBagConstraints();
    gridConstraints.gridx = 0;
    gridConstraints.gridy = 0;
    buttonsPanel.add(startStopButton, gridConstraints);
    startStopButton.addActionListener(new ActionListener()
    {
      public void actionPerformed(ActionEvent e)
      {
        startStopButtonActionPerformed(e);
      }
    });

    exitButton.setText("Exit");
```

```
   gridConstraints = new GridBagConstraints();
   gridConstraints.gridx = 0;
   gridConstraints.gridy = 1;
   gridConstraints.insets = new Insets(10, 0, 0, 0);
   buttonsPanel.add(exitButton, gridConstraints);
   exitButton.addActionListener(new ActionListener()
   {
     public void actionPerformed(ActionEvent e)
     {
       exitButtonActionPerformed(e);
     }
   });

   resultsPanel.setPreferredSize(new Dimension(200, 250));

resultsPanel.setBorder(BorderFactory.createTitledBorder("Res
ults:"));
   resultsPanel.setLayout(new GridBagLayout());
   gridConstraints = new GridBagConstraints();
   gridConstraints.gridx = 1;
   gridConstraints.gridy = 2;
   getContentPane().add(resultsPanel, gridConstraints);

   resultsTextArea.setEditable(false);
   resultsTextArea.setBackground(Color.WHITE);
   resultsPane.setPreferredSize(new Dimension(180, 220));
   resultsPane.setViewportView(resultsTextArea);
   gridConstraints = new GridBagConstraints();
   gridConstraints.gridx = 0;
   gridConstraints.gridy = 0;
   resultsPanel.add(resultsPane, gridConstraints);

   pack();
   Dimension screenSize =
Toolkit.getDefaultToolkit().getScreenSize();
   setBounds((int) (0.5 * (screenSize.width - getWidth())),
(int) (0.5 * (screenSize.height - getHeight())), getWidth(),
getHeight());

   setKeyButtons(false);
   try
   {
     wrongSound = Applet.newAudioClip(new URL("file:" +
"uhoh.wav"));
     correctSound = Applet.newAudioClip(new URL("file:" +
"tada.wav"));
   }
```

```
      catch (Exception ex)
      {
        System.out.println("Error loading sound files");
      }
  }

  private void keyButtonActionPerformed(ActionEvent e)
  {
    String n;
    int numberRight, positionRight;
    // determine which button was clicked
    // ActionCommand is text on button
    n = e.getActionCommand();
    // disable button since digits can't repeat
    keyButton[Integer.valueOf(n).intValue() -
1].setEnabled(false);
    // if first button in combo, clear out label boxes
    if (digitsEntered == 0)
    {
      comboTextField[0].setText("");
      comboTextField[1].setText("");
      comboTextField[2].setText("");
      comboTextField[3].setText("");
    }
    // add button to code
    enteredCombo += n;
    digitsEntered++;
    comboTextField[digitsEntered - 1].setText(n);
    // if all digits entered, check combo
    if (digitsEntered == numberDigits)
    {
      // reset combo buttons
      setKeyButtons(true);
      // check combination
      resultsTextArea.append("Entered: " + enteredCombo +
"\n");
      if (enteredCombo.equals(secretCombo))
      {
        correctSound.play();
        startStopButton.doClick();
      }
      else
      {
        wrongSound.play();
        numberRight = 0;
        for (int i = 0; i < numberDigits; i++)
        {
```

```
                n = String.valueOf(enteredCombo.charAt(i));
                for (int j = 0; j < numberDigits; j++)
                    if
(n.equals(String.valueOf(secretCombo.charAt(j))))
                        numberRight++;
            }
            // how many in correct position
            positionRight = 0;
            for (int i = 0; i < numberDigits; i++)
                if (secretCombo.charAt(i) ==
enteredCombo.charAt(i))
                    positionRight++;
            resultsTextArea.append(String.valueOf(numberRight) +
" digits correct" + "\n");
            resultsTextArea.append(String.valueOf(positionRight)
+ " in correct position" + "\n");
            resultsTextArea.append("Try again ..." + "\n\n");
            // clear combo to try again
            enteredCombo = "";
            digitsEntered = 0;
        }
    }
}

    private void startStopButtonActionPerformed(ActionEvent e)
    {
        if (startStopButton.getText().equals("Start Game"))
        {
            startStopButton.setText("Stop Game");
            twoDigitsRadioButton.setEnabled(false);
            threeDigitsRadioButton.setEnabled(false);
            fourDigitsRadioButton.setEnabled(false);
            exitButton.setEnabled(false);
            setKeyButtons(true);
            resultsTextArea.setText("");
            // determine number of digits and set up labels
            if (twoDigitsRadioButton.isSelected())
            {
                numberDigits = 2;
            }
            else if (threeDigitsRadioButton.isSelected())
            {
                numberDigits = 3;
            }
            else
            {
                numberDigits = 4;
```

```
      }
      for (int i = 0; i < numberDigits; i++)
      {
        comboTextField[i].setVisible(true);
        comboTextField[i].setText("");
      }
      if (numberDigits != 4)
      {
        for (int i = numberDigits; i < 4; i++)
        {
          comboTextField[i].setVisible(false);
        }
      }
      // determine combination
      secretCombo = "";
      int j;
      boolean uniqueDigit;
      for (int i = 0; i < numberDigits; i++)
      {
        // select unique digit
        do
        {
          j = myRandom.nextInt(9) + 1;
          uniqueDigit = true;
          if (i != 0)
          {
            for (int k = 0; k < i; k++)
            {
              if
(String.valueOf(secretCombo.charAt(k)).equals(String.valueOf
(j)))
                uniqueDigit = false;
            }
          }
        }
        while (!uniqueDigit);
        secretCombo += String.valueOf(j);
      }
      enteredCombo = "";
      digitsEntered = 0;
    }
    else
    {
      if (enteredCombo.equals(secretCombo))
        resultsTextArea.append("That's it!!" + "\n");
      else
        resultsTextArea.append("Game Stopped" + "\n");
```

```
      resultsTextArea.append("Combination: " + secretCombo);
      startStopButton.setText("Start Game");
      twoDigitsRadioButton.setEnabled(true);
      threeDigitsRadioButton.setEnabled(true);
      fourDigitsRadioButton.setEnabled(true);
      exitButton.setEnabled(true);
      setKeyButtons(false);
    }
  }

  private void exitButtonActionPerformed(ActionEvent e)
  {
    System.exit(0);
  }

  private void setKeyButtons(boolean a)
  {
    for (int i = 0; i < 9; i++)
    {
      keyButton[i].setEnabled(a);
    }
  }

  private void exitForm(WindowEvent evt)
  {
    System.exit(0);
  }
}

class ImagePanel extends JPanel
{
  private Image img;
  public ImagePanel(Image img)
  {
   this.img = img;
  }
  public void paintComponent(Graphics g)
  {
    g.drawImage(img, 0, 0, null);
  }
}
```

3

Tic Tac Toe Project

Review and Preview

The next project we build is the classic **Tic Tac Toe** game, where you try to line up 3 X's or 3 O's in a 3 by 3 grid. We'll develop a two player version and one where you can play against the computer.

Tic Tac Toe Project Preview

In this chapter, we will build a **Tic Tac Toe** game. This is purportedly the first game ever programmed on a computer and one of the first ever programmed by Bill Gates when he was a teenager at Lakeside School in Seattle. The object of the game is line up 3 X markers or 3 O markers in a 3 by 3 grid. The markers can run horizontally, vertically or diagonally. Turns alternate between players. The version we build here allows two players to compete against each other or to have a single player compete against a pretty smart computer.

The finished project is saved as **TicTacToe** in the **\KidGamesJava\KidGamesJava Projects** folder. Start NetBeans (or your IDE). Open the specified project group. Make **TicTacToe** the selected project. Run the project. You will see:

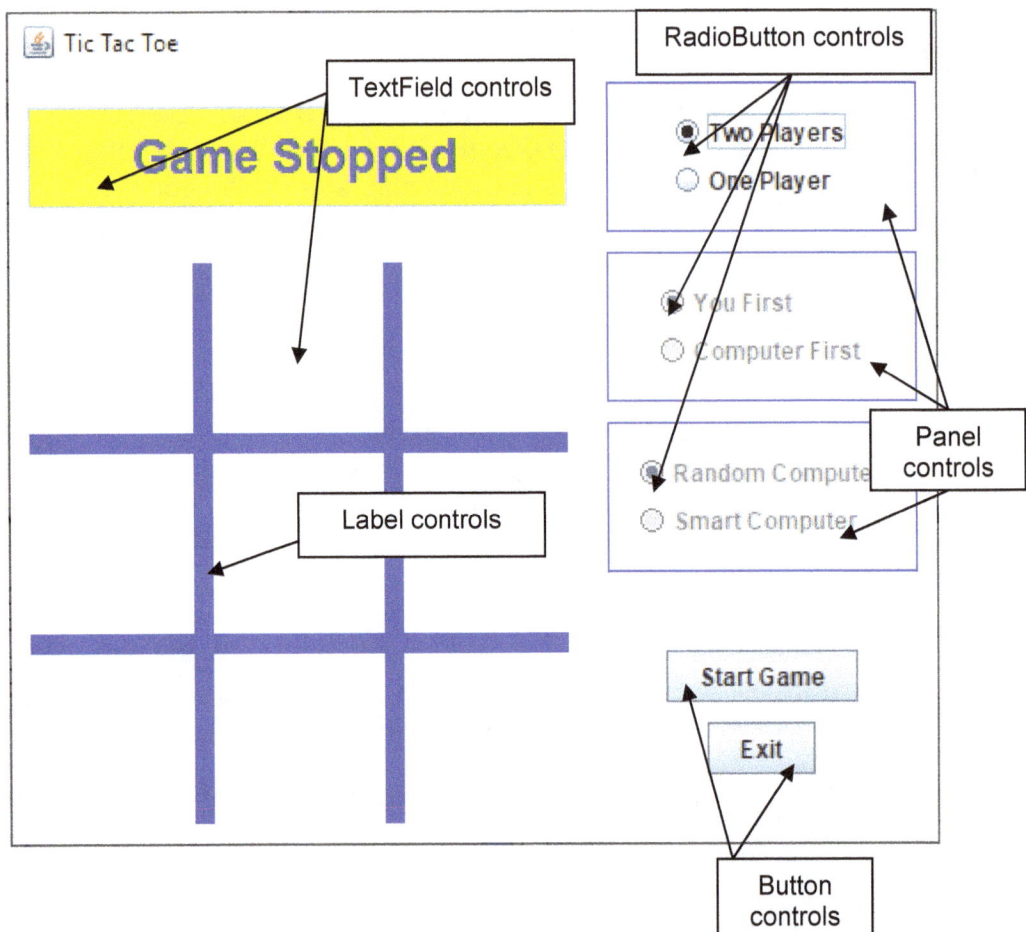

On the left is the grid for playing **Tic Tac Toe**. A text field is used to tell you whose turn it is. Text fields are also used to mark X's and O's in the grid. Skinny label controls are used to form the dark blue grid. On the right are three panel controls and two button controls. Each panel holds two radio button controls used to establish game options. The two button controls are used to start and stop the game and to exit the program.

The game appears in its 'stopped' state, the grid is cleared and waiting for you to choose game options (one or two players and, if one player, who goes first and how smart you want the computer to be). The grid is disabled – no marks can be made (by clicking the grid). I've selected a one player game, where I go first (giving me X's) and a smart computer:

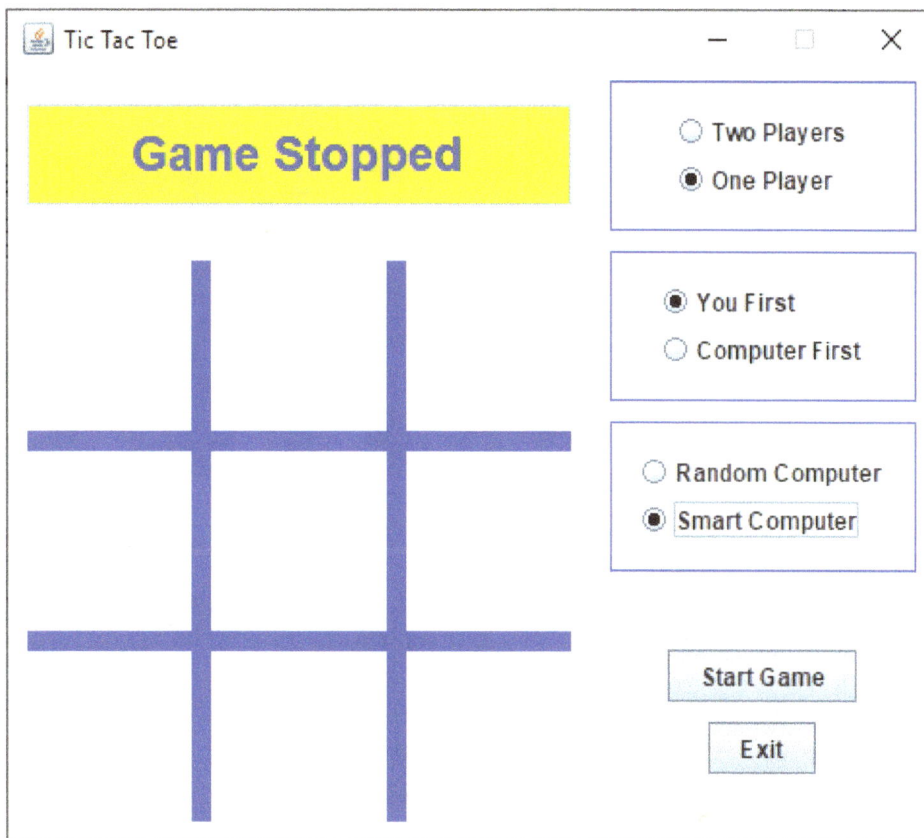

Click the **Start Game** button to start playing. Its caption will change (now reading **Stop Game**) and the options group boxes and **Exit** button will become disabled. The label at the top of the grid says **X's Turn**. X always goes first in this game (whether it's you, the human player, or the computer).

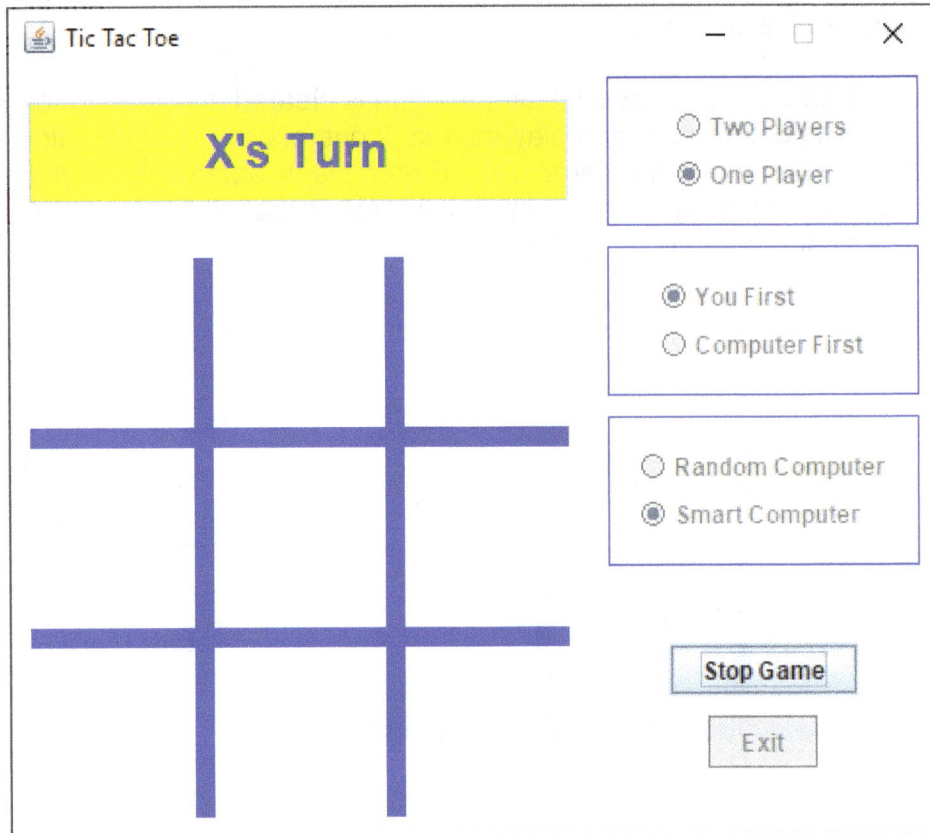

In this state, you make a mark in the grid by clicking on the desired square. The computer will then place its mark, making it your turn again. After each mark, the board is examined for a win or a draw. You keep alternating turns until there is a win, the grid is full or until you press **Stop Game**. The game works the same way for two players, with the two players alternating turns marking the grid.

Enter a mark; I chose the center square and the computer immediately placed its mark (an O) in the upper left corner:

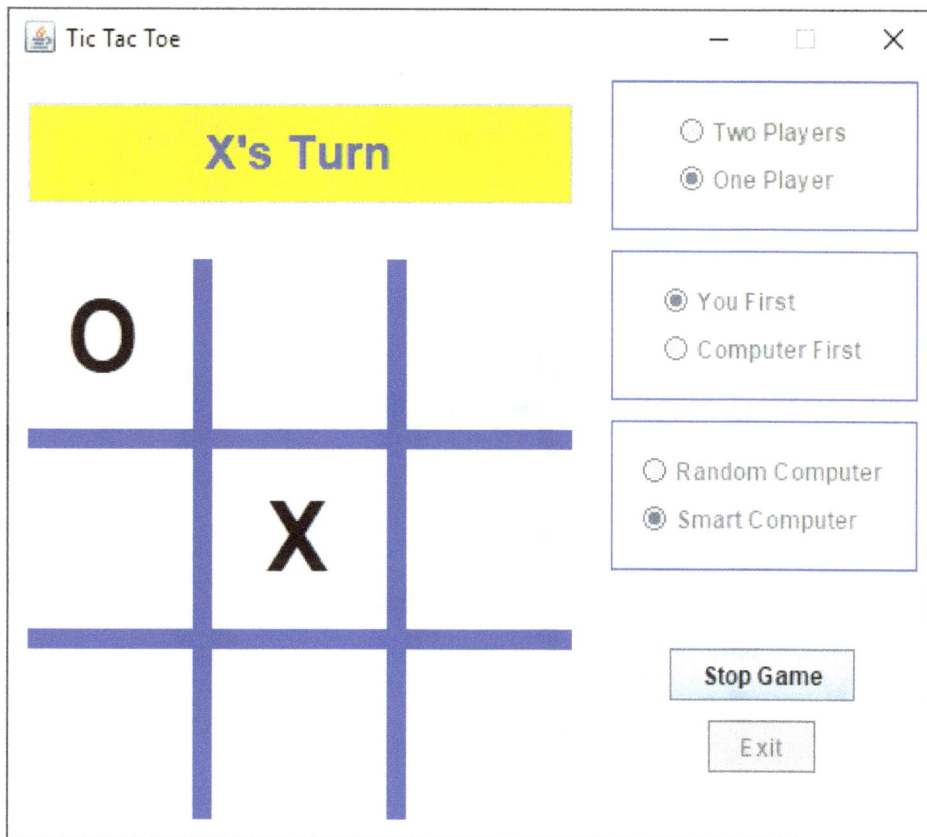

I try the lower left corner and the computer blocks me from winning:

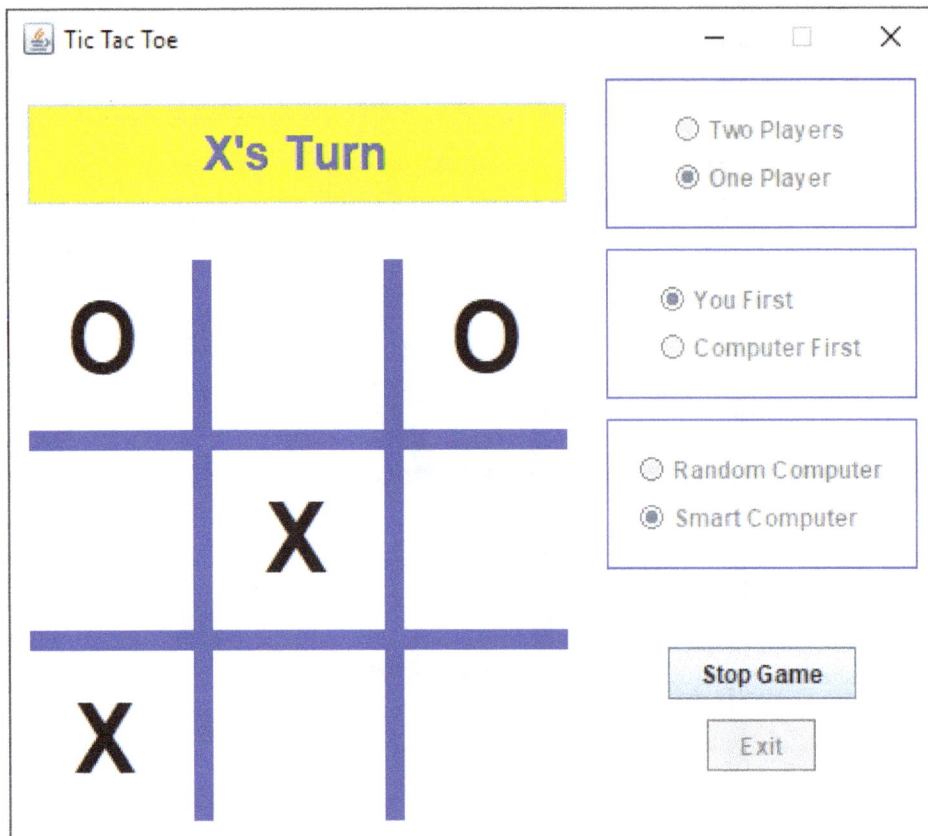

I block the computer's possible win by putting an X in the middle box of the top row. Then, the computer blocks me with a move to the middle of the bottom row:

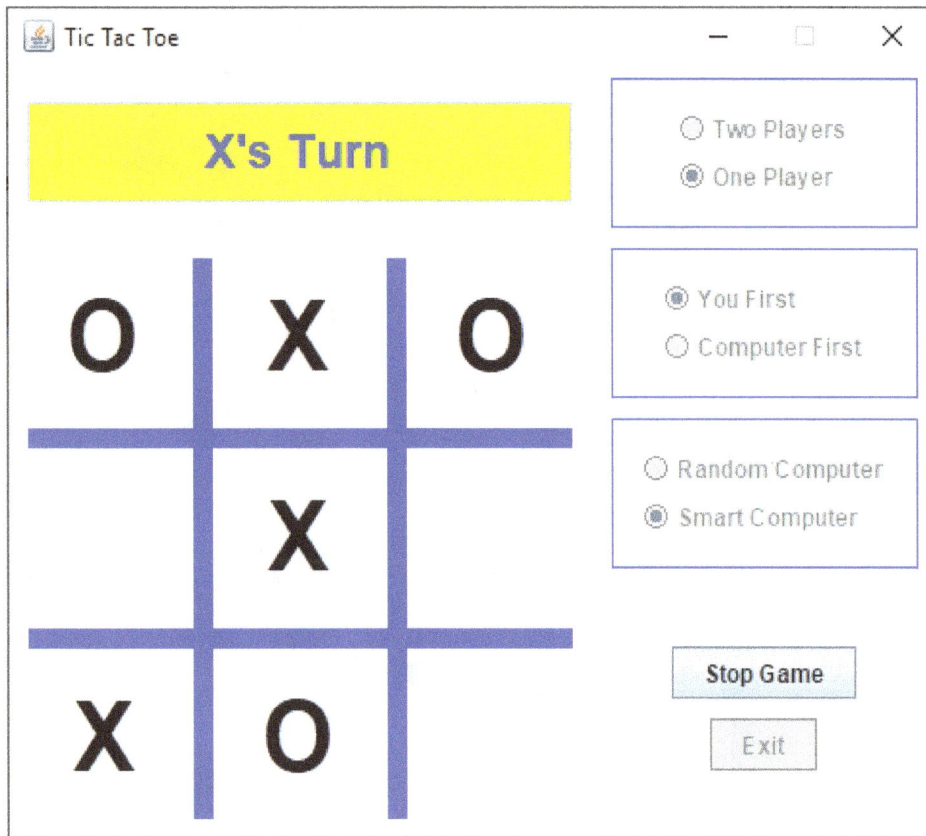

Looks like no one is going to win here.

I continued playing (moving to the right of the middle row and, following the computer's block, a move to the right of the bottom row) until finally we ended in a draw:

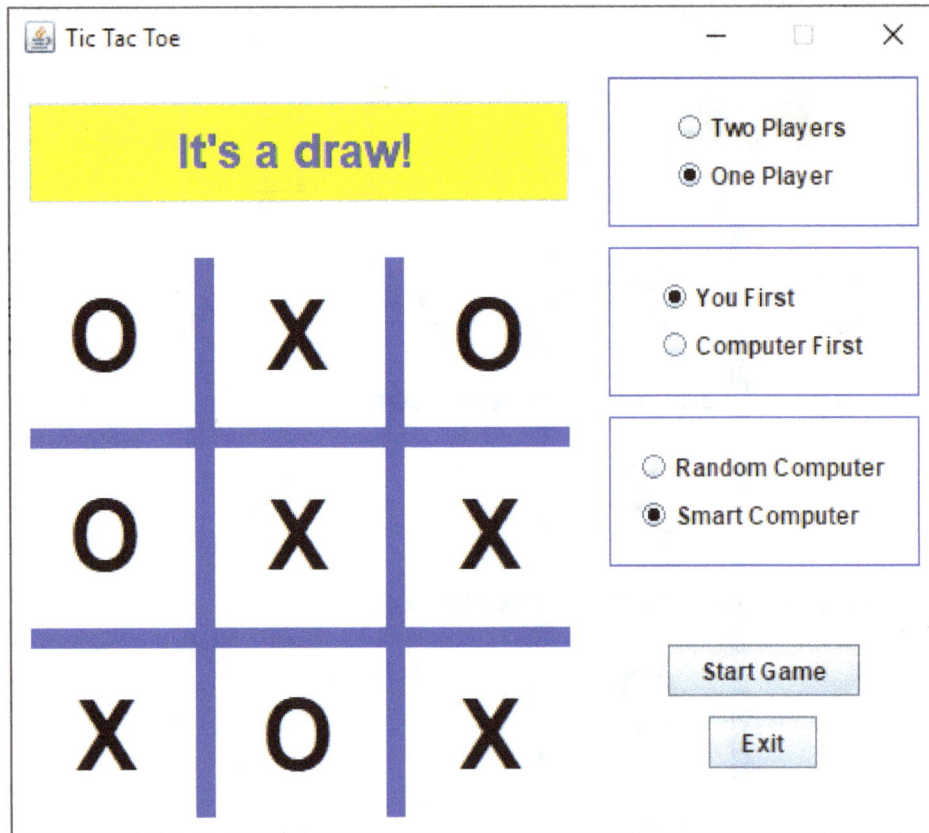

Looks like the computer is pretty smart! We'll see how this intelligence is programmed later. Notice the game returns to its stopped state to allow another game or to stop the program.

Continue playing the game to understand its operation. Try using the **Random Computer** option (the computer just makes random moves making it easier to beat). Click **Exit** when you're done to stop the game. Open the code file and look over the code, if you like.

You will now build this project in stages. As you build Java projects, we always recommend taking a slow, step-by-step process. It minimizes programming errors and helps build your confidence as things come together in a complete project.

We address **frame design**. We discuss the controls needed to build the frame, establish initial control properties and discuss how to change the state of the controls. And, we address **code design**. We discuss how to mark the grid, handle multiple players, check for a win and decide how to make computer-generated moves.

Tic Tac Toe Frame Design

We begin building the **Tic Tac Toe** game project. Let's build the frame. Start a new project in your Java Project group – name it **TicTacToe**. Delete the default code in the file named **TicTacToe.java**.   Once started, we suggest you immediately save the project with a name you choose. This sets up the folder and file structure needed for your project.

Build the basic frame with these properties:

TicTacToe Frame:
title	Tic Tac Toe
background	White
resizable	false

The code is:

```
/*
 * TicTacToe.java
 */
package tictactoe;
import javax.swing.*;
import java.awt.*;
import java.awt.event.*;

public class TicTacToe extends JFrame
{
  public static void main(String args[])
  {
    // create frame
    new TicTacToe().setVisible(true);
  }

  public TicTacToe()
  {
    // frame constructor
    setTitle("Tic Tac Toe");
    getContentPane().setBackground(Color.WHITE);
    setResizable(false);
    addWindowListener(new WindowAdapter()
    {
      public void windowClosing(WindowEvent evt)
      {
        exitForm(evt);
      }
    });
```

```
    getContentPane().setLayout(new GridBagLayout());
    GridBagConstraints gridConstraints;

    pack();
    Dimension screenSize =
Toolkit.getDefaultToolkit().getScreenSize();
    setBounds((int) (0.5 * (screenSize.width -
getWidth())), (int) (0.5 * (screenSize.height -
getHeight())), getWidth(), getHeight());
  }

  private void exitForm(WindowEvent evt)
  {
    System.exit(0);
  }
}
```

This code builds the frame, sets up the layout manager and includes code to exit the application. Run the code to make sure the frame (at least, what there is of it at this point) appears and is centered on the screen:

Let's populate our frame with other controls. All code for creating the frame and placing controls (except declarations) goes in the **TicTacToe** constructor.

We start by putting a text field control and five panel controls on the frame. The **GridBagLayout** is:

	gridx = 0	gridx = 1
gridy = 0	messageTextField	playersPanel
gridy = 1	gamePanel	firstPanel
gridy = 2		computerPanel
gridy = 3		buttonsPanel

The **messageTextField** control is used for messaging. The **gamePanel** will be used to display the marks (X and O) and to form the grid. The **playersPanel** will hold radio buttons selecting the number of players. The **firstPanel** will host radio buttons deciding who goes first in a one player game. The **computerPanel** holds radio buttons that decide how smart the computer is. And the **buttonsPanel** will hold the two button controls. We will build each panel separately. Let's begin with the first column (which includes gamePanel) in the grid layout.

Add the **messageTextField** and **gamePanel** controls to the frame with these properties:

messageTextField:

size	280, 50
editable	false
background	Yellow
foreground	Blue
text	X's Move
horizontalAlignment	Center
font	Arial, Bold, Size 24
gridx	0
gridy	0
insets	10, 10, 10, 10

gamePanel:

size	280, 280
background	White
gridx	0
gridy	1
insets	10, 10, 10, 10

These controls are declared using:

```
JTextField messageTextField = new JTextField();
JPanel gamePanel = new JPanel();
```

The controls are placed in the frame using this code:

```
messageTextField = new JTextField();
messageTextField.setPreferredSize(new Dimension(280, 50));
messageTextField.setEditable(false);
messageTextField.setBackground(Color.YELLOW);
messageTextField.setForeground(Color.BLUE);
messageTextField.setText("X's Move");
messageTextField.setHorizontalAlignment(SwingConstants.CENTER);
messageTextField.setFont(new Font("Arial", Font.BOLD, 24));
gridConstraints = new GridBagConstraints();
gridConstraints.gridx = 0;
gridConstraints.gridy = 0;
gridConstraints.insets = new Insets(10, 10, 10, 10);
getContentPane().add(messageTextField, gridConstraints);
```

```
gamePanel.setPreferredSize(new Dimension(280, 280));
gamePanel.setBackground(Color.WHITE);
gamePanel.setLayout(new GridBagLayout());
gridConstraints = new GridBagConstraints();
gridConstraints.gridx = 0;
gridConstraints.gridy = 1;
gridConstraints.gridheight = 3;
gridConstraints.insets = new Insets(10, 10, 10, 10);
getContentPane().add(gamePanel, gridConstraints);
```

Add this code in the proper locations. Run to see:

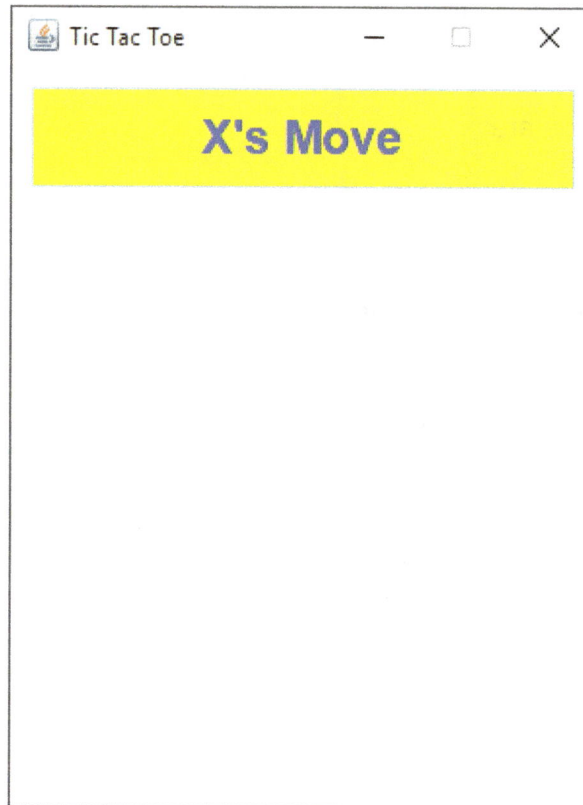

The text field and empty game panel are shown. Let's build the game panel next.

The **gamePanel** control will hold nine text field controls (to display the marks) and four skinny label controls to form a grid. The **GridBagLayout** is:

	gridx = 0	gridx = 1	gridx = 2	gridx = 3	gridx = 4
gridy = 0	boxTextField[0]	gridLabel[2]	boxTextField[1]	gridLabel[3]	boxTextField[2]
gridy = 1	gridLabel[0]				
gridy = 2	boxTextField[3]		boxTextField[4]		boxTextField[5]
gridy = 3	gridLabel[1]				
gridy = 4	boxTextField[6]		boxTextField[7]		boxTextField[8]

gridLabel[2] and **gridLabel[3]** extend to the bottom of the grid (we can't show that on this table.

The control properties are:
boxTextField[0]:

size	80, 80
editable	false
background	White
horizontalAlignment	Center
font	Arial, Bold, Size 48
border	null
gridx	0
gridy	0

boxTextField[1]:

size	80, 80
editable	false
background	White
horizontalAlignment	Center
font	Arial, Bold, Size 48
border	null
gridx	2
gridy	0

boxTextField[2]:

size	80, 80
editable	false
background	White
horizontalAlignment	Center
font	Arial, Bold, Size 48
border	null
gridx	4
gridy	0

boxTextField[3]:

size	80, 80
editable	false
background	White
horizontalAlignment	Center
font	Arial, Bold, Size 48
border	null
gridx	2
gridy	0

boxTextField[4]:

size	80, 80
editable	false
background	White
horizontalAlignment	Center
font	Arial, Bold, Size 48
border	null
gridx	2
gridy	2

boxTextField[5]:

size	80, 80
editable	false
background	White
horizontalAlignment	Center
font	Arial, Bold, Size 48
border	null
gridx	4
gridy	2

boxTextField[6]:

size	80, 80
editable	false
background	White
horizontalAlignment	Center
font	Arial, Bold, Size 48
border	null
gridx	0
gridy	4

boxTextField[7]:

size	80, 80
editable	false
background	White
horizontalAlignment	Center
font	Arial, Bold, Size 48
border	null
gridx	2
gridy	4

boxTextField[8]:

size	80, 80
editable	false
background	White
horizontalAlignment	Center
font	Arial, Bold, Size 48
border	null
gridx	4
gridy	4

gridLabel[0]:

size	280, 10
opaque	true
background	Blue
gridx	0
gridy	1
gridwidth	5
insets	5, 0, 5, 0

gridLabel[1]:

size	280, 10
opaque	true
background	Blue
gridx	0
gridy	3
gridwidth	5
insets	5, 0, 5, 0

gridLabel[2]:

size	10, 280
opaque	true
background	Blue
gridx	1
gridy	0
gridheight	5
insets	0, 5, 0, 5

gridLabel[3]:

size	10, 280
opaque	true
background	Blue
gridx	3
gridy	0
gridheight	5
insets	0, 5, 0, 5

Declare the controls using:

```
JTextField[] boxTextField = new JTextField[9];
JLabel[] gridLabel = new JLabel[4];
```

Add the controls to the **gamePanel** using:

```
for (int i = 0; i < 9; i++)
{
   boxTextField[i] = new JTextField();
   boxTextField[i].setPreferredSize(new Dimension(80, 80));
   boxTextField[i].setEditable(false);
   boxTextField[i].setBackground(Color.WHITE);

boxTextField[i].setHorizontalAlignment(SwingConstants.CENT
ER);
   boxTextField[i].setFont(new Font("Arial", Font.BOLD,
48));
   boxTextField[i].setBorder(null);
   gridConstraints = new GridBagConstraints();
   gridConstraints.gridx = 2 * (i % 3);
   gridConstraints.gridy = 2 * (i / 3);
   gamePanel.add(boxTextField[i], gridConstraints);
   boxTextField[i].addMouseListener(new MouseAdapter()
   {
public void mousePressed(MouseEvent e)
{
   boxTextFieldMousePressed(e);
}
```

```
    });
}

gridLabel[0] = new JLabel();
gridLabel[0].setPreferredSize(new Dimension(280, 10));
gridLabel[0].setOpaque(true);
gridLabel[0].setBackground(Color.BLUE);
gridConstraints = new GridBagConstraints();
gridConstraints.gridx = 0;
gridConstraints.gridy = 1;
gridConstraints.gridwidth = 5;
gridConstraints.insets = new Insets(5, 0, 5, 0);
gamePanel.add(gridLabel[0], gridConstraints);

gridLabel[1] = new JLabel();
gridLabel[1].setPreferredSize(new Dimension(280, 10));
gridLabel[1].setOpaque(true);
gridLabel[1].setBackground(Color.BLUE);
gridConstraints = new GridBagConstraints();
gridConstraints.gridx = 0;
gridConstraints.gridy = 3;
gridConstraints.gridwidth = 5;
gridConstraints.insets = new Insets(5, 0, 5, 0);
gamePanel.add(gridLabel[1], gridConstraints);

gridLabel[2] = new JLabel();
gridLabel[2].setPreferredSize(new Dimension(10, 280));
gridLabel[2].setOpaque(true);
gridLabel[2].setBackground(Color.BLUE);
gridConstraints = new GridBagConstraints();
gridConstraints.gridx = 1;
gridConstraints.gridy = 0;
gridConstraints.gridheight = 5;
gridConstraints.insets = new Insets(0, 5, 0, 5);
gamePanel.add(gridLabel[2], gridConstraints);

gridLabel[3] = new JLabel();
gridLabel[3].setPreferredSize(new Dimension(10, 280));
gridLabel[3].setOpaque(true);
gridLabel[3].setBackground(Color.BLUE);
gridConstraints = new GridBagConstraints();
gridConstraints.gridx = 3;
gridConstraints.gridy = 0;
gridConstraints.gridheight = 5;
gridConstraints.insets = new Insets(0, 5, 0, 5);
gamePanel.add(gridLabel[3], gridConstraints);
```

Notice how the loop index (**i**) is used to set the text field positioning.

This code also adds mouse listeners for each text field. The method called when a text field is clicked with the mouse **boxTextFieldMousePressed**. Add this empty method with the other methods:

```
private void boxTextFieldMousePressed(MouseEvent e)
{
}
```

Add code in the proper locations. Run to see the empty grid:

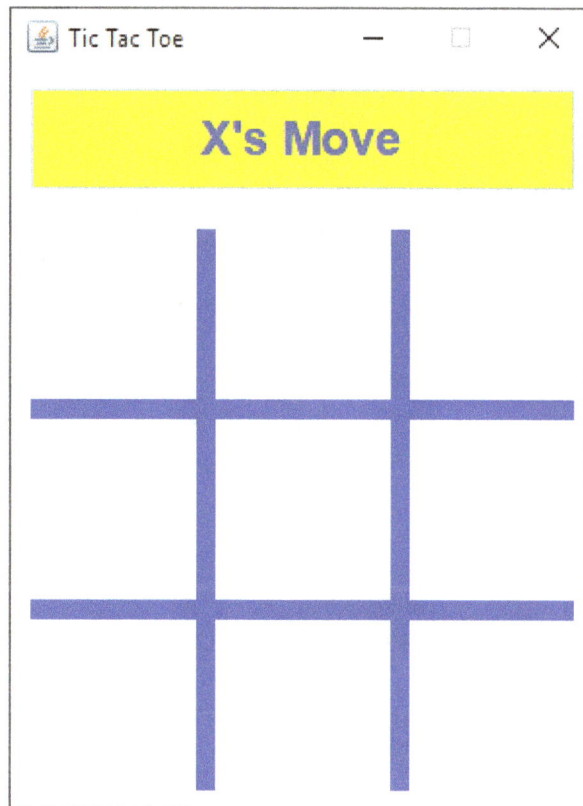

Let's add the remaining panels.

The **playersPanel** will hold two radio button controls used to select the number of players in the game. The **GridBagLayout** for optionsPanel is:

	gridx = 0
gridy = 0	**twoPlayersRadioButton**
gridy =1	**onePlayerRadioButton**

The panel and radio button properties:

playersPanel:
size	160, 75
border	Line, Blue
gridx	1 (on frame)
gridy	0 (on frame)
insets	5, 10, 5, 10

twoPlayersRadioButton:
text	Two Players
background	White
buttonGroup	playersButtonGroup
selected	true
gridx	0 (on playersPanel)
gridy	0 (on playersPanel)
anchor	WEST

onePlayerRadioButton:
text	One Player
background	White
buttonGroup	playersButtonGroup
gridx	0 (on optionsPanel)
gridy	1 (on optionsPanel)
anchor	WEST

These controls are declared using:

```
JPanel playersPanel = new JPanel();
ButtonGroup playersButtonGroup = new ButtonGroup();
JRadioButton twoPlayersRadioButton = new JRadioButton();
JRadioButton onePlayerRadioButton = new JRadioButton();
```

The radio buttons are placed in the **playersPanel** (which is placed in the frame) using:

```
playersPanel.setPreferredSize(new Dimension(160, 75));
playersPanel.setBackground(Color.WHITE);
playersPanel.setBorder(BorderFactory.createLineBorder(Colo
r.BLUE));
playersPanel.setLayout(new GridBagLayout());
gridConstraints = new GridBagConstraints();
gridConstraints.gridx = 1;
gridConstraints.gridy = 0;
gridConstraints.insets = new Insets(5, 10, 5, 10);
getContentPane().add(playersPanel, gridConstraints);

twoPlayersRadioButton.setText("Two Players");
twoPlayersRadioButton.setBackground(Color.WHITE);
twoPlayersRadioButton.setSelected(true);
playersButtonGroup.add(twoPlayersRadioButton);
gridConstraints = new GridBagConstraints();
gridConstraints.gridx = 0;
gridConstraints.gridy = 0;
gridConstraints.anchor = GridBagConstraints.WEST;
playersPanel.add(twoPlayersRadioButton, gridConstraints);
twoPlayersRadioButton.addActionListener(new
ActionListener()
{
  public void actionPerformed(ActionEvent e)
  {
    twoPlayersRadioButtonActionPerformed(e);
  }
});

onePlayerRadioButton.setText("One Player");
onePlayerRadioButton.setBackground(Color.WHITE);
playersButtonGroup.add(onePlayerRadioButton);
gridConstraints = new GridBagConstraints();
gridConstraints.gridx = 0;
gridConstraints.gridy = 1;
gridConstraints.anchor = GridBagConstraints.WEST;
playersPanel.add(onePlayerRadioButton, gridConstraints);
```

```
onePlayerRadioButton.addActionListener(new
ActionListener()
{
  public void actionPerformed(ActionEvent e)
  {
    onePlayerRadioButtonActionPerformed(e);
  }
});
```

We added listeners for the two radio buttons. Add these empty methods to handle button selections:

```
private void
twoPlayersRadioButtonActionPerformed(ActionEvent e)
{
}

private void
onePlayerRadioButtonActionPerformed(ActionEvent e)
{
}
```

Add this code in the proper locations. Run to see:

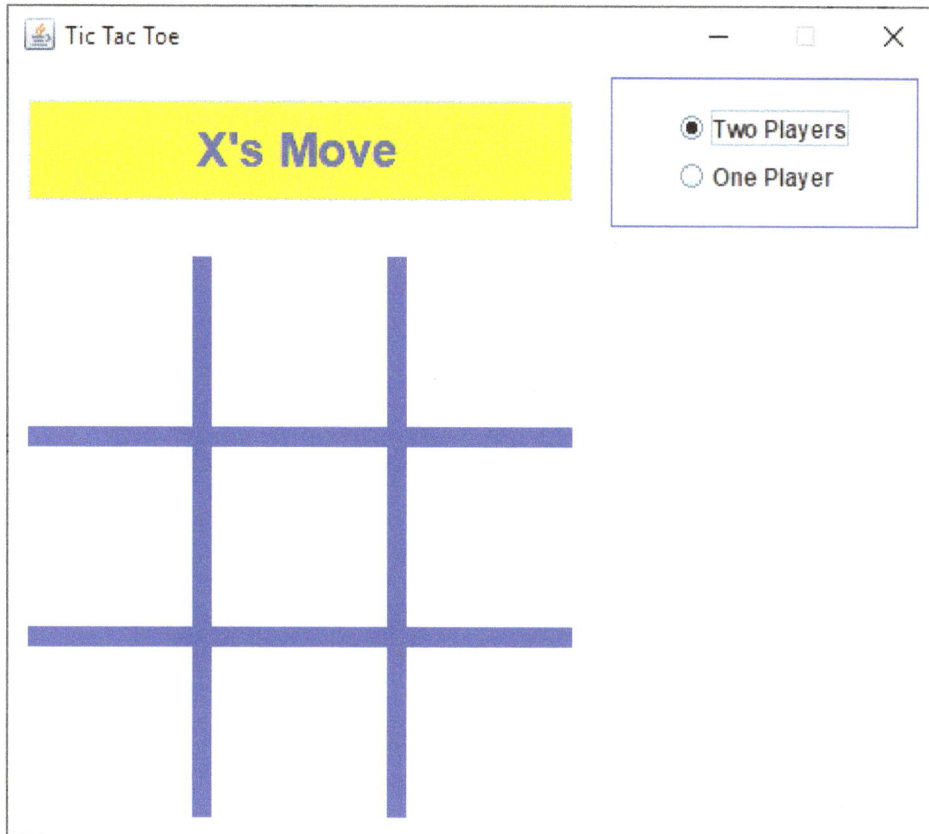

The players panel is displayed.

The **firstPanel** will hold two radio button controls used to determine who goes first in a one player game. The **GridBagLayout** for firstPanel is:

	gridx = 0
gridy = 0	**youFirstRadioButton**
gridy =1	**computerFirstRadioButton**

The panel and radio button properties:

firstPanel:
size	160, 75
border	Line, Blue
gridx	1 (on frame)
gridy	1 (on frame)
insets	5, 10, 5, 10

youFirstRadioButton:
text	You First
background	White
buttonGroup	firstButtonGroup
selected	true
gridx	0 (on firstPanel)
gridy	0 (on firstPanel)
anchor	WEST

computerFirstRadioButton:
text	Computer First
background	White
buttonGroup	firstButtonGroup
gridx	0 (on firstPanel)
gridy	1 (on firstPanel)
anchor	WEST

These controls are declared using:

```
JPanel firstPanel = new JPanel();
ButtonGroup firstButtonGroup = new ButtonGroup();
JRadioButton youFirstRadioButton = new JRadioButton();
JRadioButton computerFirstRadioButton = new
JRadioButton();
```

The radio buttons are placed in the **firstPanel** (which is placed in the frame) using:

```
firstPanel.setPreferredSize(new Dimension(160, 75));
firstPanel.setBackground(Color.WHITE);
firstPanel.setBorder(BorderFactory.createLineBorder(Color.
BLUE));
firstPanel.setLayout(new GridBagLayout());
gridConstraints = new GridBagConstraints();
gridConstraints.gridx = 1;
gridConstraints.gridy = 1;
gridConstraints.insets = new Insets(5, 10, 5, 10);
getContentPane().add(firstPanel, gridConstraints);

youFirstRadioButton.setText("You First");
youFirstRadioButton.setBackground(Color.WHITE);
youFirstRadioButton.setSelected(true);
firstButtonGroup.add(youFirstRadioButton);
gridConstraints = new GridBagConstraints();
gridConstraints.gridx = 0;
gridConstraints.gridy = 0;
gridConstraints.anchor = GridBagConstraints.WEST;
firstPanel.add(youFirstRadioButton, gridConstraints);

computerFirstRadioButton.setText("Computer First");
computerFirstRadioButton.setBackground(Color.WHITE);
firstButtonGroup.add(computerFirstRadioButton);
gridConstraints = new GridBagConstraints();
gridConstraints.gridx = 0;
gridConstraints.gridy = 1;
gridConstraints.anchor = GridBagConstraints.WEST;
firstPanel.add(computerFirstRadioButton, gridConstraints);
```

Add this code in the proper locations. Run to see:

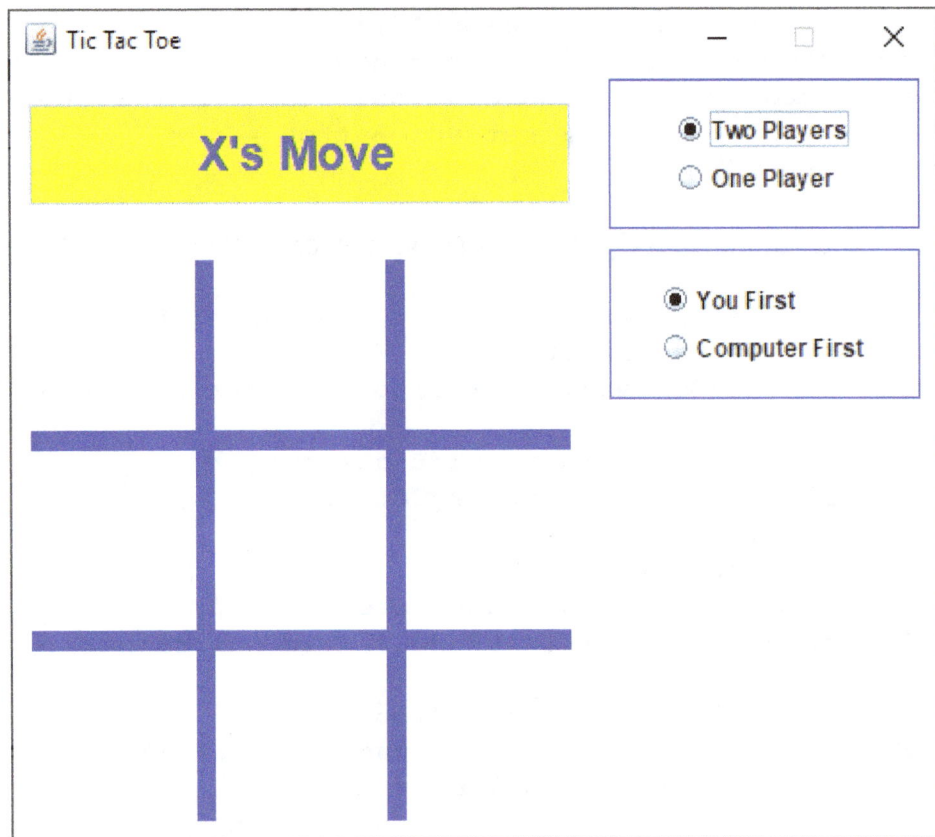

The first panel is displayed.

The **computerPanel** will hold two radio button controls used to how smart the computer is in a one player game. The **GridBagLayout** for computerPanel is:

	gridx = 0
gridy = 0	**randomRadioButton**
gridy = 1	**smartRadioButton**

The panel and radio button properties:

computerPanel:
size	160, 75
border	Line, Blue
gridx	1 (on frame)
gridy	2 (on frame)
insets	5, 10, 5, 10

randomRadioButton:
text	Random Computer
background	White
buttonGroup	computerButtonGroup
selected	true
gridx	0 (on computerPanel)
gridy	0 (on computerPanel)
anchor	WEST

smartRadioButton:
text	Smart Computer
background	White
buttonGroup	computerButtonGroup
gridx	0 (on computerPanel)
gridy	1 (on computerPanel)
anchor	WEST

These controls are declared using:

```
JPanel computerPanel = new JPanel();
ButtonGroup computerButtonGroup = new ButtonGroup();
JRadioButton randomRadioButton = new JRadioButton();
JRadioButton smartRadioButton = new JRadioButton();
```

The radio buttons are placed in the **computerPanel** (which is placed in the frame)
using:

```
computerPanel.setPreferredSize(new Dimension(160, 75));
computerPanel.setBackground(Color.WHITE);
computerPanel.setBorder(BorderFactory.createLineBorder(Col
or.BLUE));
computerPanel.setLayout(new GridBagLayout());
gridConstraints = new GridBagConstraints();
gridConstraints.gridx = 1;
gridConstraints.gridy = 2;
gridConstraints.insets = new Insets(5, 10, 5, 10);
getContentPane().add(computerPanel, gridConstraints);

randomRadioButton.setText("Random Computer");
randomRadioButton.setBackground(Color.WHITE);
randomRadioButton.setSelected(true);
computerButtonGroup.add(randomRadioButton);
gridConstraints = new GridBagConstraints();
gridConstraints.gridx = 0;
gridConstraints.gridy = 0;
gridConstraints.anchor = GridBagConstraints.WEST;
computerPanel.add(randomRadioButton, gridConstraints);

smartRadioButton.setText("Smart Computer");
smartRadioButton.setBackground(Color.WHITE);
computerButtonGroup.add(smartRadioButton);
gridConstraints = new GridBagConstraints();
gridConstraints.gridx = 0;
gridConstraints.gridy = 1;
gridConstraints.anchor = GridBagConstraints.WEST;
computerPanel.add(smartRadioButton, gridConstraints);
```

Add this code in the proper locations. Run to see:

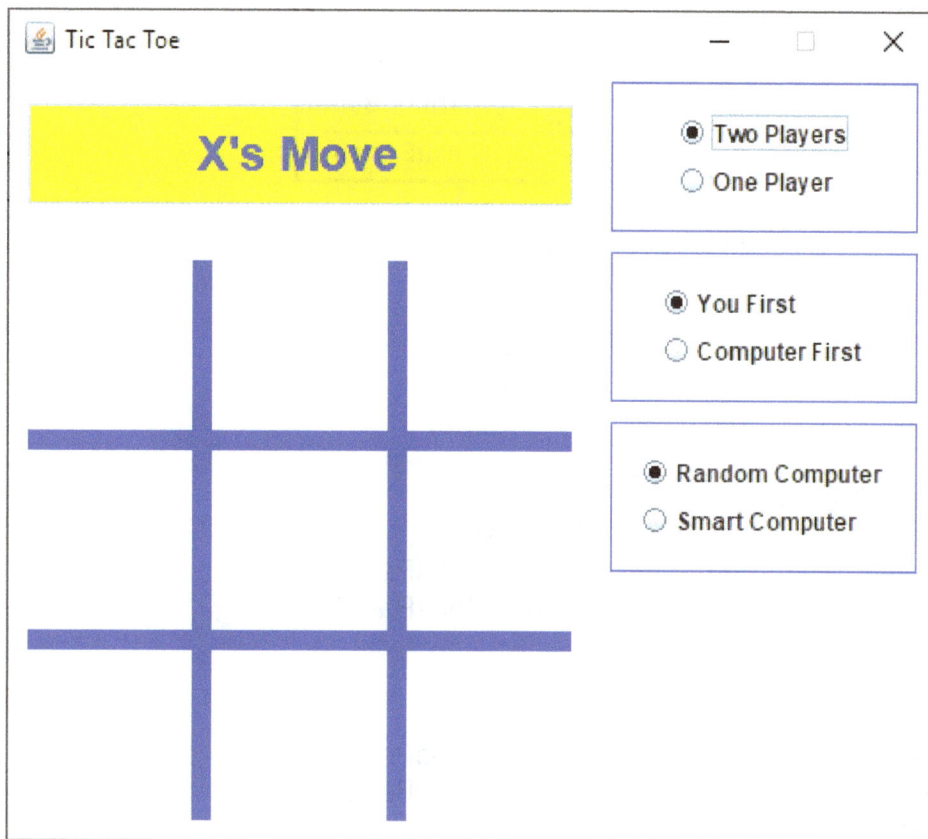

The computer panel is displayed.

The **buttonsPanel** will hold two buttons used to control game play. The **GridBagLayout** for buttonsPanel is:

	gridx = 0
gridy = 0	**startStopButton**
gridy =1	**exitButton**

The panel and button properties:

buttonsPanel:
size	160, 70
gridx	1 (on frame)
gridy	3 (on frame)

startStopButton:
text	Start Game
gridx	0 (on buttonsPanel)
gridy	0 (on buttonsPanel)

exitButton:
text	Exit
gridx	0 (on buttonsPanel)
gridy	1 (on buttonsPanel)
insets	10, 0, 0, 0

These controls are declared using:

```
JPanel buttonsPanel = new JPanel();
JButton startStopButton = new JButton();
JButton exitButton = new JButton();
```

The buttons are placed in the **buttonsPanel** (which is placed in the frame) using:

```
buttonsPanel.setPreferredSize(new Dimension(160, 70));
buttonsPanel.setBackground(Color.WHITE);
buttonsPanel.setLayout(new GridBagLayout());
gridConstraints = new GridBagConstraints();
gridConstraints.gridx = 1;
gridConstraints.gridy = 3;
getContentPane().add(buttonsPanel, gridConstraints);

startStopButton.setText("Start Game");
gridConstraints = new GridBagConstraints();
gridConstraints.gridx = 0;
gridConstraints.gridy = 0;
buttonsPanel.add(startStopButton, gridConstraints);
```

```
startStopButton.addActionListener(new ActionListener()
{
  public void actionPerformed(ActionEvent e)
  {
    startStopButtonActionPerformed(e);
  }
});

exitButton.setText("Exit");
gridConstraints = new GridBagConstraints();
gridConstraints.gridx = 0;
gridConstraints.gridy = 1;
gridConstraints.insets = new Insets(10, 0, 0, 0);
buttonsPanel.add(exitButton, gridConstraints);
exitButton.addActionListener(new ActionListener()
{
  public void actionPerformed(ActionEvent e)
  {
    exitButtonActionPerformed(e);
  }
});
```

This code also adds listeners for each button. Add these empty methods with the other methods:

```
private void startStopButtonActionPerformed(ActionEvent e)
{
}

private void exitButtonActionPerformed(ActionEvent e)
{
}
```

Add this code in the proper locations. Run to see:

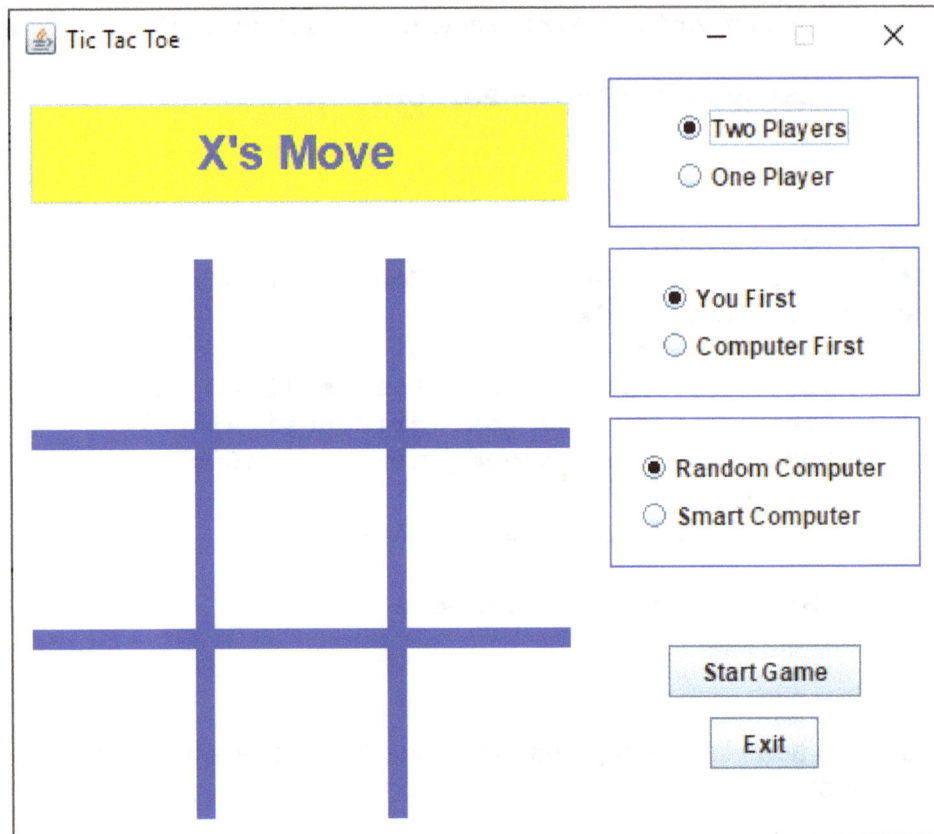

This completes the frame design. You should be able to identify all the controls in the game.

We will begin writing code for the game. We will write the code in several steps. As a first step, we will write the code that starts the game and establishes its 'stopped' state. Then, we look at how to go to 'playing' state following clicking of the **Start Game** button. During the code development process, recognize you may modify a particular method several times before arriving at the finished product.

Code Design – Initializing Stopped State

Any time we start a project, there are certain initializations that must take place. Let's look at the initializations needed in the **Tic Tac Toe** game. All initializations are done at the end of the frame's constructor method.

We want to set a message in the **messageTextField** control. And, we want the game to initially be in **Two Players** mode so we disable the radio buttons in the **firstPanel** and **computerPanel** (these are options associated with a one player game). Add this code to the end of the **TicTacToe** constructor (following the line establishing **screenSize**):

```
messageTextField.setText("Game Stopped");
youFirstRadioButton.setEnabled(false);
computerFirstRadioButton.setEnabled(false);
randomRadioButton.setEnabled(false);
smartRadioButton.setEnabled(false);
```

Run the project to make sure the frame is properly initialized. Do this and you'll see in the 'stopped' state (using default properties), the **Tic Tac Toe** game looks like this:

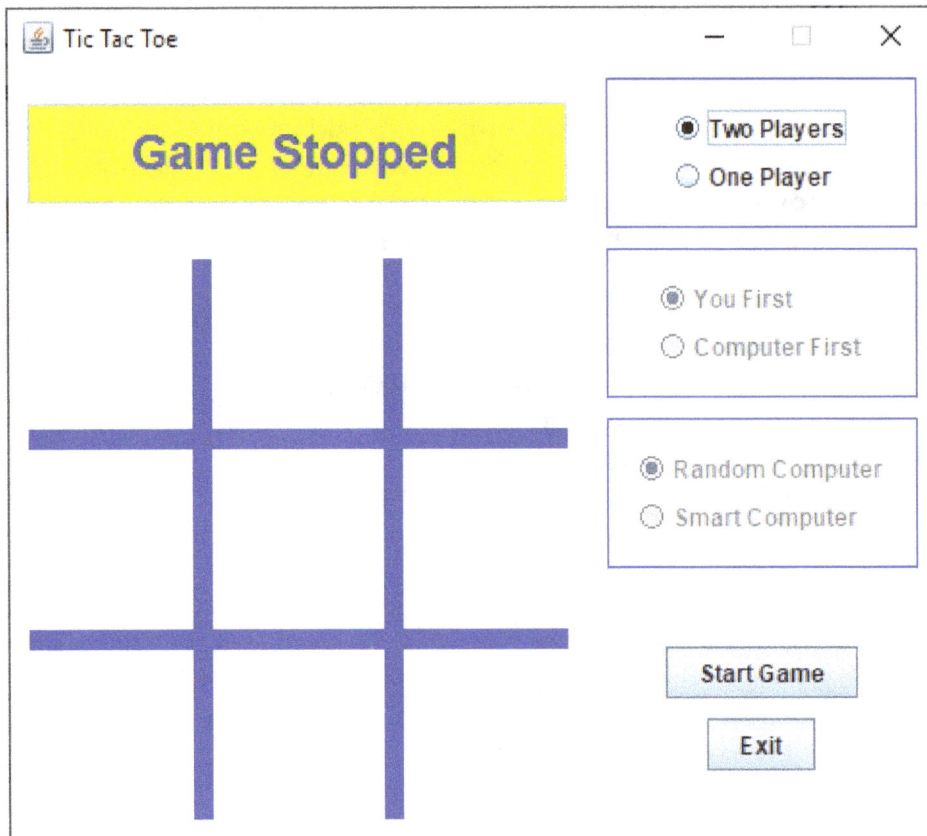

As desired, the game initializes in **Two Players** mode (you can't choose who goes first or how smart the computer is). We have two choices at this point: click **startStopButton** (the button with **Start Game**) or click **exitButton** (the button with **Exit**). We could also change to **One Player** mode – we will address this option in some detail later.

The code for exiting is simple. The **exitButtonActionPerformed** event:

```
private void exitButtonActionPerformed(ActionEvent e)
{
  System.exit(0);
}
```

This simply says whenever the **Exit** button is clicked, the project closes. Add this code to the code window.

The code for the **startStopButton** button is much more complicated. We will build it in several steps. First, we look at switching the game from stopped to playing state.

Code Design –Stopped to Playing State

When the user clicks the **Start Game** button in the 'stopped' state, several things must happen to switch the **Tic Tac Toe** game to 'playing' state:

> ➢ Change the **text** property of **startStopButton** to **Stop Game**.
> ➢ Disable all radio buttons (don't allow selection of options while playing).
> ➢ Disable **exitButton**.
> ➢ Establish this as X's turn (since X always goes first).
> ➢ Blank out text field controls displaying marks.
> ➢ Allow player to input a mark on the grid.

We establish three variables in the class level declarations to help keep track of where we are in the game:

```
boolean xTurn;
boolean canClick = false;
int numberClicks;
```

If **xTurn** is **true**, it is X's turn, otherwise it is O's turn. **canClick** is used to determine if it's okay to click on the text field controls. It is **true** when playing, **false** (the initial value) when stopped. **numberClicks** keeps track of how many of the grid labels have been clicked on (9 maximum).

The code for the **startStopButtonActionPerformed** method that implements the steps in the above method and initializes the new variables is:

```
private void startStopButtonActionPerformed(ActionEvent e)
{
  startStopButton.setText("Stop Game");
  twoPlayersRadioButton.setEnabled(false);
  onePlayerRadioButton.setEnabled(false);
  youFirstRadioButton.setEnabled(false);
  computerFirstRadioButton.setEnabled(false);
  randomRadioButton.setEnabled(false);
  smartRadioButton.setEnabled(false);
  exitButton.setEnabled(false);
  xTurn = true;
  messageTextField.setText("X's Turn");
  // reset boxes
  for (int i = 0; i < 9; i++)
    boxTextField[i].setText("");
  canClick = true;
  numberClicks = 0;
}
```

Can you see how the needed steps are implemented in code?

Save and run the project. Click **Start Game** and the game should switch to two player 'playing' state:

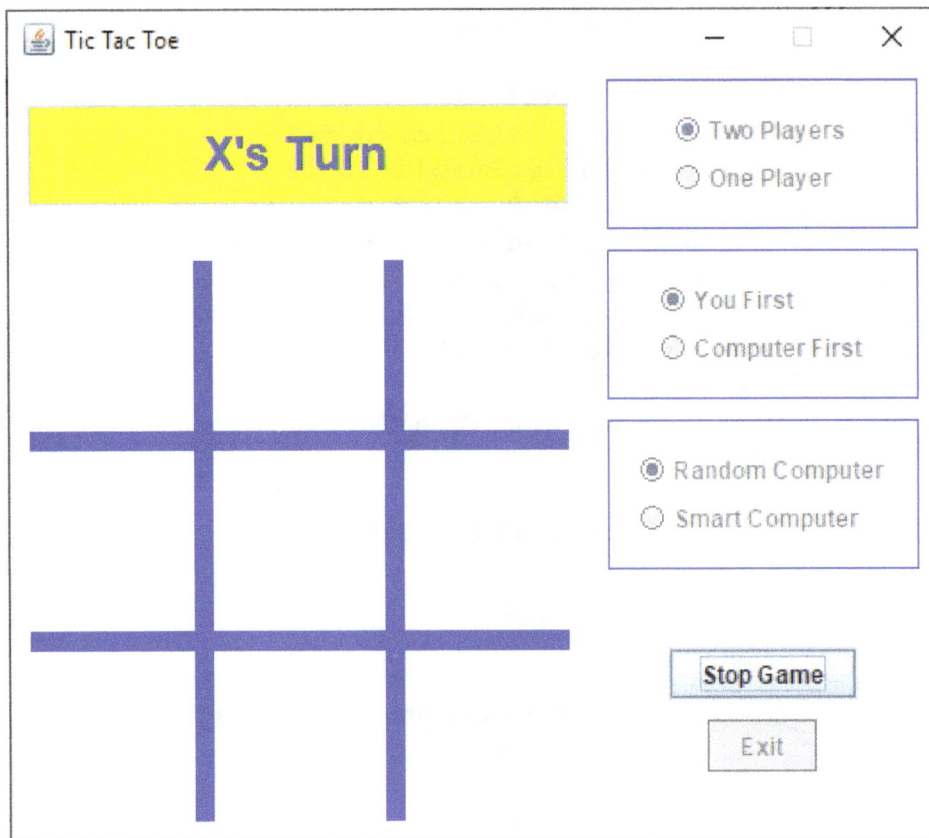

The game is waiting for the first player to click one of the grid locations (we'll write code for that soon). Notice the **Stop Game** button does nothing at the moment. Let's fix that. Stop the project.

Code Design – Playing to Stopped State

When the user clicks the **Stop Game** button in the two player 'playing' state, several things must happen to switch the **Tic Tac Toe** game to 'stopped' state:

➢ Change the **text** property of **startStopButton** to **Start Game**.
➢ Display **Game Stopped** message.
➢ Enable radio buttons in players panel.
➢ Enable radio buttons in first panel and computer panel, if one player game.
➢ Enable **exitButton**.
➢ Set **canClick** to **false.**

We use logic similar to what we did for the **Safecracker** game – modifying the code for **startStopButton**. The code that does these steps is (modifications to the current **startStopButtonActionPerformed** method code are shaded):

```
private void startStopButtonActionPerformed(ActionEvent e)
{
  if (startStopButton.getText().equals("Start Game"))
  {
    startStopButton.setText("Stop Game");
    twoPlayersRadioButton.setEnabled(false);
    onePlayerRadioButton.setEnabled(false);
    youFirstRadioButton.setEnabled(false);
    computerFirstRadioButton.setEnabled(false);
    randomRadioButton.setEnabled(false);
    smartRadioButton.setEnabled(false);
    exitButton.setEnabled(false);
    xTurn = true;
    messageTextField.setText("X's Turn");
    // reset boxes
    for (int i = 0; i < 9; i++)
      boxTextField[i].setText("");
    canClick = true;
    numberClicks = 0;
  }
  else
  {
    startStopButton.setText("Start Game");
    messageTextField.setText("Game Stopped");
    twoPlayersRadioButton.setEnabled(true);
    onePlayerRadioButton.setEnabled(true);
    if (onePlayerRadioButton.isSelected())
    {
      youFirstRadioButton.setEnabled(true);
      computerFirstRadioButton.setEnabled(true);
```

```
            randomRadioButton.setEnabled(true);
            smartRadioButton.setEnabled(true);
        }
        exitButton.setEnabled(true);
        canClick = false;
    }
}
```

Save and run the project. You should be able to now move from 'stopped' to 'playing' state and back. When stopped, make sure the proper radio buttons appear for the one and two player options. Let's write the code for the two player game, first looking at how to mark the grid.

Code Design –Marking Grid

In the **Tic Tac Toe** two player game, when a player clicks a box in the grid, we want the proper mark (X or O) to appear. After each mark, we then need to see if anyone won. If there is no win, and there are still empty locations, we switch to the next player.

So, when a grid box is clicked, we follow these steps:

> ➢ Make sure there is not a mark there already.
> ➢ Increment **numberClicks**.
> ➢ Place proper mark in corresponding text box control (**X** if **xTurn** is **true**, otherwise **O**).
> ➢ Switch to next player (not needed if there is a win or draw).
> ➢ Check for win. If there is a win, declare the winner and stop the game.
> ➢ Check if **numberClicks = 9** (board is full with no win). If so, declare the game a draw and stop.

Anticipating that a human can choose a box or the computer can choose a box (in one player game), we first write a general method that implements the above steps (not checking for a win yet, though). Add this general method (**markClickedBox**) which has an argument the index of the selected box:

```
private void markClickedBox(int i)
{
  String whoWon = "";
  // if already clicked then exit
  if (!boxTextField[i].getText().equals(""))
    return;
  numberClicks++;
  if (xTurn)
  {
    boxTextField[i].setText("X");
    xTurn = false;
    messageTextField.setText("O's Turn");
  }
  else
  {
    boxTextField[i].setText("O");
    xTurn = true;
    messageTextField.setText("X's Turn");
  }
  // check for win - will establish a value for WhoWon
  if (!whoWon.equals(""))
  {
    messageTextField.setText(whoWon + " wins!");
```

```
      startStopButton.doClick();
      return;
    }
    else if (numberClicks == 9)
    {
      // draw
      messageTextField.setText("It's a draw!");
      startStopButton.doClick();
      return;
    }
  }
```

Let's look at this code. The argument **i** is the index of the text field control (**boxTextField**) that was selected. If there is already a mark there (not blank), the method is exited. If blank, the proper mark is placed in **boxTextField[i]**. After this, we check for a win (right now just in a comment line – we'll fix that soon). If the variable **whoWon** is not blank (will be established by the check win logic), we declare the winner. Otherwise, we exit allowing other elements of the grid to be selected until the grid is full, declaring a draw.

Let's use this new method to allow selection of boxes using the mouse. The code to do this goes in the **boxTextFieldMousePressed** method (currently empty). This method is invoked whenever any of the nine text field controls are clicked by the mouse. The tricky part is – how to determine which of the nine controls was clicked. An Internet search yielded the necessary logic. The mouse press method has a **MouseEvent** argument, **e**. The following method uses this argument and returns a **Point** object (**p**) that has the coordinates of the upper left corner of the clicked component (relative to the panel hosting the component):

```
    Point p = e.getComponent().getLocation();
```

So, for our case, **p.x** and **p.y** represent the upper left corner of the clicked text field (relative to the **gamePanel** which hosts the text fields). The corresponding coordinates for the text fields can be obtained using **getX** and **getY** methods.

We can use these methods to determine which box is clicked by the mouse and, in turn, place a mark in the clicked box (using the **markClickedBox** method) Add this code to the **boxTextAreaMousePressed** method:

```
private void boxTextFieldMousePressed(MouseEvent e)
{
  if (canClick)
  {
    int i;
    // get upper left corner of clicked box
    Point p = e.getComponent().getLocation();
    // determine index based on p
    for (i = 0; i < 9; i++)
    {
      if (p.x == boxTextField[i].getX() && p.y ==
boxTextField[i].getY())
        break;
    }
    markClickedBox(i);
  }
}
```

Make sure you see how this works.

Save and run the project. You should be able to click on each of the grid locations, placing X's and O's there in alternate turns. Once you have filled all the grid locations, the game will be returned to stopped state. Wins will not be recognized. Here's what I got when I tried it:

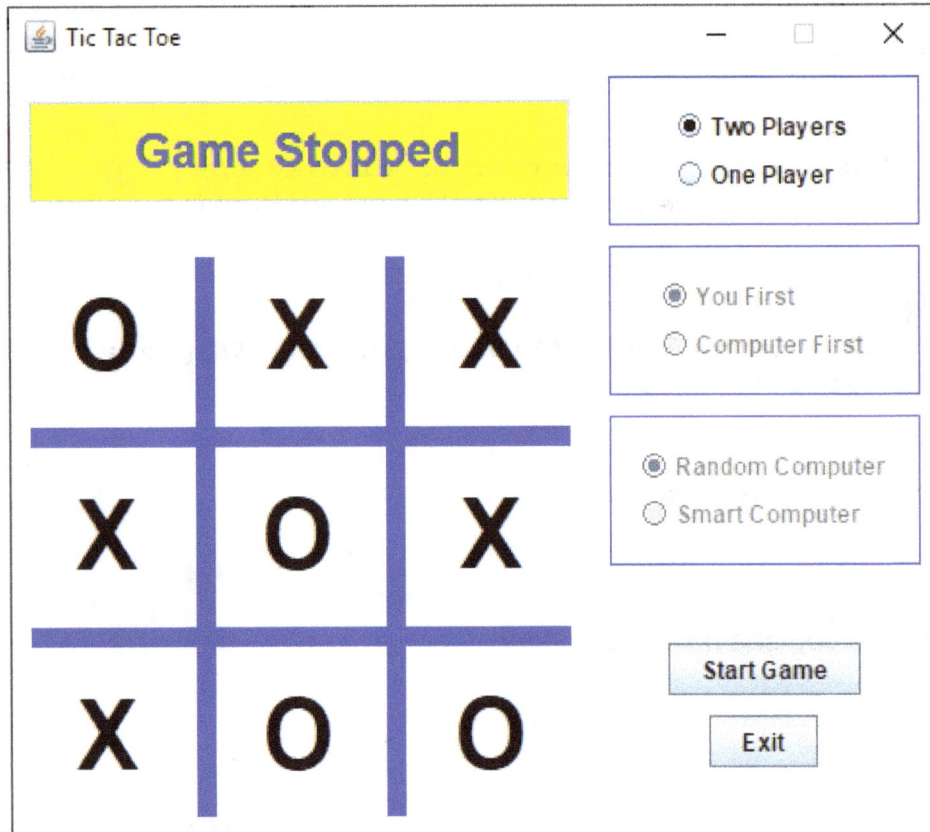

As expected, the computer completely missed the fact that O (Player 2) got a **Tic Tac Toe**!! Let's fix that. We will use a method to return a value for the **whoWon** variable used in the code.

Code Design – Checking For Win

We will build a general method (named **checkForWin**) that examines the playing grid and determines if there is a winner. If so, the win will be identified and the method will return a string variable holding the marker (**X** or **O**) for the winner or a blank if there is no winner. Let's establish a strategy for doing this.

There are eight possible ways to win (3 horizontal, 3 vertical, 2 diagonal). Recall the indices of the **boxTextField** array used in the playing grid are laid out in this manner:

0	1	2
3	4	5
6	7	8

If we declare a string array named **possibleWins**, its 8 elements would be:

```
possibleWins[0] = "012"
possibleWins[1] = "345"
possibleWins[2] = "678"
possibleWins[3] = "036"
possibleWins[4] = "147"
possibleWins[5] = "258"
possibleWins[6] = "048"
possibleWins[7] = "246"
```

So our win logic would be to go through each possible win and see if the corresponding elements of **boxTextField** all contain the same mark (**X** or **O**, but not blank). If so, a winner is declared.

Add this class level declaration to the code window:

```
String[] possibleWins = new String[8];
```

Add this code at the end of the **TicTacToe** constructor to establish values for the array:

```
// possible wins
possibleWins[0] = "012";
possibleWins[1] = "345";
possibleWins[2] = "678";
possibleWins[3] = "036";
possibleWins[4] = "147";
possibleWins[5] = "258";
possibleWins[6] = "048";
possibleWins[7] = "246";
```

Add the general method **checkForWin** to your project:

```
private String checkForWin()
{
  String winner = "";
  int[] boxNumber = new int[3];
  String[] mark = new String[3];
  // check all possible for wins
  for (int i = 0; i < 8; i++)
  {
    for (int j = 0; j < 3; j++)
    {
      boxNumber[j] =
Integer.valueOf(String.valueOf(possibleWins[i].charAt(j)))
.intValue();
      mark[j] = boxTextField[boxNumber[j]].getText();
    }
    if (mark[0].equals(mark[1]) && mark[0].equals(mark[2])
&& mark[1].equals(mark[2]) && !mark[0].equals(""))
    {
      // we have a winner
      winner = mark[0];
      for (int j = 0; j < 3; j++)

boxTextField[boxNumber[j]].setBackground(Color.RED);
    }
  }
  return (winner);
}
```

This code goes through all the possible wins. If all the marks in a particular horizontal, vertical or diagonal row match, the background color of that row is changed to red and the corresponding winner returned. Study the code to see how it works. The **boxNumber** array holds the indices of the **boxTextField** array for each possible win.

We can now modify the **markClickedbox** method to check for wins, but we need one other modification. Notice when a win or draw is declared, we stop the game by performing a click on **startStopButton**. We need some way to distinguish between this method of stopping the game and just having a player click the stop button (which stops the game before a win or draw is declared). Add this variable to the class level declarations:

```
boolean gameOver;
```

If **gameOver** is **true**, there has been a win or draw. If **false**, the **Stop Game** button was clicked before the game ended.

Make the shaded changes to the **startStopButtonActionPerformed** method:

```java
private void startStopButtonActionPerformed(ActionEvent e)
{
  if (startStopButton.getText().equals("Start Game"))
  {
    startStopButton.setText("Stop Game");
    twoPlayersRadioButton.setEnabled(false);
    onePlayerRadioButton.setEnabled(false);
    youFirstRadioButton.setEnabled(false);
    computerFirstRadioButton.setEnabled(false);
    randomRadioButton.setEnabled(false);
    smartRadioButton.setEnabled(false);
    exitButton.setEnabled(false);
    xTurn = true;
    messageTextField.setText("X's Turn");
    // reset boxes
    for (int i = 0; i < 9; i++)
    {
      boxTextField[i].setText("");
      boxTextField[i].setBackground(Color.WHITE);
    }
    canClick = true;
    numberClicks = 0;
    gameOver = false;
  }
  else
  {
    startStopButton.setText("Start Game");
    if (!gameOver)
      messageTextField.setText("Game Stopped");
    twoPlayersRadioButton.setEnabled(true);
    onePlayerRadioButton.setEnabled(true);
    if (onePlayerRadioButton.isSelected())
    {
      youFirstRadioButton.setEnabled(true);
      computerFirstRadioButton.setEnabled(true);
      randomRadioButton.setEnabled(true);
      smartRadioButton.setEnabled(true);
    }
    exitButton.setEnabled(true);
    canClick = false;
  }
}
```

These changes do several things. The text field controls' **background** is restored to **White**, in case a win was displayed. The **gameOver** variable is set to **false** when starting a new game. And, the **Game Stopped** message is not displayed if **gameOver** is **true** (meaning a winner or draw is declared).

Now, modify (changes are shaded) the **markClickedBox** method to incorporate the **checkForWin** method and the new **gameOver** variable:

```java
private void markClickedBox(int i)
{
  String whoWon = "";
  // if already clicked then exit
  if (!boxTextField[i].getText().equals(""))
    return;
  numberClicks++;
  if (xTurn)
  {
    boxTextField[i].setText("X");
    xTurn = false;
    messageTextField.setText("O's Turn");
  }
  else
  {
    boxTextField[i].setText("O");
    xTurn = true;
    messageTextField.setText("X's Turn");
  }
  // check for win - will establish a value for WhoWon
  whoWon = checkForWin();
  if (!whoWon.equals(""))
  {
    messageTextField.setText(whoWon + " wins!");
    gameOver = true;
    startStopButton.doClick();
    return;
  }
  else if (numberClicks == 9)
  {
    // draw
    messageTextField.setText("It's a draw!");
    gameOver = true;
    startStopButton.doClick();
    return;
  }
}
```

Save and run the project. You and a friend should be able to compete with wins and draws properly determined. Here is a replay of the game I tried before (notice the win by O is now declared):

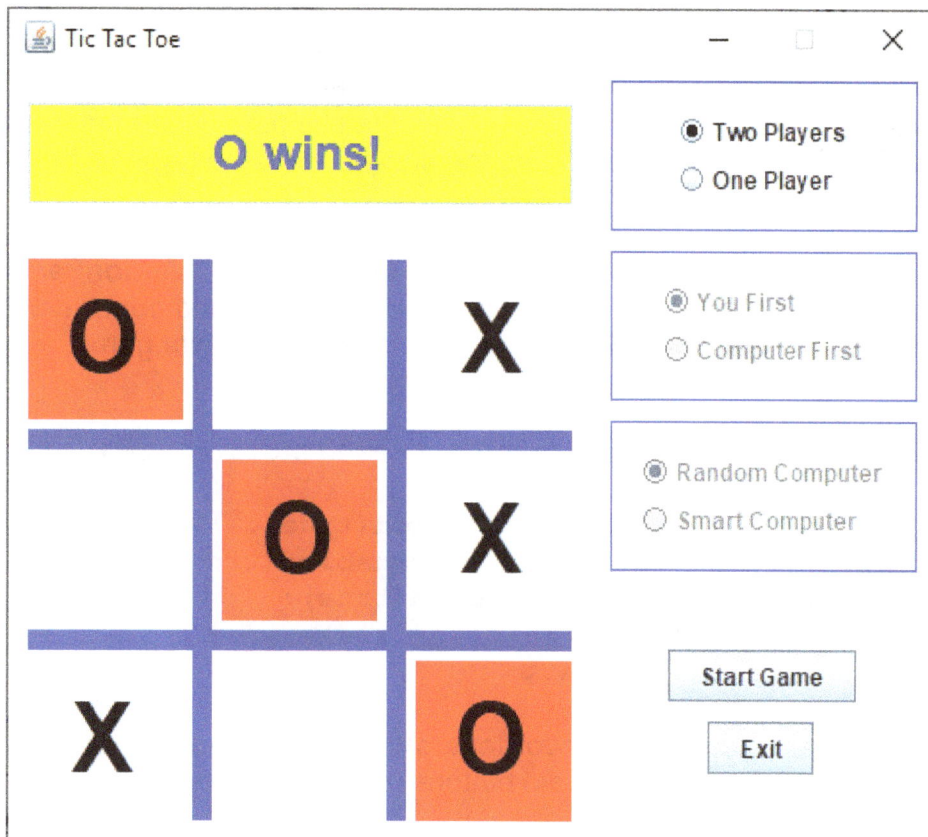

The two player game is now complete. Let's start looking at how to implement a one player game versus a computer opponent. We'll start easy, just having the computer make random moves (no brains!). This will help us establish the logic of switching players when the computer is one of them.

Code Design – Number of Players Selection

Different options are available to the player of **Tic Tac Toe** depending on the number of players selected. We have seen for the two player game that the choice of who goes first and determining how smart the computer is are not available as options. Now that we are considering the one player game (against the computer), this must change.

Place this short piece of code in the **onePlayerRadioButtonActionPerformed** method. This enables the radio buttons in the **firstPanel** and **computerPanel** controls to allow additional options available for the one player game:

```
private void
onePlayerRadioButtonActionPerformed(ActionEvent e)
{
  youFirstRadioButton.setEnabled(true);
  computerFirstRadioButton.setEnabled(true);
  randomRadioButton.setEnabled(true);
  smartRadioButton.setEnabled(true);
}
```

Likewise, place this code in the **twoPlayersRadioButtonActionPerformed** method to disable these same radio buttons (the ones in **firstPanel** and **computerPanel**) for the two player game:

```
private void
twoPlayersRadioButtonActionPerformed(ActionEvent e)
{
  youFirstRadioButton.setEnabled(false);
  computerFirstRadioButton.setEnabled(false);
  randomRadioButton.setEnabled(false);
  smartRadioButton.setEnabled(false);
}
```

Save and run the project to make sure the player choices work as desired.

Code Design – Random Computer Moves

A big part of allowing the computer to play against a human (you, the player) is to decide what "thought processes" to give the computer. We're allowing two choices: a **random computer** and a **smart computer**. We'll start by coding up the random computer. This will get all the logic of implementing computer moves along with human moves working properly. Then, we'll move on to a smart computer, developing a formidable opponent.

All of the logic behind a computer move will be implemented in a general method named **computerTurn**. For random moves, it will simply choose (at random) one of the empty boxes in the grid and place a marker in that box (X if computer goes first, O if human goes first).

Add this import statement to allow use of random numbers:

```
import java.util.Random;
```

And, add a random object to the class level declarations area of the code window:

```
Random myRandom = new Random();
```

Place this general method **computerTurn** in your project:

```
private void computerTurn()
{
  int selectedBox;
  int i, n;
  if (randomRadioButton.isSelected())
  {
    // random logic
    // put mark in Nth available square
    n = myRandom.nextInt(9 - numberClicks) + 1;
    i = 0;
    for (selectedBox = 0; selectedBox < 9; selectedBox++)
    {
      if (boxTextField[selectedBox].getText().equals(""))
        i++;
      if (i == n)
        break;
    }
    // put mark in SelectedBox
    markClickedBox(selectedBox);
  }
  else
  {
```

```
      // smart computer
   }
}
```

The logic behind the code in **computerTurn** is straightforward. At any time, we have **9 - numberClicks** empty boxes in the grid. The code selects a random number from **1** to **9 – numberClicks** and counts ahead that number of empty boxes to identify the box to mark. To mark the identified box, **boxTextField[selectedBox]**, we simulate a click on that box by calling the **markClickedBox** method with **selectedBox** as the argument. The program will know whether to place an X or O in the box based on previously implemented logic.

Now, let's implement the **computerTurn** method to allow the computer to play. We need to modify two methods. First, when we start a game, if the computer moves first, we need to invoke **computerTurn**. Make the shaded changes to the **startStopButtonActionPerformed** method:

```
private void startStopButtonActionPerformed(ActionEvent e)
{
  if (startStopButton.getText().equals("Start Game"))
  {
    startStopButton.setText("Stop Game");
    twoPlayersRadioButton.setEnabled(false);
    onePlayerRadioButton.setEnabled(false);
    youFirstRadioButton.setEnabled(false);
    computerFirstRadioButton.setEnabled(false);
    randomRadioButton.setEnabled(false);
    smartRadioButton.setEnabled(false);
    exitButton.setEnabled(false);
    xTurn = true;
    messageTextField.setText("X's Turn");
    // reset boxes
    for (int i = 0; i < 9; i++)
    {
      boxTextField[i].setText("");
      boxTextField[i].setBackground(Color.WHITE);
    }
    canClick = true;
    numberClicks = 0;
    gameOver = false;
    if (computerFirstRadioButton.isSelected())
      computerTurn();
  }
  else
  {
    startStopButton.setText("Start Game");
```

```
      if (!gameOver)
        messageTextField.setText("Game Stopped");
      twoPlayersRadioButton.setEnabled(true);
      onePlayerRadioButton.setEnabled(true);
      if (onePlayerRadioButton.isSelected())
      {
        youFirstRadioButton.setEnabled(true);
        computerFirstRadioButton.setEnabled(true);
        randomRadioButton.setEnabled(true);
        smartRadioButton.setEnabled(true);
      }
      exitButton.setEnabled(true);
      canClick = false;
    }
  }
```

And, after a mark is placed by the human player, the computer needs to take a
turn. This logic is in the **markClickedBox** method. The needed changes are
shaded:

```
  private void markClickedBox(int i)
  {
    String whoWon = "";
    // if already clicked then exit
    if (!boxTextField[i].getText().equals(""))
      return;
    numberClicks++;
    if (xTurn)
    {
      boxTextField[i].setText("X");
      xTurn = false;
      messageTextField.setText("O's Turn");
    }
    else
    {
      boxTextField[i].setText("O");
      xTurn = true;
      messageTextField.setText("X's Turn");
    }
    // check for win - will establish a value for WhoWon
    whoWon = checkForWin();
    if (!whoWon.equals(""))
    {
      messageTextField.setText(whoWon + " wins!");
      gameOver = true;
      startStopButton.doClick();
      return;
```

```
        }
        else if (numberClicks == 9)
        {
          // draw
          messageTextField.setText("It's a draw!");
          gameOver = true;
          startStopButton.doClick();
          return;
        }
      if (onePlayerRadioButton.isSelected())
          if ((xTurn && computerFirstRadioButton.isSelected()
|| (!xTurn && youFirstRadioButton.isSelected())))
            computerTurn();
}
```

With the added code, the computer takes a turn when it goes first and it's X's turn or takes a turn when the human goes first and it's O's turn.

Save and run the game. Choose the one player option and make sure **Random Computer** is selected. Try playing a few games (you go first, computer going first). Make sure things work properly, you should see the computer is pretty easy to beat! Here's a game I won when I went first:

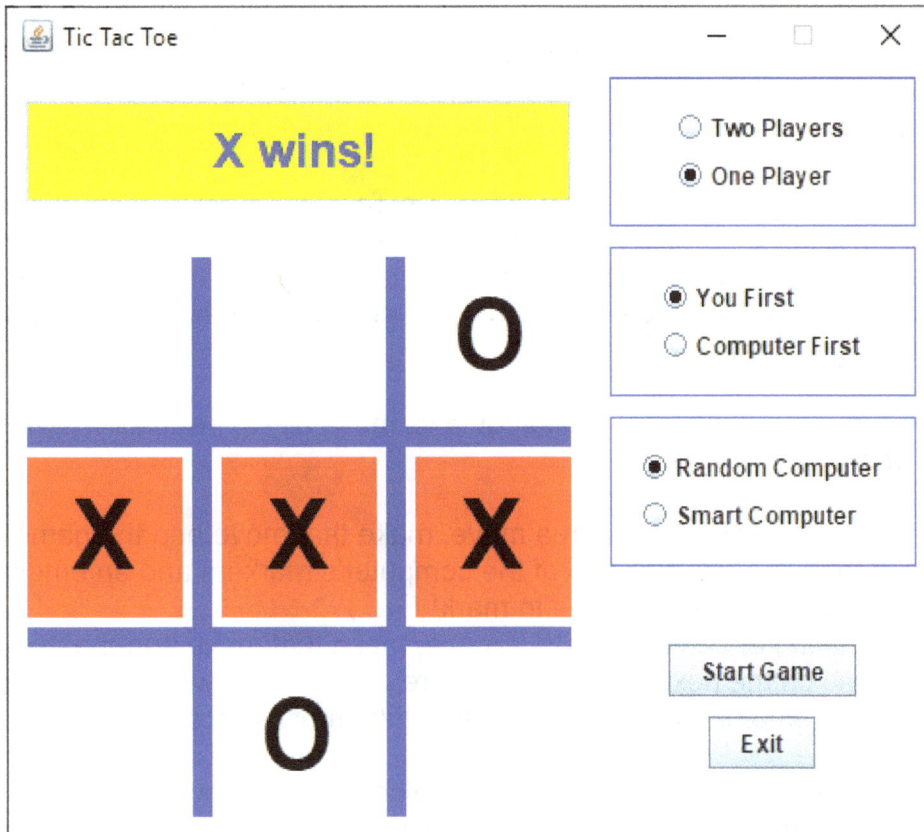

Code Design – Smart Computer Moves

We've come to one of the more fun and more challenging parts of this game project. How can we make our computer a smarter opponent? In any game where a computer is playing against a human, we must be able to write down some rules that give the computer the appearance of intelligence. Many computer opponents are unbeatable. For example, it is very hard for a human to beat a computer at the game of chess.

So how do we make our computer a better **Tic Tac Toe** player? We try to imbed choices we would make if we were playing the game. So for the computer to be a smart player, the programmer needs to be a smart player. This usually takes practice and study. For the game of **Tic Tac Toe**, we can develop a fairly simple, yet very intelligent strategy. Let's do it.

When it is the computer's turn, what should its move be? The rules we will use are (in order of choice):

1. If the computer can win with a move, make that move and the game is over. So, if there's a row with two of the computer's markers and an empty space, the empty space is the place to mark!
2. If the computer can block with a move, make that move and the opponent can't win on the next move. So, if there's a row with two of the human player's markers and an empty space, the empty space is the place to mark!
3. If there is no possible win or possible block, make a move in this order: center square, one of the four corner squares, or one of the four side squares.

I think you see this logic makes sense. You may wonder about Step 3 – why we choose that particular order. Recall there are 8 possible ways to win in **Tic Tac Toe** (3 horizontal, 3 vertical, 2 diagonal). The center square is needed in 4 of these, any one corner is involved in 3 possibilities, while any side is involved in just 2 wins. Hence, the order of choices is made on basic probabilities. Let's implement this logic in code.

Here is the modified **computerTurn** method that implements this 'smart' logic. The changes are shaded:

```java
private void computerTurn()
{
  int selectedBox;
  int i, n;
  int j, k;
  String computerMark, playerMark, markToFind;
  int[] boxNumber = new int[3];
  String[] mark = new String[3];
  int emptyBox;
  int[] bestMoves = { 4, 0, 2, 6, 8, 1, 3, 5, 7 };
  if (randomRadioButton.isSelected())
  {
    // random logic
    // put mark in Nth available square
    n = myRandom.nextInt(9 - numberClicks) + 1;
    i = 0;
    for (selectedBox = 0; selectedBox < 9; selectedBox++)
    {
      if (boxTextField[selectedBox].getText().equals(""))
        i++;
      if (i == n)
        break;
    }
    // put mark in SelectedBox
    markClickedBox(selectedBox);
  }
  else
  {
    // smart computer
    // determine who has what mark
    if (computerFirstRadioButton.isSelected())
    {
      computerMark = "X";
      playerMark = "O";
    }
    else
    {
      computerMark = "O";
      playerMark = "X";
    }
    // Step 1 (K = 1) - check for win - see if two boxes
hold computer mark and one is empty
    // Step 2 (K = 2) - check for block - see if two boxes
hold player mark and one is empty
```

```
    for (k = 1; k <= 2; k++)
    {
      if (k == 1)
        markToFind = computerMark;
      else
        markToFind = playerMark;
      for (i = 0; i < 8; i++)
      {
        n = 0;
        emptyBox = 0;
        for (j = 0; j < 3; j++)
        {
          boxNumber[j] =
Integer.valueOf(String.valueOf(possibleWins[i].charAt(j)))
.intValue();
          mark[j] = boxTextField[boxNumber[j]].getText();
          if (mark[j].equals(markToFind))
            n++;
          else if (mark[j].equals(""))
            emptyBox = boxNumber[j];
        }
        if (n == 2 && emptyBox != 0)
        {
          // mark empty box to win (K = 1) or block (K =
2)
          markClickedBox(emptyBox);
          return;
        }
      }
    }
    // Step 3 - find next best move
    for (i = 0; i < 9; i++)
    {
      if (boxTextField[bestMoves[i]].getText().equals(""))
      {
        markClickedBox(bestMoves[i]);
        return;
      }
    }
  }
}
```

In the 'smart' logic, we first find out whether the computer has X or O. Steps 1 and 2 of the computer logic are done in a for loop with k as index. In that loop, we go through all the possible wins looking for a row with 2 identical marks and an empty box. For k=1, we look for the computer's mark and an empty box – giving the computer a win on the next move. For k=2, we look for the human's mark and an empty box – giving the computer a block on the next move. If neither Step 1 or Step 2 is successful, we move to Step 3. The next best moves are listed in desired order in the array **bestMoves**. In Step 3, we go through this array, finding the first empty box available and move there.

Save and run the project. The game is now fully functional. Try playing it against the computer. You should find it can't be beat. The best you can do against the computer is a draw. Before leaving, let's add a couple of sounds.

Code Design – Adding Sounds

We know sounds make games a bit more fun. Let's add a couple to the Tick Tac Toe game. In the **\KidGamesJava\KidGamesJava Projects\TicTacToe** folder are two wav files that can be used for sound. The file **beep.wav** is a sound we'll use for games that end a draw. The **tada.wav** file is a celebratory sound we'll use for wins by either player. These files will be loaded when the project starts. Copy the two sound files to your project's folder.

Add these import statements:

```
import java.net.URL;
import java.applet.*;
```

And, add these class level declarations to represent the two sounds:

```
AudioClip drawSound;
AudioClip winSound;
```

Add these lines at the end of the **TicTacToe** constructor code to establish the sound objects:

```
try
{
  drawSound = Applet.newAudioClip(new URL("file:" +
"beep.wav"));
  winSound = Applet.newAudioClip(new URL("file:" +
"tada.wav"));
}
catch (Exception ex)
{
  System.out.println("Error loading sound files");
}
```

Make sure you copy the two sound files to your project folder.

Lastly, play the two sounds at the appropriate (shaded) locations in the **markClickedBox** method:

```
private void markClickedBox(int i)
{
  String whoWon = "";
  // if already clicked then exit
  if (!boxTextField[i].getText().equals(""))
    return;
  numberClicks++;
  if (xTurn)
  {
    boxTextField[i].setText("X");
    xTurn = false;
    messageTextField.setText("O's Turn");
  }
  else
  {
    boxTextField[i].setText("O");
    xTurn = true;
    messageTextField.setText("X's Turn");
  }
  // check for win - will establish a value for WhoWon
  whoWon = checkForWin();
  if (!whoWon.equals(""))
  {
    winSound.play();
    messageTextField.setText(whoWon + " wins!");
    gameOver = true;
    startStopButton.doClick();
    return;
  }
  else if (numberClicks == 9)
  {
    // draw
    drawSound.play();
    messageTextField.setText("It's a draw!");
    gameOver = true;
    startStopButton.doClick();
    return;
  }
  if (onePlayerRadioButton.isSelected())
    if ((xTurn && computerFirstRadioButton.isSelected())
|| (!xTurn && youFirstRadioButton.isSelected()))
      computerTurn();
}
```

Save and run the project. You should now have a complete, running version of the **Tic Tac Toe** game (the complete code listing is given at the end of the chapter). Have fun playing it! Again, you will see the computer can't be beat. Here's a game I played against a 'smart' computer where I went first, taking the middle square:

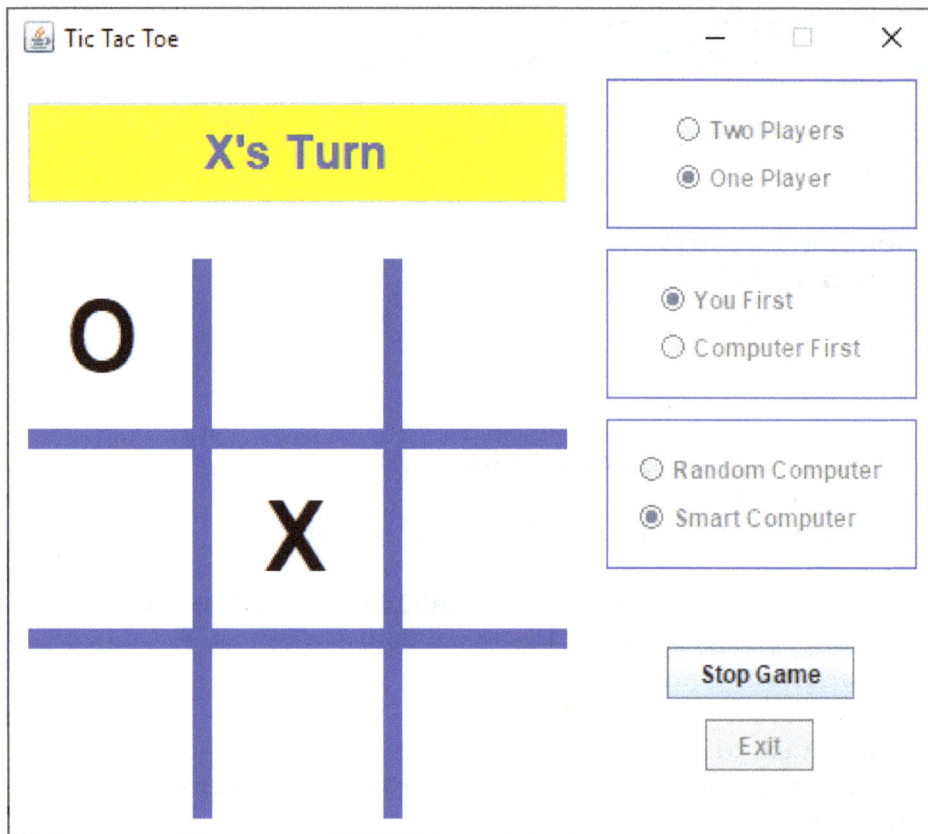

Notice, based on the logic we implemented, since the computer couldn't win or block, it took its next best move, the first available corner square.

My next move was the lower left corner:

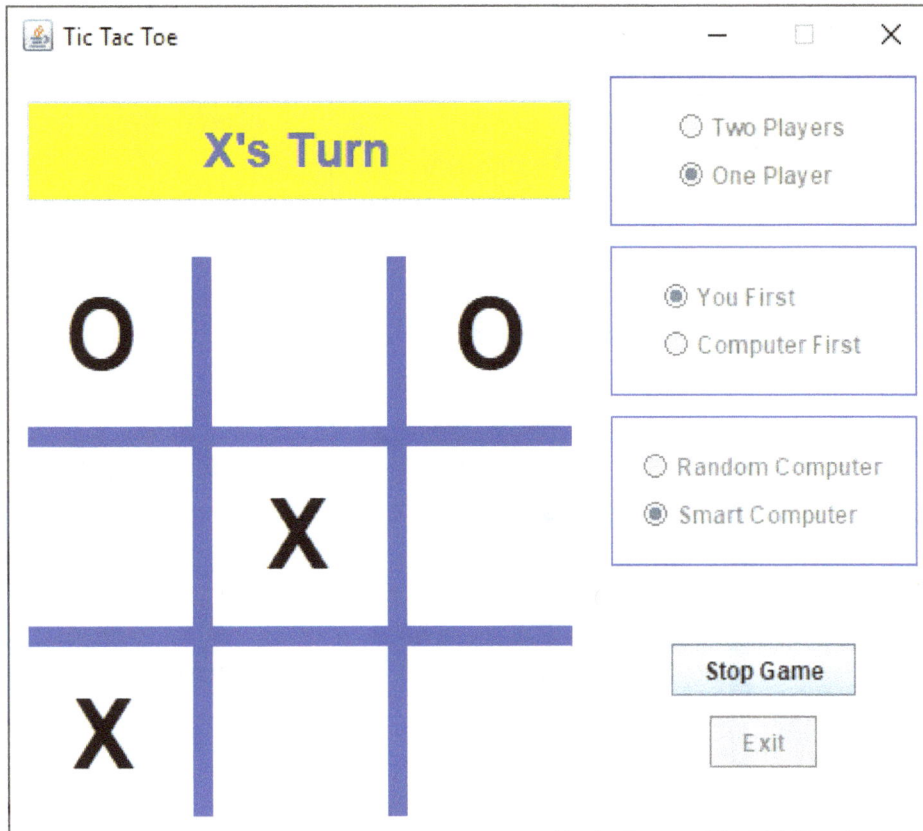

The computer logic implemented block my next move.

My next move was to block the computer, who in turn blocked me:

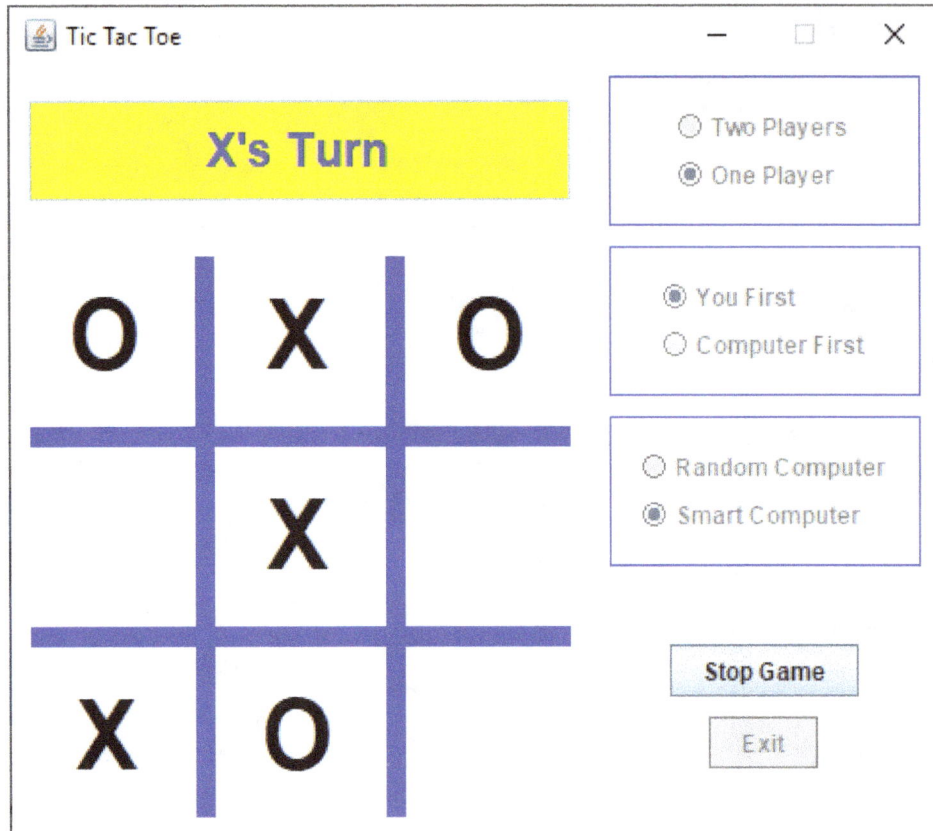

I continued playing (moving to the right of the middle row and, following the computer's block, a move to the right of the bottom row) until finally we ended in a draw:

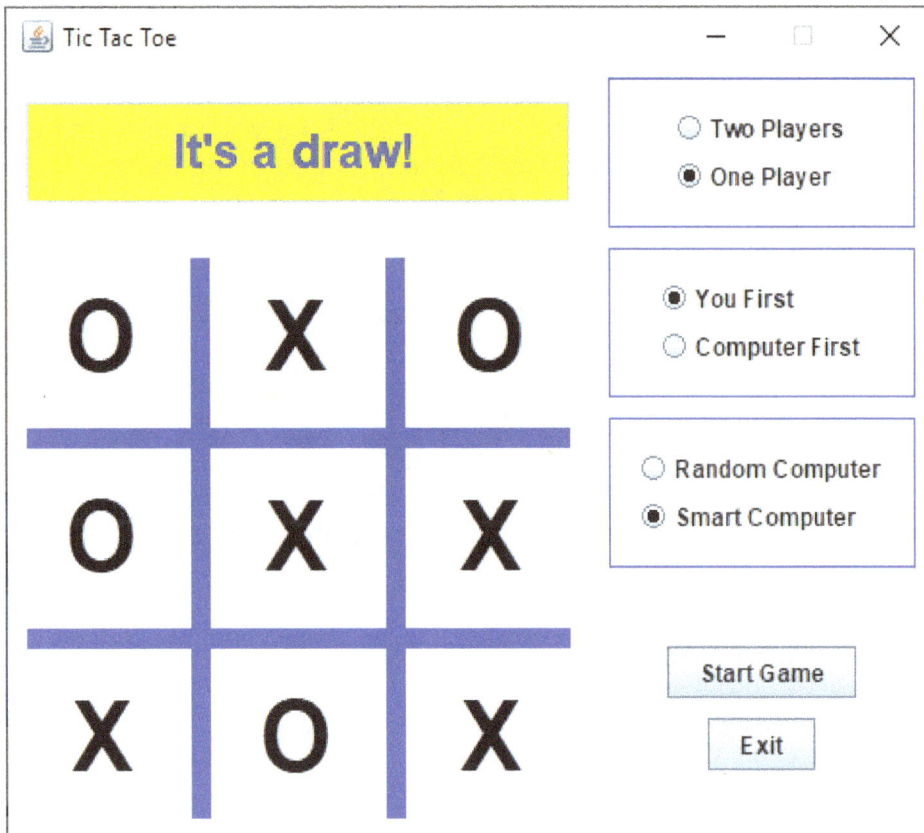

I heard the little beep and the computer's ready to play again.

Tic Tac Toe Project Review

The **Tic Tac Toe** game project is now complete. Save and run the project and make sure it works as promised. Check that all options work correctly.

If there are errors in your implementation, go back over the steps of frame and code design. Go over the developed code – make sure you understand how different parts of the project were coded. As mentioned in the beginning of this chapter, the completed project is saved as **TicTacToe** in the **\KidGamesJava\KidGamesJava Projects** folder.

While completing this project, new concepts and skills you should have gained include:

> ➢ Proper steps in project design.
> ➢ Capabilities and use of many Java controls.
> ➢ How to use general methods and methods.
> ➢ How to give the computer intelligence in playing games.

Tic Tac Toe Project Enhancements

There are several ways to improve the **Tic Tac Toe** game. Some possibilities are:

> ➤ Use label controls instead of text field controls in the grid. With such a change, you could use something other than X's and O's to mark the squares. Try using small digital photos (jpeg files).

> ➤ Add better messaging with a computer opponent. As implemented, the computer quickly makes its move. Perhaps, add a delay (see the Timer object) and perhaps some color changes in the grid so the computer has time to tell you where its move will be.

> ➤ In the current computer logic (Step 3), the computer always picks corners or sides in the same order. To make things a bit more unpredictable, add logic so the computer makes corner or side moves randomly based on the number of corner or side boxes that are empty.

> ➤ The computer in this game is pretty smart, but can be made smarter. Between Steps 2 and 3 in the current computer logic, we could add another step where the computer would be more aggressive. In this new step, have the computer search for horizontal, vertical or diagonal rows with one of its markers and two empty squares. By choosing one of the empty squares, the computer forces your next move. Even better is to find a place where with an additional mark, the computer sets up two wins, making it impossible for you to block him.

> ➤ For little kids, maybe the computer is a bit too smart. The random computer is an option, but goes to the other extreme of maybe not being smart enough. A change would be to add levels of intelligence – having the computer use its 'smart' logic sometimes and its 'random' logic sometimes. To do this, you could generate a random number from 1 to 100 and based on some threshold, determine whether to make a smart move or random move. By varying the threshold, you can make the computer extremely smart or not so smart. We implement such logic in the next game project, **Match Game**.

Tic Tac Toe Project Java Code Listing

```java
/*
 * TicTacToe.java
 */
package tictactoe;
import javax.swing.*;
import java.awt.*;
import java.awt.event.*;
import java.util.Random;
import java.net.URL;
import java.applet.*;

public class TicTacToe extends JFrame
{
  JTextField messageTextField = new JTextField();
  JPanel gamePanel = new JPanel();
  JTextField[] boxTextField = new JTextField[9];
  JLabel[] gridLabel = new JLabel[4];
  JPanel playersPanel = new JPanel();
  ButtonGroup playersButtonGroup = new ButtonGroup();
  JRadioButton twoPlayersRadioButton = new JRadioButton();
  JRadioButton onePlayerRadioButton = new JRadioButton();
  JPanel firstPanel = new JPanel();
  ButtonGroup firstButtonGroup = new ButtonGroup();
  JRadioButton youFirstRadioButton = new JRadioButton();
  JRadioButton computerFirstRadioButton = new
JRadioButton();
  JPanel computerPanel = new JPanel();
  ButtonGroup computerButtonGroup = new ButtonGroup();
  JRadioButton randomRadioButton = new JRadioButton();
  JRadioButton smartRadioButton = new JRadioButton();
  JPanel buttonsPanel = new JPanel();
  JButton startStopButton = new JButton();
  JButton exitButton = new JButton();

  boolean xTurn;
  boolean canClick = false;
  int numberClicks;
  String[] possibleWins = new String[8];
  boolean gameOver;
  Random myRandom = new Random();

  AudioClip drawSound;
  AudioClip winSound;
```

```java
public static void main(String args[])
{
  // create frame
  new TicTacToe().setVisible(true);
}

public TicTacToe()
{
  // frame constructor
  setTitle("Tic Tac Toe");
  getContentPane().setBackground(Color.WHITE);
  setResizable(false);
  addWindowListener(new WindowAdapter()
  {
    public void windowClosing(WindowEvent evt)
    {
      exitForm(evt);
    }
  });
  getContentPane().setLayout(new GridBagLayout());

  messageTextField = new JTextField();
  messageTextField.setPreferredSize(new Dimension(280,
50));
  messageTextField.setEditable(false);
  messageTextField.setBackground(Color.YELLOW);
  messageTextField.setForeground(Color.BLUE);
  messageTextField.setText("X's Move");

messageTextField.setHorizontalAlignment(SwingConstants.CENTE
R);
  messageTextField.setFont(new Font("Arial", Font.BOLD,
24));
  GridBagConstraints gridConstraints = new
GridBagConstraints();
  gridConstraints.gridx = 0;
  gridConstraints.gridy = 0;
  gridConstraints.insets = new Insets(10, 10, 10, 10);
  getContentPane().add(messageTextField, gridConstraints);

  gamePanel.setPreferredSize(new Dimension(280, 280));
  gamePanel.setBackground(Color.WHITE);
  gamePanel.setLayout(new GridBagLayout());
  gridConstraints = new GridBagConstraints();
  gridConstraints.gridx = 0;
  gridConstraints.gridy = 1;
  gridConstraints.gridheight = 3;
```

```java
   gridConstraints.insets = new Insets(10, 10, 10, 10);
   getContentPane().add(gamePanel, gridConstraints);

   for (int i = 0; i < 9; i++)
   {
     boxTextField[i] = new JTextField();
     boxTextField[i].setPreferredSize(new Dimension(80,
80));
     boxTextField[i].setEditable(false);
     boxTextField[i].setBackground(Color.WHITE);

boxTextField[i].setHorizontalAlignment(SwingConstants.CENTER
);
     boxTextField[i].setFont(new Font("Arial", Font.BOLD,
48));
     boxTextField[i].setBorder(null);
     gridConstraints = new GridBagConstraints();
     gridConstraints.gridx = 2 * (i % 3);
     gridConstraints.gridy = 2 * (i / 3);
     gamePanel.add(boxTextField[i], gridConstraints);
     boxTextField[i].addMouseListener(new MouseAdapter()
     {
       public void mousePressed(MouseEvent e)
       {
         boxTextFieldMousePressed(e);
       }
     });
   }

   gridLabel[0] = new JLabel();
   gridLabel[0].setPreferredSize(new Dimension(280, 10));
   gridLabel[0].setOpaque(true);
   gridLabel[0].setBackground(Color.BLUE);
   gridConstraints = new GridBagConstraints();
   gridConstraints.gridx = 0;
   gridConstraints.gridy = 1;
   gridConstraints.gridwidth = 5;
   gridConstraints.insets = new Insets(5, 0, 5, 0);
   gamePanel.add(gridLabel[0], gridConstraints);

   gridLabel[1] = new JLabel();
   gridLabel[1].setPreferredSize(new Dimension(280, 10));
   gridLabel[1].setOpaque(true);
   gridLabel[1].setBackground(Color.BLUE);
   gridConstraints = new GridBagConstraints();
   gridConstraints.gridx = 0;
   gridConstraints.gridy = 3;
```

```
    gridConstraints.gridwidth = 5;
    gridConstraints.insets = new Insets(5, 0, 5, 0);
    gamePanel.add(gridLabel[1], gridConstraints);

    gridLabel[2] = new JLabel();
    gridLabel[2].setPreferredSize(new Dimension(10, 280));
    gridLabel[2].setOpaque(true);
    gridLabel[2].setBackground(Color.BLUE);
    gridConstraints = new GridBagConstraints();
    gridConstraints.gridx = 1;
    gridConstraints.gridy = 0;
    gridConstraints.gridheight = 5;
    gridConstraints.insets = new Insets(0, 5, 0, 5);
    gamePanel.add(gridLabel[2], gridConstraints);

    gridLabel[3] = new JLabel();
    gridLabel[3].setPreferredSize(new Dimension(10, 280));
    gridLabel[3].setOpaque(true);
    gridLabel[3].setBackground(Color.BLUE);
    gridConstraints = new GridBagConstraints();
    gridConstraints.gridx = 3;
    gridConstraints.gridy = 0;
    gridConstraints.gridheight = 5;
    gridConstraints.insets = new Insets(0, 5, 0, 5);
    gamePanel.add(gridLabel[3], gridConstraints);

    playersPanel.setPreferredSize(new Dimension(160, 75));
    playersPanel.setBackground(Color.WHITE);

playersPanel.setBorder(BorderFactory.createLineBorder(Color.
BLUE));
    playersPanel.setLayout(new GridBagLayout());
    gridConstraints = new GridBagConstraints();
    gridConstraints.gridx = 1;
    gridConstraints.gridy = 0;
    gridConstraints.insets = new Insets(5, 10, 5, 10);
    getContentPane().add(playersPanel, gridConstraints);

    twoPlayersRadioButton.setText("Two Players");
    twoPlayersRadioButton.setBackground(Color.WHITE);
    twoPlayersRadioButton.setSelected(true);
    playersButtonGroup.add(twoPlayersRadioButton);
    gridConstraints = new GridBagConstraints();
    gridConstraints.gridx = 0;
    gridConstraints.gridy = 0;
    gridConstraints.anchor = GridBagConstraints.WEST;
```

```
    playersPanel.add(twoPlayersRadioButton,
gridConstraints);
    twoPlayersRadioButton.addActionListener(new
ActionListener()
    {
      public void actionPerformed(ActionEvent e)
      {
        twoPlayersRadioButtonActionPerformed(e);
      }
    });

    onePlayerRadioButton.setText("One Player");
    onePlayerRadioButton.setBackground(Color.WHITE);
    playersButtonGroup.add(onePlayerRadioButton);
    gridConstraints = new GridBagConstraints();
    gridConstraints.gridx = 0;
    gridConstraints.gridy = 1;
    gridConstraints.anchor = GridBagConstraints.WEST;
    playersPanel.add(onePlayerRadioButton, gridConstraints);
    onePlayerRadioButton.addActionListener(new
ActionListener()
    {
      public void actionPerformed(ActionEvent e)
      {
        onePlayerRadioButtonActionPerformed(e);
      }
    });

    firstPanel.setPreferredSize(new Dimension(160, 75));
    firstPanel.setBackground(Color.WHITE);

firstPanel.setBorder(BorderFactory.createLineBorder(Color.BL
UE));
    firstPanel.setLayout(new GridBagLayout());
    gridConstraints = new GridBagConstraints();
    gridConstraints.gridx = 1;
    gridConstraints.gridy = 1;
    gridConstraints.insets = new Insets(5, 10, 5, 10);
    getContentPane().add(firstPanel, gridConstraints);

    youFirstRadioButton.setText("You First");
    youFirstRadioButton.setBackground(Color.WHITE);
    youFirstRadioButton.setSelected(true);
    firstButtonGroup.add(youFirstRadioButton);
    gridConstraints = new GridBagConstraints();
    gridConstraints.gridx = 0;
    gridConstraints.gridy = 0;
```

```
    gridConstraints.anchor = GridBagConstraints.WEST;
    firstPanel.add(youFirstRadioButton, gridConstraints);

    computerFirstRadioButton.setText("Computer First");
    computerFirstRadioButton.setBackground(Color.WHITE);
    firstButtonGroup.add(computerFirstRadioButton);
    gridConstraints = new GridBagConstraints();
    gridConstraints.gridx = 0;
    gridConstraints.gridy = 1;
    gridConstraints.anchor = GridBagConstraints.WEST;
    firstPanel.add(computerFirstRadioButton,
gridConstraints);

    computerPanel.setPreferredSize(new Dimension(160, 75));
    computerPanel.setBackground(Color.WHITE);

computerPanel.setBorder(BorderFactory.createLineBorder(Color
.BLUE));
    computerPanel.setLayout(new GridBagLayout());
    gridConstraints = new GridBagConstraints();
    gridConstraints.gridx = 1;
    gridConstraints.gridy = 2;
    gridConstraints.insets = new Insets(5, 10, 5, 10);
    getContentPane().add(computerPanel, gridConstraints);

    randomRadioButton.setText("Random Computer");
    randomRadioButton.setBackground(Color.WHITE);
    randomRadioButton.setSelected(true);
    computerButtonGroup.add(randomRadioButton);
    gridConstraints = new GridBagConstraints();
    gridConstraints.gridx = 0;
    gridConstraints.gridy = 0;
    gridConstraints.anchor = GridBagConstraints.WEST;
    computerPanel.add(randomRadioButton, gridConstraints);

    smartRadioButton.setText("Smart Computer");
    smartRadioButton.setBackground(Color.WHITE);
    computerButtonGroup.add(smartRadioButton);
    gridConstraints = new GridBagConstraints();
    gridConstraints.gridx = 0;
    gridConstraints.gridy = 1;
    gridConstraints.anchor = GridBagConstraints.WEST;
    computerPanel.add(smartRadioButton, gridConstraints);

    buttonsPanel.setPreferredSize(new Dimension(160, 70));
    buttonsPanel.setBackground(Color.WHITE);
    buttonsPanel.setLayout(new GridBagLayout());
```

```
gridConstraints = new GridBagConstraints();
gridConstraints.gridx = 1;
gridConstraints.gridy = 3;
getContentPane().add(buttonsPanel, gridConstraints);

startStopButton.setText("Start Game");
gridConstraints = new GridBagConstraints();
gridConstraints.gridx = 0;
gridConstraints.gridy = 0;
buttonsPanel.add(startStopButton, gridConstraints);
startStopButton.addActionListener(new ActionListener()
{
  public void actionPerformed(ActionEvent e)
  {
    startStopButtonActionPerformed(e);
  }
});

exitButton.setText("Exit");
gridConstraints = new GridBagConstraints();
gridConstraints.gridx = 0;
gridConstraints.gridy = 1;
gridConstraints.insets = new Insets(10, 0, 0, 0);
buttonsPanel.add(exitButton, gridConstraints);
exitButton.addActionListener(new ActionListener()
{
  public void actionPerformed(ActionEvent e)
  {
    exitButtonActionPerformed(e);
  }
});

pack();
Dimension screenSize =
Toolkit.getDefaultToolkit().getScreenSize();
  setBounds((int) (0.5 * (screenSize.width - getWidth())),
(int) (0.5 * (screenSize.height - getHeight())), getWidth(),
getHeight());

messageTextField.setText("Game Stopped");
youFirstRadioButton.setEnabled(false);
computerFirstRadioButton.setEnabled(false);
randomRadioButton.setEnabled(false);
smartRadioButton.setEnabled(false);
// possible wins
possibleWins[0] = "012";
possibleWins[1] = "345";
```

```
      possibleWins[2] = "678";
      possibleWins[3] = "036";
      possibleWins[4] = "147";
      possibleWins[5] = "258";
      possibleWins[6] = "048";
      possibleWins[7] = "246";
      try
      {
         drawSound = Applet.newAudioClip(new URL("file:" +
"beep.wav"));
         winSound = Applet.newAudioClip(new URL("file:" +
"tada.wav"));
      }
      catch (Exception ex)
      {
         System.out.println("Error loading sound files");
      }
   }

   private void exitForm(WindowEvent evt)
   {
      System.exit(0);
   }

   private void boxTextFieldMousePressed(MouseEvent e)
   {
      if (canClick)
      {
         int i;
         // get upper left corner of clicked box
         Point p = e.getComponent().getLocation();
         // determine index based on p
         for (i = 0; i < 9; i++)
         {
            if (p.x == boxTextField[i].getX() && p.y ==
boxTextField[i].getY())
               break;
         }
         markClickedBox(i);
      }
   }

   private void
twoPlayersRadioButtonActionPerformed(ActionEvent e)
   {
      youFirstRadioButton.setEnabled(false);
      computerFirstRadioButton.setEnabled(false);
```

```
      randomRadioButton.setEnabled(false);
      smartRadioButton.setEnabled(false);
   }

   private void
onePlayerRadioButtonActionPerformed(ActionEvent e)
   {
      youFirstRadioButton.setEnabled(true);
      computerFirstRadioButton.setEnabled(true);
      randomRadioButton.setEnabled(true);
      smartRadioButton.setEnabled(true);
   }

   private void startStopButtonActionPerformed(ActionEvent e)
   {
      if (startStopButton.getText().equals("Start Game"))
      {
        startStopButton.setText("Stop Game");
        twoPlayersRadioButton.setEnabled(false);
        onePlayerRadioButton.setEnabled(false);
        youFirstRadioButton.setEnabled(false);
        computerFirstRadioButton.setEnabled(false);
        randomRadioButton.setEnabled(false);
        smartRadioButton.setEnabled(false);
        exitButton.setEnabled(false);
        xTurn = true;
        messageTextField.setText("X's Turn");
        // reset boxes
        for (int i = 0; i < 9; i++)
        {
          boxTextField[i].setText("");
          boxTextField[i].setBackground(Color.WHITE);
        }
        canClick = true;
        numberClicks = 0;
        gameOver = false;
        if (computerFirstRadioButton.isSelected())
          computerTurn();
      }
      else
      {
        startStopButton.setText("Start Game");
        if (!gameOver)
          messageTextField.setText("Game Stopped");
        twoPlayersRadioButton.setEnabled(true);
        onePlayerRadioButton.setEnabled(true);
        if (onePlayerRadioButton.isSelected())
```

```
      {
        youFirstRadioButton.setEnabled(true);
        computerFirstRadioButton.setEnabled(true);
        randomRadioButton.setEnabled(true);
        smartRadioButton.setEnabled(true);
      }
      exitButton.setEnabled(true);
      canClick = false;
    }
}

private void exitButtonActionPerformed(ActionEvent e)
{
   System.exit(0);
}

private void markClickedBox(int i)
{
   String whoWon = "";
   // if already clicked then exit
   if (!boxTextField[i].getText().equals(""))
     return;
   numberClicks++;
   if (xTurn)
   {
     boxTextField[i].setText("X");
     xTurn = false;
     messageTextField.setText("O's Turn");
   }
   else
   {
     boxTextField[i].setText("O");
     xTurn = true;
     messageTextField.setText("X's Turn");
   }
   // check for win - will establish a value for WhoWon
   whoWon = checkForWin();
   if (!whoWon.equals(""))
   {
     winSound.play();
     messageTextField.setText(whoWon + " wins!");
     gameOver = true;
     startStopButton.doClick();
     return;
   }
   else if (numberClicks == 9)
   {
```

```java
        // draw
        drawSound.play();
        messageTextField.setText("It's a draw!");
        gameOver = true;
        startStopButton.doClick();
        return;
      }
    if (onePlayerRadioButton.isSelected())
      if ((xTurn && computerFirstRadioButton.isSelected())
|| (!xTurn && youFirstRadioButton.isSelected()))
        computerTurn();
  }

  private String checkForWin()
  {
    String winner = "";
    int[] boxNumber = new int[3];
    String[] mark = new String[3];
    // check all possible for wins
    for (int i = 0; i < 8; i++)
    {
      for (int j = 0; j < 3; j++)
      {
        boxNumber[j] =
Integer.valueOf(String.valueOf(possibleWins[i].charAt(j))).i
ntValue();
        mark[j] = boxTextField[boxNumber[j]].getText();
      }
      if (mark[0].equals(mark[1]) && mark[0].equals(mark[2])
&& mark[1].equals(mark[2]) && !mark[0].equals(""))
      {
        // we have a winner
        winner = mark[0];
        for (int j = 0; j < 3; j++)

boxTextField[boxNumber[j]].setBackground(Color.RED);
      }
    }
    return (winner);
  }

  private void computerTurn()
  {
    int selectedBox;
    int i, n;
    int j, k;
    String computerMark, playerMark, markToFind;
```

```
int[] boxNumber = new int[3];
String[] mark = new String[3];
int emptyBox;
int[] bestMoves = { 4, 0, 2, 6, 8, 1, 3, 5, 7 };

if (randomRadioButton.isSelected())
{
  // random logic
  // put mark in Nth available square
  n = myRandom.nextInt(9 - numberClicks) + 1;
  i = 0;
  for (selectedBox = 0; selectedBox < 9; selectedBox++)
  {
    if (boxTextField[selectedBox].getText().equals(""))
      i++;
    if (i == n)
      break;
  }
  // put mark in SelectedBox
  markClickedBox(selectedBox);
}
else
{
  // smart computer
        // determine who has what mark
  if (computerFirstRadioButton.isSelected())
  {
    computerMark = "X";
    playerMark = "O";
  }
  else
  {
    computerMark = "O";
    playerMark = "X";
  }
  // Step 1 (K = 1) - check for win - see if two boxes
hold computer mark and one is empty
  // Step 2 (K = 2) - check for block - see if two boxes
hold player mark and one is empty
  for (k = 1; k <= 2; k++)
  {
    if (k == 1)
      markToFind = computerMark;
    else
      markToFind = playerMark;
    for (i = 0; i < 8; i++)
    {
```

```
        n = 0;
        emptyBox = 0;
        for (j = 0; j < 3; j++)
        {
          boxNumber[j] =
Integer.valueOf(String.valueOf(possibleWins[i].charAt(j))).i
ntValue();
          mark[j] = boxTextField[boxNumber[j]].getText();
          if (mark[j].equals(markToFind))
            n++;
          else if (mark[j].equals(""))
            emptyBox = boxNumber[j];
        }
        if (n == 2 && emptyBox != 0)
        {
          // mark empty box to win (K = 1) or block (K =
2)
          markClickedBox(emptyBox);
          return;
        }
      }
    }
    // Step 3 - find next best move
    for (i = 0; i < 9; i++)
    {
      if (boxTextField[bestMoves[i]].getText().equals(""))
      {
        markClickedBox(bestMoves[i]);
        return;
      }
    }
  }
}


}
```

4

Match Game Project

Review and Preview

The next project we build is a **Match Game**. This is a one or two player game - play against a friend, the computer, or play alone. Ten pairs of photos (you can use your own photos) are hidden on a playing board. The object of the game is to find matching pairs by remembering photo locations. We'll see how to generate an array of random integers and how to use the timer object for delays.

Match Game Project Preview

In this chapter, we will build a **Match Game**. Ten pairs of photos are hidden on a playing board. The object is to find matching pairs. Turns alternate between players – an extra turn is earned with each match. The version we build here allows two players to compete against each other or to have a single player play a solitaire version or compete against the computer.

The finished project is saved as **MatchGame** in the **\KidGamesJava\KidGamesJava Projects** folder. Start NetBeans (or your IDE). Open the specified project group. Make **MatchGame** the selected project. Run the project. You will see:

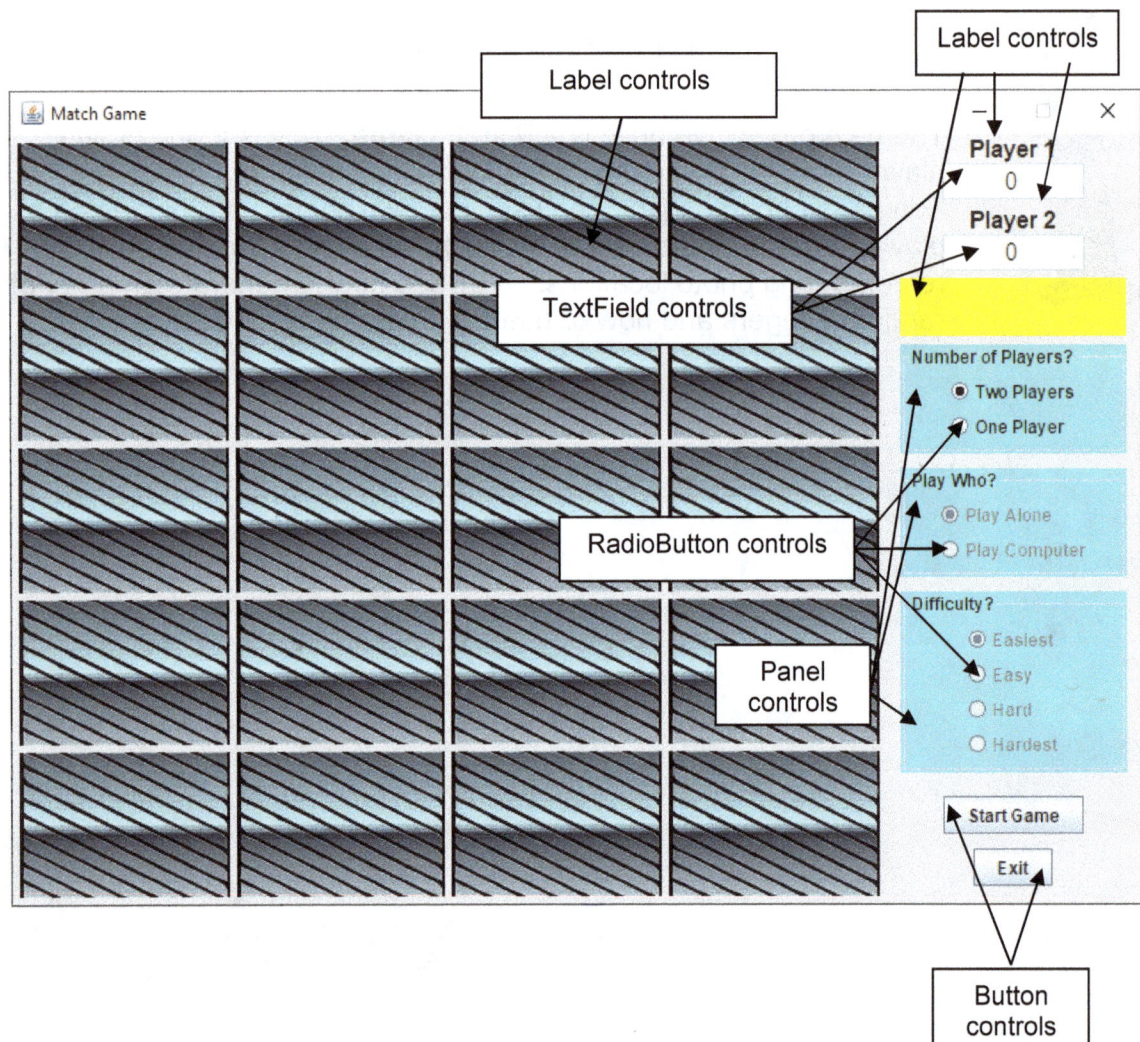

On the left is the photo display area for **Match Game**. Each photo is displayed in a label control. On the right are label and text field controls used to display scoring. There are also three panel controls and two button controls. Each panel holds radio button controls used to establish game options. The two button controls are used to start and stop the game and to exit the program.

The game appears in its 'stopped' state, the label controls holding photos are covered and waiting for you to choose game options. You can choose one or two players. If one player, you can choose to play alone or against the computer. If playing the computer, you can choose how smart you want the computer to be (**Difficulty**). As options are selected, the labels used for scoring change their headings to match the selections. I've selected a one player game, against the computer with a **Hard** difficulty:

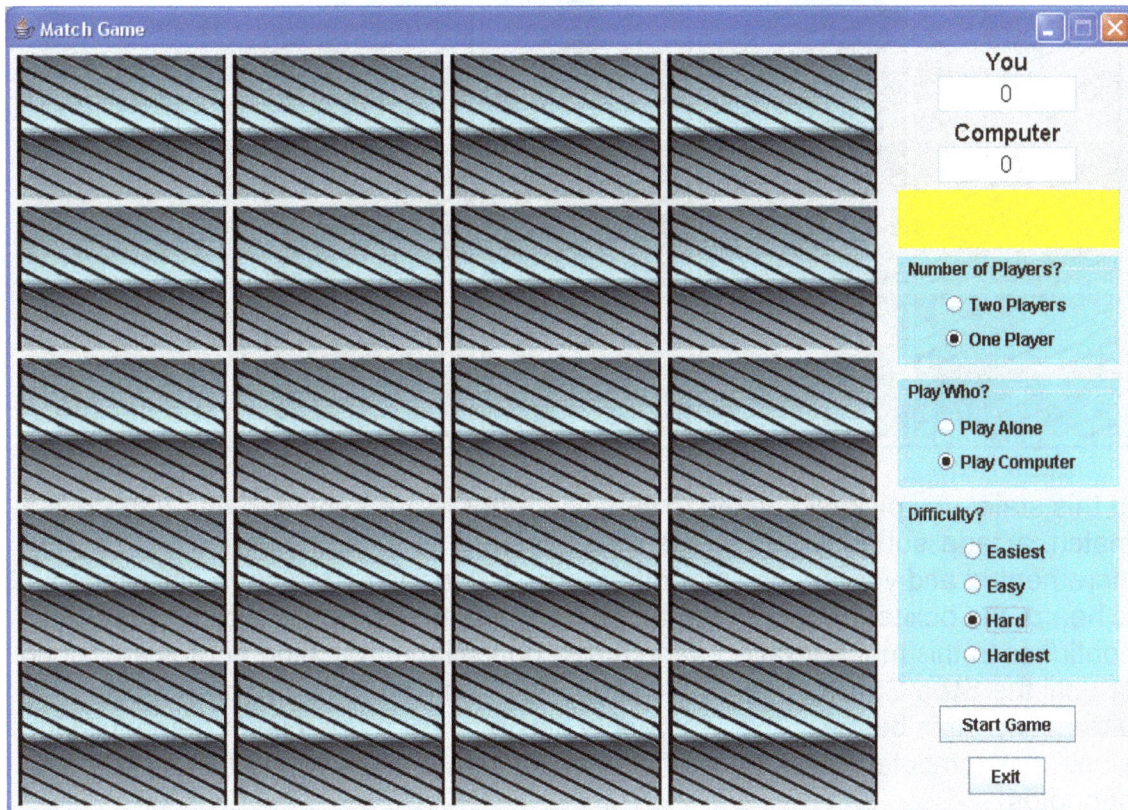

Click the **Start Game** button to start playing. Its caption will change (now reading **Stop Game**) and the options group boxes and **Exit** button will become disabled. The message area says **Pick a Box**. When playing the computer, you go first.

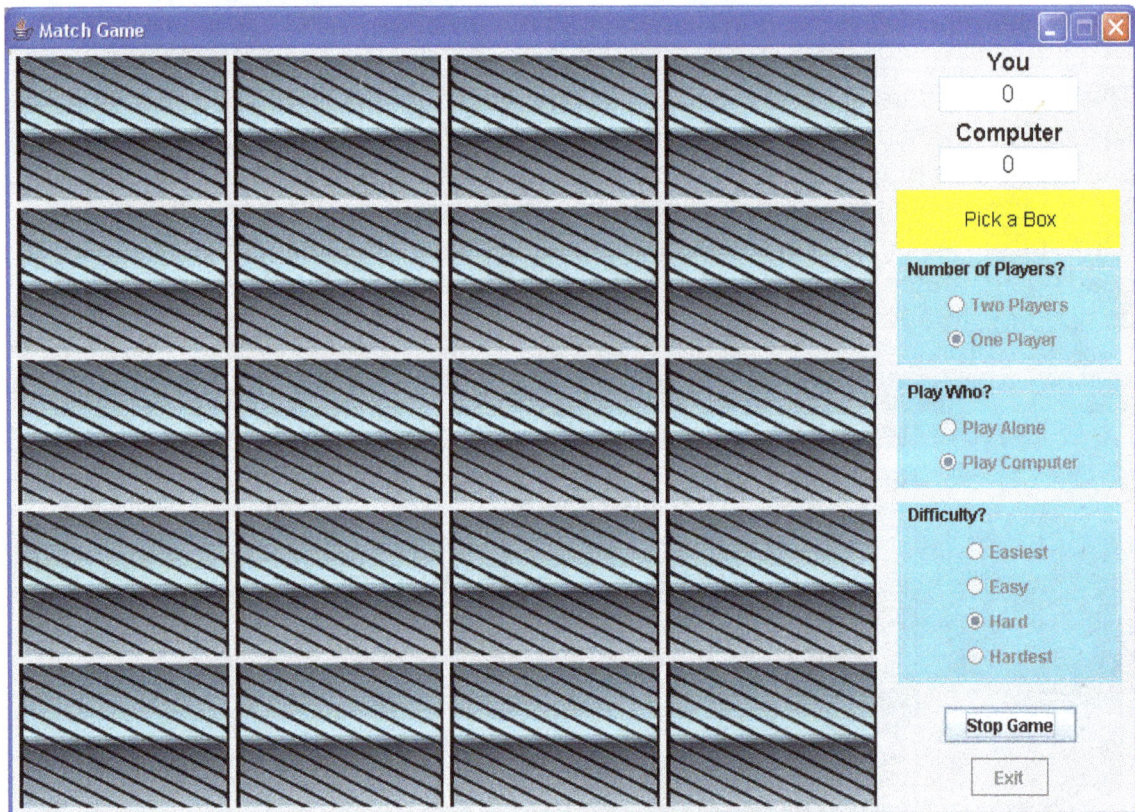

In this state, you pick two boxes to see what photos are behind them. If there is a match, a 'tada' sound will be heard, the boxes are removed, your score incremented and you are given another turn. If there is no match, a different sound is heard, the boxes are recovered and it becomes the computer's turn. Play continues in this manner (alternating turns) until all the matching photos are found or until the **Stop Game** button is clicked. Play is similar for a two player game, alternating turns between the two people playing. For a one player game, playing alone, the computer keeps track of how many tries it takes you to find all 10 pairs of photos.

I selected the first two boxes and see:

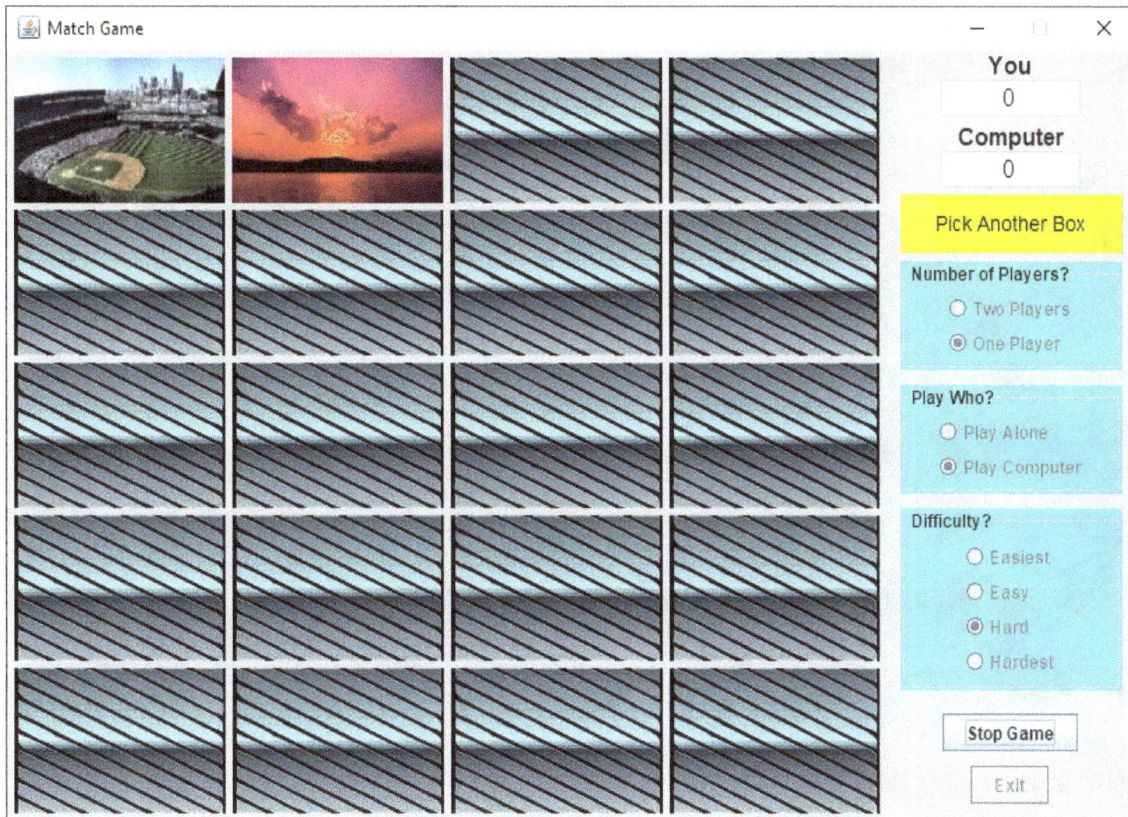

It's TMobile Park (home of the Seattle Mariners baseball team) and a pretty sunset. I hear a 'boing' sound and the board returns to it's covered state. You will most likely see different photos when you run the game because we are using random numbers.

It then becomes the computer's turn. It's choices are:

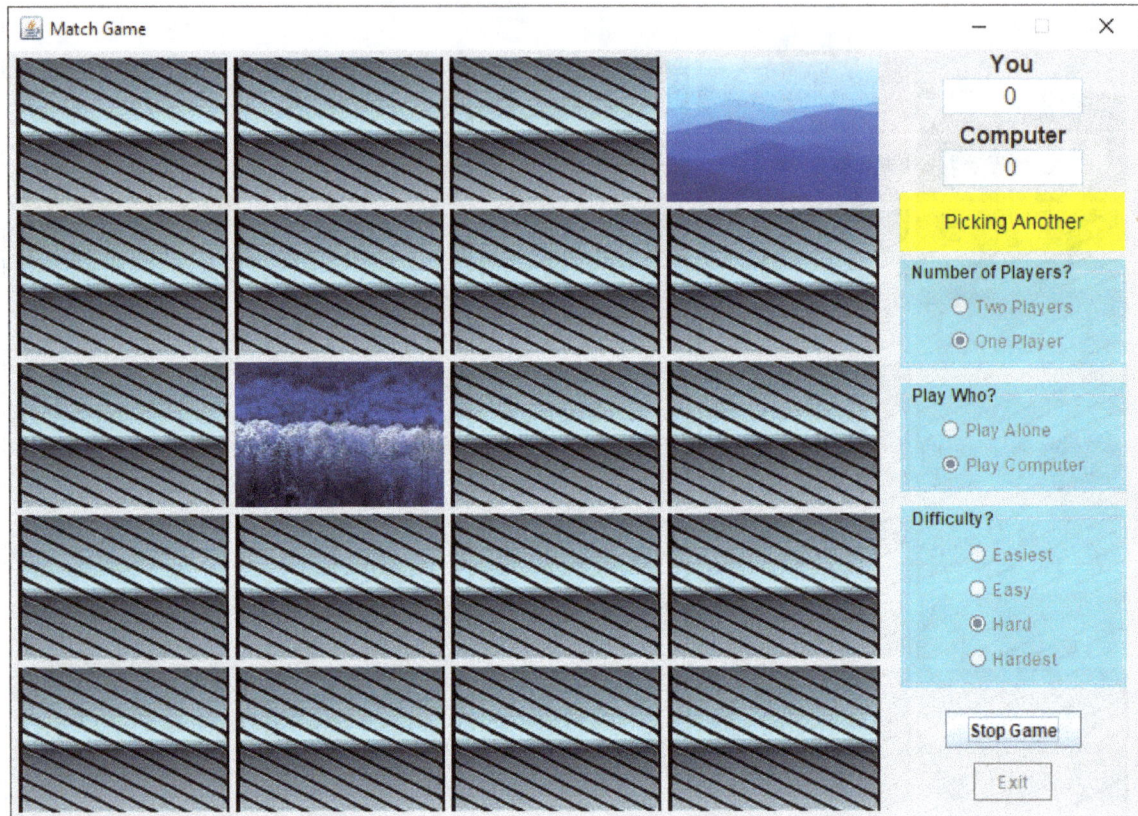

Not a match. I think you see the idea – keep looking for matches.

Picking the first box in the bottom row and the last box in the first row, I get a match. The photos are removed, my score is incremented and it's my turn again:

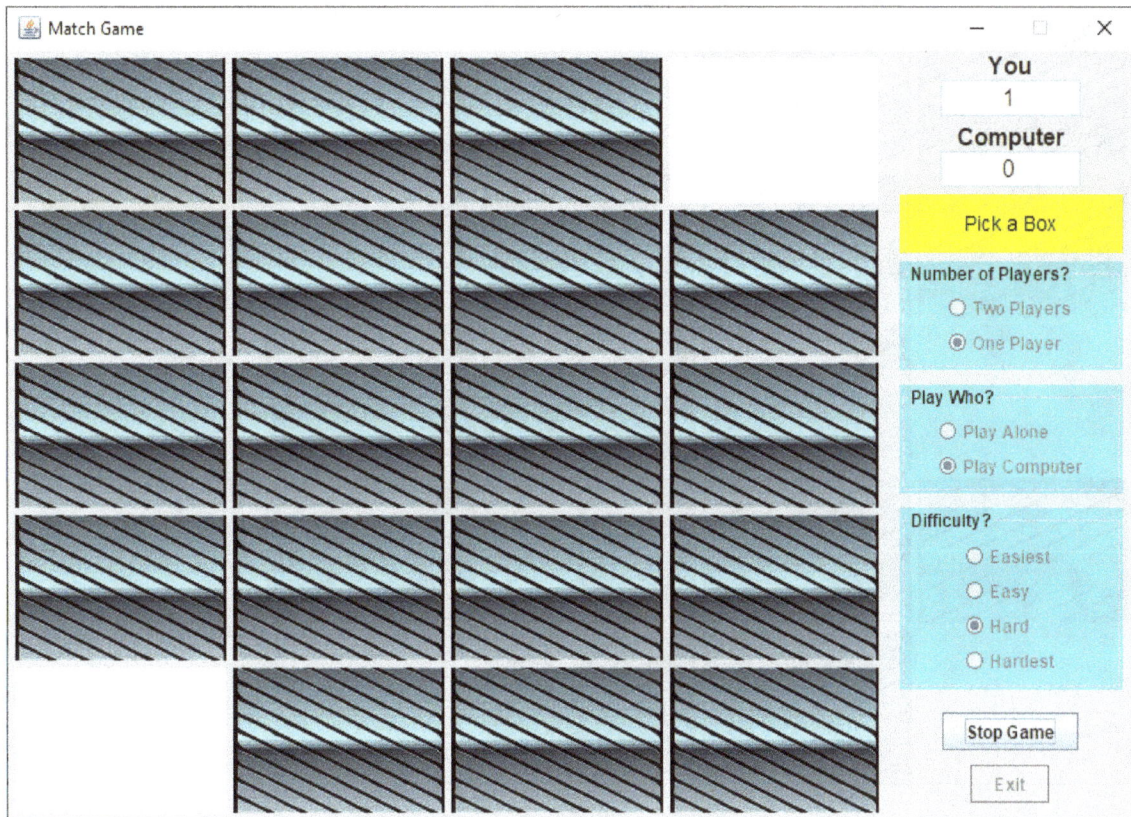

I didn't find a match, but the computer found two:

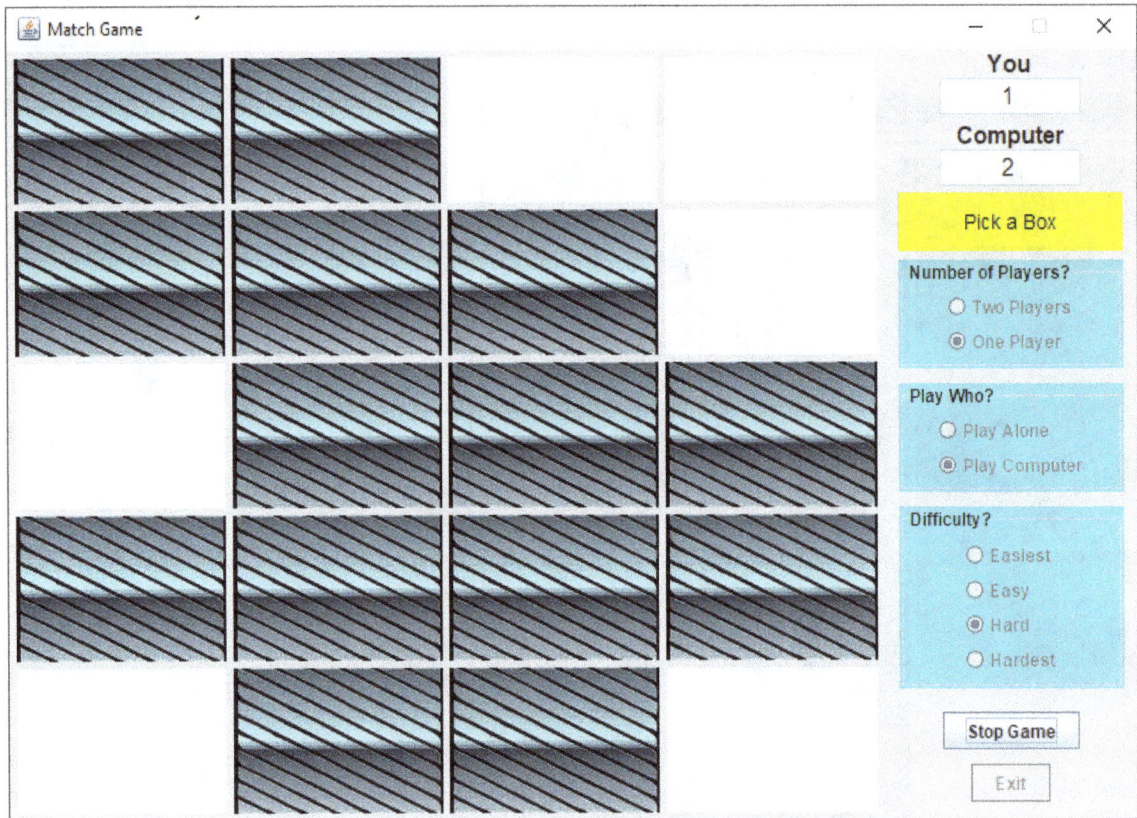

The game continues in this same manner, alternating turns between you and the computer. When there is a match, you or the computer get an additional turn. I continued playing this game against a pretty smart computer. Once all the matches were found, the final score was me 6 and the computer 4, I won!

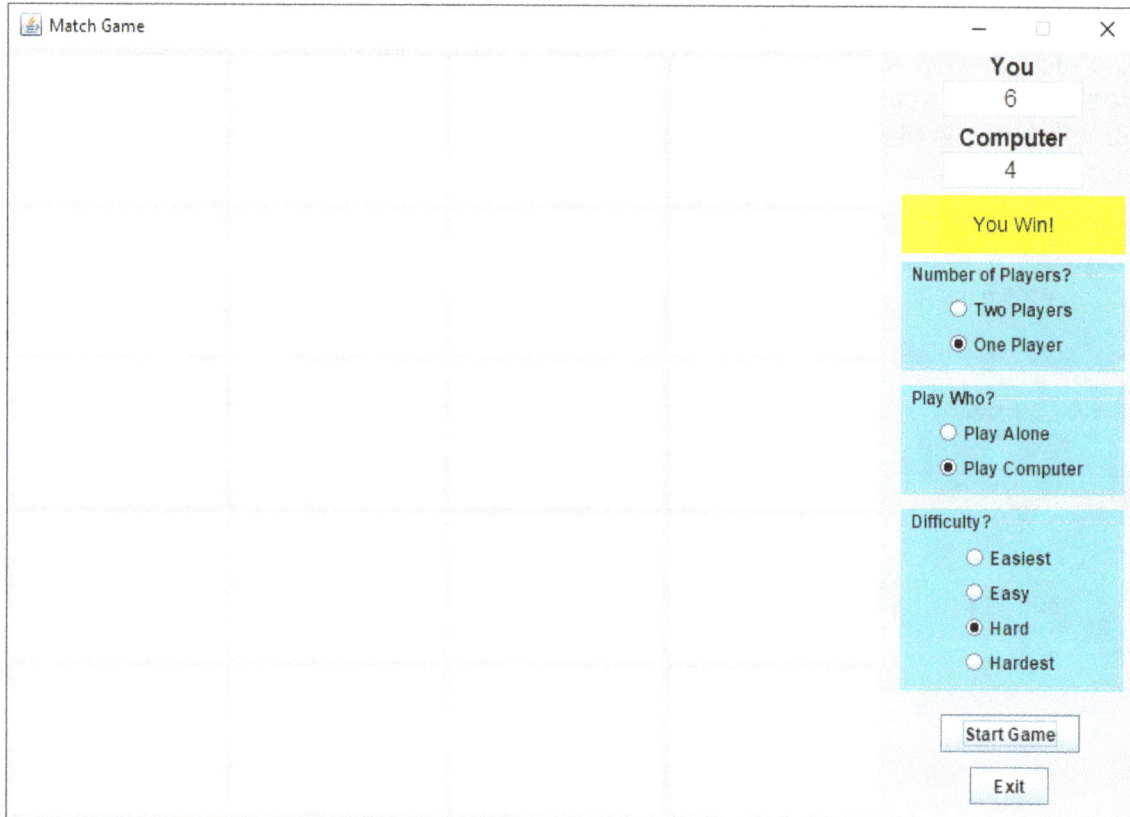

Notice the game returns to its stopped state to allow another game or to stop the program by clicking **Exit**.

Continue playing the game to understand its operation. Try using the two player game and the one player game where you **Play Alone**. Or, in the one player game against the computer, try different levels of difficulty. You will find at the **Hardest** level, the computer is nearly impossible to beat. Click **Exit** when you're done to stop the game. Open the code file and look over the code, if you like.

You will now build this project in stages. As you build Java projects, we always recommend taking a slow, step-by-step process. It minimizes programming errors and helps build your confidence as things come together in a complete project.

We address **frame design**. We discuss the controls needed to build the frame, establish initial control properties (including using your own photos in the game) and discuss how to change the state of the controls. And, we address **code design**. We discuss how to display the pairs of pictures, check for a match, handle multiple players, and decide how to make computer-generated moves. We also discuss how to "scramble" the photos and the use of timer objects for delays.

Match Game Frame Design

We begin building the **Match Game** project. Let's build the frame. Start a new project in your Java Project group – name it **MatchGame**. Delete default code in file named **MatchGame.java**.   Once started, we suggest you immediately save the project with a name you choose. This sets up the folder and file structure needed for your project.

Build the basic frame with these properties:

MatchGame Frame:
title	Match Game
resizable	false

The code is:

```java
/*
 * MatchGame.java
 */
package matchgame;
import javax.swing.*;
import java.awt.*;
import java.awt.event.*;

public class MatchGame extends JFrame
{

  public static void main(String args[])
  {
    // create frame
    new MatchGame().setVisible(true);
  }

  public MatchGame()
  {
    // frame constructor
    setTitle("Match Game");
    setResizable(false);
    addWindowListener(new WindowAdapter()
    {
      public void windowClosing(WindowEvent evt)
      {
        exitForm(evt);
      }
    });
    getContentPane().setLayout(new GridBagLayout());
```

```
      GridBagConstraints gridConstraints;

   pack();
   Dimension screenSize =
Toolkit.getDefaultToolkit().getScreenSize();
      setBounds((int) (0.5 * (screenSize.width -
getWidth())), (int) (0.5 * (screenSize.height -
getHeight())), getWidth(), getHeight());
   }

   private void exitForm(WindowEvent evt)
   {
      System.exit(0);
   }
}
```

This code builds the frame, sets up the layout manager and includes code to exit the application. Run the code to make sure the frame (at least, what there is of it at this point) appears and is centered on the screen:

Let's populate our frame with other controls. All code for creating the frame and placing controls (except declarations) goes in the **MatchGame** constructor.

We start by putting six panel controls on the frame. The **GridBagLayout** is:

	gridx = 0	gridx = 1
gridy = 0	gamePanel	resultsPanel
gridy = 1		playersPanel
gridy = 2		playWhoPanel
gridy = 3		difficultyPanel
gridy = 4		buttonsPanel

The **gamePanel** will be used to display the pictures in label controls. The **resultsPanel** will hold scoring and message controls. The **playersPanel** will hold radio buttons selecting the number of players. The **playWhoPanel** will host radio buttons deciding (in a one player game) if you play solitaire or against the computer. The **difficultyPanel** holds radio buttons that decide how smart the computer is. And the **buttonsPanel** will hold the two button controls. We will build each panel separately. Let's begin with the gamePanel.

The **gamePanel** will hold twenty label controls (in a 5 rows by 4 columns grid) used to display the hidden pictures. The **GridBagLayout** for gamePanel is:

	gridx = 0	gridx = 1	gridx = 2	gridx = 3
gridy = 0	photoLabel[0]	photoLabel[1]]	photoLabel[2]	photoLabel[3]
gridy = 1	photoLabel[4]	photoLabel[5]	photoLabel[6]	photoLabel[7]
gridy = 2	photoLabel[8]	photoLabel[9]	photoLabel[10]	photoLabel[11]
gridy = 3	photoLabel[12]	photoLabel[13]	photoLabel[14]	photoLabel[15]
gridy = 4	photoLabel[16]	photoLabel[17]	photoLabel[18]	photoLabel[19]

Add the **gamePanel** to the frame and **photoLabel** controls to the panel with these properties:

gamePanel:
size	625, 530
gridx	0 (on frame)
gridy	0 (on frame)
gridheight	5

photoLabel[0]:
size	150, 100
opaque	true
background	White
gridx	0 (on gamePanel)
gridy	0 (on gamePanel)
insets	5, 5, 0, 0

photoLabel[1]:
size	150, 100
opaque	true
background	White
gridx	0 (on gamePanel)
gridy	1 (on gamePanel)
insets	5, 5, 0, 0

photoLabel[2]:
size	150, 100
opaque	true
background	White
gridx	0 (on gamePanel)
gridy	2 (on gamePanel)
insets	5, 5, 0, 0

photoLabel[3]:
size	150, 100

opaque   true
background   White
gridx   0 (on gamePanel)
gridy   3 (on gamePanel)
insets   5, 5, 0, 5

photoLabel[4]:
size   150, 100
opaque   true
background   White
gridx   1 (on gamePanel)
gridy   0 (on gamePanel)
insets   5, 5, 0, 0

photoLabel[5]:
size   150, 100
opaque   true
background   White
gridx   1 (on gamePanel)
gridy   1 (on gamePanel)
insets   5, 5, 0, 0

photoLabel[6]:
size   150, 100
opaque   true
background   White
gridx   1 (on gamePanel)
gridy   2 (on gamePanel)
insets   5, 5, 0, 0

photoLabel[7]:
size   150, 100
opaque   true
background   White
gridx   1 (on gamePanel)
gridy   3 (on gamePanel)
insets   5, 5, 0, 5

photoLabel[8]:
size	150, 100
opaque	true
background	White
gridx	2 (on gamePanel)
gridy	0 (on gamePanel)
insets	5, 5, 0, 0

photoLabel[9]:
size	150, 100
opaque	true
background	White
gridx	2 (on gamePanel)
gridy	1 (on gamePanel)
insets	5, 5, 0, 0

photoLabel[10]:
size	150, 100
opaque	true
background	White
gridx	2 (on gamePanel)
gridy	2 (on gamePanel)
insets	5, 5, 0, 0

photoLabel[11]:
size	150, 100
opaque	true
background	White
gridx	2 (on gamePanel)
gridy	3 (on gamePanel)
insets	5, 5, 0, 5

photoLabel[12]:
size	150, 100
opaque	true
background	White
gridx	3 (on gamePanel)
gridy	0 (on gamePanel)
insets	5, 5, 0, 0

photoLabel[13]:
size	150, 100
opaque	true
background	White
gridx	3 (on gamePanel)
gridy	1 (on gamePanel)
insets	5, 5, 0, 0

photoLabel[14]:
size	150, 100
opaque	true
background	White
gridx	3 (on gamePanel)
gridy	2 (on gamePanel)
insets	5, 5, 0, 0

photoLabel[15]:
size	150, 100
opaque	true
background	White
gridx	3 (on gamePanel)
gridy	3 (on gamePanel)
insets	5, 5, 0, 5

photoLabel[16]:
size	150, 100
opaque	true
background	White
gridx	4 (on gamePanel)
gridy	0 (on gamePanel)
insets	5, 5, 5, 0

photoLabel[17]:
size	150, 100
opaque	true
background	White
gridx	4 (on gamePanel)
gridy	1 (on gamePanel)
insets	5, 5, 5, 0

photoLabel[18]:

size	150, 100
opaque	true
background	White
gridx	4 (on gamePanel)
gridy	2 (on gamePanel)
insets	5, 5, 5, 0

photoLabel[19]:

size	150, 100
opaque	true
background	White
gridx	4 (on gamePanel)
gridy	3 (on gamePanel)
insets	5, 5, 5, 5

The gamePanel size and label control insets were selected to insure 5 pixel spacing of all labels from other labels and from the edges of the panel.

These controls are declared using:

```
JPanel gamePanel = new JPanel();
JLabel[] photoLabel = new JLabel[20];
```

The controls are placed in the frame using this code:

```
gamePanel.setPreferredSize(new Dimension(625, 530));
gamePanel.setLayout(new GridBagLayout());
gridConstraints = new GridBagConstraints();
gridConstraints.gridx = 0;
gridConstraints.gridy = 0;
gridConstraints.gridheight = 5;
getContentPane().add(gamePanel, gridConstraints);
```

```
for (int i = 0; i < 20; i++)
{
  photoLabel[i] = new JLabel();
  photoLabel[i].setPreferredSize(new Dimension(150, 100));
  photoLabel[i].setOpaque(true);
  photoLabel[i].setBackground(Color.WHITE);
  gridConstraints = new GridBagConstraints();
  gridConstraints.gridx = i % 4;
  gridConstraints.gridy = i / 4;
  gridConstraints.insets = new Insets(5, 5, 0, 0);
  if (gridConstraints.gridx == 3)
    gridConstraints.insets = new Insets(5, 5, 0, 5);
  if (gridConstraints.gridy == 4)
    gridConstraints.insets = new Insets(5, 5, 5, 0);
  if (gridConstraints.gridx == 3 && gridConstraints.gridy
== 4)
    gridConstraints.insets = new Insets(5, 5, 5, 5);
  gamePanel.add(photoLabel[i], gridConstraints);
  photoLabel[i].addMouseListener(new MouseAdapter()
  {
    public void mousePressed(MouseEvent e)
    {
      photoLabelMousePressed(e);
    }
  });
}
```

Note how the loop index (**i**) is used to set proper label control properties (gridx, gridy). This code also adds mouse listeners for each label. The method called when a label is clicked with the mouse **photoLabelMousePressed**. Add this empty method with the other methods:

```
private void photoLabelMousePressed(MouseEvent e)
{
}
```

Add code in the proper locations. Run to see:

The empty label controls appear in the grid. The **gamePanel** control is complete.
Let's move to the remaining panels on the frame.

The **resultsPanel** holds three label controls and two text fields to display scores and messages. The **GridBagLayout** for resultsPanel is:

	gridx = 0
gridy = 0	player1Label
gridy = 1	scoreTextField[0]
gridy = 2	Player2Label
gridy = 3	scoreTextField[1]
gridy = 4	messageLabel

The control properties are:

resultsPanel:
size	160, 140
gridx	1 (on frame)
gridy	0 (on frame)

player1Label:
text	Player 1
font	Arial, Bold, Size 16
gridx	0 (on resultsPanel)
gridy	0 (on resultsPanel)

scoreTextField[0]:
size	100, 25
text	0
editable	false
background	White
horizontalAlignment	CENTER
font	Arial, Plain, Size 16
gridx	0 (on resultsPanel)
gridy	1 (on results Panel)

player2Label:
text	Player 2
font	Arial, Bold, Size 16
gridx	0 (on resultsPanel)
gridy	2 (on resultsPanel)

scoreTextField[1]:

size	100, 25
text	0
editable	false
background	White
horizontalAlignment	CENTER
font	Arial, Plain, Size 16
gridx	0 (on resultsPanel)
gridy	3 (on results Panel)

messageLabel:

size	160, 40
opaque	true
background	Yellow
horizontalAlignment	CENTER
text	[blank]
font	Arial, Plain, Size 14
gridx	0 (on resultsPanel)
gridy	4 (on resultsPanel)
insets	5, 0, 0, 0

Declare the controls using:

```
JPanel resultsPanel = new JPanel();
JLabel player1Label = new JLabel();
JLabel player2Label = new JLabel();
JTextField[] scoreTextField = new JTextField[2];
JLabel messageLabel = new JLabel();
```

Add the controls to the **resultsPanel** (which is placed in the frame) using:

```
resultsPanel.setPreferredSize(new Dimension(160, 140));
resultsPanel.setLayout(new GridBagLayout());
gridConstraints = new GridBagConstraints();
gridConstraints.gridx = 1;
gridConstraints.gridy = 0;
getContentPane().add(resultsPanel, gridConstraints);

player1Label.setText("Player 1");
player1Label.setFont(new Font("Arial", Font.BOLD, 16));
gridConstraints = new GridBagConstraints();
gridConstraints.gridx = 0;
gridConstraints.gridy = 0;
resultsPanel.add(player1Label, gridConstraints);

scoreTextField[0] = new JTextField();
scoreTextField[0].setPreferredSize(new Dimension(100,
25));
scoreTextField[0].setText("0");
scoreTextField[0].setEditable(false);
scoreTextField[0].setBackground(Color.WHITE);
scoreTextField[0].setHorizontalAlignment(SwingConstants.CE
NTER);
scoreTextField[0].setFont(new Font("Arial", Font.PLAIN,
16));
gridConstraints = new GridBagConstraints();
gridConstraints.gridx = 0;
gridConstraints.gridy = 1;
resultsPanel.add(scoreTextField[0], gridConstraints);

player2Label.setText("Player 2");
player2Label.setFont(new Font("Arial", Font.BOLD, 16));
gridConstraints = new GridBagConstraints();
gridConstraints.gridx = 0;
gridConstraints.gridy = 2;
gridConstraints.insets = new Insets(5, 0, 0, 0);
resultsPanel.add(player2Label, gridConstraints);

scoreTextField[1] = new JTextField();
scoreTextField[1].setPreferredSize(new Dimension(100,
25));
scoreTextField[1].setText("0");
scoreTextField[1].setEditable(false);
scoreTextField[1].setBackground(Color.WHITE);
scoreTextField[1].setHorizontalAlignment(SwingConstants.CE
NTER);
```

```
scoreTextField[1].setFont(new Font("Arial", Font.PLAIN,
16));
gridConstraints = new GridBagConstraints();
gridConstraints.gridx = 0;
gridConstraints.gridy = 3;
resultsPanel.add(scoreTextField[1], gridConstraints);

messageLabel.setPreferredSize(new Dimension(160, 40));
messageLabel.setOpaque(true);
messageLabel.setBackground(Color.YELLOW);
messageLabel.setHorizontalAlignment(SwingConstants.CENTER)
;
messageLabel.setText("");
messageLabel.setFont(new Font("Arial", Font.PLAIN, 14));
gridConstraints = new GridBagConstraints();
gridConstraints.gridx = 0;
gridConstraints.gridy = 4;
gridConstraints.insets = new Insets(5, 0, 0, 0);
resultsPanel.add(messageLabel, gridConstraints);
```

Add this code in the proper locations. Run to see:

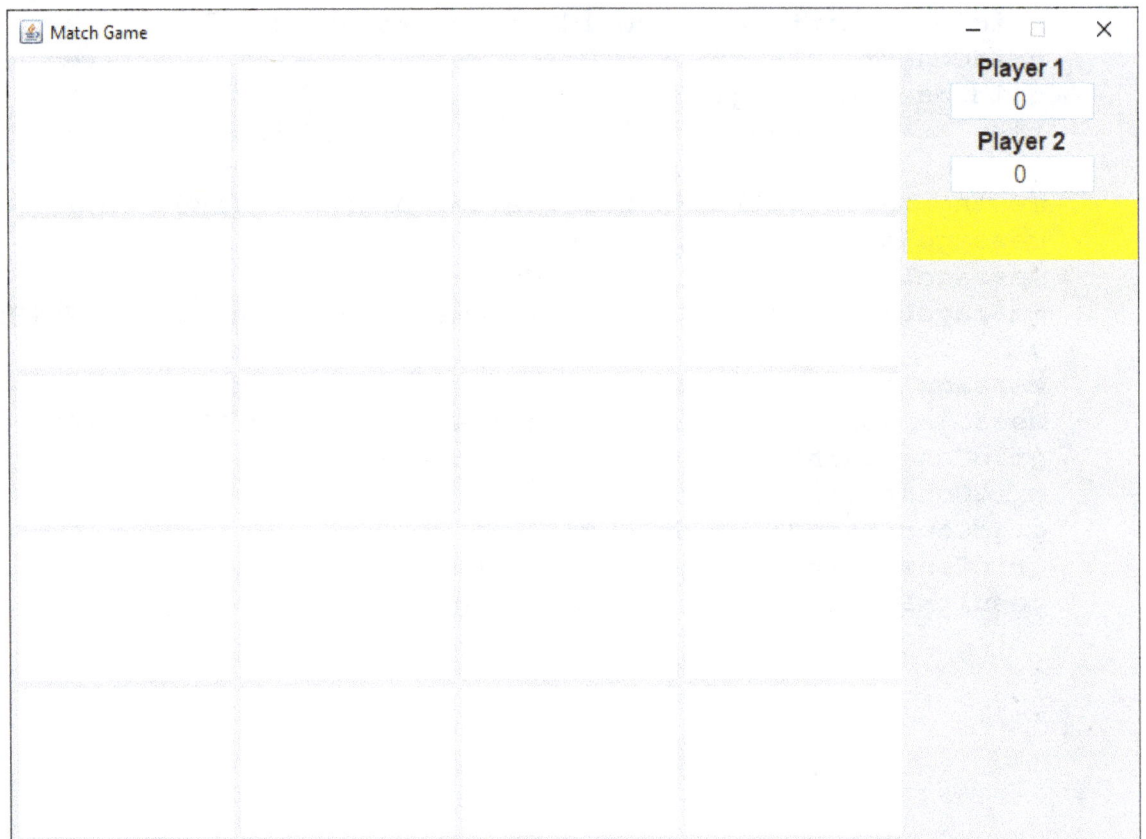

The new controls appear.

The **playersPanel** will hold two radio button controls used to select the number of players in the game. The **GridBagLayout** for optionsPanel is:

	gridx = 0
gridy = 0	twoPlayersRadioButton
gridy =1	onePlayerRadioButton

The panel and radio button properties:

playersPanel:

size	160, 75
background	Cyan
title	Number of Players?
gridx	1 (on frame)
gridy	1 (on frame)
insets	5, 10, 5, 10

twoPlayersRadioButton:

text	Two Players
background	Cyan
buttonGroup	playersButtonGroup
selected	true
gridx	0 (on playersPanel)
gridy	0 (on playersPanel)
anchor	WEST

onePlayerRadioButton:

text	One Player
background	Cyan
buttonGroup	playersButtonGroup
gridx	0 (on optionsPanel)
gridy	1 (on optionsPanel)
anchor	WEST

These controls are declared using:

```
JPanel playersPanel = new JPanel();
ButtonGroup playersButtonGroup = new ButtonGroup();
JRadioButton twoPlayersRadioButton = new JRadioButton();
JRadioButton onePlayerRadioButton = new JRadioButton();
```

The radio buttons are placed in the **playersPanel** (which is placed in the frame) using:

```
playersPanel.setPreferredSize(new Dimension(160, 75));
playersPanel.setBackground(Color.CYAN);
playersPanel.setBorder(BorderFactory.createTitledBorder("N
umber of Players?"));
playersPanel.setLayout(new GridBagLayout());
gridConstraints = new GridBagConstraints();
gridConstraints.gridx = 1;
gridConstraints.gridy = 1;
gridConstraints.insets = new Insets(5, 10, 5, 10);
getContentPane().add(playersPanel, gridConstraints);

twoPlayersRadioButton.setText("Two Players");
twoPlayersRadioButton.setBackground(Color.CYAN);
twoPlayersRadioButton.setSelected(true);
playersButtonGroup.add(twoPlayersRadioButton);
gridConstraints = new GridBagConstraints();
gridConstraints.gridx = 0;
gridConstraints.gridy = 0;
gridConstraints.anchor = GridBagConstraints.WEST;
playersPanel.add(twoPlayersRadioButton, gridConstraints);
twoPlayersRadioButton.addActionListener(new
ActionListener()
{
  public void actionPerformed(ActionEvent e)
  {
    twoPlayersRadioButtonActionPerformed(e);
  }
});

onePlayerRadioButton.setText("One Player");
onePlayerRadioButton.setBackground(Color.CYAN);
playersButtonGroup.add(onePlayerRadioButton);
gridConstraints = new GridBagConstraints();
gridConstraints.gridx = 0;
gridConstraints.gridy = 1;
gridConstraints.anchor = GridBagConstraints.WEST;
playersPanel.add(onePlayerRadioButton, gridConstraints);
```

```
onePlayerRadioButton.addActionListener(new
ActionListener()
{
  public void actionPerformed(ActionEvent e)
  {
    onePlayerRadioButtonActionPerformed(e);
  }
});
```

We added listeners for the two radio buttons. Add these empty methods to handle button selections:

```
private void
twoPlayersRadioButtonActionPerformed(ActionEvent e)
{
}

private void
onePlayerRadioButtonActionPerformed(ActionEvent e)
{
}
```

Add this code in the proper locations. Run to see:

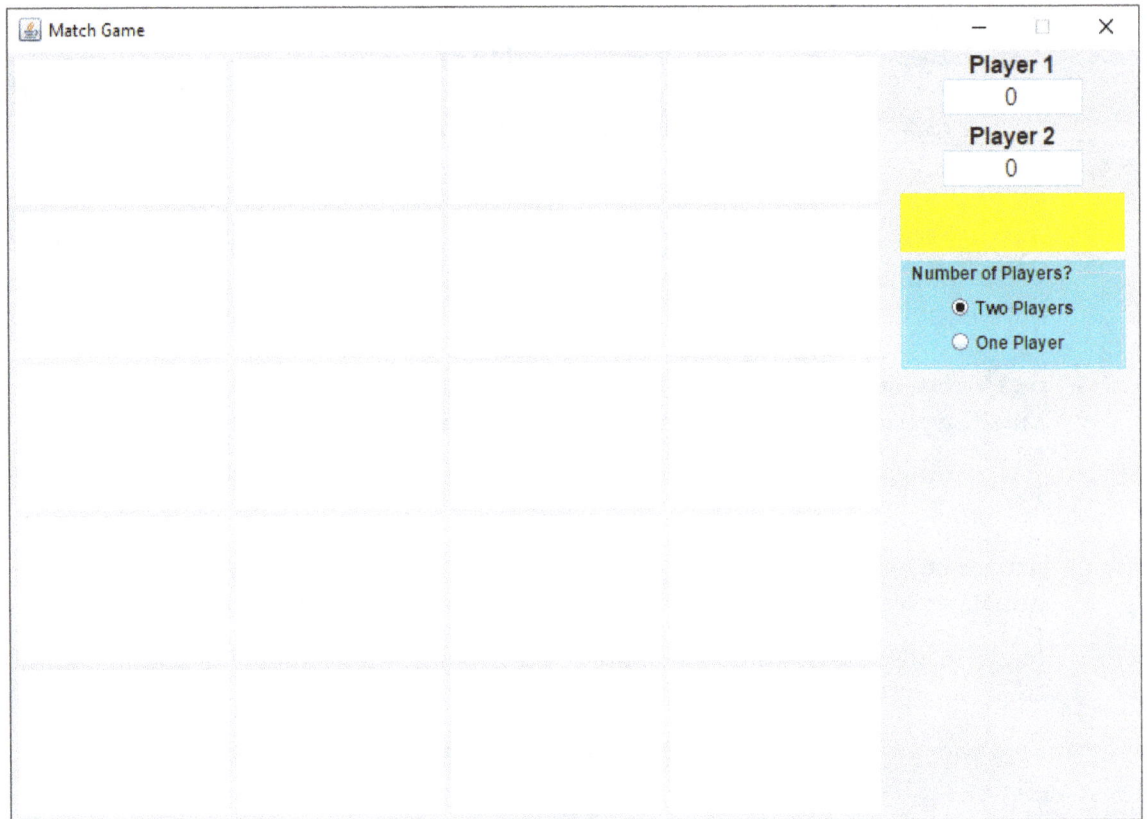

The players panel is displayed.

The **playWhoPanel** will hold two radio button controls used to determine (in a one player game) if you play alone or play against the computer. The **GridBagLayout** for playWhoPanel is:

	gridx = 0
gridy = 0	**playAloneRadioButton**
gridy =1	**playComputerRadioButton**

The panel and radio button properties:

playWhoPanel:
size	160, 75
background	Cyan
title	Play Who?
gridx	1 (on frame)
gridy	2 (on frame)
insets	5, 10, 5, 10

playAloneRadioButton:
text	Play Alone
background	Cyan
buttonGroup	playWhoButtonGroup
selected	true
gridx	0 (on playWhoPanel)
gridy	0 (on playWhoPanel)
anchor	WEST

playComputerRadioButton:
text	Play Computer
background	Cyan
buttonGroup	playWhoButtonGroup
gridx	0 (on playWhoPanel)
gridy	1 (on playWhoPanel)
anchor	WEST

These controls are declared using:

```
JPanel playWhoPanel = new JPanel();
ButtonGroup playWhoButtonGroup = new ButtonGroup();
JRadioButton playAloneRadioButton = new JRadioButton();
JRadioButton playComputerRadioButton = new JRadioButton();
```

The radio buttons are placed in the **playWhoPanel** (which is placed in the frame) using:

```
playWhoPanel.setPreferredSize(new Dimension(160, 75));
playWhoPanel.setBackground(Color.CYAN);
playWhoPanel.setBorder(BorderFactory.createTitledBorder("P
lay Who?"));
playWhoPanel.setLayout(new GridBagLayout());
gridConstraints = new GridBagConstraints();
gridConstraints.gridx = 1;
gridConstraints.gridy = 2;
gridConstraints.insets = new Insets(5, 10, 5, 10);
getContentPane().add(playWhoPanel, gridConstraints);

playAloneRadioButton.setText("Play Alone");
playAloneRadioButton.setBackground(Color.CYAN);
playAloneRadioButton.setSelected(true);
playWhoButtonGroup.add(playAloneRadioButton);
gridConstraints = new GridBagConstraints();
gridConstraints.gridx = 0;
gridConstraints.gridy = 0;
gridConstraints.anchor = GridBagConstraints.WEST;
playWhoPanel.add(playAloneRadioButton, gridConstraints);
playAloneRadioButton.addActionListener(new
ActionListener()
{
  public void actionPerformed(ActionEvent e)
  {
    playAloneRadioButtonActionPerformed(e);
  }
});

playComputerRadioButton.setText("Play Computer");
playComputerRadioButton.setBackground(Color.CYAN);
playWhoButtonGroup.add(playComputerRadioButton);
gridConstraints = new GridBagConstraints();
gridConstraints.gridx = 0;
gridConstraints.gridy = 1;
gridConstraints.anchor = GridBagConstraints.WEST;
```

```
playWhoPanel.add(playComputerRadioButton,
gridConstraints);
playComputerRadioButton.addActionListener(new
ActionListener()
{
  public void actionPerformed(ActionEvent e)
  {
    playComputerRadioButtonActionPerformed(e);
  }
});
```

We added listeners for the two radio buttons. Add these empty methods to handle button selections:

```
private void
playAloneRadioButtonActionPerformed(ActionEvent e)
{
}

private void
playComputerRadioButtonActionPerformed(ActionEvent e)
{
}
```

Add this code in the proper locations. Run to see:

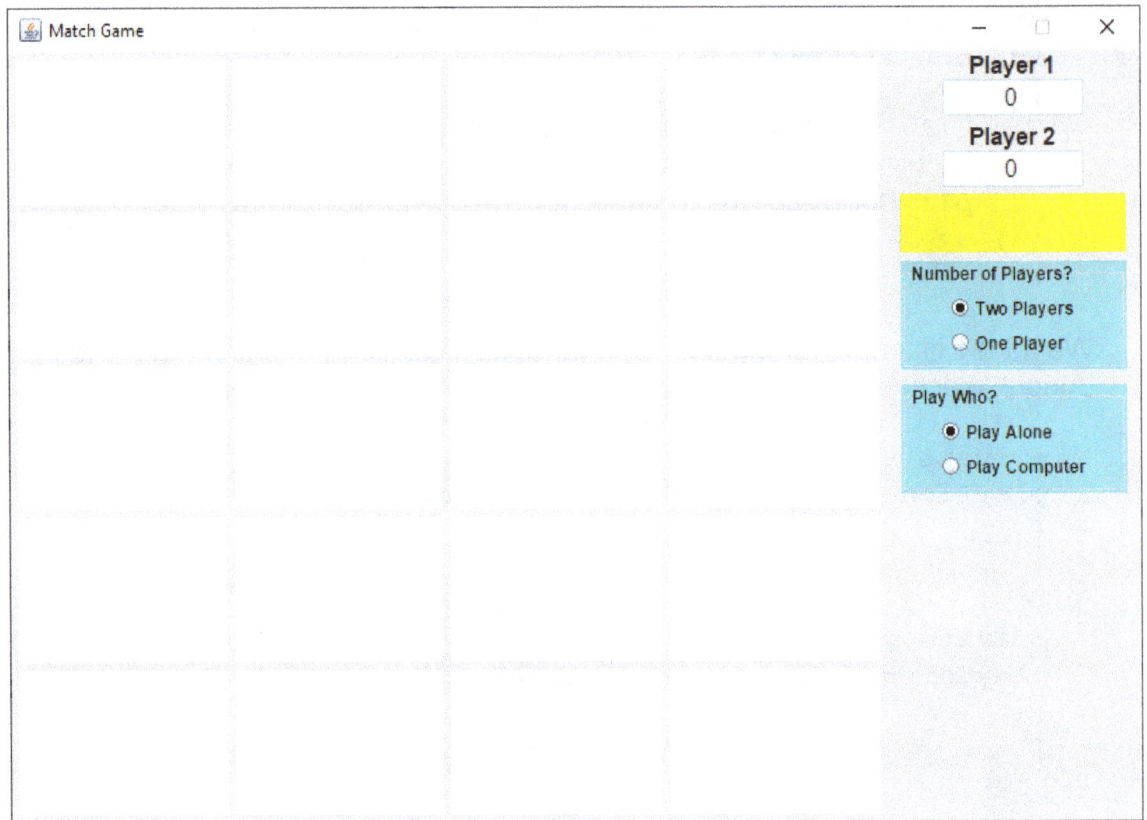

The play who panel is displayed.

The **difficultyPanel** will hold four radio button controls used to determine (in a one player game against the computer) how smart the computer is. The **GridBagLayout** for difficultyPanel is:

	gridx = 0
gridy = 0	**easiestRadioButton**
gridy =1	**easyRadioButton**
gridy = 2	**hardRadioButton**
gridy = 3	**hardestRadioButton**

The panel and radio button properties:

difficultyPanel:

size	160, 125
background	Cyan
title	Difficulty?
gridx	1 (on frame)
gridy	3 (on frame)
insets	5, 10, 5, 10

easiestRadioButton:

text	Easiest
background	Cyan
buttonGroup	difficultyButtonGroup
selected	true
gridx	0 (on difficultyPanel)
gridy	0 (on difficultyWhoPanel)
anchor	WEST

easyRadioButton:

text	Easy
background	Cyan
buttonGroup	difficultyButtonGroup
gridx	0 (on difficultyPanel)
gridy	1 (on difficultyWhoPanel)
anchor	WEST

hardRadioButton:

text	Hard
background	Cyan
buttonGroup	difficultyButtonGroup
gridx	0 (on difficultyPanel)
gridy	2 (on difficultyWhoPanel)
anchor	WEST

hardestRadioButton:

text	Hardest
background	Cyan
buttonGroup	difficultyButtonGroup
gridx	0 (on difficultyPanel)
gridy	3 (on difficultyWhoPanel)
anchor	WEST

These controls are declared using:

```
JPanel difficultyPanel = new JPanel();
ButtonGroup difficultyButtonGroup = new ButtonGroup();
JRadioButton easiestRadioButton = new JRadioButton();
JRadioButton easyRadioButton = new JRadioButton();
JRadioButton hardRadioButton = new JRadioButton();
JRadioButton hardestRadioButton = new JRadioButton();
```

The radio buttons are placed in the **difficultyPanel** (which is placed in the frame) using:

```
difficultyPanel.setPreferredSize(new Dimension(160, 125));
difficultyPanel.setBackground(Color.CYAN);
difficultyPanel.setBorder(BorderFactory.createTitledBorder
("Difficulty?"));
difficultyPanel.setLayout(new GridBagLayout());
gridConstraints = new GridBagConstraints();
gridConstraints.gridx = 1;
gridConstraints.gridy = 3;
gridConstraints.insets = new Insets(5, 10, 5, 10);
getContentPane().add(difficultyPanel, gridConstraints);

easiestRadioButton.setText("Easiest");
easiestRadioButton.setBackground(Color.CYAN);
easiestRadioButton.setSelected(true);
difficultyButtonGroup.add(easiestRadioButton);
gridConstraints = new GridBagConstraints();
gridConstraints.gridx = 0;
gridConstraints.gridy = 0;
gridConstraints.anchor = GridBagConstraints.WEST;
difficultyPanel.add(easiestRadioButton, gridConstraints);
easiestRadioButton.addActionListener(new ActionListener()
{
  public void actionPerformed(ActionEvent e)
  {
    easiestRadioButtonActionPerformed(e);
  }
});
```

```
easyRadioButton.setText("Easy");
easyRadioButton.setBackground(Color.CYAN);
easyRadioButton.setSelected(true);
difficultyButtonGroup.add(easyRadioButton);
gridConstraints = new GridBagConstraints();
gridConstraints.gridx = 0;
gridConstraints.gridy = 1;
gridConstraints.anchor = GridBagConstraints.WEST;
difficultyPanel.add(easyRadioButton, gridConstraints);
easyRadioButton.addActionListener(new ActionListener()
{
  public void actionPerformed(ActionEvent e)
  {
    easyRadioButtonActionPerformed(e);
  }
});

hardRadioButton.setText("Hard");
hardRadioButton.setBackground(Color.CYAN);
hardRadioButton.setSelected(true);
difficultyButtonGroup.add(hardRadioButton);
gridConstraints = new GridBagConstraints();
gridConstraints.gridx = 0;
gridConstraints.gridy = 2;
gridConstraints.anchor = GridBagConstraints.WEST;
difficultyPanel.add(hardRadioButton, gridConstraints);
hardRadioButton.addActionListener(new ActionListener()
{
  public void actionPerformed(ActionEvent e)
  {
    hardRadioButtonActionPerformed(e);
  }
});

hardestRadioButton.setText("Hardest");
hardestRadioButton.setBackground(Color.CYAN);
hardestRadioButton.setSelected(true);
difficultyButtonGroup.add(hardestRadioButton);
gridConstraints = new GridBagConstraints();
gridConstraints.gridx = 0;
gridConstraints.gridy = 3;
gridConstraints.anchor = GridBagConstraints.WEST;
difficultyPanel.add(hardestRadioButton, gridConstraints);
hardestRadioButton.addActionListener(new ActionListener()
{
  public void actionPerformed(ActionEvent e)
```

```
      {
        hardestRadioButtonActionPerformed(e);
      }
   });
```

We added listeners for the four radio buttons. Add these empty methods to handle button selections:

```
   private void easiestRadioButtonActionPerformed(ActionEvent e)
   {
   }

   private void easyRadioButtonActionPerformed(ActionEvent e)
   {
   }

   private void hardRadioButtonActionPerformed(ActionEvent e)
   {
   }

   private void hardestRadioButtonActionPerformed(ActionEvent e)
   {
   }
```

Add this code in the proper locations. Run to see:

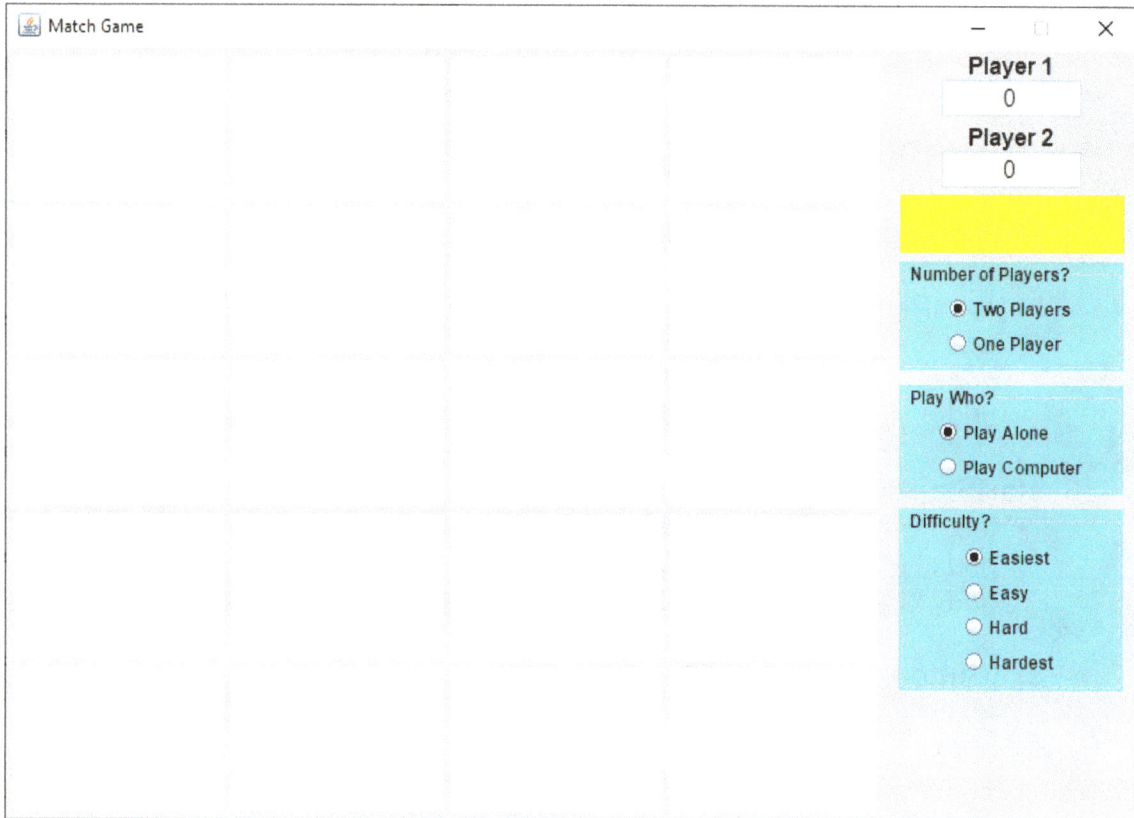

The difficulty panel is displayed.

The **buttonsPanel** will hold two buttons used to control game play. The **GridBagLayout** for buttonsPanel is:

	gridx = 0
gridy = 0	**startStopButton**
gridy =1	**exitButton**

The panel and button properties:

buttonsPanel:
size	160, 70
gridx	1 (on frame)
gridy	4 (on frame)

startStopButton:
text	Start Game
gridx	0 (on buttonsPanel)
gridy	0 (on buttonsPanel)

exitButton:
text	Exit
gridx	0 (on buttonsPanel)
gridy	1 (on buttonsPanel)
insets	10, 0, 0, 0

These controls are declared using:

```
JPanel buttonsPanel = new JPanel();
JButton startStopButton = new JButton();
JButton exitButton = new JButton();
```

The buttons are placed in the **buttonsPanel** (which is placed in the frame) using:

```
buttonsPanel.setPreferredSize(new Dimension(160, 70));
buttonsPanel.setLayout(new GridBagLayout());
gridConstraints = new GridBagConstraints();
gridConstraints.gridx = 1;
gridConstraints.gridy = 4;
getContentPane().add(buttonsPanel, gridConstraints);

startStopButton.setText("Start Game");
gridConstraints = new GridBagConstraints();
gridConstraints.gridx = 0;
gridConstraints.gridy = 0;
buttonsPanel.add(startStopButton, gridConstraints);
```

```
startStopButton.addActionListener(new ActionListener()
{
  public void actionPerformed(ActionEvent e)
  {
    startStopButtonActionPerformed(e);
  }
});

exitButton.setText("Exit");
gridConstraints = new GridBagConstraints();
gridConstraints.gridx = 0;
gridConstraints.gridy = 1;
gridConstraints.insets = new Insets(10, 0, 0, 0);
buttonsPanel.add(exitButton, gridConstraints);
exitButton.addActionListener(new ActionListener()
{
  public void actionPerformed(ActionEvent e)
  {
    exitButtonActionPerformed(e);
  }
});
```

This code also adds listeners for each button. Add these empty methods with the other methods:

```
private void startStopButtonActionPerformed(ActionEvent
e)
{
}

private void exitButtonActionPerformed(ActionEvent e)
{
}
```

Add this code in the proper locations. Run to see:

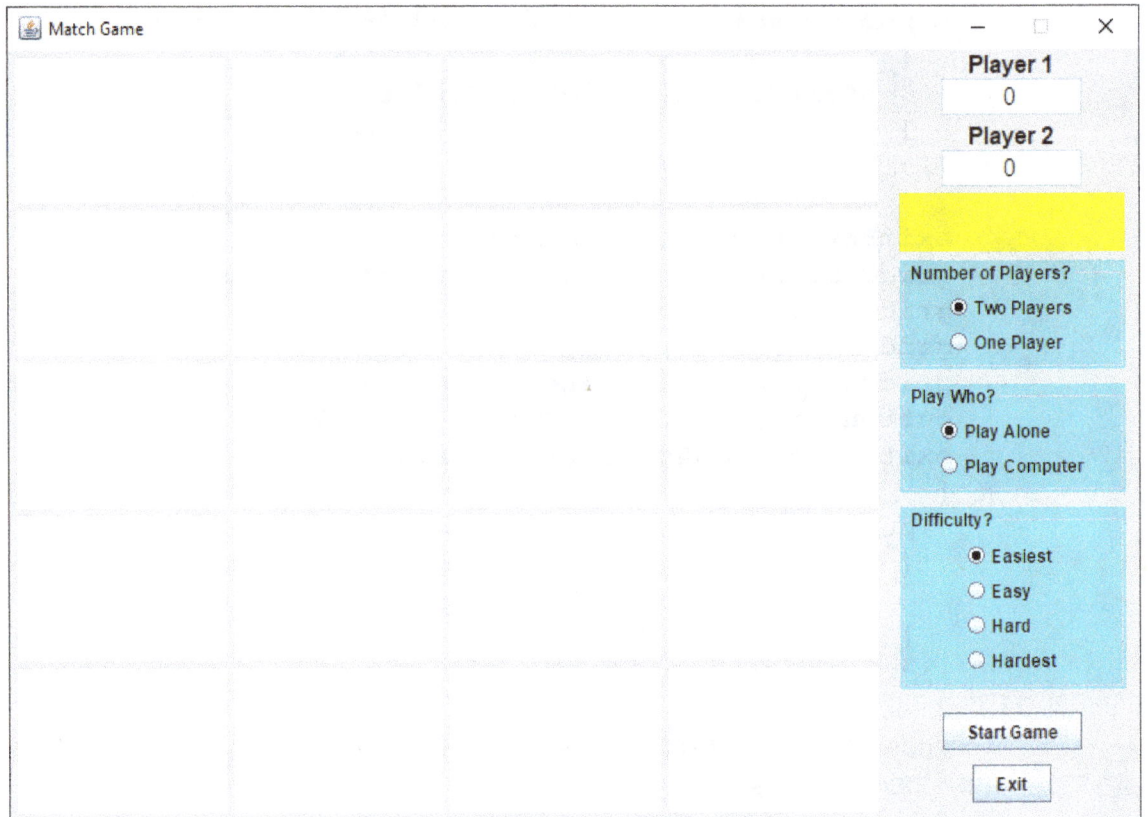

This completes the frame design. You should be able to identify all the controls in the game. Before looking at the code, let's see how to select the photos used in the game.

Photo Selection

One neat thing about this game is that you can use your own photos! This personalizes the game that makes things a lot more fun. You need to select 10 photos (jpg files from your digital camera) that you want to use. The photos should be 150 pixels wide by 100 pixels high (that's the size of the label controls and the same ratio as a typical 6 inch by 4 inch photo in horizontal orientation). If your photos are different size, they will not appear correctly. Use a photo application (like the Microsoft Windows Paint program) to resize your photos if necessary. Place the resized photos you want to use in your project's code folder. Make a note of each file's name.

If you don't have photos to use right now, we include ten sample photos in the **\KidGamesJava\KidGamesJava Projects\MatchGame** folder:

clara.jpg (one of the KIDware dogs)

toby.jpg (the other KIDware dog)

Blue hills.jpg (a stock photo of hills)

Sunset.jpg (a stock sunset photo)

Water lilies.jpg (some pretty flowers)

Winter.jpg (a winter scene)

spaceneedle.jpg (the Space Needle in Seattle)

market.jpg (the Pike Place Market in Seattle)

safeco.jpg (TMobile Park, was Safeco, in Seattle, home of the Mariners)

qwest.jpg (Century Link (was Qwest) Field in Seattle, home of the Seahawks)

Each of these photos was resized (to approximately 150 pixels by 100 pixels) from its original size using the Microsoft Paint program. These photos are used through the rest of this chapter to demonstrate game play. If you decide you use these photos (instead of your own), copy the files to your project's folder.

One additional image you need is the one used to cover a label box before it is uncovered. Also located in the **\KidGamesJava\KidGamesJava Projects\MatchGame** folder is a file named **cover.jpg** that has this picture:

Copy this file to your project folder.

We will now begin writing code for the game. After writing code for the first two projects, **Safecracker** and **Tic Tac Toe**, you should know there are certain standard steps needed to get a working project. Since you should be familiar with these steps by now, in discussing the code for **Match Game**, we will combine some steps to speed up the coding process.

We will write the code in several steps. As a first step, we will write the code that initializes the game. Then, we look at going from 'stopped' state to 'playing' state and back. During the code development process, recognize you may modify a particular method several times before arriving at the finished product.

Code Design – Initializing Stopped State

Any time we start a project, there are certain initializations that must take place. Let's look at the initializations needed in the **Match Game**. All initializations are done at the end of the frame's constructor method.

We will use an **ImageIcon** array (**photo**) to hold the 10 photos that are used in the game and an additional ImageIcon (**cover**) to hold the cover image. Add declarations for these variables in the class level declarations area:

```
ImageIcon[] photo = new ImageIcon[10];
ImageIcon cover = new ImageIcon();
```

Another initialization is to set the game in **Two Players** mode. As such, we will disable the radio buttons in the **playWhoPanel** and **difficultyPanel**. We will be enabling and disabling radio buttons many times in this game, so let's add three methods that facilitate this process. Add these three methods to your code. One is used to set the enabled property of the radio buttons in the **playersPanel**, one for the **playWhoPanel** and one for the **difficultyPanel** (in each method the boolean argument **a** specifies the desired state, true or false):

```
private void setPlayersButtons(boolean a)
{
  onePlayerRadioButton.setEnabled(a);
  twoPlayersRadioButton.setEnabled(a);
}

private void setPlayWhoButtons(boolean a)
{
  playAloneRadioButton.setEnabled(a);
  playComputerRadioButton.setEnabled(a);
}

 private void setDifficultyButtons(boolean a)
  {
  easiestRadioButton.setEnabled(a);
  easyRadioButton.setEnabled(a);
  hardRadioButton.setEnabled(a);
  hardestRadioButton.setEnabled(a);
}
```

Add this code at the end of the **MatchGame** constructor code:

```
photo[0] = new ImageIcon("clara.jpg");
photo[1] = new ImageIcon("toby.jpg");
photo[2] = new ImageIcon("Blue hills.jpg");
photo[3] = new ImageIcon("Sunset.jpg");
photo[4] = new ImageIcon("Water lilies.jpg");
photo[5] = new ImageIcon("Winter.jpg");
photo[6] = new ImageIcon("spaceneedle.jpg");
photo[7] = new ImageIcon("market.jpg");
photo[8] = new ImageIcon("safeco.jpg");
photo[9] = new ImageIcon("qwest.jpg");
cover = new ImageIcon("cover.jpg");
for (int i = 0; i < 20; i++)
  photoLabel[i].setIcon(cover);
setPlayWhoButtons(false);
setDifficultyButtons(false);
```

In the above code, if you are using your own photos, change the graphics file names as appropriate (again, make sure the files are in your project folder or they will not load).

Run the project to make sure the game is properly initialized. Do this and you'll see in the 'stopped' state (using default properties), the **Match Game** looks like this:

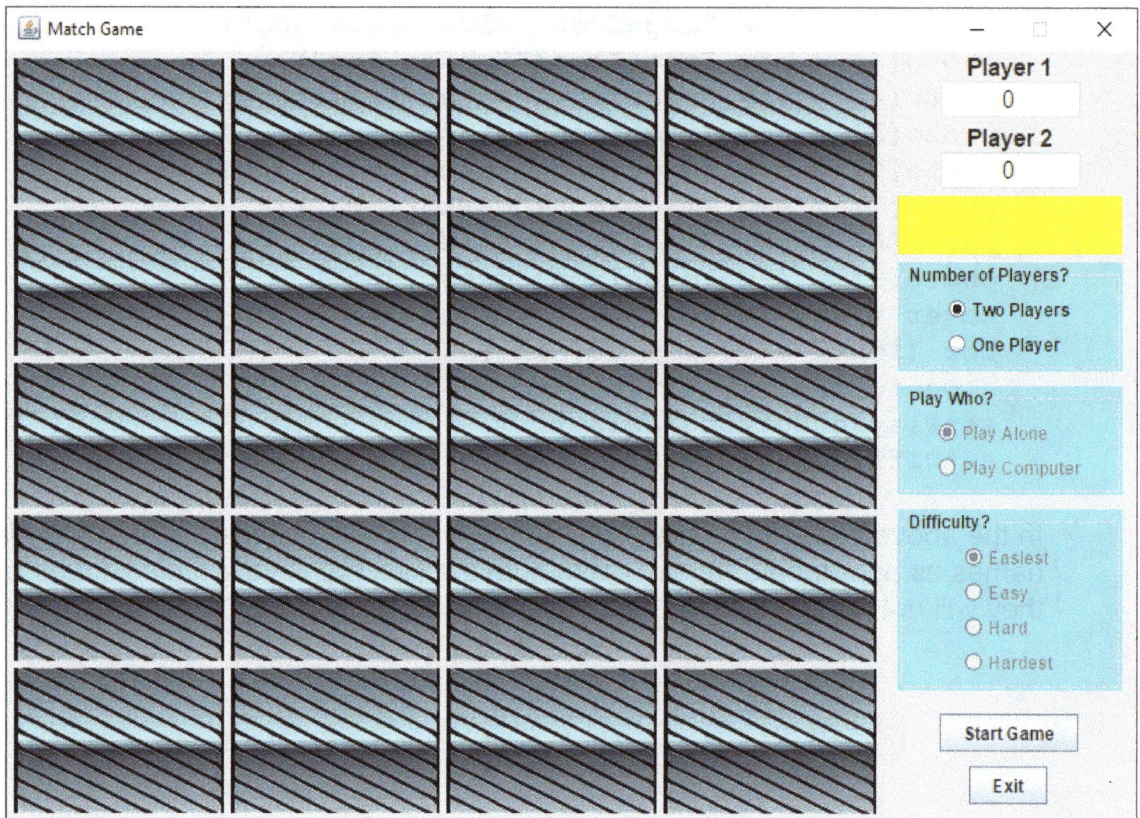

As desired, the game initializes in **Two Players** mode. The label controls are all 'covered.' We have three choices at this point: change to **One Player** mode, click **startStopButton** (the button with **Start Game**) or click **exitButton** (the button with **Exit**).

If we click on the **One Player** button, different options are available and the labels displaying the scoring information must change. The following must happen:

> ➤ Enable the radio buttons in play who panel.
> ➤ Set **player1Label text** to **You**.
> ➤ If **Play Alone** option is selected, set **player2Label text** to **Guesses**, disable radio buttons in difficulty panel.
> ➤ If **Play Computer** option is selected, set **player2Label text** to **Computer**, enable radio buttons in difficulty panel.

The code corresponding to these steps is placed in the **onePlayerRadioButtonActionPerformed** method:

```
private void
onePlayerRadioButtonActionPerformed(ActionEvent e)
{
  setPlayWhoButtons(true);
  player1Label.setText("You");
  if (playAloneRadioButton.isSelected())
  {
    player2Label.setText("Guesses");
    setDifficultyButtons(false);
  }
  else
  {
    player2Label.setText("Computer");
    setDifficultyButtons(true);
  }
}
```

In one player mode, we can select **Play Alone** or **Play Computer**. If a user clicks **Play Alone**, we need to make sure the radio buttons in the difficulty panel are disabled and that the **text** property of **player2Label** reads **Guesses**. Use this code in the **playAloneRadioButtonActionPerformed** method:

```
private void
playAloneRadioButtonActionPerformed(ActionEvent e)
{
  setDifficultyButtons(false);
  player2Label.setText("Guesses");
}
```

Conversely, if a user clicks **Play Computer**, we need to make sure the difficulty radio buttons are enabled and that the **text** property of **player2Label** reads **Computer**. Use this code in the **playComputerRadioButtonActionPerformed** method:

```
private void
playComputerRadioButtonActionPerformed(ActionEvent e)
{
  setDifficultyButtons(true);
  player2Label.setText("Computer");
}
```

Lastly, we need code for the **twoPlayersRadioButtonActionPerformed** method to return to two player mode. When this button is clicked, we disable the radio buttons in the play who panel and the difficulty radio buttons and return the label headers to their default values:

```
private void
twoPlayersRadioButtonActionPerformed(ActionEvent e)
{
  setPlayWhoButtons(false);
  setDifficultyButtons(false);
  player1Label.setText("Player 1");
  player2Label.setText("Player 2");
}
```

What about code for clicking on either of the two button controls (**Start Game** or **Exit**)? The code for exiting is simple. The **exitButtonActionPerformed** method:

```
private void exitButtonActionPerformed(ActionEvent e)
{
   System.exit(0);
}
```

This simply says whenever the **Exit** button is clicked, the project closes. Add this code.

The code for the **startStopButton** is much more complicated. We will build it in several steps. First, we look at changing the form from 'stopped' to 'playing' and back to 'stopped' state. Before doing this, let's make sure our new initialization code is working. Save and run the project. It will be in two player mode. Click **One Player**; you should see:

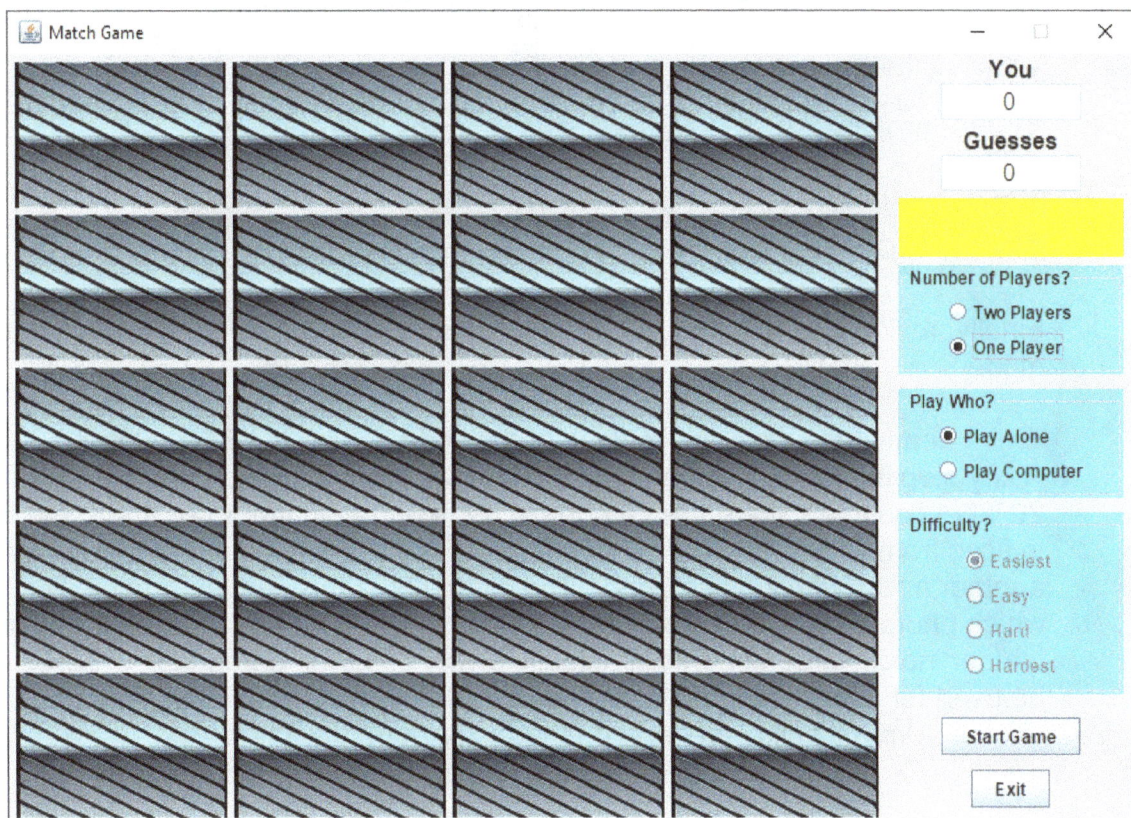

Notice the label controls change. The **Play Who** panel is enabled and the **Difficulty** panel is disabled.

Now, click **Play Computer** and the label controls again change and the
Difficulty panel is enabled:

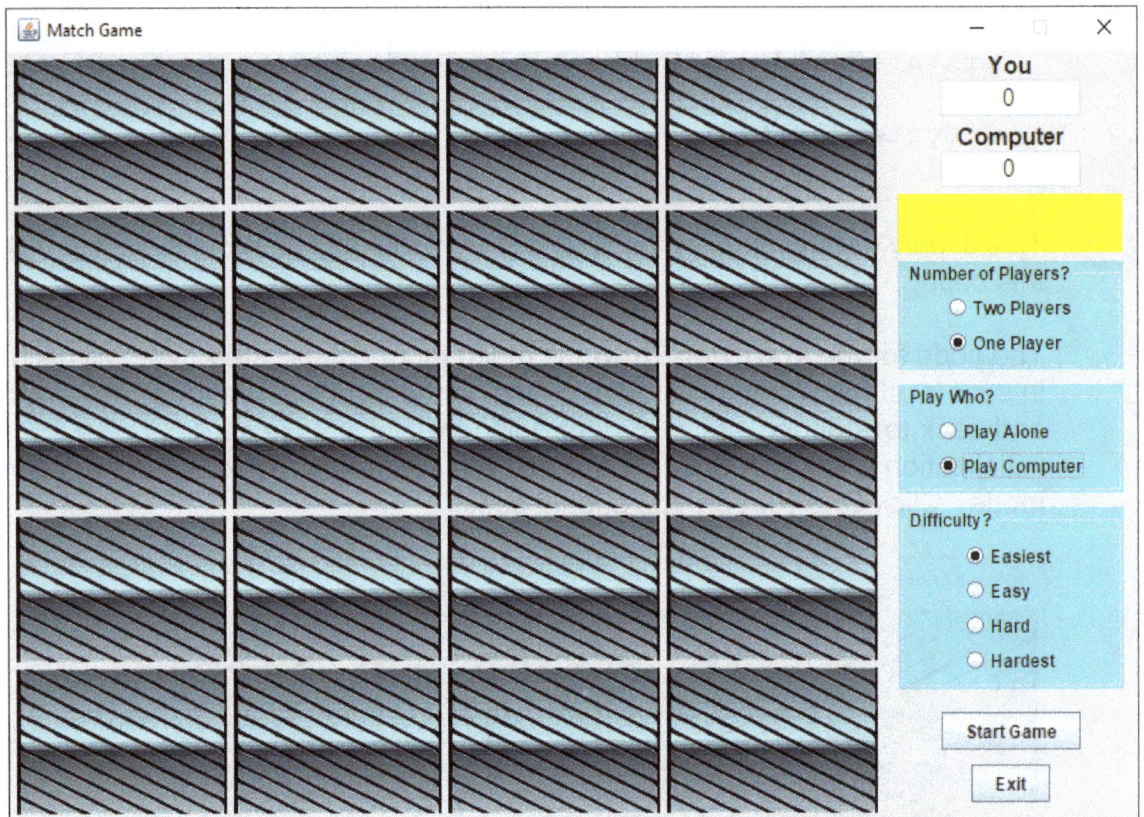

Finally, make sure when you click **Two Players**, the form returns to two player
mode.

We're nearly ready to begin looking at the code behind the **Start Game** button.
A key step in starting this game is to 'hide' two copies of each photo behind the
20 label controls. There are 10 photos, represented in the array **photo**, with
indices from 0 to 9. We want to randomly place two copies of each index in
another array (with 20 elements). The elements of this second array tell us
which photo is behind which picture box control. We need some way to shuffle
integer indices around. This is actually a very common game task which can
be used for shuffling cards, selecting multiple choice answers, or here to hide
photos. We will build a general method to perform this task.

Code Design – Integer Shuffling

We will be presenting code for a **shuffle** process, so called because it can be used to shuffle a deck of cards. Here, we'll just be shuffling 20 "cards," though the code can be generalized to any number of "cards." You might be asking, why we are shuffling 20 values, not 10, since we only have 10 photos? We need two copies of each of the 10 photo indices, hence there are 20 total items being shuffled. We propose randomly shuffling the integers from 0 to 19. After the shuffle, for any value greater than 9, we will subtract 10. This will give us a list of 20 random integers. This list will have two of each index from 0 to 9, telling us which photo is behind which picture box control. Let's see how to do this.

Usually when we need a computer version of something we can do without a computer, it is fairly easy to write down the steps taken and duplicate them in code. When we shuffle a deck of cards, we separate the deck in two parts, then interleaf the cards as we fan each part, making that familiar shuffling noise. I don't know how you could write code to do this. We'll take another approach which is hard or tedious to do off the computer, but is easy to do on a computer.

We perform what is called a "one card shuffle." In a one card shuffle, you pull a single card (at random) out of the deck and lay it aside on a pile. Repeat this 52 times and the cards are shuffled. Try it! I think you see this idea is simple, but doing a one card shuffle with a real deck of cards would be awfully time-consuming. We'll use the idea of a one card shuffle here, with a slight twist. Rather than lay the selected card on a pile, we will swap it with the bottom card in the stack of cards remaining to be shuffled. This takes the selected card out of the deck and replaces it with the remaining bottom card. The result is the same as if we lay it aside.

Here's how the shuffle works with n numbers:

➤ Start with a list of n consecutive integers.
➤ Randomly pick one item from the list. Swap that item with the last item.
   You now have one fewer items in the list to be sorted (called the
   remaining list), or n is now n - 1.
➤ Randomly pick one item from the remaining list. Swap it with the item
   on the bottom of the remaining list. Again, your remaining list now has
   one fewer items.
➤ Repeatedly remove one item from the remaining list and swap it with
   the item on the bottom of the remaining list until you have run out of
   items. When done, the list will have been replaced with the original list
   in random order.

The code to do a one card shuffle, or sort n integers, is placed in a general
method named **nRandomIntegers**. The single argument is **n** the number of
integers to sort. The method returns an array containing the randomly sorted
integers. The returned array is zero-based, returning random integers from 0
to n - 1, not 1 to n. If you need integers from 1 to n, just simply add 1 to each
value in the returned array! The code is:

```
private int[] nRandomIntegers(int n)
{
  /*
  *   Returns n randomly sorted integers 0 -> n - 1
  */
  int[] nIntegers = new int[n];
  int temp, s;
  Random sortRandom = new Random();
  //  initialize array from 0 to n - 1
  for (int i = 0; i < n; i++)
  {
    nIntegers[i] = i;
  }
  //  i is number of items remaining in list
  for (int i = n; i >= 1; i--)
  {
    s = sortRandom.nextInt(i);
    temp = nIntegers[s];
    nIntegers[s] = nIntegers[i - 1];
    nIntegers[i - 1] = temp;
  }
  return(nIntegers);
}
```

You should be able to see each step of the shuffle method. This method is general (sorting n integers) and can be used in other projects requiring random lists of integers.

Add the **nRandomIntegers** method to your **Match Game** project. Also, since we are using random numbers, we need this import statement:

```
import java.util.Random;
```

The shuffle method will be used to hide the 10 photos behind the 20 picture box controls. In the project, we will use a class level array **photoIndex** (dimensioned to 20) to hold the randomly sorted integers (the shuffled photo indices). Add this class level declaration to your project:

```
int[] photoIndex = new int[20];
```

The snippet of code that does a shuffle (and adjusts the values greater than 10) is:

```
photoIndex = nRandomIntegers(20);
for (int i = 0; i < 20; i++)
  if (photoIndex[i] > 9)
    photoIndex[i] -= 10;
```

Let's look at an example of how this works. If I run this snippet of code through a little example, the 20 elements of **photoIndex** returned from one particular call to **nRandomIntegers** are (arranged like our photo boxes):

14	11	15	1
17	2	10	0
5	18	7	8
16	12	19	13
6	4	3	9

You should see all the integers from 0 to 19. Now, subtracting 10 from each value greater than 9 yields:

4	1	5	1
7	2	0	0
5	8	7	8
6	2	9	3
6	4	3	9

As desired, we now have random pairs of the integers from 0 to 9. Matching pairs of integers represent matching pairs of photos in **Match Game**.

How do we know what photo is behind what picture box control? Say we have a label control, represented by element **i** of the array **photoLabel[i]**. To determine the photo, examine **photoIndex[i]**; call this value **j**. The photo in this label is then **photo[j]**, element **j** of the array holding the 10 photos being used. To set the **IconImage** property, the proper line of code is:

```
photoLabel[i].setIcon(photo[photoIndex[i]]);
```

We can now use the shuffling method to start building the code behind the **startStopButton** control.

Code Design – Stopped to Playing to Stopped State

In the **Safecracker** and **Tic Tac Toe** projects, the button to start and stop the game was the same control. That is also the case here. We will look at the code behind this control (**startStopButton**) to both start and stop the game.

When the user clicks the **Start Game** button in the 'stopped' state, several things must happen to switch **Match Game** to 'playing' state:

> Change the **text** property of **startStopButton** to **Stop Game**.
> Initialize scores and corresponding label controls to zero.
> Initialize number of photos remaining (20).
> Shuffle photos using **nRandomIntegers** method.
> Initialize label controls for displaying photos.
> Disable radio buttons in all panel controls (don't allow selection of options while playing).
> Disable **exitButton**.
> Establish this as Player 1's turn.
> Set message to player.
> Allow player to click on label controls.

Conversely, when the user clicks the **Stop Game** button in 'playing' state, several things must happen to switch **Match Game** to 'stopped' state:

> Change the **text** property of **startStopButton** to **Start Game**.
> Enable radio buttons in players panel.
> Enable radio buttons in play who panel, if one player game.
> Enable radio buttons in difficulty panel, if one player game and playing computer.
> Enable **exitButton**.
> Stop allowing clicking on label controls.
> If game is not over, display **Game Stopped** message.

First, let's look at the code to start the game. We establish several variables in the class level declarations to help keep track of where we are in the game:

```
int photosRemaining;
int[] score = new int[2];
boolean[] photoFound = new boolean[20];
int playerNumber, choiceNumber;
int[] choice = new int[2];
boolean canClick = false;
boolean gameOver;
```

photosRemaining tells us how many photos are still hidden, while the **score** array holds the two players scores (number of matched photos found). The **photoFound** array tells us whether a photo behind the corresponding picture box control has been uncovered (so it can't be clicked twice). **playerNumber** tells us whose turn it is and **choiceNumber** tells whether it is the player's first choice on the playing board or second choice. The **choice** array holds the indices of the two picture boxes selected. **canClick** is used to determine if it's okay to click on the picture box controls. It is **true** when playing, **false** (the initial value) when stopped. Finally, **gameOver** is used to tell us whether the game is actually over (**true** if all photos uncovered) or the **Stop Game** button was clicked before completing a game (**false**).

The code for the **startStopButtonActionPerformed** method that implements the steps for clicking on **Start Game** and initializes the new variables is:

```
private void startStopButtonActionPerformed(ActionEvent e)
{
  if (startStopButton.getText().equals("Start Game"))
  {
    startStopButton.setText("Stop Game");
    score[0] = 0;
    score[1] = 0;
    scoreTextField[0].setText("0");
    scoreTextField[1].setText("0");
    photosRemaining = 20;
    photoIndex = nRandomIntegers(20);
    for (int i = 0; i < 20; i++)
    {
      if (photoIndex[i] > 9)
        photoIndex[i] -= 10;
      photoFound[i] = false;
      photoLabel[i].setIcon(cover);
    }
    playerNumber = 1;
    choiceNumber = 1;
    if (twoPlayersRadioButton.isSelected())
```

```
          messageLabel.setText("Player 1, Pick a Box");
        else
          messageLabel.setText("Pick a Box");
        setNumberPlayersButtons(false);
        setPlayWhoButtons(false);
        setDifficultyButtons(false);
        exitButton.setEnabled(false);
        canClick = true;
        gameOver = false;
      }
      else
      {
        // stop game
      }
    }
```

The steps follow should be clear. Note especially where the "shuffling" routine was used to form the **photoIndex** array.

Save and run the project. Click on **Start Game** and you should see:

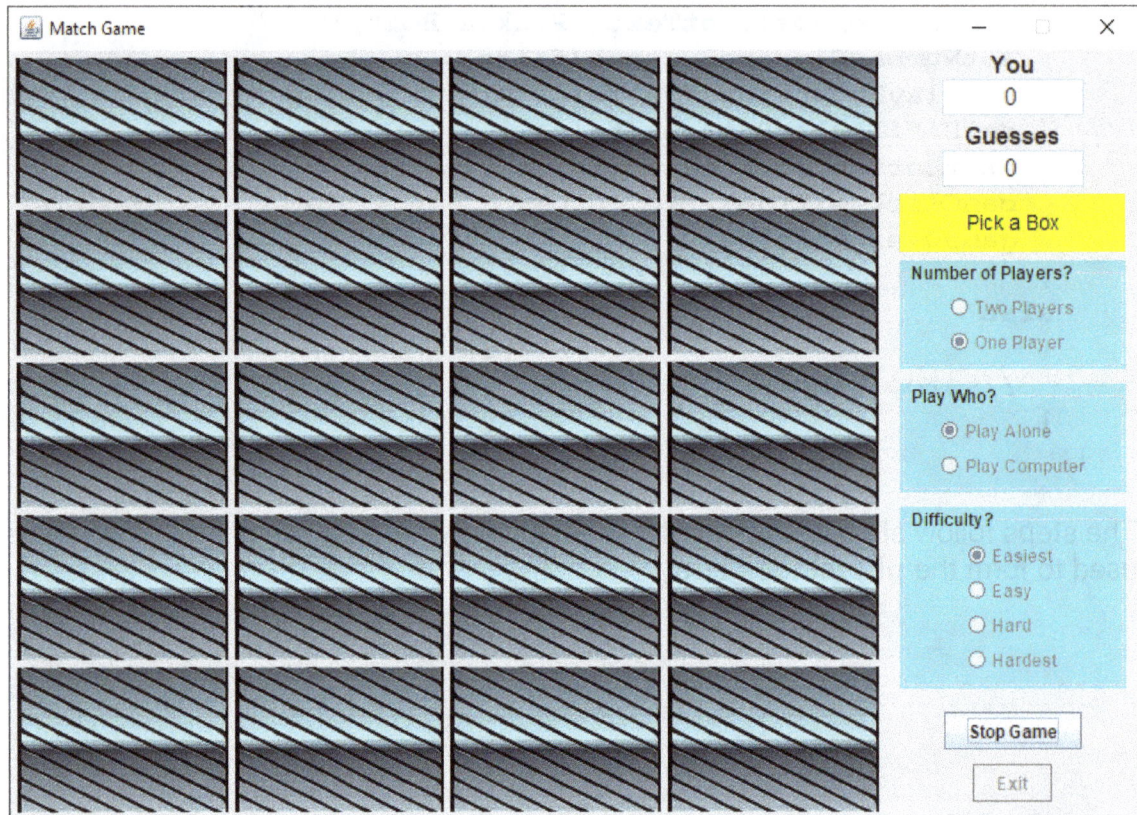

The only noticeable change is the two player message in the label control (**Player 1, Pick a Box**). Stop the project (you can't click **Stop Game** yet) and try the other options if you'd like.

The code for the **btnStartStop Click** event that implements the steps for clicking on **Stop Game** is (additions are shaded):

```
private void startStopButtonActionPerformed(ActionEvent e)
{
  if (startStopButton.getText().equals("Start Game"))
  {
    startStopButton.setText("Stop Game");
    score[0] = 0;
    score[1] = 0;
    scoreTextField[0].setText("0");
    scoreTextField[1].setText("0");
    photosRemaining = 20;
    photoIndex = nRandomIntegers(20);
    for (int i = 0; i < 20; i++)
    {
      if (photoIndex[i] > 9)
        photoIndex[i] -= 10;
      photoFound[i] = false;
      photoLabel[i].setIcon(cover);
    }
    playerNumber = 1;
    choiceNumber = 1;
    if (twoPlayersRadioButton.isSelected())
      messageLabel.setText("Player 1, Pick a Box");
    else
      messageLabel.setText("Pick a Box");
    setNumberPlayersButtons(false);
    setPlayWhoButtons(false);
    setDifficultyButtons(false);
    exitButton.setEnabled(false);
    canClick = true;
    gameOver = false;
  }
  else
  {
    // stop game
    startStopButton.setText("Start Game");
    setNumberPlayersButtons(true);
    if (onePlayerRadioButton.isSelected())
    {
      setPlayWhoButtons(true);
      if (playComputerRadioButton.isSelected())
        setDifficultyButtons(true);
    }
    exitButton.setEnabled(true);
    canClick = false;
```

```
   if (!gameOver)
     messageLabel.setText("Game Stopped");
}
}
```

Notice how we determine which panels holding radio buttons should be disabled/enabled and how we decide if the **Game Stopped** message is used. Other messages will appear (developed in later code) if a game is played to completion (**gameOver** is **True**).

Save and run the project. You should be able to now move from 'stopped' to 'playing' state and back. Make sure the panels are in the proper state for the one and two player options. Let's write the code for the two player game, first looking at how to display a photo following a click on a label control.

Code Design –Displaying Photos

In the **Match Game** two player game, when a player clicks a label on the game panel, we want the proper photo to appear. After clicking a second label, another photo is displayed and we see if there is a match. If there is a match, the photos are removed and the player is given another turn. If there is no match, the photos are hidden again and we switch to the next player.

So, when a label is clicked, we follow these steps:

➤ Make sure the box has not already been clicked.
➤ Display photo.
➤ If first choice, allow second choice and display that photo. Compare the two photos.
➤ If photos match:
   o Play matching sound.
   o Remove labels with photos from frame
   o Increment proper player score by 1.
   o Decrement **photosRemaining** by 2.
   o If **photosRemaining = 0**, set **gameOver** to **true**, determine winner, play game over sound and stop game.
   o If **photosRemaining != 0**, give player another turn.
➤ If photos do not match:
   o Play no match sound.
   o Replace photos with 'cover' graphic.
   o Swap players.

We'll code all of these steps in a bit. But first, notice we refer to playing sounds. In previous games, we added sounds at the very end. We know all games use sounds so, from now on, they will be added when needed in projects. We use three sounds in this game. In the **\KidGamesJava\KidGamesJava Projects\MatchGame** folder are three wav files that can be used for sound. The **tada.wav** file is a sound we'll use when two photos match. The **boing.wav** file is used when there is no match. And, the **wow.wav** sound is used when a game is over. Copy the three sound files to your project's folder.

Add these import statements:

```
import java.net.URL;
import java.applet.*;
```

And, add these class level declarations to represent the two sounds:

```
AudioClip matchSound;
AudioClip noMatchSound;
AudioClip gameOverSound;
```

Add ths code to the end of the **MatchGame** constructor code:

```
try
{
  matchSound = Applet.newAudioClip(new URL("file:" +
"tada.wav"));
  noMatchSound = Applet.newAudioClip(new URL("file:" +
"boing.wav"));
  gameOverSound = Applet.newAudioClip(new URL("file:" +
"wow.wav"));
}
catch (Exception ex)
{
  System.out.println("Error loading sound files");
}
```

Now the coding of displaying a photo in a selected label. Like in the **Tic Tac Toe** project, we anticipate that a human can choose a label or the computer can choose a label (in one player game versus the computer), we first write a general method that implements the above steps (not checking for a win yet, though). Add this class level variable (to indicate the selected label):

```
int labelSelected;
```

Add this general method (**showSelectedLabel**) which uses **labelSelected** to display the corresponding photo:

```
private void showSelectedLabel()
{

photoLabel[labelSelected].setIcon(photo[photoIndex[labelSe
lected]]);
  photoFound[labelSelected] = true;
  if (choiceNumber == 1)
  {
    choice[0] = labelSelected;
    choiceNumber = 2;
    if (twoPlayersRadioButton.isSelected())
    {
      messageLabel.setText("Player " +
String.valueOf(playerNumber) + ", Pick Another");
      canClick = true;
    }
    else
    {
      // one player logic
    }
  }
  else
  {
    choice[1] = labelSelected;
    choiceNumber = 1;
    if (photoIndex[choice[0]] == photoIndex[choice[1]])
    {
      // a match
      matchSound.play();
      photoLabel[choice[0]].setIcon(null);
      photoLabel[choice[1]].setIcon(null);
      score[playerNumber - 1]++;
      scoreTextField[playerNumber -
1].setText(String.valueOf(score[playerNumber - 1]));
      photosRemaining -= 2;
      if (photosRemaining == 0)
```

```
      {
        gameOver = true;
        gameOverSound.play();
        if (twoPlayersRadioButton.isSelected())
        {
          if (score[0] > score[1])
            messageLabel.setText("Player 1 Wins!");
          else if (score[1] > score[0])
            messageLabel.setText("Player 2 Wins!");
          else
            messageLabel.setText("It's a Tie!");
        }
        else
        {
          // one player logic
        }
        startStopButton.doClick();
        return;
      }
      // another turn
      if (twoPlayersRadioButton.isSelected())
      {
        messageLabel.setText("Player " +
String.valueOf(playerNumber) + ", Pick Again");
        canClick = true;
      }
      else
      {
        // one player logic
      }
    }
    else
    {
      //no match
      noMatchSound.play();
      photoFound[choice[0]] = false;
      photoFound[choice[1]] = false;
      photoLabel[choice[0]].setIcon(cover);
      photoLabel[choice[1]].setIcon(cover);
      // swap players
      if (twoPlayersRadioButton.isSelected())
      {
        if (playerNumber == 1)
          playerNumber = 2;
        else
          playerNumber = 1;
```

```
      messageLabel.setText("Player " +
String.valueOf(playerNumber) + ", Pick a Box");
      canClick = true;
    }
    else
    {
      // one player logic
    }
  }
 }
}
```

I know this is a lot of code to throw at you at once, but it's simply a straightforward implementation of the listed steps (except for determining the value of **labelSelected**; we'll look at that next). Now that you're becoming a great game programmer, you should be able to follow the logic. It's similar to that used in the **Tic Tac Toe** game. The photo behind the selected label (**photo[photoIndex[labelSelected]]**) is displayed. If this is the first choice (**choiceNumber = 1**), we tell the player to pick again (using **messageLabel**).

Following display of the second choice, we look to see if the two selections match. The selected boxes are stored in the **choice** array. If there is a match, the photos are removed, a sound is played and we check to see if all the photos have been selected. If photos remain, the same player is given another turn. Similarly, for no match, a sound is heard, the photos are recovered and players are swapped.

All of this code is for a two player game. Notice, however, we have left "hooks" (represented by comment statements) for later modifications for a one player game.

Let's use this method to allow selection of labels using the mouse. The code to do this goes in the **photoLabelMousePressed** method (currently empty). To determine which label is clicked, we use the same logic developed in the **Tic Tac Toe** game, checking the upper left corner of the clicked label. Add this code to the **photoLabelMousePressed** method:

```
private void photoLabelMousePressed(MouseEvent e)
{
  // determine which label was clicked
  // get upper left corner of clicked label
  Point p = e.getComponent().getLocation();
  // determine index based on p
  for (labelSelected = 0; labelSelected < 20;
labelSelected++)
  {
    if (p.x == photoLabel[labelSelected].getX() && p.y ==
photoLabel[labelSelected].getY())
      break;
  }
  if (!canClick || photoFound[labelSelected])
    return;
  // show image behind selected label box
  canClick = false;
  showSelectedLabel();
}
```

Clicking any of the twenty label controls used to display photos will invoke this method. The first part of the code determines the index of the element of label control array that was clicked (the variable **labelSelected**). If the box has already been clicked (or **canClick** is **false**), the method is exited. Otherwise, we show the photo behind the label using the **showSelectedLabel** method.

Save and run the project. Try playing the two player game with a friend or by yourself. You will notice a problem. When you click on the first label, the picture displays fine. When you click the second label, though, nothing is seen. You'll hear a sound indicating a match or no match, but you won't see the second photo. The code executes so quickly the display of the photos cannot keep up! We need to slow things down a bit be inserting a delay. To do this, we use the Java **timer** object. Since this may not be a familiar topic, we'll do a quick review.

Timer Object

A **timer object** generates an event every **delay** milliseconds. The code in the timer's corresponding **actionPerformed** method is executed with each such event. Other control events can be detected while the timer object processes events in the background. This multi-tasking allows more than one thing to be happening in your application.

Timer **Properties**:

delay	Number of milliseconds (there are 1000 milliseconds in one second) between each invocation of the timer object's **actionPerformed** method.
running	Boolean value indicating if timer is running.

Timer **Methods**:

start	Used to start timer object.
stop	Used to stop timer.
isRunning	Method that returns boolean value indicating whether timer is running (generating events).

Timer **Events**:

actionPerformed	Event method invoked every **delay** milliseconds while timer object's **running** property is **true**.

To use a timer object, you first declare it using the standard syntax. For a timer named **myTimer**, the code is:

```
Timer myTimer;
```

The constructor for the timer object specifies the **delay** and adds the event (**actionPerformed**) method, using an **ActionListener**, in a single step. The syntax is:

```
myTimer = new Timer(delay, new ActionListener()
{
  public void actionPerformed(ActionEvent e)
  {
    myTimerActionPerformed(e);
  }
});
```

And, the corresponding event code would be placed in a **myTimerActionPerformed** method:

```
private void myTimerActionPerformed(ActionEvent e)
{
    [method code]
}
```

To use the **timer** object, we add it to our application the same as any object. You write code in the timer object's **actionPerformed** method. This is the code you want to repeat every **delay** milliseconds

You 'turn on' a timer in code using the **start** method:

```
myTimer.start();
```

and it is turned off using the **stop** method:

```
myTimer.stop();
```

To check if the timer is on, use the **isRunning** method:

```
myTimer.isRunning();
```

If this method returns a boolean true, the timer is on.

Applications can (and many times do) have multiple timer objects. You need separate timer objects (and event methods) if you have events that occur with different regularity (different **delay** values). Timer objects are used for two primary purposes. First, as we do here, you can use a timer object to implement some 'wait time' established by the **delay** property. In this case, you simply start the timer and when the delay is reached, have the **actionPerformed** event turn its corresponding timer off. Second, you use timer objects to periodically repeat some code segment. This is very useful for graphics animation. We will do this in the remaining three projects in these notes.

Typical use of **timer** object:

> Declare timer, assigning an identifiable **name**. For **myTimer**, the statement is:

```
Timer myTimer;
```

> Establish a **delay** value. Create the timer using specified constructor, adding the **actionPerformed** method. Write the method code.
> At some point in your application, start the timer. Also, have capability to turn the timer off, when desired.

Code Design – Adding Delays

In the **Match Game**, we want to implement a delay of some duration following the code that displays a selected label. We chose to delay for 0.5 seconds (500 milliseconds). You can choose another value if you want.

To implement this delay, first declare a timer object:

```
Timer displayTimer;
```

Add it to the project (creating the event method, **displayTimerActionPerformed**) with this code:

```
displayTimer = new Timer(500, new ActionListener()
{
  public void actionPerformed(ActionEvent e)
  {
    displayTimerActionPerformed(e);
  }
});
```

Add the empty method:

```
private void displayTimerActionPerformed(ActionEvent e)
{
}
```

The way this will work is: following display of a photo, we start the timer object (**delayTimer**). This will implement a wait of **delay** milliseconds (500 milliseconds in this case) until the code in the **displayTimerActionPerformed** method is executed. The code in that method will be the code that currently follows the photo display line (the shaded code below, in **showSelectedLabel** method):

```
private void showSelectedLabel()
{

photoLabel[labelSelected].setIcon(photo[photoIndex[labelSe
lected]]);
   photoFound[labelSelected] = true;
    if (choiceNumber == 1)
   {
     choice[0] = labelSelected;
     choiceNumber = 2;
     if (twoPlayersRadioButton.isSelected())
     {
       messageLabel.setText("Player " +
String.valueOf(playerNumber) + ", Pick Another");
       canClick = true;
     }
     else
     {
       // one player logic
     }
   }
   else
   {
     choice[1] = labelSelected;
     choiceNumber = 1;
     if (photoIndex[choice[0]] == photoIndex[choice[1]])
     {
       // a match
       matchSound.play();
       photoLabel[choice[0]].setIcon(null);
       photoLabel[choice[1]].setIcon(null);
       score[playerNumber - 1]++;
       scoreTextField[playerNumber -
1].setText(String.valueOf(score[playerNumber - 1]));
       photosRemaining -= 2;
       if (photosRemaining == 0)
       {
         gameOver = true;
         gameOverSound.play();
         if (twoPlayersRadioButton.isSelected())
         {
```

```
        if (score[0] > score[1])
          messageLabel.setText("Player 1 Wins!");
        else if (score[1] > score[0])
          messageLabel.setText("Player 2 Wins!");
        else
          messageLabel.setText("It's a Tie!");
      }
      else
      {
        // one player logic
      }
      startStopButton.doClick();
      return;
    }
    // another turn
    if (twoPlayersRadioButton.isSelected())
    {
      messageLabel.setText("Player " +
String.valueOf(playerNumber) + ", Pick Again");
      canClick = true;
    }
    else
    {
      // one player logic
    }
  }
  else
  {
    //no match
    noMatchSound.play();
    photoFound[choice[0]] = false;
    photoFound[choice[1]] = false;
    photoLabel[choice[0]].setIcon(cover);
    photoLabel[choice[1]].setIcon(cover);
    // swap players
    if (twoPlayersRadioButton.isSelected())
    {
      if (playerNumber == 1)
        playerNumber = 2;
      else
        playerNumber = 1;
      messageLabel.setText("Player " +
String.valueOf(playerNumber) + ", Pick a Box");
      canClick = true;
    }
    else
    {
```

```
          // one player logic
      }
    }
  }
}
```

Before this code is executed, we stop the timer to insure the code is only processed one time.

So first replace all the above shaded code (make sure you save the deleted code) with a single line of code that turns on the timer (new line is shaded):

```
private void showSelectedLabel()
{

photoLabel[labelSelected].setIcon(photo[photoIndex[labelSe
lected]]);
  photoFound[labelSelected] = true;
  displayTimer.start();
}
```

Now, put the code you just deleted from the **showSelectedLabel** method in the **delayTimerActionPerformed** method, adding the line to turn off the timer at the beginning (shaded):

```
private void displayTimerActionPerformed(ActionEvent e)
{
  displayTimer.stop();
  if (choiceNumber == 1)
  {
    choice[0] = labelSelected;
    choiceNumber = 2;
    if (twoPlayersRadioButton.isSelected())
    {
      messageLabel.setText("Player " +
String.valueOf(playerNumber) + ", Pick Another");
      canClick = true;
    }
    else
    {
      // one player logic
    }
  }
  else
  {
    choice[1] = labelSelected;
    choiceNumber = 1;
```

```java
    if (photoIndex[choice[0]] == photoIndex[choice[1]])
    {
      // a match
      matchSound.play();
      photoLabel[choice[0]].setIcon(null);
      photoLabel[choice[1]].setIcon(null);
      score[playerNumber - 1]++;
      scoreTextField[playerNumber -
1].setText(String.valueOf(score[playerNumber - 1]));
      photosRemaining -= 2;
      if (photosRemaining == 0)
      {
        gameOver = true;
        gameOverSound.play();
        if (twoPlayersRadioButton.isSelected())
        {
          if (score[0] > score[1])
            messageLabel.setText("Player 1 Wins!");
          else if (score[1] > score[0])
            messageLabel.setText("Player 2 Wins!");
          else
            messageLabel.setText("It's a Tie!");
        }
        else
        {
          // one player logic
        }
        startStopButton.doClick();
        return;
      }
      // another turn
      if (twoPlayersRadioButton.isSelected())
      {
        messageLabel.setText("Player " +
String.valueOf(playerNumber) + ", Pick Again");
        canClick = true;
      }
      else
      {
        // one player logic
      }
    }
    else
    {
      //no match
      noMatchSound.play();
      photoFound[choice[0]] = false;
```

```
      photoFound[choice[1]] = false;
      photoLabel[choice[0]].setIcon(cover);
      photoLabel[choice[1]].setIcon(cover);
      // swap players
      if (twoPlayersRadioButton.isSelected())
      {
        if (playerNumber == 1)
          playerNumber = 2;
        else
          playerNumber = 1;
        messageLabel.setText("Player " +
String.valueOf(playerNumber) + ", Pick a Box");
        canClick = true;
      }
      else
      {
        // one player logic
      }
    }
  }
}
```

Make sure you see how this all works – it's actually kind of simple. The picture displays, the timer starts, 0.5 seconds elapses, giving time for the photo to display, the timer is turned off and the code in the timer method (**delayTimerActionPerformed**) executes.

Save and run the project. You and a friend should now be able to play a two player version of **Match Game** with the photos appearing correctly. When a match is found, you will hear a 'tada' sound and the photos will disappear. When no match is found, you will hear a 'boing' sound and the photos will be recovered. When done, you'll hear a crowd saying "wow". Give it a try. I played a two player game by myself. Here's the form after three matches have been found (2 by **Player 1**, 1 by **Player 2**) and one box has been uncovered:

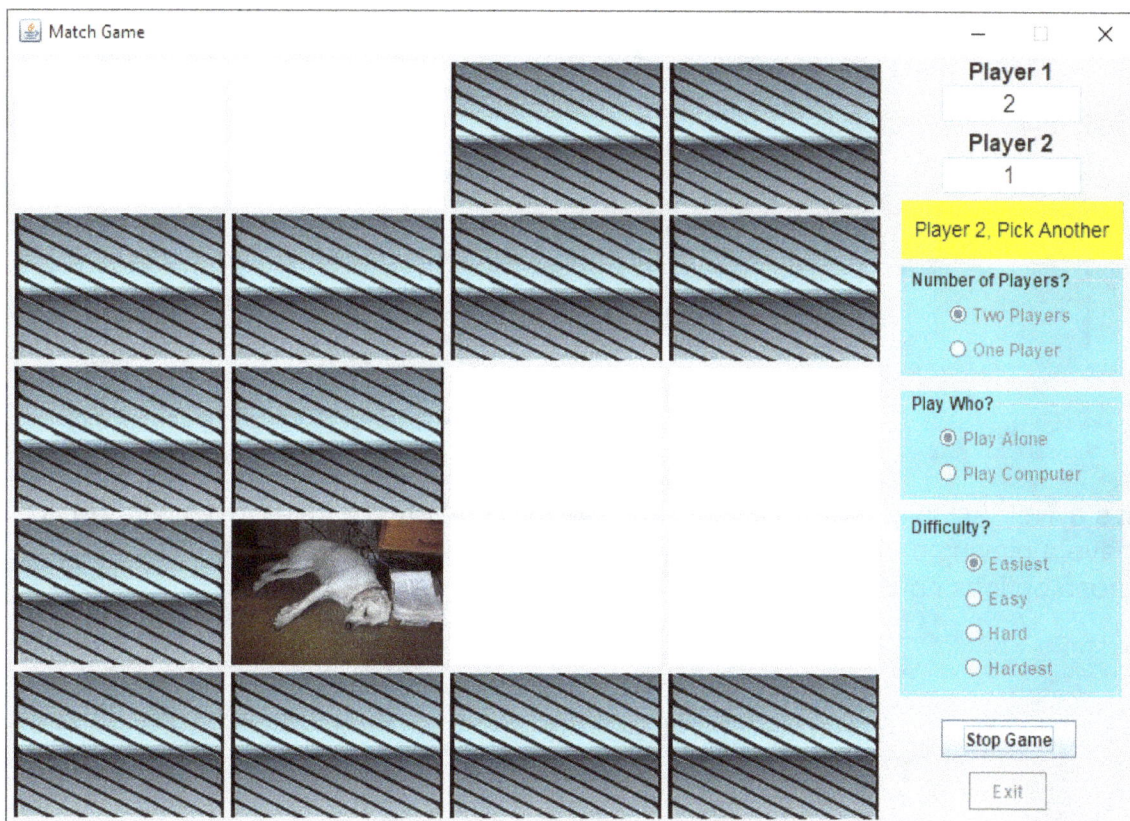

Playing the game to completion, the form looks like this, where we could now select other options and play again:

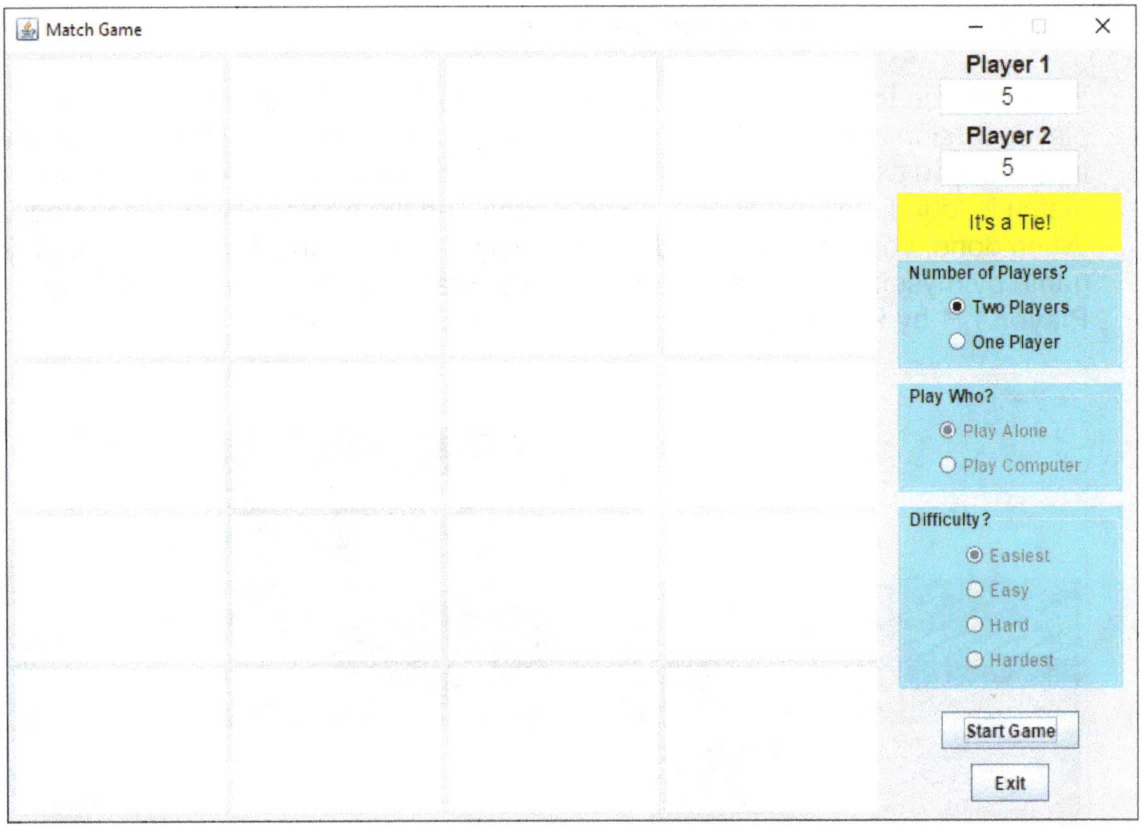

It's a Tie! Actually, I was Player 1 and Player 2. In such a case, when you don't have a playing partner, it's fun to play alone or play the computer. Let's code up those options now.

Code Design – One Player, Solitaire Game

If the **One Player**, **Play Alone** options are selected in **Match Game**, a single player tries to find matching photos on the playing form. The computer keeps track of how many guesses it takes until all matches have been found.

The steps in the one player, solitaire game following a click on a label are:

- ➢ Make sure the label has not already been selected.
- ➢ Increment number of guesses (use **scoreTextField[1]**)
- ➢ Display photo.
- ➢ If first choice, allow second choice and display that photo. Compare the two photos.
- ➢ If photos match:
  - ○ Play matching sound.
  - ○ Remove labels with photos from game panel.
  - ○ Increment number of matches by 1.
  - ○ Decrement **photosRemaining** by 2.
  - ○ If **photosRemaining = 0**, set **gameOver** to **true**, play game over sound and stop game.
  - ○ If **photosRemaining != 0**, continue playing.
- ➢ If photos do not match:
  - ○ Play no match sound.
  - ○ Replace photos with 'cover' graphic.
  - ○ Continue playing.

To implement these steps, we first make the shaded modifications to the **showSelectedMethod** method:

```
private void showSelectedLabel()
{
  // one player/solitaire game
  if (onePlayerRadioButton.isSelected() &&
playAloneRadioButton.isSelected())
  {
    score[1]++;
    scoreTextField[1].setText(String.valueOf(score[1]));
  }

photoLabel[labelSelected].setIcon(photo[photoIndex[labelSe
lected]]);
  photoFound[labelSelected] = true;
  displayTimer.start();
}
```

And we make additional modifications (shaded code) to the
displayTimerActionPerformedMethod:

```java
private void displayTimerActionPerformed(ActionEvent e)
{
  displayTimer.stop();
  if (choiceNumber == 1)
  {
    choice[0] = labelSelected;
    choiceNumber = 2;
    if (twoPlayersRadioButton.isSelected())
    {
      messageLabel.setText("Player " +
String.valueOf(playerNumber) + ", Pick Another");
      canClick = true;
    }
    else
    {
    // one player logic
      if (playerNumber == 1)
      {
        messageLabel.setText("Pick Another Box");
        canClick = true;
      }
      else
      {
        // play computer logic
      }
    }
  }
  else
  {
    choice[1] = labelSelected;
    choiceNumber = 1;
    if (photoIndex[choice[0]] == photoIndex[choice[1]])
    {
      // a match
      matchSound.play();
      photoLabel[choice[0]].setIcon(null);
      photoLabel[choice[1]].setIcon(null);
      score[playerNumber - 1]++;
      scoreTextField[playerNumber -
1].setText(String.valueOf(score[playerNumber - 1]));
      photosRemaining -= 2;
      if (photosRemaining == 0)
      {
        gameOver = true;
```

```
gameOverSound.play();
if (twoPlayersRadioButton.isSelected())
{
  if (score[0] > score[1])
    messageLabel.setText("Player 1 Wins!");
  else if (score[1] > score[0])
    messageLabel.setText("Player 2 Wins!");
  else
    messageLabel.setText("It's a Tie!");
}
else
{
  // one player logic
  if (playAloneRadioButton.isSelected())
    messageLabel.setText("All Matches Found!");
  else
  {
    // play computer logic
  }
}
startStopButton.doClick();
return;
}
// another turn
if (twoPlayersRadioButton.isSelected())
{
  messageLabel.setText("Player " +
String.valueOf(playerNumber) + ", Pick Again");
  canClick = true;
}
else
{
  // one player logic
  if (playerNumber == 1)
  {
    messageLabel.setText("Pick a Box");
    canClick = true;
  }
  else
  {
    // play computer logic
  }
}
}
else
{
  //no match
```

```
      noMatchSound.play();
      photoFound[choice[0]] = false;
      photoFound[choice[1]] = false;
      photoLabel[choice[0]].setIcon(cover);
      photoLabel[choice[1]].setIcon(cover);
      // swap players
      if (twoPlayersRadioButton.isSelected())
      {
        if (playerNumber == 1)
          playerNumber = 2;
        else
          playerNumber = 1;
        messageLabel.setText("Player " +
String.valueOf(playerNumber) + ", Pick a Box");
        canClick = true;
      }
      else
      {
        // one player logic
        if (playerNumber == 1)
        {
          messageLabel.setText("Pick a Box");
          canClick = true;
        }
        else
        {
          // play computer logic
        }
      }
    }
  }
}
```

Again, note we have left "hooks" (comment statements) for one player game versus the computer (**play computer logic**).

Save and run the game. Click **One Player** and make sure **Play Alone** is selected. Click **Start Game.** Here's the first box I uncovered:

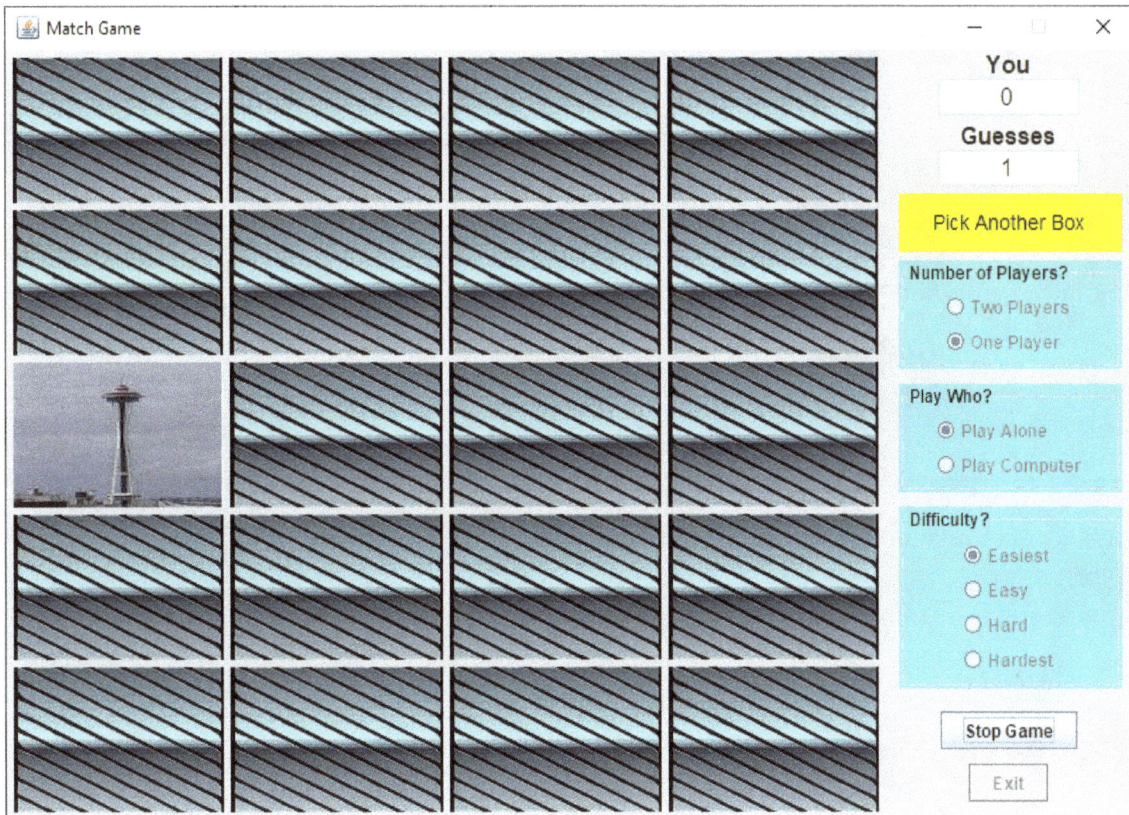

I uncovered another, but no match.

From here on, you just keep uncovering photos. The computer keeps track of how many guesses (photos uncovered) it took you to find all the matches. Here's the form once I finished (I did pretty well – it took me 42 guesses):

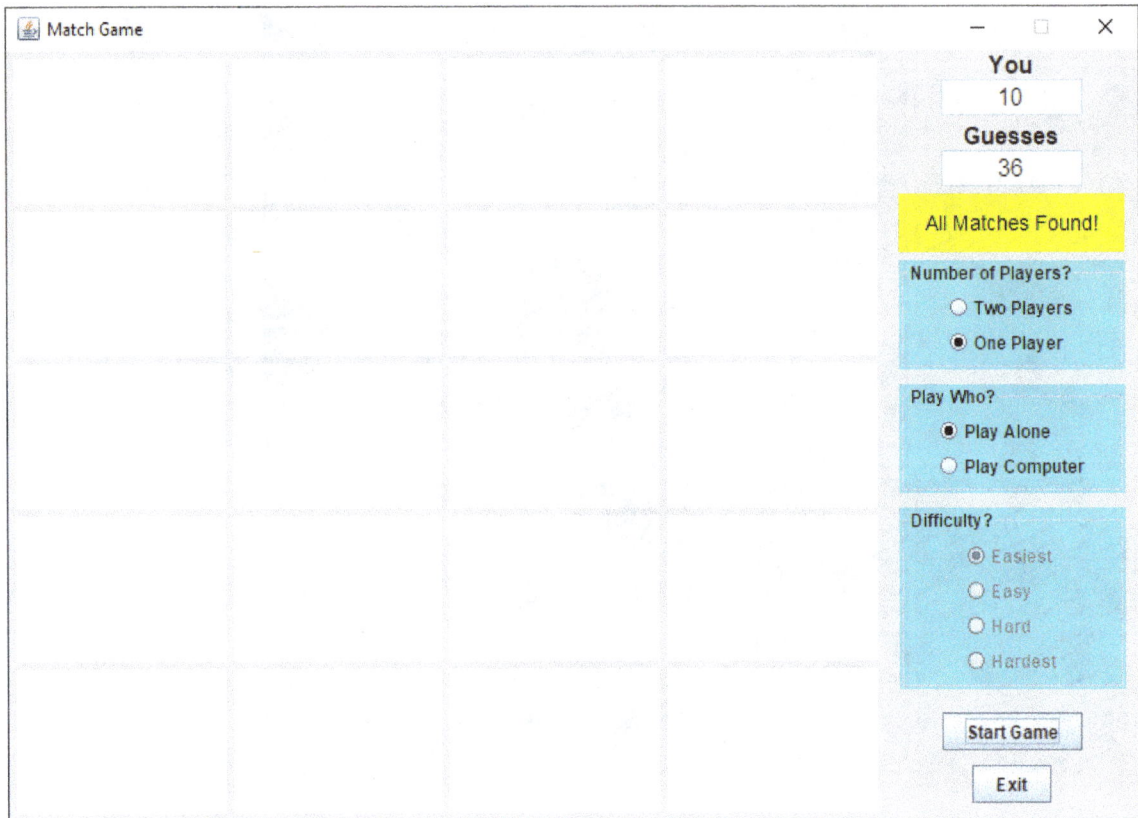

Now, let's see how to change the game to play against the computer.

Code Design – Computer Moves

It's time to give some intelligence to the computer, trying to make it a reasonable opponent in **Match Game**. Recall in the **Tic Tac Toe** game, we had two options for a computer opponent: **random** or **smart**. The random opponent was fairly easy to beat and the smart opponent was impossible to beat. As an improvement to the **Tic Tac Toe** game, we suggested graduated levels of computer intelligence. We will take that approach here.

For **Match Game**, we will still develop logic for a **random** choice (minimum intelligence) and a **smart** choice (maximum intelligence) by the computer. To give graduated levels of intelligence, we will decide how often we want the computer to make a random choice versus how often it will make a smart choice. That graduated level of intelligence is selected in the **Difficulty** panel on the **Match Game** frame.

Examine the **Difficulty** panel and you will see four levels of difficulty: **Easiest**, **Easy**, **Hard** and **Hardest**. We will set some rules for intelligence at each level. Feel free to change these if you'd like. These rules establish what percentage of computer moves are random and what percentage are smart. Obviously lower levels of intelligence will have more random choices. The rules selected are:

Easiest Difficulty: 75% Random, 25% Smart
Easy Difficulty: 50% Random, 50% Smart
Hard Difficulty: 25% Random, 75% Smart
Hardest Difficulty: 10% Random, 90% Smart

So even at the highest level of difficulty, we allow that the computer can make a mistake.

Let's build a framework for implementing a computer opponent, then develop the code for a random or a smart move. Add these class level declarations:

```
Random myRandom = new Random();
boolean smartComputer;
int difficulty = 1;
```

We will use a random number (using the **myRandom** object) to determine whether a random (**smartComputer** is **false**) or smart (**smartComputer** is **true**) move is to be made, based on the value of **difficulty** (initialized at 1, the **Easy** level). The resulting label to be uncovered will be represented by **labelSelected**.

Code the **ActionPerformed** methods for the four radio buttons used to set **difficulty**:

```
private void easiestRadioButtonActionPerformed(ActionEvent
e)
{
  difficulty = 1;
}

private void easyRadioButtonActionPerformed(ActionEvent e)
{
  difficulty = 2;
}

private void hardRadioButtonActionPerformed(ActionEvent e)
{
  difficulty = 3;
}

private void hardestRadioButtonActionPerformed(ActionEvent
e)
{
  difficulty = 4;
}
```

Code two empty methods (**randomChoice** and **smartChoice**) that return the selected box for the random and smart computer options:

```
private int randomChoice()
{
   return(0);
}

private int smartChoice()
{
   return(0);
}
```

We'll add some code to these soon.

Add a general method (**computerTurn**) that generates the computer's selection based on the selected difficulty and corresponding rules for move generation:

```
private void computerTurn()
{
   int threshold = 0;
   if (choiceNumber == 1)
   {
     switch (difficulty)
     {
       case 1:
         threshold = 25;
         break;
       case 2:
         threshold = 50;
         break;
       case 3:
         threshold = 75;
         break;
       case 4:
         threshold = 90;
         break;
     }
     if (myRandom.nextInt(100) < threshold)
       smartComputer = true;
     else
       smartComputer = false;
   }
   if (smartComputer)
     labelSelected = smartChoice();
   else
     labelSelected = randomChoice();
```

```
      showSelectedLabel();
  }
```

In this code, if it's the first choice (**choiceNumber = 1**), we decide whether we
have a smart computer for both computer selections. This is done by establishing
a **threshold** (from 0 to 100) based on difficulty. The higher the threshold, the
smarter the computer. We then generate a random number from 0 to 99. If this
number is less than the threshold, we use a smart computer (**smartComputer** is
true). In such a case, the **labelSelected** will be found using the **smartChoice**
method (which has no code yet). If **smartComputer** is **false**, we obtain
labelSelected from the **randomChoice** method (also empty). Once, we know
labelSelected, we display the corresponding photo by calling the
showSelectedLabel method.

And, we need to modify the **displayTimerActionPerformed** method to allow a
computer opponent (recall the "hooks" are marked by comment statements). In a
game against the computer, the computer is Player 2 – you always get to go first.
These shaded modifications simply call **computerTurn** at the proper time and
swap players when appropriate:

```
  private void displayTimerActionPerformed(ActionEvent e)
  {
    displayTimer.stop();
    if (choiceNumber == 1)
    {
      choice[0] = labelSelected;
      choiceNumber = 2;
      if (twoPlayersRadioButton.isSelected())
      {
        messageLabel.setText("Player " +
  String.valueOf(playerNumber) + ", Pick Another");
        canClick = true;
      }
      else
      {
      // one player logic
        if (playerNumber == 1)
        {
          messageLabel.setText("Pick Another Box");
          canClick = true;
        }
        else
        {
          // play computer logic
          messageLabel.setText("Picking Another");
          computerTurn();
          return;
```

```
        }
      }
    }
    else
    {
      choice[1] = labelSelected;
      choiceNumber = 1;
      if (photoIndex[choice[0]] == photoIndex[choice[1]])
      {
        // a match
        matchSound.play();
        photoLabel[choice[0]].setIcon(null);
        photoLabel[choice[1]].setIcon(null);
        score[playerNumber - 1]++;
        scoreTextField[playerNumber -
1].setText(String.valueOf(score[playerNumber - 1]));
        photosRemaining -= 2;
        if (photosRemaining == 0)
        {
          gameOver = true;
          gameOverSound.play();
          if (twoPlayersRadioButton.isSelected())
          {
            if (score[0] > score[1])
              messageLabel.setText("Player 1 Wins!");
            else if (score[1] > score[0])
              messageLabel.setText("Player 2 Wins!");
            else
              messageLabel.setText("It's a Tie!");
          }
          else
          {
            // one player logic
            if (playAloneRadioButton.isSelected())
              messageLabel.setText("All Matches Found!");
            else
            {
              // play computer logic
              if (score[0] > score[1])
                messageLabel.setText("You Win!");
              else if (score[1] > score[0])
                messageLabel.setText("Computer Wins!");
              else
                messageLabel.setText("It's a Tie!");
            }
          }
          startStopButton.doClick();
```

```
      return;
    }
    // another turn
    if (twoPlayersRadioButton.isSelected())
    {
      messageLabel.setText("Player " +
String.valueOf(playerNumber) + ", Pick Again");
      canClick = true;
    }
    else
    {
      // one player logic
      if (playerNumber == 1)
      {
        messageLabel.setText("Pick a Box");
        canClick = true;
      }
      else
      {
        // play computer logic
        messageLabel.setText("Picking Again");
        computerTurn();
        return;
      }
    }
  }
  else
  {
    //no match
    noMatchSound.play();
    photoFound[choice[0]] = false;
    photoFound[choice[1]] = false;
    photoLabel[choice[0]].setIcon(cover);
    photoLabel[choice[1]].setIcon(cover);
    // swap players
    if (twoPlayersRadioButton.isSelected())
    {
      if (playerNumber == 1)
        playerNumber = 2;
      else
        playerNumber = 1;
      messageLabel.setText("Player " +
String.valueOf(playerNumber) + ", Pick a Box");
      canClick = true;
    }
    else
    {
```

```
      // one player logic
      if (playComputerRadioButton.isSelected())
      {
        if (playerNumber == 1)
          playerNumber = 2;
        else
          playerNumber = 1;
      }
      if (playerNumber == 1)
      {
        messageLabel.setText("Pick a Box");
        canClick = true;
      }
      else
      {
        // play computer logic
        messageLabel.setText("Computer Picking");
        choiceNumber = 1;
        computerTurn();
        return;
      }
    }
  }
}
}
```

The framework is in place. If you trying running the game, the **Two Player** and **One Player**, **Play Alone** options will still work. Playing against the computer will not work because we need code for the **randomChoice** and **smartChoice** methods. We'll do **randomChoice** first.

Code Design – Random Computer

For random moves, the computer will simply choose (at random) one of the available labels on the game panel. This code is very similar to the random move code for the **Tic Tac Toe** game.

Replace the single line currently in the **randomChoice** method with the shaded code:

```
private int randomChoice()
{
  int count, n, rc;
  if (choiceNumber == 1)
    n = myRandom.nextInt(photosRemaining) + 1;
  else
    n = myRandom.nextInt(photosRemaining - 1) + 1;
  count = 0;
  for (rc = 0; rc < 20; rc++)
  {
    if (!photoFound[rc])
      count++;
    if (count == n)
      break;
  }
  return(rc);
}
```

The logic behind this code is straightforward. We either have **photosRemaining** unselected labels (if it's the first choice) or **photosRemaining – 1** unselected labels (if it's the second choice). The code selects a random number within this range and counts ahead that number of unselected labels to identify the index of the label to choose (returned as **rc**).

We can test our random logic, but there's one problem. If (in **computerTurn**) we select a smart computer, there is no code in the corresponding method (**smartMove**). To make things work, replace the current line in the **smartMove** method with the shaded line:

```
private int smartChoice()
{
   return(RandomChoice());
}
```

We're simply making the smart computer be random (temporarily) to allow testing of the computer move logic.

Save and run the **Match Game** project. Select the **One Player**, **Play Computer** options. **Difficulty** doesn't matter since all code is random at the moment. Click **Start Game**. You go first, trying to find matching photos. Once it's the computer's turn, notice two things. First, the photos are uncovered (in pairs) randomly, very seldom do they match. Second, the photos appear and disappear very quickly.

We can slow things down using another **timer** object (named **delayTimer**) to add some delay (we'll choose one second). Declare this timer:

```
Timer delayTimer;
```

and add it to the frame with a 1000 millisecond delay (one second):

```
delayTimer = new Timer(1000, new ActionListener()
{
   public void actionPerformed(ActionEvent e)
   {
     delayTimerActionPerformed(e);
   }
});
```

Rather than immediately display the photos in the **computerTurn** method, we will start the **timer** object. We move the line of code that displays the photo into the **delayTimerActionPerformed** method. With a 1000 millisecond **delay** property, the photos will remain on the form for 1 second. You may adjust this amount of delay if you like. So, the **delayTimerActionPerformed** event method is:

```
private void delayTimerActionPerformed(ActionEvent e)
{
  delayTimer.stop();
  showSelectedLabel();
}
```

Here we turn off the timer to stop the delay and display the photo with the line of code moved from the **computerTurn** method.

Replace the last line in the **computerTurn** method (the call to the **showSelectedLabel** method) with the single shaded line that starts the timer object:

```
private void computerTurn()
{
  int threshold = 0;
  if (choiceNumber == 1)
  {
    switch (difficulty)
    {
      case 1:
        threshold = 25;
        break;
      case 2:
        threshold = 50;
        break;
      case 3:
        threshold = 75;
        break;
      case 4:
        threshold = 90;
        break;
    }
    if (myRandom.nextInt(100) < threshold)
      smartComputer = true;
    else
      smartComputer = false;
  }
  if (smartComputer)
    labelSelected = smartChoice();
  else
    labelSelected = randomChoice();
  delayTimer.start();
}
```

Save and run the game again. Select **One Player** and **Play Computer**. Again, **Difficulty** does not matter. Click **Start Game**. You can now play against a random computer that has been slowed down a bit. You'll see the computer is not that smart, making it pretty easy for you to win. We'll fix that next by coding up a far more intelligent and formidable computer opponent. Here's a game I played (the computer did find four matches

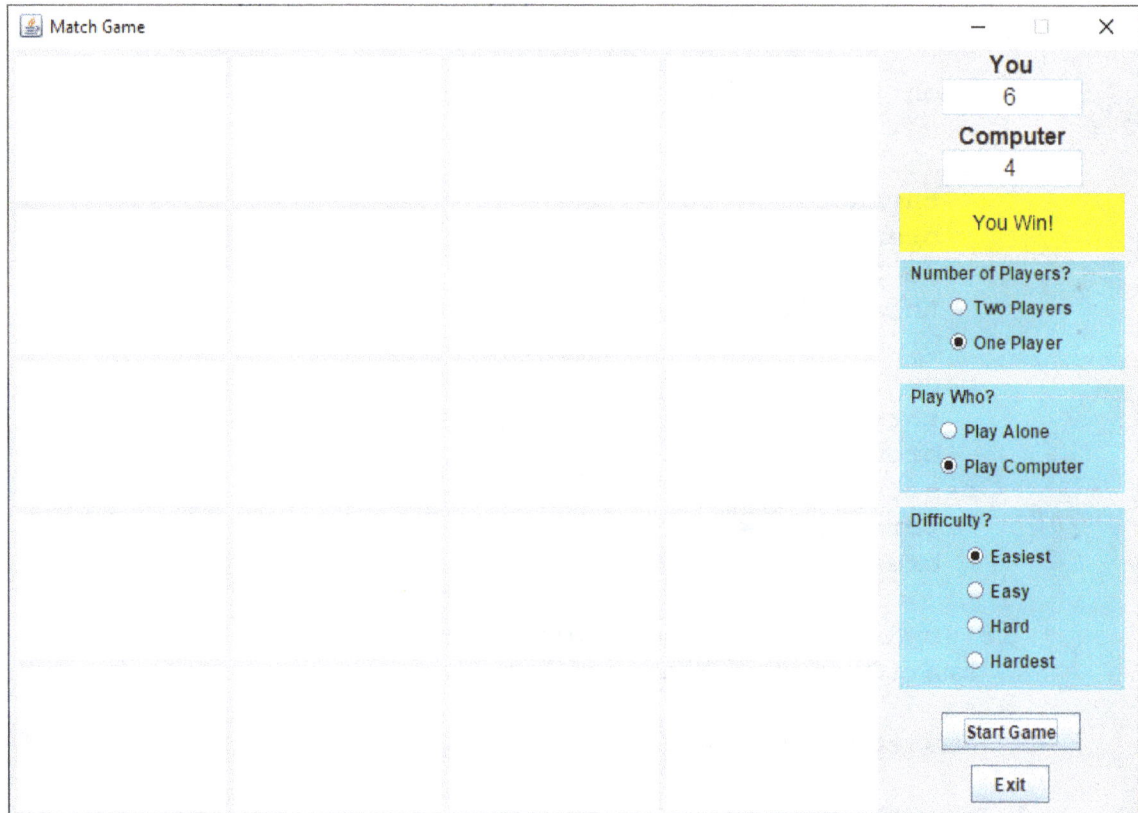

Code Design – Smart Computer

So how can we make the computer a better **Match Game** opponent? Well, we could cheat! Since the computer generated the random numbers to hide the photos behind the labels, the computer knows where everything is. Once it's the computer's turn, it could just go through that list and find all the matching pairs. You could never win. Obviously, not a good approach.

The approach we'll take is to give the computer perfect memory. In other words, once a photo has been uncovered, the computer will remember where that photo is. Then, when the computer has a turn (as a smart computer), it will search its memory for matches. If it finds a match, it will take it. First, let's code the memory.

Add this class level declaration:

```
int[] memory = new int[20];
```

This array stores the indices of photos behind the 20 label objects as each photo is uncovered. A zero value means the photo behind the label has not yet been uncovered.

The **memory** array is initialized in the **startStopButtonActionPerformed** method (the added code is shaded):

```
private void startStopButtonActionPerformed(ActionEvent e)
{
  if (startStopButton.getText().equals("Start Game"))
  {
    startStopButton.setText("Stop Game");
    score[0] = 0;
    score[1] = 0;
    scoreTextField[0].setText("0");
    scoreTextField[1].setText("0");
    photosRemaining = 20;
    photoIndex = nRandomIntegers(20);
    for (int i = 0; i < 20; i++)
    {
      if (photoIndex[i] > 9)
        photoIndex[i] -= 10;
      photoFound[i] = false;
      photoLabel[i].setIcon(cover);
      memory[i] = 0;
    }
    playerNumber = 1;
    choiceNumber = 1;
    if (twoPlayersRadioButton.isSelected())
```

```
          messageLabel.setText("Player 1, Pick a Box");
        else
          messageLabel.setText("Pick a Box");
        setNumberPlayersButtons(false);
        setPlayWhoButtons(false);
        setDifficultyButtons(false);
        exitButton.setEnabled(false);
        canClick = true;
        gameOver = false;
      }
    else
      {
        // stop game
        startStopButton.setText("Start Game");
        setNumberPlayersButtons(true);
        if (onePlayerRadioButton.isSelected())
          {
            setPlayWhoButtons(true);
            if (playComputerRadioButton.isSelected())
              setDifficultyButtons(true);
          }
        exitButton.setEnabled(true);
        canClick = false;
        if (!gameOver)
          messageLabel.setText("Game Stopped");
      }
  }
```

The values in the **memory** array are established in the
displayTimerActionPerformed method. The needed changes are shaded:

```java
private void displayTimerActionPerformed(ActionEvent e)
{
  displayTimer.stop();
  if (choiceNumber == 1)
  {
    choice[0] = labelSelected;
    choiceNumber = 2;
    memory[labelSelected] = photoIndex[labelSelected];
    if (twoPlayersRadioButton.isSelected())
    {
      messageLabel.setText("Player " +
String.valueOf(playerNumber) + ", Pick Another");
      canClick = true;
    }
    else
    {
    // one player logic
      if (playerNumber == 1)
      {
        messageLabel.setText("Pick Another Box");
        canClick = true;
      }
      else
      {
        // play computer logic
        messageLabel.setText("Picking Another");
        computerTurn();
        return;
      }
    }
  }
  else
  {
    choice[1] = labelSelected;
    choiceNumber = 1;
    memory[labelSelected] = photoIndex[labelSelected];
    if (photoIndex[choice[0]] == photoIndex[choice[1]])
    {
      // a match
      matchSound.play();
      photoLabel[choice[0]].setIcon(null);
      photoLabel[choice[1]].setIcon(null);
     // clear memory so boxes are not checked again for
match
```

```java
      memory[choice[0]] = 0;
      memory[choice[1]] = 0;
      score[playerNumber - 1]++;
      scoreTextField[playerNumber -
1].setText(String.valueOf(score[playerNumber - 1]));
      photosRemaining -= 2;
      if (photosRemaining == 0)
      {
        gameOver = true;
        gameOverSound.play();
        if (twoPlayersRadioButton.isSelected())
        {
          if (score[0] > score[1])
            messageLabel.setText("Player 1 Wins!");
          else if (score[1] > score[0])
            messageLabel.setText("Player 2 Wins!");
          else
            messageLabel.setText("It's a Tie!");
        }
        else
        {
          // one player logic
          if (playAloneRadioButton.isSelected())
            messageLabel.setText("All Matches Found!");
          else
          {
            // play computer logic
            if (score[0] > score[1])
              messageLabel.setText("You Win!");
            else if (score[1] > score[0])
              messageLabel.setText("Computer Wins!");
            else
              messageLabel.setText("It's a Tie!");
          }
        }
        startStopButton.doClick();
        return;
      }
      // another turn
      if (twoPlayersRadioButton.isSelected())
      {
        messageLabel.setText("Player " +
String.valueOf(playerNumber) + ", Pick Again");
        canClick = true;
      }
      else
      {
```

```
      // one player logic
      if (playerNumber == 1)
      {
        messageLabel.setText("Pick a Box");
        canClick = true;
      }
      else
      {
        // play computer logic
        messageLabel.setText("Picking Again");
        computerTurn();
        return;
      }
    }
  }
  else
  {
    //no match
    noMatchSound.play();
    photoFound[choice[0]] = false;
    photoFound[choice[1]] = false;
    photoLabel[choice[0]].setIcon(cover);
    photoLabel[choice[1]].setIcon(cover);
    // swap players
    if (twoPlayersRadioButton.isSelected())
    {
      if (playerNumber == 1)
        playerNumber = 2;
      else
        playerNumber = 1;
      messageLabel.setText("Player " +
String.valueOf(playerNumber) + ", Pick a Box");
      canClick = true;
    }
    else
    {
      // one player logic
      if (playComputerRadioButton.isSelected())
      {
        if (playerNumber == 1)
          playerNumber = 2;
        else
          playerNumber = 1;
      }
      if (playerNumber == 1)
      {
        messageLabel.setText("Pick a Box");
```

```
            canClick = true;
        }
        else
        {
            // play computer logic
            messageLabel.setText("Computer Picking");
            choiceNumber = 1;
            computerTurn();
            return;
        }
    }
  }
 }
}
```

Now, how do we use the **memory** array to make a smart move? The rules we will use for the computer's two choices are:

Choice 1:
1. Check **memory** array for a match.
2. If a match is found, select the first matching label control.
3. If no match is found, select a random label.

Choice 2:
1. If a match was found with Choice 1, select the second matching label.
2. If no match was found with Choice 1, check again for a match (the random choice in Choice 1 may match a photo stored in memory).
3. If a match is found, select the matching label.
4. If no match is found, select a random label.

Let's implement this logic in code.

First, add the general method **checkForMatch**. This method returns two integers in an array. If these both of these integers are non-zero, it tells the computer which two picture boxes have matching photos:

```
private int[] checkForMatch()
{
  int[] matches = new int[2];
  matches[0] = 0;
  matches[1] = 0;
  for (int i = 0; i < 20; i++)
  {
    for (int j = 0; j < 20; j++)
    {
      if (memory[i] != 0 && memory[i] == memory[j] && i !=
j)
      {
        matches[0] = i;
        matches[1] = j;
      }
    }
  }
  return (matches);
}
```

This method does a simple comparison of all labels looking for matching non-zero values in the **memory** array.

Add a class level declaration for an integer array (**matchFound**) that will be used to store the matching picture boxes:

```
int[] matchFound = new int[2];
```

Now, remove the current **return** statement from the **SmartChoice** method (the one returning a random choice). Replace that method with this code which implements the smart computer steps outlined above:

```
private int smartChoice()
{
  int sc;
  if (choiceNumber == 1)
  {
    matchFound = checkForMatch();
    if (matchFound[0] != 0 && matchFound[1] != 0)
      sc = matchFound[0];
    else
      sc = randomChoice();
  }
  else
  {
    if (matchFound[0] != 0 && matchFound[1] != 0)
      sc = matchFound[1];
    else
    {
      matchFound = checkForMatch();
      if (matchFound[0] != 0 && matchFound[1] != 0)
      {
        if (matchFound[0] != choice[0])
          sc = matchFound[0];
        else
          sc = matchFound[1];
      }
      else
        sc = randomChoice();
    }
  }
  return (sc);
}
```

Save and run the project. The game is now fully functional (the complete code listing is given at the end of the chapter). Try playing it against the computer with the **Hardest** difficulty. You should find it is very hard to beat. Continue playing seeing how the various levels of difficulty do indeed adjust the computer's intelligence. Here's a game I played with **Hard** difficulty. I selected the first two boxes and see:

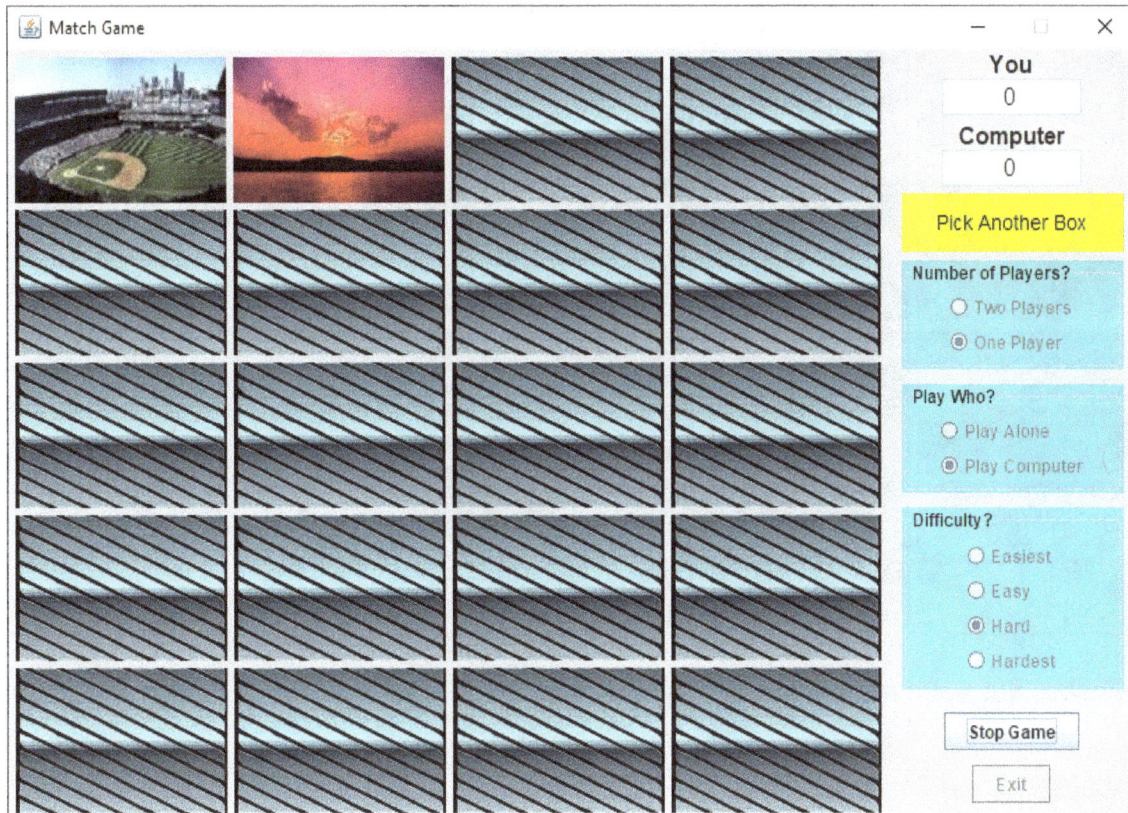

It's TMobile Park and a sunset; nice photos, but not a match.

It then becomes the computer's turn. It's choices are:

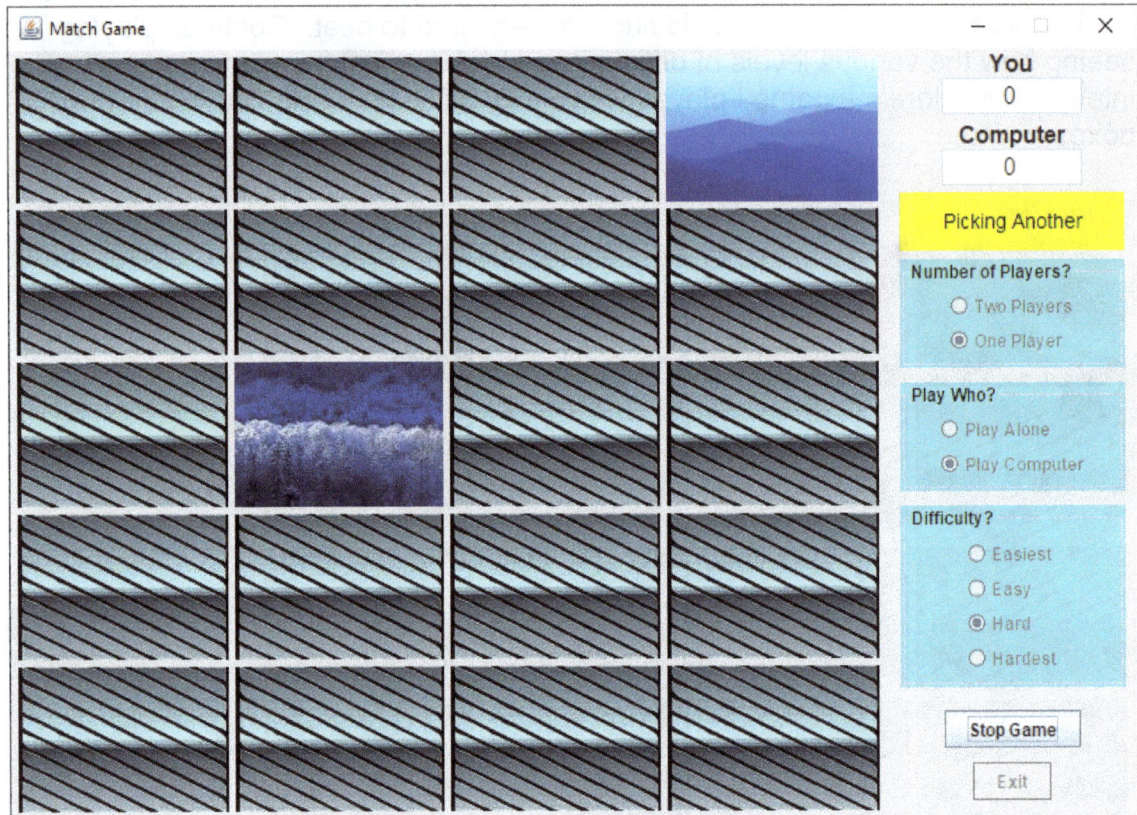

Similar, but not a match.

Picking the first box in the bottom row and the last box in the first row, I get a match. The photos are removed, my score is incremented and it's my turn again:

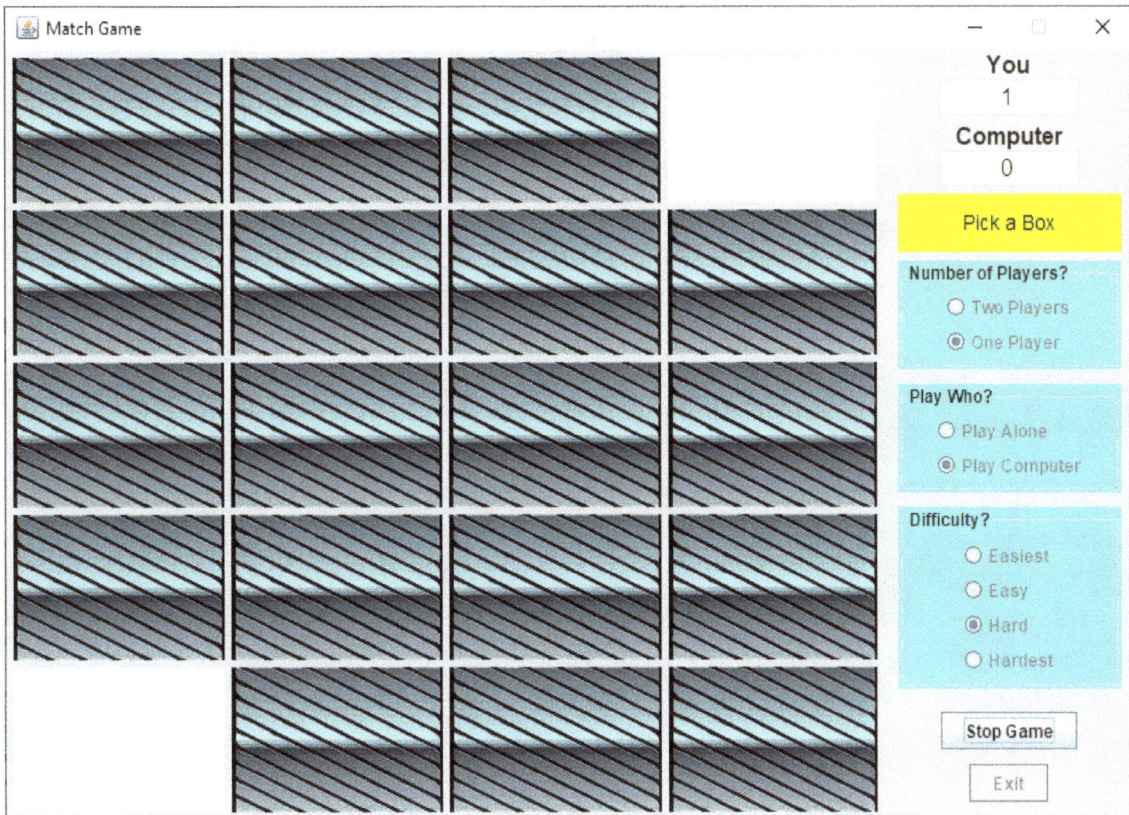

Once all the matches were found, the final score was me 6 and the computer 4, I won!

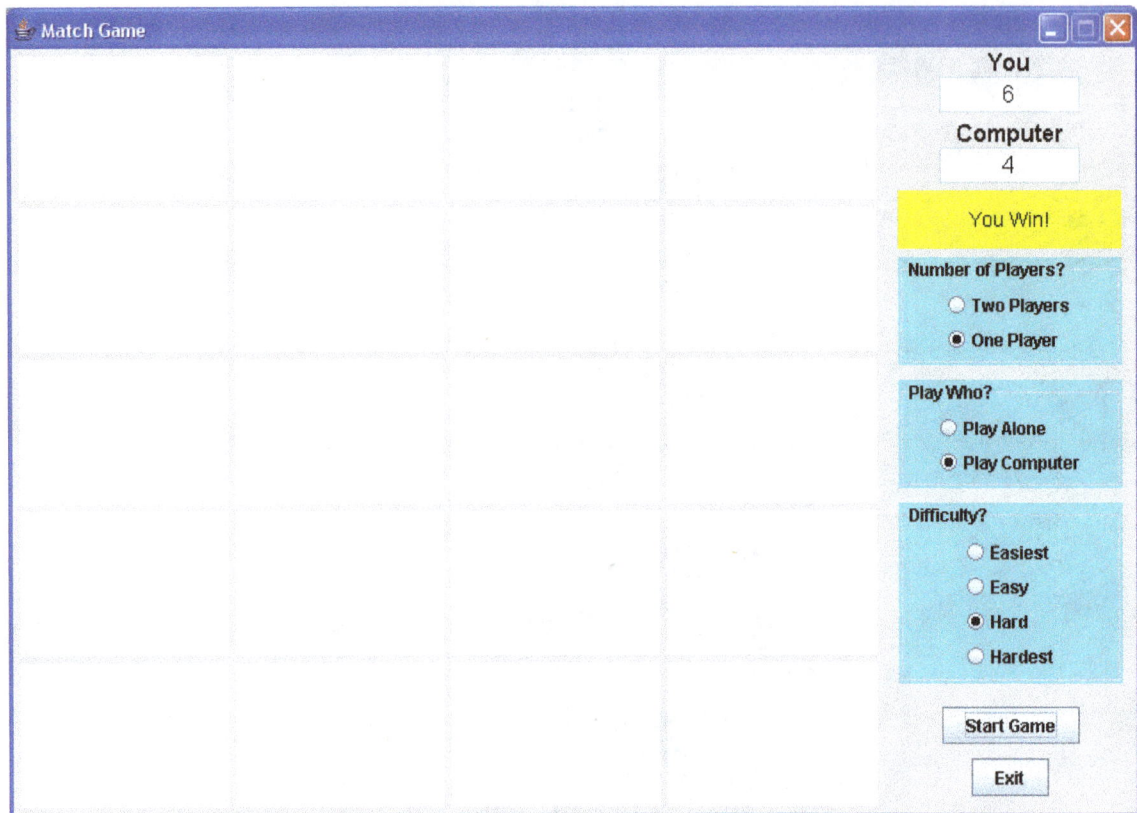

Match Game Project Review

The **Match Game** project is now complete. Save and run the project and make sure it works as promised. Check that all options work correctly.

If there are errors in your implementation, go back over the steps of frame and code design. Go over the developed code – make sure you understand how different parts of the project were coded. As mentioned in the beginning of this chapter, the completed project is saved as **MatchGame** in the **\KidGamesJava\KidGamesJava Projects** folder.

While completing this project, new concepts and skills you should have gained include:

> ➢ Proper steps in game design and game flow.
> ➢ Capabilities and use of many Java controls.
> ➢ How to randomly sort integers (shuffle numbers).
> ➢ How to implement delays in games.
> ➢ How to give the computer graduated intelligence in playing games.

Match Game Project Enhancements

There are several ways to improve the **Match Game** project. Some possibilities are:

> ➢ As written, the human player can click on labels while the computer is making a move. Implement logic to disallow this.
> ➢ Design a tool that allows for selection of photos used in the game. This requires some advanced skills. Your tool would write a file with the name of the 10 photos to use (and their location). Then when **Match Game** begins, it would open that file and automatically load the files. Reading and writing to files is briefly covered in our last game project.
> ➢ Make the number of labels displaying photos adjustable for an added difficulty adjustment (fewer boxes for little kids).
> ➢ Add additional levels of difficulty by having finer adjustments on the threshold between random and smart computer moves.
> ➢ As written, a player could theoretically find all ten pairs without giving the other player a chance. Perhaps, rewrite the game so a player only gets one extra turn after a match.
> ➢ The computer in this game is pretty smart, but it can be smarter. How you ask? If the computer uncovers a photo that has no match, its next choice could be a photo that's already been uncovered. This would not give the computer any more information about hidden photos, but it also does not give you, the opponent, any needed information either.

Match Game Project Java Code Listing

```java
/*
 * MatchGame.java
 */
package matchgame;
import javax.swing.*;
import java.awt.*;
import java.awt.event.*;
import java.util.Random;
import java.net.URL;
import java.applet.*;

public class MatchGame extends JFrame
{

    JPanel gamePanel = new JPanel();
    JLabel[] photoLabel = new JLabel[20];
    JPanel resultsPanel = new JPanel();
    JLabel player1Label = new JLabel();
    JLabel player2Label = new JLabel();
    JTextField[] scoreTextField = new JTextField[2];
    JLabel messageLabel = new JLabel();
    JPanel playersPanel = new JPanel();
    ButtonGroup playersButtonGroup = new ButtonGroup();
    JRadioButton twoPlayersRadioButton = new JRadioButton();
    JRadioButton onePlayerRadioButton = new JRadioButton();
    JPanel playWhoPanel = new JPanel();
    ButtonGroup playWhoButtonGroup = new ButtonGroup();
    JRadioButton playAloneRadioButton = new JRadioButton();
    JRadioButton playComputerRadioButton = new JRadioButton();
    JPanel difficultyPanel = new JPanel();
    ButtonGroup difficultyButtonGroup = new ButtonGroup();
    JRadioButton easiestRadioButton = new JRadioButton();
    JRadioButton easyRadioButton = new JRadioButton();
    JRadioButton hardRadioButton = new JRadioButton();
    JRadioButton hardestRadioButton = new JRadioButton();
    JPanel buttonsPanel = new JPanel();
    JButton startStopButton = new JButton();
    JButton exitButton = new JButton();

    ImageIcon[] photo = new ImageIcon[10];
    ImageIcon cover = new ImageIcon();
    int[] photoIndex = new int[20];
    int photosRemaining;
    int[] score = new int[2];
```

```java
boolean[] photoFound = new boolean[20];
int playerNumber, choiceNumber;
int[] choice = new int[2];
boolean canClick = false;
boolean gameOver;
int labelSelected;
Random myRandom = new Random();
boolean smartComputer;
int difficulty = 1;
int[] memory = new int[20];
int[] matchFound = new int[2];

AudioClip matchSound;
AudioClip noMatchSound;
AudioClip gameOverSound;

Timer displayTimer;
Timer delayTimer;

public static void main(String args[])
{
  // create frame
  new MatchGame().setVisible(true);
}

public MatchGame()
{
  // frame constructor
  setTitle("Match Game");
  setResizable(false);
  addWindowListener(new WindowAdapter()
  {
    public void windowClosing(WindowEvent evt)
    {
      exitForm(evt);
    }
  });
  getContentPane().setLayout(new GridBagLayout());
  GridBagConstraints gridConstraints;

  gamePanel.setPreferredSize(new Dimension(625, 530));
  gamePanel.setLayout(new GridBagLayout());
  gridConstraints = new GridBagConstraints();
  gridConstraints.gridx = 0;
  gridConstraints.gridy = 0;
  gridConstraints.gridheight = 5;
  getContentPane().add(gamePanel, gridConstraints);
```

```
    for (int i = 0; i < 20; i++)
    {
      photoLabel[i] = new JLabel();
      photoLabel[i].setPreferredSize(new Dimension(150,
100));
      photoLabel[i].setOpaque(true);
      photoLabel[i].setBackground(Color.WHITE);
      gridConstraints = new GridBagConstraints();
      gridConstraints.gridx = i % 4;
      gridConstraints.gridy = i / 4;
      gridConstraints.insets = new Insets(5, 5, 0, 0);
      if (gridConstraints.gridx == 3)
        gridConstraints.insets = new Insets(5, 5, 0, 5);
      if (gridConstraints.gridy == 4)
        gridConstraints.insets = new Insets(5, 5, 5, 0);
      if (gridConstraints.gridx == 3 &&
gridConstraints.gridy == 4)
        gridConstraints.insets = new Insets(5, 5, 5, 5);
      gamePanel.add(photoLabel[i], gridConstraints);
      photoLabel[i].addMouseListener(new MouseAdapter()
      {
        public void mousePressed(MouseEvent e)
        {
          photoLabelMousePressed(e);
        }
      });
    }

    resultsPanel.setPreferredSize(new Dimension(160, 140));
    resultsPanel.setLayout(new GridBagLayout());
    gridConstraints = new GridBagConstraints();
    gridConstraints.gridx = 1;
    gridConstraints.gridy = 0;
    getContentPane().add(resultsPanel, gridConstraints);

    player1Label.setText("Player 1");
    player1Label.setFont(new Font("Arial", Font.BOLD, 16));
    gridConstraints = new GridBagConstraints();
    gridConstraints.gridx = 0;
    gridConstraints.gridy = 0;
    resultsPanel.add(player1Label, gridConstraints);

    scoreTextField[0] = new JTextField();
    scoreTextField[0].setPreferredSize(new Dimension(100,
25));
    scoreTextField[0].setText("0");
```

```
    scoreTextField[0].setEditable(false);
    scoreTextField[0].setBackground(Color.WHITE);

scoreTextField[0].setHorizontalAlignment(SwingConstants.CENT
ER);
    scoreTextField[0].setFont(new Font("Arial", Font.PLAIN,
16));
    gridConstraints = new GridBagConstraints();
    gridConstraints.gridx = 0;
    gridConstraints.gridy = 1;
    resultsPanel.add(scoreTextField[0], gridConstraints);

    player2Label.setText("Player 2");
    player2Label.setFont(new Font("Arial", Font.BOLD, 16));
    gridConstraints = new GridBagConstraints();
    gridConstraints.gridx = 0;
    gridConstraints.gridy = 2;
    gridConstraints.insets = new Insets(5, 0, 0, 0);
    resultsPanel.add(player2Label, gridConstraints);

    scoreTextField[1] = new JTextField();
    scoreTextField[1].setPreferredSize(new Dimension(100,
25));
    scoreTextField[1].setText("0");
    scoreTextField[1].setEditable(false);
    scoreTextField[1].setBackground(Color.WHITE);

scoreTextField[1].setHorizontalAlignment(SwingConstants.CENT
ER);
    scoreTextField[1].setFont(new Font("Arial", Font.PLAIN,
16));
    gridConstraints = new GridBagConstraints();
    gridConstraints.gridx = 0;
    gridConstraints.gridy = 3;
    resultsPanel.add(scoreTextField[1], gridConstraints);

    messageLabel.setPreferredSize(new Dimension(160, 40));
    messageLabel.setOpaque(true);
    messageLabel.setBackground(Color.YELLOW);

messageLabel.setHorizontalAlignment(SwingConstants.CENTER);
    messageLabel.setText("");
    messageLabel.setFont(new Font("Arial", Font.PLAIN, 14));
    gridConstraints = new GridBagConstraints();
    gridConstraints.gridx = 0;
    gridConstraints.gridy = 4;
    gridConstraints.insets = new Insets(5, 0, 0, 0);
```

```
    resultsPanel.add(messageLabel, gridConstraints);

    playersPanel.setPreferredSize(new Dimension(160, 75));
    playersPanel.setBackground(Color.CYAN);

playersPanel.setBorder(BorderFactory.createTitledBorder("Num
ber of Players?"));
    playersPanel.setLayout(new GridBagLayout());
    gridConstraints = new GridBagConstraints();
    gridConstraints.gridx = 1;
    gridConstraints.gridy = 1;
    gridConstraints.insets = new Insets(5, 10, 5, 10);
    getContentPane().add(playersPanel, gridConstraints);

    twoPlayersRadioButton.setText("Two Players");
    twoPlayersRadioButton.setBackground(Color.CYAN);
    twoPlayersRadioButton.setSelected(true);
    playersButtonGroup.add(twoPlayersRadioButton);
    gridConstraints = new GridBagConstraints();
    gridConstraints.gridx = 0;
    gridConstraints.gridy = 0;
    gridConstraints.anchor = GridBagConstraints.WEST;
    playersPanel.add(twoPlayersRadioButton,
gridConstraints);
    twoPlayersRadioButton.addActionListener(new
ActionListener()
    {
      public void actionPerformed(ActionEvent e)
      {
        twoPlayersRadioButtonActionPerformed(e);
      }
    });

    onePlayerRadioButton.setText("One Player");
    onePlayerRadioButton.setBackground(Color.CYAN);
    playersButtonGroup.add(onePlayerRadioButton);
    gridConstraints = new GridBagConstraints();
    gridConstraints.gridx = 0;
    gridConstraints.gridy = 1;
    gridConstraints.anchor = GridBagConstraints.WEST;
    playersPanel.add(onePlayerRadioButton, gridConstraints);
    onePlayerRadioButton.addActionListener(new
ActionListener()
    {
      public void actionPerformed(ActionEvent e)
      {
        onePlayerRadioButtonActionPerformed(e);
```

```
      }
   });

   playWhoPanel.setPreferredSize(new Dimension(160, 75));
   playWhoPanel.setBackground(Color.CYAN);

playWhoPanel.setBorder(BorderFactory.createTitledBorder("Pla
y Who?"));
   playWhoPanel.setLayout(new GridBagLayout());
   gridConstraints = new GridBagConstraints();
   gridConstraints.gridx = 1;
   gridConstraints.gridy = 2;
   gridConstraints.insets = new Insets(5, 10, 5, 10);
   getContentPane().add(playWhoPanel, gridConstraints);

   playAloneRadioButton.setText("Play Alone");
   playAloneRadioButton.setBackground(Color.CYAN);
   playAloneRadioButton.setSelected(true);
   playWhoButtonGroup.add(playAloneRadioButton);
   gridConstraints = new GridBagConstraints();
   gridConstraints.gridx = 0;
   gridConstraints.gridy = 0;
   gridConstraints.anchor = GridBagConstraints.WEST;
   playWhoPanel.add(playAloneRadioButton, gridConstraints);
   playAloneRadioButton.addActionListener(new
ActionListener()
   {
     public void actionPerformed(ActionEvent e)
     {
       playAloneRadioButtonActionPerformed(e);
     }
   });

   playComputerRadioButton.setText("Play Computer");
   playComputerRadioButton.setBackground(Color.CYAN);
   playWhoButtonGroup.add(playComputerRadioButton);
   gridConstraints = new GridBagConstraints();
   gridConstraints.gridx = 0;
   gridConstraints.gridy = 1;
   gridConstraints.anchor = GridBagConstraints.WEST;
   playWhoPanel.add(playComputerRadioButton,
gridConstraints);
   playComputerRadioButton.addActionListener(new
ActionListener()
   {
     public void actionPerformed(ActionEvent e)
     {
```

```
        playComputerRadioButtonActionPerformed(e);
      }
    });

    difficultyPanel.setPreferredSize(new Dimension(160,
125));
    difficultyPanel.setBackground(Color.CYAN);

difficultyPanel.setBorder(BorderFactory.createTitledBorder("
Difficulty?"));
    difficultyPanel.setLayout(new GridBagLayout());
    gridConstraints = new GridBagConstraints();
    gridConstraints.gridx = 1;
    gridConstraints.gridy = 3;
    gridConstraints.insets = new Insets(5, 10, 5, 10);
    getContentPane().add(difficultyPanel, gridConstraints);

    easiestRadioButton.setText("Easiest");
    easiestRadioButton.setBackground(Color.CYAN);
    easiestRadioButton.setSelected(true);
    difficultyButtonGroup.add(easiestRadioButton);
    gridConstraints = new GridBagConstraints();
    gridConstraints.gridx = 0;
    gridConstraints.gridy = 0;
    gridConstraints.anchor = GridBagConstraints.WEST;
    difficultyPanel.add(easiestRadioButton,
gridConstraints);
    easiestRadioButton.addActionListener(new
ActionListener()
    {
      public void actionPerformed(ActionEvent e)
      {
        easiestRadioButtonActionPerformed(e);
      }
    });

    easyRadioButton.setText("Easy");
    easyRadioButton.setBackground(Color.CYAN);
    easyRadioButton.setSelected(true);
    difficultyButtonGroup.add(easyRadioButton);
    gridConstraints = new GridBagConstraints();
    gridConstraints.gridx = 0;
    gridConstraints.gridy = 1;
    gridConstraints.anchor = GridBagConstraints.WEST;
    difficultyPanel.add(easyRadioButton, gridConstraints);
    easyRadioButton.addActionListener(new ActionListener()
    {
```

```
  public void actionPerformed(ActionEvent e)
  {
    easyRadioButtonActionPerformed(e);
  }
});

hardRadioButton.setText("Hard");
hardRadioButton.setBackground(Color.CYAN);
hardRadioButton.setSelected(true);
difficultyButtonGroup.add(hardRadioButton);
gridConstraints = new GridBagConstraints();
gridConstraints.gridx = 0;
gridConstraints.gridy = 2;
gridConstraints.anchor = GridBagConstraints.WEST;
difficultyPanel.add(hardRadioButton, gridConstraints);
hardRadioButton.addActionListener(new ActionListener()
{
  public void actionPerformed(ActionEvent e)
  {
    hardRadioButtonActionPerformed(e);
  }
});

hardestRadioButton.setText("Hardest");
hardestRadioButton.setBackground(Color.CYAN);
hardestRadioButton.setSelected(true);
difficultyButtonGroup.add(hardestRadioButton);
gridConstraints = new GridBagConstraints();
gridConstraints.gridx = 0;
gridConstraints.gridy = 3;
gridConstraints.anchor = GridBagConstraints.WEST;
difficultyPanel.add(hardestRadioButton,
gridConstraints);
hardestRadioButton.addActionListener(new
ActionListener()
{
  public void actionPerformed(ActionEvent e)
  {
    hardestRadioButtonActionPerformed(e);
  }
});

buttonsPanel.setPreferredSize(new Dimension(160, 70));
buttonsPanel.setLayout(new GridBagLayout());
gridConstraints = new GridBagConstraints();
gridConstraints.gridx = 1;
gridConstraints.gridy = 4;
```

```
getContentPane().add(buttonsPanel, gridConstraints);

startStopButton.setText("Start Game");
gridConstraints = new GridBagConstraints();
gridConstraints.gridx = 0;
gridConstraints.gridy = 0;
buttonsPanel.add(startStopButton, gridConstraints);
startStopButton.addActionListener(new ActionListener()
{
  public void actionPerformed(ActionEvent e)
  {
    startStopButtonActionPerformed(e);
  }
});

exitButton.setText("Exit");
gridConstraints = new GridBagConstraints();
gridConstraints.gridx = 0;
gridConstraints.gridy = 1;
gridConstraints.insets = new Insets(10, 0, 0, 0);
buttonsPanel.add(exitButton, gridConstraints);
exitButton.addActionListener(new ActionListener()
{
  public void actionPerformed(ActionEvent e)
  {
    exitButtonActionPerformed(e);
  }
});

displayTimer = new Timer(500, new ActionListener()
{
  public void actionPerformed(ActionEvent e)
  {
    displayTimerActionPerformed(e);
  }
});

delayTimer = new Timer(1000, new ActionListener()
{
  public void actionPerformed(ActionEvent e)
  {
    delayTimerActionPerformed(e);
  }
});

pack();
```

```
      Dimension screenSize =
Toolkit.getDefaultToolkit().getScreenSize();
      setBounds((int) (0.5 * (screenSize.width - getWidth())),
(int) (0.5 * (screenSize.height - getHeight())), getWidth(),
getHeight());

      photo[0] = new ImageIcon("clara.jpg");
      photo[1] = new ImageIcon("toby.jpg");
      photo[2] = new ImageIcon("Blue hills.jpg");
      photo[3] = new ImageIcon("Sunset.jpg");
      photo[4] = new ImageIcon("Water lilies.jpg");
      photo[5] = new ImageIcon("Winter.jpg");
      photo[6] = new ImageIcon("spaceneedle.jpg");
      photo[7] = new ImageIcon("market.jpg");
      photo[8] = new ImageIcon("safeco.jpg");
      photo[9] = new ImageIcon("qwest.jpg");
      cover = new ImageIcon("cover.jpg");
      for (int i = 0; i < 20; i++)
        photoLabel[i].setIcon(cover);

      setPlayWhoButtons(false);
      setDifficultyButtons(false);
      try
      {
        matchSound = Applet.newAudioClip(new URL("file:" +
"tada.wav"));
        noMatchSound = Applet.newAudioClip(new URL("file:" +
"boing.wav"));
        gameOverSound = Applet.newAudioClip(new URL("file:" +
"wow.wav"));
      }
      catch (Exception ex)
      {
        System.out.println("Error loading sound files");
      }
  }

  private void exitForm(WindowEvent evt)
  {
    System.exit(0);
  }

  private void photoLabelMousePressed(MouseEvent e)
  {
    // determine which label was clicked
    // get upper left corner of clicked label
    Point p = e.getComponent().getLocation();
```

```
   // determine index based on p
   for (labelSelected = 0; labelSelected < 20;
labelSelected++)
   {
      if (p.x == photoLabel[labelSelected].getX() && p.y ==
photoLabel[labelSelected].getY())
         break;
   }
   if (!canClick || photoFound[labelSelected])
     return;
   // show image behind selected label box
   canClick = false;
   showSelectedLabel();
 }

 private void
twoPlayersRadioButtonActionPerformed(ActionEvent e)
 {
   setPlayWhoButtons(false);
   setDifficultyButtons(false);
   player1Label.setText("Player 1");
   player2Label.setText("Player 2");
 }

 private void
onePlayerRadioButtonActionPerformed(ActionEvent e)
 {
   setPlayWhoButtons(true);
   player1Label.setText("You");
   if (playAloneRadioButton.isSelected())
   {
     player2Label.setText("Guesses");
     setDifficultyButtons(false);
   }
   else
   {
     player2Label.setText("Computer");
     setDifficultyButtons(true);
   }
 }

 private void
playAloneRadioButtonActionPerformed(ActionEvent e)
 {
   setDifficultyButtons(false);
   player2Label.setText("Guesses");
 }
```

```
  private void
playComputerRadioButtonActionPerformed(ActionEvent e)
  {
    setDifficultyButtons(true);
    player2Label.setText("Computer");
  }

  private void easiestRadioButtonActionPerformed(ActionEvent
e)
  {
    difficulty = 1;
  }

  private void easyRadioButtonActionPerformed(ActionEvent e)
  {
    difficulty = 2;
  }

  private void hardRadioButtonActionPerformed(ActionEvent e)
  {
    difficulty = 3;
  }

  private void hardestRadioButtonActionPerformed(ActionEvent
e)
  {
    difficulty = 4;
  }

  private void startStopButtonActionPerformed(ActionEvent e)
  {
    if (startStopButton.getText().equals("Start Game"))
    {
      startStopButton.setText("Stop Game");
      score[0] = 0;
      score[1] = 0;
      scoreTextField[0].setText("0");
      scoreTextField[1].setText("0");
      photosRemaining = 20;
      photoIndex = nRandomIntegers(20);
      for (int i = 0; i < 20; i++)
      {
        if (photoIndex[i] > 9)
          photoIndex[i] -= 10;
        photoFound[i] = false;
        photoLabel[i].setIcon(cover);
```

```
      memory[i] = 0;
    }
    playerNumber = 1;
    choiceNumber = 1;
    if (twoPlayersRadioButton.isSelected())
      messageLabel.setText("Player 1, Pick a Box");
    else
      messageLabel.setText("Pick a Box");
    setNumberPlayersButtons(false);
    setPlayWhoButtons(false);
    setDifficultyButtons(false);
    exitButton.setEnabled(false);
    canClick = true;
    gameOver = false;
  }
  else
  {
    // stop game
    startStopButton.setText("Start Game");
    setNumberPlayersButtons(true);
    if (onePlayerRadioButton.isSelected())
    {
      setPlayWhoButtons(true);
      if (playComputerRadioButton.isSelected())
        setDifficultyButtons(true);
    }
    exitButton.setEnabled(true);
    canClick = false;
    if (!gameOver)
      messageLabel.setText("Game Stopped");
  }
}

private void exitButtonActionPerformed(ActionEvent e)
{
 System.exit(0);
}

private void setNumberPlayersButtons(boolean a)
{
  onePlayerRadioButton.setEnabled(a);
  twoPlayersRadioButton.setEnabled(a);
}

private void setPlayWhoButtons(boolean a)
{
  playAloneRadioButton.setEnabled(a);
```

```java
    playComputerRadioButton.setEnabled(a);
  }

  private void setDifficultyButtons(boolean a)
  {
    easiestRadioButton.setEnabled(a);
    easyRadioButton.setEnabled(a);
    hardRadioButton.setEnabled(a);
    hardestRadioButton.setEnabled(a);
  }

  private int[] nRandomIntegers(int n)
  {
    /*
    *   Returns n randomly sorted integers 0 -> n - 1
    */
    int[] nIntegers = new int[n];
    int temp, s;
    Random sortRandom = new Random();
    //   initialize array from 0 to n - 1
    for (int i = 0; i < n; i++)
    {
      nIntegers[i] = i;
    }
    //   i is number of items remaining in list
    for (int i = n; i >= 1; i--)
    {
      s = sortRandom.nextInt(i);
      temp = nIntegers[s];
      nIntegers[s] = nIntegers[i - 1];
      nIntegers[i - 1] = temp;
    }
    return(nIntegers);
  }

  private void showSelectedLabel()
  {
    // one player/solitaire game
    if (onePlayerRadioButton.isSelected() &&
playAloneRadioButton.isSelected())
    {
      score[1]++;
      scoreTextField[1].setText(String.valueOf(score[1]));
    }

photoLabel[labelSelected].setIcon(photo[photoIndex[labelSele
cted]]);
```

```
      photoFound[labelSelected] = true;
      displayTimer.start();
   }

   private void displayTimerActionPerformed(ActionEvent e)
   {
      displayTimer.stop();
      if (choiceNumber == 1)
      {
         choice[0] = labelSelected;
         choiceNumber = 2;
         memory[labelSelected] = photoIndex[labelSelected];
         if (twoPlayersRadioButton.isSelected())
         {
            messageLabel.setText("Player " +
String.valueOf(playerNumber) + ", Pick Another");
            canClick = true;
         }
         else
         {
         // one player logic
            if (playerNumber == 1)
            {
               messageLabel.setText("Pick Another Box");
               canClick = true;
            }
            else
            {
               // play computer logic
               messageLabel.setText("Picking Another");
               computerTurn();
               return;
            }
         }
      }
      else
      {
         choice[1] = labelSelected;
         choiceNumber = 1;
         memory[labelSelected] = photoIndex[labelSelected];
         if (photoIndex[choice[0]] == photoIndex[choice[1]])
         {
            // a match
            matchSound.play();
            photoLabel[choice[0]].setIcon(null);
            photoLabel[choice[1]].setIcon(null);
```

```
      // clear memory so boxes are not checked again for
match
      memory[choice[0]] = 0;
      memory[choice[1]] = 0;
      score[playerNumber - 1]++;
      scoreTextField[playerNumber -
1].setText(String.valueOf(score[playerNumber - 1]));
      photosRemaining -= 2;
      if (photosRemaining == 0)
      {
        gameOver = true;
        gameOverSound.play();
        if (twoPlayersRadioButton.isSelected())
        {
          if (score[0] > score[1])
            messageLabel.setText("Player 1 Wins!");
          else if (score[1] > score[0])
            messageLabel.setText("Player 2 Wins!");
          else
            messageLabel.setText("It's a Tie!");
        }
        else
        {
          // one player logic
          if (playAloneRadioButton.isSelected())
            messageLabel.setText("All Matches Found!");
          else
          {
            // play computer logic
            if (score[0] > score[1])
              messageLabel.setText("You Win!");
            else if (score[1] > score[0])
              messageLabel.setText("Computer Wins!");
            else
              messageLabel.setText("It's a Tie!");
          }
        }
        startStopButton.doClick();
        return;
      }
      // another turn
      if (twoPlayersRadioButton.isSelected())
      {
        messageLabel.setText("Player " +
String.valueOf(playerNumber) + ", Pick Again");
        canClick = true;
      }
```

```
    else
    {
      // one player logic
      if (playerNumber == 1)
      {
        messageLabel.setText("Pick a Box");
        canClick = true;
      }
      else
      {
        // play computer logic
        messageLabel.setText("Picking Again");
        computerTurn();
        return;
      }
    }
  }
  else
  {
    //no match
    noMatchSound.play();
    photoFound[choice[0]] = false;
    photoFound[choice[1]] = false;
    photoLabel[choice[0]].setIcon(cover);
    photoLabel[choice[1]].setIcon(cover);
    // swap players
    if (twoPlayersRadioButton.isSelected())
    {
      if (playerNumber == 1)
        playerNumber = 2;
      else
        playerNumber = 1;
      messageLabel.setText("Player " +
String.valueOf(playerNumber) + ", Pick a Box");
      canClick = true;
    }
    else
    {
      // one player logic
      if (playComputerRadioButton.isSelected())
      {
        if (playerNumber == 1)
          playerNumber = 2;
        else
          playerNumber = 1;
      }
      if (playerNumber == 1)
```

```
            {
              messageLabel.setText("Pick a Box");
              canClick = true;
            }
            else
            {
              // play computer logic
              messageLabel.setText("Computer Picking");
              choiceNumber = 1;
              computerTurn();
              return;
            }
        }
      }
    }
  }

private int randomChoice()
{
  int count, n, rc;
  if (choiceNumber == 1)
    n = myRandom.nextInt(photosRemaining) + 1;
  else
    n = myRandom.nextInt(photosRemaining - 1) + 1;
  count = 0;
  for (rc = 0; rc < 20; rc++)
  {
    if (!photoFound[rc])
      count++;
    if (count == n)
      break;
  }
  return(rc);
}

private int smartChoice()
{
  int sc;
  if (choiceNumber == 1)
  {
    matchFound = checkForMatch();
    if (matchFound[0] != 0 && matchFound[1] != 0)
      sc = matchFound[0];
    else
      sc = randomChoice();
  }
  else
```

```
    {
      if (matchFound[0] != 0 && matchFound[1] != 0)
        sc = matchFound[1];
      else
      {
        matchFound = checkForMatch();
        if (matchFound[0] != 0 && matchFound[1] != 0)
        {
          if (matchFound[0] != choice[0])
            sc = matchFound[0];
          else
            sc = matchFound[1];
        }
        else
          sc = randomChoice();
      }
    }
    return (sc);
  }

private void computerTurn()
{
  int threshold = 0;
  if (choiceNumber == 1)
  {
    switch (difficulty)
    {
      case 1:
        threshold = 25;
        break;
      case 2:
        threshold = 50;
        break;
      case 3:
        threshold = 75;
        break;
      case 4:
        threshold = 90;
        break;
    }
    if (myRandom.nextInt(100) < threshold)
      smartComputer = true;
    else
      smartComputer = false;
  }
  if (smartComputer)
    labelSelected = smartChoice();
```

```java
    else
      labelSelected = randomChoice();
    delayTimer.start();
}

private void delayTimerActionPerformed(ActionEvent e)
{
  delayTimer.stop();
  showSelectedLabel();
}

private int[] checkForMatch()
{
  int[] matches = new int[2];
  matches[0] = 0;
  matches[1] = 0;
  for (int i = 0; i < 20; i++)
  {
    for (int j = 0; j < 20; j++)
    {
      if (memory[i] != 0 && memory[i] == memory[j] && i !=
j)
      {
        matches[0] = i;
        matches[1] = j;
      }
    }
  }
  return(matches);
}
}
```

5

Pizza Delivery Project

Review and Preview

The next project we build is a **Pizza Delivery** business simulation. You have been asked to be in charge of deliveries for the neighborhood pizza parlor for one night. You take phone orders, tell the crew how many pizzas to bake, and tell the delivery car where to go.

The program teaches mental math, logical thinking skills and good business practices. We'll see how to use multiple timers, use the list box control, and build a multiple frame application.

Pizza Delivery Project Preview

In this chapter, we will build a **Pizza Delivery** game. In this simulation game, lots of decisions need to be made. The basic idea is to read the incoming phone orders and tell the delivery car where to go. You also need to make sure you always have fresh-baked pizzas ready to go out the door. The delivery area is a grid of 20 by 20 squares. The more pizzas you sell, the more money you make!

The finished project is saved as **PizzaDelivery** in the **\KidGamesJava\KidGamesJava Projects** folder. Start NetBeans (or your IDE). Open the specified project group. Make **PizzaDelivery** the selected project. Run the project. You will see:

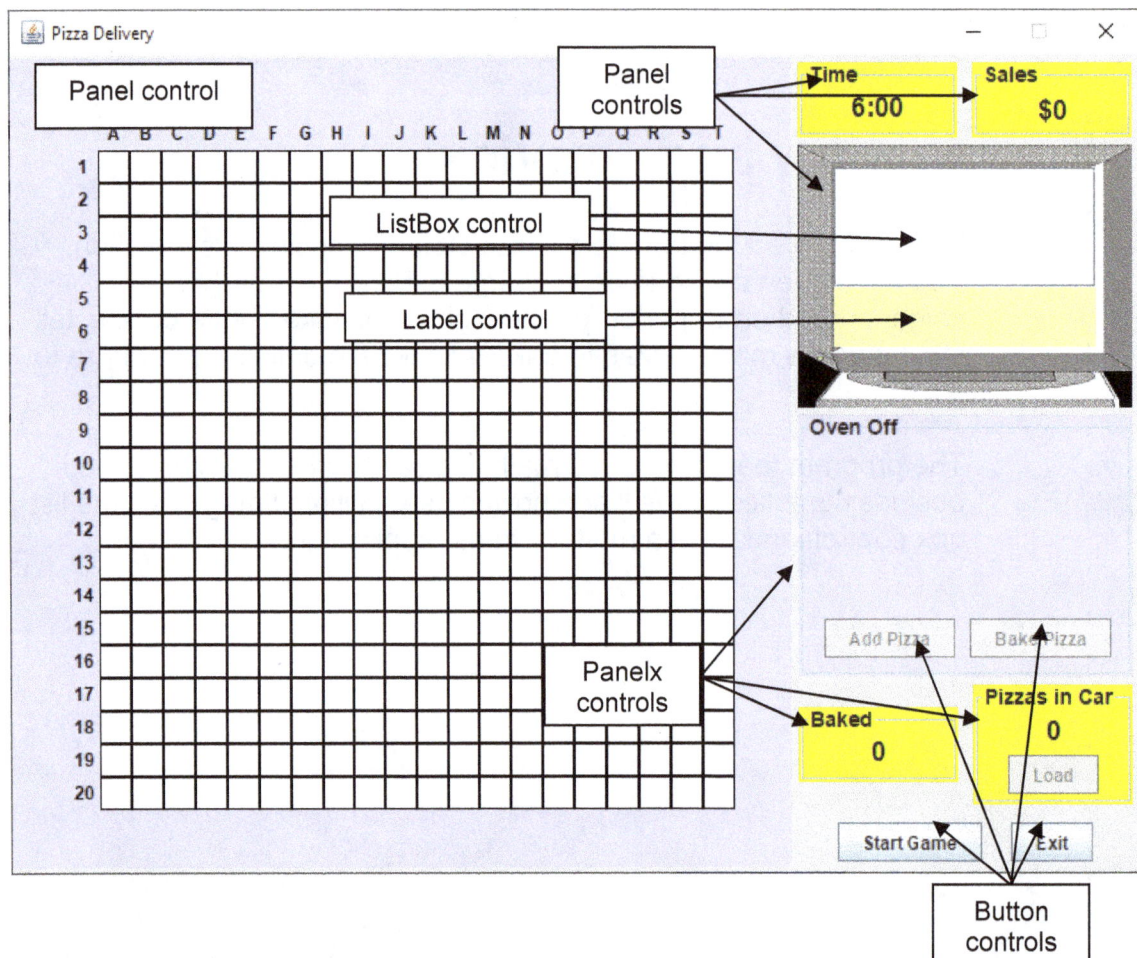

The panel control on the left of the **Pizza Delivery** frame holds the delivery grid. At the top right are panels with a single label control to display current time and current sales. The computer monitor (in a special image panel control) displays orders and status using a list box and label control. Another panel holds the pizza oven where pizzas are displayed using eight label controls. Two button controls in the panel control oven operation. The panels below the oven show how many pizzas are ready for delivery and how many are in the car (a button control loads pizzas in the car). The two button controls at the bottom are used to start/pause the game and to stop the game or exit the program.

Before running the game, let's describe its operation. You sell and deliver pizzas from 6:00 to 11:00. A clock in the upper right corner shows the time. It doesn't take 5 hours to use the program - the five hours go by in about 15 minutes, so think fast. The phone rings when an order comes in. The order box in the monitor shows what time the order was called in, the coordinates for delivery, and the number of pizzas ordered. The order is also displayed on the neighborhood grid.

In the monitor message area, you are told the current location of the car in the grid. At the beginning of the program, the car is at the pizza parlor (marked by an **X** on the grid). Panels at the bottom tell you how many pizzas are baked and ready and how many are in the car. To load pizzas in the car, click the **Load** button. To tell the car where to go, click on the grid position. The car will travel to the desired position. When it arrives, the car's horn will sound and tell you the result of the delivery. There are four possible results: (1) on-time delivery, (2) late delivery, (3) not enough pizzas in the car to make the delivery, or (4) no pizza ordered at the given location. If you make a successful delivery, the amount of sales (displayed at the top of the screen) is updated. When you need to return to the pizza parlor to load more pizzas, click the location marked by **X**.

You also need to control the pizza oven to make sure there are always pizzas available for delivery. To bake pizzas, click **Add Pizza** for each pizza you want to bake (pizzas can't be taken out once they're in). When the oven is loaded, click **Bake Pizza**. You will be told when the pizzas are ready. When the pizzas are done, a bell will ring and the pizzas are moved to the ready area. The **Baked** box always displays how many pizzas are available for loading into the car. At any time during the program, you may pause the action by clicking **Pause Game**. To restart, click **Restart Game**. To stop the program before 11:00, click **Stop Game**. Once the program stops, a summary screen will show your sales and costs results and compute your profits (if any). After reading the results, click **Return to Pizza Delivery** to play again.

This may seem like lots of instructions but the process becomes fairly obvious as you play the game. When started, the game appears in its 'stopped' state and the delivery grid will appear. At this point, you simply click **Start Game** to get things going. There are no options to select. The randomness inherent in the **Pizza Delivery** game makes each new game a different experience. Once the game starts, the first thing you notice is the phone starts ringing with orders. Here's my form after a couple of orders have come in:

At 6:01, an order for 3 pizzas was taken for delivery to column A, Row 14 (also marked on grid). At 6:06, 1 pizza was ordered at A 6. Right now, I don't have pizzas to deliver. The game starts with 8 pizzas ready to go. If I click **Load** (the car can only be loaded at the pizza parlor), those pizzas are put in the car. Then, if I click A 14 on the grid, my car goes there, beeps and makes a delivery. Then, I see:

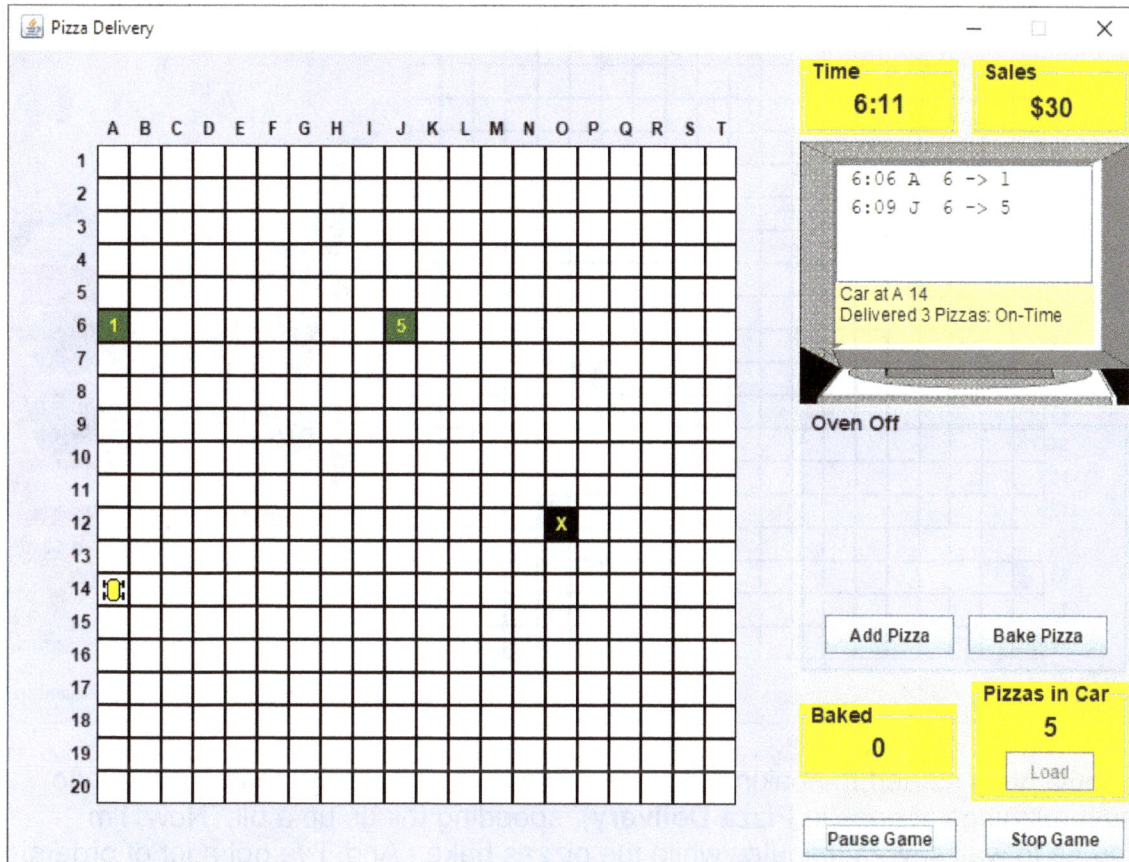

The pizzas were delivered on-time and I made $30. Notice another order came in while I was making the delivery. Next, I make the delivery at J 6. After that delivery, I'm out of pizzas and head back and stock up on more pizzas. To do this, I click the **X** mark to return to the pizza parlor.

I need more pizzas. I click the **Add Pizza** button 8 times to load the oven, then click **Bake Pizza** to start the oven (the panel turns red to show it's on):

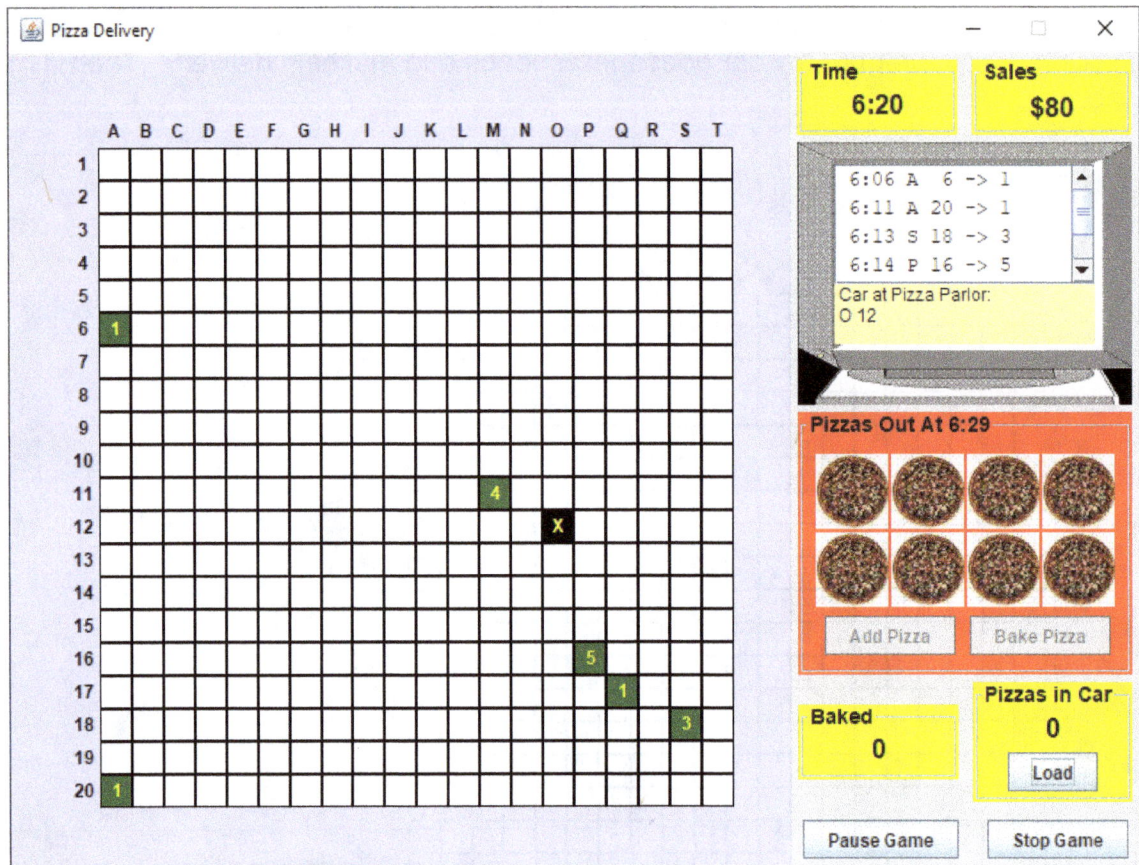

I could have started the baking process while I was out on the road (you can do several things at once in **Pizza Delivery**), speeding things up a bit. Now, I'm forced to wait several minutes while the pizzas bake. And, I've got a lot of orders! Once they're done, there are more deliveries to make and more pizzas to bake. It's a hectic night at the pizza parlor!

So, in **Pizza Delivery**, you keep baking pizzas, loading the car and sending the pizzas out to the waiting deliveries. Late deliveries are penalized and if you're too late, the customer gives up and cancels the order – just like the real world. After playing for a little over an hour, my form looks like this:

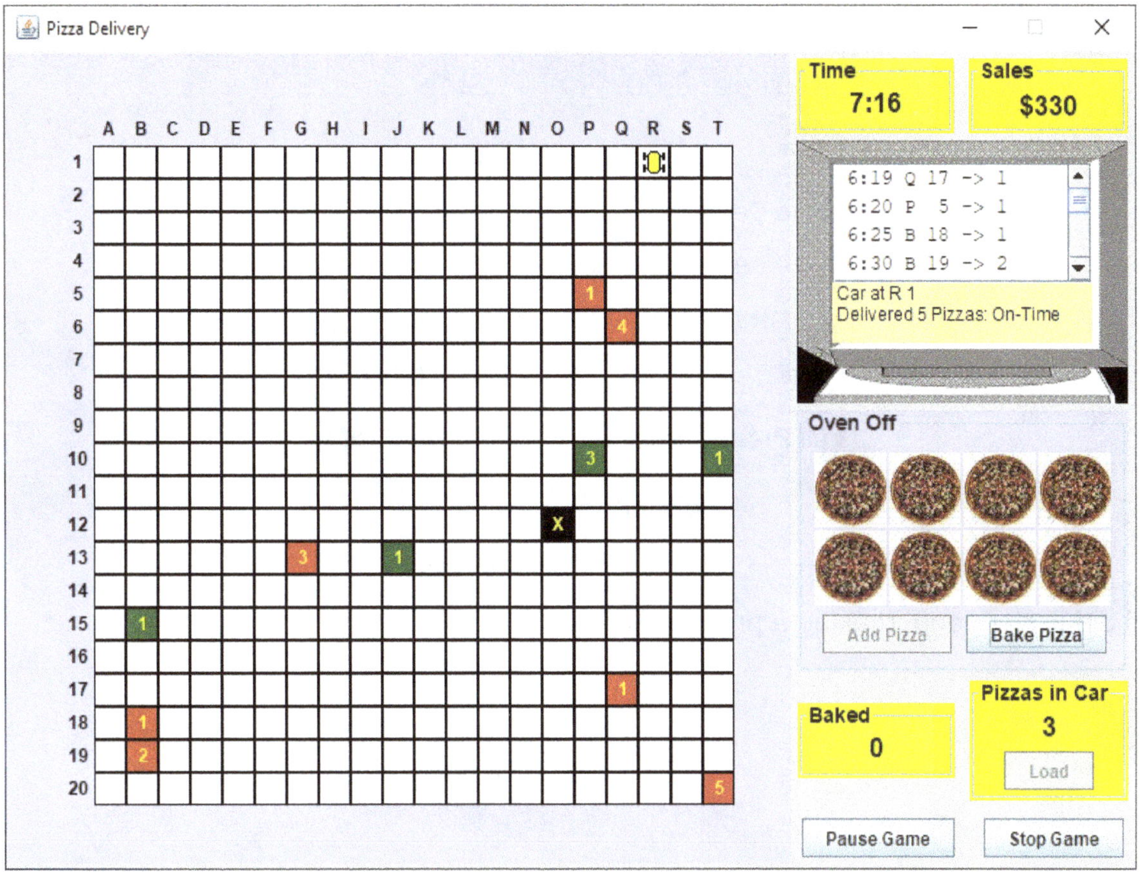

I've got lots of orders and lots of pizzas going. Order with red backgrounds indicate we're late. I need to rush those pizzas out.

I ran **Pizza Delivery** to 9:01 (closing before the usual 11:00). At that point, I clicked **Stop Game** and the following form appeared (this is the second form in the project alluded to earlier):

Pizza Delivery Sales Results   ✕

Start Time: 6:00   Stop Time: 9:01

Sales: **Costs:**

63 On-Time Deliveries $630   88 Pizzas Baked $264

10 Late Deliveries $50   360 Units Driven $36

Total Sales $680   28 Missed Deliveries $28

Total Costs $328

Total Profits: $352   **Hourly Profits: $116**

Return to Pizza Delivery

I did pretty good, making a profit of $352.

But looking at the form, I still had lots of deliveries to make and lots of wasted pizza:

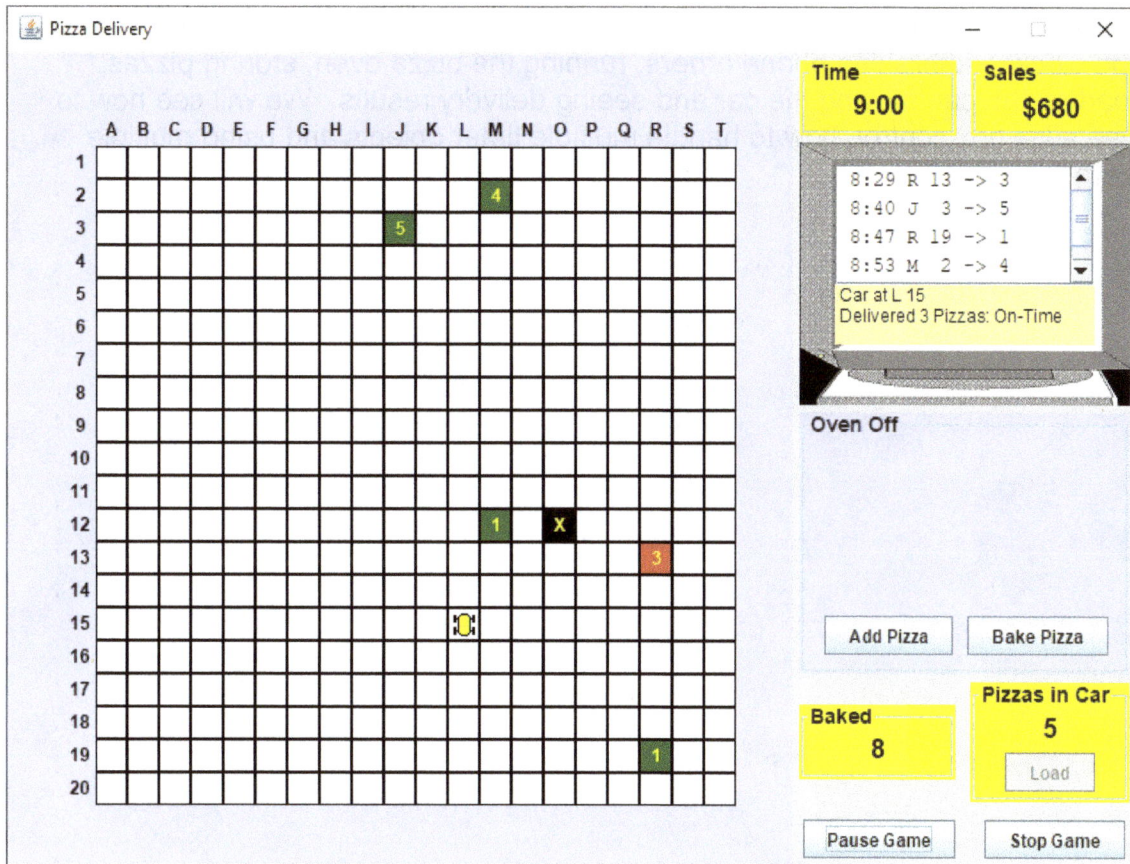

I probably could have made a lot more money in the last two hours.

Continue playing the game to understand its operation. Try playing all the way to 11:00 to see how much money you can make. Orders stop at 10:30 to allow you to finish deliveries. Click **Exit** when you're done to stop the game. Open the code file and skim over the code, if you like.

Simulations like **Pizza Delivery** are lots of fun. You get to see how your decisions affect your bottom line – net profits. And, programming such simulations are fun too – you get to make the rules to try to make the program realistic. As we build this project, we'll discuss such rules in detail. You will now build this project in stages. As you build Java projects, we always recommend taking a slow, step-by-step process. It minimizes programming errors and helps build your confidence as things come together in a complete project.

We address **frame design**. We discuss the controls needed to build both the delivery form and the results form. For the delivery form, we will show you how to build the delivery grid and establish initial conditions. And, we address **code design**. We discuss how to implement the various aspects of the game: running the clock, establishing phone orders, running the pizza oven, storing pizzas, loading the car, moving the car and seeing delivery results. We will see how to use a list box control, how to handle multiple timer objects and using multiple frames.

Pizza Delivery Frame Design

We begin building the **Pizza Delivery** project. Let's build the first frame – the one with the delivery grid, status monitor, pizza oven and car control. The results frame will be built later. Start a new project in your Java Project group – name it **PizzaDelivery**. Delete default code in file named **PizzaDelivery.java**. Once started, we suggest you immediately save the project with a name you choose. This sets up the folder and file structure needed for your project.

Build the basic frame with these properties:

PizzaDelivery Frame:
title	Pizza Delivery
resizable	false

The code is:

```java
/*
 * PizzaDelivery.java
 */
package pizzadelivery;
import javax.swing.*;
import java.awt.*;
import java.awt.event.*;

public class PizzaDelivery extends JFrame
{
  public static void main(String args[])
  {
    // create frame
    new PizzaDelivery().setVisible(true);
  }

  public PizzaDelivery()
  {
    // frame constructor
    setTitle("Pizza Delivery");
    setResizable(false);
    addWindowListener(new WindowAdapter()
    {
      public void windowClosing(WindowEvent evt)
      {
        exitForm(evt);
      }
    });
    getContentPane().setLayout(new GridBagLayout());
```

```
    GridBagConstraints gridConstraints;

    pack();
    Dimension screenSize =
Toolkit.getDefaultToolkit().getScreenSize();
    setBounds((int) (0.5 * (screenSize.width -
getWidth())), (int) (0.5 * (screenSize.height -
getHeight())), getWidth(), getHeight());
  }

  private void exitForm(WindowEvent evt)
  {
    System.exit(0);
  }
}
```

This code builds the frame, sets up the layout manager and includes code to exit the application. Run the code to make sure the frame (at least, what there is of it at this point) appears and is centered on the screen:

Let's populate our frame with other controls. All code for creating the frame and placing controls (except declarations) goes in the **PizzaDelivery** constructor.

We start by putting several panel controls on the frame. The **GridBagLayout** is:

	gridx = 0	gridx = 1	gridx = 2
gridy = 0		**timePanel**	**salesPanel**
gridy = 1		**ordersPanel**	
gridy = 2	**gridPanel**	**ovenPanel**	
gridy = 3		**readyPanel**	**inCarPanel**
gridy = 4		**buttonsPanel**	

The **gridPanel** holds the delivery grid. The **timePanel** displays the clock and the **salesPanel** shows sale figures. The **ordersPanel** displays order and car status. The **ovenPanel** is used to display and control the pizzas baking in the oven. The **readyPanel** displays the number of baked pizzas. The **inCarPanel** is used to load pizzas in the car. The **buttonsPanel** holds two buttons - one to start and pause the game and one to stop and exit the project. We will build each panel separately. Let's begin with the gridPanel.

Add the **gridPanel** to the frame with these properties:

gridPanel:

size	540, 540
color	Color(208, 208, 255), a light blue
gridx	0
gridy	0
gridheight	5

We use the Java **Color** function to define a unique color for the grid. The red, green, blue contributions were determine using the Color selection palette in the Microsoft Paint program. We use this function whenever one of the built-in colors just doesn't cut it.

The panel and its color (**gridColor**) are declared using:

```
JPanel gridPanel = new JPanel();
Color gridColor = new Color(208, 208, 255);
```

The control is placed in the frame using this code:

```
gridPanel.setPreferredSize(new Dimension(540, 540));
gridPanel.setBackground(gridColor);
gridPanel.setLayout(new GridBagLayout());
gridConstraints = new GridBagConstraints();
gridConstraints.gridx = 0;
gridConstraints.gridy = 0;
gridConstraints.gridheight = 5;
getContentPane().add(gridPanel, gridConstraints);
```

Add code in the proper locations. Run to see the empty grid panel:

Now, let's add the grid.

For the **Pizza Delivery** game, we want a delivery grid that looks like this (placed on the layout manager for the grid panel):

	A	B	C	D	E	F	G	H	I	J	K	L	M	N	O	P	Q	R	S	T
1																				
2																				
3																				
4																				
5																				
6																				
7																				
8																				
9																				
10																				
11																				
12																				
13																				
14																				
15																				
16																				
17																				
18																				
19																				
20																				

Notice we have labeling information for the columns and rows and a 20 x 20 grid used to display orders. Individual elements in the grid are referred to by a column letter and a row number (like Excel spreadsheets). We will build this grid in the **gridPanel** control using 441 (21 x 21) square label controls. Let's see how to do this.

The process is fairly straightforward. For each of the 441 label controls, we create the control, set properties and place the control in the panel control. The first row in the grid will be used to label the columns; the first column will be used to label the rows. We will ignore the label control in the upper left corner. The remaining 20 x 20 grid of label controls will be used to display orders and car motion.

First, define a class level two-dimensional array of label controls:

```
JLabel[][] deliveryGrid = new JLabel[21][21];
```

We will use the 0th elements of **deliveryGrid** to represent the column (first array index) and row (second array index) labels. We ignore **deliveryGrid[0][0]**, the upper left corner in the grid.

The code to establish this grid and display it in the grid panel control (as usual, place this after the code establishing the panel):

```
int w = (int) gridPanel.getPreferredSize().width / 24;
// j is row, i is column; build one row at a time
for (int j = 0; j < 21; j++)
{
  // start new row
  for (int i = 0; i < 21; i++)
  {
    deliveryGrid[i][j] = new JLabel();
    deliveryGrid[i][j].setPreferredSize(new Dimension(w,
w));
    deliveryGrid[i][j].setFont(new Font("Arial",
Font.BOLD, 12));

deliveryGrid[i][j].setHorizontalAlignment(SwingConstants.C
ENTER);
    gridConstraints = new GridBagConstraints();
    gridConstraints.gridy = j;
    gridConstraints.gridx =i;
    if (i == 0)
    {
      if (j != 0)
      {
        // row numbers
        deliveryGrid[i][j].setText(String.valueOf(j));
        deliveryGrid[i][j].setForeground(Color.BLACK);
      }
    }
    else if (j == 0)
    {
      if (i != 0)
      {
        // column letters
        deliveryGrid[i][j].setText(String.valueOf((char)
(i + 64)));
        deliveryGrid[i][j].setForeground(Color.BLACK);
      }
```

```
      }
      else
      {

deliveryGrid[i][j].setBorder(BorderFactory.createLineBorde
r(Color.BLACK));
        deliveryGrid[i][j].setOpaque(true);
        deliveryGrid[i][j].setBackground(Color.WHITE);
        deliveryGrid[i][j].setForeground(Color.YELLOW);
      }
      gridPanel.add(deliveryGrid[i][j], gridConstraints);
      deliveryGrid[i][j].addMouseListener(new MouseAdapter()
      {
        public void mousePressed(MouseEvent e)
        {
          deliveryGridMousePressed(e);
        }
      });
    }
  }
```

This code builds the label control grid, one row at a time. Each control is first declared, and assigned a **size**, **gridy**, and **gridx** property. We assume square controls, with the size based on the width of the panel – (1/24th of the panel, which allows for some margin space). We start at the upper left corner, working our way to the right. Other properties are assigned based on locations. Controls with column labels (**j = 0**) and row labels (**i = 0**) have no border and are given an appropriate letter or number. Internal labels (**i = 1 to 20**, **j = 1 to 20**) have a border and white background to give a grid effect. After setting properties, controls are added to the panel control. We also added a **deliveryGridMousePressed** method for each label (we will use that later to know where to move our delivery car). So add this empty method:

```
  private void deliveryGridMousePressed(MouseEvent e)
  {
  }
```

Now, let's see what the grid looks like.

Save and run the project. Like magic, you should see the grid:

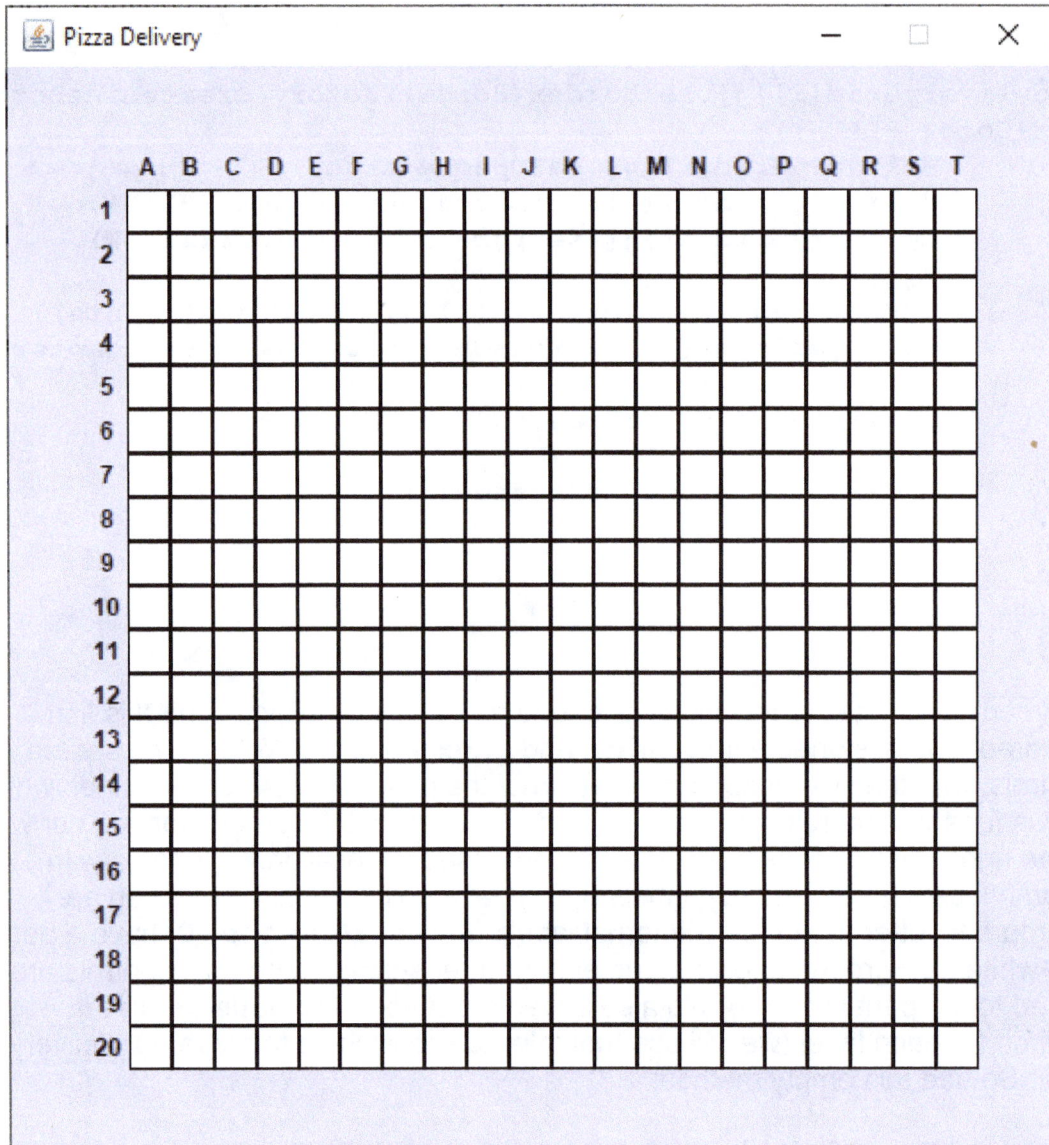

Make sure you understand how the code to add these controls work. Such code is very useful. Let's build the remaining panels.

The **timePanel** holds a single label control to display the time. The **GridBagLayout** for timePanel is:

	gridx = 0
gridy = 0	**timeLabel**

The control properties are:

timePanel:

size	110, 50
background	Yellow
title	Time
gridx	1 (on frame)
gridy	0 (on frame)
insets	5, 5, 5, 5

timeLabel:

text	6:00
font	Arial, Bold, Size 18
gridx	0 (on timePanel)
gridy	0 (on timePanel)
insets	0, 0, 5, 0

Declare the controls using:

```
JPanel timePanel = new JPanel();
JLabel timeLabel = new JLabel();
```

Add the control to the **timePanel** (which is placed in the frame) using:

```
UIManager.put("TitledBorder.font", new Font("Arial",
Font.BOLD, 14));
timePanel.setPreferredSize(new Dimension(110, 50));
timePanel.setBackground(Color.YELLOW);
timePanel.setBorder(BorderFactory.createTitledBorder("Time
"));
timePanel.setLayout(new GridBagLayout());
gridConstraints = new GridBagConstraints();
gridConstraints.gridx = 1;
gridConstraints.gridy = 0;
gridConstraints.insets = new Insets(5, 5, 5, 5);
getContentPane().add(timePanel, gridConstraints);

timeLabel.setText("6:00");
timeLabel.setFont(new Font("Arial", Font.BOLD, 18));
gridConstraints = new GridBagConstraints();
gridConstraints.gridx = 0;
gridConstraints.gridy = 0;
gridConstraints.insets = new Insets(0, 0, 5, 0);
timePanel.add(timeLabel, gridConstraints);
```

The first line here uses the **UIManager** to set the font for the panel borders.

Add this code in the proper locations. Run to see:

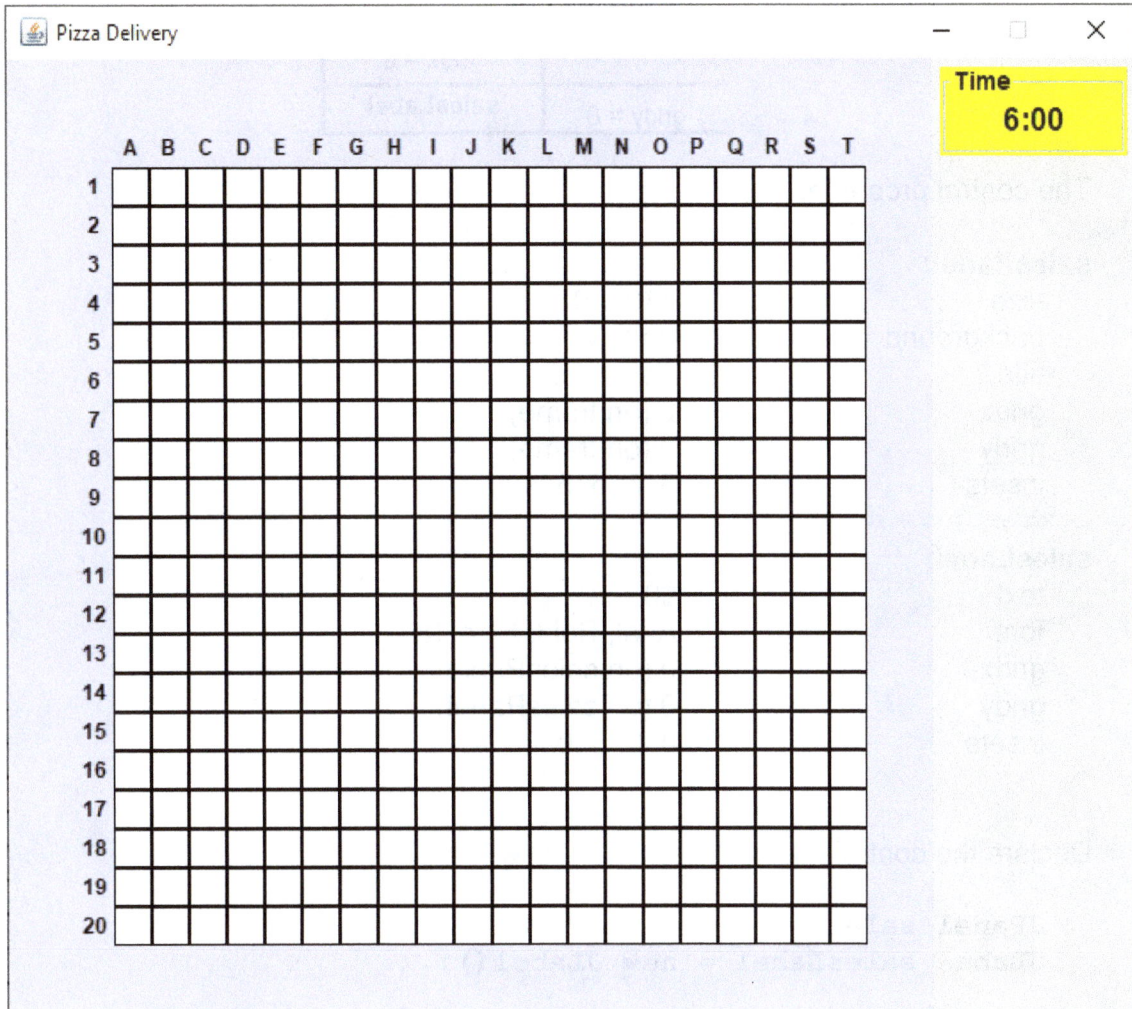

The time panel appears.

The **salesPanel** holds a single label control to show the amount of sales. The **GridBagLayout** for salesPanel is:

	gridx = 0
gridy = 0	**salesLabel**

The control properties are:

salesPanel:

size	110, 50
background	Yellow
title	Sales
gridx	2 (on frame)
gridy	0 (on frame)
insets	5, 5, 5, 5

salesLabel:

text	$0
font	Arial, Bold, Size 18
gridx	0 (on salesPanel)
gridy	0 (on salesPanel)
insets	0, 0, 5, 0

Declare the controls using:

```
JPanel salesPanel = new JPanel();
JLabel salesLabel = new JLabel();
```

Add the control to the **salesPanel** (which is placed in the frame) using:

```
salesPanel.setPreferredSize(new Dimension(110, 50));
salesPanel.setBackground(Color.YELLOW);
salesPanel.setBorder(BorderFactory.createTitledBorder("Sal
es"));
salesPanel.setLayout(new GridBagLayout());
gridConstraints = new GridBagConstraints();
gridConstraints.gridx = 2;
gridConstraints.gridy = 0;
gridConstraints.insets = new Insets(5, 5, 5, 5);
getContentPane().add(salesPanel, gridConstraints);

salesLabel.setText("$0");
salesLabel.setFont(new Font("Arial", Font.BOLD, 18));
gridConstraints = new GridBagConstraints();
gridConstraints.gridx = 0;
gridConstraints.gridy = 0;
gridConstraints.insets = new Insets(0, 0, 5, 0);
salesPanel.add(salesLabel, gridConstraints);
```

Add this code in the proper locations. Run to see:

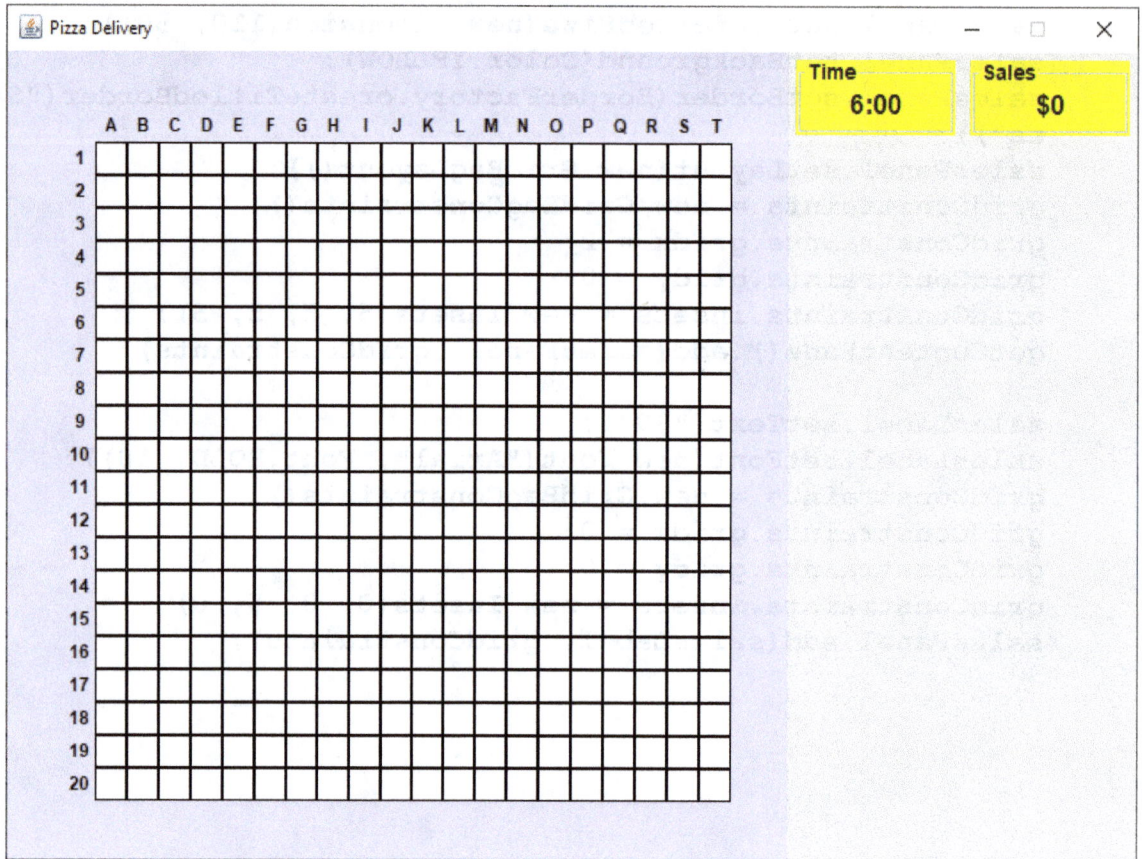

The sales panel is now in the frame.

The **ordersPanel** hosts a list box and text area control to keep you informed of order and delivery status. We also want a background image (a computer monitor) to appear in the panel. The normal panel control cannot host such a graphic, but the **ImagePanel** (seen first in the Tic Tac Toe project) can do the job. So, first add this code after the class describing the Pizza Delivery project:

```java
class ImagePanel extends JPanel
{
  private Image img;
  public ImagePanel(Image img)
  {
   this.img = img;
  }
  public void paintComponent(Graphics g)
  {
    g.drawImage(img, 0, 0, null);
  }
}
```

Recall the img property of this extended JPanel is used to define the graphic.

First, we will construct the **ordersPanel** control (with graphic) and put it in the frame. Use these properties:

ordersPanel (ImagePanel):

img	monitor.gif (included in the **\KidGamesJava\KidGamesJava Projects\PizzaDelivery** folder)
size	230, 175
gridx	1 (on frame)
gridy	1 (on frame)
gridwidth	2

Make sure to copy the monitor.gif graphic file into the folder you use to build your project. The panel size matches the size of the graphic.

Declare and create the panel:

```
ImagePanel ordersPanel = new ImagePanel(new
ImageIcon("monitor.gif").getImage());
```

The code to set the properties and place the panel in the frame:

```
ordersPanel.setPreferredSize(new Dimension(230, 175));
ordersPanel.setLayout(new GridBagLayout());
gridConstraints = new GridBagConstraints();
gridConstraints.gridx = 1;
gridConstraints.gridy = 1;
gridConstraints.gridwidth = 2;
gridConstraints.insets = new Insets(0, 5, 5, 5);
getContentPane().add(ordersPanel, gridConstraints);
```

Run. The monitor graphic should appear:

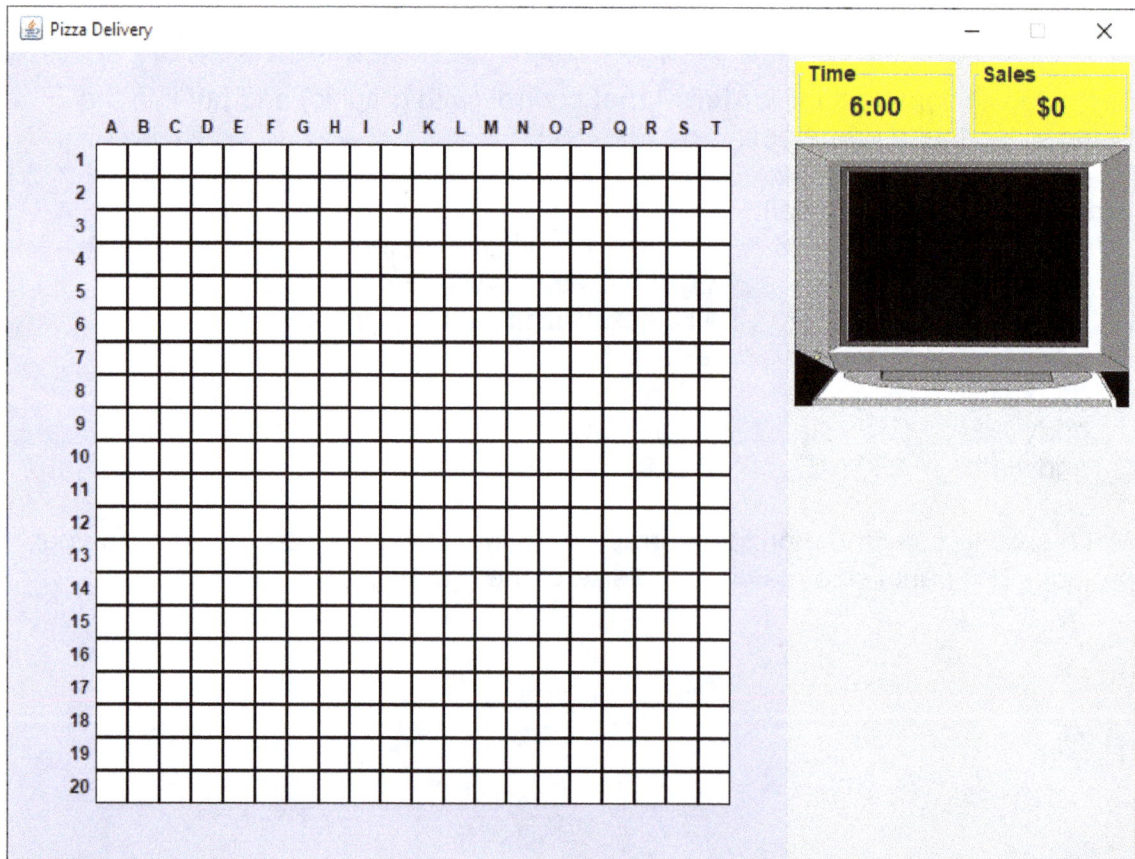

The **ordersPanel** will hold two other controls. The **GridBagLayout** for ordersPanel is:

	gridx = 0
gridy = 0	**ordersScrollPane (contains ordersList)**
gridy = 1	**messageTextArea**

The control properties:

ordersScrollPane:

size	180, 80
viewportView	ordersLlist
gridx	0
gridy	0

ordersList:

font	Courier New, PLAIN, Size 14
model	ordersListModel

messageTextArea:

size	180, 40
editable	false
opaque	true
color	Color(255, 255, 176), a pale yellow
gridx	0
gridy	1
insets	0, 0, 25, 0

The sizing and position properties were obtained via trial and error. You may want to review use of the Swing list control.

These new controls are declared using (we've also added a color declaration):

```
JScrollPane ordersScrollPane = new JScrollPane();
JList ordersList = new JList();
DefaultListModel ordersListModel = new DefaultListModel();
JTextArea messageTextArea = new JTextArea();Color
messageColor = new Color(255, 255, 176);
```

The controls are placed in the **ordersPanel** using:

```
ordersScrollPane.setPreferredSize(new Dimension(180, 80));
ordersScrollPane.setViewportView(ordersList);
ordersList.setFont(new Font("Courier New", Font.PLAIN,
14));
ordersList.setModel(ordersListModel);
gridConstraints = new GridBagConstraints();
gridConstraints.gridx = 0;
gridConstraints.gridy = 0;
ordersPanel.add(ordersScrollPane, gridConstraints);

messageTextArea.setPreferredSize(new Dimension(180, 40));
messageTextArea.setEditable(false);
messageTextArea.setOpaque(true);
messageTextArea.setBackground(messageColor);
messageTextArea.setFont(new Font("Arial", Font.PLAIN,
12));
gridConstraints = new GridBagConstraints();
gridConstraints.gridx = 0;
gridConstraints.gridy = 1;
gridConstraints.insets = new Insets(0, 0, 25, 0);
ordersPanel.add(messageTextArea, gridConstraints);
```

Add this code in the proper locations. Run to see:

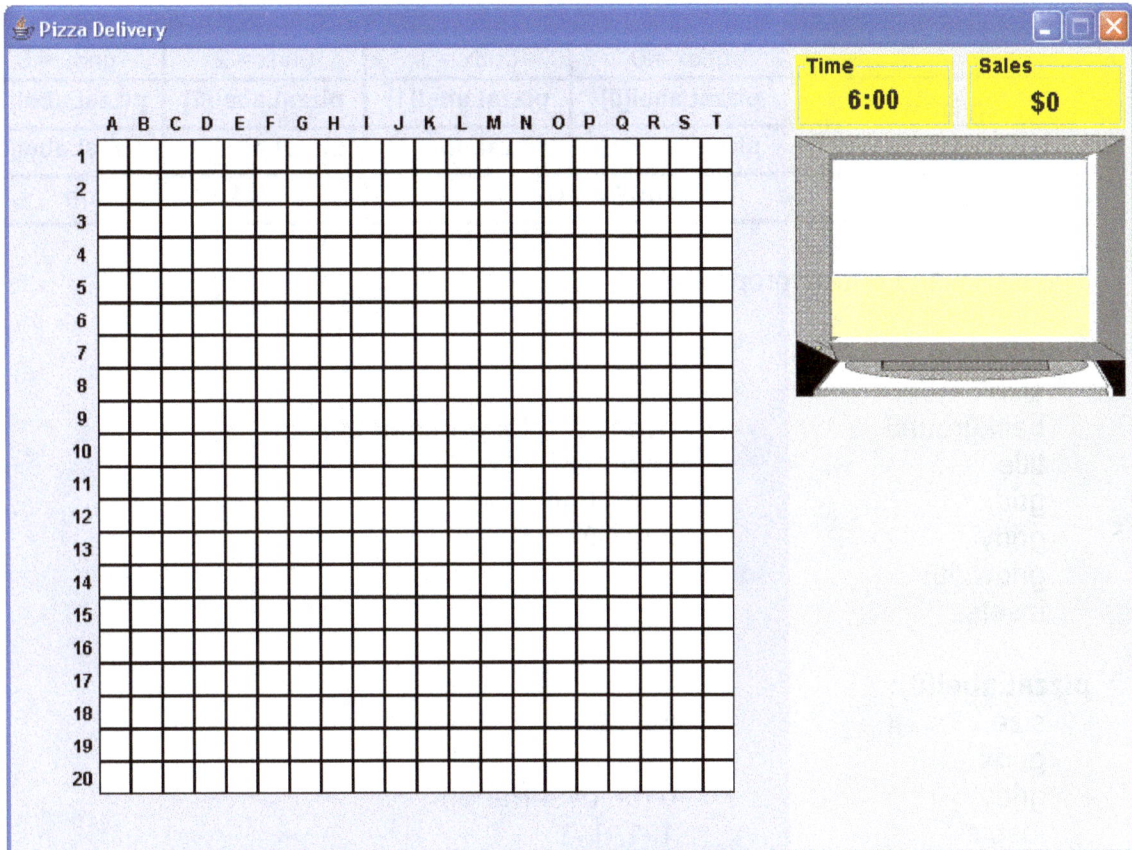

The empty list box and blank yellow text area appear on the monitor graphic.

The **ovenPanel** will hold eight label controls (to display baking pizzas) and two buttons used to control the oven. The **GridBagLayout** for ovenPanel is:

	gridx = 0	gridx = 1	gridx = 2	gridx = 3
gridy = 0	pizzaLabel[0]	pizzaLabel[1]	pizzaLabel[2]	pizzaLabel[3]
gridy =1	pizzaLabel[4]	pizzaLabel[5]	pizzaLabel[6]	pizzaLabel[7]
gridy = 2	addPizzaButton		bakePizzaButton	

The panel and button properties:

ovenPanel:
size	230, 175
background	ovenOffColor (defined in code)
title	Oven Off
gridx	1 (on frame)
gridy	2 (on frame)
gridwidth	2
insets	0, 5, 5, 5

pizzaLabel[0]:
size	50, 50
gridx	0 (on ovenPanel)
gridy	0 (on ovenPanel)
insets	1, 1, 1, 1

pizzaLabel[1]:
size	50, 50
gridx	1 (on ovenPanel)
gridy	0 (on ovenPanel)
insets	1, 1, 1, 1

pizzaLabel[2]:
size	50, 50
gridx	2 (on ovenPanel)
gridy	0 (on ovenPanel)
insets	1, 1, 1, 1

pizzaLabel[3]:
size	50, 50
gridx	3 (on ovenPanel)
gridy	0 (on ovenPanel)
insets	1, 1, 1, 1

pizzaLabel[4]:
size	50, 50
gridx	0 (on ovenPanel)
gridy	1 (on ovenPanel)
insets	1, 1, 1, 1

pizzaLabel[5]:
size	50, 50
gridx	1 (on ovenPanel)
gridy	1 (on ovenPanel)
insets	1, 1, 1, 1

pizzaLabel[6]:
size	50, 50
gridx	2 (on ovenPanel)
gridy	1 (on ovenPanel)
insets	1, 1, 1, 1

pizzaLabel[7]:
size	50, 50
gridx	3 (on ovenPanel)
gridy	1 (on ovenPanel)
insets	1, 1, 1, 1

addPizzaButton:
text	Add Pizza
enabled	false
gridx	0 (on ovenPanel)
gridy	2 (on ovenPanel)
gridwidth	2
insets	5, 0, 0, 0

bakePizzaButton:
text	Bake Pizza
enabled	false
gridx	2 (on ovenPanel)
gridy	2 (on ovenPanel)
gridwidth	2
insets	5, 0, 0, 0

These controls (and new color declaration, same as used for grid) are declared using:

```
JPanel ovenPanel = new JPanel();
JLabel[] pizzaLabel = new JLabel[8];
JButton addPizzaButton = new JButton();
JButton bakePizzaButton = new JButton();
Color ovenOffColor = new Color(208, 208, 255);
```

The controls are placed in the **ovenPanel** (which is placed in the frame) using:

```
ovenPanel.setPreferredSize(new Dimension(230, 175));
ovenPanel.setBackground(ovenOffColor);
ovenPanel.setBorder(BorderFactory.createTitledBorder("Oven
Off"));
ovenPanel.setLayout(new GridBagLayout());
gridConstraints = new GridBagConstraints();
gridConstraints.gridx = 1;
gridConstraints.gridy = 2;
gridConstraints.gridwidth = 2;
gridConstraints.insets = new Insets(0, 5, 5, 5);
getContentPane().add(ovenPanel, gridConstraints);

for (int i = 0; i < 8; i++)
{
  pizzaLabel[i] = new JLabel();
  pizzaLabel[i].setPreferredSize(new Dimension(50, 50));
  gridConstraints = new GridBagConstraints();
  gridConstraints.gridx = i % 4;
  gridConstraints.gridy = i / 4;
  gridConstraints.insets = new Insets(1, 1, 1, 1);
  ovenPanel.add(pizzaLabel[i], gridConstraints);
}

addPizzaButton.setText("Add Pizza");
addPizzaButton.setEnabled(false);
gridConstraints = new GridBagConstraints();
gridConstraints.gridx = 0;
gridConstraints.gridy = 2;
gridConstraints.gridwidth = 2;
gridConstraints.insets = new Insets(5, 0, 0, 0);
ovenPanel.add(addPizzaButton, gridConstraints);
addPizzaButton.addActionListener(new ActionListener()
{
  public void actionPerformed(ActionEvent e)
  {
    addPizzaButtonActionPerformed(e);
```

```
  }
});

bakePizzaButton.setText("Bake Pizza");
bakePizzaButton.setEnabled(false);
gridConstraints = new GridBagConstraints();
gridConstraints.gridx = 2;
gridConstraints.gridy = 2;
gridConstraints.gridwidth = 2;
gridConstraints.insets = new Insets(5, 0, 0, 0);
ovenPanel.add(bakePizzaButton, gridConstraints);
bakePizzaButton.addActionListener(new ActionListener()
{
  public void actionPerformed(ActionEvent e)
  {
    bakePizzaButtonActionPerformed(e);
  }
});
```

This code also adds listeners for each button. Add these empty methods with the other methods:

```
private void addPizzaButtonActionPerformed(ActionEvent e)
{
}

private void bakePizzaButtonActionPerformed(ActionEvent e)
{
}
```

Add this code in the proper locations. Run to see:

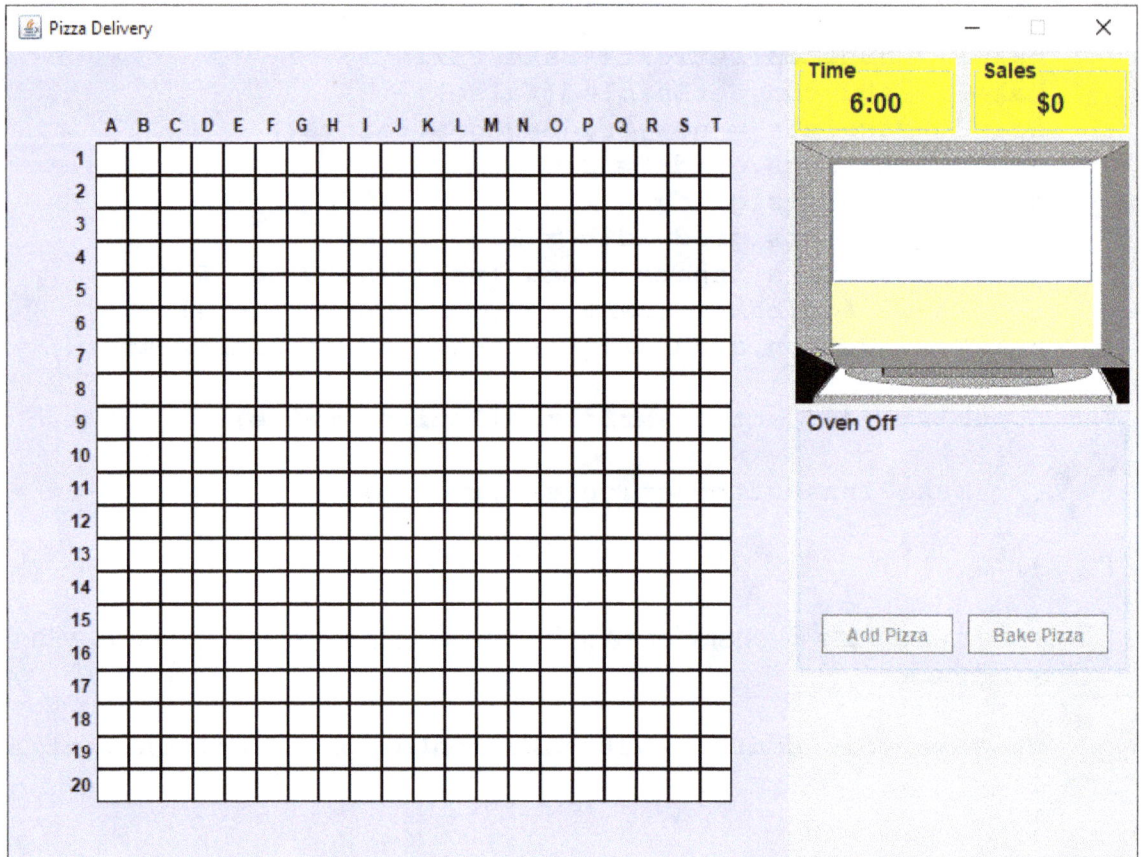

The oven (with no pizzas) appears.

The **readyPanel** holds a single label control to show the number of baked pizzas. The **GridBagLayout** for readyPanel is:

	gridx = 0
gridy = 0	**readyLabel**

The control properties are:

readyPanel:

size	110, 50
background	Yellow
title	Baked
gridx	1 (on frame)
gridy	3 (on frame)
insets	0, 5, 5, 5

readyLabel:

text	0
font	Arial, Bold, Size 18
gridx	0 (on readyPanel)
gridy	0 (on readyPanel)
insets	0, 0, 5, 0

Declare the controls using:

```
JPanel readyPanel = new JPanel();
JLabel readyLabel = new JLabel();
```

Add the control to the **readyPanel** (which is placed in the frame) using:

```
readyPanel.setPreferredSize(new Dimension(110, 50));
readyPanel.setBackground(Color.YELLOW);
readyPanel.setBorder(BorderFactory.createTitledBorder("Bak
ed"));
readyPanel.setLayout(new GridBagLayout());
gridConstraints = new GridBagConstraints();
gridConstraints.gridx = 1;
gridConstraints.gridy = 3;
gridConstraints.insets = new Insets(0, 5, 5, 5);
getContentPane().add(readyPanel, gridConstraints);

readyLabel.setText("0");
readyLabel.setFont(new Font("Arial", Font.BOLD, 18));
gridConstraints = new GridBagConstraints();
gridConstraints.gridx = 0;
gridConstraints.gridy = 0;
gridConstraints.insets = new Insets(0, 0, 5, 0);
readyPanel.add(readyLabel, gridConstraints);
```

Add this code in the proper locations. Run to see:

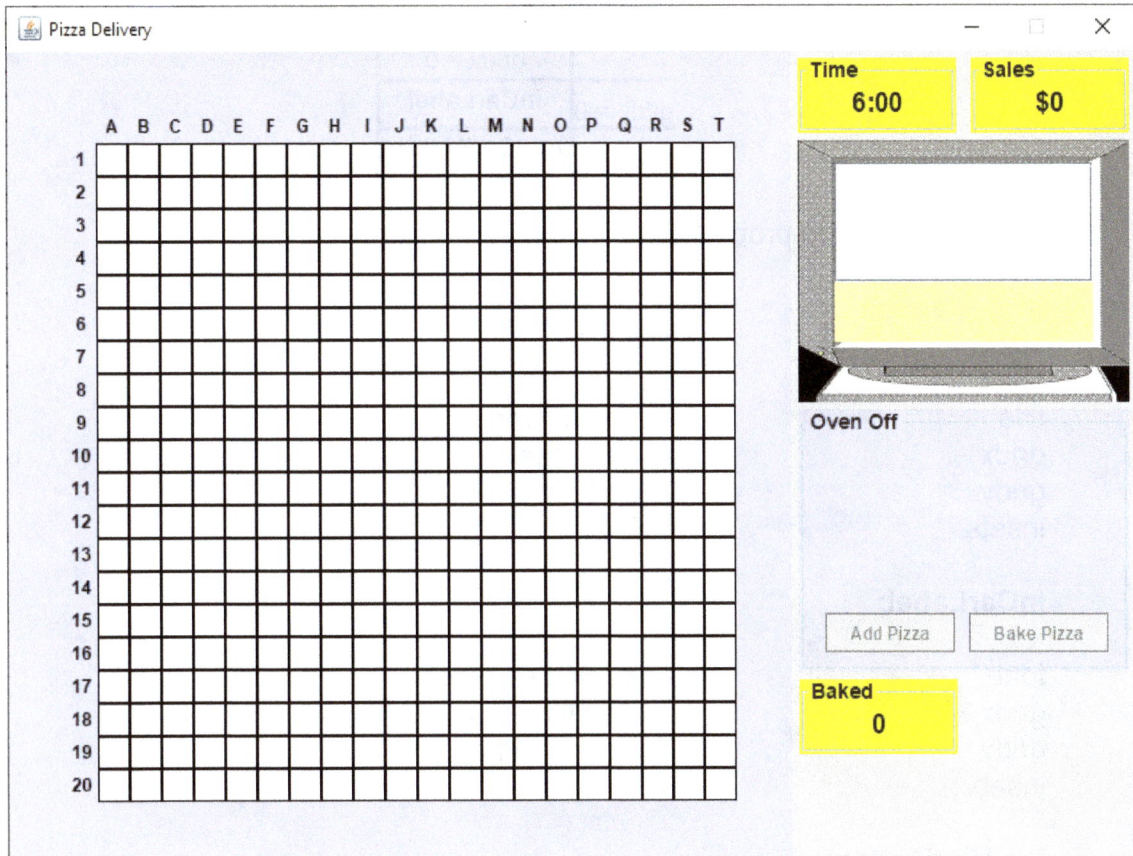

The ready panel is now in the frame.

The **inCarPanel** has a label control and a button to load pizzas in the car.. The **GridBagLayout** for inCarPanel is:

	gridx = 0
gridy = 0	**inCarLabel**
gridy =1	**loadCarButton]**

The panel and button properties:

inCarPanel:
size	110, 80
color	Yellow
title	Pizzas in Car
gridx	2 (on frame)
gridy	3 (on frame)
insets	0, 5, 5, 5

inCarLabel:
text	0
font	Arial, BOLD, Size 18
gridx	0 (on inCarPanel)
gridy	0 (on inCarPanel)
insets	0, 0, 5, 0

loadCarButton:
text	Load Car
enabled	false
gridx	0 (on inCarPanel)
gridy	1 (on inCarPanel)
gridwidth	2
insets	5, 0, 0, 0

These controls are declared using:

```
JPanel inCarPanel = new JPanel();
JLabel inCarLabel = new JLabel();
JButton loadCarButton = new JButton();
```

The controls are placed in the **inCarPanel** (which is placed in the frame) using:

```
inCarPanel.setPreferredSize(new Dimension(110, 80));
inCarPanel.setBackground(Color.YELLOW);
inCarPanel.setBorder(BorderFactory.createTitledBorder("Piz
zas in Car"));
inCarPanel.setLayout(new GridBagLayout());
gridConstraints = new GridBagConstraints();
gridConstraints.gridx = 2;
gridConstraints.gridy = 3;
gridConstraints.insets = new Insets(0, 5, 5, 5);
getContentPane().add(inCarPanel, gridConstraints);

inCarLabel.setText("0");
inCarLabel.setFont(new Font("Arial", Font.BOLD, 18));
gridConstraints = new GridBagConstraints();
gridConstraints.gridx = 0;
gridConstraints.gridy = 0;
gridConstraints.insets = new Insets(0, 0, 5, 0);
inCarPanel.add(inCarLabel, gridConstraints);

loadCarButton.setText("Load");
loadCarButton.setEnabled(false);
gridConstraints = new GridBagConstraints();
gridConstraints.gridx = 0;
gridConstraints.gridy = 1;
inCarPanel.add(loadCarButton, gridConstraints);
loadCarButton.addActionListener(new ActionListener()
{
  public void actionPerformed(ActionEvent e)
  {
    loadCarButtonActionPerformed(e);
  }
});
```

This code also adds a listeners for the button. Add this empty method with the other methods:

```
private void loadCarButtonActionPerformed(ActionEvent e)
{
}
```

Add this code in the proper locations. Run to see the new panel has been added:

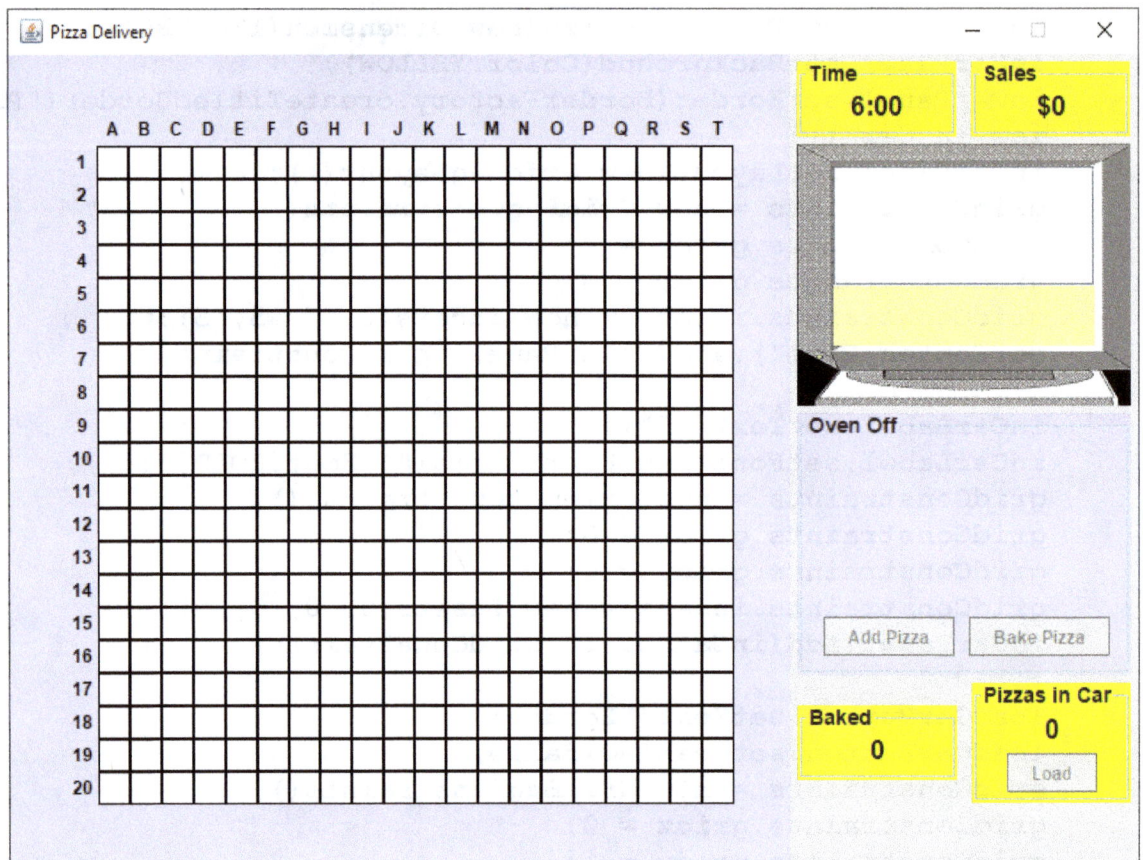

One last panel and we're done.

The **buttonsPanel** will hold two buttons used to control game play. The **GridBagLayout** for buttonsPanel is:

	gridx = 0	gridx = 1
gridy = 0	startPauseButton	exitStopButton

The panel and button properties:

buttonsPanel:
size	230, 40
gridx	1 (on frame)
gridy	4 (on frame)
gridwidth	2

startPauseButton:
text	Start Game
gridx	0 (on buttonsPanel)
gridy	0 (on buttonsPanel)
insets	0, 0, 0, 10

exitStopButton:
text	Exit
gridx	1 (on buttonsPanel)
gridy	0 (on buttonsPanel)
insets	0, 10, 0, 0

These controls are declared using:

```
JPanel buttonsPanel = new JPanel();
JButton startPauseButton = new JButton();
JButton exitStopButton = new JButton();
```

The buttons are placed in the **buttonsPanel** (which is placed in the frame) using:

```
buttonsPanel.setPreferredSize(new Dimension(230, 40));
buttonsPanel.setLayout(new GridBagLayout());
gridConstraints = new GridBagConstraints();
gridConstraints.gridx = 1;
gridConstraints.gridy = 4;
gridConstraints.gridwidth = 2;
getContentPane().add(buttonsPanel, gridConstraints);

startPauseButton.setText("Start Game");
gridConstraints = new GridBagConstraints();
gridConstraints.gridx = 0;
gridConstraints.gridy = 0;
```

```
gridConstraints.insets = new Insets(0, 0, 0, 10);
buttonsPanel.add(startPauseButton, gridConstraints);
startPauseButton.addActionListener(new ActionListener()
{
  public void actionPerformed(ActionEvent e)
  {
    startPauseButtonActionPerformed(e);
  }
});

exitStopButton.setText("Exit");
gridConstraints = new GridBagConstraints();
gridConstraints.gridx = 1;
gridConstraints.gridy = 0;
gridConstraints.insets = new Insets(0, 10, 0, 0);
buttonsPanel.add(exitStopButton, gridConstraints);
exitStopButton.addActionListener(new ActionListener()
{
  public void actionPerformed(ActionEvent e)
  {
    exitStopButtonActionPerformed(e);
  }
});
```

This code also adds listeners for each button. Add these empty methods with the other methods:

```
private void startPauseButtonActionPerformed(ActionEvent
e)
{
}

private void exitStopButtonActionPerformed(ActionEvent e)
{
}
```

Add this code in the proper locations. Run to see:

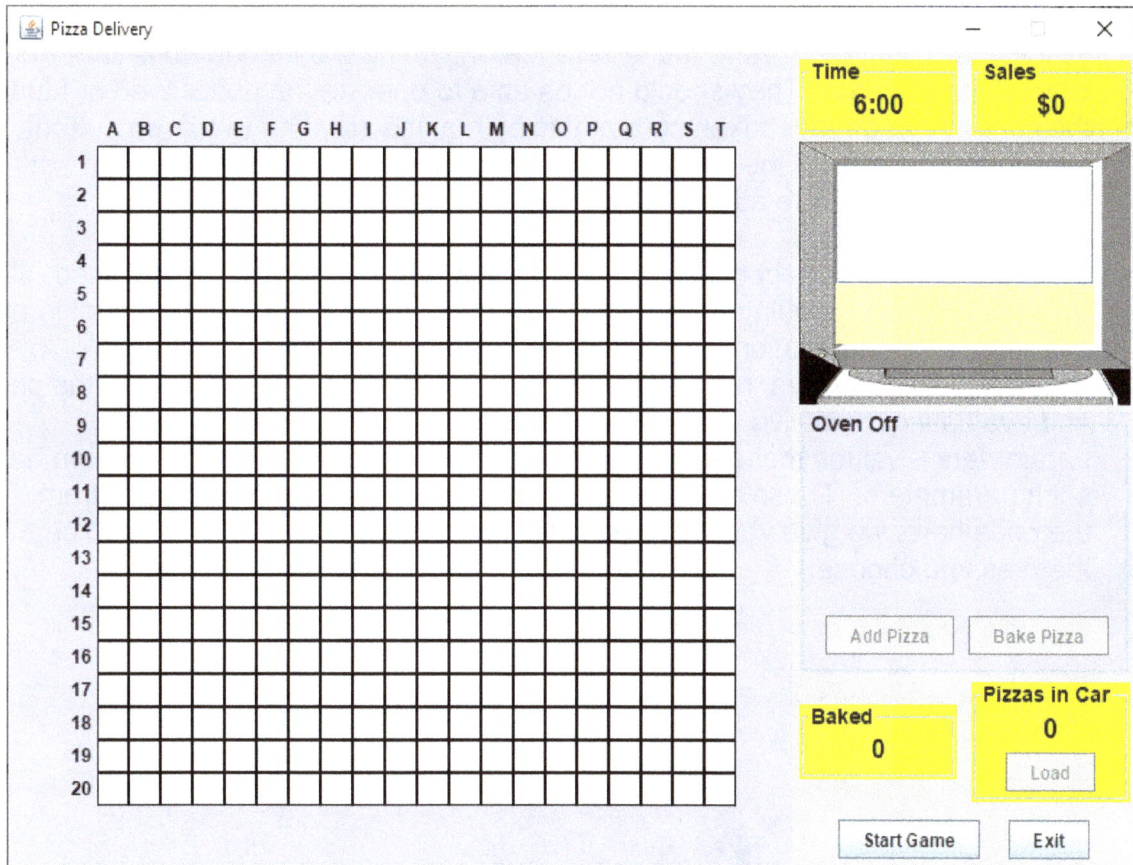

This completes the frame design. You should be able to identify all the controls in the game. We will now begin writing the remaining code for the game. We will write the code in several steps. As a first step, we will make sure the game is initialized properly. Then, we add additional elements to the game, one at a time. During the code development process, recognize you may modify a particular method several times before arriving at the finished product.

Code Design – Initializing Stopped State

When initialized, we need to make sure the only thing a user can do is click on **Start Game** or **Exit**. They should not be able to operate the pizza oven or load the car. We've already taken care of this by making sure the two oven buttons and the button to load the car are not enabled initially (the properties were set when the controls were added to the program).

Save and run the project making sure the oven and car loading are disabled. If not, set the corresponding enabled properties to false. We now begin adding other elements to our simulation, one at a time. We add code for running the clock, accepting phone orders, running the pizza oven, loading the car, moving the car and evaluating the deliveries. Each element will require certain "tuning" parameters – values that define how the simulation works. Every simulation has such parameters. These are constants you adjust as you define the program. In the code here, we give you values of such constants we use. Feel free to change them as you choose.

Code Design – Clock

The first element we add to the **Pizza Delivery** is the clock that keeps track of time. Recall the clock starts at 6:00 and stops at 11:00. We don't want the game to actually last five hours, so we speed things up a bit. We need to decide how fast we want the five hours to really go by and still be able to play the game. This is one of the tuning parameters we discussed.

The clock will be controlled by a timer object named **clockTimer**. With each event generated by this timer, we will add one minute to the clock. We want to define a constant (**mSecPerMinute**) which tells us how many milliseconds (the **delay** property of **clockTimer**) should elapse for each minute on the clock. We choose to take approximately 15 minutes to play a complete game, or to simulate 300 minutes (5 hours x 60 minutes/hour) of pizza deliveries. So, we need invoke the timer's event 300 times in 900000 milliseconds (15 minutes x 60 seconds/minute x 1000 milliseconds/second). The constant we use is thus:

> **mSecPerMinute** = 900000 / 300 = **3000** milliseconds/minute

> Add this constant to the class level declarations area:

> ```
> final int mSecPerMin = 3000;
> ```

Declare the timer object:

> ```
> Timer clockTimer;
> ```

Add the timer object to the project using a delay of **mSecPerMin**:

> ```
> clockTimer = new Timer(mSecPerMin, new ActionListener()
> {
>   public void actionPerformed(ActionEvent e)
>   {
>     clockTimerActionPerformed(e);
>   }
> });
> ```

The **clockTimerActionPerformed** method will implement the clock code.

As mentioned, with each event generated by the timer, we add one minute to the clock display. Add these class level declarations to keep track of the time:

```
int clockHour, clockMinute;
```

The corresponding code in the **clockTimerActionPerformed** method is:

```
private void clockTimerActionPerformed(ActionEvent e)
{
  clockMinute++;
  if (clockMinute > 59)
  {
    clockMinute = 0;
    clockHour++;
    if (clockHour == 11)
    {
      timeLabel.setText("11:00");
      exitStopButton.doClick();
      return;
    }
  }
  String t = String.valueOf(clockHour) + ":";
  if (clockMinute < 10)
    t += "0";
  timeLabel.setText(t + String.valueOf(clockMinute));
}
```

Note how the displayed time is formatted. Also, notice once 11:00 is reached, the game stops by clicking **exitStopButton**.

Now, we'll write the code that starts, pauses, restarts and stops the clock in **Pizza Delivery**. We also add code that exits the game. Two buttons control the game, **startPauseButton** and **exitStopButton**. These buttons have certain interactions. The **startPauseButton** control can have three possible **text** properties. If the **text** property is **Start Game** when clicked, the game is initialized and put in playing mode using:

> ➢ Change **text** to **Pause Game**.
> ➢ Initialize time to 6:00.
> ➢ Start **clockTimer**.
> ➢ Change **text** of **exitStopButton** to **Stop Game**.

When **text** property is **Pause Game** and the button is clicked, we enter pause mode:

> ➢ Change **text** to **Restart Game**.
> ➢ Stop **clockTimer**.
> ➢ Disable **exitStopButton**.

When **text** property is **Restart Game** and the button is clicked, we enter playing mode:

> ➢ Change **text** to **Pause Game**.
> ➢ Start **clockTimer**.
> ➢ Enable **exitStopButton**.

The code that covers the above steps is in the
startPauseButtonActionPerformed method:

```java
private void startPauseButtonActionPerformed(ActionEvent
e)
{
  if (startPauseButton.getText().equals("Start Game"))
  {
    startPauseButton.setText("Pause Game");
    exitStopButton.setText("Stop Game");
    clockHour = 6;
    clockMinute = 0;
    timeLabel.setText("6:00");
    clockTimer.start();
  }
  else if (startPauseButton.getText().equals("Pause
Game"))
  {
    startPauseButton.setText("Restart Game");
    exitStopButton.setEnabled(false);
    clockTimer.stop();
  }
  else
  {
    // game restarted
    startPauseButton.setText("Pause Game");
    exitStopButton.setEnabled(true);
    clockTimer.start();
  }
}
```

Save and run the project. Click **Start Game** and the clock should begin counting up the minutes. Try the pause and restart feature. How long does it take one hour to go by? It should take about 3 minutes based on our "tuning" parameter (**mSecPerMinute**). Here's the frame after running a little over one hour of game time:

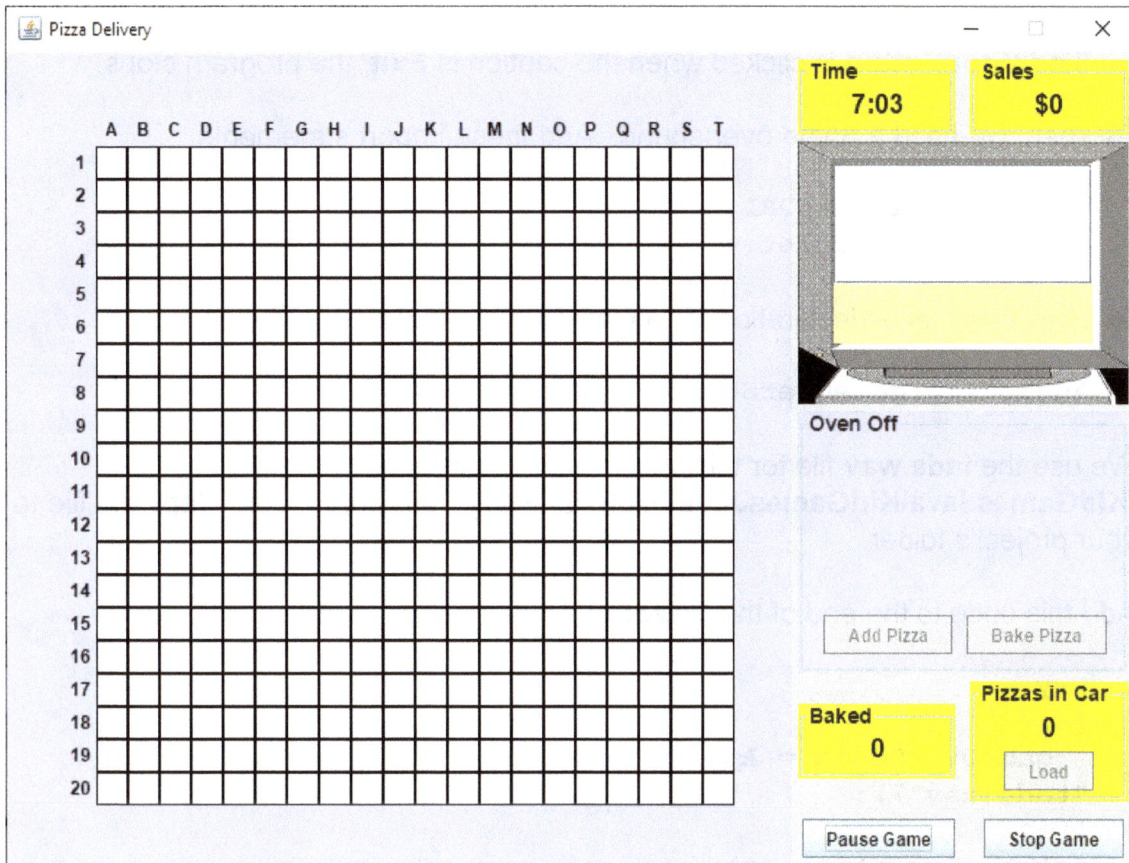

The **Stop Game** button doesn't work yet – let's fix that.

When a player clicks **Stop Game** (**exitStopButton**), the following should happen:

> ➢ Play **Game Over** sound.
> ➢ Change **text** to **Exit**.
> ➢ Change **text** of **startPauseButton** to **Start Game**.
> ➢ Stop **clockTimer**.

If **exitStopButton** is clicked when the caption is **Exit**, the program stops.

As seen, we need a game over sound. Add these import statements

```
import java.net.URL;
import java.applet.*;
```

Add this class level declaration for a **Game Over** sound:

```
AudioClip gameOverSound;
```

We use the **tada.wav** file for this sound. It is in the **\KidGamesJava\KidGamesJava Projects\PizzaDelivery** folder. Copy the file to your project's folder.

Add this code to the end of the **PizzaDelivery** constructor code:

```
try
{
  gameOverSound = Applet.newAudioClip(new URL("file:" +
"tada.wav"));
}
catch (Exception ex)
{
  System.out.println("Error loading sound files");
}
```

Now, the **exitStopButtonActionPerformed** method is:

```
private void exitStopButtonActionPerformed(ActionEvent e)
{
  if (exitStopButton.getText().equals("Stop Game"))
  {
    gameOverSound.play();
    exitStopButton.setText("Exit");
    startPauseButton.setText("Start Game");
    clockTimer.stop();
  }
  else
  {
    System.exit(0);
  }
}
```

Save and run **Pizza Delivery**. You should now be able to start the game, pause the game, restart the game and stop the game. You can also stop the program. Make sure everything works as desired. Make sure you hear a 'tada' sound when the game is ended.

You also want to make sure the program automatically stops once the clock reaches 11:00. But, you don't really want to sit around for 15 minutes to see that happen. To speed things up, temporarily set the **mSecPerMinutes** to something like 100. Then, run the program, click **Start Game** and watch time fly by! Once the clock hits 11:00, a sound will be played and the program should return to stopped state.

We often do this in programming – change parameters (even if the changes are not realistic) to test out different elements of code. Just remember, after changing the constant and making sure the clock stops at 11:00, to change the constant back to its original value of 3000. You will know it if you don't – the pizza simulation will go very quickly! Next, let's write the code to get phone orders coming in.

Code Design – Phone Orders

In **Pizza Delivery**, orders are phoned in randomly. The orders (time, location and number of pizzas) are displayed in a list box control (time sorted). The number of pizzas ordered is displayed at the proper location on the delivery grid (a dark green background is used for new orders). You then use this information to send a car to deliver the pizzas.

Here's another place where I just made up some rules for the orders – feel free to change them if you like. The rules implemented for pizza phone orders are:

- ➢ Orders arrive at random times, in 1 to 7 minute increments.
- ➢ Orders come from random locations on the delivery grid.
- ➢ Each order is for 1 to 5 pizzas, using these probabilities:
  - ▪ 1 pizza, 30 percent
  - ▪ 2 pizzas, 20 percent
  - ▪ 3 pizzas, 20 percent
  - ▪ 4 pizzas, 15 percent
  - ▪ 5 pizzas, 15 percent
- ➢ No orders are accepted after 10:30 to allow car to finish deliveries.

As mentioned, the order information will be displayed in the list box control. We use a specific format for that listing. As an example, say an order arrives at **6:20**, from grid location **G 12**, for **2 pizzas**. The order listing will appear as:

6:20 G 12 -> 2

Two arrays will be used to keep track of order information. **pizzas** is a two-dimensional array that says how many pizzas were ordered at a grid location and **pizzaTime** is a two-dimensional array holding the corresponding order time (in minutes). Add these declarations in the class level area:

```
int [][] pizzas = new int[21][21];
int [][] pizzaTime = new int[21][21];
Color onTimeDeliveryColor = new Color(0, 108, 0);
```

Notice we also defined a dark green color to indicate on-time (new) orders.

The timer object **phoneTimer** will govern how often orders arrive. Declare the timer object:

```
Timer phoneTimer;
```

Add the timer object to the project (using a **mSecPerMin delay** for now):

```
phoneTimer = new Timer(mSecPerMin, new ActionListener()
{
  public void actionPerformed(ActionEvent e)
  {
    phoneTimerActionPerformed(e);
  }
});
```

The **phoneTimerActionPerformed** method will implement the phone orders code.

In the game, the **delay** property will be set randomly. Add this import statement:

```
import java.util.Random;
```

Now, add this class level declaration to create a random object (**myRandom**):

```
Random myRandom = new Random();
```

When an order comes in, we will play a phone sound. Add this class level declaration for this sound:

```
AudioClip phoneSound;
```

We use the **phone.wav** file for this sound. It is in the **\KidGamesJava\KidGamesJava Projects\PizzaDelivery** folder. Copy the file to your project's folder.

Add this single line at the appropriate spot in the **PIzzaDelivery** constructor method to load the sound.

```
phoneSound = Applet.newAudioClip(new URL("file:" +
"phone.wav"));
```

The **phoneTimerActionPerformed** method that encodes the previously listed rules for phone orders and plays the sound is:

```
private void phoneTimerActionPerformed(ActionEvent e)
{
  int i, j, k;
  String order;
  phoneSound.play();
  if (clockHour == 10 && clockMinute >= 30)
  {
    phoneTimer.stop();
    return;
  }
  do
  {
    i = 1 + myRandom.nextInt(20);
    j = 1 + myRandom.nextInt(20);
  }
  while (pizzas[i][j] != 0);
  k = myRandom.nextInt(100);
  if (k <= 29)
    pizzas[i][j] = 1;
  else if (k <= 49)
    pizzas[i][j] = 2;
  else if (k <= 69)
    pizzas[i][j] = 3;
  else if (k <= 84)
    pizzas[i][j] = 4;
  else
    pizzas[i][j] = 5;
  pizzaTime[i][j] = clockMinute + 60 * clockHour;
  // build string listing order
```

```
order = timeLabel.getText() + " ";
if (timeLabel.getText().length() == 4)
  order = " " + order;
order += String.valueOf((char) (i + 64)) + " ";
if (j < 10)
  order += " ";
order += String.valueOf(j) + " -> " +
String.valueOf(pizzas[i][j]);
  ordersListModel.addElement(order);
  deliveryGrid[i][j].setBackground(onTimeDeliveryColor);;

deliveryGrid[i][j].setText(String.valueOf(pizzas[i][j]));
  phoneTimer.setDelay(mSecPerMin * (1 +
myRandom.nextInt(7)));
}
```

In this code, we play the phone sound. If it is past 10:30, the routine is exited. Next, we select a random unselected column (**i**) and a random row (**j**) for the order. Using the specified percentages, the number of pizzas ordered is stored in the **pizzas** array. Likewise, the order time is stored in the **pizzaTime** array. Next, the text string to put in the list box is formed and added to the list box. The corresponding grid location is marked with a dark green background (**onTimeDeliveryColor**) and the number of pizzas ordered. Before leaving the method, an new random interval value is computed. This gives us the delay (between 1 and 7 minutes) until the next order is phoned in. Make sure the added code compiles.

We need to make certain initializations for the order process. Make the shaded modifications to the **startPauseButtonActionPerformed** method to set the initial **delay** value (1 to 7 minutes), to clear any past orders from the grid and to start/stop the timer at the proper times:

```
private void startPauseButtonActionPerformed(ActionEvent
e)
{
  if (startPauseButton.getText().equals("Start Game"))
  {
    startPauseButton.setText("Pause Game");
    exitStopButton.setText("Stop Game");
    // clear grid
    for (int i = 1; i < 21; i++)
    {
      for (int j = 1; j < 21; j++)
      {
        deliveryGrid[i][j].setBackground(Color.WHITE);
        deliveryGrid[i][j].setText("");
        pizzas[i][j] = 0;
```

```
            pizzaTime[i][j] = 0;
        }
    }
    ordersListModel.removeAllElements();
    clockHour = 6;
    clockMinute = 0;
    timeLabel.setText("6:00");
    clockTimer.start();
    phoneTimer.setDelay(mSecPerMin * (1 +
MyRandom.nextInt(7)));
    phoneTimer.start();
}
else if (startPauseButton.getText().equals("Pause
Game"))
{
    startPauseButton.setText("Restart Game");
    exitStopButton.setEnabled(false);
    clockTimer.stop();
    phoneTimer.stop();
}
else
{
    // game restarted
    startPauseButton.setText("Pause Game");
    exitStopButton.setEnabled(true);
    clockTimer.start();
    phoneTimer.start();
}
}
```

We make a similar shaded change to the **exitStopButtonActionPerformed** method to turn off the timer when the game is stopped:

```java
private void exitStopButtonActionPerformed(ActionEvent e)
{
  if (exitStopButton.getText().equals("Stop Game"))
  {
    gameOverSound.play();
    exitStopButton.setText("Exit");
    startPauseButton.setText("Start Game");
    clockTimer.stop();
    phoneTimer.stop();
  }
  else
  {
    System.exit(0);
  }
}
```

Save and run the project. Click **Start Game** and the phone should start ringing, with orders in the list box and the delivery grid area. Here's what my form looked like after 5 orders:

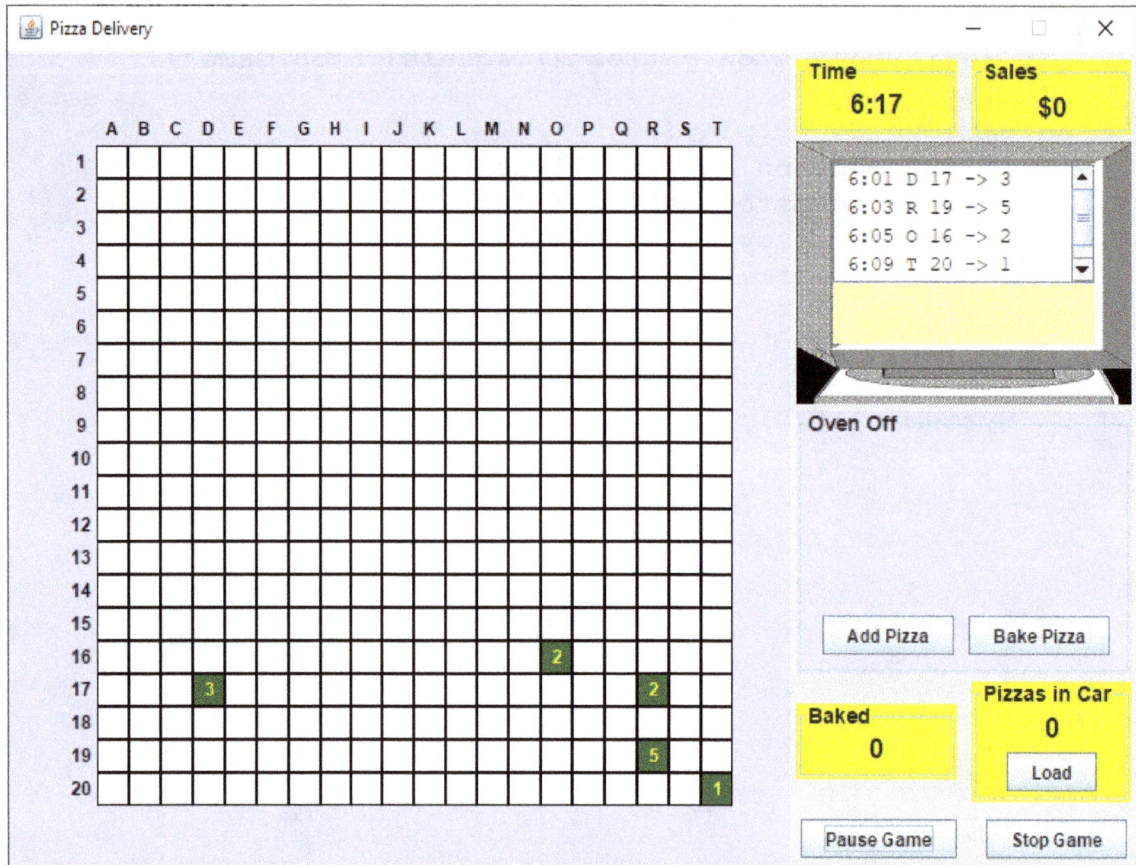

Check that you can pause, restart and stop the game. Next, we look at how to get the pizzas ready for delivery.

Code Design – Pizza Oven

Now that we know where the orders are coming from, we need to get some pizzas baked. The **ovenPanel** control holds the oven. We can bake, at most, eight pizzas at a time, using eight label controls (**pizzaLabel** array) to display the pizzas. This is another one of those rules we chose – you can change it if you like. Once the pizzas are done baking (taking 10 minutes), they are placed in the **readyPanel** for storage. Up to 20 pizzas can be stored. Any pizzas baked that cannot fit in the ready area are thrown out, costing you money. Define three constants to embody these rules:

```
final int pizzasReadyMax = 20;
final int pizzasBakingMax = 8;
final int bakingTime = 10;
```

We use one variable (**pizzasBaking**) to keep track of pizzas in the oven and another (**pizzasReady**) to specify the number of pizzas baked and stored. **totalPizzasBaked** will keep track of all pizzas baked during a single game. We use a boolean variable (**ovenGoing**) to know whether the oven is on or not – it is used for the paused state. And **pizzaIcon** holds the pizza graphic shown above. Add these declarations in the class level area:

```
int pizzasBaking, pizzasReady;
int totalPizzasBaked;
int bakingMinutesLeft;
boolean ovenGoing;
```

A pizza is pictorially represented by the **pizza.gif** file in the **\KidGamesJava\KidGamesJava Projects\PizzaDelivery** folder:

Copy this file to your project's folder. An **ImageIcon** object is used to represent the pizza. Declare the object with this line:

```
ImageIcon pizzaIcon = new ImageIcon("pizza.gif");
```

Pizzas are added to the oven by clicking the **Add Pizza** button (**addPizzaButton**) in the **ovenPanel**. With each click of the button, we follow these steps:

> ➢ Increment **pizzasBaking**.
> ➢ Set the corresponding **pizzaLabel** icon property..
> ➢ If maximum number of pizzas reached, disable **addPizzaButton**.

Note once a pizza is placed in the oven, it cannot be removed.

The **addPizzaButtonActionPerformed** method that implements these steps is:

```
private void addPizzaButtonActionPerformed(ActionEvent e)
{
  pizzasBaking++;
  pizzaLabel[pizzasBaking - 1].setIcon(pizzaIcon);
  if (pizzasBaking == pizzasBakingMax)
    addPizzaButton.setEnabled(false);
}
```

We can't quite test this new code yet since the **addPizzaButton** is disabled. We'll fix that soon.

Once loaded, a timer object **ovenTimer** will be used to time the baking process. We set the delay to **mSecPerMinute**, counting down the baking process one minute at a time. This allows proper pausing of the simulation. Declare the timer object:

```
Timer ovenTimer;
```

Add the timer object to the project:

```
ovenTimer = new Timer(mSecPerMin, new ActionListener()
{
  public void actionPerformed(ActionEvent e)
  {
    ovenTimerActionPerformed(e);
  }
});
```

The **ovenTimerActionPerformed** method will implement the pizza baking code.

With each event generated by **ovenTimer**, we will do these steps:

> ➤ If **bakingMinutesLeft != 0**, decrement **bakingMinutesLeft** and exit; else continue with next step.
> ➤ Play ding sound.
> ➤ Turn oven off.
> ➤ Increment **pizzasReady** and **totalPizzasBaked**, check limit against **pizzasReadyMax**.
> ➤ Set **ovenPanel text** to **Oven Off**; change background color to **ovenOffColor** (blue).
> ➤ Delete all pizza icons.
> ➤ Set **pizzasBaking** to 0.
> ➤ Enable **Add Pizza** and **Bake Pizza** buttons.

Notice, when the baking is done, we will play a ding sound. Add this class level declaration for the sound:

```
AudioClip dingSound;
```

We use the **ding.wav** file for this sound. It is in the **\KidGamesJava\KidGamesJava Projects\PizzaDelivery** folder. Copy the file to your project's folder.

Add this single line to the appropriate place in the **PizzaDelivery** constructor to load the sound.

```
dingSound = Applet.newAudioClip(new URL("file:" +
"ding.wav"));
```

The **ovenTimerActionPerformed** method that implements the needed steps is:

```
private void ovenTimerActionPerformed(ActionEvent e)
{
  if (bakingMinutesLeft != 0)
    bakingMinutesLeft--;
  else
  {
    dingSound.play();
    ovenTimer.stop();
    pizzasReady += pizzasBaking;
    totalPizzasBaked += pizzasBaking;
    if (pizzasReady > pizzasReadyMax)
      pizzasReady = pizzasReadyMax;
    readyLabel.setText(String.valueOf(pizzasReady));

ovenPanel.setBorder(BorderFactory.createTitledBorder("Oven
Off"));
    ovenPanel.setBackground(ovenOffColor);
    for (int i = 0; i < 8; i++)
      pizzaLabel[i].setIcon(null);
    pizzasBaking = 0;
    addPizzaButton.setEnabled(true);
    bakePizzaButton.setEnabled(true);
  }
}
```

Check that all newly added code compiles.

Baking begins by clicking the **Bake Pizza** button. The steps to follow once this button is clicked are:

> ➤ Change panel background color to **ovenOnColor** (red).
> ➤ Disable button controls.
> ➤ Display time pizzas will be done baking.
> ➤ Initialize **bakingMinutesLeft**.
> ➤ Enable **ovenTimer** to start the baking.

Add the declaration defining the oven on color:

```
Color ovenOnColor = Color.RED;
```

Now, the corresponding **bakePizzaButtonActionPerformed** method is:

```
private void bakePizzaButtonActionPerformed(ActionEvent e)
{
  int hOut, mOut;
  if (pizzasBaking == 0)
    return;
  ovenPanel.setBackground(ovenOnColor);
  addPizzaButton.setEnabled(false);
  bakePizzaButton.setEnabled(false);
  hOut = clockHour;
  mOut = clockMinute + bakingTime;
  if (mOut > 59)
  {
    mOut -= 60;
    hOut++;
  }
  String t;
  if (pizzasBaking == 1)
    t = "Pizza Out At ";
  else
    t = "Pizzas Out At ";
  t += String.valueOf(hOut) + ":";
  if (mOut < 10)
    t += "0";
  t += String.valueOf(mOut);

 ovenPanel.setBorder(BorderFactory.createTitledBorder(t));
  bakingMinutesLeft = bakingTime;
  ovenTimer.start();
}
```

Like the previous button, we can't test this code since the **bakePizzaButton** is initially disabled. We fix that now.

Make the shaded modifications to the **startPauseButtonActionPerformed** event to clear the pizza oven, initialize variables (we assume we have baked one oven load prior to opening the store) and to properly start/stop the oven timer and set oven buttons status at the proper times. This will finally allow us to test the buttons (**addPizzaButton** and **bakePizzaButton**) we coded up earlier:

```java
private void startPauseButtonActionPerformed(ActionEvent e)
{
  if (startPauseButton.getText().equals("Start Game"))
  {
    startPauseButton.setText("Pause Game");
    exitStopButton.setText("Stop Game");
    // clear grid
    for (int i = 1; i < 21; i++)
    {
      for (int j = 1; j < 21; j++)
      {
        deliveryGrid[i][j].setBackground(Color.WHITE);
        deliveryGrid[i][j].setText("");
        pizzas[i][j] = 0;
        pizzaTime[i][j] = 0;
      }
    }
    ordersListModel.removeAllElements();
    for (int i = 0; i < 8; i++)
      pizzaLabel[i].setIcon(null);
    pizzasBaking = 0;
    pizzasReady = pizzasBakingMax;
    totalPizzasBaked = pizzasReady;
    readyLabel.setText(String.valueOf(pizzasReady));
    addPizzaButton.setEnabled(true);
    bakePizzaButton.setEnabled(true);
    clockHour = 6;
    clockMinute = 0;
    timeLabel.setText("6:00");
    clockTimer.start();
    phoneTimer.setDelay(mSecPerMin * (1 +
MyRandom.nextInt(7)));
    phoneTimer.start();
  }
  else if (startPauseButton.getText().equals("Pause
Game"))
  {
    startPauseButton.setText("Restart Game");
    exitStopButton.setEnabled(false);
    clockTimer.stop();
```

```
      phoneTimer.stop();
      ovenGoing = ovenTimer.isRunning();
      ovenTimer.stop();
      addPizzaButton.setEnabled(false);
      bakePizzaButton.setEnabled(false);
    }
    else
    {
      // game restarted
      startPauseButton.setText("Pause Game");
      exitStopButton.setEnabled(true);
      clockTimer.start();
      phoneTimer.start();
      if (ovenGoing)
        ovenTimer.start();
      addPizzaButton.setEnabled(!ovenGoing);
      bakePizzaButton.setEnabled(!ovenGoing);
    }
}
```

Note how we used the **ovenGoing** variable to pause and restart the simulation. When pausing, we determine if the oven is going and disable the two buttons on the panel. Then, when restarted, if the oven was going it is restarted and the buttons are disabled. Otherwise, the buttons are enabled.

We make similar shaded changes to the **exitStopButtonActionPerformed**
method to turn off the oven timer and reset the oven when the game is stopped:

```java
private void exitStopButtonActionPerformed(ActionEvent e)
{
  if (exitStopButton.getText().equals("Stop Game"))
  {
    gameOverSound.play();
    exitStopButton.setText("Exit");
    startPauseButton.setText("Start Game");
    clockTimer.stop();
    phoneTimer.stop();
    ovenTimer.stop();

ovenPanel.setBorder(BorderFactory.createTitledBorder("Oven
Off"));
    ovenPanel.setBackground(ovenOffColor);
    for (int i = 0; i < 8; i++)
      pizzaLabel[i].setIcon(null);
  }
    addPizzaButton.setEnabled(false);
    bakePizzaButton.setEnabled(false);
  }
  else
  {
    System.exit(0);
  }
}
```

At long last, we can bake pizzas. Save and run the project. Click **Start Game**, then click **Add Pizza** some number of times. Click **Bake Pizza** and wait. After 10 minutes elapse (may be 11 minutes depending on just when you click **Bake Pizza**), you will hear a ding sound and the pizzas you baked will be moved to the **Baked** area. Here's my screen after baking five pizzas (increasing the **Baked** total to 13) and putting six more in the oven; notice, too, a few orders have come in:

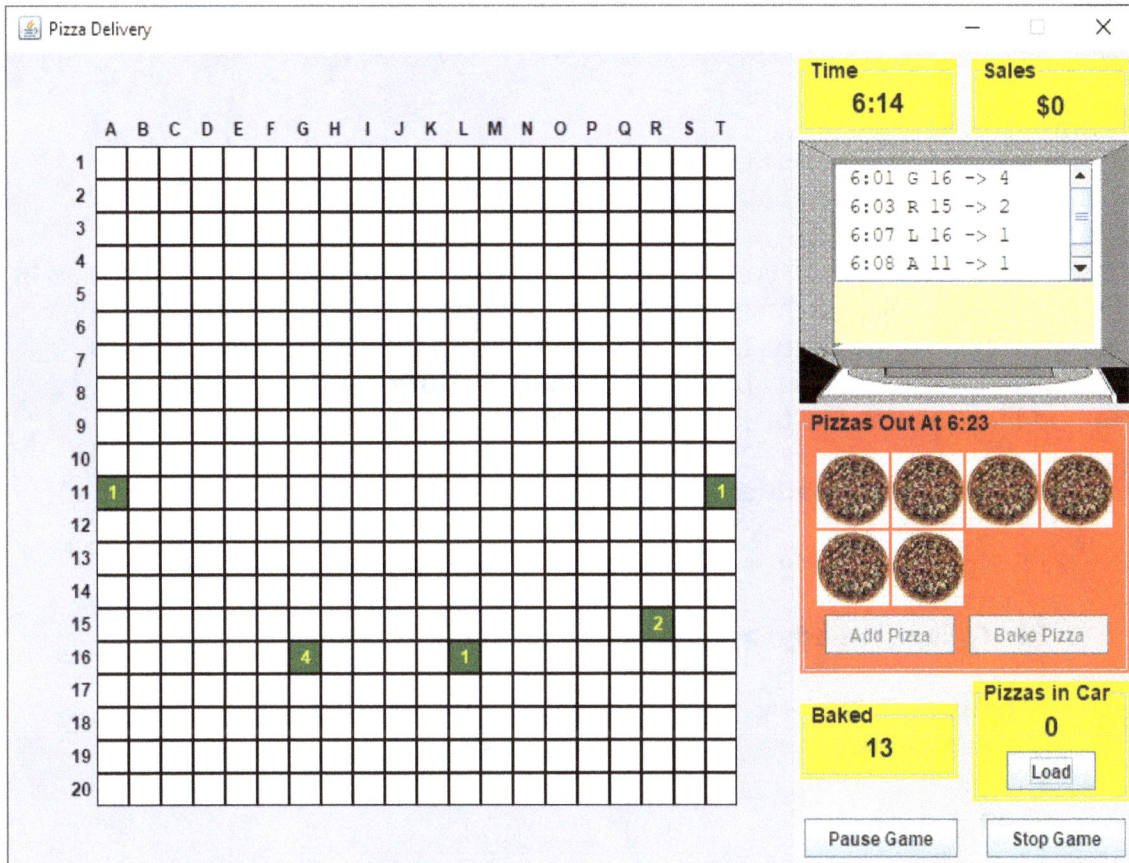

Always remember, a red oven is a baking oven; a blue oven is a cold oven. Sometimes when playing the game, you forget to start the baking process. Continue baking pizzas if you like – remember you can only store 20 pizzas. Make sure you can pause, restart and stop the game. Next, we see how to move pizzas into the car and start delivering them.

Code Design – Load Car

A delivery car is available to take pizzas from the pizza parlor to the order locations on the grid. A first step in the delivery process is to load pizzas from the **Baked** area into the car. This is done by clicking the **Load** button in the **inCarPanel** control. We use a variable **pizzasInCar** to keep track of how many pizzas are in the car. We assume a maximum of 10 pizzas can fit in the car. Add the variable declaration and another constant (**pizzasInCarMax**) to the class level declarations area:

```
int pizzasInCar;
boolean loadCarButtonEnabled;
final int pizzasInCarMax = 10;
```

As stated, to load the car, you click the **Load** button in the panel labeled **Pizzas In Car**. The steps followed (assuming there are pizzas to load) are simple. If the maximum number of pizzas to load are available, load that number in the car, otherwise load all the ready pizzas. The **loadCarButtonActionPerformed** method that handles this task (and associated labeling) is:

```
private void loadCarButtonActionPerformed(ActionEvent e)
{
  if (pizzasReady == 0)
    return;
  if (pizzasReady > pizzasInCarMax)
  {
    pizzasInCar += pizzasInCarMax;
    pizzasReady -= pizzasInCarMax;
  }
  else
  {
    pizzasInCar += pizzasReady;
    pizzasReady = 0;
  }
  readyLabel.setText(String.valueOf(pizzasReady));
  inCarLabel.setText(String.valueOf(pizzasInCar));
  loadCarButton.setEnabled(false);
}
```

Notice we disable the **Load** button once the pizzas are loaded. In the motion code, we use the **enabled** status of this button to tell us whether the car has pizzas available for delivery.

Add the shaded code to the **startPauseButtonActionPerformed method** to initialize the car variables and make sure the **Load** button is enabled and disabled properly:

```
private void startPauseButtonActionPerformed(ActionEvent
e)
{
  if (startPauseButton.getText().equals("Start Game"))
  {
    startPauseButton.setText("Pause Game");
    exitStopButton.setText("Stop Game");
    // clear grid
    for (int i = 1; i < 21; i++)
    {
      for (int j = 1; j < 21; j++)
      {
        deliveryGrid[i][j].setBackground(Color.WHITE);
        deliveryGrid[i][j].setText("");
        pizzas[i][j] = 0;
        pizzaTime[i][j] = 0;
      }
    }
    ordersListModel.removeAllElements();
    for (int i = 0; i < 8; i++)
      pizzaLabel[i].setIcon(null);
    pizzasBaking = 0;
    pizzasReady = pizzasBakingMax;
    totalPizzasBaked = pizzasReady;
    readyLabel.setText(String.valueOf(pizzasReady));
    addPizzaButton.setEnabled(true);
    bakePizzaButton.setEnabled(true);
    pizzasInCar = 0;
    inCarLabel.setText("0");
    loadCarButton.setEnabled(true);
    clockHour = 6;
    clockMinute = 0;
    timeLabel.setText("6:00");
    clockTimer.start();
    phoneTimer.setDelay(mSecPerMin * (1 +
MyRandom.nextInt(7)));
    phoneTimer.start();
  }
  else if (startPauseButton.getText().equals("Pause
Game"))
  {
    startPauseButton.setText("Restart Game");
    exitStopButton.setEnabled(false);
```

```
      clockTimer.stop();
      phoneTimer.stop();
      ovenGoing = ovenTimer.isRunning();
      ovenTimer.stop();
      addPizzaButton.setEnabled(false);
      bakePizzaButton.setEnabled(false);
      loadCarButtonEnabled = loadCarButton.isEnabled();
      loadCarButton.setEnabled(false);
   }
   else
   {
      // game restarted
      startPauseButton.setText("Pause Game");
      exitStopButton.setEnabled(true);
      clockTimer.start();
      phoneTimer.start();
      if (ovenGoing)
         ovenTimer.start();
      addPizzaButton.setEnabled(!ovenGoing);
      bakePizzaButton.setEnabled(!ovenGoing);
      loadCarButton.setEnabled(loadCarButtonEnabled);
   }
}
```

Make similar shaded changes to the **exitStopButtonActionPerformed** method to disable the load button when the game is stopped:

```
private void exitStopButtonActionPerformed(ActionEvent e)
{
  if (exitStopButton.getText().equals("Stop Game"))
  {
    gameOverSound.play();
    exitStopButton.setText("Exit");
    startPauseButton.setText("Start Game");
    clockTimer.stop();
    phoneTimer.stop();
    ovenTimer.stop();

ovenPanel.setBorder(BorderFactory.createTitledBorder("Oven
Off"));
    ovenPanel.setBackground(ovenOffColor);
    for (int i = 0; i < 8; i++)
      pizzaLabel[i].setIcon(null);
  }
    addPizzaButton.setEnabled(false);
    bakePizzaButton.setEnabled(false);
    loadCarButton.setEnabled(false);
  }
  else
  {
    System.exit(0);
  }
}
```

Save and run the project. Start the game, bake some pizzas and load the car. In this screen, I baked six pizzas, giving me 14 baked pizzas. I then clicked the **Load** button. The car now has the maximum of 10 pizzas and there are 4 pizzas remaining in the **Baked** area:

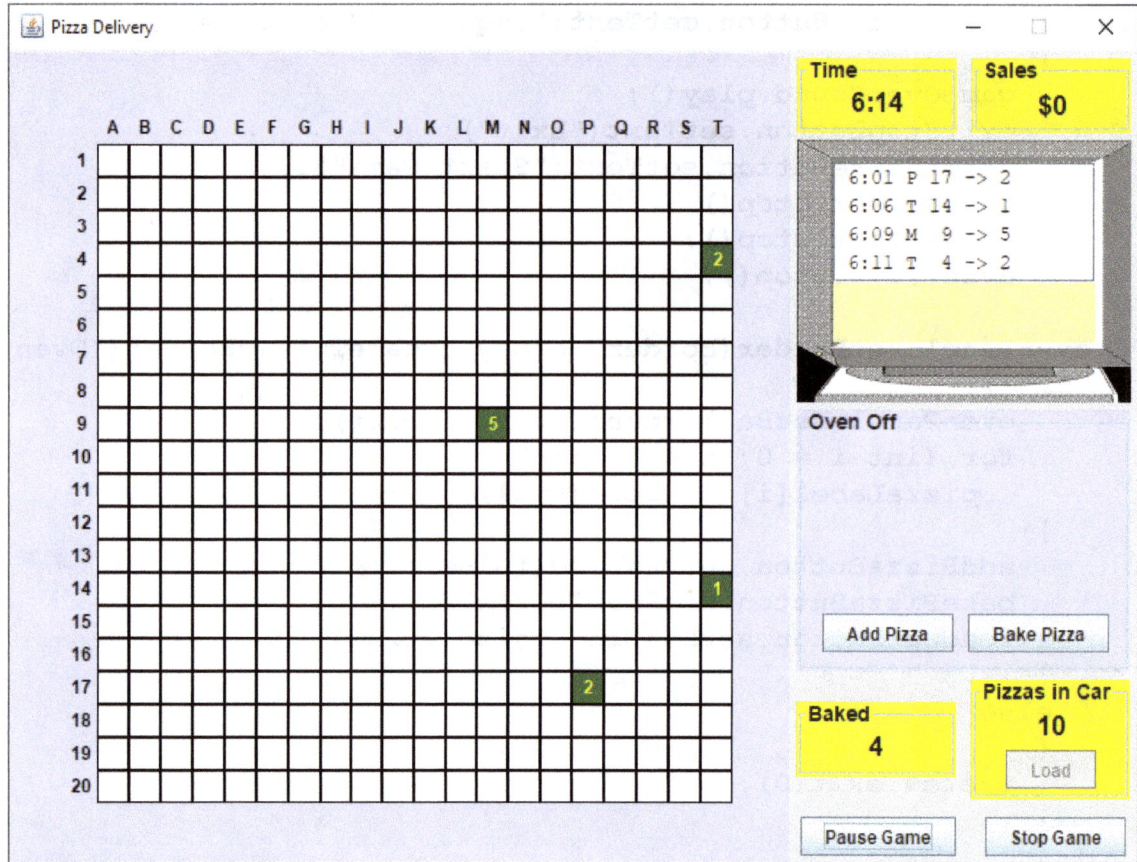

Next, let's start delivering pizzas by driving the car around the delivery grid.

Code Design – Move Car

Once there are pizzas in the car, we're ready to start deliveries. Click on a location on the delivery grid and the car (represented by a little yellow image) travels from the pizza parlor to that location. You follow the same process to have the car return to the pizza parlor when you need more pizzas. There are lots of things to do here: define the pizza parlor location (randomly set), detect clicks on the delivery grid, identify the clicked label control, and then move the car to the clicked location.

We need several variables to keep track of the car. Add these class level declarations to the code window:

```
int pizzaC, pizzaR;
int deliveryC, deliveryR;
int carC, carR;
int deltaC, deltaR;
int mileage;
bool carGoing;
```

pizzaC and **pizzaR** are the column and row numbers for the pizza parlor location in the delivery grid (marked by an **X**). **deliveryC** and **deliveryR** are the column and row numbers for the delivery (the clicked label control). **carC** and **carR** are the column and row numbers for the current car location. **deltaC** and **deltaR** are the difference between the car and delivery columns and rows. Lastly, **mileage** is the number of grid locations the car has moved through and **carGoing** indicates if the car is currently moving (used for pause mode).

The timer object **carTimer** will be used to make the car move. We define one constant to set car speed:

```
final int minPer20Squares = 3;
```

This tells us how many minutes (of clock time) we want to take for the car to travel across the delivery grid (20 squares). Declare the timer object:

```
Timer carTimer;
```

Add the timer object to the project (using a **delay** of **mSecPerMin * minPer20Squares / 20**; the number of milliseconds needed to move one square in the grid):

```
carTimer = new Timer(mSecPerMin * minPer20Squares / 20,
new ActionListener()
{
  public void actionPerformed(ActionEvent e)
  {
    carTimerActionPerformed(e);
  }
});
```

The **carTimerActionPerformed** method will implement the code to move the car.

We will use two images to represent the car, one for horizontal motion and one for vertical motion. These images are found in the **\KidGamesJava\KidGamesJava Projects\PizzaDelivery** folder:

(hcar.gif)

(vcar.gif)

Copy these files to your project's folder. **ImageIcon** objects are used to represent the car. Declare the objects

```
ImageIcon hCarIcon = new ImageIcon("hcar.gif");
ImageIcon vCarIcon = new ImageIcon("vcar.gif");
```

Clicking a grid location (we'll do that code next) will start the **carTimer**. Once started, with each event generated by this timer, we move the car one square. We do horizontal movements first, then vertical movements. The steps to accomplish this are:

> ➢ Erase car image in current position.
> ➢ If **deltaC != 0**:
>   o Increment **mileage** by 1.
>   o Set car icon to **hCarIcon.**
>   o Recompute **carC.**
>   o Recompute **deltaC.**
> ➢ If **deltaR != 0**:
>   o Increment **mileage** by 1.
>   o Set car icon to **vCarIcon.**
>   o Recompute **carR.**
>   o Recompute **deltaR.**
> ➢ Put car icon at new location.
> ➢ If **carC = deliveryC** and **carR = deliveryR**:
>   o Play beep sound.
>   o Disable **carTimer**.
>   o If **carC = pizzaC** and **carR = pizzaR**, we're back at the pizza parlor, so:
>   ➢ Establish message.
>   ➢ Delete car icon.
>   ➢ Set **pizzasInCar** to **0** (must throw extras out due to health department rules).
>   ➢ Enable **loadCarButton**.
>   o If not at pizza parlor, we're at the clicked location:
>   ➢ Establish message.
>   ➢ Check delivery status.

This may seem like a lot of steps, but they are straightforward. Notice, in particular, we re-enable **loadCarButton** when we return to the pizza parlor to allow reloading of the car.

Notice, when the car stops, we will play a beep sound. Add this class level declaration for the sound:

```
AudioClip beepSound;
```

We use the **carbeep.wav** file for this sound. It is in the **\KidGamesJava\KidGamesJava Projects\PizzaDelivery** folder. Copy the file to your project's folder.

Add this single line to the **PizzaDelivery** constructor to load the sound.

```
beepSound = Applet.newAudioClip(new URL("file:" +
"carbeep.wav"));
```

The **carTimerActionPerformed** method that implements the above steps is:

```
private void carTimerActionPerformed(ActionEvent e)
{
  ImageIcon carIcon = null;
  deliveryGrid[carC][carR].setIcon(null);
  // move horizontally first
  if (deltaC != 0)
  {
    mileage++;
    carIcon = hCarIcon;
    if (deltaC > 0)
      carC++;
    else
      carC--;
    deltaC = deliveryC - carC;
  }
  else
  {
    if (deltaR != 0)
    {
      mileage++;
      carIcon = vCarIcon;
      if (deltaR > 0)
        carR++;
      else
        carR--;
      deltaR = deliveryR - carR;
    }
  }
  deliveryGrid[carC][carR].setIcon(carIcon);
  if (carC == deliveryC && carR == deliveryR)
  {
```

```
        beepSound.play();
        carTimer.stop();
        if (carC == pizzaC && carR == pizzaR)
        {
          messageTextArea.setText(" Car at Pizza Parlor:\n " +
display(carC, carR));
          deliveryGrid[carC][carR].setIcon(null);
          pizzasInCar = 0;
          inCarLabel.setText("0");
          loadCarButton.setEnabled(true);
        }
        else
        {
          messageTextArea.setText(" Car at " + display(carC,
carR));
          // check delivery status
        }
    }
}
```

We have left a "hook" for checking delivery status (a comment statement). Also notice once the car starts moving, it doesn't stop until it reaches the clicked location.

In the above code, we use a general method **display** that converts column and row numbers to column letter and row number. Add this general method to the project:

```
private String display(int c, int r)
{
  return (String.valueOf((char)(c + 64)) + " " +
String.valueOf(r));
}
```

Note how **char** is used to convert the column number **c** to a letter (based on its Unicode). Check to make sure the new code compiles.

To move the car to a desired location on the delivery grid, we simply click that location. Remember when we built the grid? In that code, we added a **deliveryGridMousePressed** method to handle mouse clicks for all 400 (20 x 20) of the label controls in the grid. This method will be used to move the car.

Once a grid location is clicked, we follow these steps:

> ➢ Deliveries can only be made if the car is not already moving (**carTimer** is disabled), the game is in play mode (we use the **text** property of **startPauseButton** to determine this) and **loadCarButton** is disabled (pizzas have been loaded in the car). If this is not the case, exit; else continue.
> ➢ Determine column (**deliveryC**) and row (**deliveryR**) of clicked label.
> ➢ Compute **deltaC** and **deltaR**. If **deltaC = 0** and **deltaR = 0**, exit.
> ➢ Display message saying where the car is going.
> ➢ Enable **carTimer**.

We determine the column and row of the clicked label using logic similar to that in the **Tic Tac Toe** and **Match Game** projects. Recall the mouse pressed event can tell us the upper left corner of the clicked control. From this we can find **deliveryC** and **deliveryR**.

The needed steps in the **deliveryGridMousePressed** method are:

```
private void deliveryGridMousePressed(MouseEvent e)
{
  // determine which grid element was clicked
  Point p = e.getComponent().getLocation();
  // determine indicies based on p
  boolean matchFound = false;
  if (!carTimer.isRunning() && !loadCarButton.isEnabled()
&& startPauseButton.getText().equals("Pause Game"))
  {
  for (deliveryR = 1; deliveryR < 21; deliveryR++)
  {
    for (deliveryC = 1; deliveryC < 21; deliveryC++)
    {
      if (p.x == deliveryGrid[deliveryC][deliveryR].getX()
&& p.y == deliveryGrid[deliveryC][deliveryR].getY())
      {
        matchFound = true;
        break;
      }
    }
    if (matchFound)
      break;
  }
  deltaC = deliveryC - carC;
  deltaR = deliveryR - carR;
  if (deltaC == 0 && deltaR == 0)
    return;
  messageTextArea.setText(" Car Going To:\n " +
display(deliveryC, deliveryR));
    carTimer.start();
  }
}
```

Check to make sure the code still compiles. We're nearly ready to test things. We first have to take care of the starting, pausing and stopping logic, along with some more initializations.

Make the shaded modifications to the **startPauseButtonActionPerformed** method to initialize the pizza parlor location (also the initial car location) and to start/stop the timer at the proper times:

```java
private void startPauseButtonActionPerformed(ActionEvent e)
{
  if (startPauseButton.getText().equals("Start Game"))
  {
    startPauseButton.setText("Pause Game");
    exitStopButton.setText("Stop Game");
    // clear grid
    for (int i = 1; i < 21; i++)
    {
      for (int j = 1; j < 21; j++)
      {
        deliveryGrid[i][j].setBackground(Color.WHITE);
        deliveryGrid[i][j].setText("");
        pizzas[i][j] = 0;
        pizzaTime[i][j] = 0;
      }
    }
    ordersListModel.removeAllElements();
    for (int i = 0; i < 8; i++)
      pizzaLabel[i].setIcon(null);
    pizzasBaking = 0;
    pizzasReady = pizzasBakingMax;
    totalPizzasBaked = pizzasReady;
    readyLabel.setText(String.valueOf(pizzasReady));
    addPizzaButton.setEnabled(true);
    bakePizzaButton.setEnabled(true);
    pizzasInCar = 0;
    inCarLabel.setText("0");
    loadCarButton.setEnabled(true);
    // initialize pizza parlor and car location
    deliveryGrid[carC][carR].setIcon(null);
    pizzaC = 2 + myRandom.nextInt(18);
    pizzaR = 2 + myRandom.nextInt(18);

deliveryGrid[pizzaC][pizzaR].setBackground(Color.BLACK);
    deliveryGrid[pizzaC][pizzaR].setText("X");
    carC = pizzaC;
    carR = pizzaR;
    mileage = 0;
    messageTextArea.setText(" Car at Pizza Parlor:\n " +
display(carC, carR));
    clockHour = 6;
```

```
      clockMinute = 0;
      timeLabel.setText("6:00");
      clockTimer.start();
      phoneTimer.setDelay(mSecPerMin * (1 +
MyRandom.nextInt(7)));
      phoneTimer.start();
   }
   else if (startPauseButton.getText().equals("Pause
Game"))
   {
      startPauseButton.setText("Restart Game");
      exitStopButton.setEnabled(false);
      clockTimer.stop();
      phoneTimer.stop();
      ovenGoing = ovenTimer.isRunning();
      ovenTimer.stop();
      addPizzaButton.setEnabled(false);
      bakePizzaButton.setEnabled(false);
      loadCarButtonEnabled = loadCarButton.isEnabled();
      loadCarButton.setEnabled(false);
      carGoing = carTimer.isRunning();
      carTimer.stop();
   }
   else
   {
      // game restarted
      startPauseButton.setText("Pause Game");
      exitStopButton.setEnabled(true);
      clockTimer.start();
      phoneTimer.start();
      if (ovenGoing)
        ovenTimer.start();
      addPizzaButton.setEnabled(!ovenGoing);
      bakePizzaButton.setEnabled(!ovenGoing);
      loadCarButton.setEnabled(loadCarButtonEnabled);
      if (carGoing)
        carTimer.start();
   }
}
```

We first erase any previous car on the grid. Then, the pizza parlor is placed somewhere on the interior of the grid and marked by an **X**. The car is positioned at this location and the mileage initialized. A message is posted announcing the car is at the pizza parlor. Note how we used the **carGoing** variable to pause and restart the simulation.

We make a shaded change to the **exitStopButtonActionPerformed method** to turn off the car timer when the game is stopped:

```java
private void exitStopButtonActionPerformed(ActionEvent e)
{
  if (exitStopButton.getText().equals("Stop Game"))
  {
    gameOverSound.play();
    exitStopButton.setText("Exit");
    startPauseButton.setText("Start Game");
    clockTimer.stop();
    phoneTimer.stop();
    ovenTimer.stop();
    addPizzaButton.setEnabled(false);
    bakePizzaButton.setEnabled(false);

    ovenPanel.setBorder(BorderFactory.createTitledBorder("Oven Off"));
    ovenPanel.setBackground(ovenOffColor);
    for (int i = 0; i < 8; i++)
      pizzaLabel[i].setIcon(null);
    addPizzaButton.setEnabled(false);
    bakePizzaButton.setEnabled(false);
    loadCarButton.setEnabled(false);
    carTimer.stop();
  }
  else
  {
    System.exit(0);
  }
}
```

Let's test everything out. Save and run the project. Click **Start Game**. Notice the parlor is at **Column J, Row 13**. Now click **Load** to put some pizzas in the car. Now, click a location on the grid and watch the car go there. Here's my form as the car is on its way to an order for 4 pizzas at **Column O**, **Row 13**:

Once the car arrives, I hear a beep and the form is:

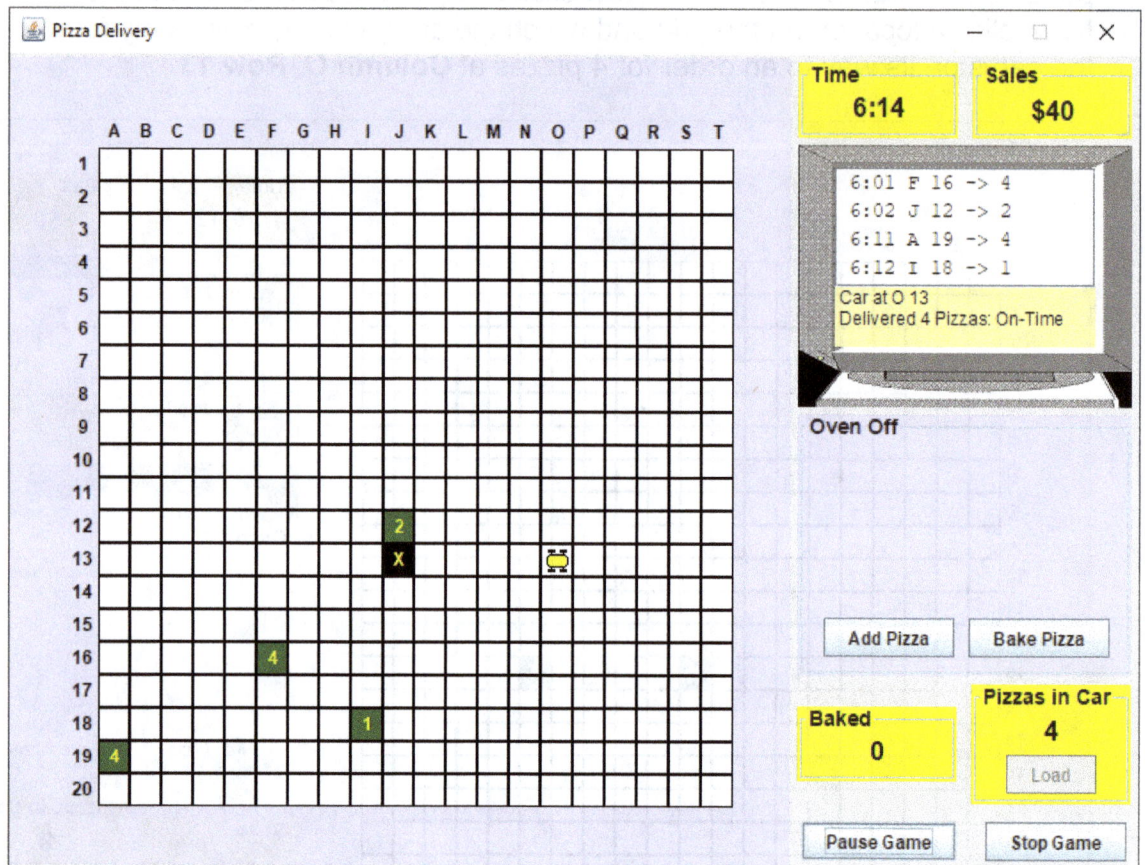

The message indicates the car is at **O 13**.

Now, click the pizza parlor (marked by an **X**) – you need to do this when you need more pizzas to deliver. The car will return and disappear from the screen:

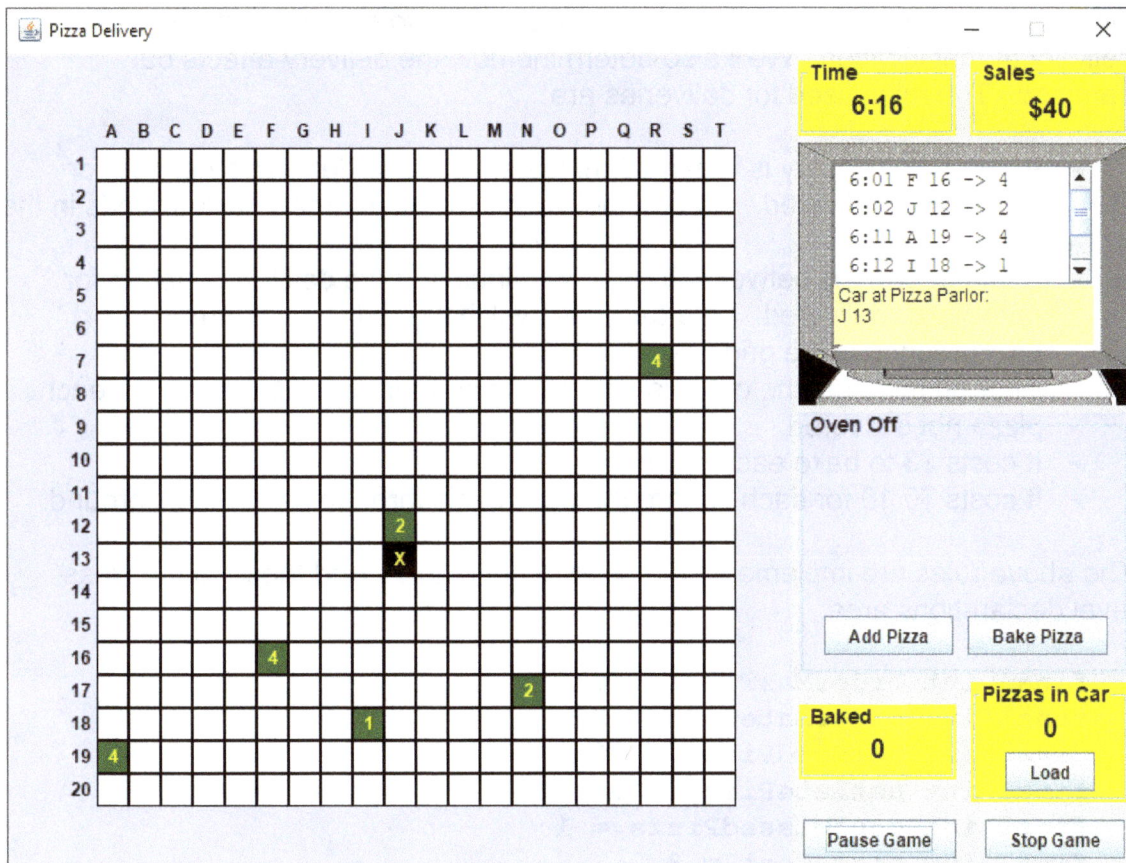

The message indicates the car is at the pizza parlor. The **Load** button is enabled and you have zero pizzas in the car. As mentioned, if the car returns with any pizzas, they must be thrown away due to health department rules. At this point, you need to bake more pizzas and reload the car if you want to go back on the road.

We're getting close to being done. Just two more steps. Notice that the order at **L 8** is still there even though we sent the car there with some pizzas. We need to check the status of any deliveries made and process it correctly. And, we need to present the final sales results when a game is stopped.

Code Design - Deliveries

Once the car arrives at a selected location, we need to check the status of the delivery at that location. We'll also determine how the delivery affects our earnings. The rules used for deliveries are:

> ➤ An on-time delivery is within 30 minutes. On-time deliveries net $10 for each pizza delivered. On-time deliveries will have green backgrounds in the grid.
> ➤ A late delivery is between 30 and 60 minutes. Late deliveries net $5 for each pizza delivered. Late deliveries will have red (**lateDeliveryColor**) backgrounds in the grid.
> ➤ After 60 minutes, the order is cancelled and there is a $1 penalty for each pizza not delivered.
> ➤ It costs $3 to bake each pizza.
> ➤ It costs $0.10 for each square the car travels through as it moves around.

The above rules are implemented in several constants. Add these to the class level declarations area:

```
final int orderMaxTime = 60;
final int orderLateTime = 30;
final int netSoldPizza = 10;
final int netLatePizza = 5;
final int costMissedPizza = 1;
final int pizzaCost = 3;
final double mileageCost = 0.1;
```

We need variables to keep track of the various delivery quantities. Add these class level declarations:

```
int pizzasOnTime;
int pizzasLate;
int missedDeliveries;
int totalSales;
Color lateDeliveryColor = new Color(224, 0, 0);
```

pizzasOnTime is the number of on-time deliveries, **pizzasLate** is the number of late deliveries, **missedDeliveries** is the number of missed deliveries, **totalSales** is the sum of all moneys taken in during deliveries, and **lateDeliveryColor** is the grid background (red) for late orders..

Make the shaded changes to the **startPauseButtonActionPerformed method**
method to initialize the new variables:

```
private void startPauseButtonActionPerformed(ActionEvent
e)
{
  if (startPauseButton.getText().equals("Start Game"))
  {
    startPauseButton.setText("Pause Game");
    exitStopButton.setText("Stop Game");
    // clear grid
    for (int i = 1; i < 21; i++)
    {
      for (int j = 1; j < 21; j++)
      {
        deliveryGrid[i][j].setBackground(Color.WHITE);
        deliveryGrid[i][j].setText("");
        pizzas[i][j] = 0;
        pizzaTime[i][j] = 0;
      }
    }
    ordersListModel.removeAllElements();
    for (int i = 0; i < 8; i++)
      pizzaLabel[i].setIcon(null);
    pizzasBaking = 0;
    pizzasReady = pizzasBakingMax;
    totalPizzasBaked = pizzasReady;
    readyLabel.setText(String.valueOf(pizzasReady));
    addPizzaButton.setEnabled(true);
    bakePizzaButton.setEnabled(true);
    pizzasInCar = 0;
    inCarLabel.setText("0");
    loadCarButton.setEnabled(true);
    // initialize pizza parlor and car location
    deliveryGrid[carC][carR].setIcon(null);
    pizzaC = 2 + myRandom.nextInt(18);
    pizzaR = 2 + myRandom.nextInt(18);

deliveryGrid[pizzaC][pizzaR].setBackground(Color.BLACK);
    deliveryGrid[pizzaC][pizzaR].setText("X");
    carC = pizzaC;
    carR = pizzaR;
    mileage = 0;
    messageTextArea.setText(" Car at Pizza Parlor:\n " +
display(carC, carR));
    pizzasOnTime = 0;
    pizzasLate = 0;
```

```
      missedDeliveries = 0;
      totalSales = 0;
      salesLabel.setText("$0");
      clockHour = 6;
      clockMinute = 0;
      timeLabel.setText("6:00");
      clockTimer.start();
      phoneTimer.setDelay(mSecPerMin * (1 +
MyRandom.nextInt(7)));
      phoneTimer.start();
    }
    else if (startPauseButton.getText().equals("Pause
Game"))
    {
      startPauseButton.setText("Restart Game");
      exitStopButton.setEnabled(false);
      clockTimer.stop();
      phoneTimer.stop();
      ovenGoing = ovenTimer.isRunning();
      ovenTimer.stop();
      addPizzaButton.setEnabled(false);
      bakePizzaButton.setEnabled(false);
      loadCarButtonEnabled = loadCarButton.isEnabled();
      loadCarButton.setEnabled(false);
      carGoing = carTimer.isRunning();
      carTimer.stop();
    }
    else
    {
      // game restarted
      startPauseButton.setText("Pause Game");
      exitStopButton.setEnabled(true);
      clockTimer.start();
      phoneTimer.start();
      if (ovenGoing)
        ovenTimer.start();
      addPizzaButton.setEnabled(!ovenGoing);
      bakePizzaButton.setEnabled(!ovenGoing);
      loadCarButton.setEnabled(loadCarButtonEnabled);
      if (carGoing)
        carTimer.start();
    }
  }
```

We indicate on-time deliveries by green backgrounds (**onTimeDeliveryColor**) in the grid and late deliveries will have red backgrounds (**lateDeliveryColor**). The backgrounds are initialized at **onTimeDeliveryColor**. Once 30 minutes elapse after an order is placed, we need to change the corresponding display grid background to red. And, once 60 minutes elapse for an order, it is removed from the grid with penalty costs incurred. All of this is done in the **clockTimerActionPerformed** method. At each event generated by the clock timer, we follow these steps:

- Check to see if 60 minutes have elapsed for the first item in the list box. This is the oldest order in the list and the only candidate for removal. If 60 minutes have elapsed, increment **missedDeliveries** by the proper number of pizzas and remove the order from the delivery grid and list box.
- For all remaining list box items, check to see if 30 minutes have elapsed. If so, and the background isn't already red, change it to red.

Make the shaded changes to the **clockTimerActionPerformed** code to implement these steps:

```
private void clockTimerActionPerformed(ActionEvent e)
{
  int clockMinutes;
  int c, r;
  String s;
  boolean expired = false;
  clockMinute++;
  if (clockMinute > 59)
  {
    clockMinute = 0;
    clockHour++;
    if (clockHour == 11)
    {
      timeLabel.setText("11:00");
      exitStopButton.doClick();
      return;
    }
  }
  String t = String.valueOf(clockHour) + ":";
  if (clockMinute < 10)
    t += "0";
  timeLabel.setText(t + String.valueOf(clockMinute));
  // check for late orders - check to if first is expired
  clockMinutes = clockMinute + 60 * clockHour;
  if (ordersListModel.getSize() != 0)
  {
    for (int i = 0; i < ordersListModel.getSize(); i++)
    {
```

```
      s = String.valueOf(ordersListModel.getElementAt(i));
      c = ((int) s.charAt(6)) - 64;
      r = Integer.valueOf(s.substring(8,
10).trim()).intValue();
      if (i == 0 && clockMinutes - pizzaTime[c][r] >=
orderMaxTime)
      {
         expired = true;
         deliveryGrid[c][r].setBackground(Color.WHITE);
         deliveryGrid[c][r].setText("");
         missedDeliveries += pizzas[c][r];
         pizzas[c][r] = 0;
      }
      else if (clockMinutes - pizzaTime[c][r] >=
orderLateTime)
      {

deliveryGrid[c][r].setBackground(lateDeliveryColor);
      }
   }
   if (expired)
      ordersListModel.removeElementAt(0);
  }
}
```

Note how we extract the column (**c**) and row (**r**) information from the list box items. In the code, we use the previously defined constants for on-time and late delivery times.

Save and run the game. Click **Start Game**. Watch as orders start out green. After 30 minutes, they should turn red. After 60 minutes, they should disappear from the grid. Make sure the program is working as desired. You might like to change the **mSecPerMinute** constant (temporarily) to a smaller number to speed things up.

As seen previously, once the car reaches a delivery location, a check on the delivery status should be done. This check is completed in the **carTimerActionPerformed** method (we left a "hook" for this code). Using our rules, the steps followed are:

> ➢ If the delivery location did not order any pizzas, post message and exit.
> ➢ If the delivery location needs more pizza than is available, post message and exit.
> ➢ If on-time delivery, increment **pizzasOnTime** by number of pizzas ordered. Increment **totalSales** accordingly.
> ➢ If late delivery, increment **pizzasLate** by number of pizzas ordered. Increment **totalSales** accordingly.
> ➢ If successful delivery (whether on-time or late), decrement **pizzasInCar** and remove order from delivery grid and list box control.

Add the shaded code to the **carTimer Click** event method to implement these steps:

```java
private void carTimerActionPerformed(ActionEvent e)
{
  int i, c, r;
  String s;
  ImageIcon carIcon = null;
  deliveryGrid[carC][carR].setIcon(null);
  // move horizontally first
  if (deltaC != 0)
  {
    mileage++;
    carIcon = hCarIcon;
    if (deltaC > 0)
      carC++;
    else
      carC--;
    deltaC = deliveryC - carC;
  }
  else
  {
    if (deltaR != 0)
    {
      mileage++;
      carIcon = vCarIcon;
      if (deltaR > 0)
        carR++;
      else
        carR--;
      deltaR = deliveryR - carR;
    }
```

```
    }
    deliveryGrid[carC][carR].setIcon(carIcon);
    if (carC == deliveryC && carR == deliveryR)
    {
      beepSound.play();
      carTimer.stop();
      if (carC == pizzaC && carR == pizzaR)
      {
        messageTextArea.setText(" Car at Pizza Parlor:\n " +
display(carC, carR));
        deliveryGrid[carC][carR].setIcon(null);
        pizzasInCar = 0;
        inCarLabel.setText("0");
        loadCarButton.setEnabled(true);
      }
      else
      {
        messageTextArea.setText(" Car at " + display(carC,
carR));
        // check delivery status
        if (pizzas[deliveryC][deliveryR] == 0)
        {
          messageTextArea.append("\n No Pizza Wanted");
        }
        else
        {
          if (pizzas[deliveryC][deliveryR] > pizzasInCar)
          {
            messageTextArea.append("\n Not Enough Pizzas");
          }
          else
          {
            messageTextArea.append("\n Delivered " +
String.valueOf(pizzas[deliveryC][deliveryR]) + " Pizza");
            if (pizzas[deliveryC][deliveryR] > 1)
              messageTextArea.append("s");
            // see if on-time
            if ((clockMinute + 60 * clockHour) -
pizzaTime[deliveryC][deliveryR] <= orderLateTime)
            {
              messageTextArea.append(": On-Time");
              totalSales += pizzas[deliveryC][deliveryR] *
netSoldPizza;
              pizzasOnTime += pizzas[deliveryC][deliveryR];
            }
            else
            {
```

```
            messageTextArea.append(": Late!");
            totalSales += pizzas[deliveryC][deliveryR] *
netLatePizza;
            pizzasLate += pizzas[deliveryC][deliveryR];
         }
         salesLabel.setText("$" +
String.valueOf(totalSales));
         pizzasInCar -= pizzas[deliveryC][deliveryR];
         inCarLabel.setText(String.valueOf(pizzasInCar));
         pizzas[deliveryC][deliveryR] = 0;

deliveryGrid[deliveryC][deliveryR].setBackground(Color.WHI
TE);
         deliveryGrid[deliveryC][deliveryR].setText("");
         // remove from list
         for (i = 0; i < ordersListModel.getSize(); i++)
         {
            s =
String.valueOf(ordersListModel.getElementAt(i));
            c = ((int) s.charAt(6)) - 64;
            r = Integer.valueOf(s.substring(8,
10).trim()).intValue();
            if (c == deliveryC && r == deliveryR)
               break;
         }
         ordersListModel.removeElementAt(i);
      }
    }
   }
}
```

Notice how we search through items in the list box to find the item corresponding (matching column and row) to the order to remove. Review the formatting of these items to see how the row and column are extracted.

Run and save the project. At long last, you can run the entire simulation. You can accept orders, bake pizzas, load the car and direct the car to orders. You can return to the pizza parlor when you need more pizzas. Try playing for a while. Here's my form after delivering pizzas for a little over an hour:

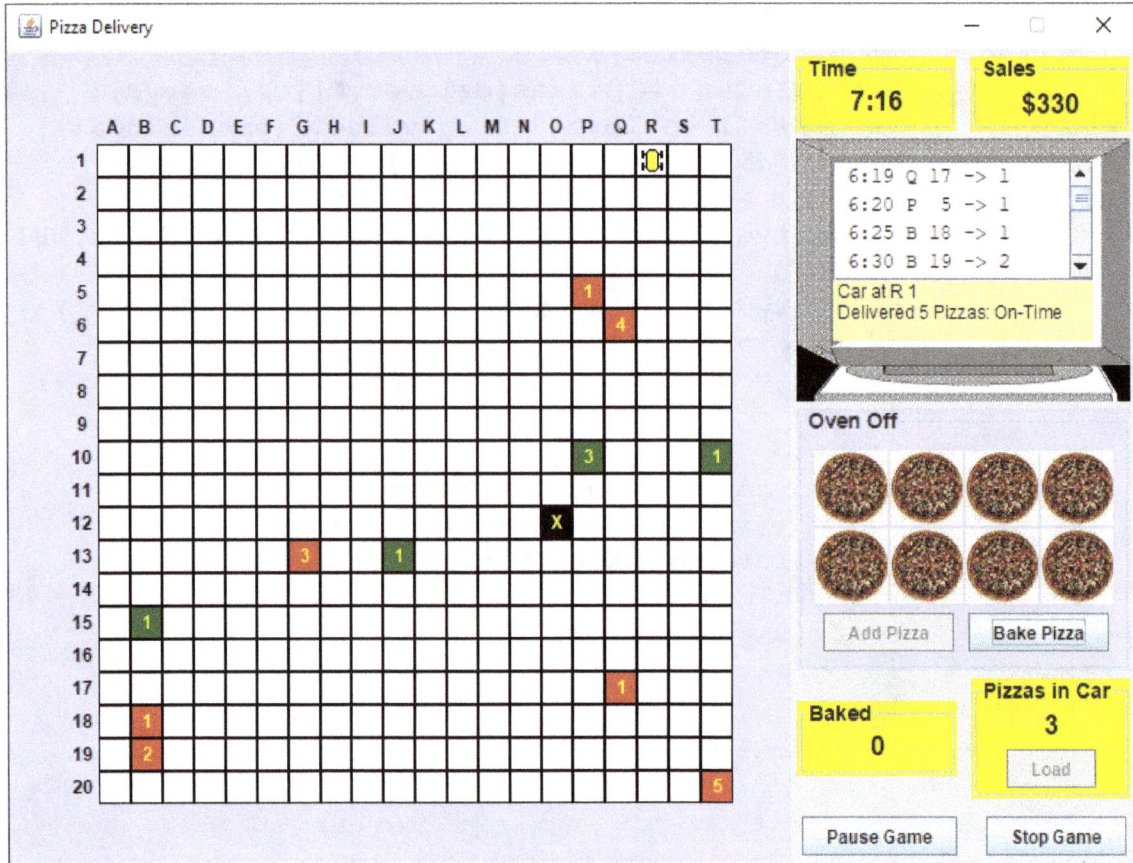

Stop the game and program when you're ready to go on. When you stop the game, the only results currently shown are the total sales. A total financial analysis should include costs to determine net profits. We'll use a separate frame to present this analysis. So let's see how to use multiple frame in a Java project.

Multiple Frame Java GUI Applications

All projects developed so far in these notes use a single frame. Many Java applications use **multiple frames**. The **About** window associated with some applications is a common example of using a second frame in an application. We want to learn how to manage multiple frames in our projects. There are three major considerations in using multiple frames:

1. Adding frames to a project
2. How to make frames appear and disappear using code
3. Transferring information to added frames

We will consider each of these points.

Before adding a new frame to a project, we assume a **main frame** has already been built. This is the frame that appears when a project begins. Such a frame has a **main** method that is invoked to start the project. Only one frame (class) in a Java project can have a main method. Hence, additional frames will not have a main method. From the main frame (**PizzaDelivery.java** in the current project), we construct and display other frames. t

To add a new frame to an application, we first add a new Java file to build the frame. Using **NetBeans**, right-click the project name and select **Add**, then **New Java Class**. In the window that appears, type the file name (**java** extension) for the new frame, select the current project **Package** name and click **Finish**. A blank pane will appear for the code. In this pane, we write the code to build the new frame using the same steps we have been using: add the controls, assign properties, and write code.

Display of different frames is handled by code you write. You need to decide when and how you want particular frames to be displayed. The user always interacts with the 'active' frame. There are two steps needed to display a frame. If the frame class is **MyFrame** (i.e. the code is in a file named **MyFrame.java**), an instance (**myFrame**) is first constructed using:

```
MyFrame myFrame  = new MyFrame();
```

Then, when desired, the frame is displayed using:

```
myFrame.setVisible(true);
```

To make a frame disappear, we use the **dispose** method. To close the current frame, use:

```
this.dispose();
```

The last consideration in a multiple frame application is to decide how (if needed) to transfer information from one frame to another. There are several ways to do this. We will look at transferring information using the **frame constructor**. Above we said to construct an instance of **myFrame**, we could use:

```
MyFrame myFrame  = new MyFrame();
```

To transfer formation to this new frame, we will not use this code, but replace it with an **overloaded** constructor for **MyFrame**:

```
MyFrame myFrame  = new MyFrame(variables);
```

where **variables** is a comma-delimited list of variables to transfer to **MyFrame**. An overloaded constructor gives us an alternate way to create an object. Once created, **myFrame** can access all the information provided by **variables**. We'll see how to do this with the **Pizza Delivery** results. You'll see it's a pretty easy modification.

Frame Design – Sales Results

When we stop the **Pizza Delivery** project, we want to display a frame of sales results. The finished frame will look like this:

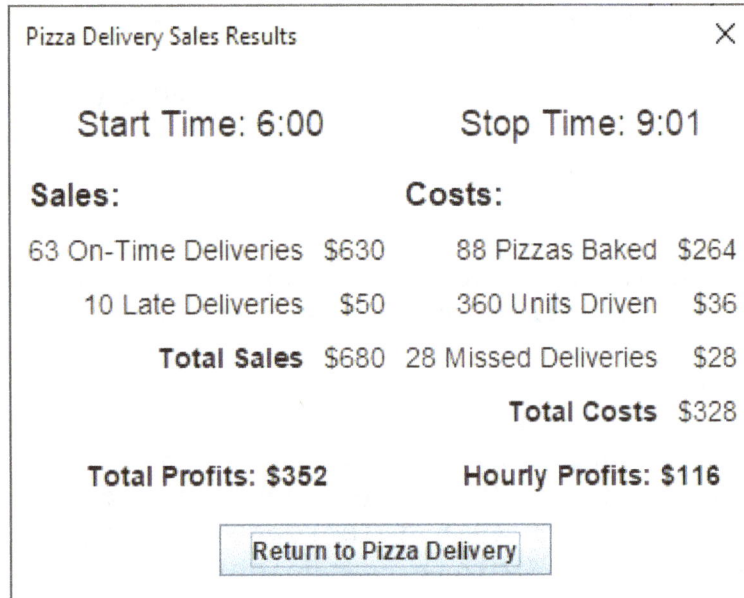

```
┌──────────────────────────────────────────────────┐
│ Pizza Delivery Sales Results                    ✕  │
│                                                    │
│     Start Time: 6:00         Stop Time: 9:01       │
│                                                    │
│   Sales:                    Costs:                 │
│                                                    │
│   63 On-Time Deliveries  $630    88 Pizzas Baked  $264 │
│                                                    │
│     10 Late Deliveries   $50    360 Units Driven   $36 │
│                                                    │
│        Total Sales  $680  28 Missed Deliveries   $28 │
│                                                    │
│                              Total Costs  $328     │
│                                                    │
│     Total Profits: $352      Hourly Profits: $116  │
│                                                    │
│            ┌──────────────────────────┐           │
│            │  Return to Pizza Delivery │           │
│            └──────────────────────────┘           │
└──────────────────────────────────────────────────┘
```

This frame is all label controls except for the single button at the bottom. Let's start building it. Add a file named **SalesResults.java** to your project's source folder (**Package pizzadelivery**). An empty code window should appear.

Build the basic frame with these properties:

PizzaDelivery Frame:
title	Pizza Delivery Sales Results
background	White
resizable	false

The code to build the basic frame is (**SalesResults.java**):

```java
/*
 * SalesResults.java
 */
package pizzadelivery;
import javax.swing.*;
import java.awt.*;
import java.awt.event.*;

public class SalesResults extends JFrame
{
```

```java
    public SalesResults()
    {
      // frame constructor
      setTitle("Pizza Delivery Sales Results");
      setResizable(false);
      getContentPane().setBackground(Color.WHITE);
      addWindowListener(new WindowAdapter()
      {
        public void windowClosing(WindowEvent evt)
        {
          exitForm(evt);
        }
      });
      getContentPane().setLayout(new GridBagLayout());
      GridBagConstraints gridConstraints;

      pack();
      Dimension screenSize =
  Toolkit.getDefaultToolkit().getScreenSize();
      setBounds((int) (0.5 * (screenSize.width -
  getWidth())), (int) (0.5 * (screenSize.height -
  getHeight())), getWidth(), getHeight());
    }

    private void exitForm(WindowEvent evt)
    {
      this.dispose();
    }
  }
```

This code is nearly identical to that used to build the Pizza Delivery frame with the exception there is <u>no main method</u>. Recall only the main frame (**PizzaDelivery.java** in this case) can have a main method. This code builds the frame, sets up the layout manager and includes code to close the frame. Even though there are no controls on the frame, let's write some code to display it.

Return to the **PizzaDelivery.java** file. Add the shaded code to
exitStopButtonActionPerformed method:

```java
private void exitStopButtonActionPerformed(ActionEvent e)
{
  if (exitStopButton.getText().equals("Stop Game"))
  {
    gameOverSound.play();
    exitStopButton.setText("Exit");
    startPauseButton.setText("Start Game");
    clockTimer.stop();
    phoneTimer.stop();
    ovenTimer.stop();
    addPizzaButton.setEnabled(false);
    bakePizzaButton.setEnabled(false);

ovenPanel.setBorder(BorderFactory.createTitledBorder("Oven
Off"));
    ovenPanel.setBackground(ovenOffColor);
    for (int i = 0; i < 8; i++)
      pizzaLabel[i].setIcon(null);
    addPizzaButton.setEnabled(false);
    bakePizzaButton.setEnabled(false);
    loadCarButton.setEnabled(false);
    carTimer.stop();
    SalesResults salesResults = new SalesResults();
    salesResults.setVisible(true);   }
  else
  {
    System.exit(0);
  }
}
```

With these lines, when the project is stopped, the sales results frame is created
and displayed.

Run the code. Click **Start Game**, then **Stop Game** to see the empty **Pizza Delivery Sales Results** frame appear::

This looks good, except for one thing. Notice you can switch back to the **Pizza Delivery** game and play again and create another results frame. We only want the possibility of one results frame that must be closed out before continuing with the Pizza Delivery game. How do we do that? It all has to do with something called **modality**.

What we currently have is a **modeless** frame. In **modeless** display, any other open application frame may be clicked and made active. Modeless frames are harder to program, because users can access them in an unpredictable order. We want a **modal** frame display, where no other open frame in the application may be accessed as long as the modal frame is open. The **About** box in most applications is an example of a **modal** display. A modal display must be closed before any other frame can be used. But there's a problem; the **JFrame** class we've been using to build frames does not allow modal displays, only modeless displays.

There is a class that does allow modal display – the **JDialog** class. We will use this class for adding frames to an existing application. For our purposes, the **JDialog** class is the same as the **JFrame** class, but with the additional optional capability of modal display. The modality of a **JDialog** object is set with the **modal** property. Make the two shaded changes to the current code for the sales results frame:

```
/*
 * SalesResults.java
 */
package pizzadelivery;
import javax.swing.*;
import java.awt.*;
import java.awt.event.*;

public class SalesResults extends JDialog
{
  public SalesResults()
  {
    // frame constructor
    setTitle("Pizza Delivery Sales Results");
    setResizable(false);
    setModal(true);
    getContentPane().setBackground(Color.WHITE);
    addWindowListener(new WindowAdapter()
    {
```

```
    public void windowClosing(WindowEvent evt)
    {
      exitForm(evt);
    }
  });
  getContentPane().setLayout(new GridBagLayout());
  GridBagConstraints gridConstraints;

  pack();
  Dimension screenSize =
Toolkit.getDefaultToolkit().getScreenSize();
    setBounds((int) (0.5 * (screenSize.width -
getWidth())), (int) (0.5 * (screenSize.height -
getHeight())), getWidth(), getHeight());
  }

  private void exitForm(WindowEvent evt)
  {
    this.dispose();;
  }
}
```

Run the project again. Click **Start Game**, then **Stop Game**. The sales results frame will appear, but you cannot switch back to the **Pizza Delivery** game until the sales results frame is closed by clicking the **X** in the upper corner. The second frame is now modal, as desired.

Let's populate the frame with controls. All code for creating the frame and placing controls (except declarations) goes in the **SalesResults** constructor. As mentioned, we need many labels and a single button control. The **GridBagLayout** is (split in two sections):

	gridx = 0	gridx = 1	gridx = 2
gridy = 0	startTimeLabel		
gridy = 1	gridTopLabel		
gridy = 2	salesHeaderLabel		gridMiddleLabel
gridy = 3	onTimeLabel	onTimeSalesLabel	gridMiddleLabel
gridy = 4	lateLabel	lateSalesLabel	gridMiddleLabel
gridy = 5	totalSalesHeaderLabel	totalSales	gridMiddleLabel
gridy = 6			gridMiddleLabel
gridy = 7	gridBottomLabel		
gridy = 8	totalProfitsLabel		
gridy = 9	returnButton		

	gridx = 3	gridx = 4
gridy = 0	stopTimeLabel	
gridy = 1	gridTopLabel (cont.)	
gridy = 2	costsHeaderLabel	
gridy = 3	bakedLabel	bakedCostsLabel
gridy = 4	milesLabel	milesCostsLabel
gridy = 5	missedLabel	missedCostsLabel
gridy = 6	totalCostsHeaderLabel	totalCosts
gridy = 7	gridBottomLabel (cont.)	
gridy = 8	hourlyProfitsLabel	
gridy = 9	returnButton (cont.)	

gridTopLabel, **gridMiddleLabel** and **gridBottomLabel** are 'skinny' labels used as borders. **startTimeLabel** and **stopTimeLabel** display the start and stop times, respectively. **salesHeaderLabel**, **onTimeLabel**, **onTimeSalesLabel**, **lateLabel**, **lateSalesLabel**, **totalSalesHeaderLabel** and **totalSales** are used to display sales information. **costHeaderLabel**, **bakedLabel**, **bakedCostsLabel**, **milesLabel**, **milesCostsLabel**, **missedLabel**, **missedCostsLabel**, **totalCostsHeaderLabel** and **totalCosts** are used to display cost information. **totalProfitsLabel** and **hourlyProfitsLabel** display profit information and **returnButton** is clicked to close the frame and return to **Pizza Delivery**.

The properties for these many controls are:

gridTopLabel:

size	375, 10
opaque	true
color	Blue
gridx	0
gridy	1
gridwidth	5
insets	5, 5, 0, 5

gridMiddleLabel:

size	10, 150
opaque	true
color	Blue
gridx	2
gridy	2
gridheight	5
insets	0, 5, 0, 5

gridBottomLabel:

size	375, 10
opaque	true
color	Blue
gridx	0
gridy	7
gridwidth	5
insets	0, 5, 5, 5

startTimeLabel:

text	Start Time: 6:00
font	Arial, PLAIN, Size 18
gridx	0
gridy	0
gridwidth	2
insets	10, 5, 0, 0

stopTimeLabel:

font	Arial, Plain, Size 18
gridx	3
gridy	0
gridwidth	2
insets	10, 0, 0, 0

salesHeaderLabel:

text	Sales:
font	Arial, Bold, Size 16
gridx	0
gridy	2
anchor	WEST
insets	10, 10, 0, 0

onTimeLabel:

font	Arial, Plain, Size 14
gridx	0
gridy	3
anchor	EAST
insets	10, 10, 0, 0

onTimeSalesLabel:

font	Arial, Plain, Size 14
gridx	1
gridy	3
anchor	EAST
insets	10, 10, 0, 0

lateLabel:

font	Arial, Plain, Size 14
gridx	0
gridy	4
anchor	EAST
insets	10, 10, 0, 0

lateSalesLabel:

font	Arial, Plain, Size 14
gridx	1
gridy	4
anchor	EAST
insets	10, 10, 0, 0

totalSalesHeaderLabel:

text	Total Sales:
font	Arial, Bold, Size 14
gridx	0
gridy	5
anchor	EAST
insets	10, 10, 0, 0

totalSalesLabel:
font	Arial, Plain, Size 14
gridx	1
gridy	5
anchor	EAST
insets	10, 10, 0, 0

costsHeaderLabel:
text	Costs:
font	Arial, Bold, Size 16
gridx	3
gridy	2
anchor	WEST
insets	10, 0, 0, 0

bakedLabel:
font	Arial, Plain, Size 14
gridx	3
gridy	3
anchor	EAST
insets	10, 0, 0, 10

bakedCostsLabel:
font	Arial, Plain, Size 14
gridx	4
gridy	3
anchor	EAST
insets	10, 0, 0, 10

milesLabel:
font	Arial, Plain, Size 14
gridx	3
gridy	4
anchor	EAST
insets	10, 0, 0, 10

milesCostsLabel:
font	Arial, Plain, Size 14
gridx	4
gridy	4
anchor	EAST
insets	10, 0, 0, 10

missedLabel:

font	Arial, Plain, Size 14
gridx	3
gridy	5
anchor	EAST
insets	10, 0, 0, 10

missedCostsLabel:

font	Arial, Plain, Size 14
gridx	4
gridy	5
anchor	EAST
insets	10, 0, 0, 10

totalCostsHeaderLabel:

text	Total Costs:
font	Arial, Bold, Size 14
gridx	3
gridy	6
anchor	EAST
insets	10, 0, 0, 10

totalCostsLabel:

font	Arial, Plain, Size 14
gridx	4
gridy	6
anchor	EAST
insets	10, 0, 0, 10

totalProfitsLabel:

font	Arial, Bold, Size 14
gridx	0
gridy	8
gridwidth	2
anchor	EAST
insets	10, 10, 10, 0

hourlyProfitsLabel:

font	Arial, Bold, Size 14
gridx	3
gridy	8
gridwidth	2
anchor	EAST
insets	10, 10, 10, 0

returnButton:

text	Return to Pizza Delivery
gridx	0
gridy	9
gridwidth	5
insets	5, 0, 5, 0

There are a lot of controls here, but the coding is straightforward. We'll add all the controls at once. Declare these controls using:

```
JLabel gridTopLabel = new JLabel();
JLabel gridMiddleLabel = new JLabel();
JLabel gridBottomLabel = new JLabel();
JLabel startTimeLabel = new JLabel();
JLabel stopTimeLabel = new JLabel();
JLabel salesHeaderLabel = new JLabel();
JLabel onTimeLabel = new JLabel();
JLabel onTimeSalesLabel = new JLabel();
JLabel lateLabel = new JLabel();
JLabel lateSalesLabel = new JLabel();
JLabel totalSalesHeaderLabel = new JLabel();
JLabel totalSalesLabel = new JLabel();
JLabel costsHeaderLabel = new JLabel();
JLabel bakedLabel = new JLabel();
JLabel bakedCostsLabel = new JLabel();
JLabel milesLabel = new JLabel();
JLabel milesCostsLabel = new JLabel();
JLabel missedLabel = new JLabel();
JLabel missedCostsLabel = new JLabel();
JLabel totalCostsHeaderLabel = new JLabel();
JLabel totalCostsLabel = new JLabel();
JLabel totalProfitsLabel = new JLabel();
JLabel hourlyProfitsLabel = new JLabel();
JButton returnButton = new JButton();
```

And add them to the frame with this code:

```
gridTopLabel.setPreferredSize(new Dimension(375, 10));
gridTopLabel.setOpaque(true);
gridTopLabel.setBackground(Color.BLUE);
gridConstraints = new GridBagConstraints();
gridConstraints.gridx = 0;
gridConstraints.gridy = 1;
gridConstraints.gridwidth = 5;
gridConstraints.insets = new Insets(5, 5, 0, 5);
getContentPane().add(gridTopLabel, gridConstraints);

gridMiddleLabel.setPreferredSize(new Dimension(10, 150));
gridMiddleLabel.setOpaque(true);
gridMiddleLabel.setBackground(Color.BLUE);
gridConstraints = new GridBagConstraints();
gridConstraints.gridx = 2;
gridConstraints.gridy = 2;
gridConstraints.gridheight = 5;
gridConstraints.insets = new Insets(0, 5, 0, 5);
getContentPane().add(gridMiddleLabel, gridConstraints);

gridBottomLabel.setPreferredSize(new Dimension(375, 10));
gridBottomLabel.setOpaque(true);
gridBottomLabel.setBackground(Color.BLUE);
gridConstraints = new GridBagConstraints();
gridConstraints.gridx = 0;
gridConstraints.gridy = 7;
gridConstraints.gridwidth = 5;
gridConstraints.insets = new Insets(0, 5, 5, 5);
getContentPane().add(gridBottomLabel, gridConstraints);

startTimeLabel.setText("Start Time: 6:00");
startTimeLabel.setFont(new Font("Arial", Font.PLAIN, 18));
gridConstraints = new GridBagConstraints();
gridConstraints.gridx = 0;
gridConstraints.gridy = 0;
gridConstraints.gridwidth = 2;
gridConstraints.insets = new Insets(10, 5, 0, 0);
getContentPane().add(startTimeLabel, gridConstraints);

stopTimeLabel.setFont(new Font("Arial", Font.PLAIN, 18));
gridConstraints = new GridBagConstraints();
gridConstraints.gridx = 3;
gridConstraints.gridy = 0;
gridConstraints.gridwidth = 2;
gridConstraints.insets = new Insets(10, 0, 0, 0);
```

```
getContentPane().add(stopTimeLabel, gridConstraints);

salesHeaderLabel.setText("Sales:");
salesHeaderLabel.setFont(new Font("Arial", Font.BOLD,
16));
gridConstraints = new GridBagConstraints();
gridConstraints.gridx = 0;
gridConstraints.gridy = 2;
gridConstraints.anchor = GridBagConstraints.WEST;
gridConstraints.insets = new Insets(10, 10, 0, 0);
getContentPane().add(salesHeaderLabel, gridConstraints);

onTimeLabel.setFont(new Font("Arial", Font.PLAIN, 14));
gridConstraints = new GridBagConstraints();
gridConstraints.gridx = 0;
gridConstraints.gridy = 3;
gridConstraints.anchor = GridBagConstraints.EAST;
gridConstraints.insets = new Insets(10, 10, 0, 0);
getContentPane().add(onTimeLabel, gridConstraints);

onTimeSalesLabel.setFont(new Font("Arial", Font.PLAIN,
14));
gridConstraints = new GridBagConstraints();
gridConstraints.gridx = 1;
gridConstraints.gridy = 3;
gridConstraints.anchor = GridBagConstraints.EAST;
gridConstraints.insets = new Insets(10, 10, 0, 0);
getContentPane().add(onTimeSalesLabel, gridConstraints);

lateLabel.setFont(new Font("Arial", Font.PLAIN, 14));
gridConstraints = new GridBagConstraints();
gridConstraints.gridx = 0;
gridConstraints.gridy = 4;
gridConstraints.anchor = GridBagConstraints.EAST;
gridConstraints.insets = new Insets(10, 10, 0, 0);
getContentPane().add(lateLabel, gridConstraints);

lateSalesLabel.setFont(new Font("Arial", Font.PLAIN, 14));
gridConstraints = new GridBagConstraints();
gridConstraints.gridx = 1;
gridConstraints.gridy = 4;
gridConstraints.anchor = GridBagConstraints.EAST;
gridConstraints.insets = new Insets(10, 10, 0, 0);
getContentPane().add(lateSalesLabel, gridConstraints);

totalSalesHeaderLabel.setText("Total Sales");
```

```
totalSalesHeaderLabel.setFont(new Font("Arial", Font.BOLD,
14));
gridConstraints = new GridBagConstraints();
gridConstraints.gridx = 0;
gridConstraints.gridy = 5;
gridConstraints.anchor = GridBagConstraints.EAST;
gridConstraints.insets = new Insets(10, 10, 0, 0);
getContentPane().add(totalSalesHeaderLabel,
gridConstraints);

totalSalesLabel.setFont(new Font("Arial", Font.PLAIN,
14));
gridConstraints = new GridBagConstraints();
gridConstraints.gridx = 1;
gridConstraints.gridy = 5;
gridConstraints.anchor = GridBagConstraints.EAST;
gridConstraints.insets = new Insets(10, 10, 0, 0);
getContentPane().add(totalSalesLabel, gridConstraints);

costsHeaderLabel.setText("Costs:");
costsHeaderLabel.setFont(new Font("Arial", Font.BOLD,
16));
gridConstraints = new GridBagConstraints();
gridConstraints.gridx = 3;
gridConstraints.gridy = 2;
gridConstraints.anchor = GridBagConstraints.WEST;
gridConstraints.insets = new Insets(10, 0, 0, 0);
getContentPane().add(costsHeaderLabel, gridConstraints);

bakedLabel.setFont(new Font("Arial", Font.PLAIN, 14));
gridConstraints = new GridBagConstraints();
gridConstraints.gridx = 3;
gridConstraints.gridy = 3;
gridConstraints.anchor = GridBagConstraints.EAST;
gridConstraints.insets = new Insets(10, 0, 0, 10);
getContentPane().add(bakedLabel, gridConstraints);

bakedCostsLabel.setFont(new Font("Arial", Font.PLAIN,
14));
gridConstraints = new GridBagConstraints();
gridConstraints.gridx = 4;
gridConstraints.gridy = 3;
gridConstraints.anchor = GridBagConstraints.EAST;
gridConstraints.insets = new Insets(10, 0, 0, 10);
getContentPane().add(bakedCostsLabel, gridConstraints);

milesLabel.setFont(new Font("Arial", Font.PLAIN, 14));
```

```
gridConstraints = new GridBagConstraints();
gridConstraints.gridx = 3;
gridConstraints.gridy = 4;
gridConstraints.anchor = GridBagConstraints.EAST;
gridConstraints.insets = new Insets(10, 0, 0, 10);
getContentPane().add(milesLabel, gridConstraints);

milesCostsLabel.setFont(new Font("Arial", Font.PLAIN,
14));
gridConstraints = new GridBagConstraints();
gridConstraints.gridx = 4;
gridConstraints.gridy = 4;
gridConstraints.anchor = GridBagConstraints.EAST;
gridConstraints.insets = new Insets(10, 0, 0, 10);
getContentPane().add(milesCostsLabel, gridConstraints);

missedLabel.setFont(new Font("Arial", Font.PLAIN, 14));
gridConstraints = new GridBagConstraints();
gridConstraints.gridx = 3;
gridConstraints.gridy = 5;
gridConstraints.anchor = GridBagConstraints.EAST;
gridConstraints.insets = new Insets(10, 0, 0, 10);
getContentPane().add(missedLabel, gridConstraints);

missedCostsLabel.setFont(new Font("Arial", Font.PLAIN,
14));
gridConstraints = new GridBagConstraints();
gridConstraints.gridx = 4;
gridConstraints.gridy = 5;
gridConstraints.anchor = GridBagConstraints.EAST;
gridConstraints.insets = new Insets(10, 0, 0, 10);
getContentPane().add(missedCostsLabel, gridConstraints);

totalCostsHeaderLabel.setText("Total Costs");
totalCostsHeaderLabel.setFont(new Font("Arial", Font.BOLD,
14));
gridConstraints = new GridBagConstraints();
gridConstraints.gridx = 3;
gridConstraints.gridy = 6;
gridConstraints.anchor = GridBagConstraints.EAST;
gridConstraints.insets = new Insets(10, 0, 0, 10);
getContentPane().add(totalCostsHeaderLabel,
gridConstraints);

totalCostsLabel.setFont(new Font("Arial", Font.PLAIN,
14));
gridConstraints = new GridBagConstraints();
```

```
gridConstraints.gridx = 4;
gridConstraints.gridy = 6;
gridConstraints.anchor = GridBagConstraints.EAST;
gridConstraints.insets = new Insets(10, 0, 0, 10);
getContentPane().add(totalCostsLabel, gridConstraints);

totalProfitsLabel.setFont(new Font("Arial", Font.BOLD,
14));
gridConstraints = new GridBagConstraints();
gridConstraints.gridx = 0;
gridConstraints.gridy = 8;
gridConstraints.gridwidth = 2;
gridConstraints.insets = new Insets(10, 10, 10, 0);
getContentPane().add(totalProfitsLabel, gridConstraints);

hourlyProfitsLabel.setFont(new Font("Arial", Font.BOLD,
14));
gridConstraints = new GridBagConstraints();
gridConstraints.gridx = 3;
gridConstraints.gridy = 8;
gridConstraints.gridwidth = 2;
gridConstraints.insets = new Insets(10, 10, 10, 0);
getContentPane().add(hourlyProfitsLabel, gridConstraints);

returnButton.setText("Return to Pizza Delivery");
gridConstraints = new GridBagConstraints();
gridConstraints.gridx = 0;
gridConstraints.gridy = 9;
gridConstraints.gridwidth = 5;
gridConstraints.insets = new Insets(5, 0, 5, 0);
getContentPane().add(returnButton, gridConstraints);
returnButton.addActionListener(new ActionListener()
{
  public void actionPerformed(ActionEvent e)
  {
    returnButtonActionPerformed(e);
  }
});
```

The above code adds a listener for the button control. We simply close the frame if this button is clicked. Add this method:

```
private void returnButtonActionPerformed(ActionEvent e)
{
  this.dispose();
}
```

Run the project. Click **Start Game**, then **Stop Game**. You should see:

```
Pizza Delivery Sales Results                          X

Start Time: 6:00


Sales:              Costs:


Total Sales


                    Total Costs



            Return to Pizza Delivery
```

The frame appears, but many of the labels (**stopTimeLabel, onTimeLabel, onTimeSalesLabel, lateLabel, lateSalesLabel, totalSalesLabel, bakedLabel, bakedCostsLabel, milesLabel, milesCostsLabel, missedLabel, missedCostsLabel, totalCostsLabel, totalProfitsLabel** and **hourlyProfitsLabel**) are blank. We need information from the main frame to fill in the text properties of these labels. We do this next. Click **Return to Pizza Delivery** to make sure the frame disappears.

Code Design – Sales Results

To fill all the listed empty label controls on the sales results form, we need these variables from the **Pizza Delivery** frame:

clockHour	**clockMinute**
pizzasOnTime	**netSoldPizza**
pizzasLate	**netLatePizza**
totalPizzasBaked	**pizzaCost**
mileage	**mileageCost**
missedDeliveries	**costMissedPizza**

We will build an overloaded constructor that passes this information into the frame and displays it in the proper label controls. Modify the header line for the **SalesResults** constructor to:

```
public SalesResults(int clockHour, int clockMinute, int
pizzasOnTime, int netSoldPizza, int pizzasLate, int
netLatePizza, int totalPizzasBaked, int pizzaCost, int
mileage, double mileageCost, int missedDeliveries, int
costMissedPizza)
```

and add this code at the end of the constructor:

```
if (clockMinute < 10)
   stopTimeLabel.setText("Stop Time: " +
String.valueOf(clockHour) + ":0" +
String.valueOf(clockMinute));
else
   stopTimeLabel.setText("Stop Time: " +
String.valueOf(clockHour) + ":" +
String.valueOf(clockMinute));
onTimeLabel.setText(String.valueOf(pizzasOnTime) + " On-
Time Deliveries");
onTimeSalesLabel.setText("$" + String.valueOf(pizzasOnTime
* netSoldPizza));
lateLabel.setText(String.valueOf(pizzasLate) + " Late
Deliveries");
lateSalesLabel.setText("$" + String.valueOf(pizzasLate *
netLatePizza));
int totalSales = pizzasOnTime * netSoldPizza + pizzasLate
* netLatePizza;
totalSalesLabel.setText("$" + String.valueOf(totalSales));
bakedLabel.setText(String.valueOf(totalPizzasBaked) + "
Pizzas Baked");
```

```
bakedCostsLabel.setText("$" +
String.valueOf(totalPizzasBaked * pizzaCost));
milesLabel.setText(String.valueOf(mileage) + " Units
Driven");
milesCostsLabel.setText("$" + String.valueOf((int)
(mileage * mileageCost)));
missedLabel.setText(String.valueOf(missedDeliveries) + "
Missed Deliveries");
missedCostsLabel.setText("$" +
String.valueOf(missedDeliveries * costMissedPizza));
int totalCosts = (int) (totalPizzasBaked * pizzaCost +
mileage * mileageCost + missedDeliveries *
costMissedPizza);
totalCostsLabel.setText("$" + String.valueOf(totalCosts));
totalProfitsLabel.setText("Total Profits: $" +
String.valueOf(totalSales - totalCosts));
if (clockHour > 6)
{
  double hours = clockHour - 6 + (double) clockMinute /
60;
  hourlyProfitsLabel.setText("Hourly Profits: $" +
String.valueOf((int) ((totalSales - totalCosts) /
hours)));
}
else
  hourlyProfitsLabel.setText("");
```

The added code in this constructor is fairly simple. It sets the **text** properties (doing intermediate calculations in some cases) for the various label controls on the **SalesResults** frame. Note we only display hourly profits if the program has been running for "one hour."

One last change – since we're using a new constructor, we need to modify the code used to create the sales results frame. Return to the code window for the **Pizza Delivery** frame. Replace the current **SalesResults** constructor with the shaded code to the **exitStopButtonActionPerformed** method:

```
private void exitStopButtonActionPerformed(ActionEvent e)
{
  if (exitStopButton.getText().equals("Stop Game"))
  {
    gameOverSound.play();
    exitStopButton.setText("Exit");
    startPauseButton.setText("Start Game");
    clockTimer.stop();
    phoneTimer.stop();
    ovenTimer.stop();
    addPizzaButton.setEnabled(false);
    bakePizzaButton.setEnabled(false);

ovenPanel.setBorder(BorderFactory.createTitledBorder("Oven
Off"));
    ovenPanel.setBackground(ovenOffColor);
    for (int i = 0; i < 8; i++)
      pizzaLabel[i].setIcon(null);
    addPizzaButton.setEnabled(false);
    bakePizzaButton.setEnabled(false);
    loadCarButton.setEnabled(false);
    carTimer.stop();
    SalesResults salesResults = new
SalesResults(clockHour, clockMinute, pizzasOnTime,
netSoldPizza, pizzasLate, netLatePizza, totalPizzasBaked,
pizzaCost, mileage, mileageCost, missedDeliveries,
costMissedPizza);
    salesResults.setVisible(true);
  }
  else
  {
    System.exit(0);
  }
}
```

The new code creates an instance of the results frame (using our new constructor). It then displays the results form.

Save and run the project one last time. It is now complete. You should be able to play a full game of **Pizza Delivery** and receive a sales report. Here's my display after a few orders have come in:

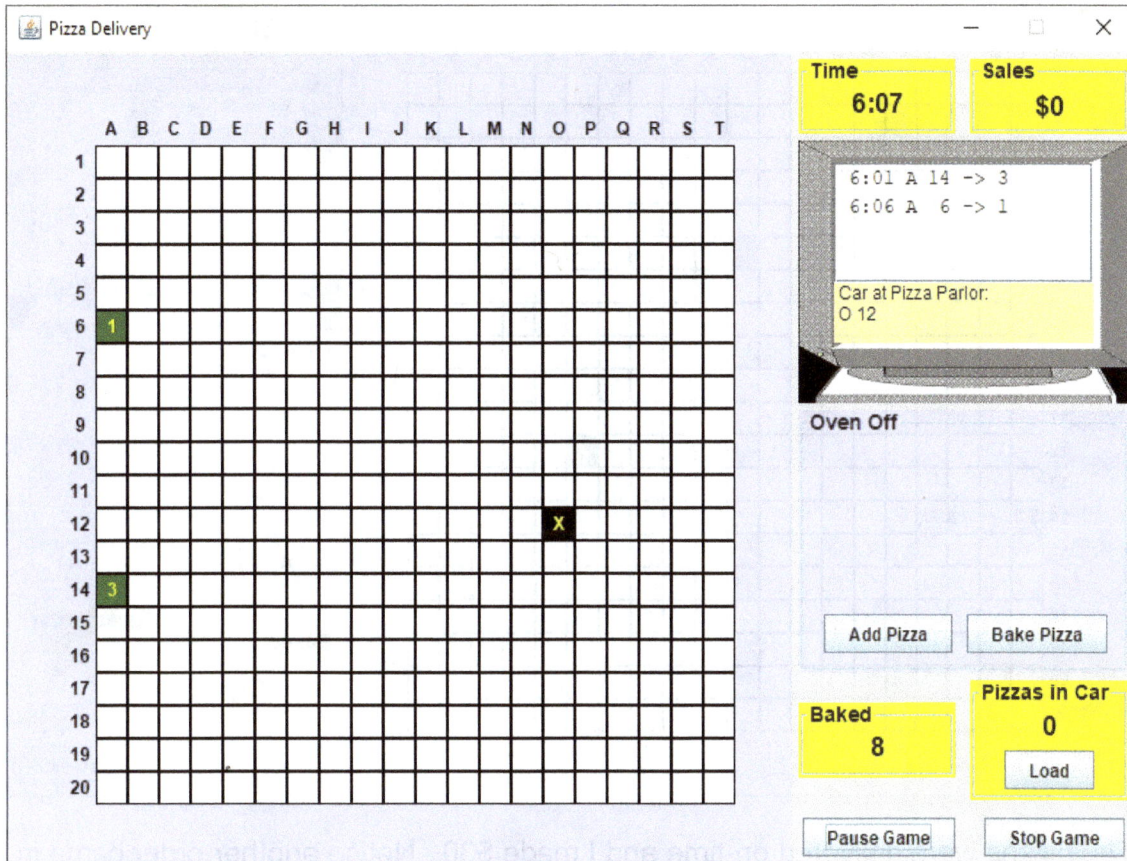

At 6:01, an order for 3 pizzas was taken for delivery to Column A, Row 14 (also marked on grid). At 6:06, 1 pizzas was ordered at A 6. I click **Load** to get some pizzas. Then, I click A 14 on the grid.

My car goes there, beeps and makes a delivery. Then, I see:

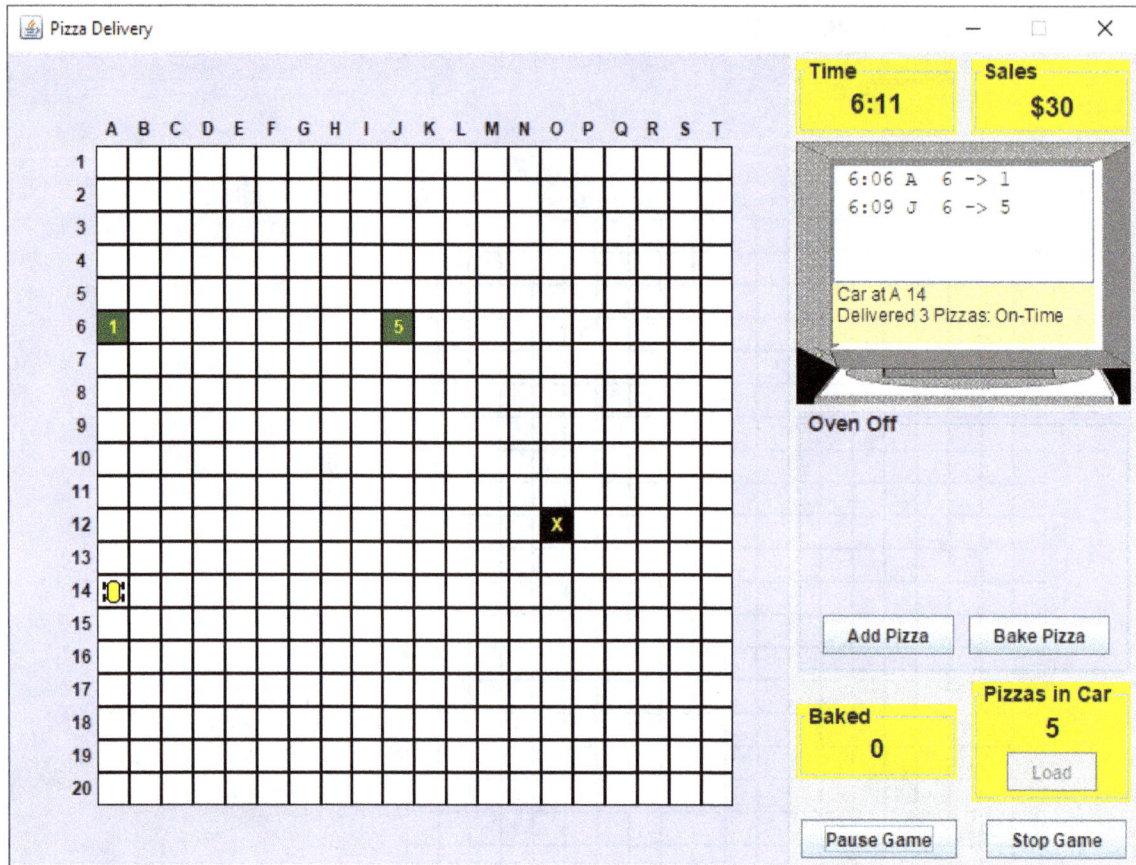

The pizzas were delivered on-time and I made $30. Notice another order came in while I was making the delivery. Next, I make the delivery at J 6. After that delivery, I'm out of pizzas and head back and stock up on more pizzas. To do this, I click the **X** mark to return to the pizza parlor.

I click the **Add Pizza** button 8 times to load the oven, then click **Bake Pizza** to start the oven:

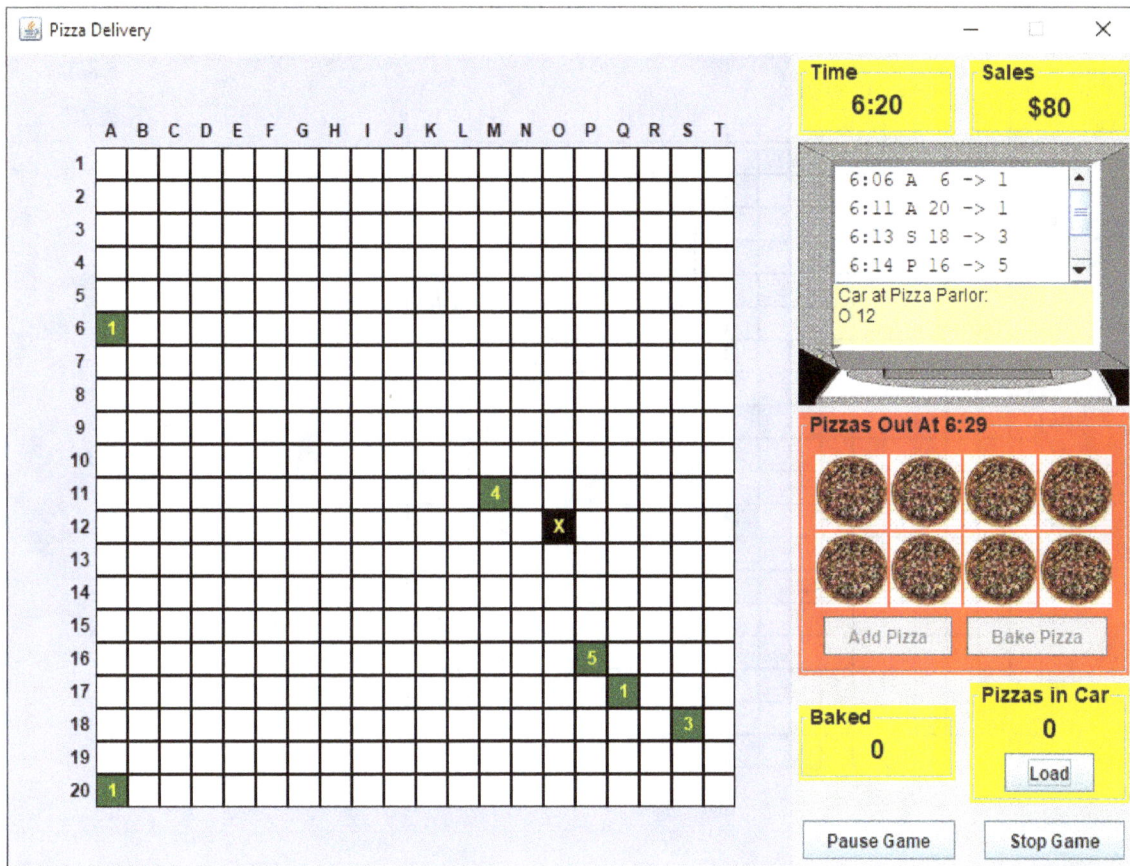

I could have started the baking process while I was out on the road, speeding things up a bit. Now, I'm forced to wait several minutes while the pizzas bake. Meanwhile, orders are waiting.

After playing for a little over an hour, my form looks like this:

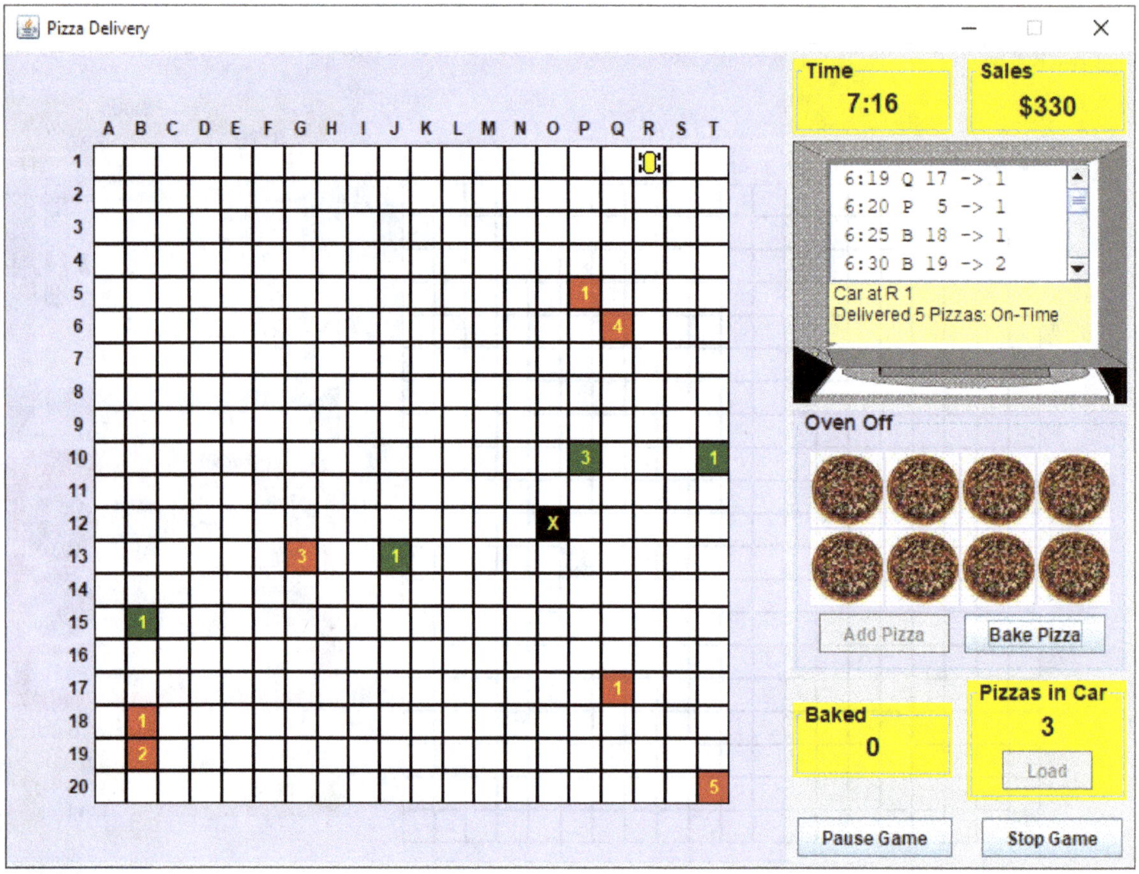

I've got lots of orders and lots of pizzas going. Order with red backgrounds indicate we're late. I need to rush those pizzas out.

I ran **Pizza Delivery** to around 9:00 (closing before the usual 11:00). At that point, I clicked **Stop Game** and the sales results form appears:

```
┌─────────────────────────────────────────────────────┐
│ Pizza Delivery Sales Results                       ✕  │
│                                                       │
│     Start Time: 6:00         Stop Time: 9:01          │
│                                                       │
│   Sales:                   Costs:                     │
│                                                       │
│   63 On-Time Deliveries  $630    88 Pizzas Baked  $264│
│       10 Late Deliveries   $50   360 Units Driven  $36│
│          Total Sales  $680  28 Missed Deliveries  $28 │
│                                   Total Costs  $328    │
│                                                       │
│   Total Profits: $352      Hourly Profits: $116       │
│            ┌─────────────────────────────┐           │
│            │  Return to Pizza Delivery   │           │
│            └─────────────────────────────┘           │
└─────────────────────────────────────────────────────┘
```

Notice how all the labels on this frame are now filled in with values. I did pretty good, making $352.

Pizza Delivery Project Review

The **Pizza Delivery** project is now complete. Save and run the project and make sure it works as promised. Check that all options work correctly.

If there are errors in your implementation, go back over the steps of frame and code design. Go over the developed code – make sure you understand how different parts of the project were coded. As mentioned in the beginning of this chapter, the completed project is saved as **PizzaDelivery** in the **\KidGamesJava\KidGamesJava Projects** folder.

While completing this project, new concepts and skills you should have gained include:

> ➢ Proper steps in game design and game flow.
> ➢ Capabilities and use of many Java controls.
> ➢ How to develop and use simulation rules.
> ➢ Use of the list box control.
> ➢ Working with multi-frame projects.

Pizza Delivery Project Enhancements

There are some ways to change the **Pizza Delivery** project. Some possibilities are:

> ➤ The game difficulty can be adjusted if you like. By varying the time between phone orders, the size of orders, the time needed to make a delivery and the speed of the car, you can make the game easier or harder. You would need some way for the player to select a difficulty.
> ➤ The current car cannot be re-routed once it starts. Modify the click logic to re-route the car if desired.
> ➤ Once business builds, you might need a second car. Think of ways you might be able to implement and control more than one car.
> ➤ This particular pizza parlor only makes one kind of pizza. This simplifies the simulation somewhat. The car can stay out on the road and deliver whatever pizzas are in the car. The oven can just keep cranking out pizzas. It would be interesting to make different types of pizzas available for order. You would have to know how many of each are ordered, bake different types and load different types into the car. This would be more like a real pizza delivery process.

Pizza Delivery Project Java Code Listing

There are two files, **PizzaDelivery.java** and **SalesResults.java**.

PizzaDelivery.java:

```java
/*
 * PizzaDelivery.java
 */
package pizzadelivery;
import javax.swing.*;
import java.awt.*;
import java.awt.event.*;
import java.net.URL;
import java.applet.*;
import java.util.Random;

public class PizzaDelivery extends JFrame
{

  JPanel gridPanel = new JPanel();
  JLabel[][] deliveryGrid = new JLabel[21][21];
  JPanel timePanel = new JPanel();
  JLabel timeLabel = new JLabel();
  JPanel salesPanel = new JPanel();
  JLabel salesLabel = new JLabel();
  ImagePanel ordersPanel = new ImagePanel(new
ImageIcon("monitor.gif").getImage());
  JScrollPane ordersScrollPane = new JScrollPane();
  JList ordersList = new JList();
  DefaultListModel ordersListModel = new DefaultListModel();
  JTextArea messageTextArea = new JTextArea();
  JPanel ovenPanel = new JPanel();
  JLabel[] pizzaLabel = new JLabel[8];
  JButton addPizzaButton = new JButton();
  JButton bakePizzaButton = new JButton();
  JPanel readyPanel = new JPanel();
  JLabel readyLabel = new JLabel();
  JPanel inCarPanel = new JPanel();
  JLabel inCarLabel = new JLabel();
  JButton loadCarButton = new JButton();
  JPanel buttonsPanel = new JPanel();
  JButton startPauseButton = new JButton();
  JButton exitStopButton = new JButton();

  Timer clockTimer;
```

```
Timer phoneTimer;
Timer ovenTimer;
Timer carTimer;

Color gridColor = new Color(208, 208, 255);
Color messageColor = new Color(255, 255, 176);
Color ovenOffColor = new Color(208, 208, 255);
Color onTimeDeliveryColor = new Color(0, 108, 0);
Color ovenOnColor = Color.RED;
Color lateDeliveryColor = new Color(224, 0, 0);

final int mSecPerMin = 3000;
final int pizzasReadyMax = 20;
final int pizzasBakingMax = 8;
final int bakingTime = 10;
final int pizzasInCarMax = 10;
final int minPer20Squares = 3;
final int orderMaxTime = 60;
final int orderLateTime = 30;
final int netSoldPizza = 10;
final int netLatePizza = 5;
final int costMissedPizza = 1;
final int pizzaCost = 3;
final double mileageCost = 0.1;


int clockHour, clockMinute;
int [][] pizzas = new int[21][21];
int [][] pizzaTime = new int[21][21];
Random myRandom = new Random();
int pizzasBaking, pizzasReady;
int totalPizzasBaked;
int bakingMinutesLeft;
boolean ovenGoing;
int pizzasInCar;
boolean loadCarButtonEnabled;
int pizzaC, pizzaR;
int deliveryC, deliveryR;
int carC, carR;
int deltaC, deltaR;
int mileage;
boolean carGoing;
int pizzasOnTime;
int pizzasLate;
int missedDeliveries;
int totalSales;
```

```java
ImageIcon pizzaIcon = new ImageIcon("pizza.gif");
ImageIcon hCarIcon = new ImageIcon("hcar.gif");
ImageIcon vCarIcon = new ImageIcon("vcar.gif");

AudioClip gameOverSound;
AudioClip phoneSound;
AudioClip dingSound;
AudioClip beepSound;

public static void main(String args[])
{
  // create frame
  new PizzaDelivery().setVisible(true);
}

public PizzaDelivery()
{
  // frame constructor
  setTitle("Pizza Delivery");
  setResizable(false);
  addWindowListener(new WindowAdapter()
  {
    public void windowClosing(WindowEvent evt)
    {
      exitForm(evt);
    }
  });
  getContentPane().setLayout(new GridBagLayout());
  GridBagConstraints gridConstraints;

  gridPanel.setPreferredSize(new Dimension(540, 540));
  gridPanel.setBackground(gridColor);
  gridPanel.setLayout(new GridBagLayout());
  gridConstraints = new GridBagConstraints();
  gridConstraints.gridx = 0;
  gridConstraints.gridy = 0;
  gridConstraints.gridheight = 5;
  getContentPane().add(gridPanel, gridConstraints);

  int w = (int) gridPanel.getPreferredSize().width / 24;
  // j is row, i is column; build one row at a time
  for (int j = 0; j < 21; j++)
  {
    // start new row
    for (int i = 0; i < 21; i++)
    {
      deliveryGrid[i][j] = new JLabel();
```

```
        deliveryGrid[i][j].setPreferredSize(new Dimension(w,
w));
        deliveryGrid[i][j].setFont(new Font("Arial",
Font.BOLD, 12));

deliveryGrid[i][j].setHorizontalAlignment(SwingConstants.CEN
TER);
        gridConstraints = new GridBagConstraints();
        gridConstraints.gridy = j;
        gridConstraints.gridx =i;
        if (i == 0)
        {
          if (j != 0)
          {
            // row numbers
            deliveryGrid[i][j].setText(String.valueOf(j));
            deliveryGrid[i][j].setForeground(Color.BLACK);
          }
        }
        else if (j == 0)
        {
          if (i != 0)
          {
            // column letters
            deliveryGrid[i][j].setText(String.valueOf((char)
(i + 64)));
            deliveryGrid[i][j].setForeground(Color.BLACK);
          }
        }
        else
        {

deliveryGrid[i][j].setBorder(BorderFactory.createLineBorder(
Color.BLACK));
          deliveryGrid[i][j].setOpaque(true);
          deliveryGrid[i][j].setBackground(Color.WHITE);
          deliveryGrid[i][j].setForeground(Color.YELLOW);
        }
        gridPanel.add(deliveryGrid[i][j], gridConstraints);
        deliveryGrid[i][j].addMouseListener(new
MouseAdapter()
        {
          public void mousePressed(MouseEvent e)
          {
            deliveryGridMousePressed(e);
          }
        });
```

```
        }
    }

    UIManager.put("TitledBorder.font", new Font("Arial",
Font.BOLD, 14));
    timePanel.setPreferredSize(new Dimension(110, 50));
    timePanel.setBackground(Color.YELLOW);

timePanel.setBorder(BorderFactory.createTitledBorder("Time")
);
    timePanel.setLayout(new GridBagLayout());
    gridConstraints = new GridBagConstraints();
    gridConstraints.gridx = 1;
    gridConstraints.gridy = 0;
    gridConstraints.insets = new Insets(5, 5, 5, 5);
    getContentPane().add(timePanel, gridConstraints);

    timeLabel.setText("6:00");
    timeLabel.setFont(new Font("Arial", Font.BOLD, 18));
    gridConstraints = new GridBagConstraints();
    gridConstraints.gridx = 0;
    gridConstraints.gridy = 0;
    gridConstraints.insets = new Insets(0, 0, 5, 0);
    timePanel.add(timeLabel, gridConstraints);

    salesPanel.setPreferredSize(new Dimension(110, 50));
    salesPanel.setBackground(Color.YELLOW);

salesPanel.setBorder(BorderFactory.createTitledBorder("Sales
"));
    salesPanel.setLayout(new GridBagLayout());
    gridConstraints = new GridBagConstraints();
    gridConstraints.gridx = 2;
    gridConstraints.gridy = 0;
    gridConstraints.insets = new Insets(5, 5, 5, 5);
    getContentPane().add(salesPanel, gridConstraints);

    salesLabel.setText("$0");
    salesLabel.setFont(new Font("Arial", Font.BOLD, 18));
    gridConstraints = new GridBagConstraints();
    gridConstraints.gridx = 0;
    gridConstraints.gridy = 0;
    gridConstraints.insets = new Insets(0, 0, 5, 0);
    salesPanel.add(salesLabel, gridConstraints);

    salesPanel.setPreferredSize(new Dimension(110, 50));
    salesPanel.setBackground(Color.YELLOW);
```

```
salesPanel.setBorder(BorderFactory.createTitledBorder("Sales
"));
    salesPanel.setLayout(new GridBagLayout());
    gridConstraints = new GridBagConstraints();
    gridConstraints.gridx = 2;
    gridConstraints.gridy = 0;
    gridConstraints.insets = new Insets(5, 5, 5, 5);
    getContentPane().add(salesPanel, gridConstraints);

    ordersPanel.setPreferredSize(new Dimension(230, 175));
    ordersPanel.setLayout(new GridBagLayout());
    gridConstraints = new GridBagConstraints();
    gridConstraints.gridx = 1;
    gridConstraints.gridy = 1;
    gridConstraints.gridwidth = 2;
    gridConstraints.insets = new Insets(0, 5, 5, 5);
    getContentPane().add(ordersPanel, gridConstraints);

    ordersScrollPane.setPreferredSize(new Dimension(180,
80));
    ordersScrollPane.setViewportView(ordersList);
    ordersList.setFont(new Font("Courier New", Font.PLAIN,
14));
    ordersList.setModel(ordersListModel);
    gridConstraints = new GridBagConstraints();
    gridConstraints.gridx = 0;
    gridConstraints.gridy = 0;
    ordersPanel.add(ordersScrollPane, gridConstraints);

    messageTextArea.setPreferredSize(new Dimension(180,
40));
    messageTextArea.setEditable(false);
    messageTextArea.setOpaque(true);
    messageTextArea.setBackground(messageColor);
    messageTextArea.setFont(new Font("Arial", Font.PLAIN,
12));
    gridConstraints = new GridBagConstraints();
    gridConstraints.gridx = 0;
    gridConstraints.gridy = 1;
    gridConstraints.insets = new Insets(0, 0, 25, 0);
    ordersPanel.add(messageTextArea, gridConstraints);

    ovenPanel.setPreferredSize(new Dimension(230, 175));
    ovenPanel.setBackground(ovenOffColor);
```

```java
ovenPanel.setBorder(BorderFactory.createTitledBorder("Oven
Off"));
    ovenPanel.setLayout(new GridBagLayout());
    gridConstraints = new GridBagConstraints();
    gridConstraints.gridx = 1;
    gridConstraints.gridy = 2;
    gridConstraints.gridwidth = 2;
    gridConstraints.insets = new Insets(0, 5, 5, 5);
    getContentPane().add(ovenPanel, gridConstraints);

    for (int i = 0; i < 8; i++)
    {
      pizzaLabel[i] = new JLabel();
      pizzaLabel[i].setPreferredSize(new Dimension(50, 50));
      gridConstraints = new GridBagConstraints();
      gridConstraints.gridx = i % 4;
      gridConstraints.gridy = i / 4;
      gridConstraints.insets = new Insets(1, 1, 1, 1);
      ovenPanel.add(pizzaLabel[i], gridConstraints);
    }

    addPizzaButton.setText("Add Pizza");
    addPizzaButton.setEnabled(false);
    gridConstraints = new GridBagConstraints();
    gridConstraints.gridx = 0;
    gridConstraints.gridy = 2;
    gridConstraints.gridwidth = 2;
    gridConstraints.insets = new Insets(5, 0, 0, 0);
    ovenPanel.add(addPizzaButton, gridConstraints);
    addPizzaButton.addActionListener(new ActionListener()
    {
      public void actionPerformed(ActionEvent e)
      {
        addPizzaButtonActionPerformed(e);
      }
    });

    bakePizzaButton.setText("Bake Pizza");
    bakePizzaButton.setEnabled(false);
    gridConstraints = new GridBagConstraints();
    gridConstraints.gridx = 2;
    gridConstraints.gridy = 2;
    gridConstraints.gridwidth = 2;
    gridConstraints.insets = new Insets(5, 0, 0, 0);
    ovenPanel.add(bakePizzaButton, gridConstraints);
    bakePizzaButton.addActionListener(new ActionListener()
```

```
    {
      public void actionPerformed(ActionEvent e)
      {
        bakePizzaButtonActionPerformed(e);
      }
    });

    readyPanel.setPreferredSize(new Dimension(110, 50));
    readyPanel.setBackground(Color.YELLOW);

readyPanel.setBorder(BorderFactory.createTitledBorder("Baked
"));
    readyPanel.setLayout(new GridBagLayout());
    gridConstraints = new GridBagConstraints();
    gridConstraints.gridx = 1;
    gridConstraints.gridy = 3;
    gridConstraints.insets = new Insets(0, 5, 5, 5);
    getContentPane().add(readyPanel, gridConstraints);

    readyLabel.setText("0");
    readyLabel.setFont(new Font("Arial", Font.BOLD, 18));
    gridConstraints = new GridBagConstraints();
    gridConstraints.gridx = 0;
    gridConstraints.gridy = 0;
    gridConstraints.insets = new Insets(0, 0, 5, 0);
    readyPanel.add(readyLabel, gridConstraints);

    inCarPanel.setPreferredSize(new Dimension(110, 80));
    inCarPanel.setBackground(Color.YELLOW);

inCarPanel.setBorder(BorderFactory.createTitledBorder("Pizza
s in Car"));
    inCarPanel.setLayout(new GridBagLayout());
    gridConstraints = new GridBagConstraints();
    gridConstraints.gridx = 2;
    gridConstraints.gridy = 3;
    gridConstraints.insets = new Insets(0, 5, 5, 5);
    getContentPane().add(inCarPanel, gridConstraints);

    inCarLabel.setText("0");
    inCarLabel.setFont(new Font("Arial", Font.BOLD, 18));
    gridConstraints = new GridBagConstraints();
    gridConstraints.gridx = 0;
    gridConstraints.gridy = 0;
    gridConstraints.insets = new Insets(0, 0, 5, 0);
    inCarPanel.add(inCarLabel, gridConstraints);
```

```
loadCarButton.setText("Load");
loadCarButton.setEnabled(false);
gridConstraints = new GridBagConstraints();
gridConstraints.gridx = 0;
gridConstraints.gridy = 1;
inCarPanel.add(loadCarButton, gridConstraints);
loadCarButton.addActionListener(new ActionListener()
{
  public void actionPerformed(ActionEvent e)
  {
    loadCarButtonActionPerformed(e);
  }
});

buttonsPanel.setPreferredSize(new Dimension(230, 40));
buttonsPanel.setLayout(new GridBagLayout());
gridConstraints = new GridBagConstraints();
gridConstraints.gridx = 1;
gridConstraints.gridy = 4;
gridConstraints.gridwidth = 2;
getContentPane().add(buttonsPanel, gridConstraints);

startPauseButton.setText("Start Game");
gridConstraints = new GridBagConstraints();
gridConstraints.gridx = 0;
gridConstraints.gridy = 0;
gridConstraints.insets = new Insets(0, 0, 0, 10);
buttonsPanel.add(startPauseButton, gridConstraints);
startPauseButton.addActionListener(new ActionListener()
{
  public void actionPerformed(ActionEvent e)
  {
    startPauseButtonActionPerformed(e);
  }
});

exitStopButton.setText("Exit");
gridConstraints = new GridBagConstraints();
gridConstraints.gridx = 1;
gridConstraints.gridy = 0;
gridConstraints.insets = new Insets(0, 10, 0, 0);
buttonsPanel.add(exitStopButton, gridConstraints);
exitStopButton.addActionListener(new ActionListener()
{
  public void actionPerformed(ActionEvent e)
  {
    exitStopButtonActionPerformed(e);
```

```
      }
    });

    clockTimer = new Timer(mSecPerMin, new ActionListener()
    {
      public void actionPerformed(ActionEvent e)
      {
        clockTimerActionPerformed(e);
      }
    });

    phoneTimer = new Timer(mSecPerMin, new ActionListener()
    {
      public void actionPerformed(ActionEvent e)
      {
        phoneTimerActionPerformed(e);
      }
    });

    ovenTimer = new Timer(mSecPerMin, new ActionListener()
    {
      public void actionPerformed(ActionEvent e)
      {
        ovenTimerActionPerformed(e);
      }
    });

    carTimer = new Timer(mSecPerMin * minPer20Squares / 20,
new ActionListener()
    {
      public void actionPerformed(ActionEvent e)
      {
        carTimerActionPerformed(e);
      }
    });

    pack();
    Dimension screenSize =
Toolkit.getDefaultToolkit().getScreenSize();
    setBounds((int) (0.5 * (screenSize.width - getWidth())),
(int) (0.5 * (screenSize.height - getHeight())), getWidth(),
getHeight());

    try
    {
      gameOverSound = Applet.newAudioClip(new URL("file:" +
"tada.wav"));
```

```
        phoneSound = Applet.newAudioClip(new URL("file:" +
"phone.wav"));
        dingSound = Applet.newAudioClip(new URL("file:" +
"ding.wav"));
        beepSound = Applet.newAudioClip(new URL("file:" +
"carbeep.wav"));
    }
    catch (Exception ex)
    {
      System.out.println("Error loading sound files");
    }
  }

  private void exitForm(WindowEvent evt)
  {
    System.exit(0);
  }

  private void addPizzaButtonActionPerformed(ActionEvent e)
  {
    pizzasBaking++;
    pizzaLabel[pizzasBaking - 1].setIcon(pizzaIcon);
    if (pizzasBaking == pizzasBakingMax)
      addPizzaButton.setEnabled(false);
  }

  private void bakePizzaButtonActionPerformed(ActionEvent e)
  {
    int hOut, mOut;
    if (pizzasBaking == 0)
      return;
    ovenPanel.setBackground(ovenOnColor);
    addPizzaButton.setEnabled(false);
    bakePizzaButton.setEnabled(false);
    hOut = clockHour;
    mOut = clockMinute + bakingTime;
    if (mOut > 59)
    {
      mOut -= 60;
      hOut++;
    }
    String t;
    if (pizzasBaking == 1)
      t = "Pizza Out At ";
    else
      t = "Pizzas Out At ";
    t += String.valueOf(hOut) + ":";
```

```
      if (mOut < 10)
        t += "0";
      t += String.valueOf(mOut);

ovenPanel.setBorder(BorderFactory.createTitledBorder(t));
      bakingMinutesLeft = bakingTime;
      ovenTimer.start();
  }

  private void loadCarButtonActionPerformed(ActionEvent e)
  {
    if (pizzasReady == 0)
      return;
    if (pizzasReady > pizzasInCarMax)
    {
      pizzasInCar += pizzasInCarMax;
      pizzasReady -= pizzasInCarMax;
    }
    else
    {
      pizzasInCar += pizzasReady;
      pizzasReady = 0;
    }
    readyLabel.setText(String.valueOf(pizzasReady));
    inCarLabel.setText(String.valueOf(pizzasInCar));
    loadCarButton.setEnabled(false);
  }

  private void startPauseButtonActionPerformed(ActionEvent
e)
  {
    if (startPauseButton.getText().equals("Start Game"))
    {
      startPauseButton.setText("Pause Game");
      exitStopButton.setText("Stop Game");
      // clear grid
      for (int i = 1; i < 21; i++)
      {
        for (int j = 1; j < 21; j++)
        {
          deliveryGrid[i][j].setBackground(Color.WHITE);
          deliveryGrid[i][j].setText("");
          pizzas[i][j] = 0;
          pizzaTime[i][j] = 0;
        }
      }
      ordersListModel.removeAllElements();
```

```
      for (int i = 0; i < 8; i++)
        pizzaLabel[i].setIcon(null);
      pizzasBaking = 0;
      pizzasReady = pizzasBakingMax;
      totalPizzasBaked = pizzasReady;
      readyLabel.setText(String.valueOf(pizzasReady));
      addPizzaButton.setEnabled(true);
      bakePizzaButton.setEnabled(true);
      pizzasInCar = 0;
      inCarLabel.setText("0");
      loadCarButton.setEnabled(true);
      // initialize pizza parlor and car location
      deliveryGrid[carC][carR].setIcon(null);
      pizzaC = 2 + myRandom.nextInt(18);
      pizzaR = 2 + myRandom.nextInt(18);

deliveryGrid[pizzaC][pizzaR].setBackground(Color.BLACK);
      deliveryGrid[pizzaC][pizzaR].setText("X");
      carC = pizzaC;
      carR = pizzaR;
      mileage = 0;
      messageTextArea.setText(" Car at Pizza Parlor:\n " +
display(carC, carR));
      pizzasOnTime = 0;
      pizzasLate = 0;
      missedDeliveries = 0;
      totalSales = 0;
      salesLabel.setText("$0");
      clockHour = 6;
      clockMinute = 0;
      timeLabel.setText("6:00");
      clockTimer.start();
      phoneTimer.setDelay(mSecPerMin * (1 +
myRandom.nextInt(7)));
      phoneTimer.start();
    }
    else if (startPauseButton.getText().equals("Pause
Game"))
    {
      startPauseButton.setText("Restart Game");
      exitStopButton.setEnabled(false);
      clockTimer.stop();
      phoneTimer.stop();
      ovenGoing = ovenTimer.isRunning();
      ovenTimer.stop();
      addPizzaButton.setEnabled(false);
      bakePizzaButton.setEnabled(false);
```

```
        loadCarButtonEnabled = loadCarButton.isEnabled();
        loadCarButton.setEnabled(false);
        carGoing = carTimer.isRunning();
        carTimer.stop();
    }
    else
    {
        // game restarted
        startPauseButton.setText("Pause Game");
        exitStopButton.setEnabled(true);
        clockTimer.start();
        phoneTimer.start();
        if (ovenGoing)
            ovenTimer.start();
        addPizzaButton.setEnabled(!ovenGoing);
        bakePizzaButton.setEnabled(!ovenGoing);
        loadCarButton.setEnabled(loadCarButtonEnabled);
        if (carGoing)
            carTimer.start();
    }
}

private void exitStopButtonActionPerformed(ActionEvent e)
{
    if (exitStopButton.getText().equals("Stop Game"))
    {
        gameOverSound.play();
        exitStopButton.setText("Exit");
        startPauseButton.setText("Start Game");
        clockTimer.stop();
        phoneTimer.stop();
        ovenTimer.stop();
        addPizzaButton.setEnabled(false);
        bakePizzaButton.setEnabled(false);

ovenPanel.setBorder(BorderFactory.createTitledBorder("Oven
Off"));
        ovenPanel.setBackground(ovenOffColor);
        for (int i = 0; i < 8; i++)
            pizzaLabel[i].setIcon(null);
        addPizzaButton.setEnabled(false);
        bakePizzaButton.setEnabled(false);
        loadCarButton.setEnabled(false);
        carTimer.stop();
        SalesResults salesResults = new
SalesResults(clockHour, clockMinute, pizzasOnTime,
netSoldPizza, pizzasLate, netLatePizza, totalPizzasBaked,
```

```
pizzaCost, mileage, mileageCost, missedDeliveries,
costMissedPizza);
    salesResults.setVisible(true);
  }
  else
  {
    System.exit(0);
  }
}

private void clockTimerActionPerformed(ActionEvent e)
{
  int clockMinutes;
  int c, r;
  String s;
  boolean expired = false;
  clockMinute++;
  if (clockMinute > 59)
  {
    clockMinute = 0;
    clockHour++;
    if (clockHour == 11)
    {
      timeLabel.setText("11:00");
      exitStopButton.doClick();
      return;
    }
  }
  String t = String.valueOf(clockHour) + ":";
  if (clockMinute < 10)
    t += "0";
  timeLabel.setText(t + String.valueOf(clockMinute));
  // check for late orders - check to if first is expired
  clockMinutes = clockMinute + 60 * clockHour;
  if (ordersListModel.getSize() != 0)
  {
    for (int i = 0; i < ordersListModel.getSize(); i++)
    {
      s = String.valueOf(ordersListModel.getElementAt(i));
      c = ((int) s.charAt(6)) - 64;
      r = Integer.valueOf(s.substring(8,
10).trim()).intValue();
      if (i == 0 && clockMinutes - pizzaTime[c][r] >=
orderMaxTime)
      {
        expired = true;
        deliveryGrid[c][r].setBackground(Color.WHITE);
```

```
            deliveryGrid[c][r].setText("");
            missedDeliveries += pizzas[c][r];
            pizzas[c][r] = 0;
          }
          else if (clockMinutes - pizzaTime[c][r] >=
orderLateTime)
          {

deliveryGrid[c][r].setBackground(lateDeliveryColor);
          }
        }
      if (expired)
        ordersListModel.removeElementAt(0);
    }
  }

  private void phoneTimerActionPerformed(ActionEvent e)
  {
    int i, j, k;
    String order;
    phoneSound.play();
    if (clockHour == 10 && clockMinute >= 30)
    {
      phoneTimer.stop();
      return;
    }
    do
    {
      i = 1 + myRandom.nextInt(20);
      j = 1 + myRandom.nextInt(20);
    }
    while (pizzas[i][j] != 0);
    k = myRandom.nextInt(100);
    if (k <= 29)
      pizzas[i][j] = 1;
    else if (k <= 49)
      pizzas[i][j] = 2;
    else if (k <= 69)
      pizzas[i][j] = 3;
    else if (k <= 84)
      pizzas[i][j] = 4;
    else
      pizzas[i][j] = 5;
    pizzaTime[i][j] = clockMinute + 60 * clockHour;
    // build string listing order
    order = timeLabel.getText() + " ";
    if (timeLabel.getText().length() == 4)
```

```
      order = " " + order;
    order += String.valueOf((char) (i + 64)) + " ";
    if (j < 10)
      order += " ";
    order += String.valueOf(j) + " -> " +
String.valueOf(pizzas[i][j]);
    ordersListModel.addElement(order);
    deliveryGrid[i][j].setBackground(onTimeDeliveryColor);;

deliveryGrid[i][j].setText(String.valueOf(pizzas[i][j]));
    phoneTimer.setDelay(mSecPerMin * (1 +
myRandom.nextInt(7)));
  }

  private void ovenTimerActionPerformed(ActionEvent e)
  {
    if (bakingMinutesLeft != 0)
      bakingMinutesLeft--;
    else
    {
      dingSound.play();
      ovenTimer.stop();
      pizzasReady += pizzasBaking;
      totalPizzasBaked += pizzasBaking;
      if (pizzasReady > pizzasReadyMax)
        pizzasReady = pizzasReadyMax;
      readyLabel.setText(String.valueOf(pizzasReady));

ovenPanel.setBorder(BorderFactory.createTitledBorder("Oven
Off"));
      ovenPanel.setBackground(ovenOffColor);
      for (int i = 0; i < 8; i++)
        pizzaLabel[i].setIcon(null);
      pizzasBaking = 0;
      addPizzaButton.setEnabled(true);
      bakePizzaButton.setEnabled(true);
    }
  }

  private void carTimerActionPerformed(ActionEvent e)
  {
    int i, c, r;
    String s;
    ImageIcon carIcon = null;
    deliveryGrid[carC][carR].setIcon(null);
    // move horizontally first
    if (deltaC != 0)
```

```
      {
        mileage++;
        carIcon = hCarIcon;
        if (deltaC > 0)
          carC++;
        else
          carC--;
        deltaC = deliveryC - carC;
      }
      else
      {
        if (deltaR != 0)
        {
          mileage++;
          carIcon = vCarIcon;
          if (deltaR > 0)
            carR++;
          else
            carR--;
          deltaR = deliveryR - carR;
        }
      }
      deliveryGrid[carC][carR].setIcon(carIcon);
      if (carC == deliveryC && carR == deliveryR)
      {
        beepSound.play();
        carTimer.stop();
        if (carC == pizzaC && carR == pizzaR)
        {
          messageTextArea.setText(" Car at Pizza Parlor:\n " +
display(carC, carR));
          deliveryGrid[carC][carR].setIcon(null);
          pizzasInCar = 0;
          inCarLabel.setText("0");
          loadCarButton.setEnabled(true);
        }
        else
        {
          messageTextArea.setText(" Car at " + display(carC,
carR));
          // check delivery status
          if (pizzas[deliveryC][deliveryR] == 0)
          {
            messageTextArea.append("\n No Pizza Wanted");
          }
          else
          {
```

```
          if (pizzas[deliveryC][deliveryR] > pizzasInCar)
          {
            messageTextArea.append("\n Not Enough Pizzas");
          }
          else
          {
            messageTextArea.append("\n Delivered " +
String.valueOf(pizzas[deliveryC][deliveryR]) + " Pizza");
            if (pizzas[deliveryC][deliveryR] > 1)
              messageTextArea.append("s");
            // see if on-time
            if ((clockMinute + 60 * clockHour) -
pizzaTime[deliveryC][deliveryR] <= orderLateTime)
              {
                messageTextArea.append(": On-Time");
                totalSales += pizzas[deliveryC][deliveryR] *
netSoldPizza;
                pizzasOnTime += pizzas[deliveryC][deliveryR];
              }
            else
              {
                messageTextArea.append(": Late!");
                totalSales += pizzas[deliveryC][deliveryR] *
netLatePizza;
                pizzasLate += pizzas[deliveryC][deliveryR];
              }
            salesLabel.setText("$" +
String.valueOf(totalSales));
            pizzasInCar -= pizzas[deliveryC][deliveryR];
            inCarLabel.setText(String.valueOf(pizzasInCar));
            pizzas[deliveryC][deliveryR] = 0;

deliveryGrid[deliveryC][deliveryR].setBackground(Color.WHITE
);
            deliveryGrid[deliveryC][deliveryR].setText("");
            // remove from list
            for (i = 0; i < ordersListModel.getSize(); i++)
            {
              s =
String.valueOf(ordersListModel.getElementAt(i));
              c = ((int) s.charAt(6)) - 64;
              r = Integer.valueOf(s.substring(8,
10).trim()).intValue();
              if (c == deliveryC && r == deliveryR)
                break;
            }
            ordersListModel.removeElementAt(i);
```

```
        }
      }
    }
  }
}

  private String display(int c, int r)
  {
    return (String.valueOf((char)(c + 64)) + " " +
String.valueOf(r));
  }

  private void deliveryGridMousePressed(MouseEvent e)
  {
    // determine which grid element was clicked
    Point p = e.getComponent().getLocation();
    // determine indicies based on p
    boolean matchFound = false;
    if (!carTimer.isRunning() && !loadCarButton.isEnabled()
&& startPauseButton.getText().equals("Pause Game"))
    {
    for (deliveryR = 1; deliveryR < 21; deliveryR++)
    {
      for (deliveryC = 1; deliveryC < 21; deliveryC++)
      {
        if (p.x == deliveryGrid[deliveryC][deliveryR].getX()
&& p.y == deliveryGrid[deliveryC][deliveryR].getY())
        {
          matchFound = true;
          break;
        }
      }
      if (matchFound)
        break;
    }
    deltaC = deliveryC - carC;
    deltaR = deliveryR - carR;
    if (deltaC == 0 && deltaR == 0)
      return;
    messageTextArea.setText(" Car Going To:\n " +
display(deliveryC, deliveryR));
    carTimer.start();
    }
  }


}
```

```java
class ImagePanel extends JPanel
{
  private Image img;
  public ImagePanel(Image img)
  {
   this.img = img;
  }
  public void paintComponent(Graphics g)
  {
    g.drawImage(img, 0, 0, null);
  }
}
```

<u>SalesResults.java:</u>

```
/*
 * SalesResults.java
 */
package pizzadelivery;
import javax.swing.*;
import java.awt.*;
import java.awt.event.*;


public class SalesResults extends JDialog
{

  JLabel gridTopLabel = new JLabel();
  JLabel gridMiddleLabel = new JLabel();
  JLabel gridBottomLabel = new JLabel();
  JLabel startTimeLabel = new JLabel();
  JLabel stopTimeLabel = new JLabel();
  JLabel salesHeaderLabel = new JLabel();
  JLabel onTimeLabel = new JLabel();
  JLabel onTimeSalesLabel = new JLabel();
  JLabel lateLabel = new JLabel();
  JLabel lateSalesLabel = new JLabel();
  JLabel totalSalesHeaderLabel = new JLabel();
  JLabel totalSalesLabel = new JLabel();
  JLabel costsHeaderLabel = new JLabel();
  JLabel bakedLabel = new JLabel();
  JLabel bakedCostsLabel = new JLabel();
  JLabel milesLabel = new JLabel();
  JLabel milesCostsLabel = new JLabel();
  JLabel missedLabel = new JLabel();
  JLabel missedCostsLabel = new JLabel();
  JLabel totalCostsHeaderLabel = new JLabel();
  JLabel totalCostsLabel = new JLabel();
  JLabel totalProfitsLabel = new JLabel();
  JLabel hourlyProfitsLabel = new JLabel();
  JButton returnButton = new JButton();

  public SalesResults(int clockHour, int clockMinute, int
pizzasOnTime, int netSoldPizza, int pizzasLate, int
netLatePizza, int totalPizzasBaked, int pizzaCost, int
mileage, double mileageCost, int missedDeliveries, int
costMissedPizza)
  {
    // frame constructor
    setTitle("Pizza Delivery Sales Results");
```

```java
setResizable(false);
setModal(true);
getContentPane().setBackground(Color.WHITE);
addWindowListener(new WindowAdapter()
{
  public void windowClosing(WindowEvent evt)
  {
    exitForm(evt);
  }
});
getContentPane().setLayout(new GridBagLayout());
GridBagConstraints gridConstraints;

gridTopLabel.setPreferredSize(new Dimension(375, 10));
gridTopLabel.setOpaque(true);
gridTopLabel.setBackground(Color.BLUE);
gridConstraints = new GridBagConstraints();
gridConstraints.gridx = 0;
gridConstraints.gridy = 1;
gridConstraints.gridwidth = 5;
gridConstraints.insets = new Insets(5, 5, 0, 5);
getContentPane().add(gridTopLabel, gridConstraints);

gridMiddleLabel.setPreferredSize(new Dimension(10,
150));
gridMiddleLabel.setOpaque(true);
gridMiddleLabel.setBackground(Color.BLUE);
gridConstraints = new GridBagConstraints();
gridConstraints.gridx = 2;
gridConstraints.gridy = 2;
gridConstraints.gridheight = 5;
gridConstraints.insets = new Insets(0, 5, 0, 5);
getContentPane().add(gridMiddleLabel, gridConstraints);

gridBottomLabel.setPreferredSize(new Dimension(375,
10));
gridBottomLabel.setOpaque(true);
gridBottomLabel.setBackground(Color.BLUE);
gridConstraints = new GridBagConstraints();
gridConstraints.gridx = 0;
gridConstraints.gridy = 7;
gridConstraints.gridwidth = 5;
gridConstraints.insets = new Insets(0, 5, 5, 5);
getContentPane().add(gridBottomLabel, gridConstraints);

startTimeLabel.setText("Start Time: 6:00");
```

```
    startTimeLabel.setFont(new Font("Arial", Font.PLAIN,
18));
    gridConstraints = new GridBagConstraints();
    gridConstraints.gridx = 0;
    gridConstraints.gridy = 0;
    gridConstraints.gridwidth = 2;
    gridConstraints.insets = new Insets(10, 5, 0, 0);
    getContentPane().add(startTimeLabel, gridConstraints);

    stopTimeLabel.setFont(new Font("Arial", Font.PLAIN,
18));
    gridConstraints = new GridBagConstraints();
    gridConstraints.gridx = 3;
    gridConstraints.gridy = 0;
    gridConstraints.gridwidth = 2;
    gridConstraints.insets = new Insets(10, 0, 0, 0);
    getContentPane().add(stopTimeLabel, gridConstraints);

    salesHeaderLabel.setText("Sales:");
    salesHeaderLabel.setFont(new Font("Arial", Font.BOLD,
16));
    gridConstraints = new GridBagConstraints();
    gridConstraints.gridx = 0;
    gridConstraints.gridy = 2;
    gridConstraints.anchor = GridBagConstraints.WEST;
    gridConstraints.insets = new Insets(10, 10, 0, 0);
    getContentPane().add(salesHeaderLabel, gridConstraints);

    onTimeLabel.setFont(new Font("Arial", Font.PLAIN, 14));
    gridConstraints = new GridBagConstraints();
    gridConstraints.gridx = 0;
    gridConstraints.gridy = 3;
    gridConstraints.anchor = GridBagConstraints.EAST;
    gridConstraints.insets = new Insets(10, 10, 0, 0);
    getContentPane().add(onTimeLabel, gridConstraints);

    onTimeSalesLabel.setFont(new Font("Arial", Font.PLAIN,
14));
    gridConstraints = new GridBagConstraints();
    gridConstraints.gridx = 1;
    gridConstraints.gridy = 3;
    gridConstraints.anchor = GridBagConstraints.EAST;
    gridConstraints.insets = new Insets(10, 10, 0, 0);
    getContentPane().add(onTimeSalesLabel, gridConstraints);

    lateLabel.setFont(new Font("Arial", Font.PLAIN, 14));
    gridConstraints = new GridBagConstraints();
```

```
    gridConstraints.gridx = 0;
    gridConstraints.gridy = 4;
    gridConstraints.anchor = GridBagConstraints.EAST;
    gridConstraints.insets = new Insets(10, 10, 0, 0);
    getContentPane().add(lateLabel, gridConstraints);

    lateSalesLabel.setFont(new Font("Arial", Font.PLAIN,
14));
    gridConstraints = new GridBagConstraints();
    gridConstraints.gridx = 1;
    gridConstraints.gridy = 4;
    gridConstraints.anchor = GridBagConstraints.EAST;
    gridConstraints.insets = new Insets(10, 10, 0, 0);
    getContentPane().add(lateSalesLabel, gridConstraints);

    totalSalesHeaderLabel.setText("Total Sales");
    totalSalesHeaderLabel.setFont(new Font("Arial",
Font.BOLD, 14));
    gridConstraints = new GridBagConstraints();
    gridConstraints.gridx = 0;
    gridConstraints.gridy = 5;
    gridConstraints.anchor = GridBagConstraints.EAST;
    gridConstraints.insets = new Insets(10, 10, 0, 0);
    getContentPane().add(totalSalesHeaderLabel,
gridConstraints);

    totalSalesLabel.setFont(new Font("Arial", Font.PLAIN,
14));
    gridConstraints = new GridBagConstraints();
    gridConstraints.gridx = 1;
    gridConstraints.gridy = 5;
    gridConstraints.anchor = GridBagConstraints.EAST;
    gridConstraints.insets = new Insets(10, 10, 0, 0);
    getContentPane().add(totalSalesLabel, gridConstraints);

    costsHeaderLabel.setText("Costs:");
    costsHeaderLabel.setFont(new Font("Arial", Font.BOLD,
16));
    gridConstraints = new GridBagConstraints();
    gridConstraints.gridx = 3;
    gridConstraints.gridy = 2;
    gridConstraints.anchor = GridBagConstraints.WEST;
    gridConstraints.insets = new Insets(10, 0, 0, 0);
    getContentPane().add(costsHeaderLabel, gridConstraints);

    bakedLabel.setFont(new Font("Arial", Font.PLAIN, 14));
    gridConstraints = new GridBagConstraints();
```

```
    gridConstraints.gridx = 3;
    gridConstraints.gridy = 3;
    gridConstraints.anchor = GridBagConstraints.EAST;
    gridConstraints.insets = new Insets(10, 0, 0, 10);
    getContentPane().add(bakedLabel, gridConstraints);

    bakedCostsLabel.setFont(new Font("Arial", Font.PLAIN,
14));
    gridConstraints = new GridBagConstraints();
    gridConstraints.gridx = 4;
    gridConstraints.gridy = 3;
    gridConstraints.anchor = GridBagConstraints.EAST;
    gridConstraints.insets = new Insets(10, 0, 0, 10);
    getContentPane().add(bakedCostsLabel, gridConstraints);

    milesLabel.setFont(new Font("Arial", Font.PLAIN, 14));
    gridConstraints = new GridBagConstraints();
    gridConstraints.gridx = 3;
    gridConstraints.gridy = 4;
    gridConstraints.anchor = GridBagConstraints.EAST;
    gridConstraints.insets = new Insets(10, 0, 0, 10);
    getContentPane().add(milesLabel, gridConstraints);

    milesCostsLabel.setFont(new Font("Arial", Font.PLAIN,
14));
    gridConstraints = new GridBagConstraints();
    gridConstraints.gridx = 4;
    gridConstraints.gridy = 4;
    gridConstraints.anchor = GridBagConstraints.EAST;
    gridConstraints.insets = new Insets(10, 0, 0, 10);
    getContentPane().add(milesCostsLabel, gridConstraints);

    missedLabel.setFont(new Font("Arial", Font.PLAIN, 14));
    gridConstraints = new GridBagConstraints();
    gridConstraints.gridx = 3;
    gridConstraints.gridy = 5;
    gridConstraints.anchor = GridBagConstraints.EAST;
    gridConstraints.insets = new Insets(10, 0, 0, 10);
    getContentPane().add(missedLabel, gridConstraints);

    missedCostsLabel.setFont(new Font("Arial", Font.PLAIN,
14));
    gridConstraints = new GridBagConstraints();
    gridConstraints.gridx = 4;
    gridConstraints.gridy = 5;
    gridConstraints.anchor = GridBagConstraints.EAST;
    gridConstraints.insets = new Insets(10, 0, 0, 10);
```

```
    getContentPane().add(missedCostsLabel, gridConstraints);

    totalCostsHeaderLabel.setText("Total Costs");
    totalCostsHeaderLabel.setFont(new Font("Arial",
Font.BOLD, 14));
    gridConstraints = new GridBagConstraints();
    gridConstraints.gridx = 3;
    gridConstraints.gridy = 6;
    gridConstraints.anchor = GridBagConstraints.EAST;
    gridConstraints.insets = new Insets(10, 0, 0, 10);
    getContentPane().add(totalCostsHeaderLabel,
gridConstraints);

    totalCostsLabel.setFont(new Font("Arial", Font.PLAIN,
14));
    gridConstraints = new GridBagConstraints();
    gridConstraints.gridx = 4;
    gridConstraints.gridy = 6;
    gridConstraints.anchor = GridBagConstraints.EAST;
    gridConstraints.insets = new Insets(10, 0, 0, 10);
    getContentPane().add(totalCostsLabel, gridConstraints);

    totalProfitsLabel.setFont(new Font("Arial", Font.BOLD,
14));
    gridConstraints = new GridBagConstraints();
    gridConstraints.gridx = 0;
    gridConstraints.gridy = 8;
    gridConstraints.gridwidth = 2;
    gridConstraints.insets = new Insets(10, 10, 10, 0);
    getContentPane().add(totalProfitsLabel,
gridConstraints);

    hourlyProfitsLabel.setFont(new Font("Arial", Font.BOLD,
14));
    gridConstraints = new GridBagConstraints();
    gridConstraints.gridx = 3;
    gridConstraints.gridy = 8;
    gridConstraints.gridwidth = 2;
    gridConstraints.insets = new Insets(10, 10, 10, 0);
    getContentPane().add(hourlyProfitsLabel,
gridConstraints);

    returnButton.setText("Return to Pizza Delivery");
    gridConstraints = new GridBagConstraints();
    gridConstraints.gridx = 0;
    gridConstraints.gridy = 9;
    gridConstraints.gridwidth = 5;
```

```
    gridConstraints.insets = new Insets(5, 0, 5, 0);
    getContentPane().add(returnButton, gridConstraints);
    returnButton.addActionListener(new ActionListener()
    {
      public void actionPerformed(ActionEvent e)
      {
        returnButtonActionPerformed(e);
      }
    });

    pack();
    Dimension screenSize =
Toolkit.getDefaultToolkit().getScreenSize();
    setBounds((int) (0.5 * (screenSize.width - getWidth())),
(int) (0.5 * (screenSize.height - getHeight())), getWidth(),
getHeight());

    if (clockMinute < 10)
      stopTimeLabel.setText("Stop Time: " +
String.valueOf(clockHour) + ":0" +
String.valueOf(clockMinute));
    else
      stopTimeLabel.setText("Stop Time: " +
String.valueOf(clockHour) + ":" +
String.valueOf(clockMinute));
    onTimeLabel.setText(String.valueOf(pizzasOnTime) + " On-
Time Deliveries");
    onTimeSalesLabel.setText("$" +
String.valueOf(pizzasOnTime * netSoldPizza));
    lateLabel.setText(String.valueOf(pizzasLate) + " Late
Deliveries");
    lateSalesLabel.setText("$" + String.valueOf(pizzasLate *
netLatePizza));
    int totalSales = pizzasOnTime * netSoldPizza +
pizzasLate * netLatePizza;
    totalSalesLabel.setText("$" +
String.valueOf(totalSales));
    bakedLabel.setText(String.valueOf(totalPizzasBaked) + "
Pizzas Baked");
    bakedCostsLabel.setText("$" +
String.valueOf(totalPizzasBaked * pizzaCost));
    milesLabel.setText(String.valueOf(mileage) + " Units
Driven");
    milesCostsLabel.setText("$" + String.valueOf((int)
(mileage * mileageCost)));
    missedLabel.setText(String.valueOf(missedDeliveries) + "
Missed Deliveries");
```

```
    missedCostsLabel.setText("$" +
String.valueOf(missedDeliveries * costMissedPizza));
    int totalCosts = (int) (totalPizzasBaked * pizzaCost +
mileage * mileageCost + missedDeliveries * costMissedPizza);
    totalCostsLabel.setText("$" +
String.valueOf(totalCosts));
    totalProfitsLabel.setText("Total Profits: $" +
String.valueOf(totalSales - totalCosts));
    if (clockHour > 6)
    {
      double hours = clockHour - 6 + (double) clockMinute /
60;
      hourlyProfitsLabel.setText("Hourly Profits: $" +
String.valueOf((int) ((totalSales - totalCosts) / hours)));
    }
    else
      hourlyProfitsLabel.setText("");
  }

  private void exitForm(WindowEvent evt)
  {
    this.dispose();;
  }

  private void returnButtonActionPerformed(ActionEvent e)
  {
    this.dispose();
  }

}
```

6

Moon Landing Project

Review and Preview

The next project we build is a **Moon Landing** simulation. You are the pilot of a lunar landing vehicle hovering over the moon. You must land it safely using your thrusters. The program uses physics and math to build a realistic simulation. You will learn how to use Java graphics for drawing lines and shapes and for complex animations with scrolling backgrounds.

Moon Landing Project Preview

In this chapter, we will build a **Moon Landing** game. In this simulation, you control horizontal and vertical thrusters to maneuver your craft over a landing pad on the surface of the moon. You want to make sure your landing speed is slow enough that you don't crash!

The finished project is saved as **MoonLanding** in the **\KidGamesJava\KidGamesJava Projects** folder. Start NetBeans (or your IDE). Open the specified project group. Make **MoonLanding** the selected project. Run the project. You will see:

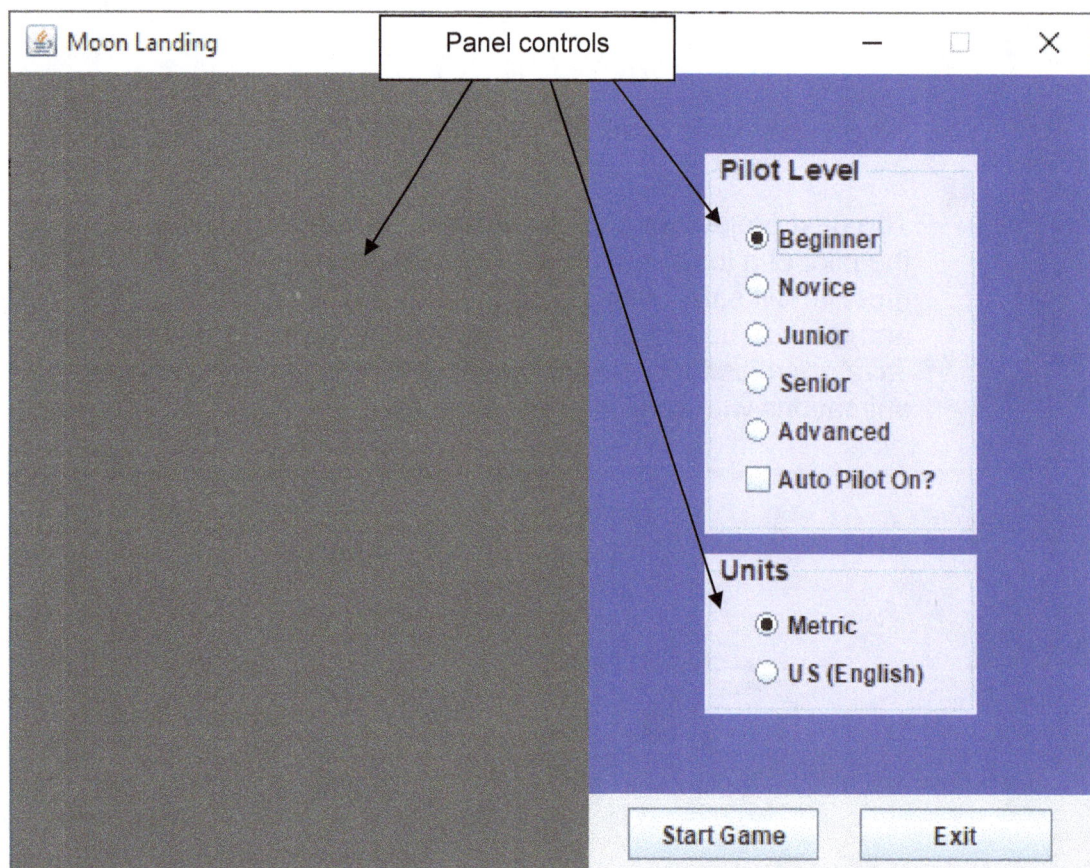

There are several panel controls. One on the left will display the moon lander. The two on the right are used to establish options for **Moon Landing**. The panel has five radio buttons and a check box control. It used to establish your level of piloting ability and whether you want to run in auto-pilot mode. The second panel (with two radio buttons) allows you to select the system of units you want information displayed in. The two button controls at the bottom are used to start the game and to exit the program.

Select **Senior** pilot level and click **Start Game**. The display changes to this:

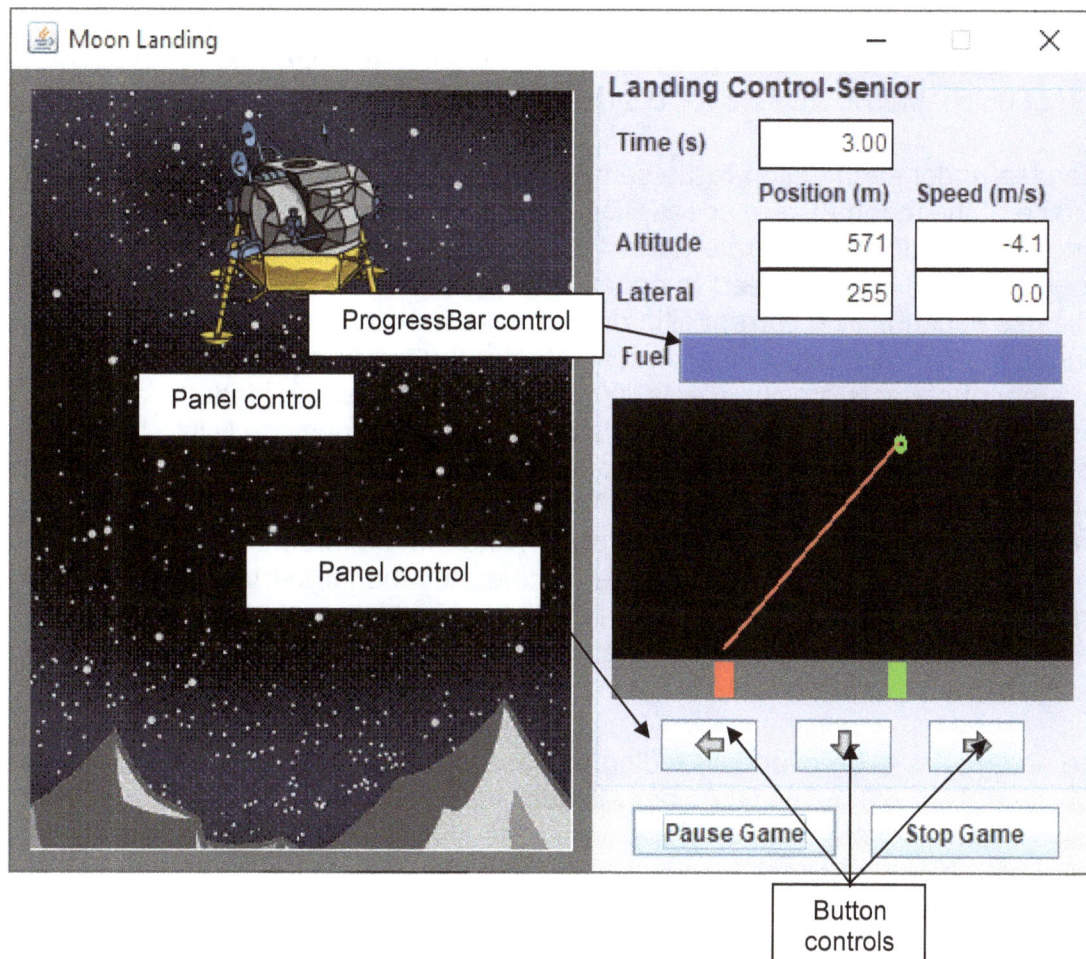

Notice the panels we saw before are gone and replaced by other panel controls. It is common in Java games to have panels stacked on top of each other to conserve frame space. Then, in code, you decide when certain frame should appear (using the **Visible** property. On the left of the **Moon Landing** frame are two panel controls (one inside the other to build a border). The inside panel displays the lunar module as it descends to the moon. On the right side is a panel holding landing control information. Several label and text field controls display time, altitude and lateral distance information. Under these is a progress bar which shows fuel remaining in the module. The black panel and smaller gray panel under the progress bar show current module position relative to the pad. The three button controls with arrows control the lander's thrusters. There is also a label (not seen) under these buttons used for messages. When running, either the label or the thrust buttons will appear. The two button controls at the bottom are used to pause/restart the game and to stop the game. Another button (not seen) lies under these buttons used to restart the game. Again, when running, either this button or the two control buttons will appear, not both.

Like the **Pizza Delivery** game in the last chapter, there's lots going on in the **Moon Landing** game. So, before running the game, let's describe its operation. Prior to starting your descent to the moon, choose your pilot level: **Beginner**, **Novice**, **Junior**, **Senior**, or **Advanced**. Decide if you want **Auto-Pilot On**. And, select the type of units: **Metric** (meters) or **US** (feet).

The idea under each option is the same. Your vehicle is some height above the surface of the moon at zero speed. Due to gravity (about one-sixth the gravity on earth), you begin to accelerate toward the surface with a corresponding change (goes negative) in your speed (a negative speed indicates descent - positive speed indicates ascent). The current altitude and speed are always displayed. You slow your descent by clicking on the vertical thruster (button with a down arrow). This thruster counteracts gravity effects. You must also adjust the lander's lateral position relative to the landing pad. Your current lateral position (- if to the left of the pad, + if to the right) and lateral speed (- if moving to the left, + if moving to the right) are displayed. Lateral motion of the lander is controlled using the two thruster controls with left and right arrows. Note the left thruster accelerates the lander to the right and the right thruster accelerates the lander to the left. All thrusters operate in 'impulse' mode. That is they just fire momentarily, changing the lander speed in the corresponding direction. In 'rocket scientist' talk, we say the thrusters impart a 'delta V' (change in velocity) to the lander.

The end goal is to be over the landing pad and going at a slow descent speed (and slow lateral speed) by the time your altitude (height above the landing pad) reaches zero. A safe landing is one where the final speed is between 0 and -3 m/s (-10.0 ft/s); higher descent speeds result in a crash! There are no crash penalties for missing the pad - your astronauts will just have a long walk back to the home base!!

The **Beginner** option provides practice in slowing the lander's vertical speed. In the **Novice** option, you get practice controlling the vehicle in the lateral direction. The computer will control the vertical thruster, you only use the left and right thrusters. The **Junior** option moves you up to having the ability to control all thrusters, and hence all motions on the lander. You now have to position the lander over its pad and make sure you are going at a slow vertical speed when landing, or else.

Then, the **Senior** option offers one more concern. With the **Senior** (and **Advanced**) option, the fuel gauge shows you how much fuel you have remaining. Each thruster burn uses some fuel (the vertical thruster uses twice as much as the left and right thrusters). So now, you must land at a safe speed, over the landing pad without running out of fuel. At low fuel levels, a beep will be heard. Once you run out of fuel, your vehicle will just accelerate toward the lunar surface, most likely resulting in a crash. The final level is **Advanced**, where your thrusters work in a random manner, removing predictability from the program. Constant adjustments are needed to keep the vehicle over the pad and within speed limits. The program offers an **Auto-Pilot** mode to demonstrate how the computer lands the vehicle. It actually does a fairly decent job.

At any time during the program, you may pause the action by clicking **Pause Game**. To restart, click **Restart Game**. To stop the program before landing, click **Stop Game**. Once a landing is complete, the program stops and you may view the final positions, speeds and fuel consumption. After reading the results, click **Landing Complete-Click to Continue** to play again.

Though this is lots of explanation – the **Moon Landing** game is simple to operate. Start it, then use the three thruster buttons to change the **Altitude** and **Lateral** position of the lander. If the game is running, stop it. Rerun the project (press <**F5**>). The game will appear in its 'stopped' state:

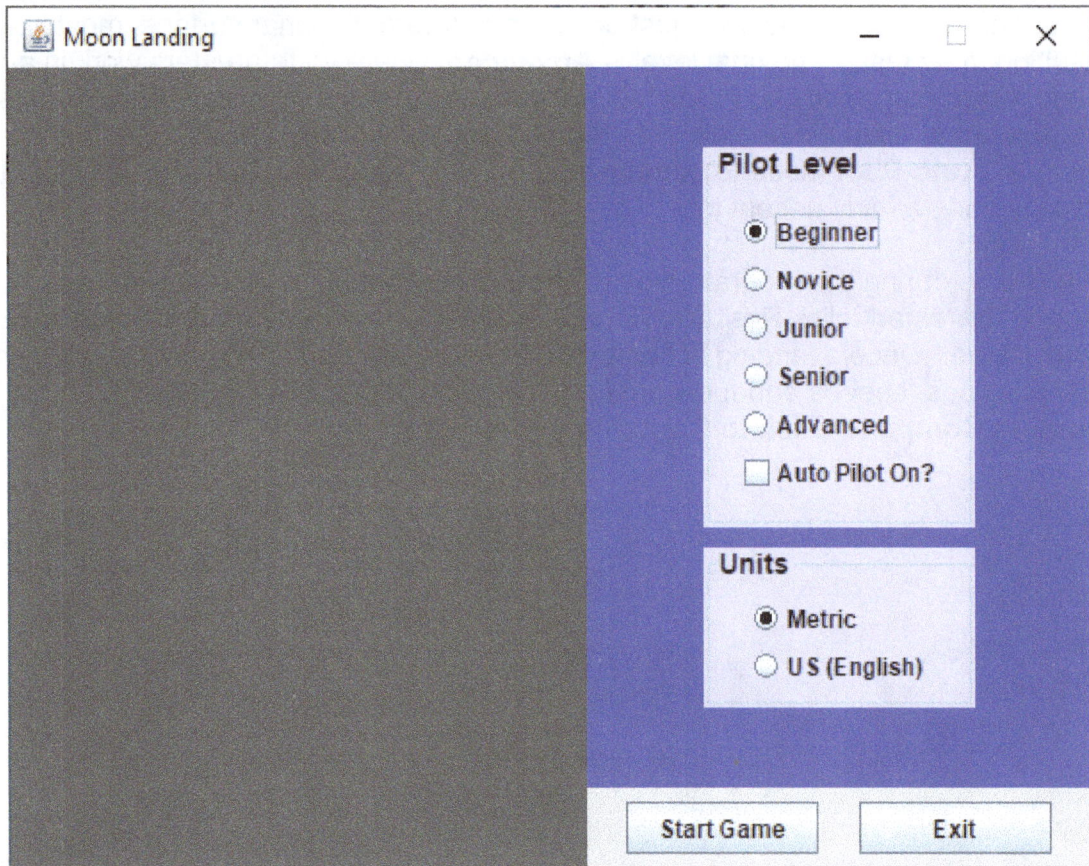

At this point, choose some options and click **Start Game** to get things going.

To demonstrate, I chose **Senior** pilot level, turned on **Auto-Pilot** and used **Metric** units. Here's the game after 8.5 seconds (an update is given every 0.5 seconds) of running (I paused at this point):

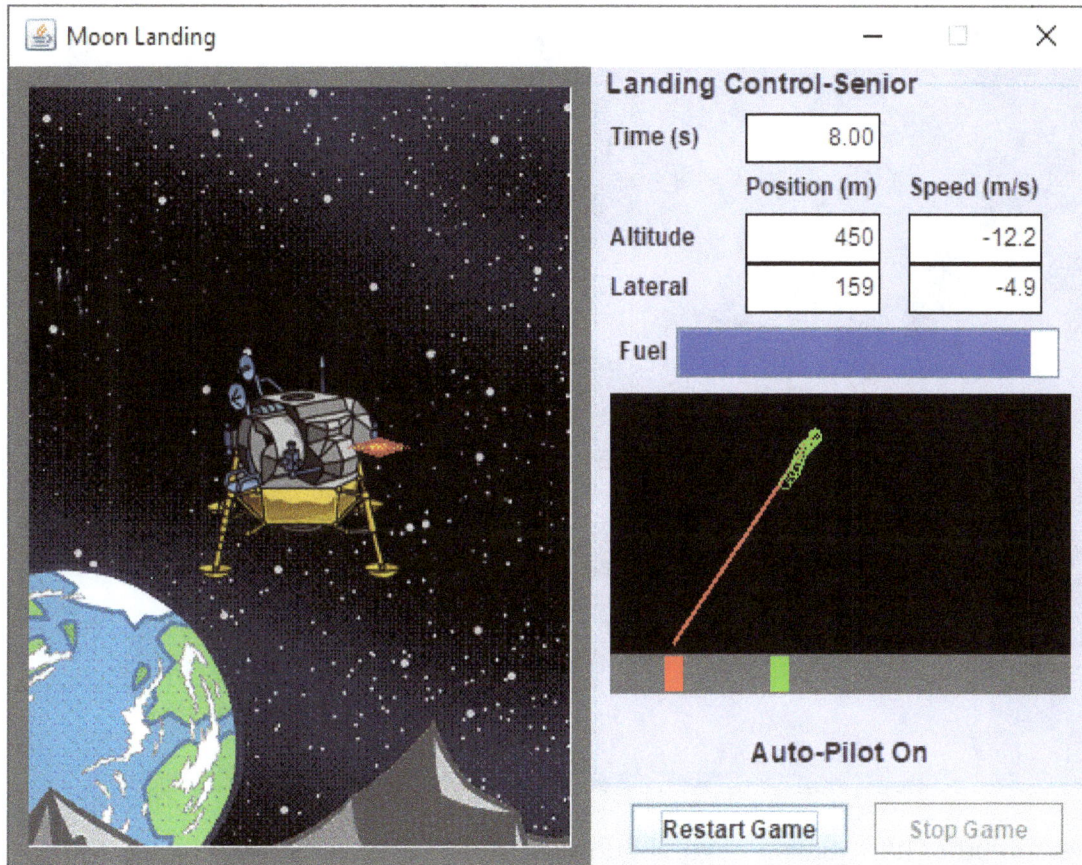

The graphic on the left shows the current position of the lander. The lander is 450 meters above the pad, dropping at 12.2 meters/second. It is 159 feet to the right (lateral position is a negative number) of the pad. The auto-pilot is applying some right thrust, accelerating the lander to a lateral speed of -4.9 meters/second. The fuel tank appears nearly full. Below the fuel gauge is a "trajectory plot," showing past vehicle positions (the circles) relative to the landing pad (with a suggested straight-line descent trajectory). Below this plot are two small boxes, one green and one red. The red box indicates the landing pad lateral location, while the green box marks the moon lander's current lateral position. When the two boxes coincide, the lander is over the pad. The thruster controls don't appear since we are using auto-pilot mode.

Here's the screen after 19.5 seconds:

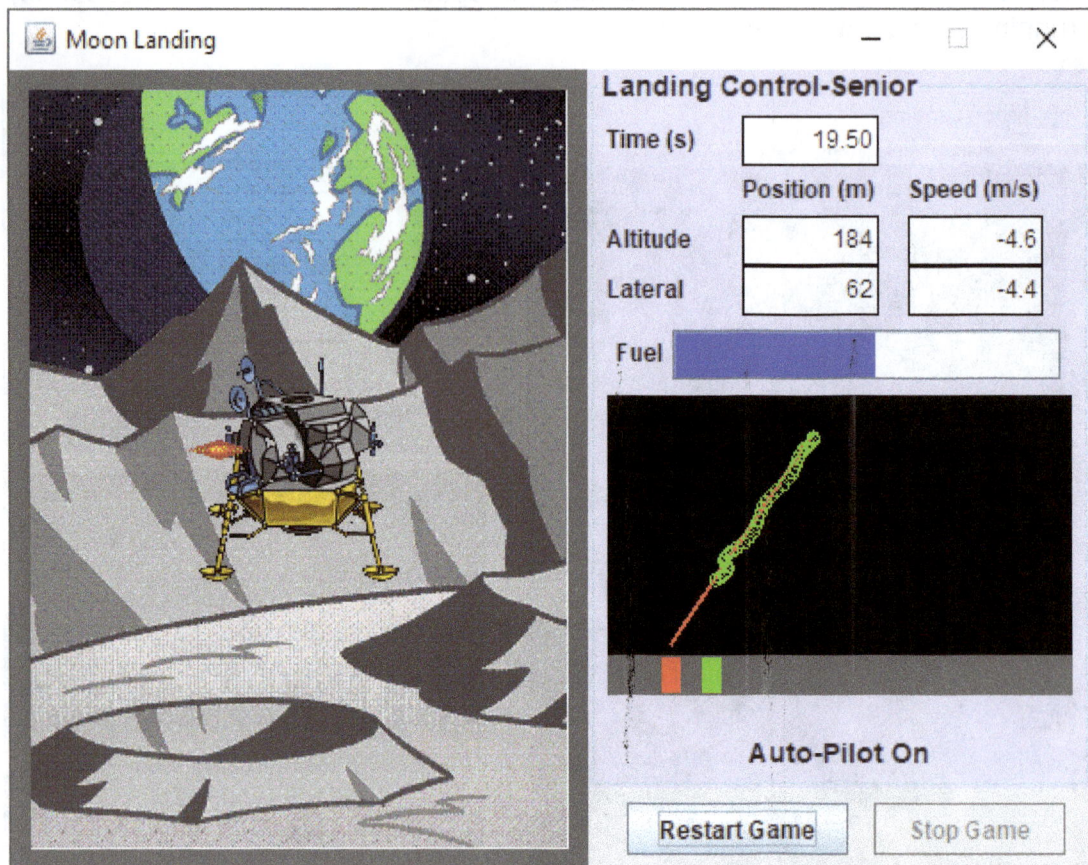

The computer has applied several bursts of vertical thrust to keep the lander vertical speed reasonable and used a few thrusts to move the lander to the left, toward the pad.

And, at 26.0 seconds:

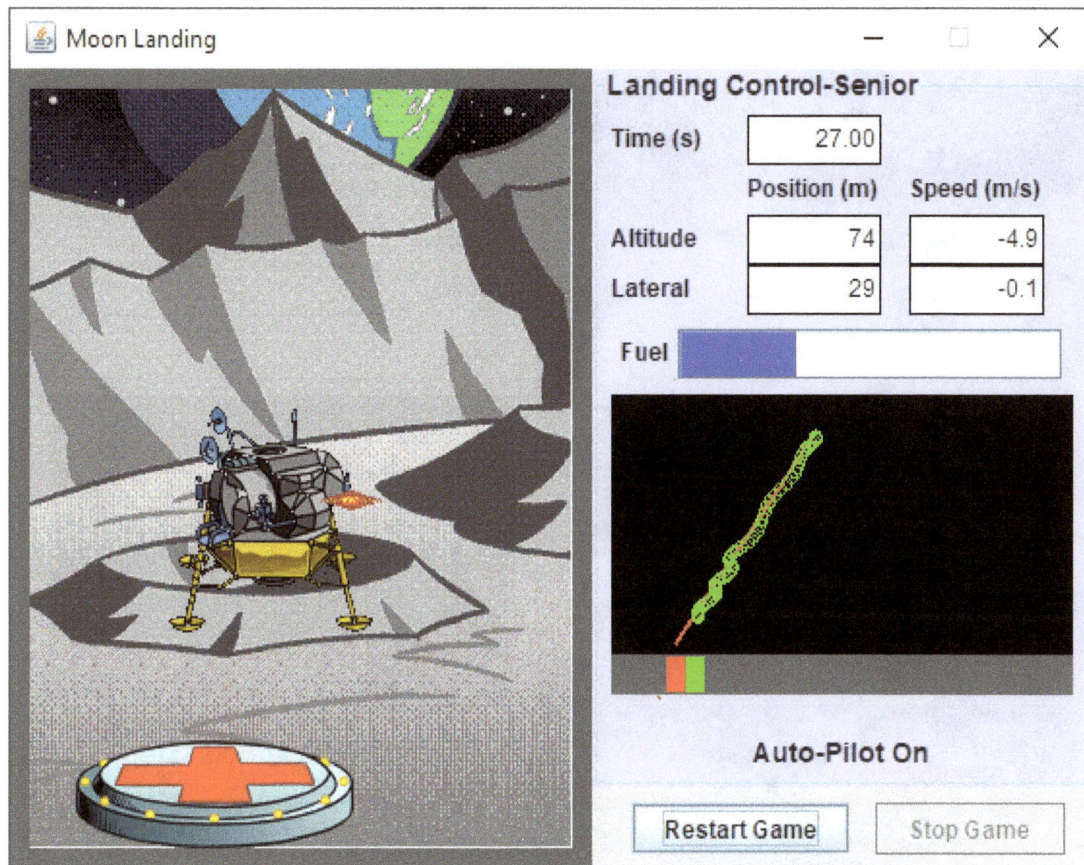

The computer is still giving thrust adjustments to finalize landing. The pad is nearby and things are looking good.

Finally, at 37.0 seconds, the lander is safely on the pad:

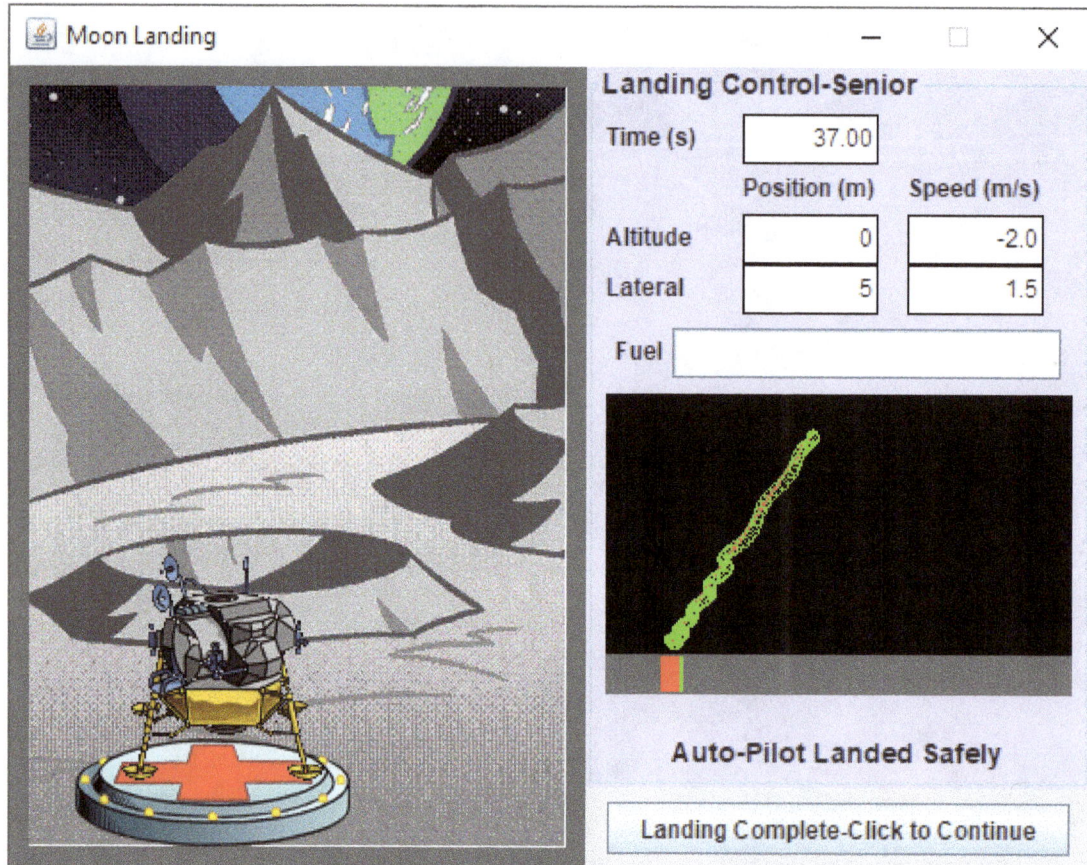

This a near perfect landing, under the safe landing speed of -3.0 m/s and nearly on top of the pad. Just in time – we were low on fuel. Notice how all the graphic depictions of lander position coincide with the numerical values. Click the button at the bottom to try again.

Continue playing **Moon Landing** to understand its operation. Try different options; try landing without the auto-pilot. Click **Exit** when you're done to stop the game. Open the code file and skim over the code, if you like.

The **Moon Landing** program demonstrates a principle used extensively in engineering and mathematics disciplines, that of computer simulation. Simulation is used to test designs and methods before actually building some device or structure. For example, we use simulators to train airline pilots - this is much safer than training them in actual planes because if they make a mistake, there is no loss of airplane or life. Before constructing a building, we simulate it on a computer to see if it can withstand winds and possible earthquakes. Using simulations, we can determine how a system operates, learn how its performance varies as we change different parameters, and develop operation methods. In building **Moon Landing**, we will use realistic numbers based on physics. You can adjust any of these parameters as you choose.

You will now build this project in stages. As you build Java projects, we always recommend taking a slow, step-by-step process. It minimizes programming errors and helps build your confidence as things come together in a complete project.

We address **frame design**. We discuss the controls needed to build the landing form, including overlapping panel controls. And, we address **code design**. We discuss how to implement the various aspects of the game: physics of motion, altitude and lateral distance calculations, line and shape graphics for the trajectory display and advanced graphics such a scrolling background and sprite animations for the lander motion display. And, we'll design a pretty good auto-pilot for demonstration and learning purposes.

Moon Landing Frame Design

We begin building the **Moon Landing** project. Start a new project in your Java project group – name it **MoonLanding**. Delete default code in file named **MoonLanding.java**. Once started, we suggest you immediately save the project with a name you choose. This sets up the folder and file structure needed for your project.

Build the basic frame with these properties:

MoonLanding Frame:
title	Moon Landing
resizable	false

The code is:

```
/*
 * MoonLanding.java
 */
package moonlanding;
import javax.swing.*;
import java.awt.*;
import java.awt.event.*;

public class MoonLanding extends JFrame
{
  public static void main(String args[])
  {
    // create frame
    new MoonLanding().setVisible(true);
  }

  public MoonLanding()
  {
    // frame constructor
    setTitle("Moon Landing");
    setResizable(false);
    addWindowListener(new WindowAdapter()
    {
      public void windowClosing(WindowEvent evt)
      {
        exitForm(evt);
      }
    });
    getContentPane().setLayout(new GridBagLayout());
    GridBagConstraints gridConstraints;
```

```
    pack();
    Dimension screenSize =
Toolkit.getDefaultToolkit().getScreenSize();
    setBounds((int) (0.5 * (screenSize.width -
getWidth())), (int) (0.5 * (screenSize.height -
getHeight())), getWidth(), getHeight());
  }

  private void exitForm(WindowEvent evt)
  {
    System.exit(0);
  }
}
```

This code builds the frame, sets up the layout manager and includes code to exit the application. Run the code to make sure the frame (at least, what there is of it at this point) appears and is centered on the screen:

Let's populate our frame with other controls. All code for creating the frame and placing controls (except declarations) goes in the **MoonLanding** constructor.

We will build the frame in stages, first establishing the panels used for lander display and control, then overlaying it with the panel used to establish options. We start by putting two panel controls and some button controls on the frame. The **GridBagLayout** is:

	gridx = 0	gridx = 1	gridx = 2
gridy = 0	framePanel	controlPanel	
gridy = 1		startPauseButtonl	exitStopButton

The **framePanel** will hold another panel to display the lander animation. The **controlPanel** will hold controls displaying landing status. **startPauseButton** is used to start and pause the game and **exitStopButton** is used to stop and exit the game. A third button (**completeButton**, initially not visible)) is placed 'under' these two buttons. It is used at the end of the game to allow viewing of landing results. We will build each panel separately. Let's begin with the **framePanel**.

The **framePanel** will hold just a single control, the **viewerPanel**. Use these properties for each:

framePanel:

size	300, 400
background	GRAY
gridx	0 (on frame)
gridy	0 (on frame)
gridwidth	2

viewerPanel:

size	280, 380
background	WHITE
gridx	0 (on framePanel)
gridy	0 (on framePanel)

Add these class level declarations:

```
JPanel framePanel = new JPanel();
JPanel viewerPanel = new JPanel();
```

The controls are placed on the frame using this code:

```
framePanel.setPreferredSize(new Dimension(300, 400));
framePanel.setBackground(Color.GRAY);
framePanel.setLayout(new GridBagLayout());
gridConstraints = new GridBagConstraints();
gridConstraints.gridx = 0;
gridConstraints.gridy = 0;
gridConstraints.gridheight = 2;
getContentPane().add(framePanel, gridConstraints);

viewerPanel.setPreferredSize(new Dimension(280, 380));
viewerPanel.setBackground(Color.WHITE);
gridConstraints = new GridBagConstraints();
gridConstraints.gridx = 0;
gridConstraints.gridy = 0;
framePanel.add(viewerPanel, gridConstraints);
```

Add code in the proper locations. Run to see the "framed" viewer panel:

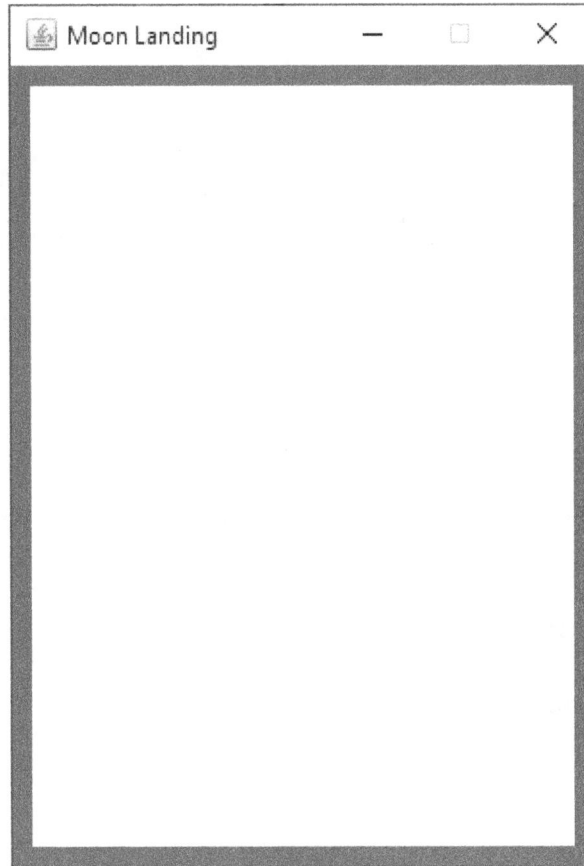

Now, let's add the control panel. Then, we'll add the buttons.

The **controlPanel** holds controls used to monitor the status of the landing. The **GridBagLayout** is:

	gridx = 0	gridx = 1	gridx = 2
gridy = 0	timeLabel	timeTextField	
gridy = 1		positionLabel	speedLabel
gridy = 2	altitudeLabel	altitudePositionLabel	altitudeSpeedLabel
gridy = 3	lateralLabel	lateralPositionLabel	lateralSpeedLabel
gridy = 4	fuelPanel		
gridy = 5	trajectoryPanel		
gridy =6	guidePanel		
gridy = 7	leftThrustButton	downThrustButton	rightThrustButton

The label and text field controls display status information. **fuelPanel** displays the remaining fuel, **trajectoryPanel** shows the descent, **guidePanel** shows the location of the lander and pad. The three button controls are used to add thrust to the lander. A label (**messageLabel**) will be hidden under the thrust buttons.

Control properties are:

controlPanel:

size	260, 360
font	Arial, Bold, Size 14
title	Landing Control-Beginner
background	Color(208, 208, 255), light blue
gridx	1 (on frame)
gridy	0 (on frame)
gridwidth	2
anchor	NORTH

timeLabel:

size	70, 25
text	Time (s)
font	Arial, Bold, Size 12
gridx	0 (on control panel)
gridy	0 (on control panel)

timeTextField:
size	70, 25
border	Black line
text	0.0
editable	false
background	White
horizontalAlignment	RIGHT
font	Arial, Plain, Size 12
gridx	1 (on control panel)
gridy	0 (on control panel)

positionLabel:
size	70, 25
text	Position (m)
font	Arial, Bold, Size 12
gridx	1 (on control panel)
gridy	1 (on control panel)

speedLabel:
size	70, 25
text	Speed (m/s)
font	Arial, Bold, Size 12
gridx	2 (on control panel)
gridy	1 (on control panel)

altitudeLabel:
size	70, 25
text	Altitude
font	Arial, Bold, Size 12
gridx	0 (on control panel)
gridy	2 (on control panel)

altitudePositionTextField:
size	70, 25
border	Black line
text	0.0
editable	false
background	White
horizontalAlignment	RIGHT
font	Arial, Plain, Size 12
gridx	1 (on control panel)
gridy	2 (on control panel)

altitudeSpeedTextField:

size	70, 25
border	Black line
text	0.0
editable	false
background	White
horizontalAlignment	RIGHT
font	Arial, Plain, Size 12
gridx	2 (on control panel)
gridy	2 (on control panel)

lateralLabel:

size	70, 25
text	Lateral
font	Arial, Bold, Size 12
gridx	0 (on control panel)
gridy	3 (on control panel)

lateralPositionTextField:

size	70, 25
border	Black line
text	0.0
editable	false
background	White
horizontalAlignment	RIGHT
font	Arial, Plain, Size 12
gridx	1 (on control panel)
gridy	3 (on control panel)

lateralSpeedTextField:

size	70, 25
border	Black line
text	0.0
editable	false
background	White
horizontalAlignment	RIGHT
font	Arial, Plain, Size 12
gridx	2 (on control panel)
gridy	3 (on control panel)

fuelPanel:
size	240, 40
background	Color(208, 208, 255), light blue
gridx	0 (on control panel)
gridy	4 (on control panel)
gridwidth	3

trajectoryPanel:
size	240, 130
background	Black
gridx	0 (on control panel)
gridy	5 (on control panel)
gridwidth	3

guidePanel:
size	240, 20
background	Gray
gridx	0 (on control panel)
gridy	6 (on control panel)
gridwidth	3

leftThrustButton:
image	leftarrow.gif (included in the **\KidGamesJava\KidGamesJava Projects\MoonLanding** folder)
gridx	0 (on control panel)
gridy	7 (on control panel)
insets	0, 25, 0, 0
anchor	WEST

downThrustButton:
image	downarrow.gif (included in the **\KidGamesJava\KidGamesJava Projects\MoonLanding** folder)
gridx	1 (on control panel)
gridy	7 (on control panel)
insets	0, 20, 0, 0
anchor	WEST

rightThrustButton:

image	rightarrow.gif (included in the **\KidGamesJava\KidGamesJava Projects\MoonLanding** folder)
gridx	2 (on control panel)
gridy	7 (on control panel)
insets	0, 20, 0, 0
anchor	WEST

messageLabel:

text	Auto-Pilot On
font	Arial, Bold, Size 14
visible	false
gridx	0 (on control panel)
gridy	7 (on control panel)
gridwidth	3
insets	11, 0, 0, 0

Make sure to copy the three button graphic files into the folder you use to build your project.

Use these declarations for the control panel (we also define the light blue color we use):

```
JPanel controlPanel = new JPanel();
JLabel timeLabel = new JLabel();
JTextField timeTextField = new JTextField();
JLabel positionLabel = new JLabel();
JLabel speedLabel = new JLabel();
JLabel altitudeLabel = new JLabel();
JTextField altitudePositionTextField = new JTextField();
JTextField altitudeSpeedTextField = new JTextField();
JLabel lateralLabel = new JLabel();
JTextField lateralPositionTextField = new JTextField();
JTextField lateralSpeedTextField = new JTextField();
JPanel fuelPanel = new JPanel();
JPanel trajectoryPanel = new JPanel();
JPanel guidePanel = new JPanel();
JButton leftThrustButton = new JButton(new
ImageIcon("leftarrow.gif"));
JButton downThrustButton = new JButton(new
ImageIcon("downarrow.gif"));
JButton rightThrustButton = new JButton(new
ImageIcon("rightarrow.gif"));
JLabel messageLabel = new JLabel();

Color lightBlue = new Color(208, 208, 255);
```

And, this code adds the controls:

```
UIManager.put("TitledBorder.font", new Font("Arial",
Font.BOLD, 14));

controlPanel.setPreferredSize(new Dimension(260, 360));
controlPanel.setBorder(BorderFactory.createTitledBorder("L
anding Control-Beginner"));
controlPanel.setBackground(lightBlue);
controlPanel.setLayout(new GridBagLayout());
gridConstraints = new GridBagConstraints();
gridConstraints.gridx = 1;
gridConstraints.gridy = 0;
gridConstraints.gridwidth = 2;
gridConstraints.anchor = GridBagConstraints.NORTH;
getContentPane().add(controlPanel, gridConstraints);

timeLabel.setPreferredSize(new Dimension(70, 25));
timeLabel.setText("Time (s)");
timeLabel.setFont(new Font("Arial", Font.BOLD, 12));
```

```
gridConstraints = new GridBagConstraints();
gridConstraints.gridx = 0;
gridConstraints.gridy = 0;
controlPanel.add(timeLabel, gridConstraints);

timeTextField.setPreferredSize(new Dimension(70, 25));
timeTextField.setBorder(BorderFactory.createLineBorder(Col
or.BLACK));
timeTextField.setText("0.0");
timeTextField.setEditable(false);
timeTextField.setBackground(Color.WHITE);
timeTextField.setHorizontalAlignment(SwingConstants.RIGHT)
;
timeTextField.setFont(new Font("Arial", Font.PLAIN, 12));
gridConstraints = new GridBagConstraints();
gridConstraints.gridx = 1;
gridConstraints.gridy = 0;
controlPanel.add(timeTextField, gridConstraints);

positionLabel.setPreferredSize(new Dimension(70, 25));
positionLabel.setText("Position (m)");
positionLabel.setFont(new Font("Arial", Font.BOLD, 12));
gridConstraints = new GridBagConstraints();
gridConstraints.gridx = 1;
gridConstraints.gridy = 1;
controlPanel.add(positionLabel, gridConstraints);

speedLabel.setPreferredSize(new Dimension(70, 25));
speedLabel.setText("Speed (m/s)");
speedLabel.setFont(new Font("Arial", Font.BOLD, 12));
gridConstraints = new GridBagConstraints();
gridConstraints.gridx = 2;
gridConstraints.gridy = 1;
controlPanel.add(speedLabel, gridConstraints);

altitudeLabel.setPreferredSize(new Dimension(70, 25));
altitudeLabel.setText("Altitude");
altitudeLabel.setFont(new Font("Arial", Font.BOLD, 12));
gridConstraints = new GridBagConstraints();
gridConstraints.gridx = 0;
gridConstraints.gridy = 2;
controlPanel.add(altitudeLabel, gridConstraints);

altitudePositionTextField.setPreferredSize(new
Dimension(70, 25));
altitudePositionTextField.setBorder(BorderFactory.createLi
neBorder(Color.BLACK));
```

```
altitudePositionTextField.setText("0.0");
altitudePositionTextField.setEditable(false);
altitudePositionTextField.setBackground(Color.WHITE);
altitudePositionTextField.setHorizontalAlignment(SwingCons
tants.RIGHT);
altitudePositionTextField.setFont(new Font("Arial",
Font.PLAIN, 12));
gridConstraints = new GridBagConstraints();
gridConstraints.gridx = 1;
gridConstraints.gridy = 2;
controlPanel.add(altitudePositionTextField,
gridConstraints);

altitudeSpeedTextField.setPreferredSize(new Dimension(70,
25));
altitudeSpeedTextField.setBorder(BorderFactory.createLineB
order(Color.BLACK));
altitudeSpeedTextField.setText("0.0");
altitudeSpeedTextField.setEditable(false);
altitudeSpeedTextField.setBackground(Color.WHITE);
altitudeSpeedTextField.setHorizontalAlignment(SwingConstan
ts.RIGHT);
altitudeSpeedTextField.setFont(new Font("Arial",
Font.PLAIN, 12));
gridConstraints = new GridBagConstraints();
gridConstraints.gridx = 2;
gridConstraints.gridy = 2;
controlPanel.add(altitudeSpeedTextField, gridConstraints);

lateralLabel.setPreferredSize(new Dimension(70, 25));
lateralLabel.setText("Lateral");
lateralLabel.setFont(new Font("Arial", Font.BOLD, 12));
gridConstraints = new GridBagConstraints();
gridConstraints.gridx = 0;
gridConstraints.gridy = 3;
controlPanel.add(lateralLabel, gridConstraints);

lateralPositionTextField.setPreferredSize(new
Dimension(70, 25));
lateralPositionTextField.setBorder(BorderFactory.createLin
eBorder(Color.BLACK));
lateralPositionTextField.setText("0.0");
lateralPositionTextField.setEditable(false);
lateralPositionTextField.setBackground(Color.WHITE);
lateralPositionTextField.setHorizontalAlignment(SwingConst
ants.RIGHT);
```

```
lateralPositionTextField.setFont(new Font("Arial",
Font.PLAIN, 12));
gridConstraints = new GridBagConstraints();
gridConstraints.gridx = 1;
gridConstraints.gridy = 3;
controlPanel.add(lateralPositionTextField,
gridConstraints);

lateralSpeedTextField.setPreferredSize(new Dimension(70,
25));
lateralSpeedTextField.setBorder(BorderFactory.createLineBo
rder(Color.BLACK));
lateralSpeedTextField.setText("0.0");
lateralSpeedTextField.setEditable(false);
lateralSpeedTextField.setBackground(Color.WHITE);
lateralSpeedTextField.setHorizontalAlignment(SwingConstant
s.RIGHT);
lateralSpeedTextField.setFont(new Font("Arial",
Font.PLAIN, 12));
gridConstraints = new GridBagConstraints();
gridConstraints.gridx = 2;
gridConstraints.gridy = 3;
controlPanel.add(lateralSpeedTextField, gridConstraints);

fuelPanel.setPreferredSize(new Dimension(240, 40));
fuelPanel.setBackground(lightBlue);
fuelPanel.setLayout(new GridBagLayout());
gridConstraints = new GridBagConstraints();
gridConstraints.gridx = 0;
gridConstraints.gridy = 4;
gridConstraints.gridwidth = 3;
controlPanel.add(fuelPanel, gridConstraints);

trajectoryPanel.setPreferredSize(new Dimension(240, 130));
trajectoryPanel.setBackground(Color.BLACK);
gridConstraints = new GridBagConstraints();
gridConstraints.gridx = 0;
gridConstraints.gridy = 5;
gridConstraints.gridwidth = 3;
controlPanel.add(trajectoryPanel, gridConstraints);

guidePanel.setPreferredSize(new Dimension(240, 20));
guidePanel.setBackground(Color.GRAY);
gridConstraints = new GridBagConstraints();
gridConstraints.gridx = 0;
gridConstraints.gridy = 6;
gridConstraints.gridwidth = 3;
```

```java
gridConstraints.insets = new Insets(0, 0, 10, 0);
controlPanel.add(guidePanel, gridConstraints);

gridConstraints = new GridBagConstraints();
gridConstraints.gridx = 0;
gridConstraints.gridy = 7;
gridConstraints.insets = new Insets(0, 25, 0, 0);
gridConstraints.anchor = GridBagConstraints.WEST;
controlPanel.add(leftThrustButton, gridConstraints);
leftThrustButton.addActionListener(new ActionListener()
{
  public void actionPerformed(ActionEvent e)
  {
    leftThrustButtonActionPerformed(e);
  }
});

gridConstraints = new GridBagConstraints();
gridConstraints.gridx = 1;
gridConstraints.gridy = 7;
gridConstraints.insets = new Insets(0, 20, 0, 0);
gridConstraints.anchor = GridBagConstraints.WEST;
controlPanel.add(downThrustButton, gridConstraints);
downThrustButton.addActionListener(new ActionListener()
{
  public void actionPerformed(ActionEvent e)
  {
    downThrustButtonActionPerformed(e);
  }
});

gridConstraints = new GridBagConstraints();
gridConstraints.gridx = 2;
gridConstraints.gridy = 7;
gridConstraints.insets = new Insets(0, 20, 0, 0);
gridConstraints.anchor = GridBagConstraints.WEST;
controlPanel.add(rightThrustButton, gridConstraints);
rightThrustButton.addActionListener(new ActionListener()
{
  public void actionPerformed(ActionEvent e)
  {
    rightThrustButtonActionPerformed(e);
  }
});

messageLabel.setText("Auto-Pilot On");
messageLabel.setFont(new Font("Arial", Font.BOLD, 14));
```

```
messageLabel.setVisible(false);
gridConstraints = new GridBagConstraints();
gridConstraints.gridx = 0;
gridConstraints.gridy = 7;
gridConstraints.gridwidth = 3;
gridConstraints.insets = new Insets(11, 0, 0, 0);
controlPanel.add(messageLabel, gridConstraints);
```

This code also adds listeners for each button. Add these empty methods with the other methods:

```
private void leftThrustButtonActionPerformed(ActionEvent
e)
{
}

private void downThrustButtonActionPerformed(ActionEvent
e)
{
}

private void rightThrustButtonActionPerformed(ActionEvent
e)
{
}
```

Save, run the project. You will see:

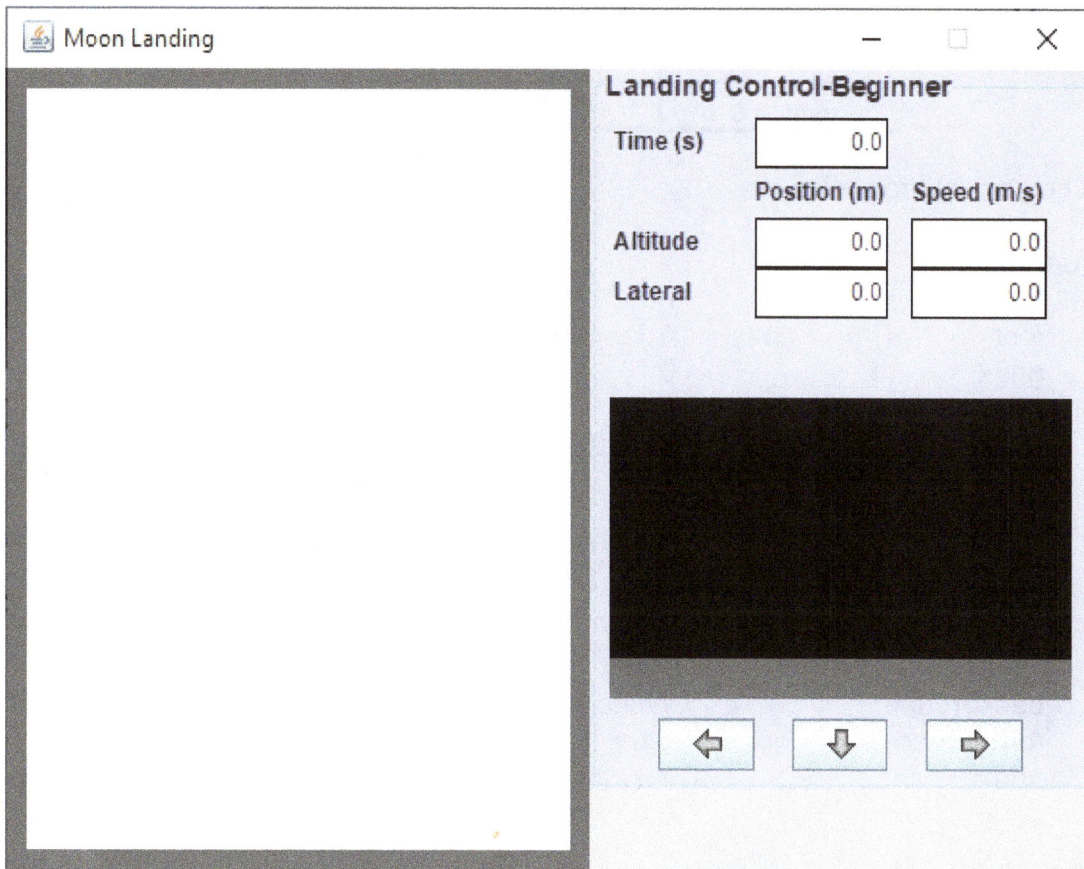

It may look like the fuel panel is not there, but it is – we just need to add some controls.

The **fuelPanel** holds a label and a progress bar. The **GridBagLayout** is:

	gridx = 0	gridx = 1
gridy = 0	**fuelLabel**	**fuelProgressBa**

The control properties are:

fuelLabel:

text	Fuel
font	Arial, Bold, Size 12
gridx	0
gridy	0
insets	0, 0, 0, 5

fuelProgressBar:

size	200, 25
minimum	0
maximum	100
value	100
background	White
foreground	Blue
gridx	1
gridy	0

Declare the controls using:

```
JLabel fuelLabel = new JLabel();
JProgressBar fuelProgressBar = new JProgressBar();
```

Add the controls to the **fuelPanel** (which is in **controlPanel**) using:

```
fuelLabel.setText("Fuel");
fuelLabel.setFont(new Font("Arial", Font.BOLD, 12));
gridConstraints = new GridBagConstraints();
gridConstraints.gridx = 0;
gridConstraints.gridy = 0;
gridConstraints.insets = new Insets(0, 0, 0, 5);
fuelPanel.add(fuelLabel, gridConstraints);
```

```
fuelProgressBar.setPreferredSize(new Dimension(200, 25));
fuelProgressBar.setMinimum(0);
fuelProgressBar.setMaximum(100);
fuelProgressBar.setValue(100);
fuelProgressBar.setBackground(Color.WHITE);
fuelProgressBar.setForeground(Color.BLUE);
gridConstraints = new GridBagConstraints();
gridConstraints.gridx = 1;
gridConstraints.gridy = 0;
fuelPanel.add(fuelProgressBar, gridConstraints);
```

Add this code in the proper locations. Run to see:

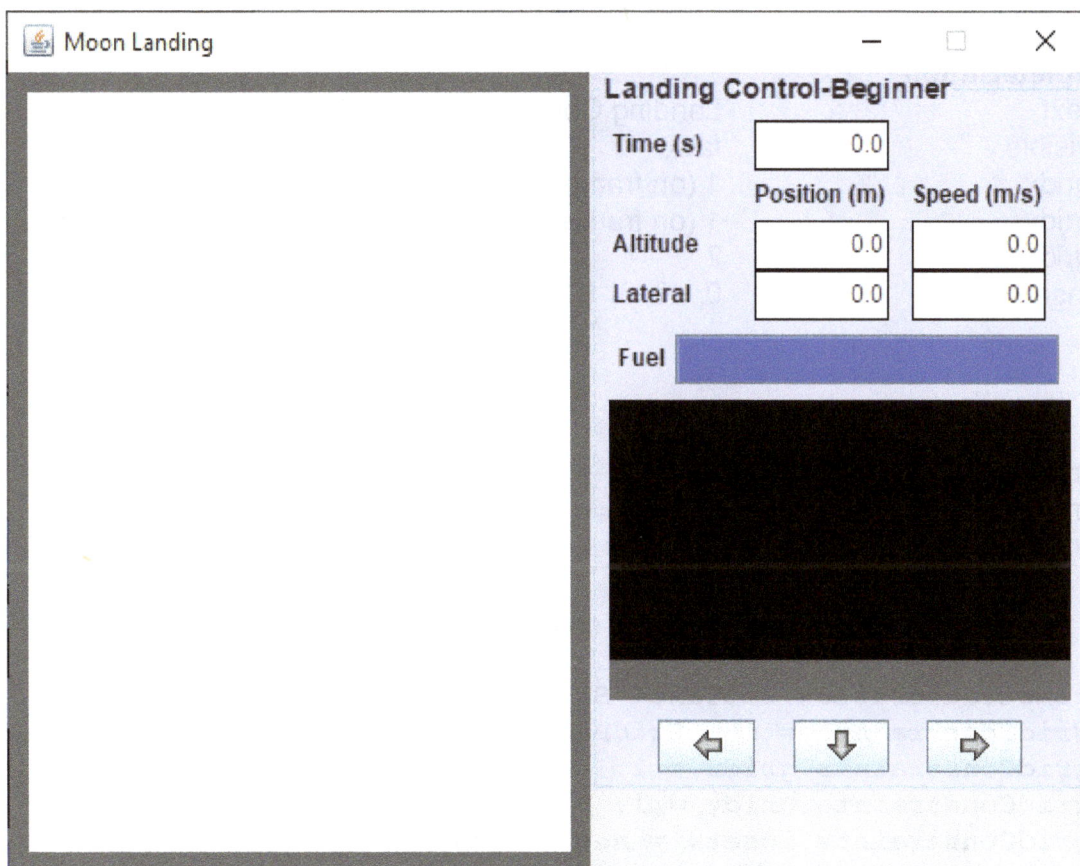

The fuel gauge is now seen – note it is initially full.

Next, we add three buttons to the frame. Properties are:

startPauseButton:

text	Start Game
gridx	1 (on frame)
gridy	1 (on frame)
insets	0, 20, 0, 0

exitStopButton:

text	Exit
gridx	2 (on frame)
gridy	1 (on frame)
insets	0, 10, 0, 10

completeButton:

text	Landing Complete-Click to Continue
visible	false
gridx	1 (on frame)
gridy	1 (on frame)
gridwidth	2
insets	0, 10, 0, 10

Use these declarations:

```
JButton startPauseButton = new JButton();
JButton exitStopButton = new JButton();
JButton completeButton = new JButton();
```

Add the buttons to the frame using this code:

```
startPauseButton.setText("Start Game");
gridConstraints = new GridBagConstraints();
gridConstraints.gridx = 1;
gridConstraints.gridy = 1;
gridConstraints.insets = new Insets(0, 20, 0, 0);
getContentPane().add(startPauseButton, gridConstraints);
startPauseButton.addActionListener(new ActionListener()
{
  public void actionPerformed(ActionEvent e)
  {
    startPauseButtonActionPerformed(e);
  }
});
```

```
exitStopButton.setText("Exit");
exitStopButton.setPreferredSize(startPauseButton.getPrefer
redSize());
gridConstraints = new GridBagConstraints();
gridConstraints.gridx = 2;
gridConstraints.gridy = 1;
gridConstraints.insets = new Insets(0, 10, 0, 10);
getContentPane().add(exitStopButton, gridConstraints);
exitStopButton.addActionListener(new ActionListener()
{
  public void actionPerformed(ActionEvent e)
  {
    exitStopButtonActionPerformed(e);
  }
});

completeButton.setText("Landing Complete-Click to
Continue");
completeButton.setVisible(false);
gridConstraints = new GridBagConstraints();
gridConstraints.gridx = 1;
gridConstraints.gridy = 1;
gridConstraints.gridwidth = 2;
gridConstraints.insets = new Insets(0, 10, 0, 10);
getContentPane().add(completeButton, gridConstraints);
completeButton.addActionListener(new ActionListener()
{
  public void actionPerformed(ActionEvent e)
  {
    completeButtonActionPerformed(e);
  }
});
```

And, add these three empty methods:

```
private void startPauseButtonActionPerformed(ActionEvent
e)
{
}

private void exitStopButtonActionPerformed(ActionEvent e)
{
}

private void completeButtonActionPerformed(ActionEvent e)
{
}
```

Run the project to see:

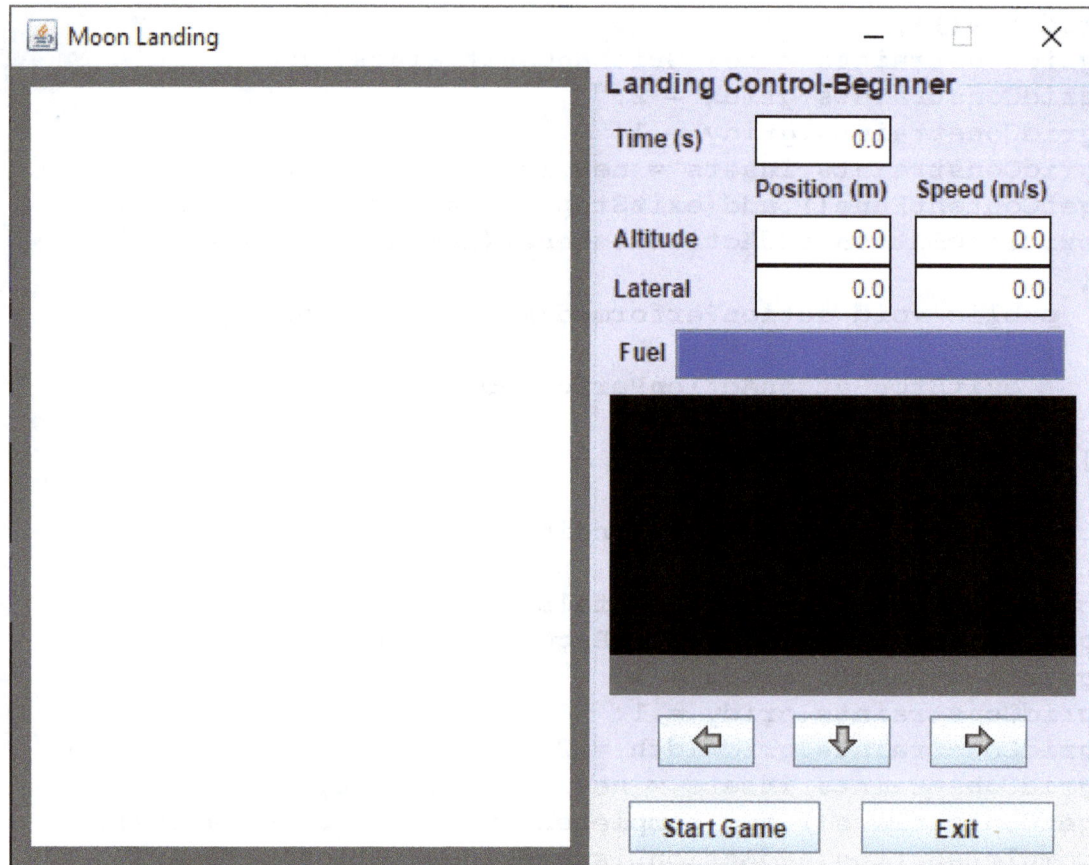

Notice the **completeButton** does not appear (its **visible** property is false). We will make this button appear, when needed, using code.

One panel remains. After all our work building the control panel, we will soon make it disappear, so the options panel will appear. The **optionsPanel** holds two panels that allow selection of game options. The **GridBagLayout** is:

	gridx = 0
gridy = 0	**pilotPanel**
gridy = 1	**unitsPanel**

pilotPanel is used to select pilot level and whether to use auto-pilot. **unitsPanel** selects the units for display.

Control properties are:

optionsPanel:

size	260, 360
background	Blue
gridx	1 (on frame)
gridy	0 (on frame)
gridwidth	2
anchor	NORTH

pilotPanel:

size	140, 190
background	Color(208, 208, 255), light blue
font	Arial, Bold, Size 14
text	Pilot Level
gridx	0 (on options panel)
gridy	0 (on options panel)

pilotPanel:

size	140, 180
background	Color(208, 208, 255), light blue
font	Arial, Bold, Size 14
text	Units
gridx	0 (on options panel)
gridy	1 (on options panel)
insets	10, 0, 0, 0

Use these declarations:

```
JPanel optionsPanel = new JPanel();
JPanel pilotPanel = new JPanel();
JPanel unitsPanel = new JPanel();
```

And, this code makes the control panel invisible (**visible** is **false**) and adds the new panels:

```
controlPanel.setVisible(false);

optionsPanel.setPreferredSize(new Dimension(260, 360));
optionsPanel.setBackground(Color.BLUE);
optionsPanel.setLayout(new GridBagLayout());
gridConstraints = new GridBagConstraints();
gridConstraints.gridx = 1;
gridConstraints.gridy = 0;
gridConstraints.gridwidth = 2;
gridConstraints.anchor = GridBagConstraints.NORTH;
getContentPane().add(optionsPanel, gridConstraints);

pilotPanel.setBorder(BorderFactory.createTitledBorder("Pil
ot Level"));
pilotPanel.setPreferredSize(new Dimension(140, 190));
pilotPanel.setBackground(lightBlue);
pilotPanel.setLayout(new GridBagLayout());
gridConstraints = new GridBagConstraints();
gridConstraints.gridx = 0;
gridConstraints.gridy = 0;
optionsPanel.add(pilotPanel, gridConstraints);

unitsPanel.setBorder(BorderFactory.createTitledBorder("Uni
ts"));
unitsPanel.setPreferredSize(new Dimension(140, 80));
unitsPanel.setBackground(lightBlue);
unitsPanel.setLayout(new GridBagLayout());
gridConstraints = new GridBagConstraints();
gridConstraints.gridx = 0;
gridConstraints.gridy = 1;
gridConstraints.insets = new Insets(10, 0, 0, 0);
optionsPanel.add(unitsPanel, gridConstraints);
UIManager.put("TitledBorder.font", new Font("Arial",
Font.BOLD, 14));
```

Save, run the project. You will see:

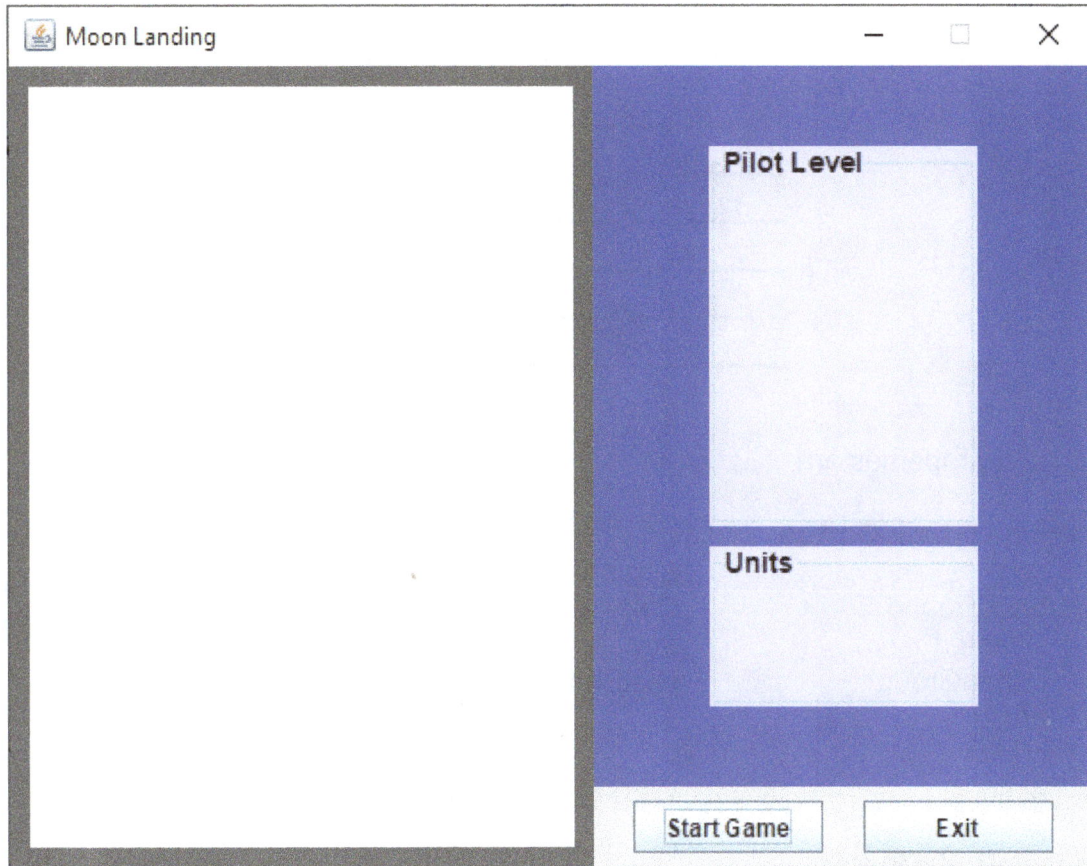

The control panel is gone and the empty pilot level and units panels appear. Let's add controls to these panels to complete the frame design.

The **pilotPanel** allows selection of pilot level and whether auto-pilot is on. The **GridBagLayout** is:

	gridx = 0
gridy = 0	**beginnerRadioButton**
gridy = 1	**noviceRadioButton**
gridy = 2	**juniorRadioButton**
gridy = 3	**seniorRadioButton**
gridy = 4	**advancedRadioButton**
gridy =5	**autoPilotCheckBox**

Control properties are:

beginnerRadioButton:
text	Beginner
background	Color(208, 208, 255), light blue
selected	true
buttonGroup	pilotButtonGroup
gridx	0
gridy	0
anchor	WEST

noviceRadioButton:
text	Novice
background	Color(208, 208, 255), light blue
buttonGroup	pilotButtonGroup
gridx	0
gridy	1
anchor	WEST

juniorRadioButton:
text	Junior
background	Color(208, 208, 255), light blue
buttonGroup	pilotButtonGroup
gridx	0
gridy	2
anchor	WEST

seniorRadioButton:

text	Senior
background	Color(208, 208, 255), light blue
buttonGroup	pilotButtonGroup
gridx	0
gridy	3
anchor	WEST

advancedRadioButton:

text	Advanced
background	Color(208, 208, 255), light blue
buttonGroup	pilotButtonGroup
gridx	0
gridy	4
anchor	WEST

autoPilotCheckBox:

text	Auto-Pilot On?
background	Color(208, 208, 255), light blue
gridx	0
gridy	5
anchor	WEST

Use these declarations:

```
ButtonGroup pilotButtonGroup = new ButtonGroup();
JRadioButton beginnerRadioButton = new JRadioButton();
JRadioButton noviceRadioButton = new JRadioButton();
JRadioButton juniorRadioButton = new JRadioButton();
JRadioButton seniorRadioButton = new JRadioButton();
JRadioButton advancedRadioButton = new JRadioButton();
JCheckBox autoPilotCheckBox = new JCheckBox();
```

And, this code adds the controls:

```
beginnerRadioButton.setText("Beginner");
beginnerRadioButton.setBackground(lightBlue);
beginnerRadioButton.setSelected(true);
pilotButtonGroup.add(beginnerRadioButton);
gridConstraints = new GridBagConstraints();
gridConstraints.gridx = 0;
gridConstraints.gridy = 0;
gridConstraints.anchor = GridBagConstraints.WEST;
pilotPanel.add(beginnerRadioButton, gridConstraints);
beginnerRadioButton.addActionListener(new ActionListener()
{
  public void actionPerformed(ActionEvent e)
  {
pilotRadioButtonActionPerformed(e);
  }
});

noviceRadioButton.setText("Novice");
noviceRadioButton.setBackground(lightBlue);
pilotButtonGroup.add(noviceRadioButton);
gridConstraints = new GridBagConstraints();
gridConstraints.gridx = 0;
gridConstraints.gridy = 1;
gridConstraints.anchor = GridBagConstraints.WEST;
pilotPanel.add(noviceRadioButton, gridConstraints);
noviceRadioButton.addActionListener(new ActionListener()
{
  public void actionPerformed(ActionEvent e)
  {
pilotRadioButtonActionPerformed(e);
  }
});

juniorRadioButton.setText("Junior");
juniorRadioButton.setBackground(lightBlue);
pilotButtonGroup.add(juniorRadioButton);
gridConstraints = new GridBagConstraints();
gridConstraints.gridx = 0;
gridConstraints.gridy = 2;
gridConstraints.anchor = GridBagConstraints.WEST;
pilotPanel.add(juniorRadioButton, gridConstraints);
juniorRadioButton.addActionListener(new ActionListener()
{
  public void actionPerformed(ActionEvent e)
  {
```

```
pilotRadioButtonActionPerformed(e);
   }
});

seniorRadioButton.setText("Senior");
seniorRadioButton.setBackground(lightBlue);
pilotButtonGroup.add(seniorRadioButton);
gridConstraints = new GridBagConstraints();
gridConstraints.gridx = 0;
gridConstraints.gridy = 3;
gridConstraints.anchor = GridBagConstraints.WEST;
pilotPanel.add(seniorRadioButton, gridConstraints);
seniorRadioButton.addActionListener(new ActionListener()
{
  public void actionPerformed(ActionEvent e)
  {
pilotRadioButtonActionPerformed(e);
  }
});

advancedRadioButton.setText("Advanced");
advancedRadioButton.setBackground(lightBlue);
pilotButtonGroup.add(advancedRadioButton);
gridConstraints = new GridBagConstraints();
gridConstraints.gridx = 0;
gridConstraints.gridy = 4;
gridConstraints.anchor = GridBagConstraints.WEST;
pilotPanel.add(advancedRadioButton, gridConstraints);
advancedRadioButton.addActionListener(new ActionListener()
{
  public void actionPerformed(ActionEvent e)
  {
pilotRadioButtonActionPerformed(e);
  }
});

autoPilotCheckBox.setText("Auto Pilot On?");
autoPilotCheckBox.setBackground(lightBlue);
gridConstraints = new GridBagConstraints();
gridConstraints.gridx = 0;
gridConstraints.gridy = 5;
gridConstraints.anchor = GridBagConstraints.WEST;
pilotPanel.add(autoPilotCheckBox, gridConstraints);
```

This code also adds a listener for each radio button. Add this empty method:

```
private void pilotRadioButtonActionPerformed(ActionEvent
e)
{
}
```

Save, run the project. You will see:

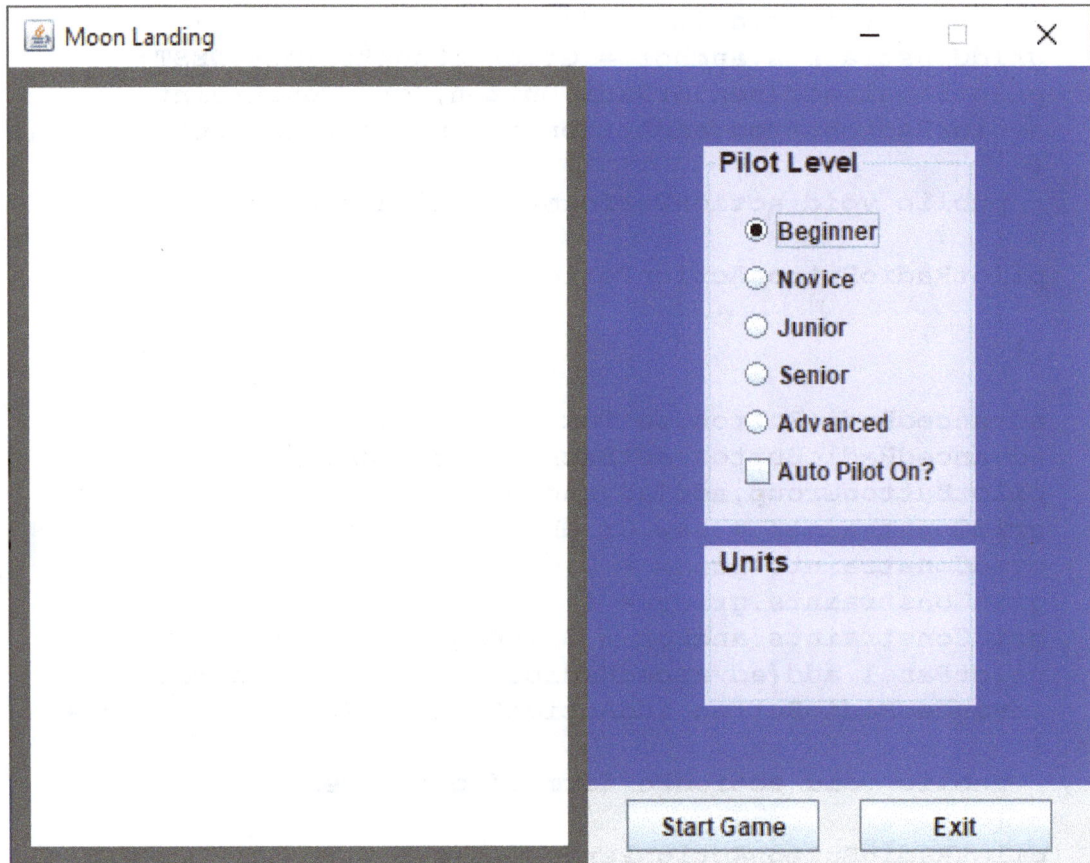

The radio buttons and check box appear in the pilot level panel. Now, the units panel.

The **unitsPanel** allows selection between metric and US units of measure. The **GridBagLayout** is:

	gridx = 0
gridy = 0	**metricRadioButton**
gridy = 1	**usRadioButton**

Control properties are:

metricRadioButton:

text	Metric
background	Color(208, 208, 255), light blue
selected	true
buttonGroup	unitsButtonGroup
gridx	0
gridy	0
anchor	WEST

usRadioButton:

text	US (English)
background	Color(208, 208, 255), light blue
buttonGroup	unitsButtonGroup
gridx	0
gridy	1
anchor	WEST

Use these declarations:

```
ButtonGroup unitsButtonGroup = new ButtonGroup();
JRadioButton metricRadioButton = new JRadioButton();
JRadioButton usRadioButton = new JRadioButton();
```

And, this code adds the controls:

```
metricRadioButton.setText("Metric");
metricRadioButton.setBackground(lightBlue);
metricRadioButton.setSelected(true);
unitsButtonGroup.add(metricRadioButton);
gridConstraints = new GridBagConstraints();
gridConstraints.gridx = 0;
gridConstraints.gridy = 0;
gridConstraints.anchor = GridBagConstraints.WEST;
unitsPanel.add(metricRadioButton, gridConstraints);
metricRadioButton.addActionListener(new ActionListener()
{
  public void actionPerformed(ActionEvent e)
  {
unitsRadioButtonActionPerformed(e);
  }
});

usRadioButton.setText("US (English)");
usRadioButton.setBackground(lightBlue);
unitsButtonGroup.add(usRadioButton);
gridConstraints = new GridBagConstraints();
gridConstraints.gridx = 0;
gridConstraints.gridy = 1;
gridConstraints.anchor = GridBagConstraints.WEST;
unitsPanel.add(usRadioButton, gridConstraints);
usRadioButton.addActionListener(new ActionListener()
{
  public void actionPerformed(ActionEvent e)
  {
unitsRadioButtonActionPerformed(e);
  }
});
```

This code also adds a listener for each radio button. Add this empty method:

```
private void unitsRadioButtonActionPerformed(ActionEvent
e)
{
}
```

Save, run the project. You will see:

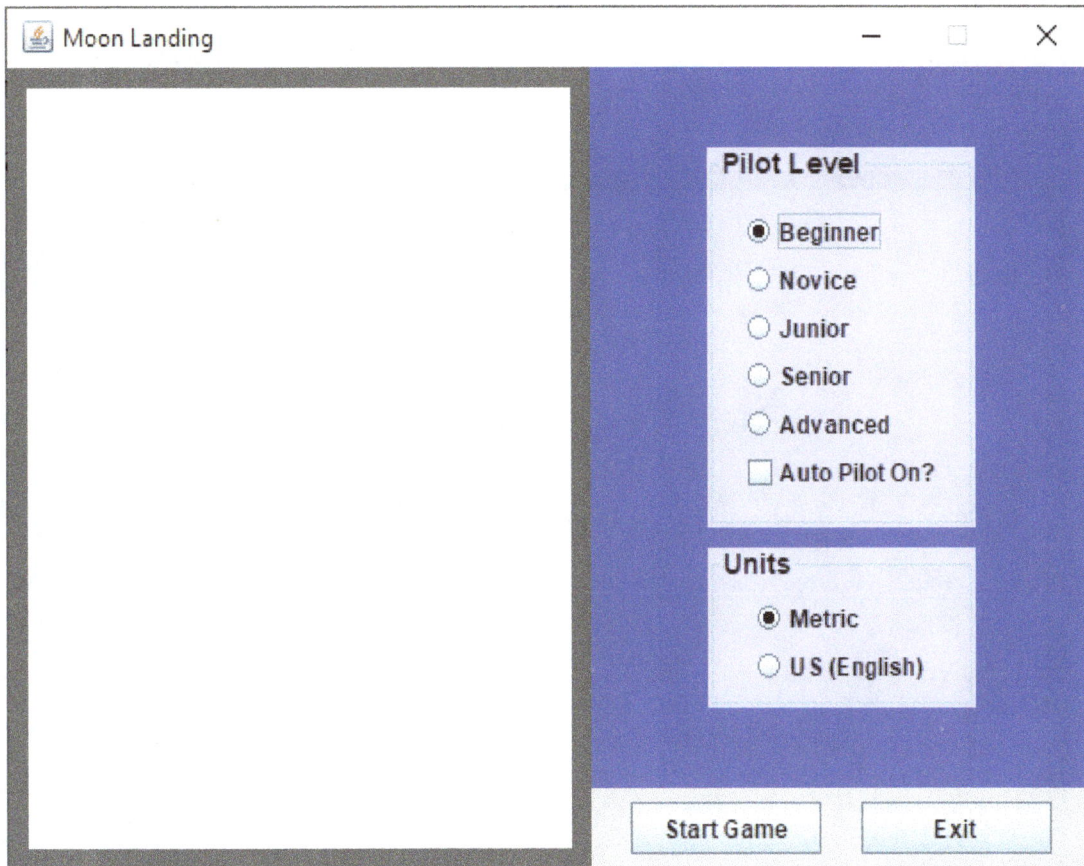

The frame is complete.

We will now begin writing the remaining code for the game. We will write the code in several steps. As a first step, we will write the code that sets the options and do some initial coding for the start/pause and exit/stop buttons. Then, we add additional elements to the game, one at a time. During the code development process, recognize you may modify a particular method several times before arriving at the finished product.

Code Design – Initializing Options, Clock

Even though we have no code, notice we can run the game. It appears as:

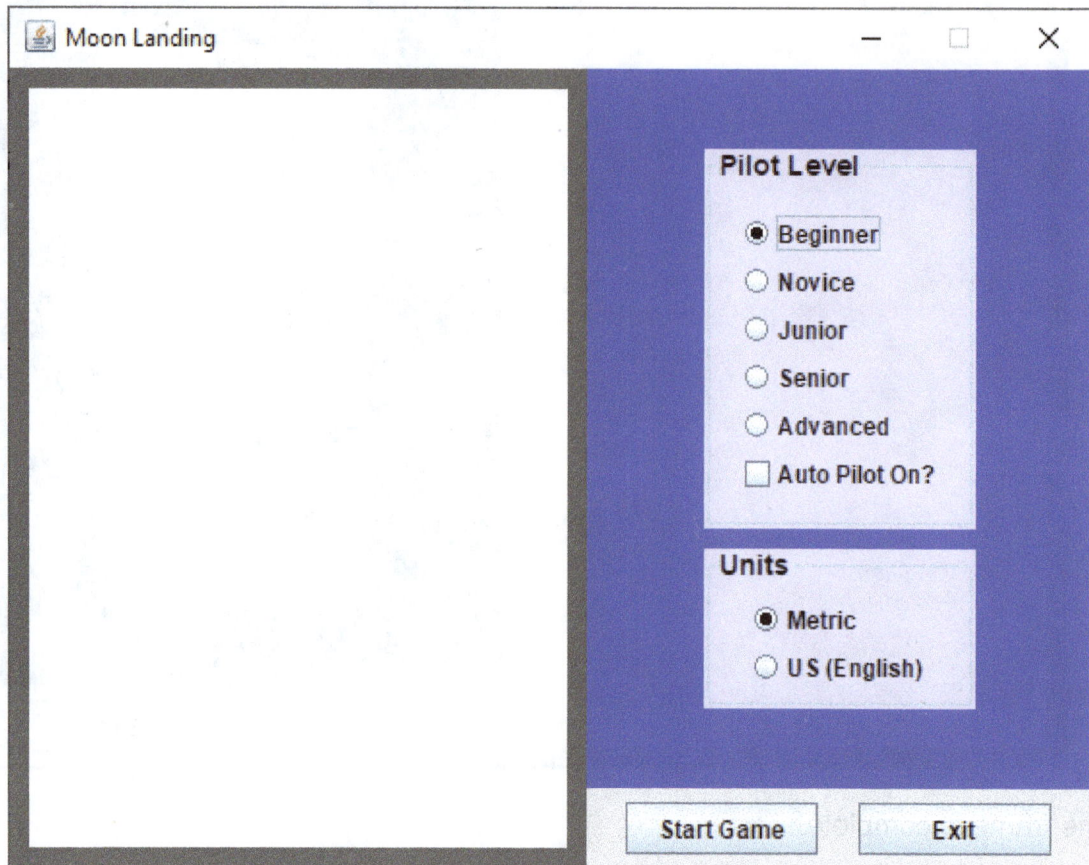

In this 'stopped' state, all a user can do is choose one of the two options (**Pilot Level** or **Units**) or click on **Start Game** or **Exit**. You can also decide if you want **Auto-Pilot On**. If a user chooses to start a game, the options panel (**optionsPanel**) should disappear and the control panel (**panelControl**) appears.

We will use a variable (**pilotLevel**) that ranges from 1 to 5 to keep track of the selected pilot level. Add this class level declaration to the code window:

```
int pilotLevel = 1;
```

We initialize this to **Beginner** (**pilotLevel = 1**) level to match the initially checked radio button.

The code to set **pilotLevel** is in the **pilotRadioButtonActionPerformed** method (handles clicks on any of the five radio buttons):

```
private void pilotRadioButtonActionPerformed(ActionEvent
e)
{
  String t = e.getActionCommand();
  if (t.equals("Beginner"))
    pilotLevel = 1;
  else if (t.equals("Novice"))
    pilotLevel = 2;
  else if (t.equals("Junior"))
    pilotLevel = 3;
  else if (t.equals("Senior"))
    pilotLevel = 4;
  else if (t.equals("Advanced"))
    pilotLevel = 5;
}
```

We will do the calculations in this program in **Metric** units. This means all positions will be in meters and all speeds will be in meters/second. If a user selects **US (English)** units, we need to multiply all results by the number than converts meters to feet. This number will be stored in a variable **multiplier**. Add this class level declaration and initialize it to 1.0 since for metric units (the default choice), we just multiply everything by 1.0:

```
double multiplier = 1.0;
```

The **multiplier** is set in the **unitsRadioButtonActionPerformed** method:

```
private void unitsRadioButtonActionPerformed(ActionEvent
e)
{
  String t = e.getActionCommand();
  if (t.equals("Metric"))
    multiplier = 1.0;
  else
    multiplier = 3.2808;
}
```

This says there are 3.2808 feet in a meter.

We use a timer object (**landingTimer**) in the **Moon Landing** program to update the elapsed time, all computed values and all graphics elements of the program. In this initialization stage, we'll just use it to update the time. Declare the timer object:

```
Timer landingTimer;
```

Add the timer object to the project using a delay of 500 msec (0.5 seconds) and add a listener for the **landingTimerActionPerformed** method:

```
landingTimer = new Timer(500, new ActionListener()
{
  public void actionPerformed(ActionEvent e)
  {
    landingTimerActionPerformed(e);
  }
});
```

Add this class level declaration for the variable (**time**) to represent elapsed time (in seconds):

```
double time;
```

The time is then updated in the **landingTimerActionPerformed** method:

```
private void landingTimerActionPerformed(ActionEvent e)
{
  time += (double) (landingTimer.getDelay()) / 1000;
  timeTextField.setText(new
DecimalFormat("0.00").format(time));
}
```

As mentioned, the **delay** isy set to 500 milliseconds, hence an update will be obtained every 0.5 seconds. You need to add this **import** statement to use the **DecimalFormat** class:

```
import java.text.*;
```

This might be a good time to compile your code to make sure things are okay. Fix any errors you might encounter.

Now, we'll begin writing the code that starts, pauses, restarts and stops **Moon Landing**. We also write code that exits the program. Before doing this, however, let's review what each **Pilot Level** entails:

> ➢ **Beginner** – No lateral thrust control; no fuel usage.
> ➢ **Novice** – No vertical thrust control; no fuel usage.
> ➢ **Junior** – All thrust controls; no fuel usage.
> ➢ **Senior**, **Advanced** – All thrust controls; fuel usage.

If **Auto-Pilot** is on, we have no thrust controls, but want the label specifying **Auto-Pilot On** visible. Hence, when a game starts, different controls may or not appear in the group box displaying the lander control information.

Two buttons control the game, **startPauseButton** and **exitStopButton**. These buttons have certain interactions. The **startPauseButton** control can have three possible **text** properties. If the **text** property is **Start Game** when clicked, the game is initialized and put in playing mode using:

> ➢ Change **text** to **Pause Game**.
> ➢ Change **text** of **exitStopButton** to **Stop Game**.
> ➢ Set **optionsPanel visible** property to **false**.
> ➢ Set **controlPanel visible** property to **true**.
> ➢ If **pilotLevel = 1**:
>> o Set **controlPanel text** property to **Beginner.**
>> o Remove **leftThrustButton, rightThrustbutton, fuelLabel, fuelProgressBar**.
> ➢ If **pilotLevel = 2**:
>> o Set **controlPanel text** property to **Novice.**
>> o Remove **downThrustButton, , fuelLabel, fuelProgressBar**.
> ➢ If **pilotLevel = 3**:
>> o Set **controlPanel text** property to **Junior.**
>> o Remove **fuelLabel, fuelProgressBar**.
> ➢ If **pilotLevel = 4**:
>> o Set **controlPanel text** property to **Senior.**
> ➢ If **pilotLevel = 5**:
>> o Set **controlPanel text** property to **Advanced.**
> ➢ If **Auto-Pilot On** is checked:
>> o Remove **leftThrustButton, downThrustButton, rightThrustButton.**
>> o Set **messageLabel visible** property to **true** (with appropriate **text**)
> ➢ Set **positionLabel** and **speedLabel** based on units selection.
> ➢ Initialize **time** to zero
> ➢ Set **viewerPanel visible** property to **true**.
> ➢ Start **landingTimer**.

When **text** property is **Pause Game** and the button is clicked, we enter pause mode:

> ➢ Change **text** to **Restart Game**.
> ➢ Disable **exitStopButton**.
> ➢ Disable **leftThrustButton, downThrustButton, rightThrustButton.**.
> ➢ Stop **landingTimer**.

When **text** property is **Restart Game** and the button is clicked, we enter playing mode:

> ➢ Change **text** to **Pause Game**.
> ➢ Enable **exitStopButton.**.
> ➢ Enable **leftThrustButton, downThrustButton, rightThrustButton.**.
> ➢ Start **landingTimer**.

The code that covers the above steps is in the **startPauseButtonActionPerformed** method:

```
private void startPauseButtonActionPerformed(ActionEvent
e)
{
  if (startPauseButton.getText().equals("Start Game"))
  {
    startPauseButton.setText("Pause Game");
    exitStopButton.setText("Stop Game");
    optionsPanel.setVisible(false);
    controlPanel.setVisible(true);
    switch (pilotLevel)
    {
      case 1:

controlPanel.setBorder(BorderFactory.createTitledBorder("L
anding Control-Beginner"));
        leftThrustButton.setVisible(false);
        rightThrustButton.setVisible(false);
        downThrustButton.setVisible(true);
        fuelLabel.setVisible(false);
        fuelProgressBar.setVisible(false);
        break;
      case 2:

controlPanel.setBorder(BorderFactory.createTitledBorder("L
anding Control-Novice"));
        leftThrustButton.setVisible(true);
        rightThrustButton.setVisible(true);
        downThrustButton.setVisible(false);
```

```
            fuelLabel.setVisible(false);
            fuelProgressBar.setVisible(false);
            break;
         case 3:

controlPanel.setBorder(BorderFactory.createTitledBorder("L
anding Control-Junior"));
            leftThrustButton.setVisible(true);
            rightThrustButton.setVisible(true);
            downThrustButton.setVisible(true);
            fuelLabel.setVisible(false);
            fuelProgressBar.setVisible(false);
            break;
         case 4:

controlPanel.setBorder(BorderFactory.createTitledBorder("L
anding Control-Senior"));
            leftThrustButton.setVisible(true);
            rightThrustButton.setVisible(true);
            downThrustButton.setVisible(true);
            fuelLabel.setVisible(true);
            fuelProgressBar.setVisible(true);
            break;
         case 5:

controlPanel.setBorder(BorderFactory.createTitledBorder("L
anding Control-Advanced"));
            leftThrustButton.setVisible(true);
            rightThrustButton.setVisible(true);
            downThrustButton.setVisible(true);
            fuelLabel.setVisible(true);
            fuelProgressBar.setVisible(true);
            break;
      }
      if (autoPilotCheckBox.isSelected())
      {
        leftThrustButton.setVisible(false);
        rightThrustButton.setVisible(false);
        downThrustButton.setVisible(false);
        messageLabel.setText("Auto-Pilot On");
        messageLabel.setVisible(true);
      }
      else
      {
        messageLabel.setVisible(false);
      }
      if (metricRadioButton.isSelected())
```

```
    {
      positionLabel.setText("Position (m)");
      speedLabel.setText("Speed (m/s)");
    }
    else
    {
      positionLabel.setText("Position (ft)");
      speedLabel.setText("Speed (ft/s)");
    }
    time = 0.0;
    timeTextField.setText("0.0");
    viewerPanel.setVisible(true);
    landingTimer.start();
  }
  else if (startPauseButton.getText().equals("Pause
Game"))
  {
    startPauseButton.setText("Restart Game");
    exitStopButton.setEnabled(false);
    leftThrustButton.setEnabled(false);
    downThrustButton.setEnabled(false);
    rightThrustButton.setEnabled(false);
    landingTimer.stop();
  }
  else
  {
    startPauseButton.setText("Pause Game");
    exitStopButton.setEnabled(true);
    leftThrustButton.setEnabled(true);
    downThrustButton.setEnabled(true);
    rightThrustButton.setEnabled(true);
    landingTimer.start();
  }
}
```

When a player clicks **Stop Game** (**exitStopButton**), the following should happen:

> ➢ Change **text** to **Exit**.
> ➢ Change **text** of **startPauseButton** to **Start Game**.
> ➢ Set **optionsPanel visible** property to **true**.
> ➢ Set **controlPanel visible** property to **false**.
> ➢ Set **viewerPanel visible** property to **true**.
> ➢ Stop **landingTimer**.

If **exitStopButton** is clicked when the caption is **Exit**, the program stops.

The corresponding code goes in the **exitStopButton ActionPerformed** method:

```
private void exitStopButtonActionPerformed(ActionEvent e)
{
  if (exitStopButton.getText().equals("Stop Game"))
  {
    exitStopButton.setText("Exit");
    startPauseButton.setText("Start Game");
    optionsPanel.setVisible(true);
    controlPanel.setVisible(false);
    viewerPanel.setVisible(false);
    landingTimer.stop();
  }
  else
  {
    System.exit(0);
  }
}
```

Save and run the project. You should be able to start the game, pause the game, restart the game and stop the game. Make sure everything works as desired. Try each combination of **Pilot Level**, **Auto-Pilot On** and **Units** selection. Make sure after clicking **Start Game**, the lander control panel displays the proper controls. Make sure the clock time is increasing in 0.5 second increments. Here's the form for a **Senior** level, no auto-pilot and **US** units after 4.5 seconds:

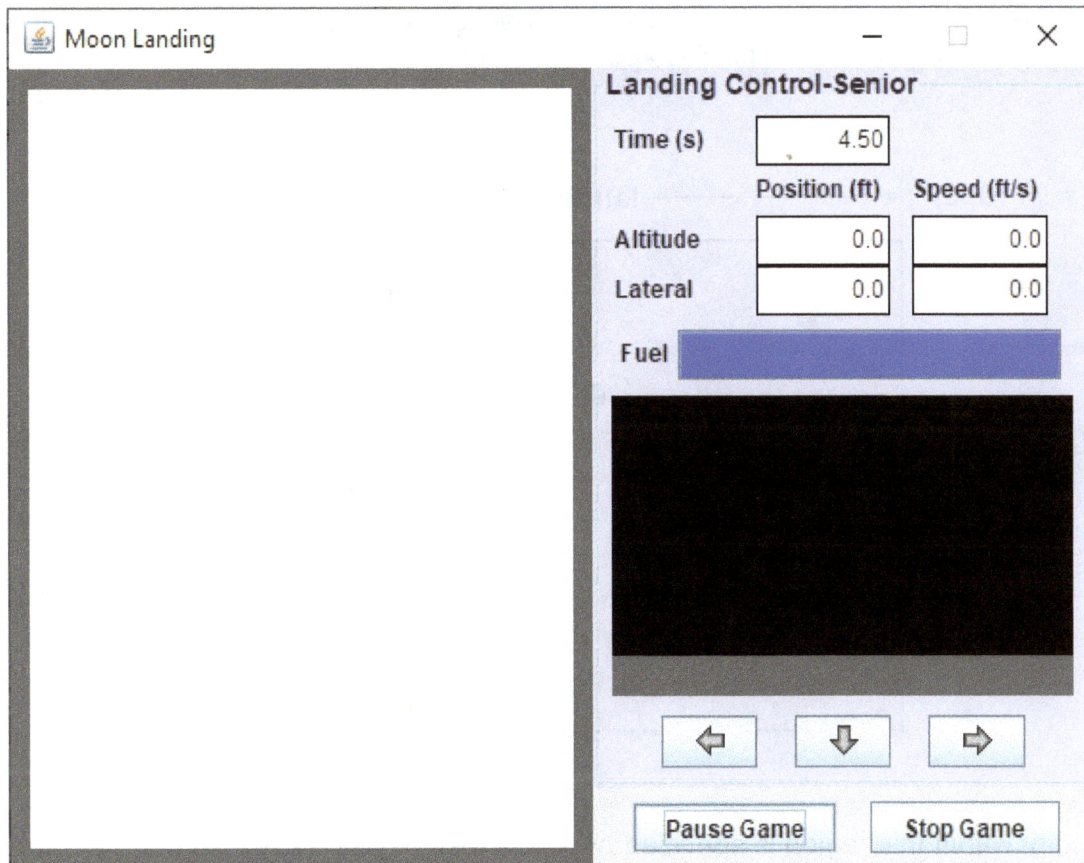

As desired, all thruster controls appear, as does the fuel gauge. Make sure the **Pause Game** and **Restart Game** buttons affect the clock correctly. Next, let's write the code that implements the math and physics behind the lunar module motion.

Code Design – Physics of Moon Landing

Are you ready for a little physics and math? Don't worry it won't be too scary.
We want to write the equations that describe the position and speed of the
landing vehicle as it descends to the moon. As a first step, we need to define a
coordinate system to do our computations. We assume all graphics elements
(the lander, the thrust flames, the pad, the background) are contained within a
rectangular region named **landscape**:

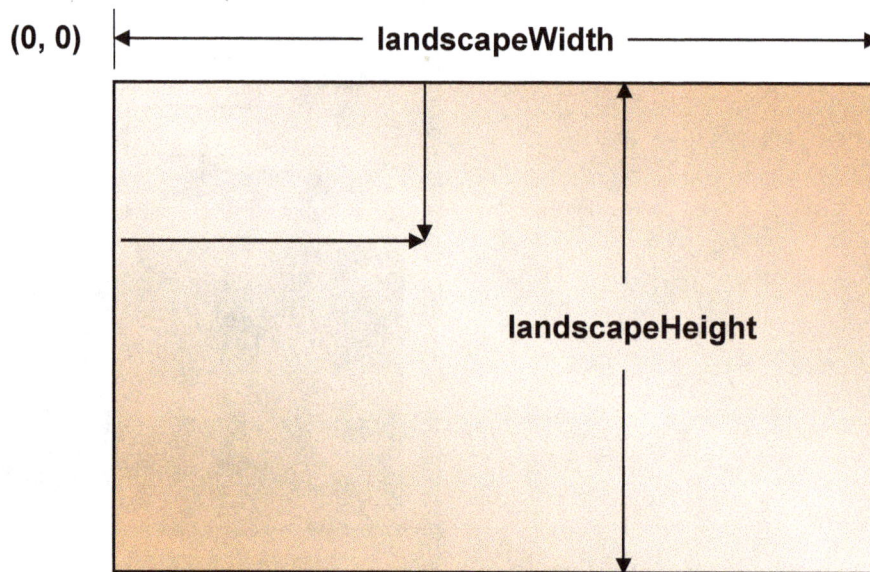

A point within this region is specified by a "Cartesian" pair, **(x, y)**. In the diagram,
note the **x** (horizontal) coordinate increases from left to right, starting at **0** and
extending to **landscapeWidth - 1**. The **y** (vertical) coordinate increases from top
to bottom, starting at **0** and ending at **landscapeHeight - 1**. All measurements are
integers and in units of **pixels**. In this program, we will assume one pixel
corresponds to one meter of distance.

Each graphic element is also contained within a rectangle. The lander element (**lander**) is located at the Cartesian pair **(landerX, landerY)** within the **landscape** rectangle:

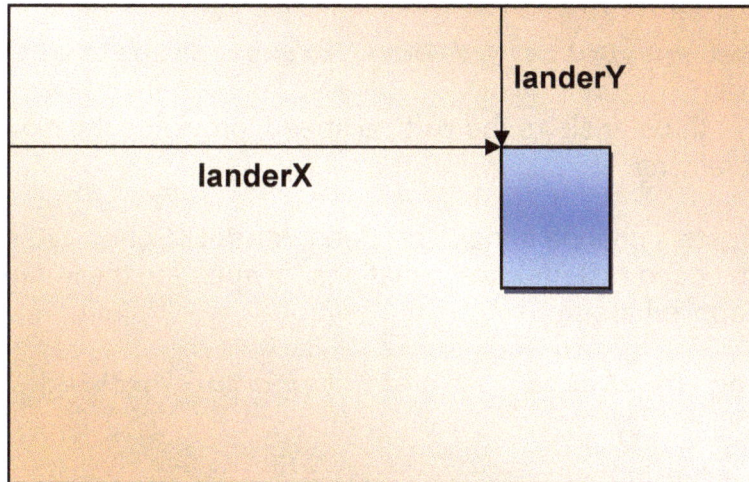

The **lander** has width **landerWidth** and height **landerHeight**. **landerX** and **landerY** are assigned some initial values (at **time = 0**). The lander speeds are **landerXSpeed** and **landerYSpeed**, in the respective directions. **landerXSpeed** and **landerYSpeed** are initialized at zero.

Once we have initial values for **landerX**, **landerY**, **landerXSpeed** and **landerYSpeed**, they are "updated" (incremented or decremented) at various times. The speeds are updated whenever thrust is used. Both the speeds and positions are updated with each change of the running clock, governed by **landingTimer**. Let's look at the "update" equations, first seeing how thrust affects speed.

The vertical thruster affects only the vertical speed, **landerYSpeed**. We assume this, and the horizontal thrusters, work in what rocket scientists call "impulse mode," imparting an immediate speed change (delta) in the opposite direction. If that change in speed is called **yDelta**, the equation for changing speed in the y-direction when the thruster is applied is:

```
landerYSpeed -= yDelta; // Down thruster applied
```

The vertical (down) thruster slows the vertical speed, providing the slowing we need for a proper landing.

The horizontal thrusters change horizontal speed, **landerXSpeed**. Assuming an impulse change in speed (**xDelta**), the equations for speed in the x-direction when the thrusters are applied are:

```
landerXSpeed += xDelta; // Left thruster applied
```

and

```
landerXSpeed -= xDelta; // Right thruster applied
```

The left thruster slows the lander toward the right; the right thruster slows the lander to the right.

Knowing the horizontal (**landerXSpeed**) and vertical (**landerYSpeed**) speeds of the lander, how do we determine the positions **landerX** and **landerY**? We use the classic formula that tells us:

Distance Traveled = Speed x Time Traveled

This equation is derived using a branch of mathematics known as calculus. Use that fact to impress your friends. This computation is done every time the clock updates its time (in the **landingTimerActionPerformed** method). Let **t** be the interval of the timer control in seconds:

```
t = (double) (landingTimer.getDelay()) / 1000;
```

The 1000 divisor converts the **delay** property (in milliseconds) to seconds.

Knowing **t**, the X and Y position of the lander are updated each clock cycle using:

```
landerX += speedX * t;

landerY += speedY * t;
```

You should see that **speedX * t** is the horizontal distance traveled by the lander in one clock cycle and **speedY * t** is the corresponding vertical distance.

The vertical speed of the lander (**landerYSpeed**) also changes with each clock cycle. Gravity tends to accelerate (increase speed) the lander toward the moon surface. If the gravitational acceleration is **gravity**, in **g** seconds, the speed is increased according to:

```
landerYSpeed += gravity * t;
```

The gravity on the moon is about 1/6th the gravity on earth (which is 9.8 meters per second per second; the vertical speed changes 9.8 m/s every second). So, in our program, we will use:

```
gravity = 9.8 / 6.0;
```

You can change this if you like to simulate other planets or see how fast a lander descends on the earth (just use 9.8).

We will also allow for possible changes in the horizontal speed (**landerXSpeed**) with each clock cycle. If we apply a horizontal thrust in one direction, the lander will continue to move in that direction until a thrust is applied in the opposite direction. To counteract that effect, if the lander is moving horizontally, we will apply a "drag" term that tends to slow it down, even without thrust. If this amount of slowing is **drag**, the corresponding speed corrections are:

```
landerXSpeed -= drag; // landerXSpeed > 0

landerXSpeed += drag; // landerXSpeed < 0
```

Notice there is no slowing if the lander is not moving (**landerXSpeed = 0**).

This completes the "update" equations for the lunar lander's position and speed. Let's modify the project to include these equations and get the lander moving. Add four form level variables to compute position and speed:

```
double landerX, landerY;
double landerXSpeed, landerYSpeed;
```

Initialize these variables in the **startPauseButtonActionPerformed** method. For now, we set all the variables to zero. Later, we will randomly assign **landerX**. The shaded changes are:

```
private void startPauseButtonActionPerformed(ActionEvent
e)
{
  if (startPauseButton.getText().equals("Start Game"))
  {
    startPauseButton.setText("Pause Game");
    exitStopButton.setText("Stop Game");
    optionsPanel.setVisible(false);
    controlPanel.setVisible(true);
    switch (pilotLevel)
    {
      case 1:

controlPanel.setBorder(BorderFactory.createTitledBorder("L
anding Control-Beginner"));
        leftThrustButton.setVisible(false);
        rightThrustButton.setVisible(false);
        downThrustButton.setVisible(true);
        fuelLabel.setVisible(false);
        fuelProgressBar.setVisible(false);
        break;
      case 2:

controlPanel.setBorder(BorderFactory.createTitledBorder("L
anding Control-Novice"));
        leftThrustButton.setVisible(true);
        rightThrustButton.setVisible(true);
        downThrustButton.setVisible(false);
        fuelLabel.setVisible(false);
        fuelProgressBar.setVisible(false);
        break;
      case 3:

controlPanel.setBorder(BorderFactory.createTitledBorder("L
anding Control-Junior"));
        leftThrustButton.setVisible(true);
```

```
               rightThrustButton.setVisible(true);
               downThrustButton.setVisible(true);
               fuelLabel.setVisible(false);
               fuelProgressBar.setVisible(false);
               break;
            case 4:

controlPanel.setBorder(BorderFactory.createTitledBorder("L
anding Control-Senior"));
               leftThrustButton.setVisible(true);
               rightThrustButton.setVisible(true);
               downThrustButton.setVisible(true);
               fuelLabel.setVisible(true);
               fuelProgressBar.setVisible(true);
               break;
            case 5:

controlPanel.setBorder(BorderFactory.createTitledBorder("L
anding Control-Advanced"));
               leftThrustButton.setVisible(true);
               rightThrustButton.setVisible(true);
               downThrustButton.setVisible(true);
               fuelLabel.setVisible(true);
               fuelProgressBar.setVisible(true);
               break;
         }
         if (autoPilotCheckBox.isSelected())
         {
           leftThrustButton.setVisible(false);
           rightThrustButton.setVisible(false);
           downThrustButton.setVisible(false);
           messageLabel.setText("Auto-Pilot On");
           messageLabel.setVisible(true);
         }
         else
         {
           messageLabel.setVisible(false);
         }
         if (metricRadioButton.isSelected())
         {
           positionLabel.setText("Position (m)");
           speedLabel.setText("Speed (m/s)");
         }
         else
         {
           positionLabel.setText("Position (ft)");
           speedLabel.setText("Speed (ft/s)");
```

```
         }
         time = 0.0;
         timeTextField.setText("0.0");
         viewerPanel.setVisible(true);
         landerX = 0;
         landerY = 0;
         landerXSpeed = 0;
         landerYSpeed = 0;
         landingTimer.start();
      }
      else if (startPauseButton.getText().equals("Pause
Game"))
      {
         startPauseButton.setText("Restart Game");
         exitStopButton.setEnabled(false);
         leftThrustButton.setEnabled(false);
         downThrustButton.setEnabled(false);
         rightThrustButton.setEnabled(false);
         landingTimer.stop();
      }
      else
      {
         startPauseButton.setText("Pause Game");
         exitStopButton.setEnabled(true);
         leftThrustButton.setEnabled(true);
         downThrustButton.setEnabled(true);
         rightThrustButton.setEnabled(true);
         landingTimer.start();
      }
   }
```

Next, add four form level constants to define speed changes, gravity and drag effects:

```
final double xDelta = 1.2;
final double yDelta = 2.4;
final double gravity = 9.8 / 6.0;
final double drag = 0.1;
```

Each of these numbers (except **gravity**) was found by trial and error. You may want to make changes – feel free.

Vertical thrust is control by the button control **downThrustButton**. The **ActionPerformed** method for this control is:

```
private void downThrustButtonActionPerformed(ActionEvent
e)
```

```
   {
      landerYSpeed -= yDelta;
   }
```

This is the update of vertical speed due to thrust.

Horizontal thrust is control by **leftThrustButton** and **rightThrustbutton**. The **ActionPerformed** methods for these controls are:

```
   private void leftThrustButtonActionPerformed(ActionEvent
   e)
   {
      landerXSpeed += xDelta;
   }

   private void rightThrustButtonActionPerformed(ActionEvent
   e)
   {
      landerXSpeed -= xDelta;
   }
```

These routines update horizontal speed due to thrust.

Recall both lander position and speed are updated in the **landingTimer ActionPerformed** method. The steps to follow in this method are:

 ➢ Update time display (already implemented).
 ➢ Update **landerX** and **landerY**.
 ➢ Display status of lander.
 ➢ Update **landerXSpeed** and **landerYSpeed**.

We will use a general method (**updateStatus**) to display lander status. For now, this method simply displays position and speed information (converting to proper units using the **multiplier** variable):

```
private void updateStatus()
{
  altitudePositionTextField.setText(new
DecimalFormat("0").format(landerY * multiplier));
  lateralPositionTextField.setText(new
DecimalFormat("0").format(landerX * multiplier));
  altitudeSpeedTextField.setText(new
DecimalFormat("0.0").format(landerYSpeed * multiplier));
  lateralSpeedTextField.setText(new
DecimalFormat("0.0").format(landerXSpeed * multiplier));
}
```

The altitude text fields display **Y** motion, while the lateral text fields display **X** motion.

With the above method, the shaded changes to the **landingTimer ActionPerformed** method that implement the new steps are:

```
private void landingTimerActionPerformed(ActionEvent e)
{
  time += (double) (landingTimer.getDelay()) / 1000;
  timeTextField.setText(new
DecimalFormat("0.00").format(time));
  landerX += landerXSpeed * (double)
(landingTimer.getDelay()) / 1000;
  landerY += landerYSpeed * (double)
(landingTimer.getDelay()) / 1000;
  updateStatus();
  landerX += landerXSpeed;
  landerY += landerYSpeed;
  // horizontal drag
  if (landerXSpeed > 0)
    landerXSpeed -= drag;
  else if (landerXSpeed < 0)
    landerXSpeed += drag;
  // gravity
  landerYSpeed += gravity * (double)
(landingTimer.getDelay()) / 1000;
}
```

Also, return to the **startPauseButton ActionPerformed** method and add this one line following the initialization of the lander position and speed:

```
updateStatus();
```

This initializes the displays properly.

Save and run the project. Select **Junior Pilot Level**. Click **Start Game**. The time will increment, as will the position and speed in the vertical direction (labeled as **Altitude**). Click the down thrust button and see the vertical speed decrease. Try the horizontal thrusters to make sure you can move the lander left and right (labeled as **Lateral**). Here's the middle of a run I made:

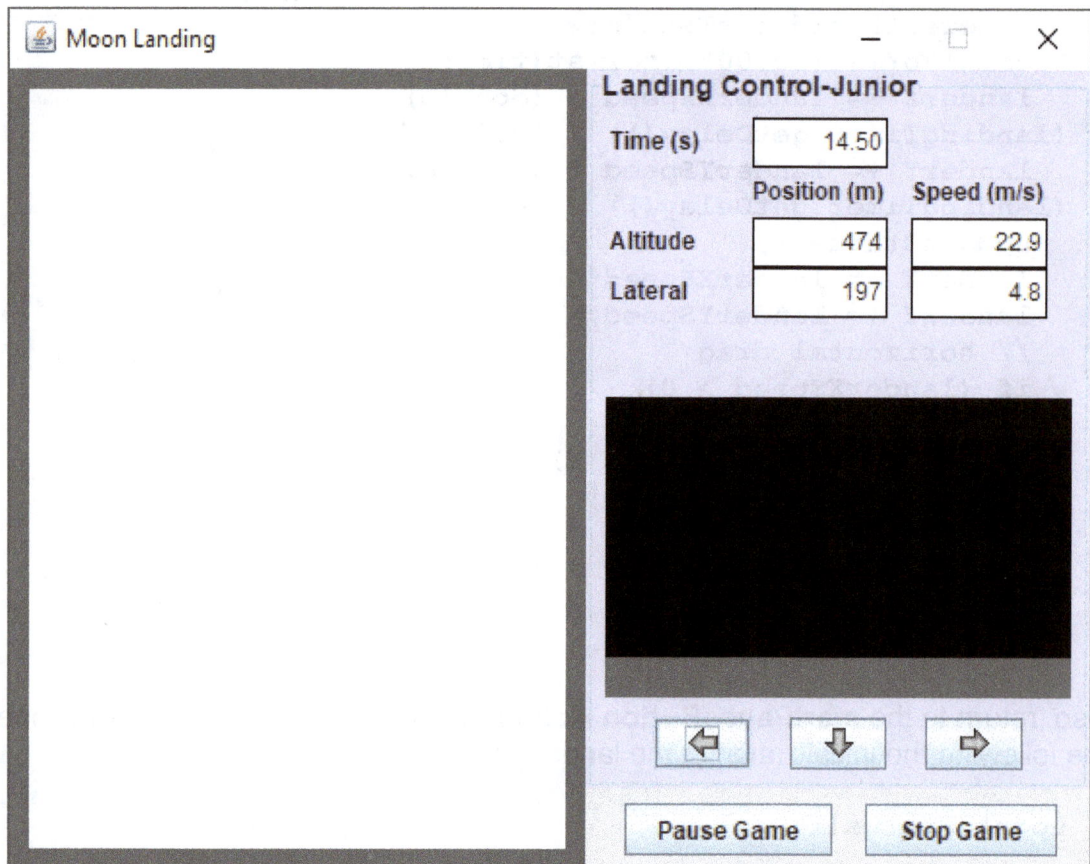

The module has moved down 474 meters and is traveling at 22.9 meters/second downward. The lander has moved 197 meters to the right (positive number) and is moving at 4.8 m/s to the right. Make sure you can move the lander left and right, up and down.

Remaining Work

Believe it or not, the basics of the moon landing program are done – we can control the lander and see its location and speed (in label controls). But there is still a lot of work to be done to make this an appealing, useful game. Let's outline the needed work, then get started.

As implemented, the displayed information is not very useful. Knowing the distance from the left of the landscape rectangle (**landerX**) and the distance from the top of the rectangle (**landerY**) does not tell us what we really need to know – how far we are from the landing pad. So, as a first task, we will place the landing pad on the landscape and display distances and speeds relative to the pad. To do this, we need to know image sizes, so we will load the images used in the program (though we won't display them yet). We will add landing detection logic.

We need to modify the game to account for differences among the various pilot levels, including monitoring fuel consumption. And, of course, we need some sounds. After this, we will have a working 'text version' of the game.

The text version of the game is acceptable, but graphics elements add that extra flair. The first graphic element we add is the trajectory display under the label controls. To add this element, we need to first discuss how to use Java graphics objects. In particular, we will learn how to draw colored lines and circles. We will also implement a graphic indication of lander and pad locations (using the panel under the trajectory display panel).

After tackling these displays, we move on to the animated display of the lander moving across the landscape to the landing pad. To do this, we need more discussion of Java graphics. We will learn how to use scrolling backgrounds and how to move objects around in a smooth fashion.

And the final addition to **Moon Landing** will be development of an auto-pilot. This serves two purposes. First, the auto-pilot is actually needed for the **Novice** pilot level (where you control horizontal thrust, while the computer handles the vertical thrust). Second, auto-pilot mode is a good way to learn how to control the landing vehicle.

As we said, there's a lot of work to do. Let's get going.

Code Design – Landing Pad Distances

As noted, the current displayed values do not answer the question – how far are we from the landing pad? Let's add the **pad** graphic element to the landscape element and determine what these distances are. The **pad** element (another rectangle; shown in red) is located at **(padX, padY)**, has width **padWidth** and height **padHeight**:

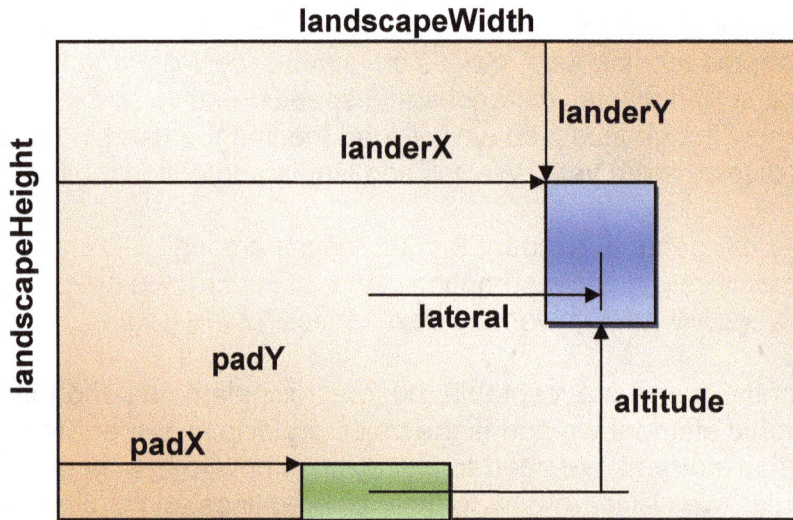

In this sketch, we've added two distances. **altitude** specifies how far the lander is above the pad. It is the distance from the bottom of the lander to the middle of the pad:

```
altitude = (landscapeHeight - padHeight / 2) - (landerY +
landerHeight);
```

Notice **altitude** decreases as the lander goes down (**landerY** increases). This is opposite of our basic coordinate system, but it makes sense here. **altitude** represents the height above the pad – it approaches zero as the lander gets closer to the pad.

The other distance, **lateral**, specifies the horizontal distance from the lander to the pad. It is the distance from the middle of the lander to the middle of the pad:

```
lateral = (landerX + landerWidth) - (padX + padWidth);
```

Notice **lateral** is positive if the lander is the right of the pad, negative if it is to the left of the pad. **lateral** is zero if the lander is directly centered over the pad.

We can add these equations to our program to get proper indication of **altitude** and **lateral**, but there's one problem. We don't know the sizes of our images. We'll fix that now. We will use five images in the program: **landscape**, **lander**, **pad**, **hThrust**, and **vThrust**. Each image is included as a **gif** file in the **\KidGamesJava\KidGamesJava Projects\MoonLanding** folder. Let's take a look at each image. You can open them in the Windows Paint program or any other drawing program you might have.

The **landscape** image (**landscape.gif**) is 676 pixels wide by 732 pixels high (shown 60 percent of actual size here):

Such images can be created in painting programs. The dimensions of each image was determined using Microsoft **Paint**.

The **lander** image (**lander.gif**) is 105 pixels wide by 115 pixels high (shown actual size):

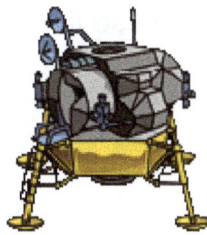

The **pad** image (**pad.gif**) is 143 pixels wide by 64 pixels high (also actual size):

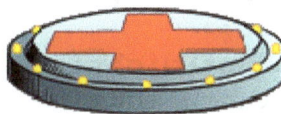

And, the **hThrust** image (**hthrust.gif**) is 32 pixels by 16 pixels (twice actual size):

while the **vThrust** (**vthrust.gif**) image is 24 pixels by 32 pixels (also twice actual size):

In the **Moon Landing** program, each of these images is represented by a Java **Image** object. For now, we will just load them into the program to obtain the needed dimensions (**Width** and **Height**). Later, we will use the images in the animation of the moon landing. Add these five class level declarations to the code window:

```
Image landscape;
Image lander;
Image pad;
Image hThrust;
Image vThrust;
int landscapeWidth, landscapeHeight;
int landerWidth, landerHeight;
int padWidth, padHeight;
int hThrustWidth, hThrustHeight;
int vThrustWidth, vThrustHeight;
```

To establish an **Image** object using a graphics file and obtain the width and height of the images, use this code at the end of the frame constructor method:

```
landscape = new ImageIcon("landscape.gif").getImage();
landscapeWidth = landscape.getWidth(this);
landscapeHeight = landscape.getHeight(this);
lander = new ImageIcon("lander.gif").getImage();
landerWidth = lander.getWidth(this);
landerHeight = lander.getHeight(this);
pad= new ImageIcon("pad.gif").getImage();
padWidth = pad.getWidth(this);
padHeight = pad.getHeight(this);
hThrust = new ImageIcon("hThrust.gif").getImage();
hThrustWidth = hThrust.getWidth(this);
hThrustHeight = hThrust.getHeight(this);
vThrust = new ImageIcon("vThrust.gif").getImage();
vThrustWidth = vThrust.getWidth(this);
vThrustHeight = vThrust.getHeight(this);
```

This code assumes the graphics files are in your project's folder. Copy the five gif files to that folder.

Having the images and their dimensions now allows us to modify the code to include computations and display of **altitude** and **lateral**. First, add these class level declarations for the pad location and the new variables:

```
double padX, padY;
double altitude, lateral;
```

The computations of **altitude** and **lateral** will be placed in the **updateStatus** general method. Make the shaded changes to this method:

```
private void updateStatus()
{
  altitude = (landscapeHeight - padHeight / 2) - (landerY
+ landerHeight);
  lateral = (landerX + landerWidth / 2) - (padX + padWidth
/ 2);
  if (altitude > 0)
    altitudePositionTextField.setText(new
DecimalFormat("0").format(altitude * multiplier));
  else
    altitudePositionTextField.setText("0");
  if (Math.abs(lateral) < 1)
    lateralPositionTextField.setText("Above");
  else
    lateralPositionTextField.setText(new
DecimalFormat("0").format(lateral * multiplier));
  altitudeSpeedTextField.setText(new
DecimalFormat("0.0").format(-landerYSpeed * multiplier));
  lateralSpeedTextField.setText(new
DecimalFormat("0.0").format(landerXSpeed * multiplier));
  }
```

We have the equations for **altitude** and **lateral**. For the altitude position text field, **landerY** has been replaced by **altitude** (limiting the value to zero). For lateral position, **landerX** has been replaced by **lateral** (with a note of **Above** if within 1 meter). In the vertical speed text field, a negative sign has been added to show negative speed is altitude descent.

We can almost test the changes. We need to place the pad on the landscape. With each new game, we will randomly set the horizontal position of the pad (and the lander) within the landscape rectangle. The pad will be placed on the bottom of the rectangle.

Add this import statement:

```
import java.util.Random;
```

And, add a class level random object to the code:

```
Random myRandom = new Random();
```

Then, make the shaded changes in the **startPauseButton ActionPerformed** method:

```
private void startPauseButtonActionPerformed(ActionEvent
e)
{
  if (startPauseButton.getText().equals("Start Game"))
  {
    startPauseButton.setText("Pause Game");
    exitStopButton.setText("Stop Game");
       .

       .
    time = 0.0;
    timeTextField.setText("0.0");
    landerX = (landscapeWidth - landerWidth) *
myRandom.nextDouble();
    landerY = 0;
    landerXSpeed = 0;
    landerYSpeed = 0;
    padX = (landscapeWidth - padWidth) *
myRandom.nextDouble();
    padY = landscapeHeight - padHeight;
    updateStatus();
    landingTimer.start();
  }
  else if (startPauseButton.getText().equals("Pause
Game"))
  {
    startPauseButton.setText("Restart Game");
    exitStopButton.setEnabled(false);
    leftThrustButton.setEnabled(false);
    downThrustButton.setEnabled(false);
    rightThrustButton.setEnabled(false);
    landingTimer.stop();
```

```
      }
      else
      {
        startPauseButton.setText("Pause Game");
        exitStopButton.setEnabled(true);
        leftThrustButton.setEnabled(true);
        downThrustButton.setEnabled(true);
        rightThrustButton.setEnabled(true);
        landingTimer.start();
      }
    }
```

These new lines randomly place the lander and pad within the bounds of the **landscape** image width.

Save and run the project. Again, chose **Junior** level pilot and click **Start Game**. You will now see the altitude drop as the speed becomes larger in a negative sense (descent). The lateral position will approach zero as the lander gets closer to the pad. Here's my screen after 9.5 seconds:

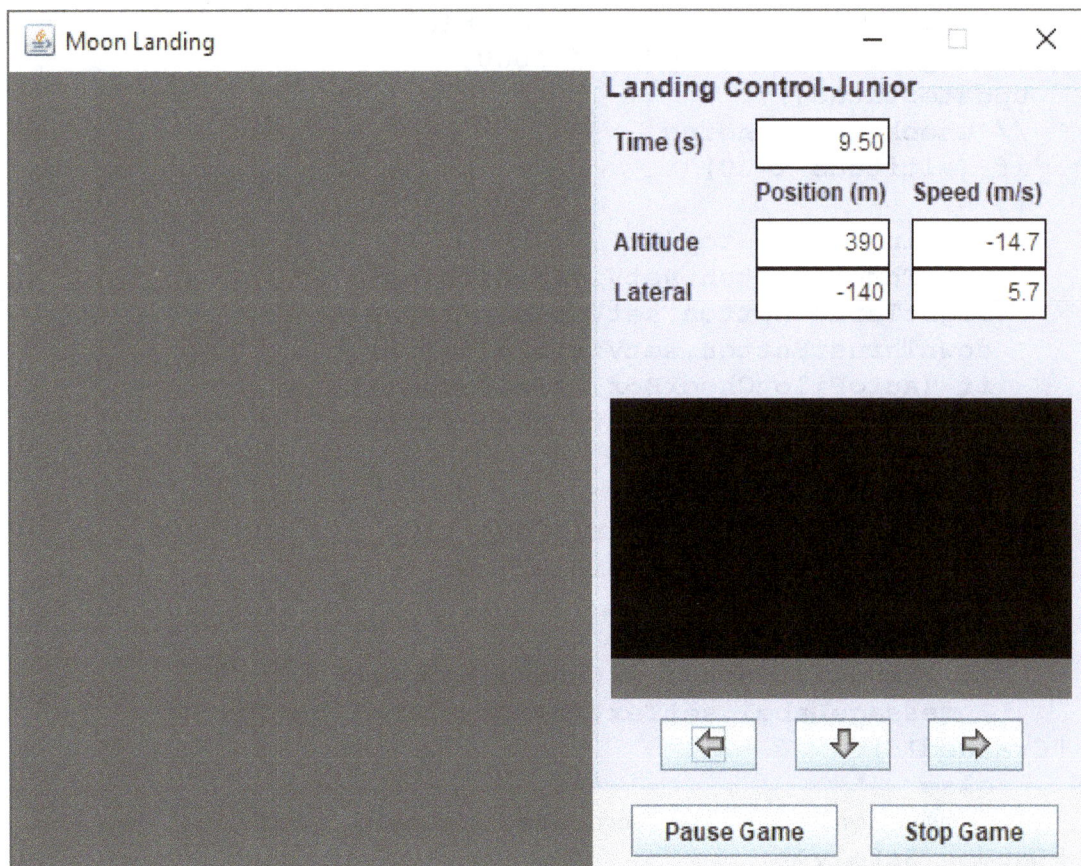

Code Design – Landing Detection

If you continue to run the game as programmed, **altitude** will stop at zero, but the speed will continue to increase and you can still apply thrust. We need someway to detect a landing and determine if it is a safe landing. We will do this in the **landingTimer ActionPerformed** method. Add a constant declaration defining the maximum acceptable landing speed:

```
final double safeLandingSpeed = 3.0;
```

Now, add the shaded changes to the **landingTimer ActionPerformed** method:

```
private void landingTimerActionPerformed(ActionEvent e)
{
  time += (double) (landingTimer.getDelay()) / 1000;
  timeTextField.setText(new
DecimalFormat("0.00").format(time));
  landerX += landerXSpeed * (double)
(landingTimer.getDelay()) / 1000;
  landerY += landerYSpeed * (double)
(landingTimer.getDelay()) / 1000;
  updateStatus();
  // check for landing
  if (altitude <= 0)
  {
    landingTimer.stop();
    leftThrustButton.setVisible(false);
    rightThrustButton.setVisible(false);
    downThrustButton.setVisible(false);
    if (autoPilotCheckBox.isSelected())
      messageLabel.setText("Auto-Pilot ");
    else
    {
      messageLabel.setText("You ");
      messageLabel.setVisible(true);
    }
    // crash?
    if (landerYSpeed > safeLandingSpeed)
      messageLabel.setText(messageLabel.getText() +
"Crashed!");
    else
      messageLabel.setText(messageLabel.getText() +
"Landed Safely");
    // bring up complete button
    startPauseButton.setVisible(false);
    exitStopButton.setVisible(false);
```

```
    completeButton.setVisible(true);
    return;
  }
  landerX += landerXSpeed;
  landerY += landerYSpeed;
  // horizontal drag
  if (landerXSpeed > 0)
    landerXSpeed -= drag;
  else if (landerXSpeed < 0)
    landerXSpeed += drag;
  // gravity
  landerYSpeed += gravity * (double)
(landingTimer.getDelay()) / 1000;
}
```

In this code, once **altitude** reaches zero, **landingTimer** is disabled, the thruster buttons are removed and the appropriate landing message is displayed based on the vertical speed (and based on whether auto-pilot is on). Then, the **completeButton** is displayed. No penalty is incurred for missing the landing pad (large value of **lateral**).

Add this code to the **completeButton ActionPerformed** method:

```
private void completeButtonActionPerformed(ActionEvent e)
{
  completeButton.setVisible(false);
  startPauseButton.setVisible(true);
  exitStopButton.setVisible(true);
  exitStopButton.doClick();
}
```

This code simply re-establishes the buttons to control the game and allows options to be selected again (via clicking **exitStopButton**).

Save and run the project again. Now, once the lander altitude reaches zero, the program will stop and display status upon landing. Here's my screen:

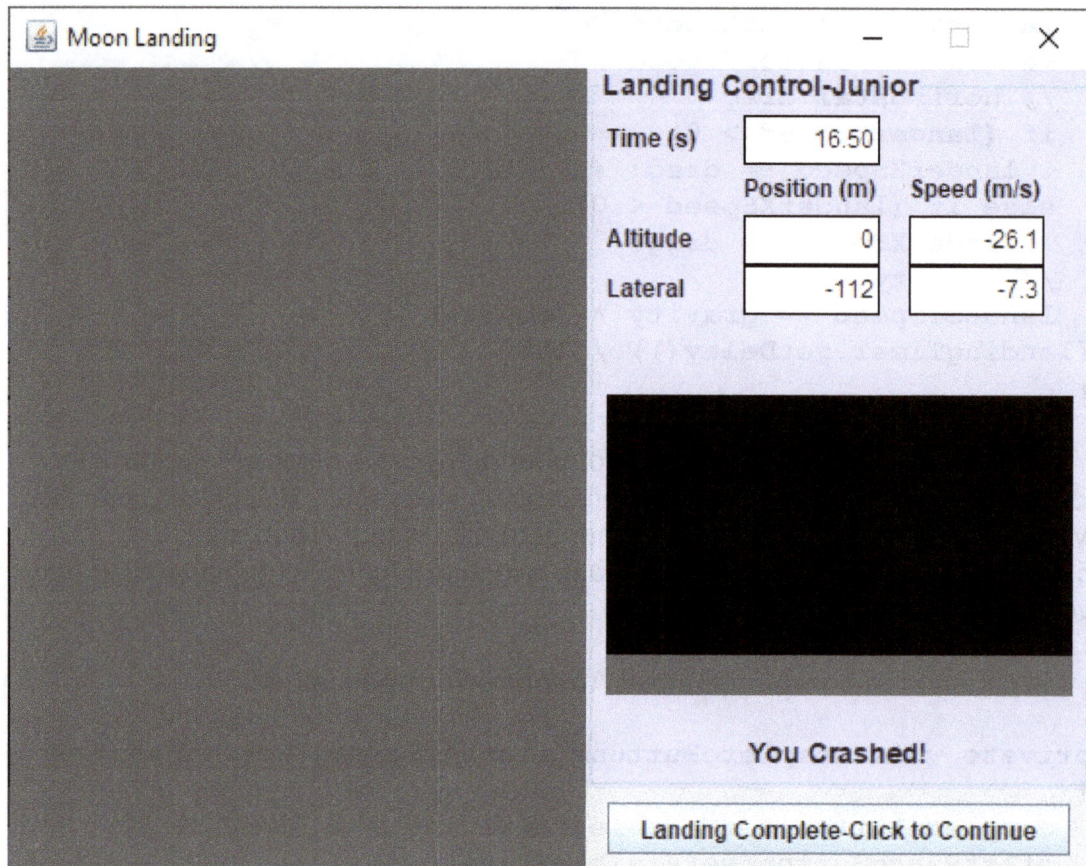

I crashed badly. Note the button (**completeButton**) at the bottom that you click to continue playing the game

Code – Pilot Levels and Sounds

The **Moon Landing** game is becoming more complete. The last big change is adding the graphics features. Before doing that we need to add just a few other changes.

Some changes related to selected **Pilot Level** need implementation. First, the two highest levels (**Senior** and **Advanced**) have fuel limitations. We have added the code that displays the fuel gauge for these levels. We now need code that computes fuel usage and displays remaining fuel in the gauge. Add this class level declaration for the variable that keeps track of remaining fuel:

```
static double fuelRemaining;
```

And, add three constants:

```
static final double maximumFuel = 100;
final double hFuel = 1.0;
final double vFuel = 2.0;
```

maximumFuel is the amount of initial fuel, **hFuel** is the fuel used by a burst on a horizontal thruster and **vFuel** is fuel used by a vertical thruster burst.

The amount of fuel and fuel gauge are initialized in the **startPauseButton ActionPerformed** method (changes are shaded):

```
private void startPauseButtonActionPerformed(ActionEvent e)
{
  if (startPauseButton.getText().equals("Start Game"))
  {
    startPauseButton.setText("Pause Game");
    exitStopButton.setText("Stop Game");
    .

    .
    time = 0.0;
    timeTextField.setText("0.0");
    landerX = (landscapeWidth - landerWidth) *
myRandom.nextDouble();
    landerY = 0;
    landerXSpeed = 0;
    landerYSpeed = 0;
    padX = (landscapeWidth - padWidth) *
myRandom.nextDouble();
    padY = landscapeHeight - padHeight;
    fuelRemaining = maximumFuel;
```

```
      fuelProgressBar.setValue(100);
   updateStatus();
   landingTimer.start();
}
else if (startPauseButton.getText().equals("Pause
Game"))
{
   startPauseButton.setText("Restart Game");
   exitStopButton.setEnabled(false);
   leftThrustButton.setEnabled(false);
   downThrustButton.setEnabled(false);
   rightThrustButton.setEnabled(false);
   landingTimer.stop();
}
else
{
   startPauseButton.setText("Pause Game");
   exitStopButton.setEnabled(true);
   leftThrustButton.setEnabled(true);
   downThrustButton.setEnabled(true);
   rightThrustButton.setEnabled(true);
   landingTimer.start();
}
}
```

Notice we set the **fuelProgressBar** value to **100** (100% full) regardless of pilot level. For levels other than **Senior** and **Advanced**, **fuelProgressBar** does not appear on the panel, so this line of code has no effect. Also for those levels, we will leave **fuelRemaining** at **maximumFuel**, so the fuel tank is always full.

Fuel is used with each burst of a thruster. Modify each thruster (**downThrustButton**, **leftThrustButton**, **rightThrustButton**) **ActionPerformed** method as follows (changes are shaded):

```
private void downThrustButtonActionPerformed(ActionEvent e)
{
  if (fuelRemaining > 0)
  {
    landerYSpeed -= yDelta;
    if (pilotLevel > 3)
      fuelRemaining -= vFuel;
  }
}

private void leftThrustButtonActionPerformed(ActionEvent e)
{
  if (fuelRemaining > 0)
  {
    landerXSpeed += xDelta;
    if (pilotLevel > 3)
      fuelRemaining -= hFuel;
  }
}

private void rightThrustButtonActionPerformed(ActionEvent e)
{
  if (fuelRemaining > 0)
  {
    landerXSpeed -= xDelta;
    if (pilotLevel > 3)
      fuelRemaining -= hFuel;
  }
}
```

With these changes, thrust is not allowed if there is no fuel and **fuelRemaining** is decremented only for pilot levels greater than 3 (**Senior** and **Advanced**).

Lastly, the fuel gauge is updated in the **updateStatus** method. To give some audio feedback, we emit a beep when fuel is below 10% full. The changes to the method are shaded:

```java
private void updateStatus()
{
  altitude = (landscapeHeight - padHeight / 2) - (landerY
+ landerHeight);
  lateral = (landerX + landerWidth / 2) - (padX + padWidth
/ 2);
  if (altitude > 0)
    altitudePositionTextField.setText(new
DecimalFormat("0").format(altitude * multiplier));
  else
    altitudePositionTextField.setText("0");
  if (Math.abs(lateral) < 1)
    lateralPositionTextField.setText("Above");
  else
    lateralPositionTextField.setText(new
DecimalFormat("0").format(lateral * multiplier));
  altitudeSpeedTextField.setText(new
DecimalFormat("0.0").format(-landerYSpeed * multiplier));
  lateralSpeedTextField.setText(new
DecimalFormat("0.0").format(landerXSpeed * multiplier));
  // update fuel guage
  int fuelPercent = (int) (100 * fuelRemaining /
maximumFuel);
  fuelProgressBar.setValue(fuelPercent);
  if (fuelPercent <= 10)
    Toolkit.getDefaultToolkit().beep();
}
```

Save and run the project. Select **Senior** pilot level. As the lander descends, apply horizontal and vertical thrust and watch the fuel gauge drop. Here's my form after several bursts of thrust:

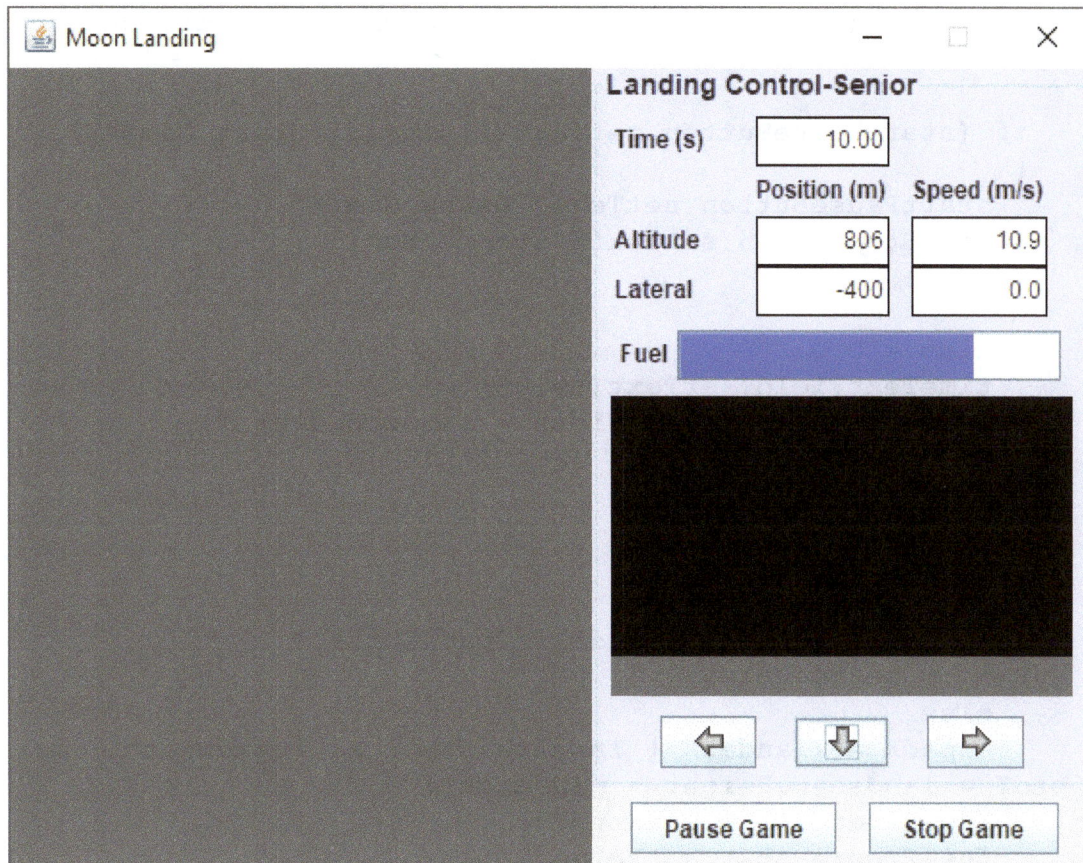

In the lowest pilot level (**Beginner**; **pilotLevel = 1**), the landing pad needs to be directly under the lander, since horizontal thrusters are not available. This is done in the **startPauseButton ActionPerformed** method (new code shaded):

```
private void startPauseButtonActionPerformed(ActionEvent
e)
{
  if (startPauseButton.getText().equals("Start Game"))
  {
    startPauseButton.setText("Pause Game");
    exitStopButton.setText("Stop Game");
        .

        .

    time = 0.0;
    timeTextField.setText("0.0");
    landerX = (landscapeWidth - landerWidth) *
myRandom.nextDouble();
    landerY = 0;
    landerXSpeed = 0;
    landerYSpeed = 0;
    if (pilotLevel != 1)
       padX = (landscapeWidth - padWidth) *
myRandom.nextDouble();
    else
       padX = (landerX + landerWidth / 2) - padWidth / 2;
padY = landscapeHeight - padHeight;
    fuelRemaining = maximumFuel;
    fuelProgressBar.setValue(100);
    updateStatus();
    landingTimer.start();
  }
  else if (startPauseButton.getText().equals("Pause
Game"))
  {
    startPauseButton.setText("Restart Game");
    exitStopButton.setEnabled(false);
    leftThrustButton.setEnabled(false);
    downThrustButton.setEnabled(false);
    rightThrustButton.setEnabled(false);
    landingTimer.stop();
  }
  else
  {
    startPauseButton.setText("Pause Game");
    exitStopButton.setEnabled(true);
    leftThrustButton.setEnabled(true);
    downThrustButton.setEnabled(true);
```

```
      rightThrustButton.setEnabled(true);
      landingTimer.start();
   }
}
```

Save and run the project. Select **Beginner** level. Click **Start Game**. Make sure the pad is under the lander. Here's what I see:

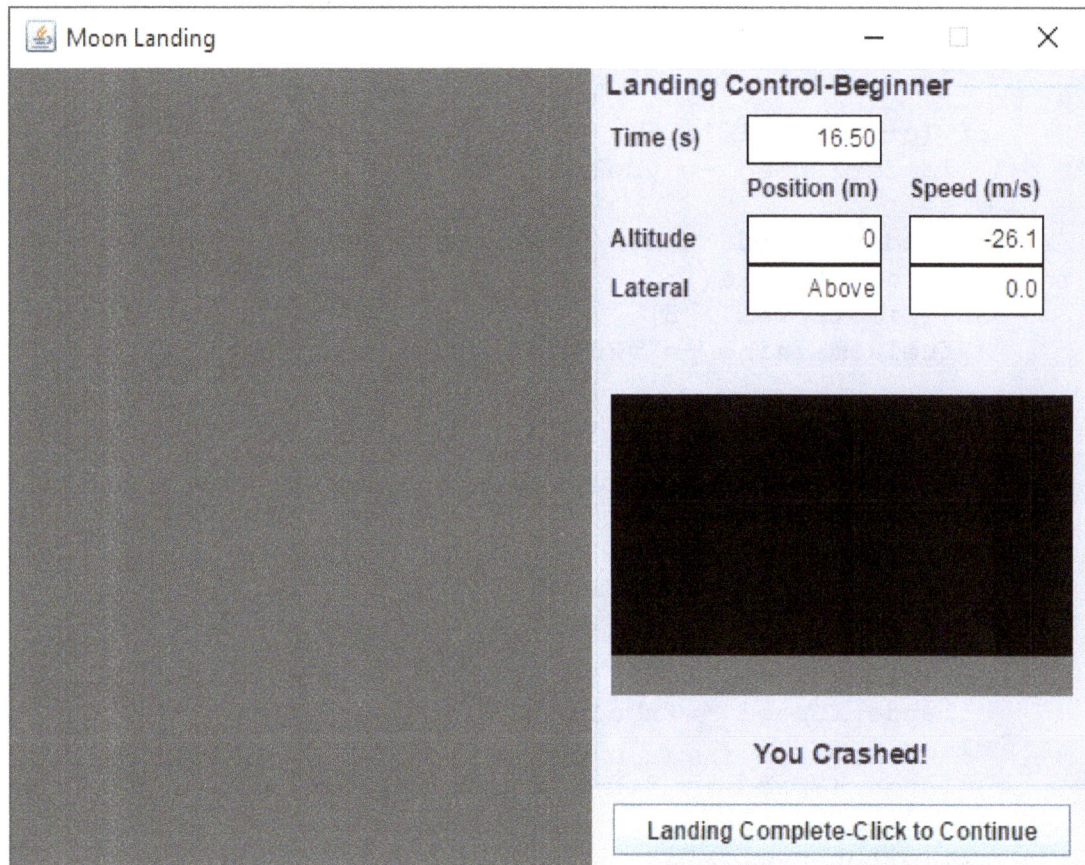

Notice **Lateral** position is listed as **Above**.

The last change we need to make regarding pilot level is with the **Advanced** level. In this level, we want the thrusters to be unpredictable, generating random amounts of thrust. For horizontal and vertical thrust, we will have anywhere from 0 to twice the maximum available delta in speed. These changes are made in the thruster button **ActionPerformed** methods. The changes are shaded:

```
private void downThrustButtonActionPerformed(ActionEvent
e)
{
  if (fuelRemaining > 0)
  {
    if (pilotLevel != 5)
      landerYSpeed -= yDelta;
    else
      landerYSpeed -= 2.0 * yDelta *
myRandom.nextDouble();
    if (pilotLevel > 3)
      fuelRemaining -= vFuel;
  }
}

private void leftThrustButtonActionPerformed(ActionEvent
e)
{
  if (fuelRemaining > 0)
  {
    if (pilotLevel != 5)
      landerXSpeed += xDelta;
    else
      landerXSpeed += 2.0 * xDelta *
myRandom.nextDouble();
    if (pilotLevel > 3)
      fuelRemaining -= hFuel;
  }
}
```

```
private void rightThrustButtonActionPerformed(ActionEvent
e)
{
  if (fuelRemaining > 0)
  {
    if (pilotLevel != 5)
      landerXSpeed -= xDelta;
    else
      landerXSpeed -= 2.0 * xDelta *
myRandom.nextDouble();
    if (pilotLevel > 3)
      fuelRemaining -= hFuel;
  }
}
```

Save and run the project. Try the **Advanced** level and watch the fuel go down very fast. This completes all but one change needed for pilot level. The one change still needed is related to the **Novice** level (**pilotLevel = 2**). At that level, you only control the horizontal thrusters to practice moving in the lateral direction. The vertical thrust is controlled by the computer auto-pilot. Since we haven't coded the auto-pilot yet, you are guaranteed to crash at **Novice** level (until we've completed the **Moon Landing** program, that is).

One last change before tackling all the graphic effects – let's add sounds. In the **\KidGamesJava\KidGamesJava Projects\MoonLanding** folder are four **wav** files. The file **vthrust.wav** is played when vertical thrust is applied, **hthrust.wav** is played when horizontal thrust is applied, **safe.wav** is played following a safe landing, while **crash.wav** is played is you crash. These files are loaded when the project starts. Copy the four files to your project's folder. Add these import statements:

```
import java.net.URL;
import java.applet.*;
```

Add these class level declarations for the four sounds:

```
AudioClip vThrustSound;
AudioClip hThrustSound;
AudioClip goodLandingSound;
AudioClip badLandingSound;
```

The sounds are loaded at the end of the frame constructor method. Add the code to establish the sound objects:

```
try
{
  vThrustSound = Applet.newAudioClip(new URL("file:" +
"vthrust.wav"));
  hThrustSound = Applet.newAudioClip(new URL("file:" +
"hthrust.wav"));
  goodLandingSound = Applet.newAudioClip(new URL("file:" +
"safe.wav"));
  badLandingSound = Applet.newAudioClip(new URL("file:" +
"crash.wav"));
}
catch (Exception ex)
{
  System.out.println("Error loading sound files");
}
```

Again, note the sounds are assumed to be in the same folder with the graphics. Make sure you copy the wav files to your project folder.

The vertical thrust sound (**vThrustSound**) is played when vertical (down) thrust is applied. Add the single shaded line to the **downThrustButton ActionPerformed** method:

```
private void downThrustButtonActionPerformed(ActionEvent
e)
{
  if (fuelRemaining > 0)
  {
    vThrustSound.play();
    if (pilotLevel != 5)
      landerYSpeed -= yDelta;
    else
      landerYSpeed -= 2.0 * yDelta *
mYRandom.nextDouble();
    if (pilotLevel > 3)
      fuelRemaining -= vFuel;
  }
}
```

The horizontal thrust sound (**hThrustSound**) is played when either left or right thrust is applied. Add the shaded lines to the **leftThrustButton** and **rightThrustButton ActionPerformed** methods:

```
private void leftThrustButtonActionPerformed(ActionEvent
e)
{
  if (fuelRemaining > 0)
  {
    hThrustSound.play();
    if (pilotLevel != 5)
      landerXSpeed += xDelta;
    else
      landerXSpeed += 2.0 * xDelta *
myRandom.nextDouble();
    if (pilotLevel > 3)
      fuelRemaining -= hFuel;
  }
}

private void rightThrustButton_Click(object sender,
EventArgs e)
{
  if (fuelRemaining > 0)
  {
    hThrustSound.Play();
    if (pilotLevel != 5)
        landerXSpeed -= xDelta;
    else
        landerXSpeed -= 2.0 * xDelta *
myRandom.NextDouble();
    if (pilotLevel > 3)
        fuelRemaining -= hFuel;
  }
}
```

The landing sounds (**goodLandingSound**, **badLandingSound**) are played following landing. Add the shaded changes to the **landingTimer ActionPerformed** method (where the landing is evaluated):

```
private void landingTimerActionPerformed(ActionEvent e)
{
  time += (double) (landingTimer.getDelay()) / 1000;
  timeTextField.setText(new
DecimalFormat("0.00").format(time));
  landerX += landerXSpeed * (double)
(landingTimer.getDelay()) / 1000;
  landerY += landerYSpeed * (double)
(landingTimer.getDelay()) / 1000;
  updateStatus();
  // check for landing
  if (altitude <= 0)
  {
    landingTimer.stop();
    leftThrustButton.setVisible(false);
    rightThrustButton.setVisible(false);
    downThrustButton.setVisible(false);
    if (autoPilotCheckBox.isSelected())
      messageLabel.setText("Auto-Pilot ");
    else
    {
      messageLabel.setText("You ");
      messageLabel.setVisible(true);
    }
    // crash?
    if (landerYSpeed > safeLandingSpeed)
    {
      badLandingSound.play();
      messageLabel.setText(messageLabel.getText() +
"Crashed!");
    }
    else
    {
      goodLandingSound.play();
      messageLabel.setText(messageLabel.getText() +
"Landed Safely");
    }
    // bring up complete button
    startPauseButton.setVisible(false);
    exitStopButton.setVisible(false);
    completeButton.setVisible(true);
    return;
  }
```

```
  landerX += landerXSpeed;
  landerY += landerYSpeed;
  // horizontal drag
  if (landerXSpeed > 0)
    landerXSpeed -= drag;
  else if (landerXSpeed < 0)
    landerXSpeed += drag;
  // gravity
  landerYSpeed += gravity * (double)
(landingTimer.getDelay()) / 1000;
}
```

Save and run the project. Select a pilot level and play a game. Make sure you hear sounds when the thrusters are applied. Make sure the proper landing sound plays. You'll have to figure out how to do a safe landing (speed under -3 meters/second) to hear the safe landing sound!

At this point in the development of **Moon Landing**, we have a fully-functional (except for auto-pilot) 'text version' of the game, meaning we need to carefully watch numerical values in the label controls to monitor our lander's location. Way back in the earliest days of home computing, similar programs (using only vertical thrust, with names like **Rocket**, **Lunar**, **LEM**, **Apollo**) were among the most popular computer games. Since then, great strides have been made in the graphics capabilities of computers. Let's take advantage of those capabilities and develop ways to graphically follow our lander's excursion to the moon's surface.

The first display we will develop is the 'trajectory panel' under the label and text field controls on the right side of the form. In this panel, we will draw a line indicating the desired path from the lander to the pad. We will also draw the path followed by the lander as it descends. Before adding this panel, we need to review some basic graphics capabilities. We will look at graphics methods, graphics objects, colors, stroke and paint objects, drawing lines, and drawing ellipses and rectangles.

Graphics Methods

Java offers a wealth of **graphics methods** that let us draw lines, rectangles, ellipses, pie shapes and polygons. With these methods, you can draw anything! These methods are provided by the **Graphics2D** class.

Using graphics objects is a little detailed, but worth the time to learn. There is a new vocabulary with many new objects to study. We'll cover every step. The basic approach to drawing with graphics objects will always be:

➢ Create a **Graphics2D** object.
➢ Establish the **Stroke** and **Paint** objects needed for drawing.
➢ Establish the **Shape** object for drawing.
➢ Draw shape to **Graphics2D** object using drawing methods
➢ Dispose of graphics object when done.

In the next few sections, we will learn about **Graphics2D** objects, **Stroke** and **Paint** objects (use of **colors**) and **Shape** objects. We'll learn how to draw **lines**, and how to draw **ellipses**, and how to draw and fill **rectangles**. This will give use the skills needed to construct the trajectory panel. We'll also build the guide panel under the trajectory panel. Let's get started.

Graphics2D Object

As mentioned, graphics methods (drawing methods) are applied to graphics objects. **Graphics2D objects** provide the "surface" for drawing methods. In this project, we will use the panel control for drawing.

A **Graphics2D object** (**g2D**) is created using:

```
Graphics g2D = (Graphics2D) hostControl.getGraphics();
```

where **hostControl** is the control hosting the graphics object. Note the **getGraphics** method returns a **Graphics** object that must be cast (converted) to a **Graphics2D** object. Placement of this statement depends on scope. Place it in a method for method level scope. Place it with other class level declarations for class level scope.

Once a graphics object is created, all graphics methods are applied to this object. Hence, to apply a drawing method named **drawingMethod** to the **g2D** object, use:

```
g2D.drawingMethod(arguments);
```

where **arguments** are any needed arguments.

Once you are done drawing to an object and need it no longer, it should be properly disposed to clear up system resources. The syntax for disposing of our example graphics object uses the **dispose** method:

```
g2D.dispose();
```

Stroke and Paint Objects

The attributes of lines (either lines or borders of shapes) drawn using **Graphics2D** objects are specified by the **stroke**. Stroke can be used to establish line style, such as solid, dashed or dotted lines, line thickness and line end styles. By default, a solid line, one pixel in width is drawn. In this class, we will only look at how to change the line thickness. Stroke is changed using the **setStroke** method. To set the thickness (**width**) of the line for a graphics object **g2D**, use a **BasicStroke** object:

```
g2D.setStroke(new BasicStroke(width));
```

After this method, all lines will be drawn with the new **width** attribute.

To change the color of lines being drawn, use the **setPaint** method. For our example graphics object, the color is changed using:

```
g2D.setPaint(color);
```

where **color** is either a built-in color or one set using RGB values. After this line of code, all lines are drawn with the new color.

The **setPaint** method can also be used to establish the color and pattern used to fill a graphics region.

Shapes and Drawing Methods

We will learn to draw various **shapes**. Shapes will include lines, rectangles, and ellipses. The classes used to do this drawing are in the **java.awt.geom.*** package, so we need to include an import statement for this package.

Shape objects are specified with the **user coordinates** of the hosting panel control (**myPanel**):

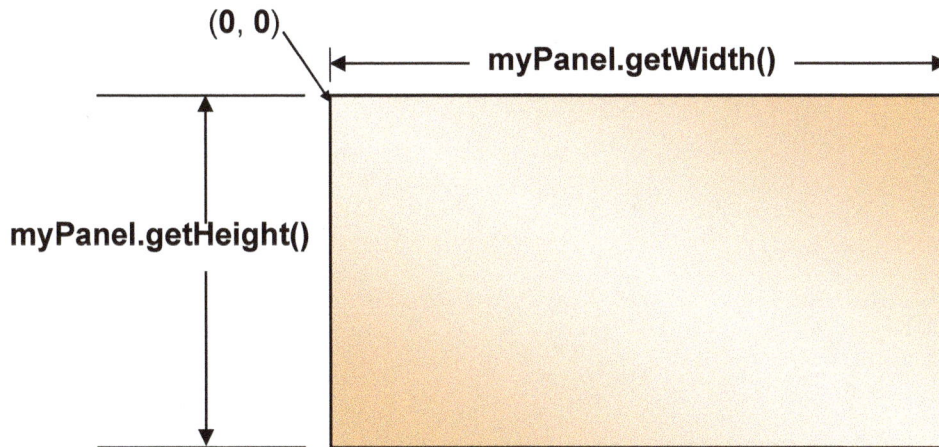

The host dimensions, **myPanel.getWidth()** and **myPanel.getHeight()** represent the "graphics" region of the control hosting the graphics object.

This is the same coordinate system we have been using for the **Moon Landing** program. Points are referred to by a Cartesian pair, **(x, y)**. In the diagram, note the **x** (horizontal) coordinate runs from left to right, starting at **0** and extending to **myPanel.getWidth() - 1**. The **y** (vertical) coordinate goes from top to bottom, starting at **0** and ending at **myPanel.getHeight() - 1**. All measurements are integers and in units of **pixels**.

Once a **shape** object is created (we will see how to do that next), the shape is drawn using the draw method. For a shape **myShape** using our example graphics object (**g2D**), the code is:

```
g2D.draw(myShape);
```

The shape will be drawn using the current **stroke** and **paint** attributes.

For shape objects that encompass some two-dimensional region, that region can be filled using the fill method. For our example, the code is:

```
g2D.fill(myShape);
```

The shape will be filled using the current **paint** attribute.

Let's define our first shape – a **line** – yes, a line is a shape.

Line2D Shape

The first shape we learn to draw is a line, or the **Line2D** shape. This shape is used to connect two Cartesian points with a straight-line segment:

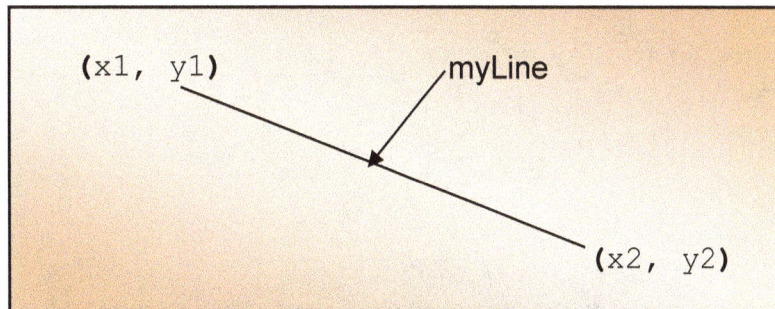

If we wish to connect the point (**x1**, **y1**) with (**x2**, **y2**), the shape (**myLine**) is created using:

```
Line2D.Double myLine = new Line2D.Double(x1, y1, x2, y2);
```

Each coordinate value is a **double** type (there is also a **Line2D.Float** shape, where each coordinate is a **float** type). Once created, the line is drawn (in a previously created Graphics2D object, **g2D**) using the **draw** method:

```
g2D.draw(myLine);
```

The line will be drawn using the current **stroke** and **paint** attributes.

Say we have a panel control (**myPanel**) of dimension (300, 200). To draw a black line (**myLine**) in that panel, with a line width of 1 (the default stroke) from (20, 20) to (280, 180), the Java code would be:

```
Graphics2D g2D = (Graphics2D) myPanel.getGraphics();
Line2D.Double myLine = new Line2D.Double(20, 20, 280,
180);
g2D.setPaint(Color.BLACK);
g2D.draw(myLine);
g2D.dispose();
```

This produces:

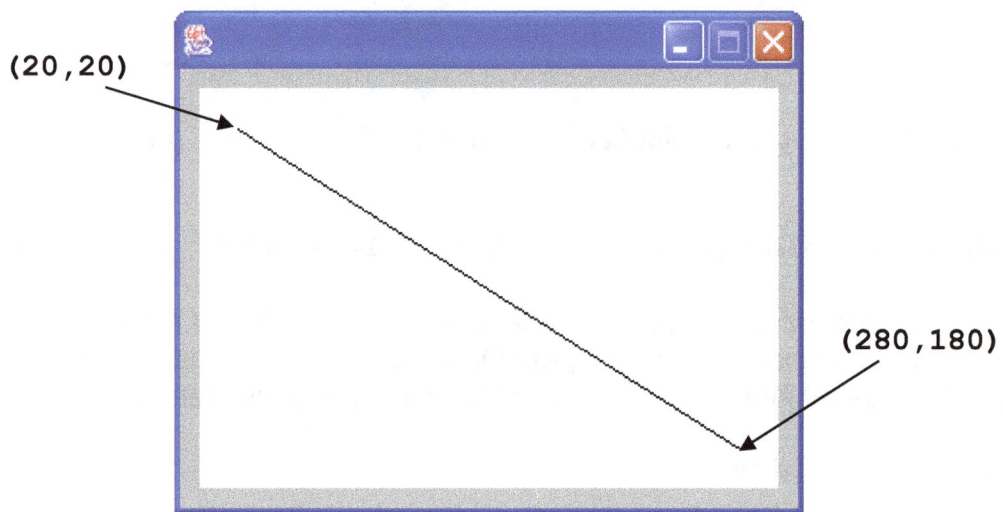

For every line segment you need to draw, you will need a separate **Line2D** shape and **draw** statement. Of course, you can choose to change color (**setPaint**) or width (**setStroke**) at any time you wish.

Code Design – Trajectory Display, Suggested Path

Believe it or not, after all this new material, we're finally ready to draw a line on the trajectory panel in **Moon Landing**. This line will connect the initial lander position with the landing pad position to give you (and later the auto-pilot) a suggested trajectory (path) to follow while landing. Let's review all the steps necessary to do this. Recall the trajectory panel is named **trajectoryPanel**.

Steps to draw the suggested trajectory:

- ➢ Declare a graphics object **trajectoryGraphics**.
- ➢ Create the graphics object.
- ➢ Create **stroke** object with width of 2.
- ➢ At **time = 0.0**, clear the graphics object and draw a line (using **draw**) connecting initial lander position with pad position.

These steps are straightforward. The only thing not clear is the coordinates of the line. Let's look a sketch of the initial lander and pad location on the **landscape** element:

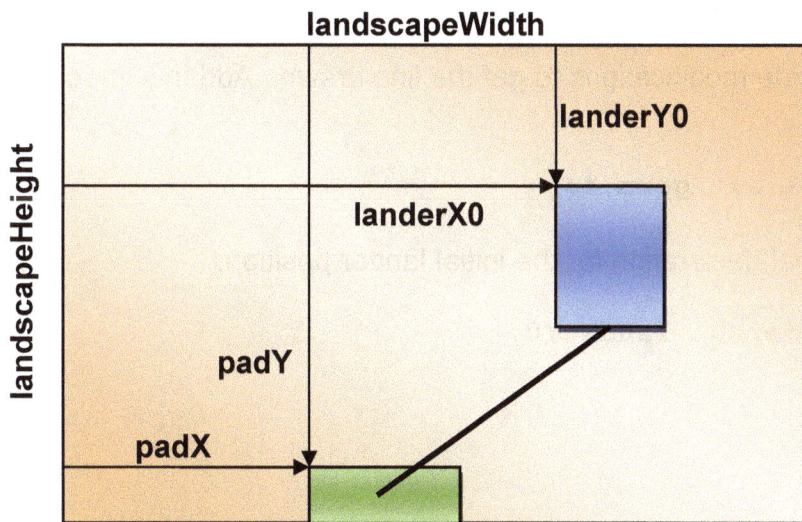

where **landerX0** and **landerY0** are the lander position at time = 0.0.

The line we want to draw is shown in black, connecting the bottom middle of the lander with the center of the pad. The Cartesian pair at the bottom of the lander is:

```
X = landerX0 + landerWidth / 2;
Y = landerY0 + landerHeight;
```

And the middle of the landing pad:

```
X = padX + padWidth / 2;
Y = padY + padHeight / 2;
```

The coordinates given above are relative to the size of the **landscape** element and we want to draw the line in **trajectoryPanel**. Hence, prior to drawing the line, we need to scale the X and Y coordinates to fit the points within the trajectory panel. Each X coordinate should be multiplied by **trajectoryXScale**:

```
trajectoryXScale  = trajectoryPanel.getWidth() /
landscapeWidth;
```

and the Y coordinates should be multiplied by **trajectoryYScale**:

```
trajectoryYScale = trajectory.getHeight() /
landscapeHeight;
```

Let's make the code modifications to get the line drawn. Add this import statement:

```
import java.awt.geom.*;
```

Add this class level declaration for the initial lander position:

```
double landerX0, landerY0;
```

Create a new general method (**updateTrajectory**) with the code to draw the trajectory line:

```
private void updateTrajectory()
{
  Graphics2D trajectoryGraphics = (Graphics2D)
trajectoryPanel.getGraphics();
  double trajectoryXScale = (double)
(trajectoryPanel.getWidth()) / landscapeWidth;
  double trajectoryYScale = (double)
(trajectoryPanel.getHeight()) / landscapeHeight;
  if (time == 0.0)
  {
    landerX0 = landerX;
    landerY0 = landerY;
    trajectoryGraphics.setStroke(new BasicStroke(2));
    trajectoryGraphics.setPaint(Color.RED);
    Line2D.Double trajectoryLine = new
Line2D.Double(trajectoryXScale * (landerX0 + landerWidth /
2), trajectoryYScale * (landerY0 + landerHeight),
trajectoryXScale * (padX + padWidth / 2), trajectoryYScale
* (padY + padHeight / 2));
    trajectoryGraphics.draw(trajectoryLine);
  }
  trajectoryGraphics.dispose();
}
```

This code is a straightforward implementation of the previously derived equations. The code building the line shape (**trajectoryLine**) is very long!. Right now, this method is only used for the initial line. We will modify it soon to display the trajectory followed by the lander.

Add the one shaded line to the **startPauseButton ActionPerformed** method to draw the initial suggested trajectory using **UpdateTrajectory**:

```java
private void startPauseButtonActionPerformed(ActionEvent
e)
{
  if (startPauseButton.getText().equals("Start Game"))
  {
    startPauseButton.setText("Pause Game");
    exitStopButton.setText("Stop Game");
         .

         .

    time = 0.0;
    timeTextField.setText("0.0");
    landerX = (landscapeWidth - landerWidth) *
myRandom.nextDouble();
    landerY = 0;
    landerXSpeed = 0;
    landerYSpeed = 0;
    if (pilotLevel != 1)
      padX = (landscapeWidth - padWidth) *
myRandom.nextDouble();
    else
      padX = (landerX + landerWidth / 2) - padWidth / 2;
padY = landscapeHeight - padHeight;
    fuelRemaining = maximumFuel;
    fuelProgressBar.setValue(100);
    updateStatus();
    updateTrajectory();
    landingTimer.start();
  }
  else if (startPauseButton.getText().equals("Pause
Game"))
  {
    startPauseButton.setText("Restart Game");
    exitStopButton.setEnabled(false);
    leftThrustButton.setEnabled(false);
    downThrustButton.setEnabled(false);
    rightThrustButton.setEnabled(false);
    landingTimer.stop();
  }
  else
  {
    startPauseButton.setText("Pause Game");
    exitStopButton.setEnabled(true);
    leftThrustButton.setEnabled(true);
    downThrustButton.setEnabled(true);
```

```
      rightThrustButton.setEnabled(true);
      landingTimer.start();
    }
  }
```

Save and run the project. Select a pilot level and click **Start Game**. Here's my example:

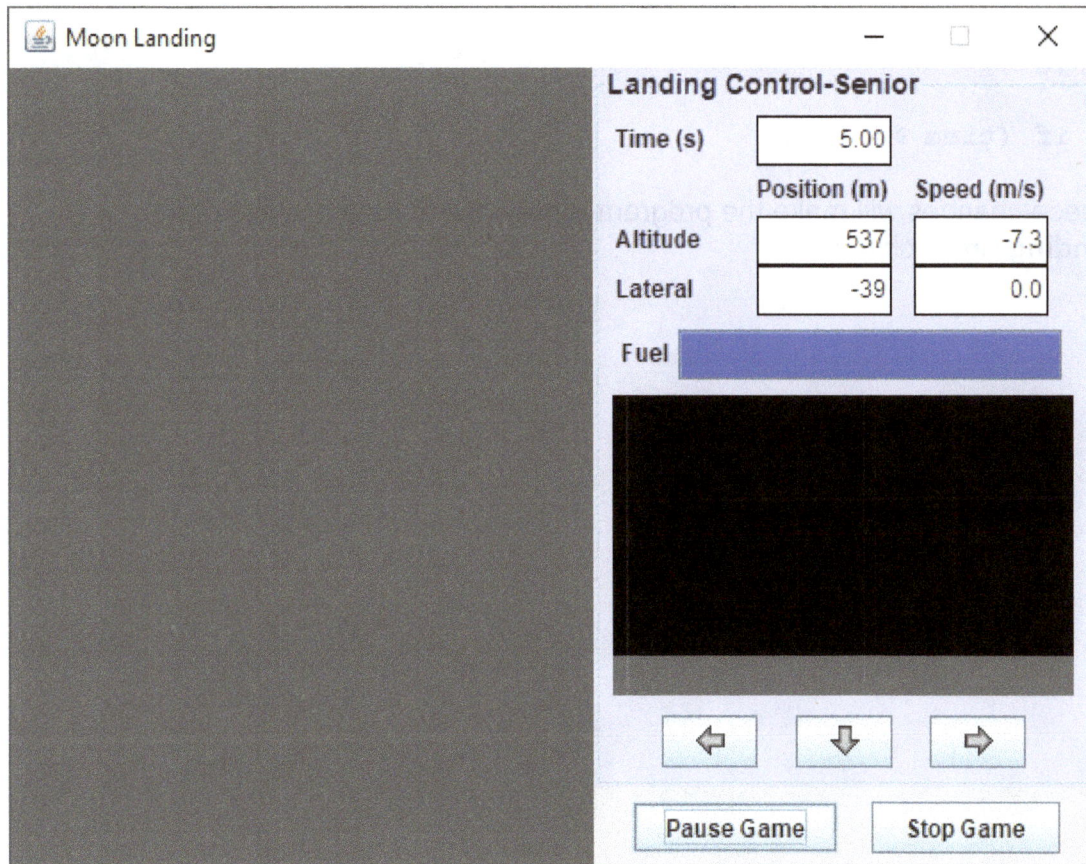

Hey - where's the trajectory line? Let's see what's going on.

Try this. In the **landingTimerActionPerformed** method, add this line after the call to **updateStatus**:

```
updateTrajectory();
```

Now, in the **updateTrajectory** method, change this line:

```
if (time == 0.0)
```

To

```
if (time >= 0.0)
```

These changes will make the program redraw the line each cycle of the **landingTimer** object.

Run the project again. **Click Start** Game. After a cycle of the timer, you will see:

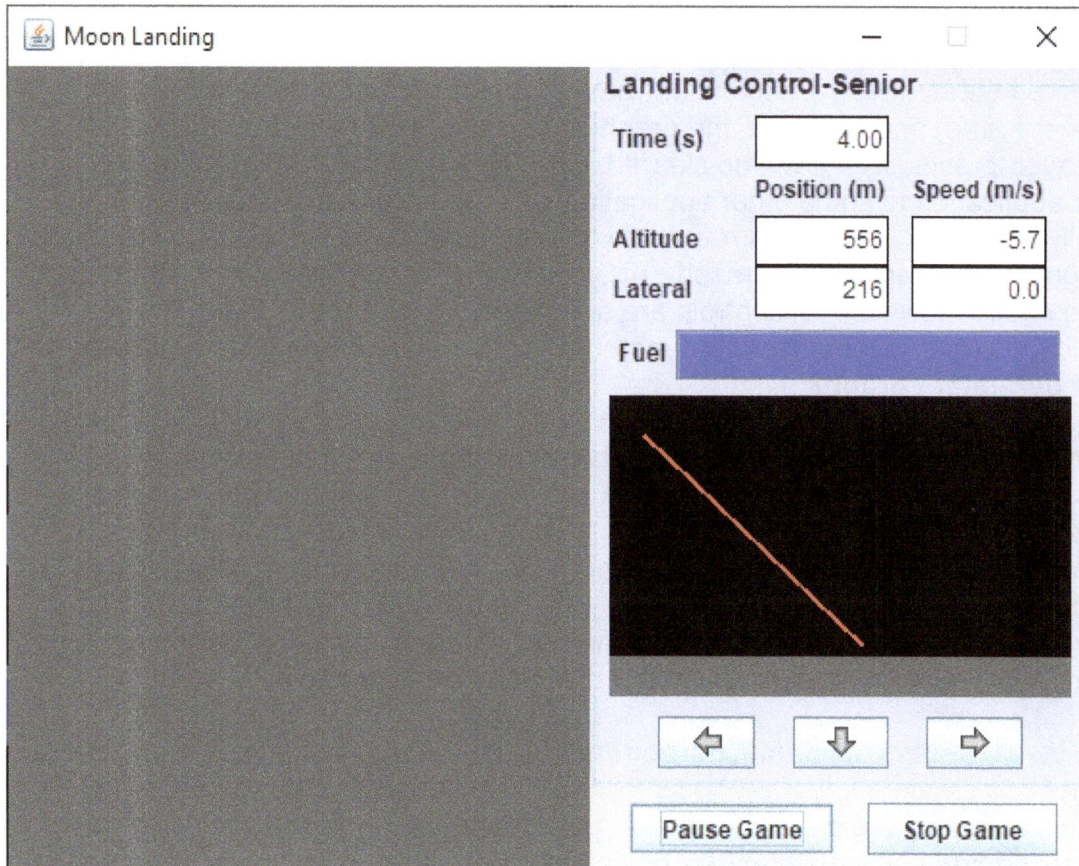

The line is there. Click **Pause Game**. Reduce the frame to an icon (click the underscore button in the upper right corner). Restore the frame and the line will be gone again. It will redraw when you restart the game. So why didn't the line appear the first time we draw it and why did it disappear while paused? The answer to these questions has to do with something called **persistent graphics**.

Before going further, don't forget to change the line of code in **updateTrajectory** back to:

```
if (time == 0.0)
```

You can leave the added call to **updateTrajectory** in the **landingTimer** method. We will use it as we continue.

Persistent Graphics

Java graphics objects have <u>no</u> memory. They only display what has been last drawn on them. If you reduce your frame to an icon (or it becomes obscured by another frame) and restore it, the graphics object cannot remember what was displayed previously – it will be cleared. Similarly, if you switch from an active Java application to some other application, your Java form may become partially or fully obscured. When you return to your Java application, the obscured part of any graphics object will be erased. Again, there is no memory. Notice in both these cases, however, all controls are automatically restored to the form. Your application remembers these, fortunately! The controls are persistent. We also want **persistent graphics**.

To maintain persistent graphics, we need to build memory into our graphics objects using code. In this code, we must be able to recreate, when needed, the current state of a graphics object. This 'custom' code is placed in the host control's **paintComponent** method. This event method is called whenever an obscured object becomes unobscured. The **paintComponent** method will be called for each object when a frame is first activated and when a frame is restored from an icon or whenever an obscured object is viewable again.

How do we access the **paintComponent** method for a control? For such access, we need to create a separate **class** for the control that **extends** the particular control. Creating the class is a simple. We define a **GraphicsPanel** class (a **JPanel** control hosting a graphics object, each panel needing persistent graphics would use a different name) using the following code framework:

```
class GraphicsPanel extends JPanel
{
  public void paintComponent(Graphics g)
  {
      [Painting code goes here]
  }
}
```

This class is placed after the main class in a program. A **GraphicsPanel** object is then declared and created using:

```
GraphicsPanel myPanel = new GraphicsPanel();
```

With this declaration, the "painting" of the control is now handled by the **paintComponent** method. Notice this method passes a **Graphics** object **g**. The first step in painting the component is to cast this object to a **Graphics2D** object:

```
Graphics2D g2D = (Graphics2D) g;
```

After this, we place code in the **paintComponent** method that describes the current state of the graphics object. In particular, make sure the first statement is:

```
super.paintComponent(g2D);
```

This will reestablish any background color (the keyword **super** refers to the 'inherited' control, the panel in this case).

Maintaining persistent graphics does require a bit of work on your part. You need to always know what is in your graphics object and how to recreate the object, when needed. This usually involves developing some program variables that describe how to recreate the graphics object. And, you usually need to develop some ad hoc rules for recreation. As you build your first few **paintComponent** events, you will begin to develop your own ways for maintaining persistent graphics. At certain times, you'll need to force a "repaint" of your control. To do this, for a host control named **hostControl** use:

```
hostControl.repaint();
```

You will often need to have your **paintComponent** method access variables from your main class. If your main class is named **mainClass** and you want the value of **myVariable**, the variable is accessed using:

```
mainClass.myVariable
```

Any variables accessed in this manner must have class level scope and, when declared, be prefaced with the keyword **static**. This is due to the way the **paintComponent** method works.

This all may sound difficult, but it really isn't and an example should clear things up. Let's see how to maintain persistent graphics in our trajectory display panel. First, add the framework for a new class named **TrajectoryPanel** class at the end of the main class (**MoonLanding**) code:

```
class TrajectoryPanel extends JPanel
{
  public void paintComponent(Graphics g)
  {
    Graphics2D g2D = (Graphics2D) g;
    super.paintComponent(g2D);
  }
}
```

Change the line of code in the main class creating **trajectoryPanel** to:

```
TrajectoryPanel trajectoryPanel = new TrajectoryPanel();
```

Next, move all the graphics statements out of the **updateTrajectory** method into the **paintComponent** method. For now, **updateTrajectory** will have no code, but don't delete the method. The **paintComponent** method will be (the added lines are shaded – make sure these lines are no longer in the **updateTrajectory** method):

```
public void paintComponent(Graphics g)
{
  Graphics2D g2D = (Graphics2D) g;
  super.paintComponent(g2D);
  Graphics2D trajectoryGraphics = (Graphics2D)
trajectoryPanel.getGraphics();
  double trajectoryXScale = (double)
(trajectoryPanel.getWidth()) / landscapeWidth;
  double trajectoryYScale = (double)
(trajectoryPanel.getHeight()) / landscapeHeight;
  if (time == 0.0)
  {
    landerX0 = landerX;
    landerY0 = landerY;
    trajectoryGraphics.setStroke(new BasicStroke(2));
    trajectoryGraphics.setPaint(Color.RED);
    Line2D.Double trajectoryLine = new
Line2D.Double(trajectoryXScale * (landerX0 + landerWidth /
2), trajectoryYScale * (landerY0 + landerHeight),
trajectoryXScale * (padX + padWidth / 2), trajectoryYScale
* (padY + padHeight / 2));
    trajectoryGraphics.draw(trajectoryLine);
  }
```

```
    trajectoryGraphics.dispose();
}
```

We need to make some modifications to make this code work:

> Delete the line creating **trajectoryGraphics** using **trajectoryPanel**. This line is not needed because the graphics object is provided when the method is called. Change all **trajectoryGraphics** references to this new object **g2D**.
> Remove the references to **trajectoryPanel** in code computing the scale factors. The use of this control is implicit in the class definition.
> We want to draw the line any time the **paintComponent** method is called, so remove the **if** block (requiring time == 0.0). Delete the two lines setting **landerX0** and **landerY0** (we will set these in the main class).
> Several variables are from the main class.:

landscapeWidth	**landscapeHeight**
landerX0	**landerY0**
landerWidth	**landerHeight**
padX	**padY**
padWidth	**padHeight**

Preface all instances of these variables in the **paintComponent** method with **MoonLanding.** – also, in the main class, preface the declarations of each of these variables with the keyword **static**.

The modified method is (changes are shaded):

```
public void paintComponent(Graphics g)
{
  Graphics2D g2D = (Graphics2D) g;
  super.paintComponent(g2D);
  double trajectoryXScale = (double) (getWidth()) /
MoonLanding.landscapeWidth;
  double trajectoryYScale = (double) (getHeight()) /
MoonLanding.landscapeHeight;
  g2D.setStroke(new BasicStroke(2));
  g2D.setPaint(Color.RED);
  Line2D.Double trajectoryLine = new
Line2D.Double(trajectoryXScale * (MoonLanding.landerX0 +
MoonLanding.landerWidth / 2), trajectoryYScale *
(MoonLanding.landerY0 + MoonLanding.landerHeight),
trajectoryXScale * (MoonLanding.padX +
MoonLanding.padWidth / 2), trajectoryYScale *
(MoonLanding.padY + MoonLanding.padHeight / 2));
  g2D.draw(trajectoryLine);
  g2D.dispose();
}
```

With this code, the trajectory line will be drawn each time the method is invoked.

Return to the **updateTrajectory** method in the main class. Modify it so it looks like this (we establish the initial lander position):

```
private void updateTrajectory()
{
  if (time == 0.0)
  {
    landerX0 = landerX;
    landerY0 = landerY;
  }
}
```

Run the game again. Select a pilot level and click **Start Game**. A line will be there and will persist:

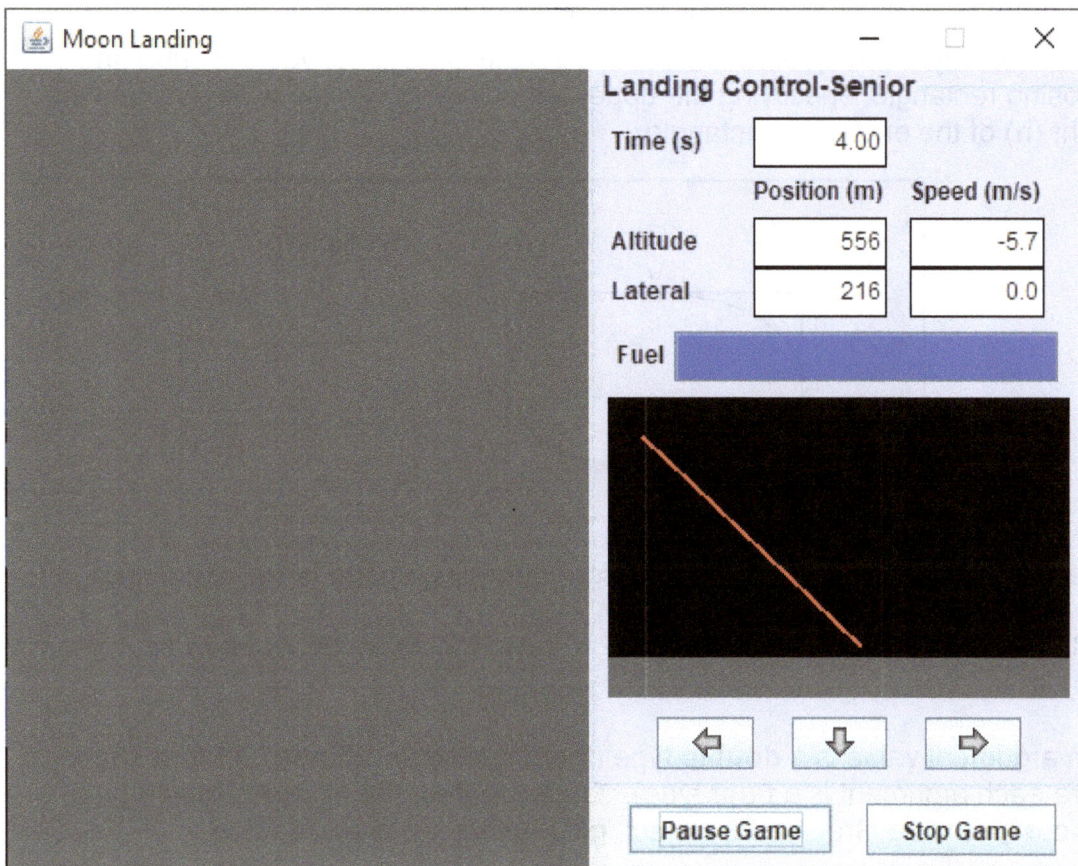

From now on, we will develop only persistent graphics using similar techniques.

We will use circles (ellipses) to mark this trajectory, so let's see how to add these graphic elements using the **Ellipse2D** shape.

Ellipse2D Shape

We now begin looking at two-dimensional shapes. The first is an ellipse, represented by the **Ellipse2D** shape. To specify an ellipse, you describe an enclosing rectangle, specifying the upper left corner (**x, y**), the width (**w**) and the height (**h**) of the enclosing rectangle:

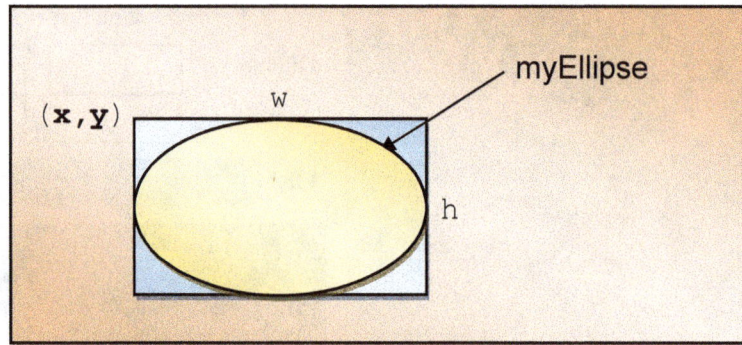

If the ellipse is named **myEllipse**, the corresponding shape is created using:

```
Ellipse2D.Double myEllipse = new Ellipse2D.Double(x, y, w,
h);
```

Each argument value is a **double** type (there is also an **Ellipse2D.Float** shape, where each argument is a **float** type). Once created, the ellipse is drawn (in a previously created Graphics2D object, **g2D**) using the **draw** method:

```
g2D.draw(myEllipse);
```

The ellipse will be drawn using the current **stroke** and **paint** attributes.

Say we have a panel (**myPanel**) of dimension (300, 200). To draw a black ellipse (**myEllipse**) in that panel, with a line width of 1 (the default stroke), starting at (40, 40), with width 150 and height 100, the Java code would be:

```
Graphics2D g2D = (Graphics2D) myPanel.getGraphics();
Ellipse2D.Double myEllipse = new Ellipse2D.Double(40, 40,
150, 100);
g2D.setPaint(Color.BLACK);
g2D.draw(myEllipse);
g2D.dispose();
```

This produces:

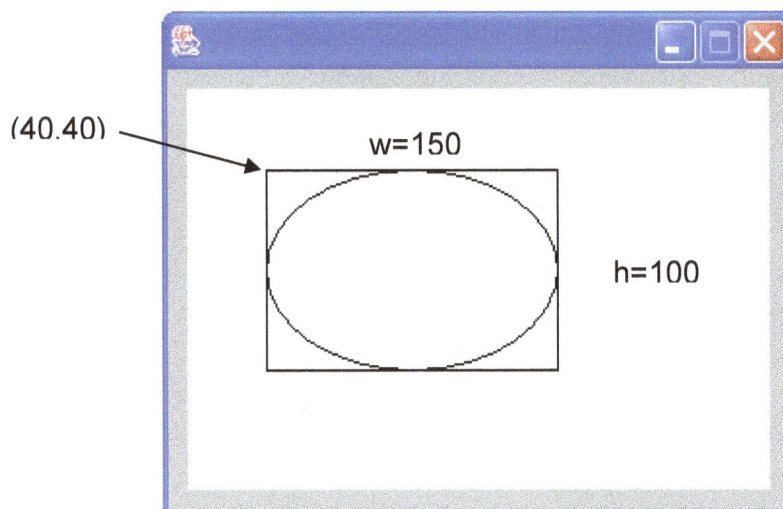

The surrounding rectangle is shown to display how the ellipse fits.

The ellipse we just drew is pretty boring. It would be nice to have the capability to fill it with a color and/or pattern. Filling of shapes in Java2D is done with the **fill** method. If the graphics object is **g2D**, and the shape **myShape**, the syntax to fill the shape is:

```
g2D.fill(myEllipse);
```

The ellipse will be filled with the current **paint** attribute. For now, we will just fill the shapes with solid colors

To fill our example ellipse with yellow, we use this code:

```
Graphics2D g2D = (Graphics2D) myPanel.getGraphics();
Ellipse2D.Double myEllipse = new Ellipse2D.Double(40, 40,
150, 100);
g2D.setPaint(Color.YELLOW);
g2D.fill(myEllipse);
g2D.dispose();
```

This produces:

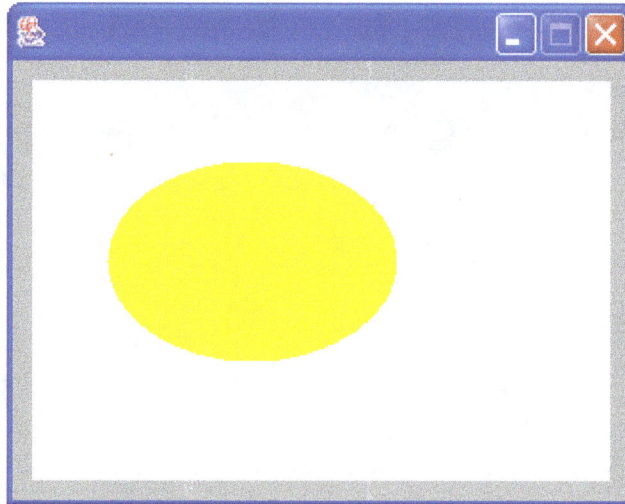

Notice the fill method fills the entire region with the selected color. If you had previously used the **draw** method to form a bordered ellipse, the fill will blot out that border. If you want a bordered, filled region, do the **fill** operation **first**, **then** the **draw** operation.

Code Design – Trajectory Display, Actual Path

We now modify the **updateTrajectory** method to draw a circle at the lander position as time elapses. With this, we will have a graphic depiction of the path followed by the lander as it descends. Such a depiction improves our ability to monitor the lander position with respect to the pad. It is a simple modification since we have already created the **trajectoryGraphics** graphics object.

The circle is centered at the bottom of the lander graphic element. That point was earlier defined by:

```
X = landerX + landerWidth / 2;
Y = landerY + landerHeight;
```

Recall this position is relative to the landscape element hence each point needs to be scaled to fit within **trajectoryPanel**. We want to draw a position circle at each event generated by the **landingTimer**. To reconstruct these circles in the **paintComponent** method, we need to somehow save each circle drawn. This may sound like a daunting task, but it's not too bad (fortunately).

The Java **Vector** class stores a collection of objects that works like an array, but has a special feature of being able to grow and shrink as needed. We will use a **Vector** object to store every circle drawn in the trajectory display. Then, when needed, the **paintComponent** method will use this vector object to recreate the points. Let's look at how to use the **Vector** class. This class useds the **java.util.Vector** package..

If I am storing a vector of points called **myPoints**, the required vector object is created using this constructor:

```
Vector myPoints = new Vector(50, 10);
```

This will create a vector of 50 initial elements, with 10 elements added every time new elements are needed (these numbers can be changed if desired). The size of **myPoints** is handled by Java – you never have to worry about it, unlike arrays.

Once created, a point is added to the vector using the **add** method. If the point object to add is named **myPoint**, the syntax is:

```
myPoints.add(myPoint);
```

The vector object (**myPoints**) keeps every object stored and accounted for.

In the **paintComponent** method, we need to recover all of the points we have stored so they can be redrawn on the graphics panel. To do this, we need to know how many objects there are and how to recover each one. The number of elements in a vector object is given by the **size** property. For our example object (**myPoints**), that value is found using:

```
myPoints.size()
```

The objects are stored like a zero-based array, ranging from object **0** to object **size** **– 1**. To retrieve object **n** from our example, use the **elementAt** method:

```
myPoint = myPoints.elementAt(n);
```

Having retrieved the colored line object, we can redraw it in the graphics panel control.

One last thing you might like to do with the vector object is to remove all the elements to do a reinitialization. We would do this in our game when we initialize things. The code that does this is:

```
myPoints.removeAllElements();
```

This line should be followed by a **repaint** of the control hosting the graphics panel.

So, we can now use a vector object to store and retrieve points in our Moon Landing game. One question that remains is how to specify a point object. Java has the solution – a **Point2D** object. You will see it is very easy to use. Each trajectory circle will be represented by a **Point2D** object. And our **Vector** object will be a vector of such objects. Let's draw some ellipses.

Add this **import** statement so we can use the Vector class:

```
import java.util.Vector;
```

In the class level declarations, create a vector of **trajectoryPoints**:

```
static Vector trajectoryPoints = new Vector(50, 10);
```

We anticipate needing this in the **paintComponent** method, hence have declared it **static**.

In the **startPauseButtonActionPerformed** method, add this line right before the **updateTrajectory** for initialization of **trajectoryPoints**:

```
trajectoryPoints.removeAllElements();
```

Make the shaded changes to the **updateTrajectory** to add the current trajectory point to the **Vector** object and repaint the panel:

```
private void updateTrajectory()
{
  if (time == 0.0)
  {
    landerX0 = landerX;
    landerY0 = landerY;
  }
  trajectoryPoints.add(new Point2D.Double(landerX +
landerWidth / 2 , landerY + landerYHeight));
  trajectoryPanel.repaint();
}
```

Lastly, modify the **paintComponent** method of the **TrajectoryPanel** class to redraw the points (changes are shaded):

```
public void paintComponent(Graphics g)
{
  Graphics2D g2D = (Graphics2D) g;
  super.paintComponent(g2D);
  double trajectoryXScale = (double) (getWidth()) /
MoonLanding.landscapeWidth;
  double trajectoryYScale = (double) (getHeight()) /
MoonLanding.landscapeHeight;
  g2D.setStroke(new BasicStroke(2));
  g2D.setPaint(Color.RED);
  Line2D.Double trajectoryLine = new
Line2D.Double(trajectoryXScale * (MoonLanding.landerX0 +
MoonLanding.landerWidth / 2), trajectoryYScale *
(MoonLanding.landerY0 + MoonLanding.landerHeight),
trajectoryXScale * (MoonLanding.padX +
MoonLanding.padWidth / 2), trajectoryYScale *
(MoonLanding.padY + MoonLanding.padHeight / 2));
  g2D.draw(trajectoryLine);

  g2D.setStroke(new BasicStroke(1));
  for (int i = 0; i < MoonLanding.trajectoryPoints.size();
i++)
  {
    Point2D.Double thisPoint = (Point2D.Double)
MoonLanding.trajectoryPoints.elementAt(i);
    Ellipse2D.Double trajectoryCircle = new
Ellipse2D.Double(trajectoryXScale * thisPoint.getX() - 3,
trajectoryYScale * thisPoint.getY() - 3, 6, 6);
    g2D.setPaint(Color.GREEN);
    g2D.draw(trajectoryCircle);
  }
  g2D.dispose();
}
```

In the added code, for each point in the **trajectoryPoints** object, we get the x and y values, then draw a green circle, 6 pixels in diameter, centered at the corresponding point.

Save and run the project. Select a pilot level, click **Start Game**. Try to land safely using the thrusters. You should see that the trajectory panel provides a useful indication of where the lander is located relative to the pad. And you get a plot of the trajectory followed to landing. Here's a run I made (**Junior** pilot level):

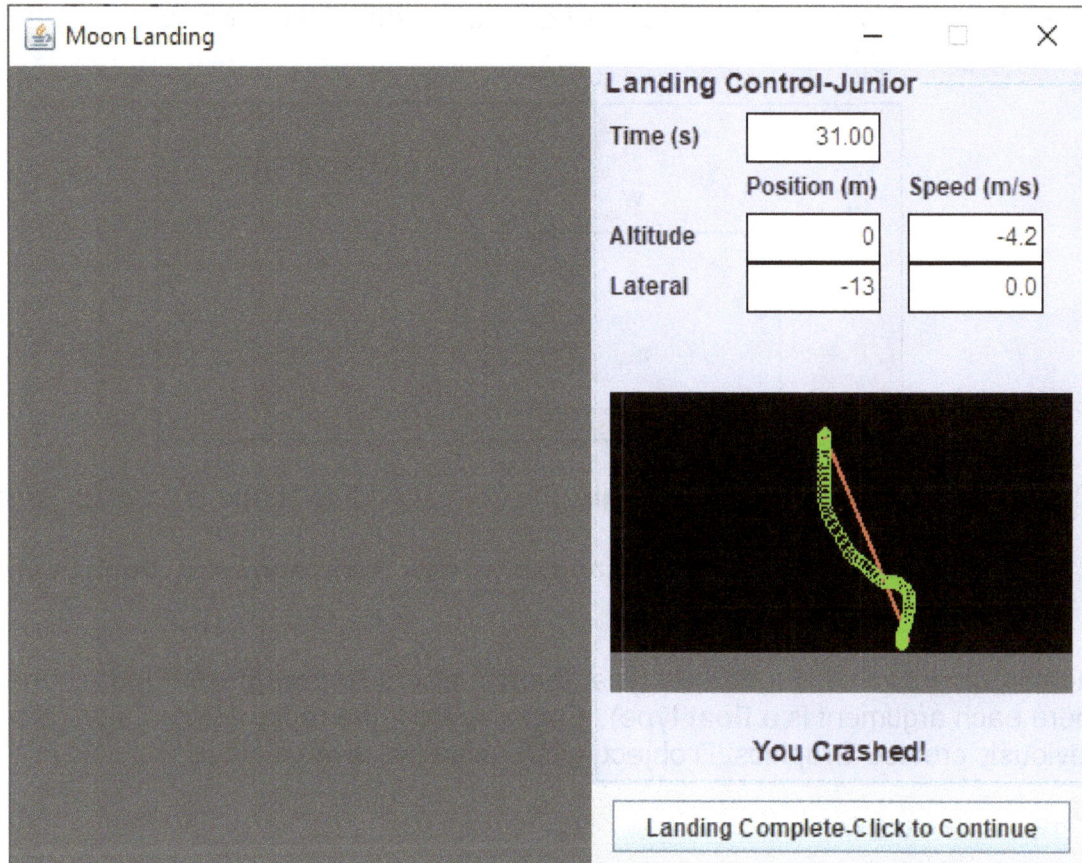

I didn't stay real close to the suggested trajectory, missing the pad by 13 meters and I crashed!

Though no penalty is assessed for missing the pad in the horizontal direction, it is useful to know during and after flight how close the lander is to the pad. One indication is the position value displayed in the text field control. And the trajectory plot gives an indication near the end of a landing. Direct graphic indicators of relative positions would be an improvement. We will use small rectangles in the guide panel under the trajectory panel for such indicators. Let's see how to draw rectangles.

Rectangle2D Shape

Rectangles can be defined, drawn and filled using methods nearly identical to the ellipse methods. To specify this shape, you need to know the Cartesian location of the upper left corner of the rectangle (**x, y**), the width of the rectangle, **w**, and the rectangle height, **h**:

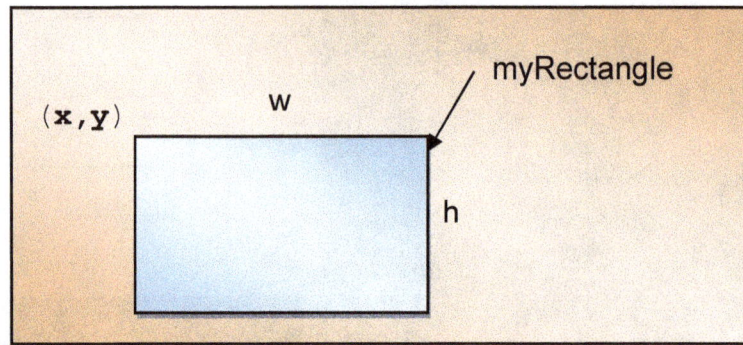

If the rectangle is named **myRectangle**, the corresponding shape is created using:

```
Rectangle2D.Double myRectangle = new Rectangle2D.Double(x,
y, w, h);
```

Each argument value is a **double** type (there is also a **Rectangle2D.Float** shape, where each argument is a **float** type). Once created, the rectangle is drawn (in a previously created Graphics2D object, **g2D**) using the **draw** method:

```
g2D.draw(myRectangle);
```

The rectangle will be drawn using the current **stroke** and **paint** attributes.

Again, we have a panel (**myPanel**) of dimension (300, 200). To draw a black rectangle (**myRectangle**) in that panel, with a line width of 1 (the default stroke), starting at (40, 40), with width 150 and height 100, the Java code would be:

```
Graphics2D g2D = (Graphics2D) myPanel.getGraphics();
Rectangle2D.Double myRectangle = new
Rectangle2D.Double(40, 40, 150, 100);
g2D.setPaint(Color.BLACK);
g2D.draw(myRectangle);
g2D.dispose();
```

This produces:

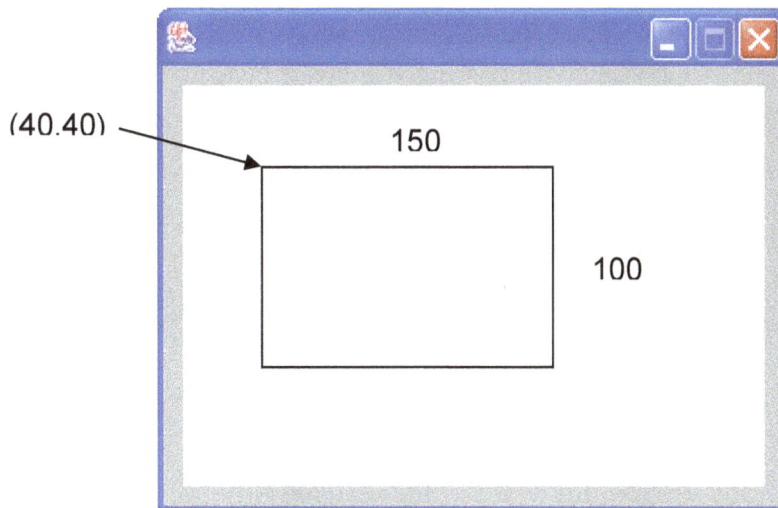

The rectangle is filled with the fill method:

```
g2D.fill(myRectangle);
```

The shape will be filled with the current **paint** attribute.

To fill our example rectangle with red, we use this code:

```
Graphics2D g2D = (Graphics2D) myPanel.getGraphics();
Rectangle2D.Double myRectangle = new
Rectangle2D.Double(40, 40, 150, 100);
g2D.setPaint(Color.RED);
g2D.fill(myRectangle);
g2D.dispose();
```

This produces:

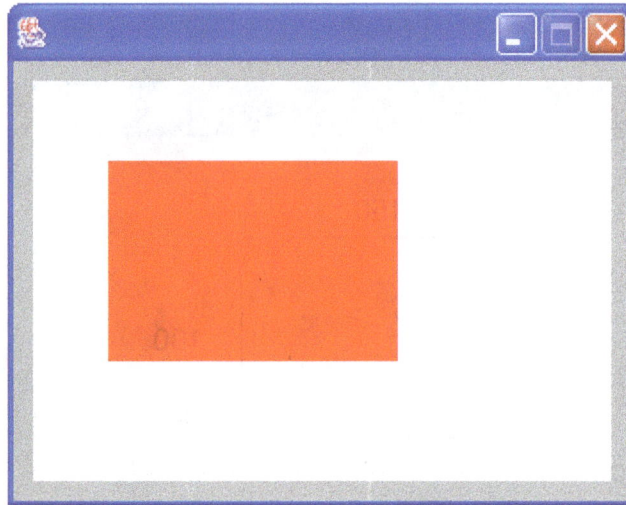

Like the ellipse methods, notice the fill operation erases any border that may have been there after a draw operation. For a bordered, filled ellipse, do the fill, then the draw.

Code Design – Guide Display

In the guide display (**guidePanel**), a green rectangle will represent the lander horizontal position, while a red rectangle will represent the landing pad. The center of each rectangle within **guidePanel** should coincide with the center of the lander and pad images within the landscape background. Or, using simple proportion, the corresponding **X** positions are:

```
landerRectangleCenter = (landerX + lander.Width / 2) *
guidePanel.getWidth() / landscapeWidth;

padRectangleCenter = (padX + pad.Width / 2) *
guidePanel.getWidth() / landscapeWidth;
```

We will have the rectangle be 10 pixels wide and have the height of the guide panel (minus room for the border). Let's develop the **Rectangle2D** shape for such a rectangle. A drawing will help:

guidePanel

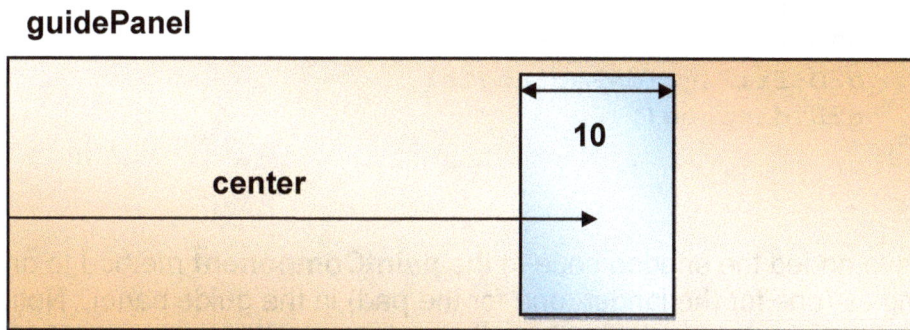

Assuming the border is one pixel wide, you should see this rectangle is created within **guidePanel** using:

```
new Rectangle2D.Double(center – 5, 1, 10,
guidePanel.getHeight() – 2);
```

We want the guide panel graphics to be persistent. Add a new class named **GuidePanel** with the same structure as the **TrajectoryPanel**:

```
class GuidePanel extends JPanel
{
  public void paintComponent(Graphics g)
  {
    Graphics2D g2D = (Graphics2D) g;
    super.paintComponent(g2D);
    int x = (int) ((MoonLanding.landerX +
MoonLanding.landerWidth / 2) * getWidth() /
MoonLanding.landscapeWidth - 5);
    Rectangle2D.Double guideRectangle = new
Rectangle2D.Double(x, 1, 10, getHeight() - 2);
    g2D.setPaint(Color.GREEN);
    g2D.fill(guideRectangle);
    x = (int) ((MoonLanding.padX + MoonLanding.padWidth /
2) * getWidth() / MoonLanding.landscapeWidth - 5);
    guideRectangle = new Rectangle2D.Double(x, 1, 10,
getHeight() - 2);
    g2D.setPaint(Color.RED);
    g2D.fill(guideRectangle);
    g2D.dispose();
  }
}
```

We have added the shaded code in the **paintComponent** method to draw the two rectangles (one for the lander, one for the pad) in the guide panel. Notice the method uses several variables from the main class. Most were used by the **TrajectoryPanel** hence already have the **static** designation. One exception is the variable **landerX**. Add the preface **static** to its declaration. And, add it to **landerY** too – we'll need it for future work.

In the main class, change the declaration statement for **guidePanel** to:

```
GuidePanel guidePanel = new GuidePanel();
```

And add these two lines at the end of the **updateStatus** method (to draw the guide panel):

```
// update guide display
guidePanel.repaint();
```

Save and run the project. The green and red boxes will show the relative horizontal location of the lander to the pad. Here's my screen:

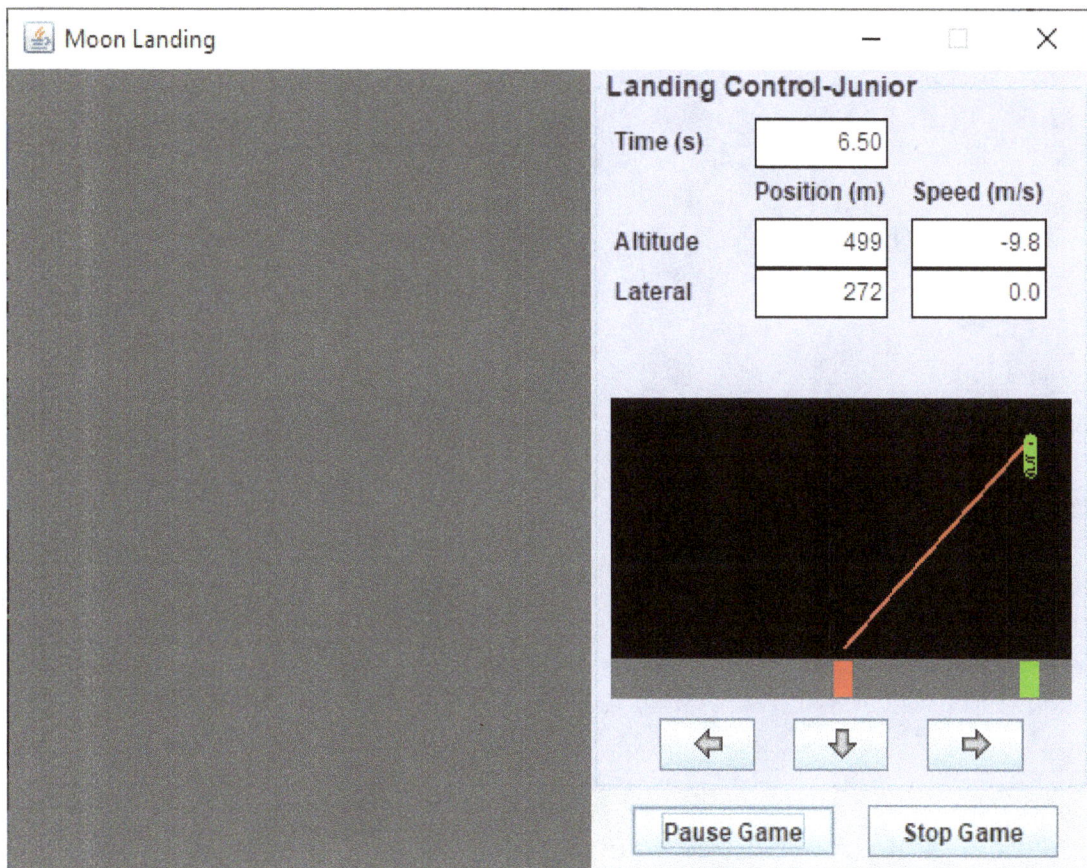

The lander (green) is to the right of the pad (red). This is also reflected in the positive **Lateral** value of 272 meters.

If I apply right thrust, the lander will move to the left nearing the pad. Here's the screen a little later:

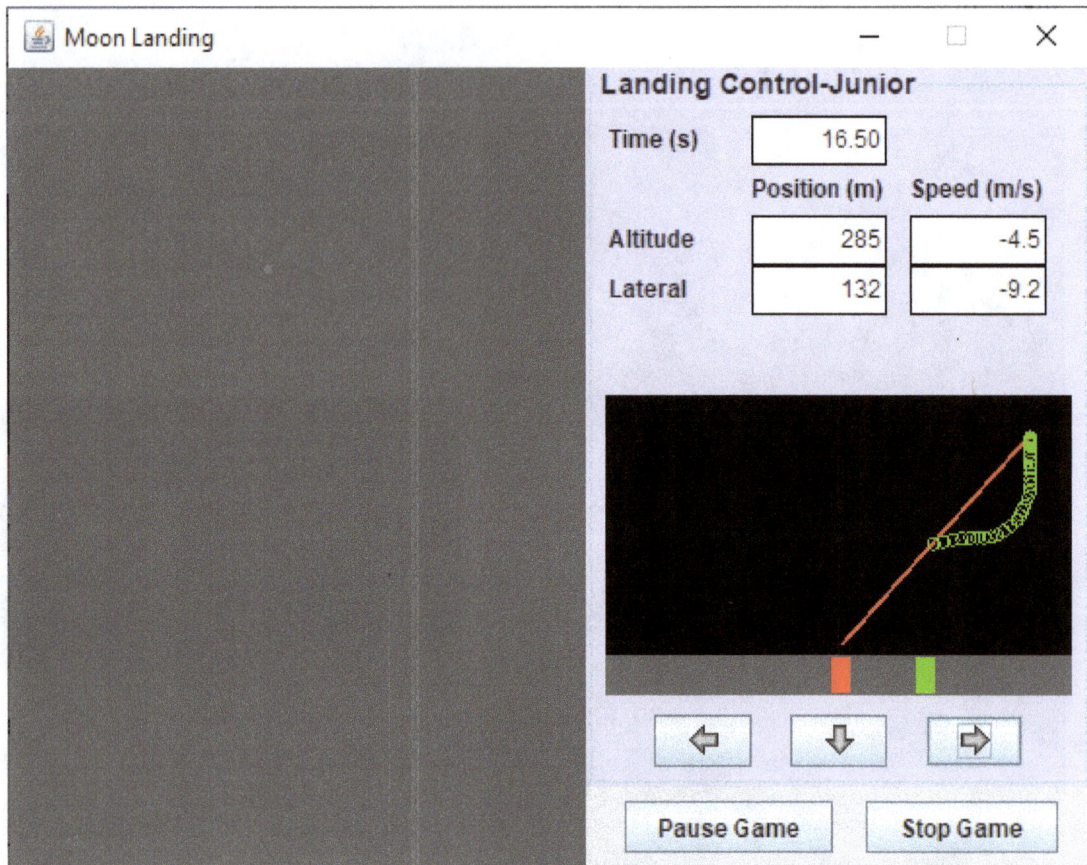

I'm now 132 meters to the right, moving to the left. I think you see how the graphic indicators are really nice

The trajectory display and guide displays are useful in helping land on the moon safely. But, we can do better. Let's use the graphic elements (landscape, lander, pad, thrust graphics) we saw earlier and develop an animated display of the lander as it descends across the landscape onto the landing pad. We place this animation in the viewer panel (**viewerPanel**) on the left of the form. To do this, we need to look at a few more graphics topics: scrolling backgrounds and sprite animation.

Scrolling Background – drawImage Method

Most action games employ scrolling or moving backgrounds. In our program, we will use the viewer panel (**viewerPanel**) to display the lander as it moves across the landscape toward the landing pad. We will center the lander graphic in the panel (if possible). Then, to give the appearance of motion, we will move or scroll the landscape behind the lander. What looks like a very sophisticated effect is really just a simple application of the **drawImage** graphics method. This method allows us to take a region of an image and "draw" it into a display area.

The **drawImage** graphics method for establishing a background is fairly simple. Assume you an **Image** object (**myImage**). Within this object is a rectangular region (**source**) that you wish to copy to a rectangular region (**destination**) in a graphic object **g2D**. The syntax for such an operation is:

```
g2D.drawImage(myImage, dx1, dy1, dx2, dy2, sx1, sy1, sx2,
sy2, null);
```

where:

(**dx1, dy1**)	Coordinate of the upper left corner within the graphics object (the destination rectangle) where the image will be drawn.
(**dx2, dy2**)	Coordinate of the lower right corner within the graphics object (the destination rectangle) where the image will be drawn.
(**sx1, sy1**)	Coordinate of the upper left corner of the image object (the source rectangle) defining the portion of the image to draw in the graphics object.
(**sx2, sy2**)	Coordinate of the upper right corner of the image object (the source rectangle) defining the portion of the image to draw in the graphics object.

All the above coordinates must be **int** type. The final argument (set to **null**) is an **ImageObserver** object we won't need.

For scrolling backgrounds, the 'destination' rectangle encompasses the entire control (**myControl**) hosting the graphics object used as the viewing area. Hence, the corresponding coordinates are:

```
(dx1,dy1) = (0, 0)
(dx2,dy2) = (myControl.getWidth() -1,
myControl.getHeight() - 1)
```

The 'source' rectangle contains the portion of the image we want to copy into the graphics object. This rectangle has the same dimensions (width and height) as the destination rectangle, with the corners shifted by a desired position (x, y) within the source image:

```
(sx1,sy1) = (x, y)
(sx2,sy2) = (x + myControl.getWidth() - 1, y +
myControl.getHeight() - 1)
```

Code Design – Scrolling Landscape

Let's see how **drawImage** works with our **landscape** image object and viewer panel (**viewerPanel**). Here is the viewer panel we will use to watch the animation:

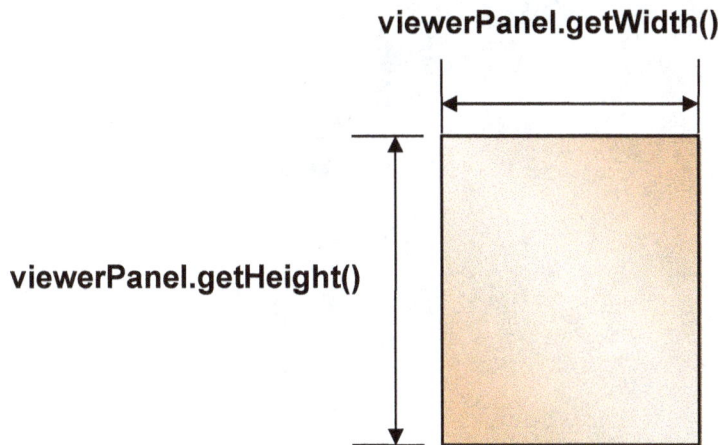

viewerPanel.getWidth()

viewerPanel.getHeight()

The panel area is defined the **destination** area for the **drawImage** method, with coordinates:

```
(dx1,dy1) = (0, 0)
(dx2,dy2) = (viewerPanel.getWidth() -1,
viewerPanel.getHeight() - 1)
```

Here is the **landscape** image we loaded a while back (shown 60 percent of full-size):

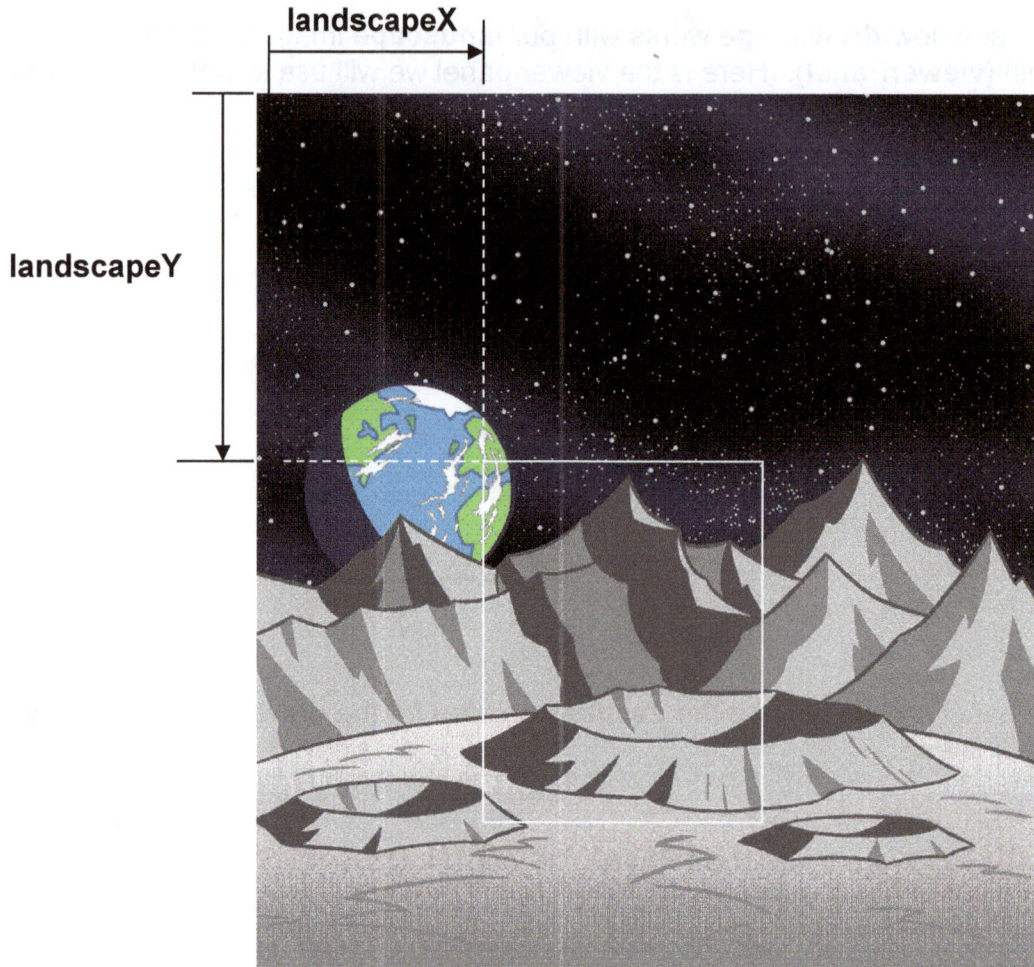

Shown on the image is a rectangular region located at **(landscapeX, landscapeY)**. This region has the same width as the viewer panel (**viewerPanel**) and the same height. This defines our **source** area, with coordinates:

```
(sx1,sy1) = (landscapeX, landscapeY)
(sx2,sy2) = (landscapeX + viewerPanel.getWidth() - 1,
landscapeY + viewerPanel.getHeight() - 1)
```

Assuming the **viewerPanel** hosts a graphics object **g2D**, the source image is copied into the panel using:

```
g2D.drawImage(landscape, 0, 0, viewerPanel.getWidth() -1,
viewerPanel.getHeight() - 1, landscapeX, landscapeY,
landscapeX + viewerPanel.getWidth() - 1, landscapeY +
viewerPanel.getHeight() - 1, null);
```

The viewer display will then appear as:

By varying **landscapeX** and **landscapeY**, the background landscape will appear to move (or scroll) within the viewer panel. So, the question is how do you determine **landscapeX** and **landscapeY** to give the lander this appearance of motion?

We choose to keep the lander image centered within the panel viewer (if possible). Superimposing the viewer panel on the landscape image (also showing the lander in the gray box, we have:

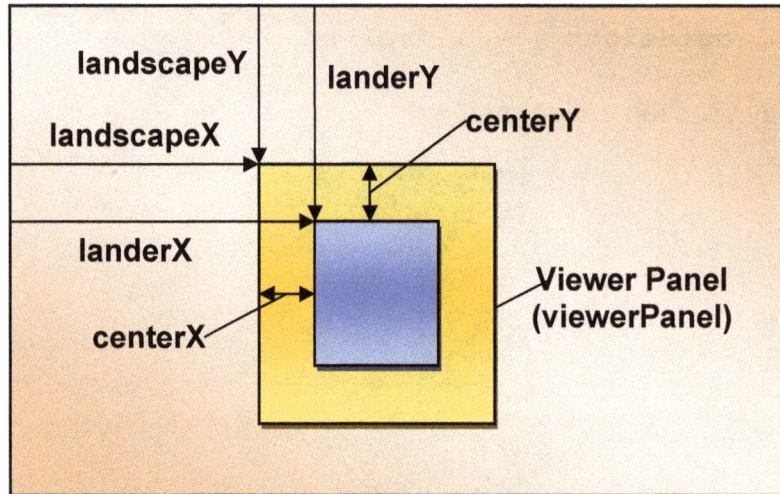

Let's do the math. We have two variables (**centerX** and **centerY**) that specify the distance from the edges of the viewer panel to the lander image to keep the lander centered:

```
centerX = (viewerPanel.getWidth() - landerWidth) / 2;
centerY = (viewerPanel.getHeight() - landerHeight) / 2;
```

With these, the values of **landscapeX** and **landscapeY** (knowing **landerX** and **landerY**) are seen to be:

```
landscapeX = landerX - centerX;
landscapeY = landerY - centerY;
```

So, as the lander moves (varying **landerX** and **landerY**), we compute **landscapeX** and **landscapeY**. This defines the region of the landscape image to copy into the viewer panel to give the scrolling effect.

Notice we said we would center the lander in the viewer panel, <u>if possible</u>. There are four cases where we will not be able to center the lander, each related to being beyond one of the four borders of the landscape image. Let's look at each border and the limiting values of **landscapeX** and **landscapeY**:

Left border, **landscapeX > 0**
Right border, **landscapeX < landscapeWidth – viewerPanel.getWidth()**
Top border, **landscapeY > 0**
Bottom border, **landscapeY < landscapeHeight – viewerPanel.getHeight()**

In these limiting cases, we will relax the need to center the lander and allow it to move freely (sometimes even out of the viewer).

Now, let's code up the scrolling background, then once it's working, we'll add the lander (and the pad and thrust flames). We want the graphics to be persistent, so time to define and add a 'graphics' panel class named **ViewerPanel**:

```
class ViewerPanel extends JPanel
{
  public void paintComponent(Graphics g)
  {
    Graphics2D g2D = (Graphics2D) g;
    super.paintComponent(g2D);
    g2D.drawImage(MoonLanding.landscape, 0, 0, getWidth()
- 1, getHeight() - 1, (int) MoonLanding.landscapeX, (int)
MoonLanding.landscapeY, (int) (MoonLanding.landscapeX +
getWidth() - 1), (int) (MoonLanding.landscapeY +
getHeight() - 1), null);
    g2D.dispose();
  }
}
```

This code uses the **drawImage** method we developed earlier.

Return to the **MoonLanding** class. Change the declaration for **viewerPanel** to:

```
ViewerPanel viewerPanel = new ViewerPanel();
```

Change the declarations for the **landscape Image** object and **landscapeX** and **landscapeY** so they are **static** (they are used in **paintComponent**):

```
static Image landscape;
static double landscapeX, landscapeY;
```

Add the class level declarations for new positioning variables:

```
static double landerXView, landerYView;
double centerX, centerY;
```

landerXView and **landerYView** will be the position of the lander within the viewing region (**centerX** and **centerY**, unless one of the limiting conditions discussed is met).

Add these lines at the end of the frame constructor to compute **centerX** and **centerY** and to make the viewer panel initially invisible so we don't see any graphics features until properly situated:

```
centerX = (viewerPanel.getWidth() - landerWidth) / 2;
centerY = (viewerPanel.getHeight() - landerHeight) / 2;
viewerPanel.setVisible(false);
```

Add a general method (**updateViewer**) where we place the code associated with landing animation. Add this code to the method:

```
private void updateViewer()
{
  // adjust landscape background
  landscapeX = landerX - centerX;
  landerXView = centerX;
  if (landscapeX <= 0)
  {
    landscapeX = 0;
    landerXView = landerX;
  }
  if (landscapeX >= landscapeWidth -
viewerPanel.getWidth())
  {
    landscapeX = landscapeWidth - viewerPanel.getWidth();
    landerXView = landerX - landscapeX;
  }
  landscapeY = landerY - centerY;
  landerYView = centerY;
  if (landscapeY <= 0)
  {
    landscapeY = 0;
    landerYView = landerY;
  }
  if (landscapeY >= landscapeHeight -
viewerPanel.getHeight())
  {
    landscapeY = landscapeHeight -
viewerPanel.getHeight();
    landerYView = landerY - landscapeY;
  }
  // draw landscape
  viewerPanel.repaint();
}
```

The code above determines **landscapeX**, **landscapeY** and **landerXViewer**, **landerYViewer** (being cognizant of the borders), then repaints the viewer panel.

Initialize the viewer and make it visible with the shaded lines in the
startPauseButton ActionPerformed method:

```java
private void startPauseButtonActionPerformed(ActionEvent
e)
{
  if (startPauseButton.getText().equals("Start Game"))
  {
    startPauseButton.setText("Pause Game");
    exitStopButton.setText("Stop Game");

    time = 0.0;
    timeTextField.setText("0.0");
    landerX = (landscapeWidth - landerWidth) *
myRandom.nextDouble();
    landerY = 0;
    landerXSpeed = 0;
    landerYSpeed = 0;
    if (pilotLevel != 1)
      padX = (landscapeWidth - padWidth) *
myRandom.nextDouble();
    else
      padX = (landerX + landerWidth / 2) - padWidth / 2;
    padY = landscapeHeight - padHeight;
    fuelRemaining = maximumFuel;
    fuelProgressBar.setValue(100);
    trajectoryPoints.removeAllElements();
    updateStatus();
    updateTrajectory();
    updateViewer();
    viewerPanel.setVisible(true);
    landingTimer.start();
  }
  else if (startPauseButton.getText().equals("Pause
Game"))
  {
    startPauseButton.setText("Restart Game");
    exitStopButton.setEnabled(false);
    leftThrustButton.setEnabled(false);
    downThrustButton.setEnabled(false);
    rightThrustButton.setEnabled(false);
    landingTimer.stop();
  }
  else
  {
    startPauseButton.setText("Pause Game");
    exitStopButton.setEnabled(true);
```

```
    leftThrustButton.setEnabled(true);
    downThrustButton.setEnabled(true);
    rightThrustButton.setEnabled(true);
    landingTimer.start();
  }
}
```

And, the viewer updates are done in the **landingTimer ActionPerformed** event (add shaded line):

```
private void landingTimerActionPerformed(ActionEvent e)
{
  time += (double) (landingTimer.getDelay()) / 1000;
  timeTextField.setText(new
DecimalFormat("0.00").format(time));
  landerX += landerXSpeed * (double)
(landingTimer.getDelay()) / 1000;
  landerY += landerYSpeed * (double)
(landingTimer.getDelay()) / 1000;
  updateStatus();
  updateTrajectory();
  updateViewer();
  // check for landing
  if (altitude <= 0)
  {
    .

    .

  }
  landerX += landerXSpeed;
  landerY += landerYSpeed;
  // horizontal drag
  if (landerXSpeed > 0)
    landerXSpeed -= drag;
  else if (landerXSpeed < 0)
    landerXSpeed += drag;
  // gravity
  landerYSpeed += gravity * (double)
(landingTimer.getDelay()) / 1000;
}
```

Save and run the game. Choose a pilot level, click **Start Game**. As you move the lander around using thrusters, the landscape will now scroll. Here's what my form looks like after crashing:

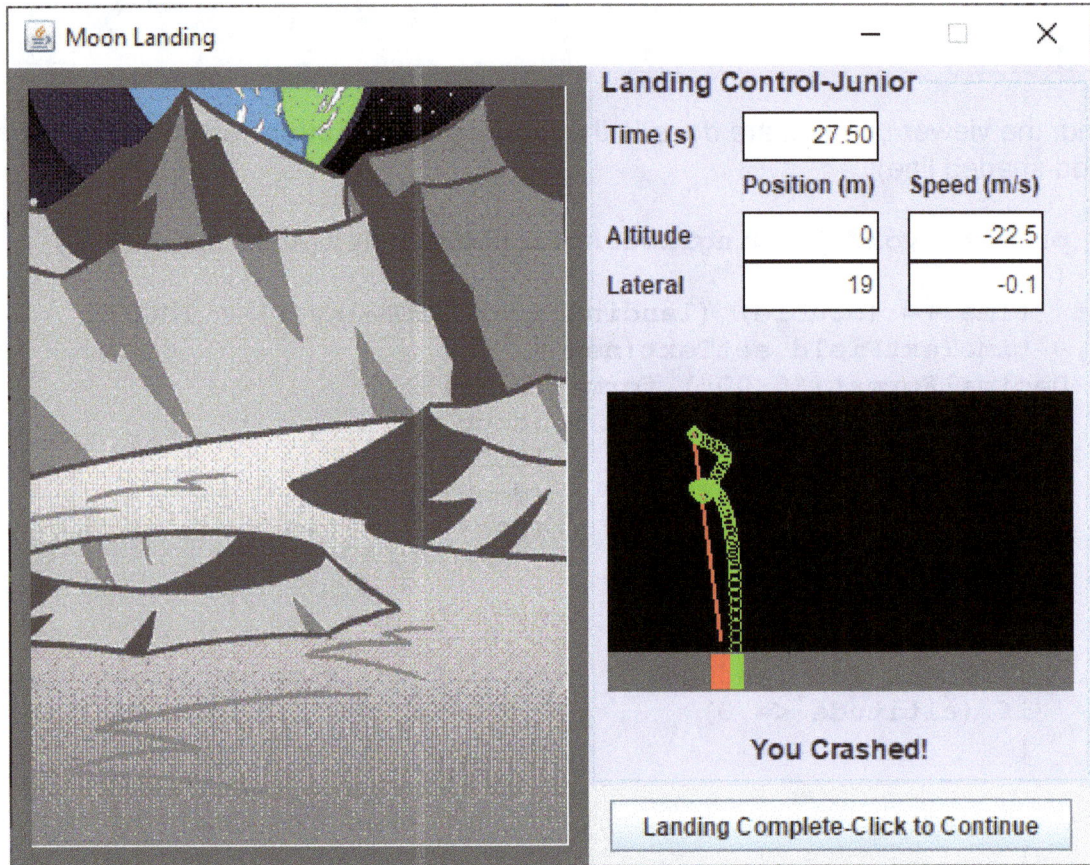

After lots of explanation, you should see that the scrolling is really fairly simple. We can finish the animation now by adding other graphic elements – the lander, the pad and the thruster flames.

Sprite Animation

We complete the animation by adding the **lander** image and other graphic elements to the viewer panel. Recall the lander image appears as:

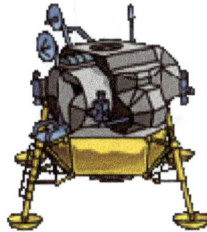

We use another version of the **drawImage** graphics method to place this on the background image in the viewer panel. If the viewer panel graphics object is **g2D**, we use:

```
g2D.drawImage(lander, x, y, w, h, null);
```

In this method, the lander image will be positioned at (**x, y**) with width **w** and height **h**. The width and height arguments are optional and can be the original image size or scaled up or down. It's your choice. To draw the image at (**x, y**) in its original size, simply use:

```
g2D.drawImage(lander, x, y, null);
```

A picture illustrates what's going on with **drawImage**:

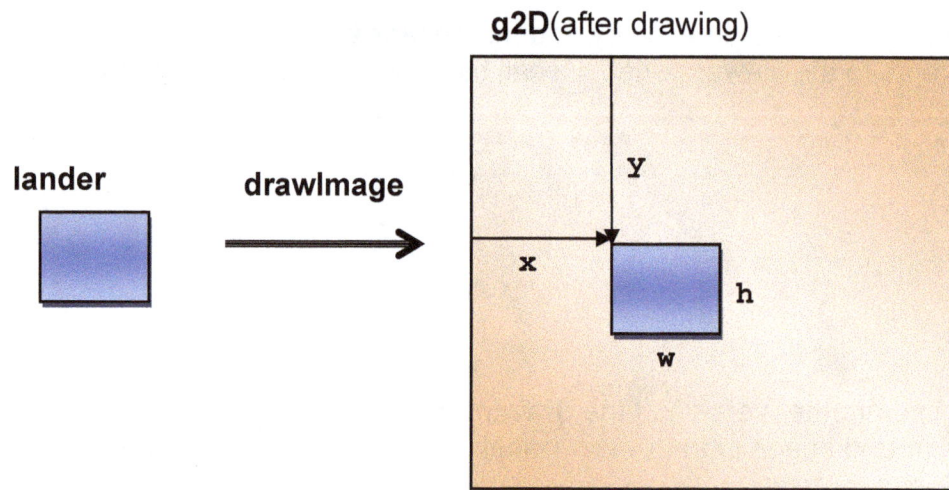

g2D(after drawing)

lander   drawImage

Note how the transfer of the rectangular region occurs. Successive transfers gives the impression of motion, or animation. Recall **w** and **h** in the graphics object do not have to necessarily match the width and height of the **image** object. Scaling (up or down) is possible.

If you copy the lander onto the landscape background using the **drawImage** method, the lander will be there, but the background will be black, obliterating any part of the landscape behind it. We want whatever background the lander is over to "come through." To do this, we want to define the black color in the background to be transparent. Let's look at two ways of doing this.

Many graphics programs allow you to define a color within a **gif** image to be transparent. A program I use to do this is Corel's Paint Shop Pro. If you have such software, you can load the lander, pad and thrust images and define the black background to be transparent, the resave the images.

We'll take another approach - using Java code to define an image with a transparent color. Doing an Internet search turned up this cool Java class (**Transparency.java**, saved in the **\KidGamesJava\KidGamesJava Projects** folder):

```
/*
 *   From:
 *http://www.rgagnon.com/javadetails/java-0265.html
 *
 */

import java.awt.*;
import java.awt.image.*;
```

```
public class Transparency
{
  public static Image makeColorTransparent(Image im, final
Color color)
  {
    ImageFilter filter = new RGBImageFilter()
    {
      // the color we are looking for... Alpha bits are
set to opaque
      public int markerRGB = color.getRGB() | 0xFF000000;
      public final int filterRGB(int x, int y, int rgb)
      {
        if ( ( rgb | 0xFF000000 ) == markerRGB )
        {
          // Mark the alpha bits as zero - transparent
          return 0x00FFFFFF & rgb;
        }
        else
        {
          // nothing to do
          return rgb;
        }
      }
    };
    ImageProducer ip = new
FilteredImageSource(im.getSource(), filter);
    return Toolkit.getDefaultToolkit().createImage(ip);
  }
}
```

This **Transparency** class allows the creation of an **Image** object with a transparent color. Look through the code if you'd like. It does some 'bitwise' math to define a transparent color in an image.

Add **Transparency.java** to your project's source folder (add a line at the top that says `package moonlanding;`)

To use the **Transparency** class, assume you have an image (**myImage**) with a background color (**myColor**) you want changed to transparent. The following line of code will return the same image, with the input background color set to transparent (**myTransparentImage**):

```
myTransparentImage =
Transparency.makeColorTransparent(myImage, myColor);
```

We have noted one problem with using the **Transparency** class. Though the returned image retains the size of the original image, It seems to destroy **width** and **height** information. So, to obtain the width and height of your image, always refer to the original image.

One question is lingering – how do you determine the desired color to make transparent? In our lander example, it is black, or appears to be, but that's not a real definite specification. The argument used in the **makeColorTransparent** method must be a Java **Color** object, using values for the red, green and blue contributions. How do you come up with such values? I'll give you one approach using the lander image as an example.

Here's a snippet of code to identify the background color in the lander image (I also found this code on the Internet – there's lots of neat code out there):

```
Image landerTemp= new ImageIcon("lander.gif").getImage();
BufferedImage landerTempB = new
BufferedImage(landerTemp.getWidth(null),
landerTemp.getHeight(null), BufferedImage.TYPE_INT_RGB);
// Copy image to buffered image
Graphics g = landerTempB.createGraphics();
// Paint the image onto the buffered image
g.drawImage(landerTemp, 0, 0, null);
int c = landerTempB.getRGB(0, 0);
int  red = (c & 0x00ff0000) >> 16;
int  green = (c & 0x0000ff00) >> 8;
int  blue = c & 0x000000ff;
System.out.println("red " + red);
System.out.println("green " + green);
System.out.println("blue " + blue);
```

First, the lander image is loaded from its file. Next, the **Image** object (**landerTemp**) is converted to a **BufferedImage** object (**landerTempB**). We can determine the color of individual pixels in such objects. That is what is done in the remaining lines of code – we read the color, using **getRGB**, of the pixel in the upper left corner of **landerTempB** (part of the background), convert it to its red, green and blue components and print these to the output window.

To use this code, you need to add this import statement:

```
import java.awt.image.BufferedImage;
```

Running this snippet results in:

```
General Output
-----------------------Configuration: Moc
red 0
green 0
blue 0

Process completed.
```

This tells us the red, green and blue contributions are each 0. Hence, the transparent background color can be represented by:

```
new Color(0, 0, 0)
```

This is the color argument (black, by the way) we would use in the **makeColorTransparent** method to make the background of the lander (and, later the pad and thruster flames) transparent. Let's add these images to the viewer panel.

Code Design – Lander Animation

Placing the lander, pad and thrust graphics in the viewer panel is straightforward once we know the background color. Add these lines in the main class frame constructor code (after the code reading in the **Image** objects and determining widths and heights of each):

```
lander = Transparency.makeColorTransparent(lander, new
Color(0, 0, 0));
pad = Transparency.makeColorTransparent(pad, new Color(0,
0, 0));
hThrust = Transparency.makeColorTransparent(hThrust, new
Color(0, 0, 0));
vThrust = Transparency.makeColorTransparent(vThrust, new
Color(0, 0, 0));
```

These lines create new versions of the **Image** objects with transparent backgrounds.

The animation code goes in panel's **paintComponent** method. Main class variables will be needed in this method to do the animation. Modify the declarations for these variables to be **static**:

```
static Image lander;
static Image pad;
static Image hThrust;
static Image vThrust;
static int hThrustWidth, hThrustHeight;
static int vThrustWidth, vThrustHeight;
```

To add thruster graphics to the animation, we need to know if thrust is being applied. Define three class level boolean variables (make them **static** since they will be used for drawing) that will tell us if thrust is on:

```
static boolean vThrustOn, lThrustOn, rThrustOn;
```

Then, in each of the corresponding thrust control button **ActionPerformed** methods, set the value of these variables (shaded lines):

```
private void downThrustButtonActionPerformed(ActionEvent
e)
{
  if (fuelRemaining > 0)
  {
    vThrustOn = true;
    vThrustSound.play();
    if (pilotLevel != 5)
      landerYSpeed -= yDelta;
    else
      landerYSpeed -= 2.0 * yDelta *
myRandom.nextDouble();
    if (pilotLevel > 3)
      fuelRemaining -= vFuel;
  }
}

private void leftThrustButtonActionPerformed(ActionEvent e)
  {
  if (fuelRemaining > 0)
  {
    lThrustOn = true;
    hThrustSound.play();
    if (pilotLevel != 5)
      landerXSpeed += xDelta;
    else
      landerXSpeed += 2.0 * xDelta *
MyRandom.nextDouble();
    if (pilotLevel > 3)
      fuelRemaining -= hFuel;
  }
}
```

```java
private void rightThrustButtonActionPerformed(ActionEvent
e)
{
  if (fuelRemaining > 0)
  {
    rThrustOn = true;
    hThrustSound.play();
    if (pilotLevel != 5)
      landerXSpeed -= xDelta;
    else
      landerXSpeed -= 2.0 * xDelta *
myRandom.nextDouble();
    if (pilotLevel > 3)
      fuelRemaining -= hFuel;
  }
}
```

Upon landing, we want to make sure the thrusters are off. Add the shaded code change to the **landingTimer ActionPerformed** method:

```
private void landingTimerActionPerformed(ActionEvent e)
{
  time += (double) (landingTimer.getDelay()) / 1000;
  timeTextField.setText(new
DecimalFormat("0.00").format(time));
  landerX += landerXSpeed * (double)
(landingTimer.getDelay()) / 1000;
  landerY += landerYSpeed * (double)
(landingTimer.getDelay()) / 1000;
  updateStatus();
  updateTrajectory();
  updateViewer();
  // check for landing
  if (altitude <= 0)
  {
      vThrustOn = false;
      lThrustOn = false;
      rThrustOn = false;
      updateViewer();
    .
    .
    .
  }
  landerX += landerXSpeed;
  landerY += landerYSpeed;
  // horizontal drag
  if (landerXSpeed > 0)
    landerXSpeed -= drag;
  else if (landerXSpeed < 0)
    landerXSpeed += drag;
  // gravity
  landerYSpeed += gravity * (double)
(landingTimer.getDelay()) / 1000;
}
```

Note we need to update the viewer panel after turning the thrusters off to make sure they do not appear.

Now, make the shaded changes to the **viewerPanel paintComponent** method to draw the lander, the pad and the thrusts (when on):

```
public void paintComponent(Graphics g)
{
  Graphics2D g2D = (Graphics2D) g;
  super.paintComponent(g2D);
  g2D.drawImage(MoonLanding.landscape, 0, 0, getWidth() -
1, getHeight() - 1, (int) MoonLanding.landscapeX, (int)
MoonLanding.landscapeY, (int) (MoonLanding.landscapeX +
getWidth() - 1), (int) (MoonLanding.landscapeY +
getHeight() - 1), null);
  // add pad
  g2D.drawImage(MoonLanding.pad, (int) (MoonLanding.padX -
MoonLanding.landscapeX), (int) (MoonLanding.padY -
MoonLanding.landscapeY), null);
  // add lander
  g2D.drawImage(MoonLanding.lander, (int)
MoonLanding.landerXView, (int) MoonLanding.landerYView,
null);
  //add thrusters if on
  if (MoonLanding.vThrustOn)      {
    g2D.drawImage(MoonLanding.vThrust, (int)
(MoonLanding.landerXView + 0.5 * MoonLanding.landerWidth -
0.5 * MoonLanding.vThrustWidth), (int)
(MoonLanding.landerYView + MoonLanding.landerHeight -
MoonLanding.vThrustHeight), null);
    MoonLanding.vThrustOn = false;
  }
  if (MoonLanding.lThrustOn)
  {
    g2D.drawImage(MoonLanding.hThrust, (int)
(MoonLanding.landerXView - 5), (int)
(MoonLanding.landerYView + 40), null);
    MoonLanding.lThrustOn = false;
  }
  if (MoonLanding.rThrustOn)
  {
    g2D.drawImage(MoonLanding.hThrust, (int)
(MoonLanding.landerXView + MoonLanding.landerWidth -
MoonLanding.hThrustWidth + 5), (int)
(MoonLanding.landerYView + 40), null);
    MoonLanding.rThrustOn = false;
  }
  g2D.dispose();
}
```

We first place the pad at (**padX – landscapeX**, **padY – landscapeY**), its position within the viewer panel. We add the landing pad even though it may not be seen in the viewer. Then the lander image is placed in the viewer. We add the pad before the lander so the lander will be 'on top' of the pad graphic. Lastly, each of the thrust images are added to the viewer (if the corresponding thruster is on). The locations of the thrust images relative to the lander were obtained by trial and error.

Save and run the project. Pick **Junior** pilot level. Start a game. Immediately click **Pause Game**. Here's my screen:

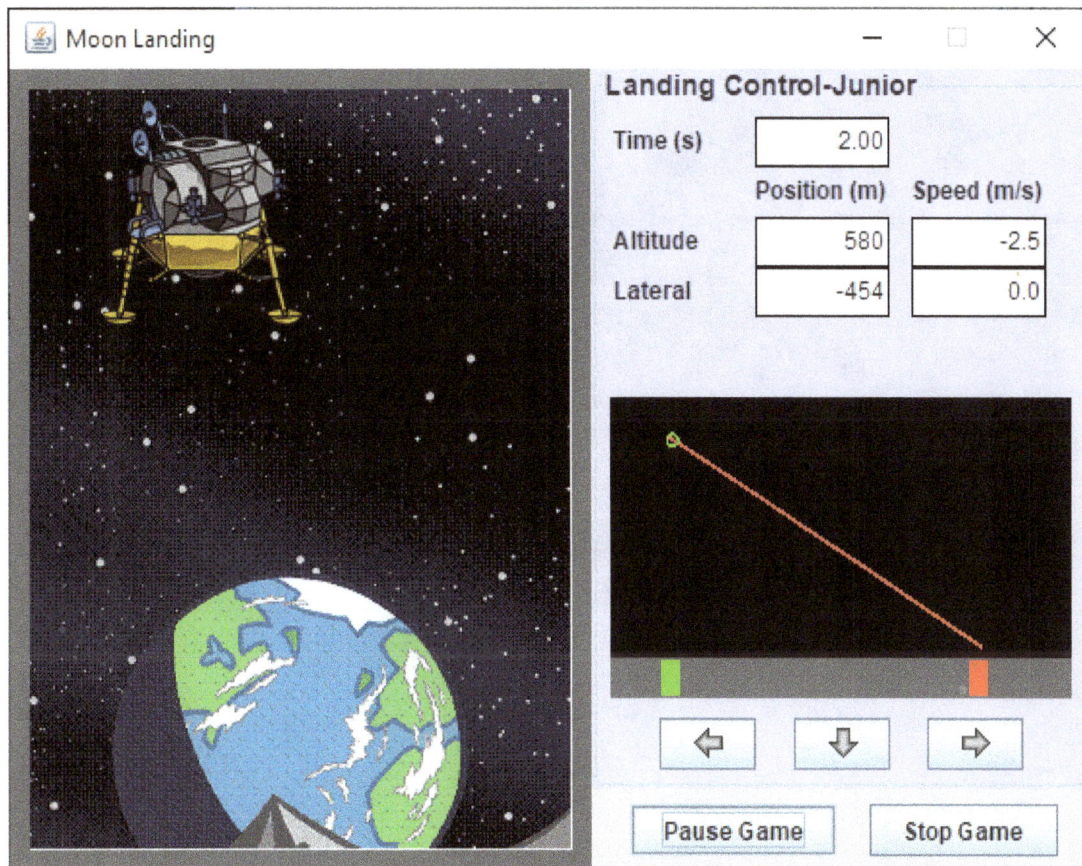

Notice the lander is <u>not</u> centered in the viewer panel. This is because the landscape is at its upper limit (**landscapeY = 0**). Click **Restart Game**. Let the lander drop. Try the thrusters. Pause the game again once the lander appears in the middle of the viewer.

You should now see a very nice animation of the landing process. Here's my screen:

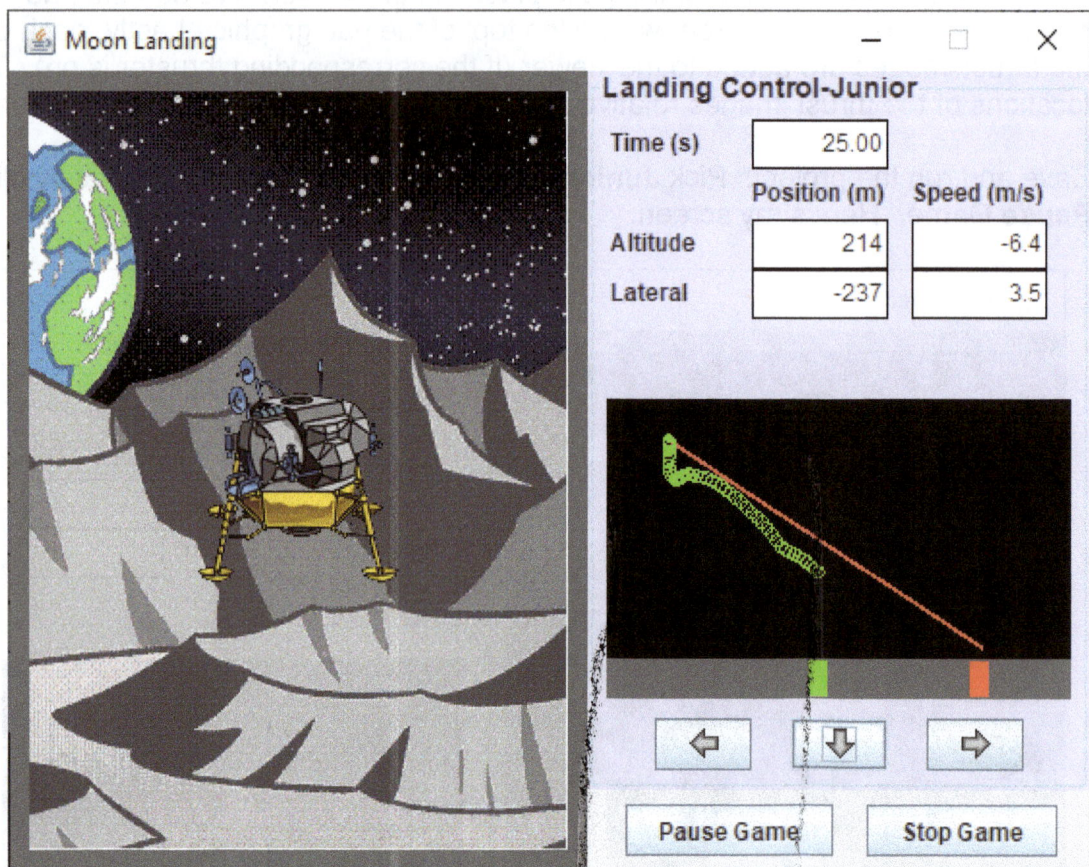

Continue toward the pad. As the lander nears the pad, it will no longer be centered in the panel since the landscape is near its lower limit. Here's my screen right before a crash landing:

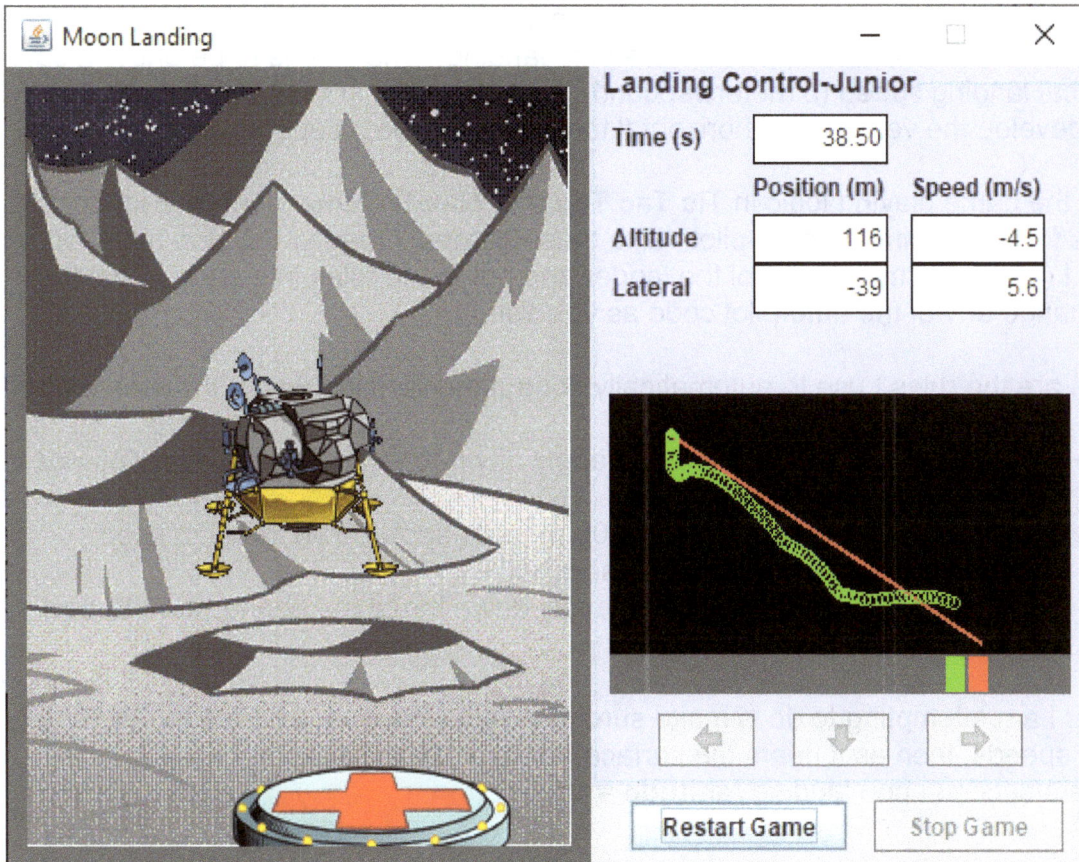

I think you'll agree you have a nice game by now. The graphics effects are pretty amazing! We need one last change to make it complete. We need to code the auto-pilot option.

Code Design - Autopilot

The auto-pilot option allows you to see how the computer controls the lander as it descends to the moon. With auto-pilot, the computer controls the horizontal and vertical thrusters in attempt to make a safe landing. The goal is to be under a safe vertical landing speed (3 meters/second), while being near the landing pad. We will develop the vertical and horizontal thruster auto-pilots separately.

Like the game playing logic in **Tic Tac Toe** and **Match Game**, there are no rigid rules for developing an auto-pilot. Like those games, I tried to develop rules for how I (a human) might control the lander and put those rules into code. Feel free to change any of the auto-pilot code as you see fit.

Here are the rules I use to automatically control the vertical (down) thruster control:

> ➢ If **altitude** is above 300 meters, apply down thrust to keep **landerYSpeed** under 12 meters/second.
> ➢ If **altitude** is between 100 and 300 meters, apply down thrust to keep **landerYSpeed** under 6 meters/second.
> ➢ If **altitude** is under 100 meters, apply down thrust to keep **landerYSpeed** under **2 + 0.04 * altitude**.

What I am attempting to do is make sure the lander never accelerates to extremely high speeds, then as it nears the surface, ramp down the speed to have it near 2 meters/second upon landing (**altitude = 0**).

The code for the vertical auto-pilot is placed in the **landingTimer ActionPerformed** event. The additions are noted by the shaded code:

```
private void landingTimerActionPerformed(ActionEvent e)
{
  time += (double) (landingTimer.getDelay()) / 1000;
  timeTextField.setText(new
DecimalFormat("0.00").format(time));
  landerX += landerXSpeed * (double)
(landingTimer.getDelay()) / 1000;
  landerY += landerYSpeed * (double)
(landingTimer.getDelay()) / 1000;
  updateStatus();
  updateTrajectory();
  updateViewer();
  // check for landing
  if (altitude <= 0)
  {
    .
    .
    .
  }
  // autopilot or Novice level - adjust vertical thrust
  if (autoPilotCheckBox.isSelected() || pilotLevel == 2)
  {
    if (altitude > 300)
    {
      if (landerYSpeed > 12)
        downThrustButton.doClick();
    }
    else if (altitude > 100)
    {
      if (landerYSpeed > 6)
        downThrustButton.doClick();
    }
    else
    {
      if (landerYSpeed > (2 + 0.04 * altitude))
        downThrustButton.doClick();
    }
  }
  landerX += landerXSpeed;
  landerY += landerYSpeed;
  // horizontal drag
  if (landerXSpeed > 0)
    landerXSpeed -= drag;
  else if (landerXSpeed < 0)
    landerXSpeed += drag;
```

```
  // gravity
  landerYSpeed += gravity * (double)
(landingTimer.getDelay()) / 1000;
}
```

In this new code, when the computer needs to apply thrust, it performs a **doClick** method on the corresponding thrust button. Notice we use this auto-pilot when the auto-pilot check box is checked <u>and</u> when **pilotLevel = 2** (when you, the human, only control horizontal thrust).

Save and run the project. Select **Beginner** pilot level. Select the **Auto-Pilot On** option. Click **Start Game**. The computer takes over (the first burst of thrust will occur when the downward speed exceeds 12 meters/sec) and brings the lander to a safe landing:

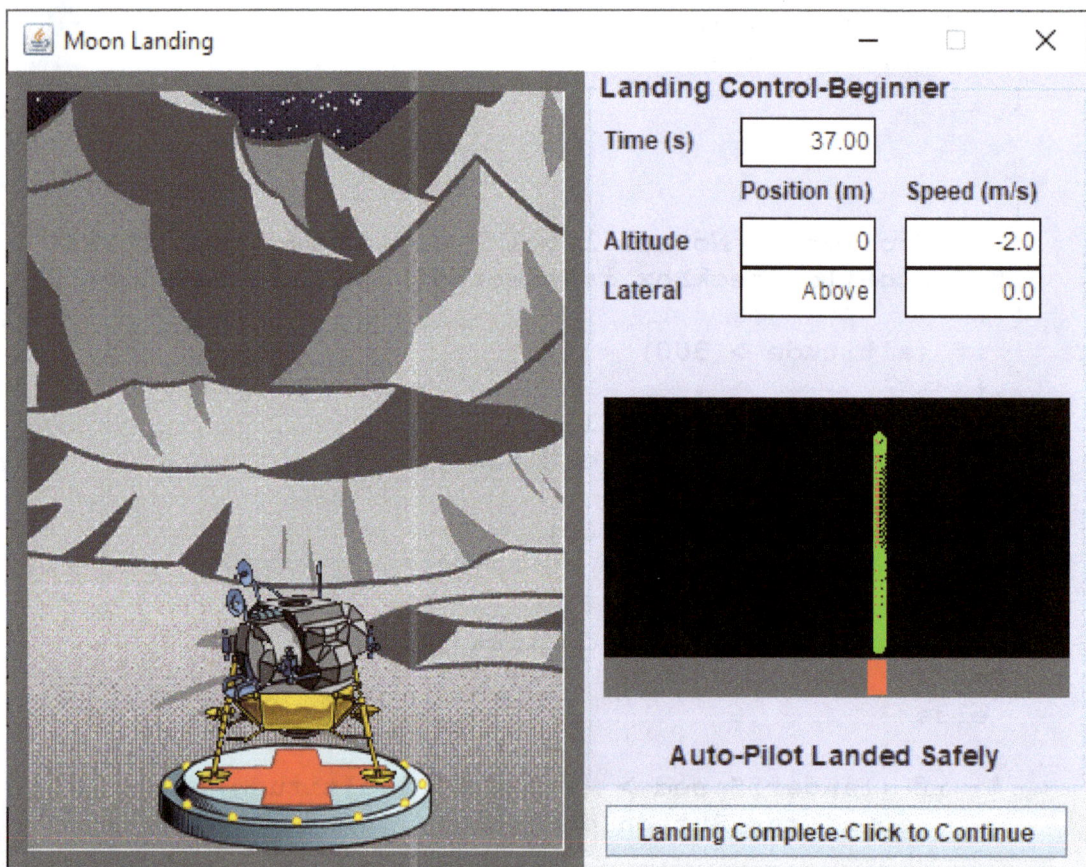

Run the game again, this time with **Novice** pilot level and auto-pilot off. Make sure the computer provides the needed vertical thrust as you control the horizontal thrust. Here's my run with **Novice** level (not a bad job):

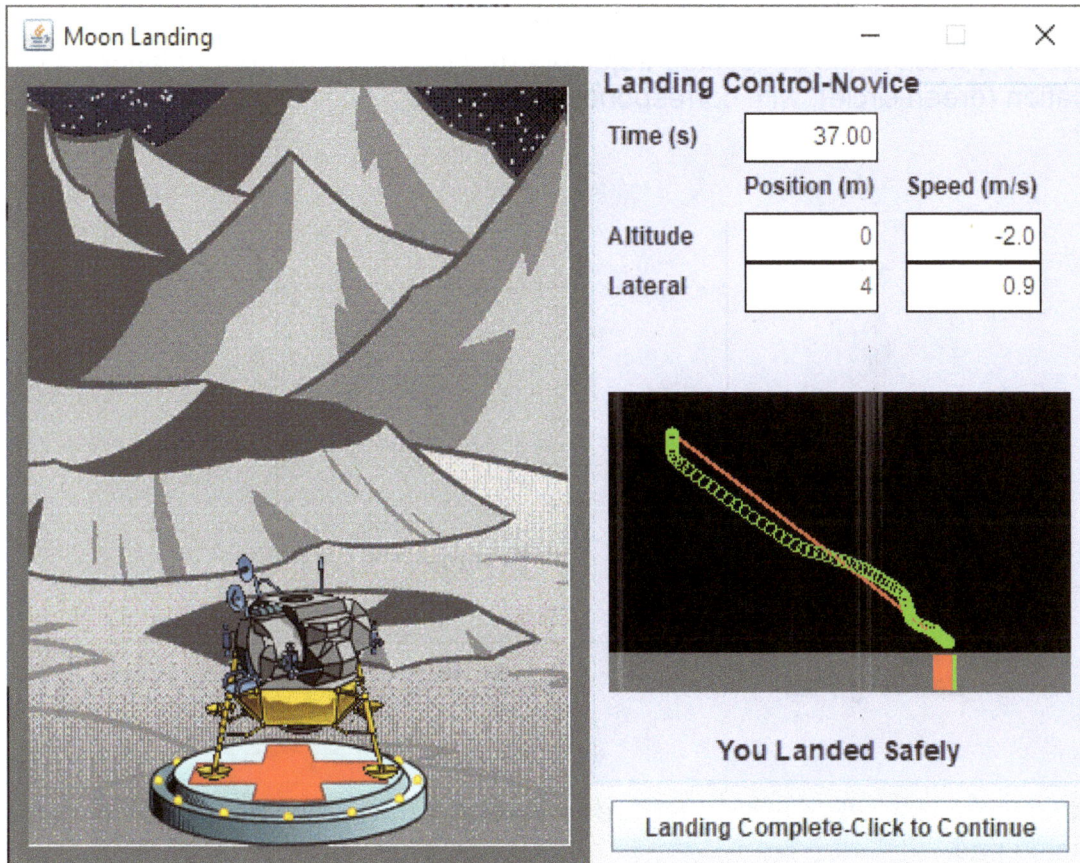

Now, let's complete this game with some automatic horizontal thrust control.

To automatically control the horizontal thrusters, we will use the suggested path (the red line) drawn in the trajectory panel. The idea is to apply thrust such that the lander stays near this path, leading to the landing pad. Engineers call this approach "**trajectory following**." Let the altitude at **time = 0.0** be **altitude0** and the corresponding lateral distance be **lateral0** (the starting point on the trajectory). Here's a sketch of the suggested trajectory (red line) and the current lander location (green circle), with corresponding variables:

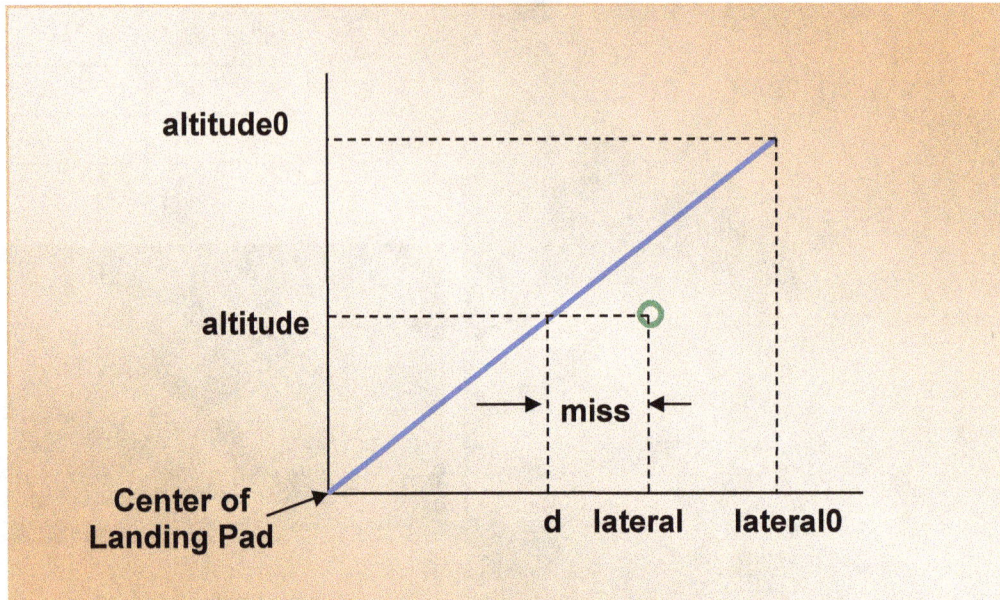

In this graph, the origin (where **altitude = lateral = 0**) represents the center of the landing pad.

In this sketch, the lander lateral position is **lateral**, yet we want it to be **d**, the point on the trajectory line corresponding to the lander altitude (**altitude**). We define a "miss" distance (**miss**) as:

```
miss = lateral - d;
```

Using the idea of similar triangles, we can write:

```
d / lateral0 = altitude / altitude0
```

Or

```
d = lateral0 * (altitude / altitude0);
```

Then, the **miss** distance is:

```
miss = lateral - lateral0 * (altitude / altitude0);
```

If **miss** is a positive number, we want the lander to move to the left (or apply right thrust). Conversely, is **miss** is negative, we want the lander to move to the right (or apply left thrust). A good question to ask is how big does **miss** need to be before applying thrust? Zero would not be a good answer. In such a case, the right thruster would move the lander to the left of the path, then the left thruster would move it back to the right. The horizontal thrusters would just keep alternating, burning lots of fuel. In our game, we will not apply any horizontal thrust until the lander is at least two meters away from the suggested trajectory path.

As an aside, this is similar to logic used in the thermostat used to heat your home. When the temperature is lower than the thermostat setting, the furnace is turned on. When the temperature exceeds the setting, the furnace is turned off. But, the furnace doesn't turn on if the temperature is just below the setting. It waits until the temperature difference (**miss**) is about 2 degrees or so. The same difference in temperature is used before turning the furnace back off. This keeps your furnace from just cycling on and off.

Let's code the final element of the **Moon Landing** game – the horizontal auto-pilot. Add this class level declaration for the three new variables:

```
double altitude0, lateral0, miss;
```

The initial altitude and lateral distance are established in the **updateTrajectory** general method (shaded changes):

```
private void updateTrajectory()
{
  if (time == 0.0)
  {
    landerX0 = landerX;
    landerY0 = landerY;
    altitude0 = altitude;
    lateral0 = lateral;
  }
  trajectoryPoints.add(new Point2D.Double(landerX +
landerWidth / 2 , landerY + landerHeight));
  trajectoryPanel.repaint();
}
```

The code for the horizontal auto-pilot is placed under the vertical auto-pilot code in the **landingTimer ActionPerformed** method. The additions are noted by the shaded code:

```
private void landingTimerActionPerformed(ActionEvent e)
{
  time += (double) (landingTimer.getDelay()) / 1000;
  timeTextField.setText(new
DecimalFormat("0.00").format(time));
  landerX += landerXSpeed * (double)
(landingTimer.getDelay()) / 1000;
  landerY += landerYSpeed * (double)
(landingTimer.getDelay()) / 1000;
  updateStatus();
  updateTrajectory();
  updateViewer();
  // check for landing
  if (altitude <= 0)
  {
    .
    .
  }
  // autopilot or Novice level - adjust vertical thrust
  if (autoPilotCheckBox.isSelected() || pilotLevel == 2)
  {
```

```
  if (altitude > 300)
  {
    if (landerYSpeed > 12)
      downThrustButton.doClick();
  }
  else if (altitude > 100)
  {
    if (landerYSpeed > 6)
      downThrustButton.doClick();
  }
  else
  {
    if (landerYSpeed > (2 + 0.04 * altitude))
      downThrustButton.doClick();
  }
}
// autopilot - adjust horizontal thrust
if (autoPilotCheckBox.isSelected())
{
  miss = lateral - altitude * (lateral0 / altitude0);
  if (miss > 2)
    rightThrustButton.doClick();
   else if (miss < -2)
    leftThrustButton.doClick();
}
landerX += landerXSpeed;
landerY += landerYSpeed;
// horizontal drag
if (landerXSpeed > 0)
  landerXSpeed -= drag;
else if (landerXSpeed < 0)
  landerXSpeed += drag;
// gravity
landerYSpeed += gravity * (double)
(landingTimer.getDelay()) / 1000;
}
```

Save the project one last time. Run the project. Select **Senior** pilot level, and turn **Auto-Pilot On**. Here's the game after 8.5 seconds of running (I paused at this point):

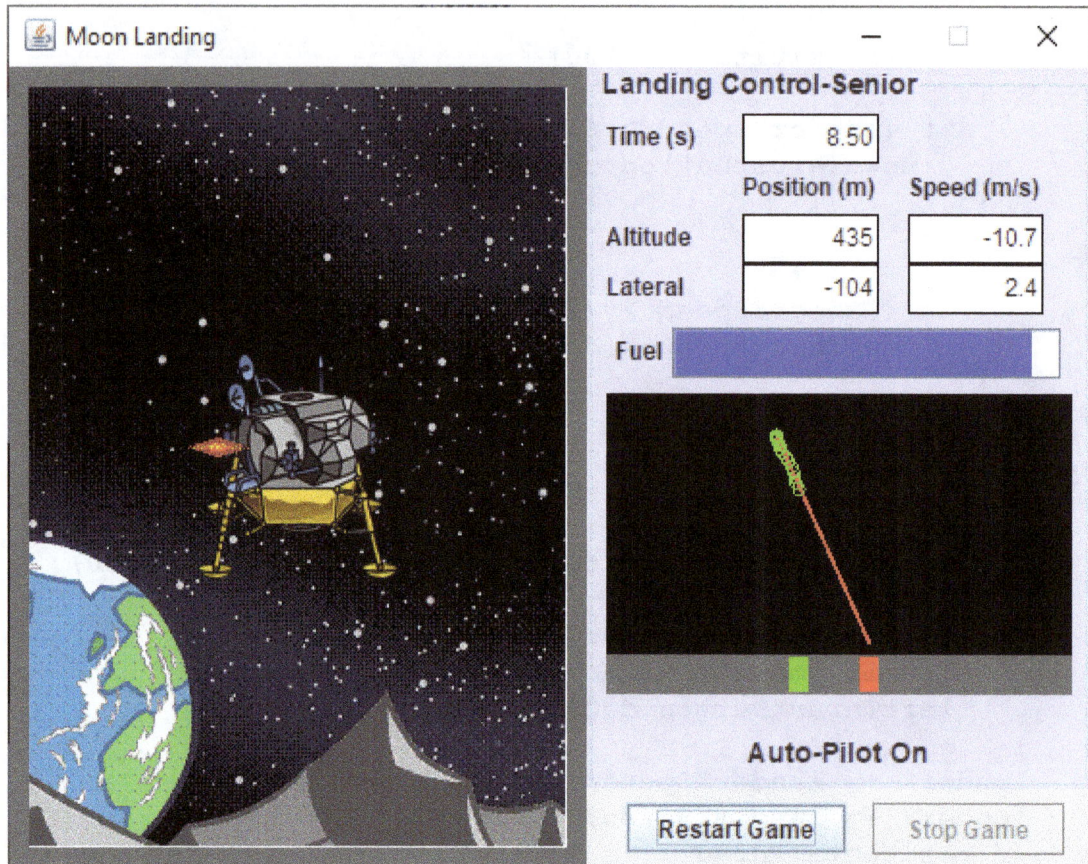

The auto-pilot is applying some left thrust, accelerating the lander to a lateral speed of 2.4 meters/second, moving the lander toward the trajectory line (see trajectory panel).

Here's the screen after 19.5 seconds:

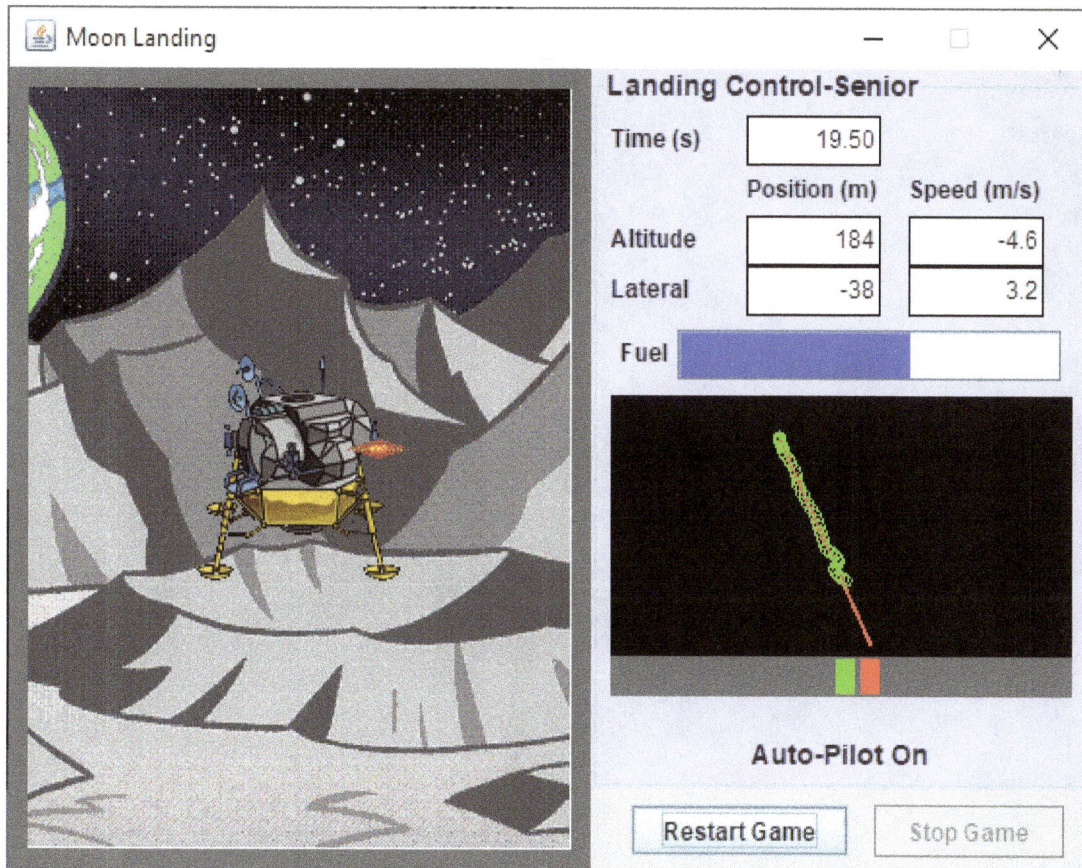

The computer has applied several bursts of vertical thrust to keep the lander vertical speed reasonable and used a few horizontal thrusts to keep the lander near the desired trajectory.

Now, at 26.0 seconds:

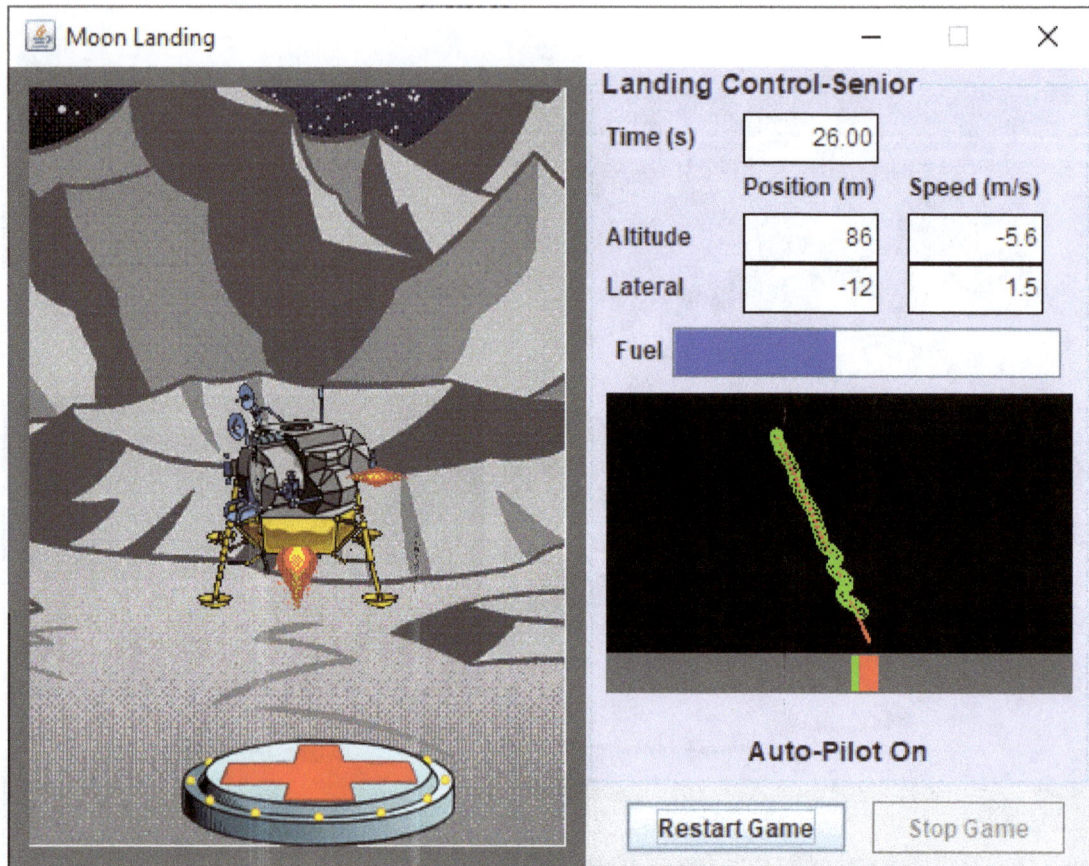

The computer is still giving thrust adjustments to finalize landing. The pad is nearby and things are looking good.

Finally, at 37.0 seconds, the lander is safely on the pad:

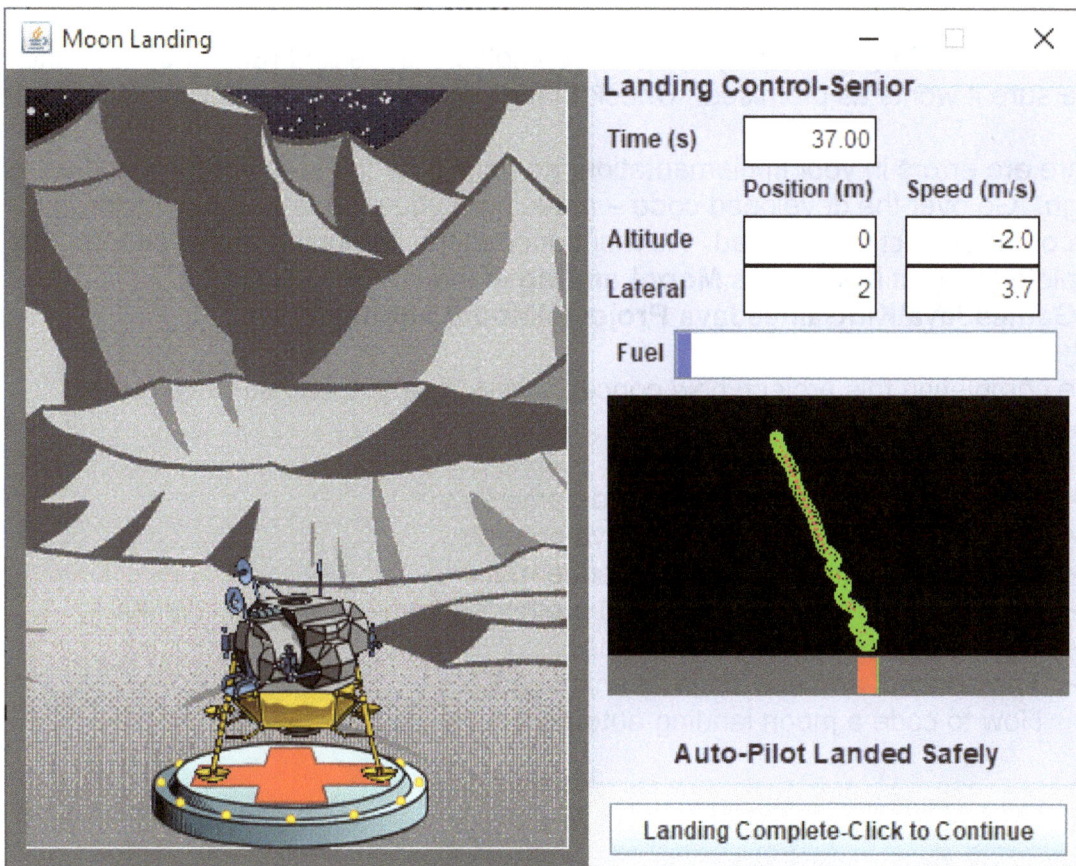

A near perfect landing under the safe landing speed of -2.0 m/s and almost right on top of the pad. Click the button at the bottom if you want to play again.

The game is now complete. As you play, it will become obvious that there are many ways to obtain a safe landing with the vehicle. Without a fuel constraint, you can take forever to land. A more interesting problem is to try to land as fast as possible. This is the so-called **minimum time problem**. Or try to land using the least fuel possible - an important problem in space travel where you don't want to launch a lot of unnecessary weight.

Try a so-called '**coast and burn**' approach. That is, let your lander keep dropping until some point where you apply nearly constant vertical thrust until landed. This approach needs to be used in space vehicles where thrusters can only be turned on, but never off (like solid rocket motors).

Moon Landing Project Review

The **Moon Landing** game project is now complete. Save and run the project and make sure it works as promised. Check that all options work correctly.

If there are errors in your implementation, go back over the steps of form and code design. Go over the developed code – make sure you understand how different parts of the project were coded. As mentioned in the beginning of this chapter, the completed project is saved as **MoonLanding** in the **\KidGamesJava\KidGamesJava Projects\MoonLanding** folder.

While completing this project, new concepts and skills you should have gained include:

> ➢ Proper steps in game design and game flow.
> ➢ Capabilities and use of many Java controls.
> ➢ Use of math and physics to describe motion.
> ➢ How to use graphics objects and methods to draw lines and ellipses.
> ➢ How to use scrolling backgrounds.
> ➢ The concept and use of sprite animation.
> ➢ How to code a moon landing auto-pilot.

Moon Landing Project Improvements

There are some ways to change the **Moon Landing** project. Some possibilities are:

> ➤ It would be nice if the options selections you make are saved from one game to the next. This requires the use of files which are discussed in the next chapter.
> ➤ Add more elaborate graphic effects upon crash landings.
> ➤ Add keyboard control for the thrusters (this is discussed in the next chapter).
> ➤ Add a way to graphically see how close you are to a safe landing speed (rather than just display the number).
> ➤ As implemented, you may notice a bit of a delay between hearing a thruster and seeing the graphic display. This delay is because the sound and drawing of the thrust are in two different methods. I kind of like the delay – you hear the sound, then pretty soon the flames start flying. If the delay bothers you, try to put the sound and graphics in the same routine.
> ➤ The current game gives minimal evaluation of the landing, just checking to see if the vertical speed is acceptable. Expand the definition of a safe landing to include horizontal position and speed. You might like to add some comments. In the original text versions of this game, comments on the landing were quite cynical. Some example comments for bad landings from these old programs are:

> "Sorry, there were no survivors – you blew it!"
> "Appropriate condolences will be sent to your next of kin."
> "The space program hates to lose experienced astronauts."

Moon Landing Project Java Code Listing

There are two files, **MoonLanding.java** and **Transparency.java**.

MoonLanding.java:

```java
/*
 * MoonLanding.java
 */
package moonlanding;
import javax.swing.*;
import java.awt.*;
import java.awt.event.*;
import java.text.*;
import java.util.Random;
import java.net.URL;
import java.applet.*;
import java.awt.geom.*;
import java.util.Vector;

public class MoonLanding extends JFrame
{

    JPanel framePanel = new JPanel();
    ViewerPanel viewerPanel = new ViewerPanel();

    JPanel controlPanel = new JPanel();
    JLabel timeLabel = new JLabel();
    JTextField timeTextField = new JTextField();
    JLabel positionLabel = new JLabel();
    JLabel speedLabel = new JLabel();
    JLabel altitudeLabel = new JLabel();
    JTextField altitudePositionTextField = new JTextField();
    JTextField altitudeSpeedTextField = new JTextField();
    JLabel lateralLabel = new JLabel();
    JTextField lateralPositionTextField = new JTextField();
    JTextField lateralSpeedTextField = new JTextField();
    JPanel fuelPanel = new JPanel();
    TrajectoryPanel trajectoryPanel = new TrajectoryPanel();
    GuidePanel guidePanel = new GuidePanel();
    JButton leftThrustButton = new JButton(new
ImageIcon("leftarrow.gif"));
    JButton downThrustButton = new JButton(new
ImageIcon("downarrow.gif"));
    JButton rightThrustButton = new JButton(new
ImageIcon("rightarrow.gif"));
```

```
JLabel messageLabel = new JLabel();
JLabel fuelLabel = new JLabel();
JProgressBar fuelProgressBar = new JProgressBar();
JButton startPauseButton = new JButton();
JButton exitStopButton = new JButton();
JButton completeButton = new JButton();

JPanel optionsPanel = new JPanel();
JPanel pilotPanel = new JPanel();
JPanel unitsPanel = new JPanel();
ButtonGroup pilotButtonGroup = new ButtonGroup();
JRadioButton beginnerRadioButton = new JRadioButton();
JRadioButton noviceRadioButton = new JRadioButton();
JRadioButton juniorRadioButton = new JRadioButton();
JRadioButton seniorRadioButton = new JRadioButton();
JRadioButton advancedRadioButton = new JRadioButton();
JCheckBox autoPilotCheckBox = new JCheckBox();
ButtonGroup unitsButtonGroup = new ButtonGroup();
JRadioButton metricRadioButton = new JRadioButton();
JRadioButton usRadioButton = new JRadioButton();
Timer landingTimer;

Color lightBlue = new Color(208, 208, 255);

int pilotLevel = 1;
double multiplier = 1.0;
double time;
static double landerX, landerY;
static double landerX0, landerY0;
double landerXSpeed, landerYSpeed;
static double padX, padY;
double altitude, lateral;
Random myRandom = new Random();

static Image landscape;
static Image lander;
static Image pad;
static Image hThrust;
static Image vThrust;

static int landscapeWidth, landscapeHeight;
static int landerWidth, landerHeight;
static int padWidth, padHeight;
static int hThrustWidth, hThrustHeight;
static int vThrustWidth, vThrustHeight;
double fuelRemaining;
static Vector trajectoryPoints = new Vector(50, 10);
```

```java
static double landscapeX, landscapeY;
static double landerXView, landerYView;
double centerX, centerY;
static boolean vThrustOn, lThrustOn, rThrustOn;
double altitude0, lateral0, miss;


final double xDelta = 1.2;
final double yDelta = 2.4;
final double gravity = 9.8 / 6.0;
final double drag = 0.1;
final double safeLandingSpeed = 3.0;
final double maximumFuel = 100;
final double hFuel = 1.0;
final double vFuel = 2.0;

AudioClip vThrustSound;
AudioClip hThrustSound;
AudioClip goodLandingSound;
AudioClip badLandingSound;

public static void main(String args[])
{
  // create frame
  new MoonLanding().setVisible(true);
}

public MoonLanding()
{
  // frame constructor
  setTitle("Moon Landing");
  setResizable(false);
  addWindowListener(new WindowAdapter()
  {
    public void windowClosing(WindowEvent evt)
    {
      exitForm(evt);
    }
  });
  getContentPane().setLayout(new GridBagLayout());
  GridBagConstraints gridConstraints;

  framePanel.setPreferredSize(new Dimension(300, 400));
  framePanel.setBackground(Color.GRAY);
  framePanel.setLayout(new GridBagLayout());
  gridConstraints = new GridBagConstraints();
  gridConstraints.gridx = 0;
```

```
        gridConstraints.gridy = 0;
        gridConstraints.gridheight = 2;
        getContentPane().add(framePanel, gridConstraints);

        viewerPanel.setPreferredSize(new Dimension(280, 380));
        viewerPanel.setBackground(Color.WHITE);
        gridConstraints = new GridBagConstraints();
        gridConstraints.gridx = 0;
        gridConstraints.gridy = 0;
        framePanel.add(viewerPanel, gridConstraints);

        UIManager.put("TitledBorder.font", new Font("Arial",
Font.BOLD, 14));

        controlPanel.setPreferredSize(new Dimension(260, 360));
        //controlPanel.setVisible(false);

controlPanel.setBorder(BorderFactory.createTitledBorder("Lan
ding Control-Beginner"));
        controlPanel.setBackground(lightBlue);
        controlPanel.setLayout(new GridBagLayout());
        gridConstraints = new GridBagConstraints();
        gridConstraints.gridx = 1;
        gridConstraints.gridy = 0;
        gridConstraints.gridwidth = 2;
        gridConstraints.anchor = GridBagConstraints.NORTH;
        getContentPane().add(controlPanel, gridConstraints);

        timeLabel.setPreferredSize(new Dimension(70, 25));
        timeLabel.setText("Time (s)");
        timeLabel.setFont(new Font("Arial", Font.BOLD, 12));
        gridConstraints = new GridBagConstraints();
        gridConstraints.gridx = 0;
        gridConstraints.gridy = 0;
        controlPanel.add(timeLabel, gridConstraints);

        timeTextField.setPreferredSize(new Dimension(70, 25));

timeTextField.setBorder(BorderFactory.createLineBorder(Color
.BLACK));
        timeTextField.setText("0.0");
        timeTextField.setEditable(false);
        timeTextField.setBackground(Color.WHITE);

timeTextField.setHorizontalAlignment(SwingConstants.RIGHT);
        timeTextField.setFont(new Font("Arial", Font.PLAIN,
12));
```

```
gridConstraints = new GridBagConstraints();
gridConstraints.gridx = 1;
gridConstraints.gridy = 0;
controlPanel.add(timeTextField, gridConstraints);

positionLabel.setPreferredSize(new Dimension(70, 25));
positionLabel.setText("Position (m)");
positionLabel.setFont(new Font("Arial", Font.BOLD, 12));
gridConstraints = new GridBagConstraints();
gridConstraints.gridx = 1;
gridConstraints.gridy = 1;
controlPanel.add(positionLabel, gridConstraints);

speedLabel.setPreferredSize(new Dimension(70, 25));
speedLabel.setText("Speed (m/s)");
speedLabel.setFont(new Font("Arial", Font.BOLD, 12));
gridConstraints = new GridBagConstraints();
gridConstraints.gridx = 2;
gridConstraints.gridy = 1;
controlPanel.add(speedLabel, gridConstraints);

altitudeLabel.setPreferredSize(new Dimension(70, 25));
altitudeLabel.setText("Altitude");
altitudeLabel.setFont(new Font("Arial", Font.BOLD, 12));
gridConstraints = new GridBagConstraints();
gridConstraints.gridx = 0;
gridConstraints.gridy = 2;
controlPanel.add(altitudeLabel, gridConstraints);

altitudePositionTextField.setPreferredSize(new
Dimension(70, 25));

altitudePositionTextField.setBorder(BorderFactory.createLine
Border(Color.BLACK));
altitudePositionTextField.setText("0.0");
altitudePositionTextField.setEditable(false);
altitudePositionTextField.setBackground(Color.WHITE);

altitudePositionTextField.setHorizontalAlignment(SwingConsta
nts.RIGHT);
altitudePositionTextField.setFont(new Font("Arial",
Font.PLAIN, 12));
gridConstraints = new GridBagConstraints();
gridConstraints.gridx = 1;
gridConstraints.gridy = 2;
controlPanel.add(altitudePositionTextField,
gridConstraints);
```

```
    altitudeSpeedTextField.setPreferredSize(new
Dimension(70, 25));

altitudeSpeedTextField.setBorder(BorderFactory.createLineBor
der(Color.BLACK));
    altitudeSpeedTextField.setText("0.0");
    altitudeSpeedTextField.setEditable(false);
    altitudeSpeedTextField.setBackground(Color.WHITE);

altitudeSpeedTextField.setHorizontalAlignment(SwingConstants
.RIGHT);
    altitudeSpeedTextField.setFont(new Font("Arial",
Font.PLAIN, 12));
    gridConstraints = new GridBagConstraints();
    gridConstraints.gridx = 2;
    gridConstraints.gridy = 2;
    controlPanel.add(altitudeSpeedTextField,
gridConstraints);

    lateralLabel.setPreferredSize(new Dimension(70, 25));
    lateralLabel.setText("Lateral");
    lateralLabel.setFont(new Font("Arial", Font.BOLD, 12));
    gridConstraints = new GridBagConstraints();
    gridConstraints.gridx = 0;
    gridConstraints.gridy = 3;
    controlPanel.add(lateralLabel, gridConstraints);

    lateralPositionTextField.setPreferredSize(new
Dimension(70, 25));

lateralPositionTextField.setBorder(BorderFactory.createLineB
order(Color.BLACK));
    lateralPositionTextField.setText("0.0");
    lateralPositionTextField.setEditable(false);
    lateralPositionTextField.setBackground(Color.WHITE);

lateralPositionTextField.setHorizontalAlignment(SwingConstan
ts.RIGHT);
    lateralPositionTextField.setFont(new Font("Arial",
Font.PLAIN, 12));
    gridConstraints = new GridBagConstraints();
    gridConstraints.gridx = 1;
    gridConstraints.gridy = 3;
    controlPanel.add(lateralPositionTextField,
gridConstraints);
```

```java
    lateralSpeedTextField.setPreferredSize(new Dimension(70,
25));

lateralSpeedTextField.setBorder(BorderFactory.createLineBord
er(Color.BLACK));
    lateralSpeedTextField.setText("0.0");
    lateralSpeedTextField.setEditable(false);
    lateralSpeedTextField.setBackground(Color.WHITE);

lateralSpeedTextField.setHorizontalAlignment(SwingConstants.
RIGHT);
    lateralSpeedTextField.setFont(new Font("Arial",
Font.PLAIN, 12));
    gridConstraints = new GridBagConstraints();
    gridConstraints.gridx = 2;
    gridConstraints.gridy = 3;
    controlPanel.add(lateralSpeedTextField,
gridConstraints);

    fuelPanel.setPreferredSize(new Dimension(240, 40));
    fuelPanel.setBackground(lightBlue);
    fuelPanel.setLayout(new GridBagLayout());
    gridConstraints = new GridBagConstraints();
    gridConstraints.gridx = 0;
    gridConstraints.gridy = 4;
    gridConstraints.gridwidth = 3;
    controlPanel.add(fuelPanel, gridConstraints);

    trajectoryPanel.setPreferredSize(new Dimension(240,
130));
    trajectoryPanel.setBackground(Color.BLACK);
    gridConstraints = new GridBagConstraints();
    gridConstraints.gridx = 0;
    gridConstraints.gridy = 5;
    gridConstraints.gridwidth = 3;
    controlPanel.add(trajectoryPanel, gridConstraints);

    guidePanel.setPreferredSize(new Dimension(240, 20));
    guidePanel.setBackground(Color.GRAY);
    gridConstraints = new GridBagConstraints();
    gridConstraints.gridx = 0;
    gridConstraints.gridy = 6;
    gridConstraints.gridwidth = 3;
    gridConstraints.insets = new Insets(0, 0, 10, 0);
    controlPanel.add(guidePanel, gridConstraints);

    gridConstraints = new GridBagConstraints();
```

```
gridConstraints.gridx = 0;
gridConstraints.gridy = 7;
gridConstraints.insets = new Insets(0, 25, 0, 0);
gridConstraints.anchor = GridBagConstraints.WEST;
controlPanel.add(leftThrustButton, gridConstraints);
leftThrustButton.addActionListener(new ActionListener()
{
  public void actionPerformed(ActionEvent e)
  {
    leftThrustButtonActionPerformed(e);
  }
});

gridConstraints = new GridBagConstraints();
gridConstraints.gridx = 1;
gridConstraints.gridy = 7;
gridConstraints.insets = new Insets(0, 20, 0, 0);
gridConstraints.anchor = GridBagConstraints.WEST;
controlPanel.add(downThrustButton, gridConstraints);
downThrustButton.addActionListener(new ActionListener()
{
  public void actionPerformed(ActionEvent e)
  {
    downThrustButtonActionPerformed(e);
  }
});

gridConstraints = new GridBagConstraints();
gridConstraints.gridx = 2;
gridConstraints.gridy = 7;
gridConstraints.insets = new Insets(0, 20, 0, 0);
gridConstraints.anchor = GridBagConstraints.WEST;
controlPanel.add(rightThrustButton, gridConstraints);
rightThrustButton.addActionListener(new ActionListener()
{
  public void actionPerformed(ActionEvent e)
  {
    rightThrustButtonActionPerformed(e);
  }
});

messageLabel.setText("Auto-Pilot On");
messageLabel.setFont(new Font("Arial", Font.BOLD, 14));
messageLabel.setVisible(false);
gridConstraints = new GridBagConstraints();
gridConstraints.gridx = 0;
gridConstraints.gridy = 7;
```

```
    gridConstraints.gridwidth = 3;
    gridConstraints.insets = new Insets(11, 0, 0, 0);
    controlPanel.add(messageLabel, gridConstraints);

    fuelLabel.setText("Fuel");
    fuelLabel.setFont(new Font("Arial", Font.BOLD, 12));
    gridConstraints = new GridBagConstraints();
    gridConstraints.gridx = 0;
    gridConstraints.gridy = 0;
    gridConstraints.insets = new Insets(0, 0, 0, 5);
    fuelPanel.add(fuelLabel, gridConstraints);

    fuelProgressBar.setPreferredSize(new Dimension(200,
25));
    fuelProgressBar.setMinimum(0);
    fuelProgressBar.setMaximum(100);
    fuelProgressBar.setValue(100);
    fuelProgressBar.setBackground(Color.WHITE);
    fuelProgressBar.setForeground(Color.BLUE);
    gridConstraints = new GridBagConstraints();
    gridConstraints.gridx = 1;
    gridConstraints.gridy = 0;
    fuelPanel.add(fuelProgressBar, gridConstraints);

    startPauseButton.setText("Start Game");
    gridConstraints = new GridBagConstraints();
    gridConstraints.gridx = 1;
    gridConstraints.gridy = 1;
    gridConstraints.insets = new Insets(0, 20, 0, 0);
    getContentPane().add(startPauseButton, gridConstraints);
    startPauseButton.addActionListener(new ActionListener()
    {
      public void actionPerformed(ActionEvent e)
      {
        startPauseButtonActionPerformed(e);
      }
    });

    exitStopButton.setText("Exit");

exitStopButton.setPreferredSize(startPauseButton.getPreferre
dSize());
    gridConstraints = new GridBagConstraints();
    gridConstraints.gridx = 2;
    gridConstraints.gridy = 1;
    gridConstraints.insets = new Insets(0, 10, 0, 10);
    getContentPane().add(exitStopButton, gridConstraints);
```

```
exitStopButton.addActionListener(new ActionListener()
{
  public void actionPerformed(ActionEvent e)
  {
    exitStopButtonActionPerformed(e);
  }
});

completeButton.setText("Landing Complete-Click to
Continue");
completeButton.setVisible(false);
gridConstraints = new GridBagConstraints();
gridConstraints.gridx = 1;
gridConstraints.gridy = 1;
gridConstraints.gridwidth = 2;
gridConstraints.insets = new Insets(0, 10, 0, 10);
getContentPane().add(completeButton, gridConstraints);
completeButton.addActionListener(new ActionListener()
{
  public void actionPerformed(ActionEvent e)
  {
    completeButtonActionPerformed(e);
  }
});

controlPanel.setVisible(false);

optionsPanel.setPreferredSize(new Dimension(260, 360));
optionsPanel.setBackground(Color.BLUE);
optionsPanel.setLayout(new GridBagLayout());
gridConstraints = new GridBagConstraints();
gridConstraints.gridx = 1;
gridConstraints.gridy = 0;
gridConstraints.gridwidth = 2;
gridConstraints.anchor = GridBagConstraints.NORTH;
getContentPane().add(optionsPanel, gridConstraints);


pilotPanel.setBorder(BorderFactory.createTitledBorder("Pilot
Level"));
pilotPanel.setPreferredSize(new Dimension(140, 190));
pilotPanel.setBackground(lightBlue);
pilotPanel.setLayout(new GridBagLayout());
gridConstraints = new GridBagConstraints();
gridConstraints.gridx = 0;
gridConstraints.gridy = 0;
optionsPanel.add(pilotPanel, gridConstraints);
```

```java
unitsPanel.setBorder(BorderFactory.createTitledBorder("Units
"));
    unitsPanel.setPreferredSize(new Dimension(140, 80));
    unitsPanel.setBackground(lightBlue);
    unitsPanel.setLayout(new GridBagLayout());
    gridConstraints = new GridBagConstraints();
    gridConstraints.gridx = 0;
    gridConstraints.gridy = 1;
    gridConstraints.insets = new Insets(10, 0, 0, 0);
    optionsPanel.add(unitsPanel, gridConstraints);

    beginnerRadioButton.setText("Beginner");
    beginnerRadioButton.setBackground(lightBlue);
    beginnerRadioButton.setSelected(true);
    pilotButtonGroup.add(beginnerRadioButton);
    gridConstraints = new GridBagConstraints();
    gridConstraints.gridx = 0;
    gridConstraints.gridy = 0;
    gridConstraints.anchor = GridBagConstraints.WEST;
    pilotPanel.add(beginnerRadioButton, gridConstraints);
    beginnerRadioButton.addActionListener(new
ActionListener()
    {
      public void actionPerformed(ActionEvent e)
      {
        pilotRadioButtonActionPerformed(e);
      }
    });

    noviceRadioButton.setText("Novice");
    noviceRadioButton.setBackground(lightBlue);
    pilotButtonGroup.add(noviceRadioButton);
    gridConstraints = new GridBagConstraints();
    gridConstraints.gridx = 0;
    gridConstraints.gridy = 1;
    gridConstraints.anchor = GridBagConstraints.WEST;
    pilotPanel.add(noviceRadioButton, gridConstraints);
    noviceRadioButton.addActionListener(new ActionListener()
    {
      public void actionPerformed(ActionEvent e)
      {
        pilotRadioButtonActionPerformed(e);
      }
    });
```

```
juniorRadioButton.setText("Junior");
juniorRadioButton.setBackground(lightBlue);
pilotButtonGroup.add(juniorRadioButton);
gridConstraints = new GridBagConstraints();
gridConstraints.gridx = 0;
gridConstraints.gridy = 2;
gridConstraints.anchor = GridBagConstraints.WEST;
pilotPanel.add(juniorRadioButton, gridConstraints);
juniorRadioButton.addActionListener(new ActionListener()
{
  public void actionPerformed(ActionEvent e)
  {
    pilotRadioButtonActionPerformed(e);
  }
});

seniorRadioButton.setText("Senior");
seniorRadioButton.setBackground(lightBlue);
pilotButtonGroup.add(seniorRadioButton);
gridConstraints = new GridBagConstraints();
gridConstraints.gridx = 0;
gridConstraints.gridy = 3;
gridConstraints.anchor = GridBagConstraints.WEST;
pilotPanel.add(seniorRadioButton, gridConstraints);
seniorRadioButton.addActionListener(new ActionListener()
{
  public void actionPerformed(ActionEvent e)
  {
    pilotRadioButtonActionPerformed(e);
  }
});

advancedRadioButton.setText("Advanced");
advancedRadioButton.setBackground(lightBlue);
pilotButtonGroup.add(advancedRadioButton);
gridConstraints = new GridBagConstraints();
gridConstraints.gridx = 0;
gridConstraints.gridy = 4;
gridConstraints.anchor = GridBagConstraints.WEST;
pilotPanel.add(advancedRadioButton, gridConstraints);
advancedRadioButton.addActionListener(new
ActionListener()
{
  public void actionPerformed(ActionEvent e)
  {
    pilotRadioButtonActionPerformed(e);
  }
```

```
});

autoPilotCheckBox.setText("Auto Pilot On?");
autoPilotCheckBox.setBackground(lightBlue);
gridConstraints = new GridBagConstraints();
gridConstraints.gridx = 0;
gridConstraints.gridy = 5;
gridConstraints.anchor = GridBagConstraints.WEST;
pilotPanel.add(autoPilotCheckBox, gridConstraints);

metricRadioButton.setText("Metric");
metricRadioButton.setBackground(lightBlue);
metricRadioButton.setSelected(true);
unitsButtonGroup.add(metricRadioButton);
gridConstraints = new GridBagConstraints();
gridConstraints.gridx = 0;
gridConstraints.gridy = 0;
gridConstraints.anchor = GridBagConstraints.WEST;
unitsPanel.add(metricRadioButton, gridConstraints);
metricRadioButton.addActionListener(new ActionListener()
{
  public void actionPerformed(ActionEvent e)
  {
    unitsRadioButtonActionPerformed(e);
  }
});

usRadioButton.setText("US (English)");
usRadioButton.setBackground(lightBlue);
unitsButtonGroup.add(usRadioButton);
gridConstraints = new GridBagConstraints();
gridConstraints.gridx = 0;
gridConstraints.gridy = 1;
gridConstraints.anchor = GridBagConstraints.WEST;
unitsPanel.add(usRadioButton, gridConstraints);
usRadioButton.addActionListener(new ActionListener()
{
  public void actionPerformed(ActionEvent e)
  {
    unitsRadioButtonActionPerformed(e);
  }
});

landingTimer = new Timer(500, new ActionListener()
{
  public void actionPerformed(ActionEvent e)
  {
```

```
            landingTimerActionPerformed(e);
        }
    });


    pack();
    Dimension screenSize =
Toolkit.getDefaultToolkit().getScreenSize();
    setBounds((int) (0.5 * (screenSize.width - getWidth())),
(int) (0.5 * (screenSize.height - getHeight())), getWidth(),
getHeight());

    landscape = new ImageIcon("landscape.gif").getImage();
    landscapeWidth = landscape.getWidth(this);
    landscapeHeight = landscape.getHeight(this);
    lander = new ImageIcon("lander.gif").getImage();
    landerWidth = lander.getWidth(this);
    landerHeight = lander.getHeight(this);
    pad= new ImageIcon("pad.gif").getImage();
    padWidth = pad.getWidth(this);
    padHeight = pad.getHeight(this);
    hThrust = new ImageIcon("hThrust.gif").getImage();
    hThrustWidth = hThrust.getWidth(this);
    hThrustHeight = hThrust.getHeight(this);
    vThrust = new ImageIcon("vThrust.gif").getImage();
    vThrustWidth = vThrust.getWidth(this);
    vThrustHeight = vThrust.getHeight(this);
    lander = Transparency.makeColorTransparent(lander, new
Color(0, 0, 0));
    pad = Transparency.makeColorTransparent(pad, new
Color(0, 0, 0));
    hThrust = Transparency.makeColorTransparent(hThrust, new
Color(0, 0, 0));
    vThrust = Transparency.makeColorTransparent(vThrust, new
Color(0, 0, 0));

    try
    {
      vThrustSound = Applet.newAudioClip(new URL("file:" +
"vthrust.wav"));
      hThrustSound = Applet.newAudioClip(new URL("file:" +
"hthrust.wav"));
      goodLandingSound = Applet.newAudioClip(new URL("file:"
+ "safe.wav"));
      badLandingSound = Applet.newAudioClip(new URL("file:"
+ "crash.wav"));
    }
```

```java
    catch (Exception ex)
    {
      System.out.println("Error loading sound files");
    }
    centerX = (viewerPanel.getWidth() - landerWidth) / 2;
    centerY = (viewerPanel.getHeight() - landerHeight) / 2;
    viewerPanel.setVisible(false);
  }

  private void exitForm(WindowEvent evt)
  {
    System.exit(0);
  }

  private void downThrustButtonActionPerformed(ActionEvent
e)
  {
    if (fuelRemaining > 0)
    {
      vThrustOn = true;
      vThrustSound.play();
      if (pilotLevel != 5)
        landerYSpeed -= yDelta;
      else
        landerYSpeed -= 2.0 * yDelta *
myRandom.nextDouble();
      if (pilotLevel > 3)
        fuelRemaining -= vFuel;
    }
  }

  private void leftThrustButtonActionPerformed(ActionEvent
e)
  {
    if (fuelRemaining > 0)
    {
      lThrustOn = true;
      hThrustSound.play();
      if (pilotLevel != 5)
        landerXSpeed += xDelta;
      else
        landerXSpeed += 2.0 * xDelta *
myRandom.nextDouble();
      if (pilotLevel > 3)
        fuelRemaining -= hFuel;
    }
  }
```

```
   private void rightThrustButtonActionPerformed(ActionEvent
e)
   {
     if (fuelRemaining > 0)
     {
       rThrustOn = true;
       hThrustSound.play();
       if (pilotLevel != 5)
         landerXSpeed -= xDelta;
       else
         landerXSpeed -= 2.0 * xDelta *
myRandom.nextDouble();
       if (pilotLevel > 3)
         fuelRemaining -= hFuel;
     }
   }




   private void startPauseButtonActionPerformed(ActionEvent
e)
   {
     if (startPauseButton.getText().equals("Start Game"))
     {
       startPauseButton.setText("Pause Game");
       exitStopButton.setText("Stop Game");
       optionsPanel.setVisible(false);
       controlPanel.setVisible(true);
       switch (pilotLevel)
       {
         case 1:

controlPanel.setBorder(BorderFactory.createTitledBorder("Lan
ding Control-Beginner"));
           leftThrustButton.setVisible(false);
           rightThrustButton.setVisible(false);
           downThrustButton.setVisible(true);
           fuelLabel.setVisible(false);
           fuelProgressBar.setVisible(false);
           break;
         case 2:

controlPanel.setBorder(BorderFactory.createTitledBorder("Lan
ding Control-Novice"));
           leftThrustButton.setVisible(true);
           rightThrustButton.setVisible(true);
```

```
          downThrustButton.setVisible(false);
          fuelLabel.setVisible(false);
          fuelProgressBar.setVisible(false);
          break;
        case 3:

controlPanel.setBorder(BorderFactory.createTitledBorder("Lan
ding Control-Junior"));
          leftThrustButton.setVisible(true);
          rightThrustButton.setVisible(true);
          downThrustButton.setVisible(true);
          fuelLabel.setVisible(false);
          fuelProgressBar.setVisible(false);
          break;
        case 4:

controlPanel.setBorder(BorderFactory.createTitledBorder("Lan
ding Control-Senior"));
          leftThrustButton.setVisible(true);
          rightThrustButton.setVisible(true);
          downThrustButton.setVisible(true);
          fuelLabel.setVisible(true);
          fuelProgressBar.setVisible(true);
          break;
        case 5:

controlPanel.setBorder(BorderFactory.createTitledBorder("Lan
ding Control-Advanced"));
          leftThrustButton.setVisible(true);
          rightThrustButton.setVisible(true);
          downThrustButton.setVisible(true);
          fuelLabel.setVisible(true);
          fuelProgressBar.setVisible(true);
          break;
      }
      if (autoPilotCheckBox.isSelected())
      {
        leftThrustButton.setVisible(false);
        rightThrustButton.setVisible(false);
        downThrustButton.setVisible(false);
        messageLabel.setText("Auto-Pilot On");
        messageLabel.setVisible(true);
      }
      else
      {
        messageLabel.setVisible(false);
      }
```

```
      if (metricRadioButton.isSelected())
      {
        positionLabel.setText("Position (m)");
        speedLabel.setText("Speed (m/s)");
      }
      else
      {
        positionLabel.setText("Position (ft)");
        speedLabel.setText("Speed (ft/s)");
      }
      time = 0.0;
      timeTextField.setText("0.0");
      landerX = (landscapeWidth - landerWidth) *
myRandom.nextDouble();
      landerY = 0;
      landerXSpeed = 0;
      landerYSpeed = 0;
      if (pilotLevel != 1)
        padX = (landscapeWidth - padWidth) *
myRandom.nextDouble();
      else
        padX = (landerX + landerWidth / 2) - padWidth / 2;
      padY = landscapeHeight - padHeight;
      fuelRemaining = maximumFuel;
      fuelProgressBar.setValue(100);
      trajectoryPoints.removeAllElements();
      updateStatus();
      updateTrajectory();
      updateViewer();
      viewerPanel.setVisible(true);
      landingTimer.start();
    }
    else if (startPauseButton.getText().equals("Pause
Game"))
    {
      startPauseButton.setText("Restart Game");
      exitStopButton.setEnabled(false);
      leftThrustButton.setEnabled(false);
      downThrustButton.setEnabled(false);
      rightThrustButton.setEnabled(false);
      landingTimer.stop();
    }
    else
    {
      startPauseButton.setText("Pause Game");
      exitStopButton.setEnabled(true);
      leftThrustButton.setEnabled(true);
```

```
            downThrustButton.setEnabled(true);
            rightThrustButton.setEnabled(true);
            landingTimer.start();
        }
    }

    private void exitStopButtonActionPerformed(ActionEvent e)
    {
        if (exitStopButton.getText().equals("Stop Game"))
        {
            exitStopButton.setText("Exit");
            startPauseButton.setText("Start Game");
            optionsPanel.setVisible(true);
            controlPanel.setVisible(false);
            viewerPanel.setVisible(false);
            landingTimer.stop();
        }
        else
        {
            System.exit(0);
        }
    }
    private void completeButtonActionPerformed(ActionEvent e)
    {
        completeButton.setVisible(false);
        startPauseButton.setVisible(true);
        exitStopButton.setVisible(true);
        exitStopButton.doClick();
    }

    private void pilotRadioButtonActionPerformed(ActionEvent
e)
    {
        String t = e.getActionCommand();
        if (t.equals("Beginner"))
            pilotLevel = 1;
        else if (t.equals("Novice"))
            pilotLevel = 2;
        else if (t.equals("Junior"))
            pilotLevel = 3;
        else if (t.equals("Senior"))
            pilotLevel = 4;
        else if (t.equals("Advanced"))
            pilotLevel = 5;
    }
```

```java
  private void unitsRadioButtonActionPerformed(ActionEvent
e)
  {
    String t = e.getActionCommand();
    if (t.equals("Metric"))
      multiplier = 1.0;
    else
      multiplier = 3.2808;
  }

  private void landingTimerActionPerformed(ActionEvent e)
  {
    time += (double) (landingTimer.getDelay()) / 1000;
    timeTextField.setText(new
DecimalFormat("0.00").format(time));
    landerX += landerXSpeed * (double)
(landingTimer.getDelay()) / 1000;
    landerY += landerYSpeed * (double)
(landingTimer.getDelay()) / 1000;
    updateStatus();
    updateTrajectory();
    updateViewer();
    // check for landing
    if (altitude <= 0)
    {
      vThrustOn = false;
      lThrustOn = false;
      rThrustOn = false;
      updateViewer();
      landingTimer.stop();
      leftThrustButton.setVisible(false);
      rightThrustButton.setVisible(false);
      downThrustButton.setVisible(false);
      if (autoPilotCheckBox.isSelected())
        messageLabel.setText("Auto-Pilot ");
      else
      {
        messageLabel.setText("You ");
        messageLabel.setVisible(true);
      }
      // crash?
      if (landerYSpeed > safeLandingSpeed)
      {
        badLandingSound.play();
        messageLabel.setText(messageLabel.getText() +
"Crashed!");
      }
```

```java
    else
    {
      goodLandingSound.play();
      messageLabel.setText(messageLabel.getText() +
"Landed Safely");
    }
    // bring up complete button
    startPauseButton.setVisible(false);
    exitStopButton.setVisible(false);
    completeButton.setVisible(true);
    return;
  }
  // autopilot or Novice level - adjust vertical thrust
  if (autoPilotCheckBox.isSelected() || pilotLevel == 2)
  {
    if (altitude > 300)
    {
      if (landerYSpeed > 12)
        downThrustButton.doClick();
    }
    else if (altitude > 100)
    {
      if (landerYSpeed > 6)
        downThrustButton.doClick();
    }
    else
    {
      if (landerYSpeed > (2 + 0.04 * altitude))
        downThrustButton.doClick();
    }
  }
  // autopilot - adjust horizontal thrust
  if (autoPilotCheckBox.isSelected())
  {
    miss = lateral - altitude * (lateral0 / altitude0);
    if (miss > 2)
      rightThrustButton.doClick();
     else if (miss < -2)
      leftThrustButton.doClick();
  }
  landerX += landerXSpeed;
  landerY += landerYSpeed;
  // horizontal drag
  if (landerXSpeed > 0)
    landerXSpeed -= drag;
  else if (landerXSpeed < 0)
    landerXSpeed += drag;
```

```
    // gravity
    landerYSpeed += gravity * (double)
(landingTimer.getDelay()) / 1000;
  }

  private void updateStatus()
  {
    altitude = (landscapeHeight - padHeight / 2) - (landerY
+ landerHeight);
    lateral = (landerX + landerWidth / 2) - (padX + padWidth
/ 2);
    if (altitude > 0)
      altitudePositionTextField.setText(new
DecimalFormat("0").format(altitude * multiplier));
    else
      altitudePositionTextField.setText("0");
    if (Math.abs(lateral) < 1)
      lateralPositionTextField.setText("Above");
    else
      lateralPositionTextField.setText(new
DecimalFormat("0").format(lateral * multiplier));
    altitudeSpeedTextField.setText(new
DecimalFormat("0.0").format(-landerYSpeed * multiplier));
    lateralSpeedTextField.setText(new
DecimalFormat("0.0").format(landerXSpeed * multiplier));
    // update fuel guage
    int fuelPercent = (int) (100 * fuelRemaining /
maximumFuel);
    fuelProgressBar.setValue(fuelPercent);
    if (fuelPercent <= 10)
      Toolkit.getDefaultToolkit().beep();
    // update guide display
    guidePanel.repaint();
  }

  private void updateTrajectory()
  {
    if (time == 0.0)
    {
      landerX0 = landerX;
      landerY0 = landerY;
      altitude0 = altitude;
      lateral0 = lateral;
    }
    trajectoryPoints.add(new Point2D.Double(landerX +
landerWidth / 2 , landerY + landerHeight));
    trajectoryPanel.repaint();
```

```
    }

  private void updateViewer()
  {
    // adjust landscape background
    landscapeX = landerX - centerX;
    landerXView = centerX;
    if (landscapeX <= 0)
    {
      landscapeX = 0;
      landerXView = landerX;
    }
    if (landscapeX >= landscapeWidth -
viewerPanel.getWidth())
    {
      landscapeX = landscapeWidth - viewerPanel.getWidth();
      landerXView = landerX - landscapeX;
    }
    landscapeY = landerY - centerY;
    landerYView = centerY;
    if (landscapeY <= 0)
    {
      landscapeY = 0;
      landerYView = landerY;
    }
    if (landscapeY >= landscapeHeight -
viewerPanel.getHeight())
    {
      landscapeY = landscapeHeight -
viewerPanel.getHeight();
      landerYView = landerY - landscapeY;
    }
    // draw landscape
    viewerPanel.repaint();
  }

}


class TrajectoryPanel extends JPanel
{
  public void paintComponent(Graphics g)
  {
    Graphics2D g2D = (Graphics2D) g;
    super.paintComponent(g2D);
    double trajectoryXScale = (double) (getWidth()) /
MoonLanding.landscapeWidth;
```

```
     double trajectoryYScale = (double) (getHeight()) /
MoonLanding.landscapeHeight;
     g2D.setStroke(new BasicStroke(2));
     g2D.setPaint(Color.RED);
     Line2D.Double trajectoryLine = new
Line2D.Double(trajectoryXScale * (MoonLanding.landerX0 +
MoonLanding.landerWidth / 2), trajectoryYScale *
(MoonLanding.landerY0 + MoonLanding.landerHeight),
trajectoryXScale * (MoonLanding.padX + MoonLanding.padWidth
/ 2), trajectoryYScale * (MoonLanding.padY +
MoonLanding.padHeight / 2));
     g2D.draw(trajectoryLine);

     g2D.setStroke(new BasicStroke(1));
     for (int i = 0; i < MoonLanding.trajectoryPoints.size();
i++)
     {
       Point2D.Double thisPoint = (Point2D.Double)
MoonLanding.trajectoryPoints.elementAt(i);
       Ellipse2D.Double trajectoryCircle = new
Ellipse2D.Double(trajectoryXScale * thisPoint.getX() - 3,
trajectoryYScale * thisPoint.getY() - 3, 6, 6);
       g2D.setPaint(Color.GREEN);
       g2D.draw(trajectoryCircle);
     }
     g2D.dispose();
   }
}

class GuidePanel extends JPanel
{
  public void paintComponent(Graphics g)
  {
    Graphics2D g2D = (Graphics2D) g;
    super.paintComponent(g2D);
    int x = (int) ((MoonLanding.landerX +
MoonLanding.landerWidth / 2) * getWidth() /
MoonLanding.landscapeWidth - 5);
    Rectangle2D.Double guideRectangle = new
Rectangle2D.Double(x, 1, 10, getHeight() - 2);
    g2D.setPaint(Color.GREEN);
    g2D.fill(guideRectangle);
    x = (int) ((MoonLanding.padX + MoonLanding.padWidth / 2)
* getWidth() / MoonLanding.landscapeWidth - 5);
    guideRectangle = new Rectangle2D.Double(x, 1, 10,
getHeight() - 2);
    g2D.setPaint(Color.RED);
```

```
      g2D.fill(guideRectangle);
      g2D.dispose();
  }
}


class ViewerPanel extends JPanel
{
  public void paintComponent(Graphics g)
  {
    Graphics2D g2D = (Graphics2D) g;
    super.paintComponent(g2D);
    g2D.drawImage(MoonLanding.landscape, 0, 0, getWidth() -
1, getHeight() - 1, (int) MoonLanding.landscapeX, (int)
MoonLanding.landscapeY, (int) (MoonLanding.landscapeX +
getWidth() - 1), (int) (MoonLanding.landscapeY + getHeight()
- 1), null);
    // add pad
    g2D.drawImage(MoonLanding.pad, (int) (MoonLanding.padX -
MoonLanding.landscapeX), (int) (MoonLanding.padY -
MoonLanding.landscapeY), null);
    // add lander
    g2D.drawImage(MoonLanding.lander, (int)
MoonLanding.landerXView, (int) MoonLanding.landerYView,
null);
    //add thrusters if on
    if (MoonLanding.vThrustOn)        {
      g2D.drawImage(MoonLanding.vThrust, (int)
(MoonLanding.landerXView + 0.5 * MoonLanding.landerWidth -
0.5 * MoonLanding.vThrustWidth), (int)
(MoonLanding.landerYView + MoonLanding.landerHeight -
MoonLanding.vThrustHeight), null);
      MoonLanding.vThrustOn = false;
    }
    if (MoonLanding.lThrustOn)
    {
      g2D.drawImage(MoonLanding.hThrust, (int)
(MoonLanding.landerXView - 5), (int)
(MoonLanding.landerYView + 40), null);
      MoonLanding.lThrustOn = false;
    }
    if (MoonLanding.rThrustOn)
    {
      g2D.drawImage(MoonLanding.hThrust, (int)
(MoonLanding.landerXView + MoonLanding.landerWidth -
MoonLanding.hThrustWidth + 5), (int)
(MoonLanding.landerYView + 40), null);
      MoonLanding.rThrustOn = false;
```

```
        }

    g2D.dispose();
    }
}
```

Transparency.java:

```java
/*
 *   From:
 *http://www.rgagnon.com/javadetails/java-0265.html
 *
 */
package moonlanding;
import java.awt.*;
import java.awt.image.*;

public class Transparency
{
  public static Image makeColorTransparent(Image im, final
Color color)
  {
    ImageFilter filter = new RGBImageFilter()
    {
      // the color we are looking for... Alpha bits are set
to opaque
      public int markerRGB = color.getRGB() | 0xFF000000;
      public final int filterRGB(int x, int y, int rgb)
      {
        if ( ( rgb | 0xFF000000 ) == markerRGB )
        {
          // Mark the alpha bits as zero - transparent
          return 0x00FFFFFF & rgb;
        }
        else
        {
          // nothing to do
          return rgb;
        }
      }
    };
    ImageProducer ip = new
FilteredImageSource(im.getSource(), filter);
    return Toolkit.getDefaultToolkit().createImage(ip);
  }
}
```

Appendix - Installing Java and NetBeans

Downloading and Installing Java

To write and run programs using Java, you need the **Java Development Kit** (JDK) and the **NetBeans Integrated Development Environment** (IDE). These are free products that you can download from the Internet. This simply means we will copy a file onto our computer to allow installation of Java. Each product requires a separate download and installation process.

<u>Java Development Kit</u>

1. Start up your web browser (Internet Explorer, Chrome, Firefox, Safari or other browser) and go to Java web site:

https://www.oracle.com/technetwork/java/javase/downloads/jdk11-downloads-5066655.html

This web site has lots of useful Java information. As you become more proficient in your programming skills, you will go to this site often for answers to programming questions, interaction with other Java programmers, and lots of sample programs.

2. Once on the page with the JDK download links, accept the Licensing Agreement and choose the link corresponding to your computer's operating system.

For Microsoft Windows: select the Windows exe file

Java SE Development Kit 11.0.3

You must accept the Oracle Technology Network License Agreement for Oracle Java SE to download this software.
Thank you for accepting the Oracle Technology Network License Agreement for Oracle Java SE; you may now download this software.

Product / File Description	File Size	Download
Linux	147.31 MB	jdk-11.0.3_linux-x64_bin.deb
Linux	154.04 MB	jdk-11.0.3_linux-x64_bin.rpm
Linux	171.37 MB	jdk-11.0.3_linux-x64_bin.tar.gz
macOS	166.2 MB	jdk-11.0.3_osx-x64_bin.dmg
macOS	166.52 MB	jdk-11.0.3_osx-x64_bin.tar.gz
Solaris SPARC	186.85 MB	jdk-11.0.3_solaris-sparcv9_bin.tar.gz
Windows	150.98 MB	jdk-11.0.3_windows-x64_bin.exe
Windows	171 MB	jdk-11.0.3_windows-x64_bin.zip

Instructions for installing Java on other platforms such as Linux or Solaris can also be found on the website. My screenshots in these notes will be Microsoft Windows.

For Mac OS: click on the macOS dmg file

Java SE Development Kit 11.0.3

You must accept the Oracle Technology Network License Agreement for Oracle Java SE to download this software.
Thank you for accepting the Oracle Technology Network License Agreement for Oracle Java SE; you may now download this software.

Product / File Description	File Size	Download
Linux	147.31 MB	⬇ jdk-11.0.3_linux-x64_bin.deb
Linux	154.04 MB	⬇ jdk-11.0.3_linux-x64_bin.rpm
Linux	171.37 MB	⬇ jdk-11.0.3_linux-x64_bin.tar.gz
macOS	166.2 MB	⬇ jdk-11.0.3_osx-x64_bin.dmg
macOS	166.52 MB	⬇ jdk-11.0.3_osx-x64_bin.tar.gz
Solaris SPARC	186.85 MB	⬇ jdk-11.0.3_solaris-sparcv9_bin.tar.gz
Windows	150.98 MB	⬇ jdk-11.0.3_windows-x64_bin.exe
Windows	171 MB	⬇ jdk-11.0.3_windows-x64_bin.zip

For Linux OS: click on the Linux deb file

Java SE Development Kit 11.0.3

You must accept the Oracle Technology Network License Agreement for Oracle Java SE to download this software.
Thank you for accepting the Oracle Technology Network License Agreement for Oracle Java SE; you may now download this software.

Product / File Description	File Size	Download
Linux	147.31 MB	⬇ jdk-11.0.3_linux-x64_bin.deb
Linux	154.04 MB	⬇ jdk-11.0.3_linux-x64_bin.rpm
Linux	171.37 MB	⬇ jdk-11.0.3_linux-x64_bin.tar.gz
macOS	166.2 MB	⬇ jdk-11.0.3_osx-x64_bin.dmg
macOS	166.52 MB	⬇ jdk-11.0.3_osx-x64_bin.tar.gz
Solaris SPARC	186.85 MB	⬇ jdk-11.0.3_solaris-sparcv9_bin.tar.gz
Windows	150.98 MB	⬇ jdk-11.0.3_windows-x64_bin.exe
Windows	171 MB	⬇ jdk-11.0.3_windows-x64_bin.zip

Once you select a file, you may be asked to create an Oracle Account – follow the requested steps.

3. You will be asked what you want to do with the selected download file. Click **Run**. The installation begins.

4. The Java installer will unpack some files and an introductory window will appear:

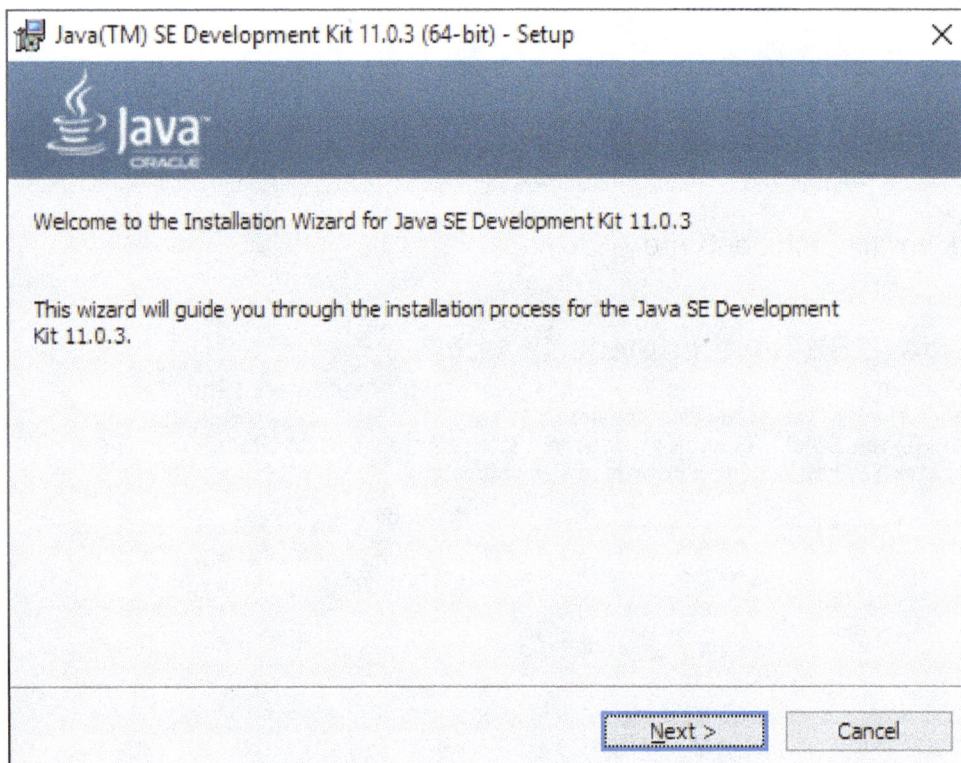

Click **Next** to start the installation. Several windows will appear in sequence. Accept the default choices by clicking **Next** at each window.

When complete (it will take a while), you will see this window:

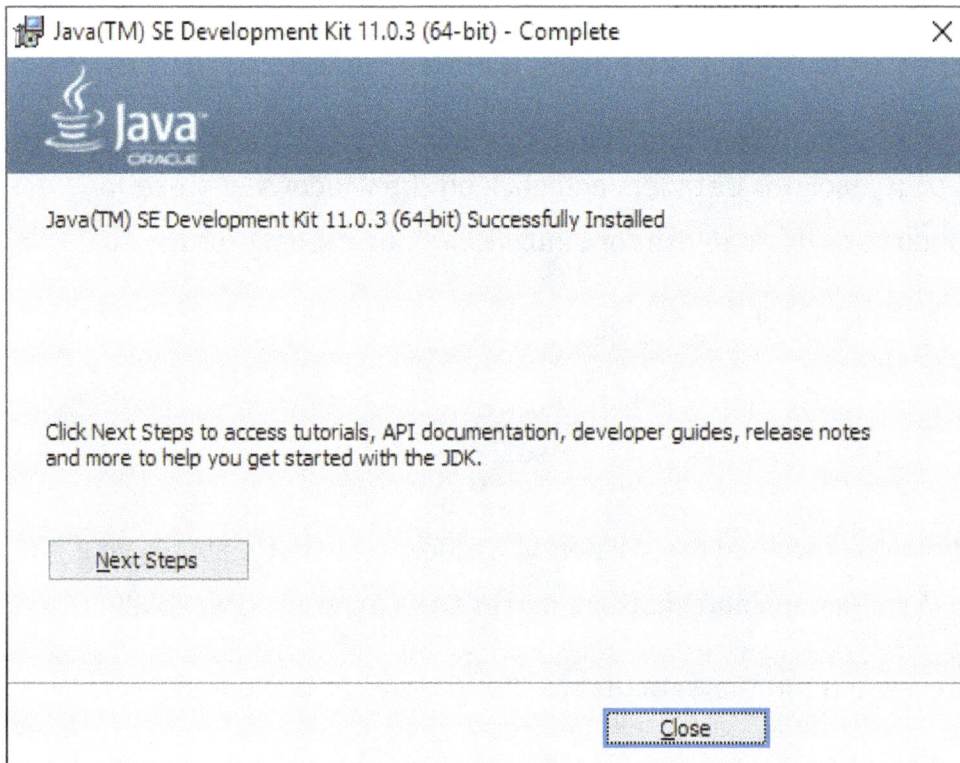

Click **Close** and the installation will complete. Next, let's install NetBeans.

NetBeans Integrated Development Environment

1. Go to this website:

2. https://netbeans.apache.org/download/nb111/nb111.html

3. On this web page, look for Installers and click on the windows-x64.exe for Microsoft Windows or linux-x64.sh for Linux OS or macosx.dmg for the MAC OS:

- Apache-NetBeans-11.1-bin-windows-x64.exe (SHA-512, PGP ASC)
- Apache-NetBeans-11.1-bin-linux-x64.sh (SHA-512, PGP ASC)
- Apache-NetBeans-11.1-bin-macosx.dmg (SHA-512, PGP ASC)

Click on the link above to download the version of NetBeans 11 that matches your Operating System. Click the link and choose a mirror site to use for downloading.

Once downloaded, click and run the **executable** file to install it on your system.

Running NetBeans

You now have Java and the **NetBeans** IDE installed on your computer. All of our programming work will be done using NetBeans. Let's make sure **NetBeans** installed correctly. To start using NetBeans under Microsoft Windows,

- Double-click the **NetBeans** shortcut on your computer's desktop

You can rename this shortcut if you choose. To start using NetBeans under the MAC OS,

- Click on the **Finder** and go to the **Applications Folder.**

The NetBeans program should start (several windows and menus will appear).

We will learn more about NetBeans in the notes. For now, we want to make some formatting changes. In Java programming, indentations in the code we write are used to delineate common blocks. The NetBeans IDE uses four spaces for indentations as a default. This author (and these notes) uses two spaces. To make this change, choose the **Tools** menu item and click **Options**. In the window that appears, choose the **Editor** option and the **Formatting** tab:

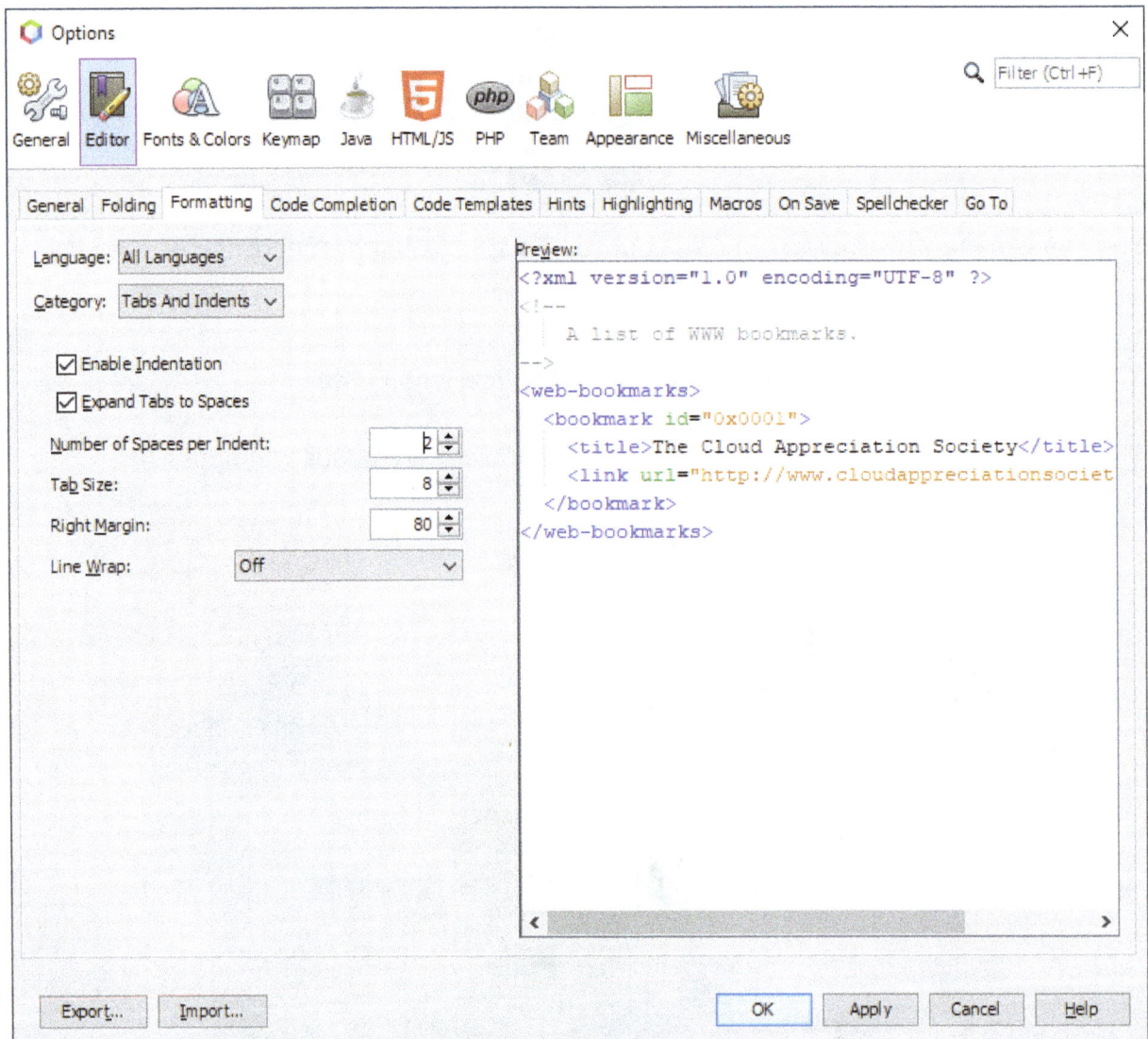

As shown, choose the **Tabs and Indents Category** and set the **Number of Spaces per Indent** to **2**.

Before leaving this window, we make another change. Braces (curly brackets) are used to start and stop blocks of code. We choose to have these brackets always be on a separate line – it makes checking code much easier.

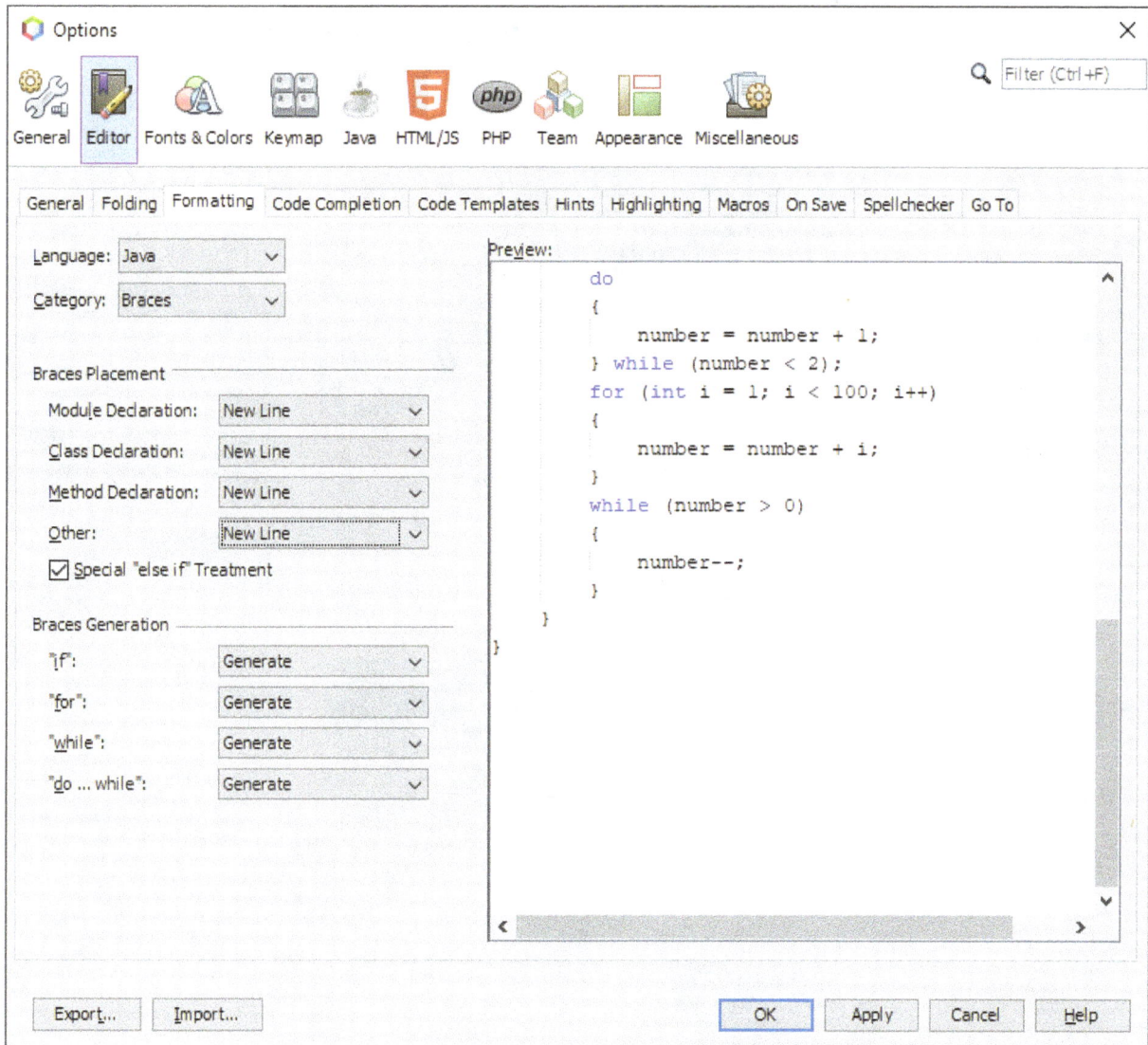

As shown, choose the **Braces Category** and under **Braces Placement**, set all choices to **New Line**. Click **Apply**, then **OK**. Stop **NetBeans** – you're ready to go!

More Self-Study or Instructor-Led Computer Programming Tutorials by Kidware Software

ORACLE JAVA PROGRAMMING TUTORIALS

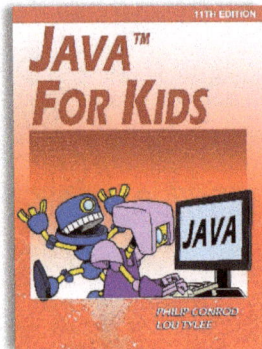

Java™ For Kids is a beginning programming tutorial consisting of 10 chapters explaining (in simple, easy-to-follow terms) how to build a Java application. Students learn about project design, object-oriented programming, console applications, graphics applications and many elements of the Java language. Numerous examples are used to demonstrate every step in the building process. The projects include a number guessing game, a card game, an allowance calculator, a state capitals game, Tic-Tac-Toe, a simple drawing program, and even a basic video game. Designed for kids ages 12 and up.

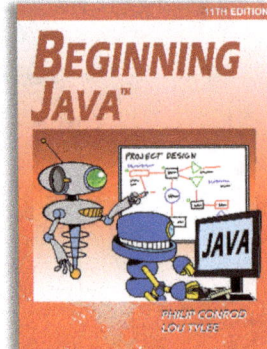

Beginning Java™ is a semester long "beginning" programming tutorial consisting of 10 chapters explaining (in simple, easy-to-follow terms) how to build a Java application. The tutorial includes several detailed computer projects for students to build and try. These projects include a number guessing game, card game, allowance calculator, drawing program, state capitals game, and a couple of video games like Pong. We also include several college prep bonus projects including a loan calculator, portfolio manager, and checkbook balancer. Designed for students age 15 and up.

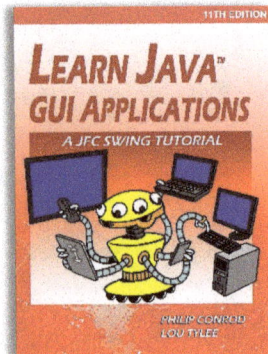

Learn Java™ GUI Applications is a 9 lesson Tutorial covering object-oriented programming concepts, using an integrated development environment to create and test Java projects, building and distributing GUI applications, understanding and using the Swing control library, exception handling, sequential file access, graphics, multimedia, advanced topics such as printing, and help system authoring. Our Beginning Java or Java For Kids tutorial is a pre-requisite for this tutorial

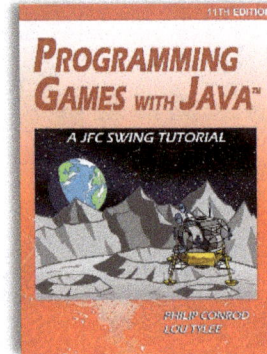

Programming Games with Java™ is a semester long "intermediate" programming tutorial consisting of 10 chapters explaining (in simple, easy-to-follow terms) how to build a Visual C# Video Games. The games built are non-violent, family-friendly and teach logical thinking skills. Students will learn how to program the following Visual C# video games: Safecracker, Tic Tac Toe, Match Game, Pizza Delivery, and Moon Landing. This intermediate level self-paced tutorial can be used at home or school. The tutorial is simple enough for kids yet engaging enough for beginning adults. Our Learn Java GUI Applications tutorial is a required pre-requisite for this tutorial.

Java™ Homework Projects is a Java GUI Swing tutorial covering object-oriented programming concepts. It explains (in simple, easy-to-follow terms) how to build Java GUI project to use around the home. Students learn about project design, the Java Swing controls, many elements of the Java language, and how to distribute finished projects. The projects built include a Dual-Mode Stopwatch, Flash Card Math Quiz, Multiple Choice Exam, Blackjack Card Game, Weight Monitor, Home Inventory Manager and a Snowball Toss Game. Our Learn Java GUI Applications tutorial is a pre-requisite for this tutorial

MICROSOFT SMALL BASIC PROGRAMMING TUTORIALS

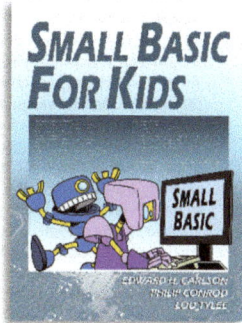

Small Basic For Kids is an illustrated introduction to computer programming that provides an interactive, self-paced tutorial to the new Small Basic programming environment. The book consists of 30 short lessons that explain how to create and run a Small Basic program. Elementary students learn about program design and many elements of the Small Basic language. Numerous examples are used to demonstrate every step in the building process. The tutorial also includes two complete games (Hangman and Pizza Zapper) for students to build and try. Designed for kids ages 8+.

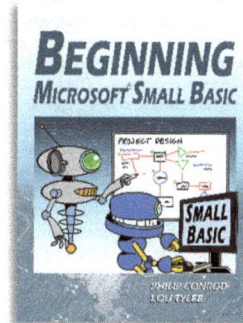

The Beginning Microsoft Small Basic Programming Tutorial is a self-study first semester "beginner" programming tutorial consisting of 11 chapters explaining (in simple, easy-to-follow terms) how to write Microsoft Small Basic programs. Numerous examples are used to demonstrate every step in the building process. The last chapter of this tutorial shows you how four different Small Basic games could port to Visual Basic, Visual C# and Java. This beginning level self-paced tutorial can be used at home or at school. The tutorial is simple enough for kids ages 10+ yet engaging enough for adults.

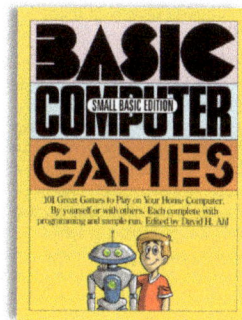

Basic Computer Games - Small Basic Edition is a re-make of the classic BASIC COMPUTER GAMES book originally edited by David H. Ahl. It contains 100 of the original text based BASIC games that inspired a whole generation of programmers. Now these classic BASIC games have been re-written in Microsoft Small Basic for a new generation to enjoy! The new Small Basic games look and act like the original text based games. The book includes all the original spaghetti code and GOTO commands!

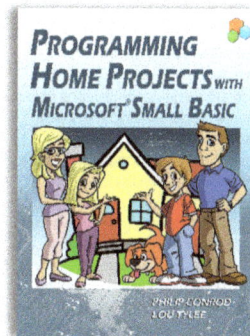

Programming Home Projects with Microsoft Small Basic is a self-paced programming tutorial explains (in simple, easy-to-follow terms) how to build Small Basic Windows applications. Students learn about program design, Small Basic objects, many elements of the Small Basic language, and how to debug and distribute finished programs. Sequential file input and output is also introduced. The projects built include a Dual-Mode Stopwatch, Flash Card Math Quiz, Multiple Choice Exam, Blackjack Card Game, Weight Monitor, Home Inventory Manager and a Snowball Toss Game.

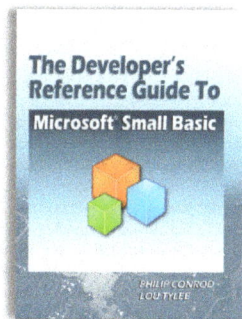

The Developer's Reference Guide to Microsoft Small Basic While developing all the different Microsoft Small Basic tutorials we found it necessary to write The Developer's Reference Guide to Microsoft Small Basic. The Developer's Reference Guide to Microsoft Small Basic is over 500 pages long and includes over 100 Small Basic programming examples for you to learn from and include in your own Microsoft Small Basic programs. It is a detailed reference guide for new developers.

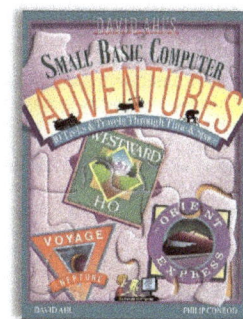

David Ahl's Small Basic Computer Adventures is a Microsoft Small Basic re-make of the classic *Basic Computer Games* programming *book* originally written by David H. Ahl. This new book includes the following classic adventure simulations; Marco Polo, Westward Ho!, The Longest Automobile Race, The Orient Express, Amelia Earhart: Around the World Flight, Tour de France, Subway Scavenger, Hong Kong Hustle, and Voyage to Neptune. Learn how to program these classic computer simulations in Microsoft Small Basic.

MICROSOFT VISUAL STUDIO 2019 PROGRAMMING TUTORIALS

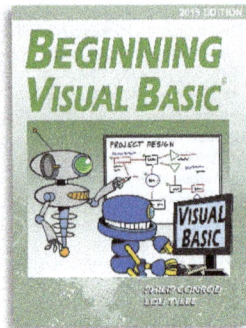

Beginning Visual Basic® is a semester long self-paced "beginner" programming tutorial consisting of 10 chapters explaining (in simple, easy-to-follow terms) how to build a Visual Basic Windows application. The tutorial includes several detailed computer projects for students to build and try. These projects include a number guessing game, card game, allowance calculator, drawing program, state capitals game, and a couple of video games like Pong. We also include several college prep bonus projects including a loan calculator, portfolio manager, and checkbook balancer. Designed for students age 15 and up.

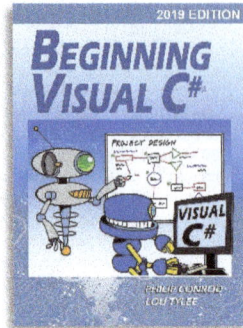

Beginning Visual C#® is a semester long "beginning" programming tutorial consisting of 10 chapters explaining (in simple, easy-to-follow terms) how to build a C# Windows application. The tutorial includes several detailed computer projects for students to build and try. These projects include a number guessing game, card game, allowance calculator, drawing program, state capitals game, and a couple of video games like Pong. We also include several college prep bonus projects including a loan calculator, portfolio manager, and checkbook balancer. Designed for students ages 15+.

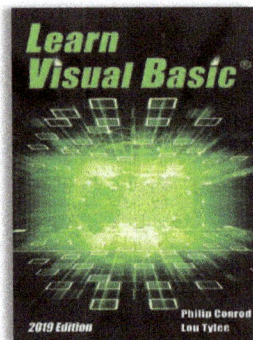

LEARN VISUAL BASIC is a comprehensive college level programming tutorial covering object-oriented programming, the Visual Basic integrated development environment, building and distributing Windows applications using the Windows Installer, exception handling, sequential file access, graphics, multimedia, advanced topics such as web access, printing, and HTML help system authoring. The tutorial also introduces database applications (using ADO .NET) and web applications (using ASP.NET).

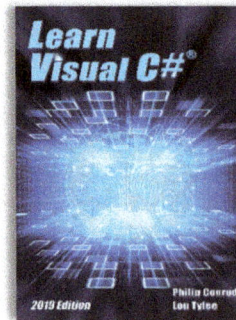

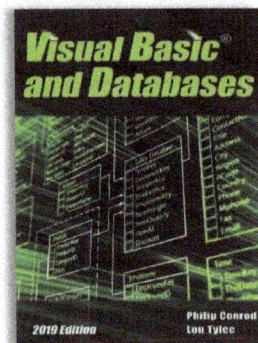

LEARN VISUAL C# is a comprehensive college level computer programming tutorial covering object-oriented programming, the Visual C# integrated development environment and toolbox, building and distributing Windows applications (using the Windows Installer), exception handling, sequential file input and output, graphics, multimedia effects (animation and sounds), advanced topics such as web access, printing, and HTML help system authoring. The tutorial also introduces database applications (using ADO .NET) and web applications (using ASP.NET).

VISUAL BASIC AND DATABASES is a tutorial that provides a detailed introduction to using Visual Basic for accessing and maintaining databases for desktop applications. Topics covered include: database structure, database design, Visual Basic project building, ADO .NET data objects (connection, data adapter, command, data table), data bound controls, proper interface design, structured query language (SQL), creating databases using Access, SQL Server and ADOX, and database reports. Actual projects developed include a book tracking system, a sales invoicing program, a home inventory system and a daily weather monitor.

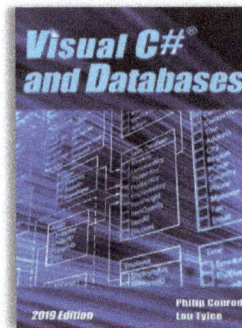

VISUAL C# AND DATABASES is a tutorial that provides a detailed introduction to using Visual C# for accessing and maintaining databases for desktop applications. Topics covered include: database structure, database design, Visual C# project building, ADO .NET data objects (connection, data adapter, command, data table), data bound controls, proper interface design, structured query language (SQL), creating databases using Access, SQL Server and ADOX, and database reports. Actual projects developed include a book tracking system, a sales invoicing program, a home inventory system and a daily weather monitor.

www.ingramcontent.com/pod-product-compliance
Lightning Source LLC
Chambersburg PA
CBHW080342220326
41598CB00030B/4578